Lecture Notes in Computer Science 2515

Edited by G. Goos, J. Hartmanis, and J. van Leeuwen

W0106759

Springer
Berlin
Heidelberg
New York
Barcelona
Hong Kong
London
Milan
Paris
Tokyo

Fernando Boavida   Edmundo Monteiro
João Orvalho (Eds.)

Protocols and Systems for Interactive Distributed Multimedia

Joint International Workshops
on Interactive Distributed Multimedia Systems
and Protocols for Multimedia Systems, IDMS/PROMS 2002
Coimbra, Portugal, November 26-29, 2002
Proceedings

 Springer

Series Editors

Gerhard Goos, Karlsruhe University, Germany
Juris Hartmanis, Cornell University, NY, USA
Jan van Leeuwen, Utrecht University, The Netherlands

Volume Editors

Fernando Boavida
Edmundo Monteiro
Universidade de Coimbra, Departamento de Engenharia Informática
Pólo II, 3030-290 Coimbra, Portugal
E-mail: {boavida,edmundo}@dei.uc.pt

João Orvalho
Instituto Politécnico de Coimbra, Escola Superior de Educação
Praça Heróis do Ultramar, 3030 Coimbra, Portugal
E-mail: orvalho@dei.uc.pt

Cataloging-in-Publication Data applied for

A catalog record for this book is available from the Library of Congress

Bibliographic information published by Die Deutsche Bibliothek
Die Deutsche Bibliothek lists this publication in the Deutsche Nationalbibliographie;
detailed bibliographic data is available in the Internet at <http://dnb.ddb.de>.

CR Subject Classification (1998): H.5.1, C.2, H.4, H.5, H.3

ISSN 0302-9743
ISBN 3-540-00169-7 Springer-Verlag Berlin Heidelberg New York

Springer-Verlag Berlin Heidelberg New York
a member of BertelsmannSpringer Science+Business Media GmbH

http://www.springer.de

© Springer-Verlag Berlin Heidelberg 2002

Typesetting: Camera-ready by author, data conversion by PTP-Berlin, Stefan Sossna e.K.
Printed on acid-free paper   SPIN: 10870978   06/3142   5 4 3 2 1 0

Preface

Interactive Distributed Multimedia Systems (IDMS) and Protocols for Multimedia Systems (PROMS) have been two successful series of international events bringing together researchers, developers, and practitioners from academia and industry in all areas of multimedia systems. In 2002, for the first time, these two workshops were held jointly, in what we hope was the first of a new series of challenging and topical international workshops.

IDMS/PROMS 2002 contributed to scientific, strategic, and practical advances in the area of distributed multimedia applications, protocols, and intelligent management tools, with emphasis on their provision over broadband networks. Along with tutorials, regular papers and technical demonstrations, IDMS/PROMS 2002 resulted in high-quality original work.

The areas of interest of IDMS/PROMS cover mobile multimedia systems, multimedia middleware, multimedia communication protocols, quality-of-service issues, resource management, next-generation Internet, active and programmable networking for multimedia applications, multimedia-specific mobile agents, multimedia distribution and transport, multimedia traffic engineering, multimedia encoding and compression, ubiquitous computing, multimedia applications, development tools for distributed multimedia applications, performance of protocols and applications, multimedia content management, service access, accounting and tariff policing for multimedia teleservices, and standards (e.g., MPEG) and related issues.

The IDMS/PROMS 2002 call for papers attracted 112 submissions from Asian, Australian, European, North American, and South American countries. These were subject to thorough review work by the Program Committee members and additional reviewers who carried out their work using a specially built conference system, WebChairing, developed in Coimbra by Flor de Utopia, which allowed full control of the submission and reviewing processes.

A high-quality selection of 30 full papers organized in 9 single-track sessions made up the IDMS/PROMS 2002 main technical program, which included topics such as performance of protocols and applications, mobile multimedia systems, standards and related issues, quality-of-service issues, video systems and applications, resource management, and multimedia support. This was complemented by one invited keynote talk by Andrew T. Campbell, from Columbia University, USA, who opened the workshop with a presentation on wireless IP.

In addition to the main technical program, the day preceding the workshop was dedicated to four excellent tutorials on Internet Multimedia Streaming, Internet Middleware, IP Network Monitoring and Measurements, and Media Representation Standards for the New Millennium, respectively, given by Henning Schulzrinne (Columbia University, USA), Mikhail Smirnow (Fraunhofer FOKUS, Germany), Philippe Owezarski (LAAS-CNRS, France), and Fernando Pereira (IST, Portugal).

We wish to record our appreciation of the efforts of many people in bringing about the IDMS/PROMS 2002 workshop: to all the authors who submitted their papers to the workshop, we regret that it was not possible to accept more papers; to the Program Committee and to all associated reviewers; to our sponsors and supporting institutions; and to ESEC for the multimedia coverage of the workshop. Finally, we would like to thank all the people who helped us at the University of Coimbra, namely Jorge Sá Silva, Paulo Simões, Marília Oliveira, João Cunha, João Sá Marta, and all the volunteers from the Laboratory of Communications and Telematics.

September 2002   Fernando Boavida
                                                        Edmundo Monteiro
                                                           João Orvalho

Organization

Program Chair

Fernando Boavida, University of Coimbra, Portugal

Tutorial Chair

Edmundo Monteiro, University of Coimbra, Portugal

Program Committee

Alexandre Santos, University of Minho, Portugal
Andrew Campbell, Columbia University, USA
Arnaldo Martins, University of Aveiro, Portugal
Arturo Azcorra, Carlos III University, Madrid, Spain
Augusto Casaca, INESC, Portugal
Burkhard Stiller, ETH Zurich, Switzerland
David Hutchison, Lancaster University, United Kingdom
Edmundo Madeira, University of Campinas, Brazil
Edmundo Monteiro, University of Coimbra, Portugal
Fernando Boavida, University of Coimbra, Portugal
Fernando Pereira, Instituto Superior Técnico, Portugal
Francisco Fontes, Portugal Telecom Inovação, SA, Portugal
Frank Eliassen, University of Oslo, Norway
Fred Stentiford, UCL, United Kingdom
Giorgio Ventre, University Frederico II, Napoli, Italy
Greg O'Shea, Microsoft Research, Cambridge, United Kingdom
Gregor v. Bochmann, University of Ottawa, Canada
Guy Leduc, University of Liege, Belgium
Hans Scholten, Twente University, The Netherlands
Henk Eertink, Telematica Instituut, The Netherlands
Jan Bormans, IMEC, Belgium
Jason Nieh, Columbia University, USA
Jean-Luc Raffy, Institut National des Télécommunications, France
Joao Orvalho, IPC/CISUC, Portugal
Joe Finney, Lancaster University, United Kingdom
Jordi Domingo-Pascual, Universitat Politècnica de Catalunya, Spain
Ketan Mayer-Patel, University of North Carolina, USA
Lars Wolf, Technical University Braunschweig, Germany
Laurent Mathy, Lancaster University, United Kingdom
Marten van Sinderen, University of Twente, The Netherlands

Martin Mauve, University of Mannheim, Germany
Michel Diaz, LAAS-CNRS, France
Nick Race, Lancaster University, United Kingdom
Patrick Senac, ENSICA, France
Paul D. Amer, University of Delaware, USA
Philippe Owezarski, LAAS-CNRS, France
Radu Popescu-Zeletin, GMD-FOKUS, Germany
Ralf Steinmetz, TU Darmstadt, Germany
Roberto Canonico, University Frederico II, Napoli, Italy
Serge Fdida, LiP6, France
Sergio Palazzo, University of Catania, Italy
Thomas Plagemann, University of Oslo, Unik, Norway
Tim Chown, University of Southampton, United Kingdom
Timothy Roscoe, Intel Research, Berkeley, USA
Tobias Helbig, Philips Research Laboratories, Germany
Ulrich Hofmann, University of Salzburg, Austria
Vera Goebel, University of Oslo, Norway
Winfried Kalfa, TU Chemnitz, Germany
Wolfgang Effelsberg, University of Mannheim, Germany
Zdzislaw Papir, AGH University of Technology, Poland

Additional Reviewers

Ahmed Sehrouchni, ENST
Alberto Garcia-Martinez, University Carlos III of Madrid
Amaro Sousa, University of Aveiro
Anders Andersen, University of Tromsø
Antonio Pescapè, University of Napoli
António Pereira, Polytechnic Institute of Leiria
Bernard Laurent, Institut National des Télécommunications
Caro Armando, University of Delaware
Carsten Griwodz, University of Oslo
Christophe Chassot, LAAS/CNRS
Eleri Cardozo, UNICAMP, University of Campinas
Erich Plasser, FTW
Fabrice Frances, ENSICA
Gauthier Lafruit, IMEC
Geoff Morrison, BTexact Technologies
Gonçalo Quadros, Critical Software
Halvorsen Pål, University of Oslo
Hans Ole Rafaelsen, University of Tromsø
Hänselmann Thomas, University of Mannheim
Ignacio Soto, Universidad Carlos III de Madrid
Ilidio Chaves, Pedro Nunes Institute
Jerome Lacan, ENSICA

Joaquim Macedo, University of Minho
Joaquim Sousa Pinto, University of Aveiro
Johan Garcia, Karlstad University
Jorge Sa Silva, University of Coimbra
José Carlos López Ardao, Universidad de Vigo
Josep Mangues-Bafalluy, Universitat Politecnica de Catalunya
Josep Sole Pareta, Universitat Politecnica de Catalunya
Juszkiewicz Krzysztof, Department of Telecommunications
Karel Van Oudheusden, IMEC
Ken Chen, University Paris 13, L2TI
Klaas Tack, IMEC
Kristof Denolf, IMEC
Laurent Dairaine, ENSICA
Leszczuk Mikolaj, Department of Telecommunications
Lila Boukhatem, University Paris 6, LIP6
Luís Silva, University of Coimbra
Marília Curado, University of Coimbra
Matt Walker, BTexact Technologies
Mauricio Magalhaes, UNICAMP, University of Campinas
Natkaniec Marek, Department of Telecommunications
Nelson Fonseca, UNICAMP, University of Campinas
Nils Damm Christophersen, University of Oslo
Olav Lysne, Simula Research Laboratory
Pacyna Piotr, Department of Telecommunications
Paul Smith, Lancaster University
Paulo Carvalho, University of Coimbra
Paulo Marques, University of Coimbra
Paulo Martins de Carvalho, University of Minho
Paulo Mendes, University of Coimbra
Paulo Simoes, University of Coimbra
Perennou Tanguy, ENSICA
Richard Staehli, Simula Research Laboratory
Rui Valadas, University of Aveiro
Rui Aguiar, University of Aveiro
Rui Lopes, Lancaster University
Salvatore D'Antonio, CINI-ITEM
Simon Pietro Romano, University of Napoli "Federico II"
Stefan Schmid, Lancaster University
Steven Simpson
Thomas Ziegler, FTW
Tim Chart, Lancaster University
Tomasz Orzechowski, Department of Telecommunications
Velthausz Daan, Telematica Instituut
Watza Rafal, Department of Telecommunications

Local Organizing Committee

João Orvalho (Chair), IPC/CISUC, Portugal
Jorge Sá Silva, University of Coimbra, Portugal
Marília Oliveira, University of Coimbra, Portugal
Paulo Simões, University of Coimbra, Portugal

Steering Committee

Thomas Plagemann, University of Oslo, UniK, Norway
Patrick Senac, ENSICA, France
Hans Scholten, Twente University, The Netherlands
Marten van Sinderen, Twente University, The Netherlands
Joe Finney, Lancaster University, United Kingdom
Laurent Mathy, Lancaster University, United Kingdom
Zdzislaw Papir, AGH University of Technology, Poland
Arturo Azcorra, Carlos III University, Madrid, Spain

Supporting and Sponsoring Organizations (alphabetically)

3Com
Association for Computing Machinery, ACM
Escola Superior de Educação de Coimbra, ESEC
Fundação para a Ciência e a Tecnologia, FCT
Instituto Pedro Nunes, IPN-LIS
Instituto Politécnico de Coimbra, IPC
Operational Program for Science, Technology and Innovation of the III European
    Framework
University of Coimbra

Table of Contents

Performance of Protocols and Applications

Mobile Multimedia Systems I

Standards and Related Issues

Quality of Service Issues I

Video Systems and Applications

Quality of Service Issues II

Mobile Multimedia Systems II

Resource Management

Multimedia Support

Tutorials and Invited Program

Optimal Traffic Shaping with Deterministic Guarantees Using GPS Scheduling

Enrique Hernández, Joan Vila, Sergio Saez, and Silvia Terrasa

Departamento de Informática de Sistemas y Computadores (DISCA)
Universidad Politécnica de Valencia,
Camino de Vera s/n, 46022 Valencia, SPAIN
{ehernandez,jvila,ssaez,sterrasa}@disca.upv.es

Abstract[1]. The transmission of video over a high-speed network implies guaranteeing a Quality of Service (QoS). This transmission requires a very demanding reservation of network resources, so optimisation becomes a key issue. Traffic shaping has been proposed as a means for improving network utilisation. This paper introduces a fast and bounded method to obtain the leaky bucket shaper parameters that optimises network reservations (bandwidth and buffers) with deterministic guarantees using GPS scheduling. The algorithm presented finds the optimal solution in 5 or 6 iterations. Another important contribution of this paper is comparing this new admission scheme with different EDF control admission tests. Results show that although GPS is a little less efficient than the optimal EDF scheduler for one node (as expected), it is as efficient as the best RC-EDF known policies for several nodes, or even better when the number of network hops is high.

1 Introduction

Transporting multimedia traffic while guaranteeing a required Quality of Service is a challenging problem that has received a lot of attention in recent years [1]. The approach for guaranteeing Quality of Service is usually based on reserving network resources. Designing efficient algorithms for traffic control and resource allocation [2] is very difficult since VBR (Variable Bit Rate) video traffic is both delay-sensitive and has a high degree of burstiness.

An approach to reduce the utilisation of network resources is traffic smoothing. The goal of traffic smoothing is to reduce the variability of the traffic transmission. This smoothing can be done either *offline*: prior to transmission, the traffic is analysed and smoothed based on some criteria, or *online*: the traffic is smoothed using a buffer in the sender node so it does not violate a given constraint. Online smoothing is usually called shaping [3]. Traffic shaping introduces a new queue to hold the stream of packets while they are waiting to be injected in the network. This implies that the

---

[1] This work has been supported by the Spanish Government Research Office (CYCYT) under grant TIC99-1043-C03-02.

F. Boavida et al. (Eds.): IDMS/PROMS 2002, LNCS 2515, pp. 1-14, 2002.

sender prefetches video frames to a queue in advance. This queue smoothes the original bursty traffic so that the network resources requirements can be reduced.

Several works about optimal smoothing have been reported in the literature. Some solutions (typically *offline* smoothing) try to find an optimal transmission schedule (that is, a set of transmission rates) with several criteria for optimality, including minimising the transmission peak rate, number of rate changes and start-up delay [4,5,6] (see a good comparison in [7]). The main problem with these schemes is that transmission rate changes in time, so guaranteeing the quality of service of the transmission would require renegotiation of the network resources reservation. However, in VBR transmission environments with deterministic guarantees it seems more realistic to place only an initial reservation that is maintained during the whole transmission. Common solutions for optimising resources in such a scenario are usually based on traffic shaping. In [8] the authors found an expression of the minimal buffer size for a given rate drain. In [3], the objective was to minimise the playback delay D and the buffer size at the receiver.

Different packet-scheduling disciplines have been devised in order to guarantee this QoS. The most widely used among them, are those based on Generalised Processor Sharing (GPS) and on Earliest Deadline First (EDF).

The GPS[2] [9,10] theory has been widely used and low-cost implementations have become available on the market. This policy guarantees throughput to individual connections and also provides smaller end-to-end delay bounds to connections crossing several nodes than other policies. A key factor in obtaining these smaller delay bounds is the ability to take into account dependencies in the successive nodes that a connection has to traverse. In GPS lower delays imply higher bandwidth reservations. Its main attraction is its simplicity, both in the admission test as well as in the scheduler.

In the EDF theory there is no simple or direct relation between bandwidth and delay, but it allows achieving low delays with high bandwidths in one node. As a matter of fact, it has been proven to be optimal in terms of the schedulable region at a single node [11]. However, in a network, the end-to-end delay is obtained as the sum of the delays at each node, so the total delay is usually high. In order to reduce this network delay, per-hop traffic shaping was introduced (this is known as Rate-Controlled EDF or RC-EDF) [12]. In theory, RC-EDF can offer substantial performance gains over GPS. However, the admission control tests for this policy are considerably more complex than those for GPS, requiring the use of approximation techniques [13,14,15]. Sivaraman et al. [16] studied how to select the shaping parameters that maximise network utilisation for an RC-EDF scheduler. The conclusion of this paper is that except in trivial cases, it is infeasible to identify "optimal" shapers that maximise RC-EDF schedulable regions.

A common issue that has not been resolved satisfactorily in previous works is the selection of the appropriate flow specification parameters of a traffic workload that optimise network resources. In GPS, this can be done using an iterative and costly

---

[2] In this paper when we use the term GPS we refer to its packetized version (also known as WFQ (Weighted Fair Queuing) or PGPS (Packetized GPS)).

process based on scanning the video every iteration and for every transmission (note that a movie of 100 minutes is about 2 Gbytes in length). Therefore, this reservation is usually calculated approximately. In [17,18], the authors introduced a fast and bounded method to optimise bandwidth reservation. However, this optimisation has a drawback: the buffer required in the nodes for large deadlines is very high. Reducing this buffer requirement implies using a traffic shaper in the sender node. According to this, this paper introduces a different optimisation method to obtain the shaper parameters based on the concept of envelope points. This method minimises the bandwidth and buffer requirements of the network.

Results for the one node case show that this new scheme practically offers the same efficiency as the optimal EDF scheduler. But with several nodes, the proposed scheme is as efficient as the best known RC-EDF policies, using much more simple implementations. Another advantage of this new method is that it only affects the sender and receiver nodes. No modification needs to be done in the nodes. Therefore, this can be applied to a wide range of networks using GPS scheduling in the nodes.

The simulations performed in this paper use two sets of VBR traffic. The first one is the well-known MPEG-1 traces studied by O. Rose [19] from the University of Wurzburg. Recently, a new set of MPEG-4 and H.263 traces (with different quality codifications levels) from the Technical University of Berlin have been placed on the web [20]. This variety of traffic traces proves the applicability of our new algorithms.

2 Background

2.1 EDF Scheduling

The EDF (Earliest Deadline First) scheduling discipline is well known in the context of real-time processor scheduling. The adaptation of this scheduler to Real-Time transmission works as follows [21,16]: each flow i at switch m is associated with a local delay bound d_i^m; when a packet of flow i arrives to the scheduler at time t, a deadline $t + d_i^m$ is assigned, and packets are dispatched by increasing order of deadline.

Georgiadis *et al.* [11] demonstrated that EDF is the optimal scheduling policy at a single node in terms of the schedulable region for a set of flows with given deterministic delay requirements. This kind of service has one great drawback: the end-to-end delay in a network is obtained as the sum of the worst-case delay at each node, so the total delay is usually quite high. In order to reduce this network delay, per-hop traffic shaping was introduced (known as Rate-Controlled EDF or RC-EDF) [12]. In these service disciplines, the traffic of each connection is reshaped at every node to ensure that the traffic offered to the scheduler conforms to specific characteristics.

Using these disciplines, Georgiadis *et al.*, obtained an expression for the end-to-end delay in terms of the shaper envelope $E_i(t)$ and the local delays d_i. The total delay is computed as the sum of the shaper delay d_i^{sh} and the sum of the local delay of the switches d_i^m: $d_i = d_i^{sh} + \sum_{m-1}^{M} d_i^m$.

The efficiency of these schemes critically depends on the choice of shaper E_i. Sivaraman et al. [16] demonstrated that identifying the "optimal" shaper is in general infeasible, as it requires the entire network state to be known. One solution, proposed by the authors in [12] is the use of the leaky bucket parameters induced by GPS.

Some necessary and sufficient conditions for EDF schedulability on a single node have been proposed in [12]. The theoretical optimality of EDF and the existence of those necessary conditions for schedulability make EDF an attractive choice for real-time transmission. However, the EDF scheduler has two drawbacks: first, the implementation of EDF has a high computational cost. The second drawback is that, although the EDF schedulability condition can be expressed simply, the procedure used to test it can be computationally very complex.

In order to simplify this test, *Firoui et al.* [13] uses a piecewise linear traffic envelope that provides a low computational complexity control admission test. Each traffic is characterised by a multiple-leaky-bucket $(\sigma_k, \rho_k)_{k=1..m}$, where m is the number of segments. This traffic characterisation (which is concave, increasing, and piecewise linear) provides a simplification on the calculus of the control admission tests.

Sivaraman et al. [16] proposed a new heuristic to improve the method of Firoui et al. The results in [22] show that smoothing is not convenient for flow traversing a single hop. Nevertheless, when the numbers of hops is high it is more efficient to smooth the traffic entirely at the ingress to the network. According to this, Sivaraman et al. have proposed an heuristic to obtain the shaper delay.

2.2 GPS Scheduling

The Generalised Processor Sharing scheduler is an idealised fluid discipline that is easy to implement and has been widely used. A seminal work by Parekh and Gallager [9,10] introduces an equation to obtain the maximum delay when the traffic is leaky-bucket regulated at the input. This means that the traffic is constrained by the following function $\alpha(t) = \sigma + \rho t$ (σ is the bucket depth and ρ drain rate). The end-to-end delay bound is a function of the reserved bandwidth in the links and is usually calculated using a traffic and network model. The maximum end-to-end queuing delay bound can be calculated using this equation:

$$D_i = \frac{\sigma + nL_i}{R} + \sum_{j=1}^{n} \frac{Lmax_j}{C_j} \qquad R \le p \qquad (1)$$

where L_i is the maximum packet size for session i, $Lmax_j$ is the maximum packet size in node j, C_j the bandwidth of the link j, and n the number of nodes. The buffer size in the jth node is $\sigma + jL_i$. In order to simplify this delay expression, we can use the C_{tot} and D_{tot} parameters for defining the network as described in [23]. C_{tot} is nL_i, D_{tot} is $\sum_{j=1}^{n} Lmax_j / C_j$, and M is maximum packet size. Note that equation (1) can be used only when the bandwidth reservation R is smaller than the peak reservation p. When $R > p$ another expression that does not depend on the flow parameters must be used. In summary, the delay equations are:

$$D = \frac{\sigma + C_{tot}}{R} + D_{tot} \quad \rho \leq R \leq p \tag{2}$$

$$D = \frac{M + C_{tot}}{R} + D_{tot} \quad R \geq p \geq \rho \tag{3}$$

With these equations, the control admission test becomes very simple. For a new connection i with a given end-to-end delay D_i, it is necessary to calculate the bandwidth reservation that makes equation (2) or (3) less than D, and the sum of the bandwidth reservation for all channels at the node less than the total link bandwidth C_j.

From equations (2) and (3) it is easy to see that the network resource reservation depends mainly on the selection of appropriate flow specification parameters from a traffic workload (the σ and ρ parameters) for a given delay D and network configuration. The optimal bandwidth reservation can be found using an iterative method over traffic traces which is costly and not bounded.

However, a much more convenient and faster method based on the concept of empirical envelope was introduced in [17,18]. Using the empirical envelope, a set of points, so called *envelope points*, which give a condensed description of the traffic flow, is calculated. These points are used to obtain the σ value depending on ρ for a given traffic. The number of points obtained has been proven to be very low (between 34 and 84 points using Rose MPEG-1 sample traffic and between 20 and 123 for the Berlin set using MPEG-4, H.261 and H263 traffic). The optimal bandwidth reservation of the nodes can be obtained using these points in a fast and bounded way. The computational cost of this algorithm is $O(log\ m)$ where m is the number of envelope points.

This approach comprises two phases. During the first phase the video is analysed off-line in order to obtain its empirical envelope and to extract a reduced set of points from this envelope (the envelope points). The second phase occurs at channel establishment time and, at this point, the former set of points is used together with channel parameters to estimate the optimal reservations.

3   Obtaining Optimal Shaper Parameters

A drawback of the GPS bandwidth reservation schemes is that it becomes necessary to increment the use of the network buffers in order to reduce network bandwidth (by incrementing the total delay). The buffer requirements increase dramatically when deadlines of more than one second are used. The main reason for this problem is that the traffic is injected into the network with no delay, so the network has to cope directly with the high variability of video traffics. However, if a leaky-bucket traffic shaper is introduced, previous to the network traffic injection, the network buffer utilisation is highly reduced (the traffic is smoothed). Therefore, the problem scenario is the one depicted in Figure 1.

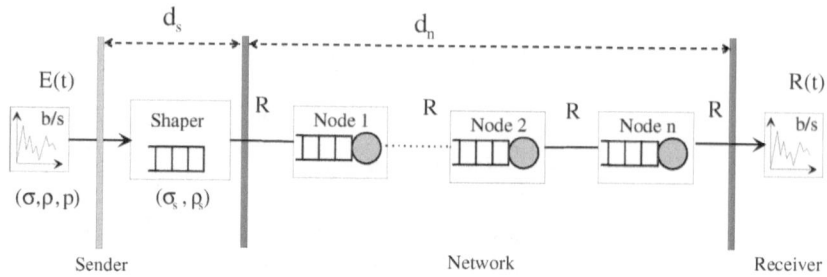

Fig. 1. Traffic shaping scenario

Shaping is the standard method used to make an arbitrary flow conform to some traffic envelope $\alpha(t)$[3]. A shaper, with a shaping curve α, takes a flow as input, stores the bits in a buffer, and outputs the bits to the network conforming to the traffic envelope $\alpha(t)$. The leaky bucket shaper has two parameters: the buffer size σ_s and the output rate ρ_s, so $\alpha(t) = \rho_s t$. The goal of this section is to obtain the traffic shaper parameters (σ_s, ρ_s) that minimise the bandwidth and buffer reservation of the network for a given delay D and a known traffic. This is a different goal from the optimisation scheme presented in [17,18], whose aim is to obtain the flow specification parameters (σ, ρ) without a shaper. However, the following proofs show that the optimisation scheme is very similar for both scenarios.

As shown in Figure 1, the total delay D is (replacing d_n by equation 2):

$$D = d_n + d_s = \frac{\sigma + C_{tot}}{R} + D_{tot} + d_s \quad (R \geq \rho) \tag{4}$$

Working out the value of σ:

$$\sigma = (D - D_{tot} - d_s)R - C_{tot} \quad (R \geq \rho) \tag{5}$$

If the terms C_{tot} and D_{tot} were 0 (a perfect GPS flow) then $\sigma = (D - d_s)R$, so the root of the last equation would be $d_s = D$. In other words total smoothing, so $\rho_s = R$. This is logical as Zhang demonstrated [24]: introducing a leaky-bucket shaper in a network does not affect the maximum end-to-end delay. As C_{tot} and D_{tot} are not 0, the network delay d_n cannot be 0, and the bandwidth reservation must be slightly increased. A leaky bucket shaper produces a new traffic with a peak rate $p_s = \rho_s$. If 0 is used as the network σ value, then the network bandwidth reservation R must be ρ_s (in order to avoid packets loss). Then, equation (3) can be used to obtain the network delay. This implies that buffer requirement in the network is minimal: jL_i in the jth node.

A leaky bucket shaper with parameter ρ_s introduces the following delay:

$$d_s = \frac{\sigma_s}{\rho_s} \quad (\rho_s \geq R) \tag{6}$$

so the total delay is:

$$D = d_n + d_s = \frac{M + C_{tot}}{\rho_s} + D_{tot} + \frac{\sigma_s}{\rho_s} \quad (R = \rho_S) \tag{7}$$

The value of σ_s depends on ρ_s for a particular traffic. Assume that encoded video sequences have n frames and the number of encoded bits produced by frame i is B_i. If there are f frames per second, and the finite capacity of the bucket is not taken into consideration, then the bucket fullness (in bits) at the end of frame period i is [8]:

$$\sigma_i = \max\{0, \sigma_{i-1} + B_i - \frac{\rho_s}{f}\} \tag{8}$$

In order to calculate the shaper capacity σ_s so that the bucket does not overflow, σ_s is chosen such that $\sigma_i \leq \sigma_s \; \forall i$. The value of σ_s can be thus written as a function of ρ_s:

$$\sigma_s(\rho_s) = \max_{0 < i \leq n} \sigma_i \tag{9}$$

Therefore, we can obtain the σ_s for a given ρ_s value. Then, the buffering delay is:

$$d_s(\rho_s) = \frac{\sigma_s(\rho_s)}{\rho_s} \tag{10}$$

As $\sigma_s(\rho_s)$ is a decreasing function, $d_s(\rho)$ is also decreasing and the total delay can be written as a function of ρ_s:

$$D(\rho_s) = \frac{M + C_{tot}}{R} + D_{tot} + \frac{\sigma_s(\rho_s)}{\rho_s} = \frac{M + C_{tot} + \sigma_s(\rho_s)}{\rho_s} + D_{tot} \tag{11}$$

Lemma 1: $D(\rho_s)$ is a decreasing function in the domain $[0,p]$.

Proof: This is straightforward. The terms M, C_{tot} and D_{tot} are constants. Provided that $\sigma_s(\rho_s)$ is decreasing and the denominator is increasing, the first term is decreasing so $D(\rho_s)$ is also decreasing. ∎

However, our goal is to obtain ρ_s for a given delay. Equation (11) can be used to find the shaper parameters using, for example, an iterative method to find the values of ρ_s and σ_s that optimise this reservation. However, this equation can be used when ρ_s ranges from 0 to p. It is important to determine if we can use this equation for a given maximum delay D, that is, when the following condition $D(\rho_s) \leq D$ holds:

Lemma 2: $D(\rho_s) \leq D$ when $D \geq \dfrac{M + C_{tot}}{p} + D_{tot}$.

Proof: Given that the range of ρ_s is $[0,p]$, and $\sigma_s(p)$ is 0, then the minimal value of $D(\rho_s)$ will occur when ρ_s is p (by Lemma 1 $D(\rho_s)$ is decreasing). So, the following holds:

$$D(p) = \frac{M + C_{tot}}{p} + D_{tot} \leq D$$ ∎

If this condition is not satisfied, it is necessary to reserve a higher bandwidth than the peak rate in order to transmit with the required delay. In this case, an equation like (3) which does not depend on the traffic characteristics should be used, so that no shaper would be needed.

A new algorithm to obtain ρ_s that uses envelope points will be now introduced. The *Envelope Points* [18] are the subset of points $\{ t_1 < t_2 < \ldots t_m \}$ of the Empirical Envelope $E(t)$ such that the slopes ρ_i of the straight lines $l_i(t) \geq E(t) \ \forall t$ that joins $E(t_i)$ with $E(t_{i+1})$ are always decreasing. Therefore, each *Envelope Point i* is defined by the following 3-tuple $EP_i = \{t_i, E(t_i), \rho\}$ where:

$$\rho_i = \begin{cases} \dfrac{E(t_{i+1}) - E(t_i)}{t_{i+1} - t_i} & \text{for } i < m \\[2mm] 0 & \text{for } i = m \end{cases}$$

From the envelope points, we can obtain a function equivalent to $\sigma_s(\rho_s)$ as a composition of linear functions. Each linear function is defined as:

$$\sigma_i(\rho) = E(t_i) - t_i \rho \qquad \rho_{i-1} \geq \rho \geq \rho_i \qquad (12)$$

Then, $\sigma'(\rho)$ is the composition of linear functions $\sigma(\rho)$ for each interval defined by the m envelope points.

$$\sigma'(\rho) = \sigma_i(\rho) \qquad \rho_{i-1} \geq \rho \geq \rho_i \qquad i = 1..m \qquad (13)$$

To calculate $\sigma'(\rho)$, we have to find the interval where ρ is located and then apply equation (12). Thus, $\sigma'(\rho)$ is equivalent to $\sigma_s(\rho_s)$ although it has one great advantage: it is not necessary to traverse all the traffic to calculate the σ_s for a given ρ_s. Since $\sigma'(\rho)$ is formed by linear segments, this allows us to develop a fast and direct method to find the optimal shaper:

Theorem 1: If the root $R = \rho$ is in the interval $[\rho_{i-1}, \rho_i]$, then

$$\rho_s = \frac{M + C_{tot} + E(t_i)}{D - D_{tot} + t_i} \qquad (14)$$

Proof: If the root $R = \rho$ is in the interval $[\rho_{i-1}, \rho_i]$, then $\sigma_i(\rho) = E(t_i) - Rt_i$. We then replace $\sigma_s(\rho_s)$ by this expression in (11) and work out the value of ρ_s yielding:

$$D(\rho_s) = \frac{M + C_{tot} + E(t_i) - \rho_s t_i}{\rho_s} + D_{tot} \Rightarrow \rho_s = \frac{M + C_{tot} + E(t_i)}{D - D_{tot} + t_i} \qquad \blacksquare$$

This implies that if we know the interval, the value of ρ_s can be obtained directly. The search of this interval is easy and bounded: a binary search among the envelope points can be done to find the interval. When the interval is found, Theorem 1 can be applied to obtain R. Lemma 2 allows checking whether this method can be applied for a given delay D. An algorithm for finding the solution is detailed in Figure (2). This algorithm finds the solution very quickly and is bounded to *log m* steps, so it has a computational cost of *O(log m)*, where *m* is the number of points. As mentioned in the previous section, the value of m is very small (between 20 and 120 points for the analysed videos), so the solution can be found in 5 or 6 iterations.

```
GetOptimalShaper(
            Input: Ctot, Dtot, M, EPi = (ti, ρs, Ei) i = 0..n
            { Network parameters and Envelope points }
            Output: σs,ρs,R  { Shaper and reservation} )
begin
            i0 = 0; i1 = n;
            do
              i = (i0 + i1)/2;
              Di = (M + Ctot + Ei - ρs*ti)/ρs + Dtot;
              If Di < D then i0 = i;
              If Di > D then i1 = i;
            while (i1 - i0) > 1;
            R = ρs = (M + Ctot + E(ti))/(D - Dtot + ti);
            σs = Ei - R*ti;
end;
```

Fig. 2. An algorithm to calculate the optimal shaper

4   Performance and Network Resources Utilisation

This section is devoted to evaluate the network resources utilisation of the proposed scheme and to compare it with other known schemes, mainly EDF. The EDF schemes are based on the test proposed in [13] that gives an index of the accepted connections is used. The algorithms described in the previous sections were implemented in a test program called RTNOU (Real-Time Network Optimisation Utilities). This program can read traffic traces (for example the Rose and Berlin sets) and allows obtaining the envelope points, the optimal bandwidth reservation and other interesting operations. This program and the C source code of the algorithms can be freely downloaded from the authors' web page[3].

Using the algorithm of Figure (2) and the network of Figure (3a) the obtained shaper parameters for a delay of 0.5s are: (ρ_s = 597,048b/s, σ_s= 245,837). Therefore, the network reservation is $R=\rho_s$=597,048b/s. This is slightly higher than the optimal reservation with no shaping, which is 592,183 b/s. By Lemma (2), the minimal permitted delay can be calculated as $D = (M+C_{tot})/p+D_{tot}$= 0.0296s. Figure (3b) shows the optimal shaper parameters ρ_s and σ_s as a function of the required delay ranging from 0s to 5s. This pattern is very similar to the one obtained with no shaper. The greater the required delay is, the higher the value of σ_s is. This is because frames have to be stored in the shaper buffer. The increase of σ_s versus time is quite linear. On the other hand, ρ_s decreases exponentially to 0.1s and later decreases linearly.

Figure (4a) shows the efficiency of the shaped bandwidth reservations R versus the unshaped optimal bandwidth reservation R_u (the quotient R/R_u in percentage). As

---

[3] web page: `http://www.disca.upv.es/enheror/RTNOU.html`

expected, the efficiency grows when the delay is higher, practically reaching 100% for delays greater than 2 seconds. This behaviour is very interesting because, for low delays, the buffer reservation in the unshaped scheme is low. Hence, there is no buffer problem in the nodes. Nevertheless, for high delays, where the buffer needs grow dramatically in the unshaped scheme, the efficiency of the shaped scheme is very high, so it can be used with a very small increment of the network bandwidth requirements.

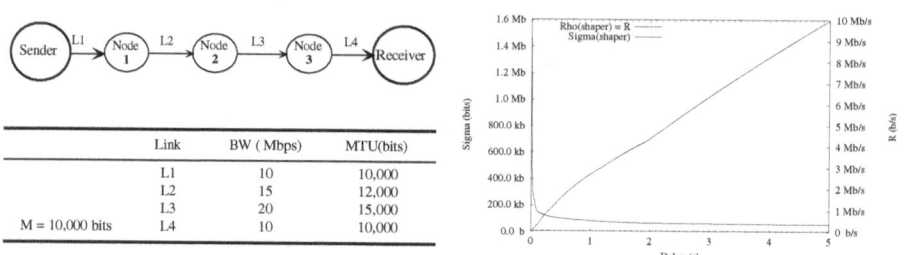

	Link	BW (Mbps)	MTU(bits)
	L1	10	10,000
	L2	15	12,000
	L3	20	15,000
M = 10,000 bits	L4	10	10,000

Fig. 3. a) Sample network, b) Optimal shaper parameters for Terminator traffic

The bandwidth utilisation level is defined as the ratio R/m, where m is the mean rate of the traffic [2]. This ratio gives clear evidence of the network utilisation for a given traffic. This level was calculated for the MPEG-1 Rose traffics: *Terminator*, *Soccer*, *Lambs* and MTV and MPEG-4 Berlin traffic *Soccer* depending on the maximum delay (see Figure 4b). As stated in the previous section, higher delays provide better utilisations. With delays of about 5 seconds, utilisations ranging from 35% to 85% can be obtained. For lower delays, the utilisation is also quite good (for a 1-second delay, it ranges from 25% to 60%). The bandwidth utilisation depends mainly on the traffic burstiness. Using the peak/mean ratio as a level of burstiness, it is easy to see that traffics with a low burstiness ratio have a greater bandwidth utilisation level.

The level of utilisation is useful for comparing a single traffic. Nevertheless, for a network it is more useful to obtain an index of the number of accepted connections for a given workload (a set of VBR traffics). For this reason, the call blocking probabilities were obtained via simulations. This evaluation was proposed in [13] and has been used in [16]. It obtains the probability that a new traffic may not be admitted because there are not enough network resources to transmit this traffic.

The proposed simulations focus on one switch of the network and it is assumed that the chosen switch is the bottleneck for all the flows passing through it. The chosen switch determines, therefore, whether an incoming flow can be accepted into the network or not. Furthermore, the chosen switch operates at 155 Mbps (corresponding to an OC-3 ATM link) and multiplexes a traffic mix consisting of six types of video flows (the following MPEG1 Rose traffic: Video, Jurassic, MTV, Lambs, Soccer and Terminator).

Flow arrivals are generated according to a Poisson process with parameter α, ψ and their durations are exponentially distributed with mean $1/\beta$. The ratio α/β characterises the load offered to the link (the average number of flows that would exist at any time at a link with no capacity limitation). Each flow has traffic characteristics which are chosen randomly from the characteristics of the six types of traffic. A million flows were generated in each simulation run and we were interested in the link-blocking probability (the ratio between the number of rejected flows and the total number of generated flows).

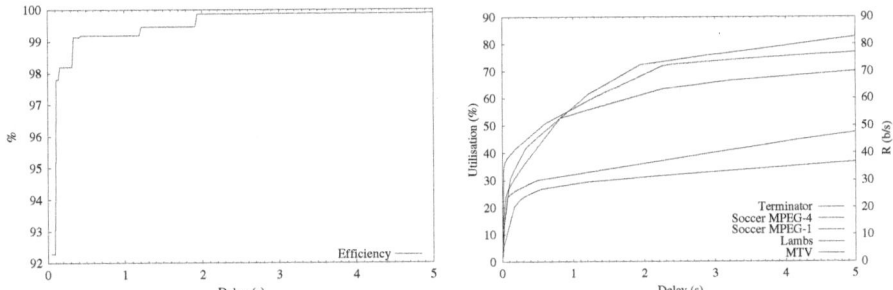

Fig. 4. a) Optimal shaper Efficiency. b) Bandwidth utilisation depending on delay.

For these simulations, we implemented the admission control of GPS and four EDF schemes:

1. EDF(Exact): EDF exact call acceptance test. It uses complete traffic traces to test acceptance,
2. RC-EDF(STS): Segment Total Smoothing RC-EDF, a simplified (and usable) new test for RC-EDF using four segments and total smoothing designed in [13],
3. RC-EDF(SHS): Segment Hop Smoothing RC-EDF, an improved version of 2 devised in [16],
4. GPS: Optimal bandwidth reservation as described in section 2, and
5. GPS(TS): Total shaping as described in section 3.

The first simulation tested a single link. The goal was to compare the admission control in one node. The end-to-end delay requirement d (excluding propagation delays) of the flow was uniformly distributed in [50ms, 1s] and the offered load was varied from 110 to 150 calls. The results are shown in Figure (5a). With a single node, the values for GPS and GPS(TS) are practically the same (although GPS(TS) is a little worse than GPS, as expected). As stated above, the best acceptance test is the EDF(Exact). The RC-EDF(SHS) curve is a little worse but follows the pattern of EDF(Exact) curve. The RC-EDF(STS) is the worst test, as stated in [16] (for one node, traffic shaping is not effective). As expected, the results for GPS are worse than those for EDF(Exact).

The goal of the second simulation was to compare admission control in a network of nodes. The following parameters were used: the end-to-end delay requirement d (excluding propagation delays) of the flow was uniformly distributed in [100ms, 1s], and its hop-length was uniformly chosen in [1,10][4]. The total delay (minus shaping delay) was divided equally among the hops, and the call acceptance test was performed at the switch to determine whether the flow could be accepted into the

---

[4] We repeated the test in [16] with the same results. In this article, we present another test with other parameters. We incremented the number of hops from 5 to 10, and the results varied significantly. This led us to believe that the number of hops is determinant in the efficiency of the different admission tests.

network. The results are shown in Figure (5b). In this case, the results for EDF(Exact) are very bad because it is not appropriate for a network of nodes. The other three curves present a similar pattern. In this case, the GPS[5] curve is between the RC-EDF(STS) and RC-EDF(SHS) curves.

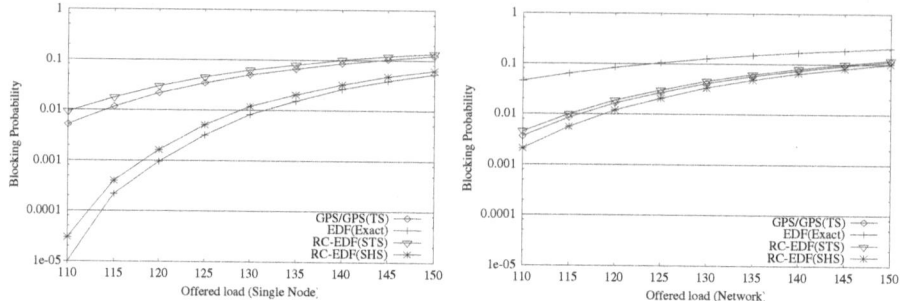

Fig. 5. Call blocking probability in a) a single node, b) a network

The main factor that affects these results is the number of hops. Thus, Figure (6a) represents the results of the admission test varying the numbers of hops. Using a workload of 130, the numbers of hops was varied from 1 to 15 (the delay range was the same as the previous experiment). This figure shows that GPS is the best test when the number of hops is moderately high (more than 4). Although the RC-EDF blocking probability is very low for one or two nodes, this probability increments rapidly for three nodes or more. Nevertheless, the GPS curve grows very slowly as compared to RC-EDF(SHS). This is the effect of the GPS optimisation scheme which obtains the shaper parameters that optimise the bandwidth depending on the delay and network parameters (the number of hops). In the RC-EDF segment-based test, the shapers are selected before the network is known, so this optimisation cannot be done. The results for load 170 in Figure (6b) follow the pattern of load 130 although the blocking probability is higher.

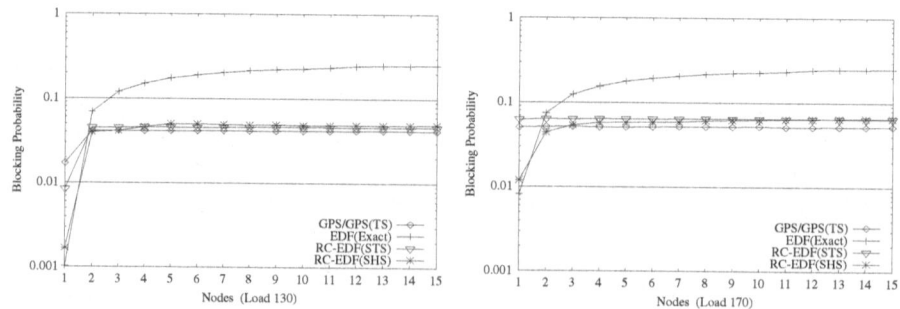

Fig. 6. Call blocking probability for load 130 and 170 depending on network nodes.

---

[5] The results for the GPS(TS) are a little worse than for GPS, but these differences cannot be appreciated in the graphics.

5 Conclusions

Traffic shaping has been proven to be an efficient way to reduce network resources requirements for VBR transmission. This paper introduces a fast and bounded method to obtain the shaper leaky bucket parameters which optimise the bandwidth reservation and minimise the use of buffer nodes for GPS schedulers for a given end-to-end delay. This new method can be applied to any network that uses a leaky-bucket or token-bucket traffic model and only affects the sender and receiver nodes. No modification needs to be done in the nodes, so this can be applied to a wide range of networks.

Two different comparisons have been done to test the efficient of this shaping approach. The first one compares its efficiency versus the unshaped optimal scheme and shows that is practically the same, although highly reducing the buffer needs. The goal of the second comparison is to evaluate the efficiency of the admission control tests of different EDF and GPS schedulers. The results show that for one node it is a little less efficient than the optimal EDF scheduler (as expected). However, in a network with several nodes, the simulations show that our scheme is nearly as good as the RC-EDF policies, and when the number of hops is moderately high (greater than 4) the GPS is better.

Although RC-EDF has been proposed as being more efficient than GPS, the performance of RC-EDF crucially depends upon the choice of the shaping parameters. With this new optimisation scheme, the GPS can achieve efficiency similar to that of EDF schedulers, but without their complexities. In summary, GPS is an excellent choice for real-time transmission: it is simple, efficient and there are commercial implementations.

References

1. M. Krunz, "Bandwidth Allocation Strategies for Transporting Variable-Bit-Rate Video Traffic", *IEEE Communications Magazine*, pp. 40-46, Jan. 1999.
2. M. Conti and E. Gregori, "Bandwidth Allocation for the Transmission of Scalable MPEG Video Traffic with Deterministic Guarantees", *Real Time Imaging 7*, 237-253 (2001). doi: 10.1006/rtim.2000.0225.
3. J.Y. Le Boudec and O. Verscheure "Optimal Smoothing for Guaranteed Service" *IEEE/ACM Transactions on Networking*. VoL. 8, No. 6, Dec 2000
4. J.D. Salehi, Z.L. Zhang, J. Kurose and D. Towsley, "Supporting Stored Video : Reducing Rate Variability and End-to-End Resource Requirements Through Optimal Smoothing", *IEEE/ACM Transactions on Networking*, vol. 6, N° 4, pp. 397-410,Aug. 1998.
5. J. Rexford and D. Towsley "Smoothing Variable-Bit-Rate Video in an Internetwork" IEEE/ACM Transactions on Networking. Vol 7, N° 2, April 1999, pp. 202-215.
6. J. Zhang, J. Hui, "Applying traffic smoothing techniques for quality of service control in VBR video". Computer Communications. August 1997.
7. W. C. Feng and J. Rexford, "A Comparison of Bandwidth Smoothing Techniques for the Transmission of Prerecorded Compressed Video". IEEE Infocom Apr. 1997, pp. 58-66

8. A.R. Reibman and A.W.Berger "Traffic Descriptors for VBR Video Teleconferencing Over ATM Networks". *IEEE/ACM Trans. On Networking*. Vol 3, N° 3, June 1995 pp. 329-339.
9. A.Parekh and R.Gallager, "A generalised processor sharing approach to flow control in integrated services networks: The single node case", *IEEE/ACM Trans. on Networking*, vol. 1, n° 3, pp.344-357, June 1993
10. A.Parekh and R.Gallager, "A generalised processor sharing approach to flow control in integrated services networks: The multiple node case", *IEEE/ACM Trans. on Networking*, vol. 2, n° 2, pp.137-150, April 1994
11. L. Georgiadis, R. Guerin, and A. Parekh. "Optimal multiplexing on a single link: Delay and Buffer Requiriment". *IEEE/ACM Transactions on Information Theory*, 43(5):1518-1535, September 1997. Previous version in Proceeding of INFOCOM'94.
12. L. Georgiadis, R. Guerin, V. Peris and K.N. Sivarajan. "Efficient Network QoS Provisioning Based on per Node Traffic Shaping". *IEEE/ACM Transactions on Networking*, 4(4):482-501, August 1996
13. V. Firoiu, J. Kurose, and D. Towsley. "Efficient admission control of piecewise linear traffic envelopes at edf schedulers". *IEEE/ACM Transactions on Networking*, 6(5):558–570, October 1998.
14. F. M. Chiussi and V. Sivaraman; "Achieving High Utilization in Guaranteed Services Networks Using Early-Deadline-First Scheduling" IWQoS '98, Napa Valley, California, May 1998, pp.209-217.
15. D. E. .Wrege, and J. Liebeherr. "Video Traffic Characterization for Multimedia Networks with a Deterministic Service", *IEEE Infocom 96*, pp. 537-544, April 1996.
16. V. Sivaraman, F. Chiussi, M. Gerla, "Traffic Shaping for End-to-End Delay Guarantees with EDF Scheduling", *In proceedings of IWQoS'00.*
17. E. Hernández, J.Vila , "A fast method to optimise network resources for Video-on-demand Transmission". *IEEE Proceedings of Euromicro 2000*, pp. 440-447. Sep. 2000
18. E. Hernández, J.Vila, "A New Approach to Optimise Bandwith Reservation for Real-Time Video Transmission with Deterministic Guarantees".*Real-Time Imaging*. Academic Press. In press.
19. O. Rose, "Statistical properties of MPEG video traffic and their impact on traffic modeling in ATM systems", *Proceedings of the 20th Annual Conference on Local Computer Networks, Minneapolis. 1995, pp. 397-406.*
20. F.H.P. Fitzek, M. Reisslein, "MPEG-4 and H.263 Video Traces for Network Performance Evaluation", *IEEE Network*, vol 15, N° 6, pp. 40-54. Nov/Dec. 2001.
21. D. Ferrari and D. Verma, "A scheme for real-time channel establishment in wide-area networks", *IEEE Journal on Selected areas in Communications*, 8(3):368-379, April 1990.
22. E. Knightly and P. Rossaro. "On the effects of smoothing for deterministic QoS". *Distributed Systems Engineering Journal: Special Issue on QoS*, 4(1):3–15, March 1997.
23. S. Schenker, C.Partridge, R.Guerinm, Specification of Guaranteed Quality of Service, RFC 2212
24. H. Zhang, "Service Disciplines for integrated services packet-switching networks". PhD Dissertation. UCB/CSD-94-788. University of California at Berkeley. November 1993.

Evaluation of Video Server Capacity with Regard to Quality of the Service in Interactive News-On-Demand Systems

J.R. Arias, F.J. Suárez, D.F. García, X.X. García, and V.G. García

Departamento de Informática, Universidad de Oviedo, Spain
{arias, fran, daniel, xabiel}@atc.uniovi.es, victor@correo.uniovi.es

Abstract. A key issue in any system for distribution of continuous media-on-demand is the capacity of the system with regard to quality of the service specifications, that is, the number of simultaneous streams the system can provide until degradation of the quality of reproduction and interactivity perceived by the users. This work presents the evaluation of interactive video-on-demand systems, with special attention to limitations caused by the video server. The evaluation is based on a set of metrics designed to determine the number of streams a video server can support under specific requirements of the quality of the service as perceived by the users. To validate the utility of these metrics, a prototype of a news-on-demand service has been built and the load for this kind of systems has been characterised. In addition, a load generator which emulates the concurrent access of several users to the system has been built. The evaluation establishes the relationship between the video server limitations and the quality of the service perceived by the users.

1 Introduction

Recent advances in computer and telecommunication areas have made several remote multimedia services through LANs or Internet viable. Some examples are tele-education, tele-working, digital libraries, video-on-demand and entertainment services. Examples of commercial video-on-demand services are movies-on-demand and news-on-demand, where the user can interact with the streams through the typical fast-forward, rewind, pause and stop functions. Thera are two main factors that define the capacity of this kind of system: the service capacity or number of simultaneous streams the system can serve, and the quality of the service perceived by users, both at reproduction of streams and inter-activity levels. The greater the number of streams the system can serve, and the higher the quality of reproduction and short response times to interactive functions, the more economically feasible it becomes.

The principle elements of the system that limit its capacity are the video server and the communication network. In this work, the influence of the video server, which provides news-on-demand service, is studied using a communication network with sufficient bandwith to carry all the traffic without significative

F. Boavida et al. (Eds.): IDMS/PROMS 2002, LNCS 2515, pp. 15–25, 2002.

additional delays. Thus, the server's influence on the behaviour of the system can be isolated. The main goal is to design a set of metrics to measure and relate the video server capacity and the quality of the service as perceived by the users. These metrics help in dimensioning the server capacity in function of the required quality of the service. The utility of the metrics is validated through experimental analysis of a service prototype.

2   Related Work

General and valuable references for distribution of continuous media and video-on-demand systems are [9] (continuous media-on-demand) [18] (streaming video) [15] (interactive video-on-demand systems) and [10] (quality of service in networked multimedia systems).

Interest in the quality of the service provided by multimedia-on-demand systems has increased over the last years. Examples are [3], which studies the design of this kind of systems with quality of service (QoS) guarantees and [13], which defines a protocol to improve the quality of presentation by controlling the quality of the service in the network, based on the properties of the multimedia flows.

The main contribution of this work is the proposal of a set of metrics as support for analysis of interactive systems, and the way they relate server capacity to the quality of the service perceived by users. In this specific context, related works only address the problem partially. In [17] an empirical study of video performance across the internet is developed, also using a set of metrics for evaluation. Nevertheless, the metrics are design to study the performance of the network, not of the server. In [12] adaptive multimedia content delivery as a way to achieve scalability is studied and a set of metrics to evaluate server load is developed. Drawbacks in this case are the low weight of multimedia content in the study and the poor set of quality of the service metrics. Nor do these two works consider metrics of interactivity, very important in systems like news-on-demand. In [16] the problem of interactivity is addressed, analysing the performance of video servers under initial delay bounds. Nevertheless, the study is based on theoretical models of the server (not in measurement and metrics) and does not consider other quality of the service properties.

3   Prototype of Service

News-on-demand is one of the most popular on-demand services. To built a prototype representative of real systems, one of the most important news-on-demand services in Internet has been selected as a reference, the BBC Audio/Video News [5].

The synthetic prototype implemented emulates a daily service to which 50 news items are incorporated each day. The initial version of the prototype contains news for one week. The news items have varying popularity and consequently different probability of access. The news items are classified according

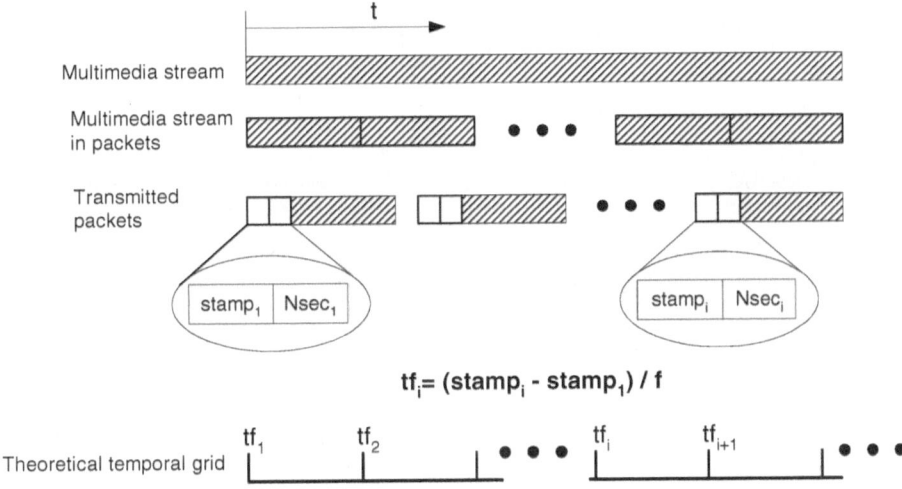

Fig. 1. Theoretical temporal grid of the stream

to their length: a) Short (30 sec.-1 min., 6% of total), b) Medium (1min. -3:30 min., 84% of total) or c) Long (3:30 min.-1 hour, 10% of total). News is available at three transmission speeds: a) Low (28 kbps. maximum), b) Medium (28-56 kbps.) and c) High (more than 56 kbps.). Frame size is always 176x144, so transmission speed relates directly to frame speed (8-30 fps). For all the news, the video server stores streams coded for the three possible transmission speeds.

4   Quality of the Service Metrics

To evaluate the quality of the service, several measures are taken in the client. These measures are used to calculate a set of metrics of the quality of the service that help in evaluating video server capacity.

Multimedia information has to be prepared to be emitted and reproduced continuously and in real-time (*streaming*). As shown in Figure 1, each multimedia stream must be divided in packets for transmission. Information is added into the packets to properly place them in the stream for a correct reproduction in the client. *Streaming* implies that packets are emitted in the same order, and with the same intervals, as used in normal reproduction. This temporal behaviour may be partially lost at reproduction, and so diminish the quality of reproduction, due to emission delays in the server or transmission delays in the network.

The metrics used to measure the quality of the service are based on two fields carried with each packet of the stream transmitted: the sequence number and the timestamp. The sequence number marks the order in which the packet was emitted from the video server. The first sequence number is generated randomly to assure that a client can differentiate between two streams from different

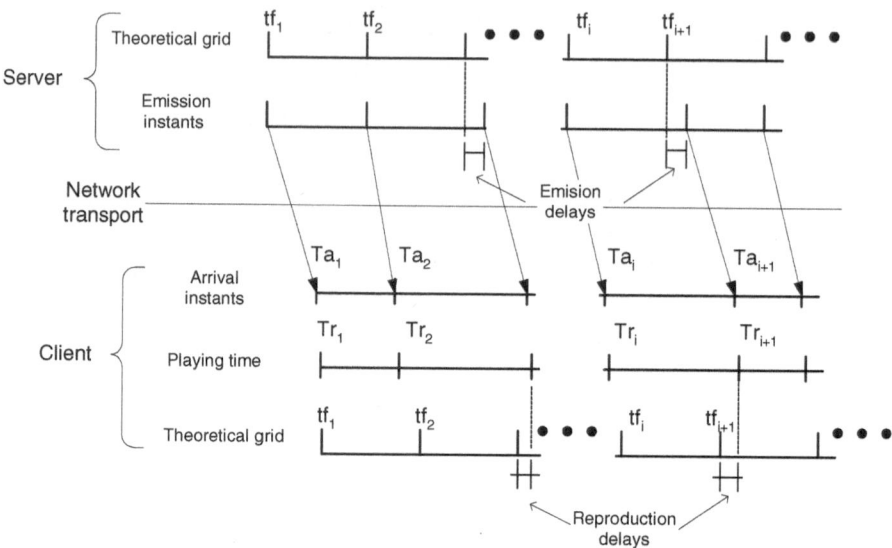

Fig. 2. Multimedia stream reproduction

sources, and is increased monotonically with each packet. It is possible to use the sequence number to calculate the total number of packets emitted by a multimedia server. The timestamp of the packet indicates its place in the temporal ordination of the stream. The stamp is calculated using the sampling frequency at which the multimedia stream was created.

The timestamp places each packet in its temporal position in the stream. These positions form the *theoretical temporal grid* of emission or playing of the stream. The more the emission/playing of the stream conforms to the theoretical temporal grid, the better the quality of the service obtained. The temporal position of the ith packet in the stream is denoted with tf_i and is calculated as follows:

$$tf_i = \frac{stamp_i - stamp_1}{f} \qquad (1)$$

where $stamp_1$ and $stamp_i$ are the timestamps of the first and ith packets respectively, and f is the sampling frequency.

4.1   Metrics of Quality of Reproduction

Using the value of tf_i of the ith packet, and the arrival time, Ta_i, of this packet, several metrics of quality of reproduction of the stream can be defined.

Percentage of delayed packets: This shows how well the stream received conforms to the theoretical temporal grid (Fig. 2). To obtain this metric, the playing time of the ith packet, Tr_i, is calculated, as follows:

$$Tr_i = Ta_1 + (tf_i - tf_1) \tag{2}$$

where Ta_1 is the arrival time of the first packet and tf_i and tf_1 come from (1). When $Ta_i > Tr_i$ the packet does not arrive in time to be played so there is a delay in the reproduction of the stream. For each packet the delay is calculated with

$$D_i = Tr_i - Ta_i \tag{3}$$

When $D_i < 0$ there are discontinuities in the stream. Based on the delay of each packet, if N_D is the number of packets delayed, it is possible to calculate the total percentage of delayed packets, D, using the total number of packets received, N_r.

$$D = \frac{N_D}{N_r} * 100 \tag{4}$$

Mean packet delay: This is the arithmetic mean of the delays:

$$\bar{R} = \frac{\sum D_i}{N_r} \tag{5}$$

Percentage of packets lost: If N_e is the number of packets emitted, this metric is obtained with

$$L = \frac{N_e - N_r}{N_e} * 100$$

Number of client buffer reloads: The client buffer tries to compensate for the transmission delays suffered by the packets. The buffer stores a number of packets previous to their playing times. When delays are too long, the packet to play can not be in the buffer. In this case, there is a *buffer failure* and it must be reloaded completely. The greater the number of reloads, the worse the quality of reproduction of the stream. When the client has a buffer, the new playing time of each packet (see Fig. 3) is

$$Tr_{ib} = Ta_{lb} + (tf_i - tf_{1b}) \tag{6}$$

where Ta_{lb} is the arrival time of the packet which fills the buffer in the last complete reload, and tf_{1b} is the temporal position of the first packet to arrive at the buffer in the last reload. This packet will have the playing time: $Tr_{lb} = Tr_{1b} + BT$, where Tr_{1b} is the playing time of the first packet in the buffer and BT is the length of the buffer. To determine when a buffer failure is taking place, the arrival time of each packet must be checked:

$$Fb = Tr_{ib} - Ta_i \tag{7}$$

When $Fb < 0$ there is a buffer failure and the buffer must be reloaded.

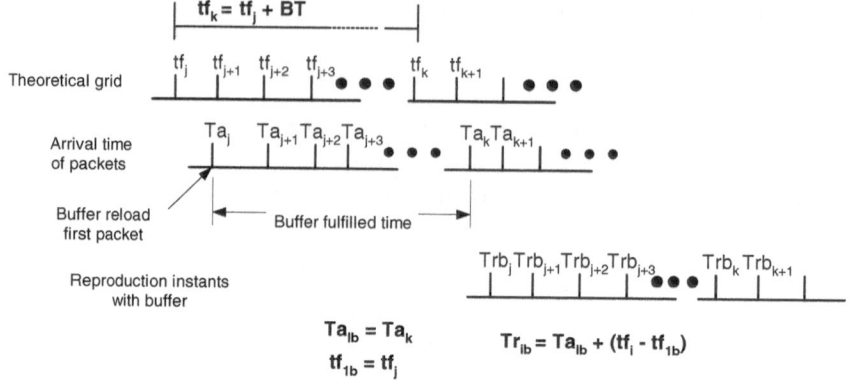

Fig. 3. Multimedia stream reproduction with buffer

4.2 Metrics of Quality of Interactivity

These metrics measure the quality of the communication established between client and server, and whether the server load can affect the client's interaction with the stream (pause, forward, rewind, etc). The metrics are:

Mean start response time: This metric quantifies the time a user has to wait between a request for the start of a stream and confirmation of the transmission from the server. If this length becomes too long, the client is often led to abandon the reproduction.

Mean interaction response time: This measures the waiting time between client interaction (pause, stop, rewind, etc) and the response by the server.

5 Metrics of Server Capacity

The aim of these metrics is to measure the load of the server with an increased number of client requests.

5.1 Throughput

Streams served per hour: This counts the number of streams emitted by the server in a given period of time.

5.2 Resource Utilization

By monitoring the server, the load of its resources (CPU, hard disk, network) and the utilization of each of them can be measured.

CPU utilization: This is the percentage of server processor utilization.

Hard disk utilization: This is the rate between the disk blocks read from the hard disk and the maximum number of disk blocks that can be read.

Network utilization: This is the percentage of network utilization measured in the server network interface.

6   Workload Characterization

Previous works has been used to characterize the workload. In [4] the streaming workload generated by a large university is compared to traditional web objects. In [11], [1] and [2] analysis of the workload generated on educational multimedia servers in European and American universities are presented. In [8] a tool to specify characteristics of the access to multimedia information is presented. The characteristics include popularity of the objects, temporal correlation among requests, seasonal patterns of access and the duration of user sessions.

In the service model proposed in this paper the user can request as much news as he wants. The choice of news is made randomly among all available news. The access probability to each piece of news is driven by the Zipf law [19], which establishes that access frequency is proportional to the popularity, and the more recent the news, the greater its popularity.

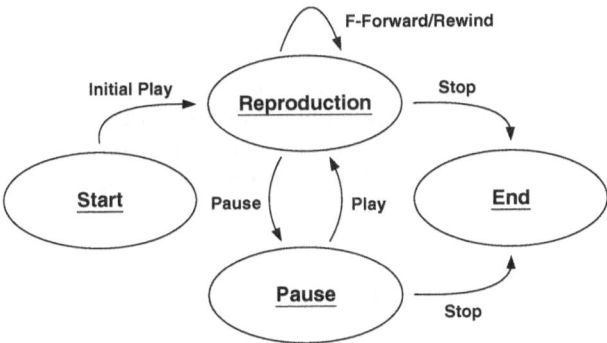

Fig. 4. User interactions

Table 1. Probability of user actions

Action	After pause	Rest
F-Forward	0	0.2
Rewind	0	0.2
Reproduction	0.7	0
Pause	0	0.3
Stop	0.3	0.3

In the Figure 4 the state diagram of user behaviour is shown. The diagram shows the possible states of a client and the interactions of the client with the server that make the client change state. Table 1 shows the probabilities of each interaction. According to [8], the probability of a transaction lasting from the initial play to the end state is established at 0.5: half of the requests are abandoned before completion due to lack of interest on the part of the user.

Each one of the client states and the thinking time before the selection of a new stream has a length which follows constant statistical distributions. These distributions are based on the work presented in [8] and are shown in Table 2.

Table 2. Statistical distributions.

State	Distribution	Short stream parameters	Long stream parameters
Initial Play	Exponential	mean=100 sec	mean=100 sec
Other Play	Exponential	mean=100 sec	mean=420 sec
Pause	Weibull	shape=0.5 scale=40	shape=0.5 scale=120
Thinking time	Exponential	mean=10 sec	

Although a Pareto distribution to the playing times is proposed in [8], it was observed that this distribution does not fit the characteristics of the service well: the length of the reproductions obtained are too short. The playing times were therefore adjusted by a exponential with a mean of 100 seconds. To best emulate the behaviour of the clients a differentiation was introduced when the clients ask for a long-play stream. In these cases the parameters of the distributions are slightly modified as shown in Table 2. Obviously, this differentiation is not necessary in the case of the thinking time.

7   Experimental Procedure

The experimental procedure was carried out with two computers, one of them working as the news server and the other playing the role of multiple clients by running a specific emulation tool. The computers were linked by a dedicated 100 Mb/s Fast-Ethernet. Measurements were taken in both computers: in the server using the sar system utility [7] and in the client using the specific tool built.

The video server software used for news distribution under *streaming* technology is the *Darwin Streaming Server* [6], which is free distribution software from Apple for platforms based on Intel processors. This server uses RTSP (*Real Time Streaming Protocol*) [14].

8   Current Results and Future Work

Some results have been obtained from a preliminary analysis of the prototype, without considering the use of buffers in the clients. Figure 5 shows the values of some metrics as a function of the number of users simultaneously connected to the server. A curve is generated for each transmission speed.

The quality of interactivity (Figure 5a) shows how the response times of server to user actions increase progressively with the number of users. Figure 5c

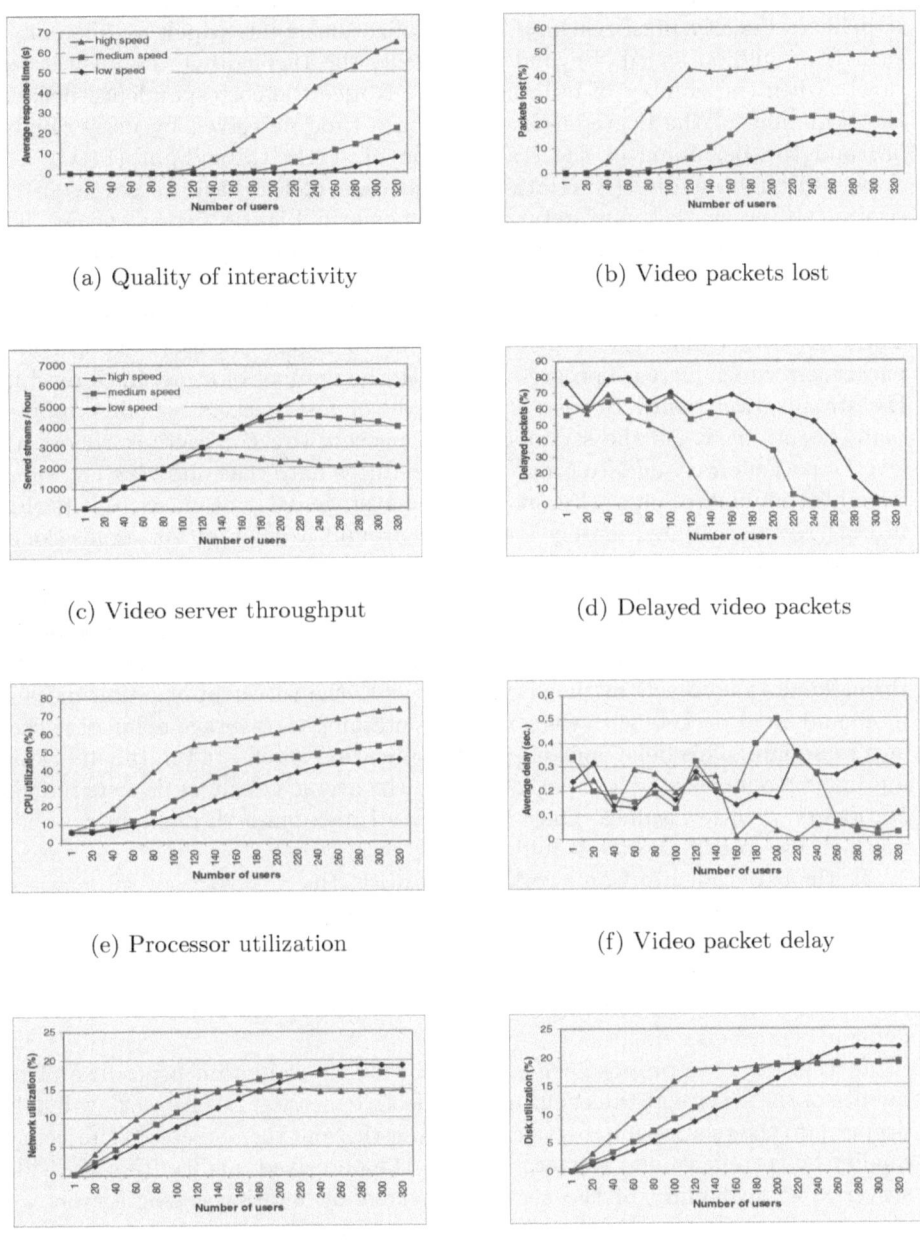

(a) Quality of interactivity

(b) Video packets lost

(c) Video server throughput

(d) Delayed video packets

(e) Processor utilization

(f) Video packet delay

(g) Network interface utilization

(h) Disk utilization

Fig. 5. Metric values for prototype

shows the evolution of server throughput as a function of the number of users. It behaves linearly until reaching the stabilization point, which is different for each transmission speed. Beyond that point, the throughput diminishes very slowly when the number of users increases. Notice the correspondence between the beginning of the degradation of response time perceived by users (Figure 5a) and the beginning of the stabilization of server throughput (Figure 5c). Server throughput directly relates to utilization of the basic resources of the server (processor, disk and network), as shown in Figures 5e, 5f and 5g. The utilisation levels of these resources remain approximately stationary beyond the stabilization point, but none of them show a utilization level near saturation.

The quality of reproduction corresponding to video is shown in Figure 5, the audio relatives being very similar. According to Figure 5b, users experiment a packet loss which increase progressively with the number of users, until reaching the stabilization point. Beyond it, the level of lost packets remains approximately stationary. As the server discards packets (by not sending them), the level of packets arriving late progressively reduces until reaching very low values for a high number of users (Figure 5d). The average delay of video packets (Figure 5f) remains approximately stationary around a value of 200 milliseconds, independently of the number of users.

It can be concluded that the server application (Darwing server) does not go beyond a certain level of throughput, even if the hardware resources do not reach saturation levels. Just before reaching the maximum throughput, as the throughput (load level) of the server increases, the server application discards more and more packets with the goal of maintaining the average delay of packets at a minimum. This behaviour of server application is reflected in the metrics as a progressive increase in lost packets, while the average delay of packets remains stationary with low values. Once the point of maximum throughput has been reached, the loss of packets stabilizes.

In the experimental framework of this work, the prototype of the news-on-demand service used has capacity for: a) 120 users for high speed, b) 200 users for medium speed, and c) 260 users for low speed, while maintaining an acceptable quality of the service. With these numbers of supported users using economical personal computers as servers, the economic feasibility of interactive video-on-demand services is evident.

In this work we propose a measurement-based evaluation procedure of the quality of the service at the client using objective metrics. Future work will delve deeper into the relationship between these metrics and the perceived (subjective) quality by the client, and ways to improve the perceived quality from the video server. The scalability of the service provided by multiprocessor servers and clusters will also be explored.

References

1. S. Acharya, B. Smith, and P. Parnes. Characterizing user access to videos on the world wide web. In *ACM/SPIE Multimedia Computing and Networking*, 1998. http://citeseer.nj.nec.com/acharya98experiment.html.

2. J.M. Almeida, J. Krueger, D.L. Eager, and M.K. Vernon. Analysis of educational media server workloads. In *Workshop on Network and Operating System Support (NOSSDAV)*, 2001. http://citeseer.nj.nec.com/493220.html.

3. M. Buddhikot, G. Parulkar, and R. Gopalakrishnan. Scalable multimedia-on-demand via world-wideweb (www) with qos guarantees. In *NOSSDAV*, April 1996. citeseer.nj.nec.com/buddhikot96scalable.html.

4. M. Chesire, A. Wolman, G. Voelker, and H. Levy. Measurement and analysis of a streaming media workload. In *USENIX Symposium on Internet Technologies and Systems (USITS)*, San Francisco, CA, USA, March 2001. http://citeseer.nj.nec.com/chesire01measurement.html.

5. British Broadcast Corporation. Bbc news - audiovideo section. News-on-demand service, 2002. http://news.bbc.co.uk.

6. Apple Computer Inc. Open source streaming server, 2002. http://www.publicsource.apple.com/projects/streaming/.

7. Imperial Technology Inc. Testing unix system performance. White paper, 2002. http://www.imperialtech.com/technology_whitepapers.htm.

8. S. Jin and A. Bestavros. A generator of internet streaming media objects and workloads. Technical report, Boston University. Computer Science Department, October 2001. http://citeseer.nj.nec.com/jin01generator.html.

9. Computer Journal. Continuous media on demand. Collection of Articles, September 2001.

10. K. Nahrstedt and R. Steinmetz. Resource management in networked multimedia systems. *IEEE Computer*, 28(5):52–63, 1995. http://citeseer.nj.nec.com/nahrstedt95resource.html.

11. J. Padhye and J. Kurose. An empirical study of client interactions with a continuous-media courseware server. In *Workshop on Network and Operating System Support (NOSSDAV)*, 1998. http://citeseer.nj.nec.com/padhye97empirical.html.

12. R. Pradhan. Adaptive multimedia content delivery for scalable web servers. Master's thesis, Worcester Polytechnic Institute, Computer Science Department, May 2001. http://www.cs.wpi.edu/~claypool/ms/web-load/.

13. L. Rojas-Córdenas, E. Chaput, L. Dairaine, P. Sónac, and M. Diaz. Transport of video over partial order connections. *Computer Networks*, 31(7):709–725, April 1999. http://citeseer.nj.nec.com/316559.html.

14. H. Schulzrinne, A. Rao, and R. Lanphier. Real time streaming protocol (rtsp). The Internet Society (RFC 2326), April 1998. http://citeseer.nj.nec.com/schulzrinne98real.html.

15. T.P.J. To and B. Hamidzadeh. *Interactive Video-On-Demand Systems*. Kluwer, 1998.

16. S. Tsao, Y. Huang, and J. Ding. Performance analysis of video storage server under initial delay bounds. *Journal of Systems Architecture*, 46(2):163–179, 2000.

17. Y. Wang, M. Claypool, and et al. An empirical study of realvideo performance across the internet. In *ACM SIGCOMM Internet Measurement Workshop*, 2001. http://citeseer.nj.nec.com/wang01empirical.html.

18. D. Wu and et al. Streaming video over the internet: Approaches and directions. *IEEE Transactions on Circuits and Systems for Video Technology*, 11(1):1–20, February 2001. http://citeseer.nj.nec.com/wu01streaming.html.

19. G.K. Zipf. *The human behaviour and the principle of least effort*. Addison Wesley, 1949.

When FEC Speed up Data Access
in P2P Networks

J. Lacan, L. Lancérica, and L. Dairaine

ENSICA,
1, Place Emile Blouin
31052 Toulouse cedex 5, France
{Jerome.Lacan, Laurent.Lancerica, Laurent.Dairaine}@ensica.fr

Abstract. Peer to peer (P2P) Network is a high level logical network architecture build over end-user nodes interconnected by a physical network infrastructure. The performance in data access over the P2P networks is one of the main issues because the downloading of data is often the longest phase of P2P usage by end-user. In the present effort, we propose an approach based on Forward Error Correction (FEC) to speed-up data access into P2P networks. The main idea is to use FEC to dilute the information over the peers. This dilution allows a greater and flexible choice among downloadable disseminated parts of the FEC-encoded data and then enhances the speed up of the transfer. A case study illustrates the technique and a performance evaluation shows that for the same amount of information disseminated into the P2P network, this solution is more efficient in terms of data access performance compared to classical file replications.

1 Introduction

The popularity of P2P file sharing applications offers new prospects to Internet end-users. In this context, users can move from the simple consumer state to the active state of publisher, sharing their contents through the network. Peer to peer (P2P) Network is a high level logical network architecture build over end-user nodes interconnected by a physical network infrastructure. Main P2P systems services are storage, finding and download of data. The main characteristic of P2P network is to avoid any centralized point, allowing the building of new distributed services that are not built on classical models such as master-slave, consumer-supplier or client-server.

The main benefits of P2P networks are to enhance the utilization of information, bandwidth, and computing resources [7]. The classical client-server model reduces the information resource usage because it makes difficult to find all the information from centralised servers. Allowing peers to collaborate in such a way to find the information is a decentralised solution avoiding those difficulties. The centralisation of information onto servers that attract so many requests from clients introduces bottleneck at network and system level, leading to the building of large web farms and broadband network resources. The dissemination of information over a set of peers allows distributing the load over the physical network and the end-systems. Bandwidth resources can be also enhanced because the P2P systems may introduce high level routing function allowing speed up data access by load balancing or other

F. Boavida et al. (Eds.): IDMS/PROMS 2002, LNCS 2515, pp. 26-37, 2002.

approaches. Finally, computing resources are shared over the P2P network allowing e.g. a file to be replicated over a big number of peers.

As a result, numerous research level issues are related to the building of such a system. Scalability, fault tolerance, authentification, routing or data finding are examples of hot topics associated to this domain. The performance in data access over the P2P networks is also a crucial aspect because the downloading of data is often the longest phase of P2P usage by end-user. The contribution of this paper concerns this last issue.

A classical approach in this domain consists in enhancing the localization of replicated copies [1] [11] and downloading one them from the closest server. In the present effort, we propose a complementary approach consisting in using these optimized searching techniques over a set of Forward Error Correction (FEC) encoded blocks, to speed-up the data access into the P2P network. The FEC usage allows the information to be diluted over a number of different data blocks. Those blocks being disseminated over the P2P network, the FEC properties induce that only subparts of the total set of blocks are needed to reconstitute the original information. This allows the client to better choose the closest blocks among the multiple FEC blocks copies in such a way to reconstitute the original information. We show in this paper that for the same amount of information disseminated into the P2P network, this solution is more efficient in terms of data access performance compared to classical file replications.

The paper is structured as follows. The next section proposes a related work onto the FEC usage into P2P networks. Forward Error encoding is firstly described, and main applications are given in the context of P2P networks. The next section explains how the FEC are used into the P2P network. The technique is illustrated into a specific case study. Section 4 presents a performance evaluation, based both on analytical and simulation study. Section 5 proposes concluding remarks.

2   Related Works

2.1   Forward Error Correction (FEC)

The error correcting codes or Forward Error Correction (FEC) techniques are a classical mechanism to protect the information against errors or losses in transmissions. The principle of FEC is to add redundancy to the transmitted information, so that it is still possible for receivers to recover the whole transmitted data, even after experiencing error transmissions.

The main class of FEC used in network domain is the block codes. These codes consider a group of k packets and compute n-k redundancy packets. In an erasure channel, *i.e.* a channel where the positions of the errors are known, the fundamental property of FEC permits to the receiver to reconstruct the k initial packets as soon as it receives k packets among the n emitted ones. Note that this property holds only for maximum distance separable (MDS) codes, *e.g.* Reed-Solomon codes [12][13]. Other classical codes used in erasure channels, e.g. Tornado codes [2], need generally more than k received packets.

FEC are used in several kinds of applications: wireless transmissions (e.g., satellite, cellular phone) data storage (e.g., CD-ROM, DVD.) or computer memory (e.g., RDRAM). In networking context, FEC are classically used at lower layers (hardware) in detection/correction mode. In higher layers, similar software techniques such as CRC or checksums are used to detect corrupted packets. Since few years, with the improvements of the performance of personal computers, it is possible to implement encoding and decoding of the FEC in software at user level (i.e., transport or application layer). For example, most of reliable multicast transport protocols use FEC [16]. In data storage area, FEC are used to protect data against the failures of storage devices. Small scratches on CD-ROM are corrected by FEC directly implemented on the encoded information. Failures of hard disks can be protected by FEC-based systems such as RAID technology [10].

2.2   Use of FEC in the Context of Distributed Storage

A classical concept on fault-tolerant systems consists in replicating data on several servers. FEC can improve the reliability of these systems by encoding the data, splitting up the encoded data and distributing the fragments over various servers [4]. The basic idea is that a redundant fragment situated on a server can compensate for the loss of any other fragment (of same size) due to the failure of another server. From a fault-tolerance point of view, the use of FEC reduces "mean time of failures by many orders of magnitude compared to replication systems with similar storage and bandwidth requirements" [17].

In the Internet context, the replication is used to speedup data access in mirror sites. A FEC-based alternative is proposed in [3] with a parallel access scheme for open-loop multicast distributions. The data are encoded on each mirror site with Tornado codes and are distributed in multicast mode. A user receives FEC-encoded parts of the data from several servers and is able to reconstruct the data as soon as it obtains a sufficient number of different packets. However, this solution can only be applied in particular contexts (such as software distribution) and presents several drawbacks such as, for example, the ending of the connections or the management of the network congestions.

3   Using FEC to Enhance Downloading Performances

3.1   Context

P2P files sharing systems have very specific characteristics compared to classical distributed storage systems. An important point concerns the potential number of peers (e.g., up to 1.5 million users online at any time for Kazaa System in May 2002 [8]). Moreover, these peers strongly differ from storage system concerning the lifetime in the P2P network, the available throughput and the quantity of stored data. These parameters can vary between three and five orders of magnitude across the peers in the systems [15]. In this context, the design of decentralized systems which takes in account all these properties is a difficult problem.

Our proposal is particularly well suited in this heterogeneous and moving context. Indeed, the usage of FEC allows enhancing the dissemination of the (parts of) files in the P2P networks. In addition to an enhancement of the global reliability of the data (like in distributed storage area [17]), this dissemination amazingly permits to improve the downloading performance of the users.

This section defines the use of FEC in such system and presents on a case study the basic principle which permits to speed up the data access.

3.2 Principle

A P2P system uses a peering architecture that offers the support for various P2P services such as file sharing between the various peers. Examples of such system are Napster, Gnutella, Kazaa or Edonkey [5][6][8][9]. Using these systems, each node is able to determine its peers and to localize data over the peer network. The peering algorithms allow furthermore determining the effective cost, in terms of bandwidth, for transferring data directly between two considered peers ([8][9]).

Our approach is based on the following method. Before the publication, the shared file is cut into n blocks. These various blocks are then FEC-encoded (see Fig. 1).

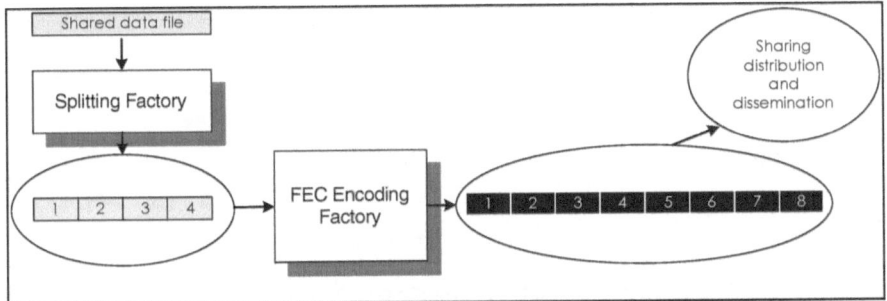

Fig. 1. Encoding and sharing mechanism of the data.

The shared files then become a sets of n+m blocks. Depending on FEC encoding technique, the n first blocks can or not be the n original blocks. In first case, they just result from the original file splitting. The m next blocks integrate the redundancy introduced by the FEC encoding. In the second case, the original information contained into the n blocks is diluted into the n+m blocks. The last phase of publication is the distribution of the various blocks over the P2P network. This distribution is ensured using a native service of the P2P architecture. This dissemination algorithm can be based either on the natural dissemination due to the user downloads between the peers or on a more specific dissemination algorithm of the P2P system. However, we are aware that this second solution, which is more efficient, can induce additional bandwidth usage.

Considering the various blocks disseminated into the network, downloading a complete file is equivalent to download any of n distinct blocks among the n+m ones. As there are greater choices between the different blocks to get, the availability and the robustness of the system is increased. When these blocks are disseminated over the P2P network, the searching service helps to determine the closest ones by considering a certain cost function (e.g., the biggest bandwidth). Then, the n closest blocks are downloaded in a classical way. The original data file can be finally obtained from the decoding of those n blocks. The next section proposes a concrete illustration of the performance gain obtained using such a technique.

3.3 Case Study

To illustrate the concept and the benefits resulting from a P2P file sharing system using FEC mechanism, we present a case study based on a (very simple) P2P network. In this case study, the file transfer between two peers in ensured by a direct connection with a given cost. For sake of simplicity, we assume that the P2P structure is organized such as this cost is proportional to the total number of P2P hops between the two nodes in the peer tree. This cost does not take into account the time due to the localization algorithm. Moreover this inferred time is usually negligible compared to the downloading time. The network structure is fixed and different blocks or files distributions schemes are compared according to their downloading cost (see Fig. 2).

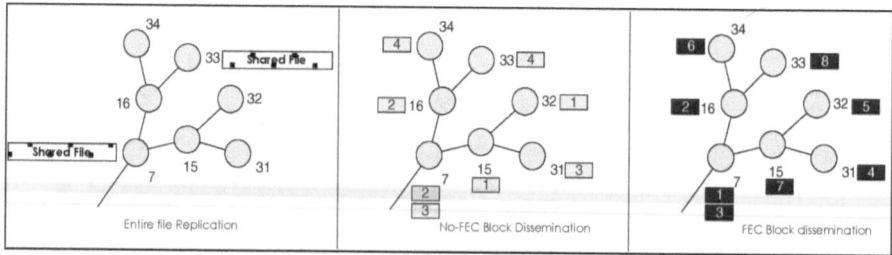

Fig. 2. Simple example to compute cost to recover entire file

We suppose the node 31 wants to recover the file.

The first approach, named *Entire File Replication*, consists in keeping the entire file which is simply replicated into 2 random nodes of the network (e.g., node 33 and node 7). When split into blocks (see next approach), the considered file is supposed to be cut in 4 blocks of the same size. Then the cost to download the file is equivalent to download 4 blocks situated at 2 hops (i.e., from node 7 to node 31), then $C = 4*2 = 8$.

This approach can be compared to the *No-FEC Block Dissemination* that considers the same file split up into 4 blocks. In this case, the 4 different blocks are duplicated 2 times so that the total load is always 8 blocks. In this case, 1block is at 0 hop, 1 block is at 1 hop, 1 block is at 2 hops, and 1 block is at 4 hops then $C = 1*0 + 1*1 + 1*2 + 1*4 = 7$.

In the last approach, the *FEC Block Dissemination* there is still 8 blocks disseminated over the P2P network, but these blocks are FEC encoded. This encoding permits to choose any 4 over the 8 blocks of data, allowing a better choice of Peers. *As a result, the FEC Block Dissemination* cost is: 1block is at 0 hop, 1 block is at 1 hop, and 2 blocks are at 2 hops then $C = 1*0 + 1*1 + 2*2 = 5$

The results obtained in the example of Fig. 2 illustrates that the use of FEC can reduce the downloading cost for downloading a file. We are conscious that some P2P systems allow parallel connections to download the various blocks. In this case, the file downloading cost is now greatly influenced by the block the most expensive to download. In a perfect parallel context (bottleneck-disjoint), the *no-FEC Block dissemination* cost would be equal to 4. This cost must be compared to the *FEC Block Dissemination* cost equal to 2. Note that in the remaining of this article, we only consider serial (no parallel) downloading.

In order to generalize these results, we then consider the topology illustrated in Fig. 3.

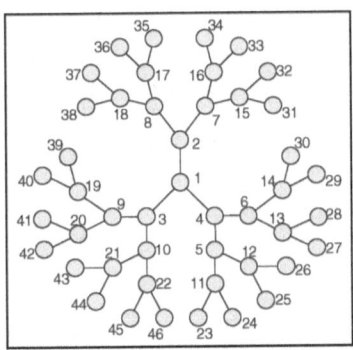

Fig. 3. The simple network topology used in the case study

Given this topology and cost computation technique, let us compare the downloading cost of a file for the different approaches. We consider that the file is split up into 10 blocks and that the rate of the FEC code is ½. Then, each encoded file is a set of 20 blocks. One will consider furthermore that each of these blocks is duplicated 5 times to constitute a set of 100 blocks to be spread in the network. This replication is operated randomly among all nodes. This cost is compared to two other approaches. 10,000 tests are processed to obtain a qualitative average.

– *FEC Block Dissemination*: **File downloading average cost per peer : 13.99**
  - 10 blocks file, FEC encoding rate ½, each block duplicate 5 times : total 100 blocks
– *No-FEC Block Dissemination* : **File downloading average cost per peer: 17.03**
  - 10 blocks file, no FEC encoding, each block duplicate 10 times : total 100 blocks
– *Entire file Replication* : **File downloading average cost per peer : 16.85**
  - 10 blocks file, no FEC encoding, each block duplicate 10 times : total 100 blocks

These early results show that on average, the use of a system using FEC increases (up to 17%) the access speed to the data shared in a P2P network with regard to classical approaches.

Furthermore the use of the FEC increases the presence probability of a file in the network by offering besides an improved reliability. The following section proposes a more general and realistic model to quantify the performance obtained by a P2P system implementing such a FEC technique.

4 Data Access Performance Evaluation

4.1 Problem Modeling

The main objective of the current section is to quantify the improvement of using the technique presented in the previous paragraph. We propose a simple model allowing computing the cost to get an entire file over the three dissemination approaches (a) *Entire File Replication*, (b) *no-FEC Block Dissemination* and (c) *FEC-block Dissemination*. This cost refers to the downloading time of the file. Note that the time needed for the localization of the data is not taken into account because it is usually much lower than the downloading time. However, it must be remarked that the localization of the different blocks (approaches (b) and (c)) will take generally more time than the localization of a single file.

The reference cost concerns the entire file replication cost. In this approach, the file is entirely replicated r times over the network. The cost C then can be computed from the following expression.

$$C = \min_{j=1..r}(C_j) \tag{1}$$

Where C_j is the cost of getting the jth replication of the entire file.

The *no-FEC Block Dissemination* supposes the file to be split up into n blocks $b_1, b_2, ... b_n$; each block is supposed to have the same size. In this experience, the cost of getting the entire file consists in summing the costs to download each of the n blocks. If r replicas of the blocks are disseminated into the peer network, C becomes:

$$C = \sum_{i=1}^{n} \min_{j=1..r}(c_{i,j}) \tag{2}$$

Where $c_{i,j}$ is the cost of download of the jth replica of the ith block.

We finally consider the *FEC-Block Dissemination*. The n original blocks constituting the file become now $n + m$ blocks due to FEC redundancy. Getting the file consists now in downloading the n distinct blocks of minimum costs over the $n + m$ blocks. If the $n + m$ blocks are replicated r' times over the network, if we define $m_i = \min_{j=1..r'}(c_{i,j})$, for $i = 1, ..., m + n$, and the function

$f : \{1, ..., n + m\} \rightarrow \{1, ..., n + m\}$ such as $m_{f(1)} < m_{f(2)} < ... < m_{f(n+m)}$, then the cost to get the entire file is given:

$$C = \sum_{i=1}^{n} m_{f(i)} \tag{3}$$

To be fair with the previous approaches in term of data storage load over the P2P network, we assume the total number of blocks disseminated into the network to be constant, then:

$$r' = \frac{(n * r)}{(n + m)} \tag{4}$$

4.2 Simulation Study

Implementation. The simple model given in the previous section has been implemented. The main idea is to consider 3 arrays of size *r* for *entire file dissemination* and of size *n.r* and *n.m.r* 'for respectively *no-FEC block dissemination* and *FEC-block dissemination*. The arrays are filled by random numbers following a certain probability law. Each value of the arrays represents the cost of getting the corresponding block (or file for the first array). Equations (1) and (2) allow an easy and quick computing of the download cost for the entire file. Each experience is done 100.000 times and gain percentages compared of the two last approaches are compared to the first one.

Probability Law. The characteristics of the probability law are a central issue for the last model. Indeed, depending on the probability law, the model previously presented can be adapted to any kinds of networks. In order to build a probability law as close to the reality as possible, we make two assumptions:
– the delay of the transmission between two peers is proportional to their distance;
– the distribution of the peers in the world is uniform.
It follows that the number of peers contained in a given surface is proportional to the area of this surface. By considering a particular peer, the number of peers which are at a distance greater than d and less than d+1 corresponds to the area of the corresponding ring (see Fig. 4).

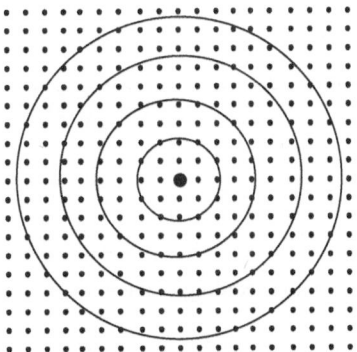

Fig. 4. Distribution of the peers

It may be observed that the area of the ring bounded by r and r+1, denoted by $A(R_{r,r+1})$ grows linearly, i.e., $A(R_{r,r+1}) - A(R_{r-1,r}) = 2\Pi$, for every r. On Fig. 4, the number of points included in $R_{0,1}$, $R_{1,2}$, $R_{2,3}$, $R_{3,4}$ is respectively 13, 44, 72 and 104. On this example, it can be verified that the number of points is increased of roughly 30 at each step.

Therefore, in order to randomly generate peers, we fix a maximum distance *d* between the central peer and the other peers (this distance corresponds to the radius of the greatest disk) and we consider that the discrete random variable X used in the simulations is such that $\Pr(X = x)$ corresponds to the probability that a peer randomly chosen is in $R_{x-1,x}$, i.e. $\Pr(X = x) = (2x-1)/d^2$, for $x = 1,...,d$.

This distribution is used to fill the costs arrays of the model implementation.

Impact on number of blocks onto the performance gain. Model implementation is used to evaluate the gain of splitting up the file into a variable number of blocks using or not FEC (from 1 to 100 blocks). For each simulation, we compute the cost of getting an entire file replicated 10 times. The mean cost is computed over 100.000 simulations.

The first curve results from the cost comparison between getting the entire file when it is entirely replicated 10 times in the network (*entire file replication*), and when it is split up into a number of blocks, those blocks being replicated 10 times (*No FEC block dissemination*).

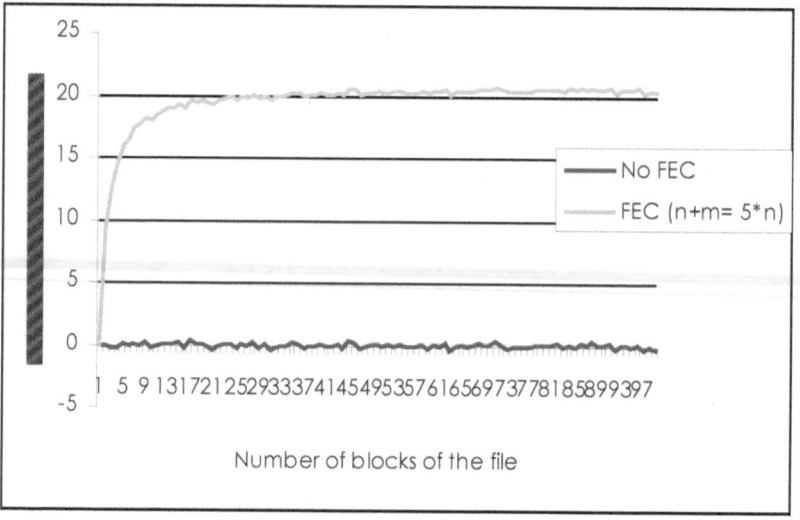

Fig. 5. Performance gain according to the number of blocks of the file.

We first notice in Fig. 5 that the *No FEC* curve shows that no performance gain is obtained when using a simple No-FEC Block dissemination. This result is not amazing and the equivalence of the two approaches can be mathematically proved (if parallel connections are not used).

The second curve presents the cost gain when using Bloc-FEC dissemination technique versus File Replication. The FEC redundancy rate used in this simulation is 5 FEC blocks for 1 original block (n+m=5*n). Due to this redundancy, each of the resulting blocks is only replicated 2 times (see Equation (4)). In this case, we can see that the gain quickly reaches approx. 20% when the file is split up into a minimum number of blocks (approx. 15 blocks). The cost of splitting a file into several blocks is the control information needed to localize the different blocks. The curve also shows that no more gain is obtained when the file is split up into a number of blocks larger than 30.

Impact of FEC redundancy on performance gain. The original file is now supposed to be split up into 20 blocks replicated 40 times. The total number of blocks is then fixed to 800. The cost of getting the entire file represents the reference cost. From this basis, we compute the gain for different values of FEC redundancy. The abscissa represents the redundancy rate R of the FEC, and is given by $R = (n + m) / n$. The redundancy rate is then computed so that Equation (4) is verified. The next Figure presents the obtained gain according to FEC redundancy rate.

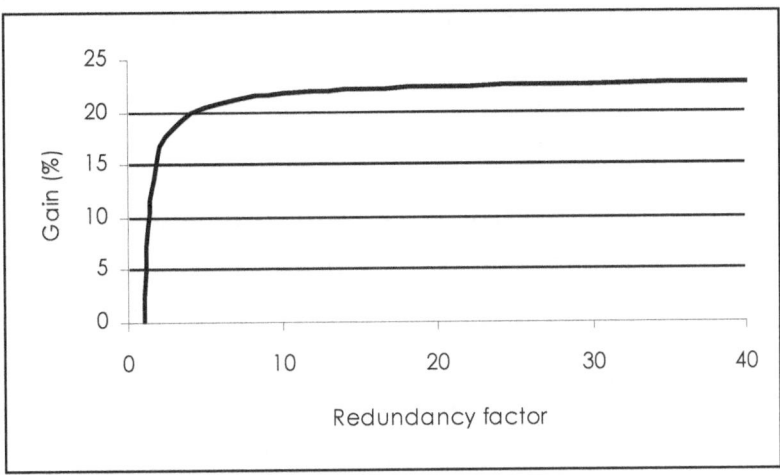

Fig. 6. Gain according to FEC redundancy rate.

The curve shows that up to a FEC rate of 5, the gain progresses quickly from 0 to approx. 22%. Then the gain is stable, and never goes beyond 24%. The recommended value for FEC redundancy factor is about 5 in this scenario.

An important point is that all these results are closely related to the probability law. For example, by using a uniform probability law (i.e. $\Pr(X = x_i) = \Pr(X = x_j)$, $\forall i, j$), the gain can easily reach up to 30%. Unfortunately, the Uniform law does not seem very realistic.

5 Concluding Remarks

In this paper, we have presented a P2P file sharing system using a FEC scheme to disseminate information over the peers. Profits were estimated by comparing our system to classical approaches of various P2P systems.

Several lessons emerged from the obtained results. First, the use of FEC allows increasing the average availability of data and decreasing the access time. Secondly, although the obtained results depend on the probability law of date distribution over the peer network, there is a set of values optimizing the peering architecture by using a number of blocks and a FEC redundancy rate couple. Finally, the use of such a

FEC-based system enhances system robustness, data availability and data access time reduction, while keeping constant the storage capacity of every peer.

In the sights of the obtained results, future works concern studies of different realistic probability laws of peers distribution to obtain optimum benefits. We plan to study in more details the behavior of our technique in the case of parallel downloadings (early simulations show a gain up to 25% of *FEC block dissemination* compared to *FEC block dissemination*). A study of dissemination and localization algorithms well-adapted to FEC-encoded blocks management is also envisaged. A mathematical proof of the interest of the FEC based on the presented model is also under study.

References

1. K. Aberer, M. Punceva, M. Hauswirth, R. Schmidt, "Improving Data Access in P2P Systems", IEEE Internet Computing 6, 1, pp. 58-67, Jan./Feb. 2002.
2. J. W. Byers, M. Luby, M. Mitzenmacher, A. Rege, "A Digital Fountain Approach to Reliable Distribution of Bulk Data", ACM SIGCOMM '98, September 2-4, 1998.
3. J. W. Byers, M. Luby, M. Mitzenmacher, "Accessing Multiple Mirror Sites in Parallel: Using Tornado Codes to Speed Up Downloads", in INFOCOM 99, 1999.
4. Y. Chen, J. Edler, A. Goldberg, A. Goettlieb, S. Sobti, P. Yianilos "Prototype Implementation of Archival Intermemory", in *Proc. of IEEE ICDE*, February 1996.
5. Edonkey2000 Peer-to-peer system, www.edonkey2000.com, May 2002,
6. Gnutella Peer-to-peer system, www.gnutella.com, May 2002,
7. Li Gong, "Peer-to-Peer Networks in Action", IEEE Internet Computing, January-February 2002
8. Kazaa Peer-to-peer system, www.kazaa.com, May 2002,
9. Napster Peer-to-peer system, www.napster.com, May 2002,
10. D. Patterson, G. Gibson, R. Katz, "A case for redundant arrays of inexpensive disks (RAID).,", *Proceedings of ACM SIGMOD '88*, 1988.
11. C. G. Plaxton, R. Rajaraman, A. W. Richa, "Accessing Nearby Copies of Replicated Objects in Distributed Environment", Proc. ACM Symp. Parallel Algorithms and Architectures, ACM Press, New York, June 1997.
12. I. S. Reed, G. Solomon, "Polynomial Codes Over Certain Finite Field", J. SIAM, vol. 8, pp. 300-304, 1960.
13. L. Rizzo, "Effective Erasure Codes for Reliable Computer Communication Protocols", In *Computer Communication Review*, April 1997.
14. P. Rodriguez, A. Kirpal, E. W. Biersack, "Parallel-Access for Mirror Sites in the Internet", *In Proceedings of IEEE/Infocom'2000*, Tel-Aviv, Israel. March 2000.
15. S. Saroiu, P. Gummadi, S. Gribble, "A Measurement Study of Peer-to-Peer File Sharing Systems", Technical Report, UW-CSE-01-06-02, University of Washington, Department of Computer Science and Engineering, Seattle, WA 98195-2350, July 2001
16. T. Speakman, D. Farinacci, J. Crowcroft, J. Gemmell, S. Lin, A. Tweedly, D. Leshchiner, M. Luby, N. Bhaskar, R. Edmonstone, K. Morse Johnson, T. Montgomery, L. Rizzo, R. Sumanasekera, L. Vicisano, "PGM Reliable Transport Protocol", April 2000
17. H.Weatherspoon, J. D. Kubiatowicz, "Erasure Coding vs. Replication : A Quantitative Comparison", *inProc. of IPTPS '02*, March 2002.

Scalable Independent Multi-level Distribution in Multimedia Content Analysis

Viktor S. Wold Eide[1,2], Frank Eliassen[2],
Ole-Christoffer Granmo[1,2], and Olav Lysne[2]* **

[1] Department of Informatics, P.O. Box 1080 Blindern, N-0316 Oslo, Norway
{viktore,olegr}@ifi.uio.no
[2] Simula Research Laboratory, P.O. Box 134 N-1325 Lysaker, Norway
{viktore,frank,olegr,olavly}@simula.no

Abstract. Due to the limited processing resources available on a typical host, monolithic multimedia content analysis applications are often restricted to simple content analysis tasks, covering a small number of media streams. This limitation on processing resources can often be reduced by parallelizing and distributing an application, utilizing the processing resources on several hosts. However, multimedia content analysis applications consist of multiple logical levels, such as streaming, filtering, feature extraction, and classification. This complexity makes parallelization and distribution a difficult task, as each logical level may require special purpose techniques. In this paper we propose a component-based framework where each logical level can be parallelized and distributed independently. Consequently, the available processing resources can be focused on the processing bottlenecks at hand. An event notification service based interaction mechanism is a key factor for achieving this flexible parallelization and distribution. Experiments demonstrate the scalability of a real-time motion vector based object tracking application implemented in the framework.

1 Introduction

The technical ability to generate volumes of digital media data is becoming increasingly "main stream". To utilize the growing number of media sources, both the ease of use and the computational flexibility of methods for content-based access must be addressed.

In order to make media content more accessible, pattern classification systems which automatically classify media content in terms of high-level concepts have been taken into use. Roughly stated, the goal of such pattern classification systems is to bridge the gap between the low-level features produced through signal processing (filtering and feature extraction) and the high-level concepts desired by the end-user. Automatic visual surveillance [1], automatic indexing of TV Broadcast News [2] (e.g. into Newscaster, Report, Weather Forecast, and Commercial segments), and remote sensing image interpretation [3] are examples of popular application domains.

---

* Authors are listed alphabetically
** The DMJ project is funded by the Norwegian Research Council under grant no. 126103/431

F. Boavida et al. (Eds.): IDMS/PROMS 2002, LNCS 2515, pp. 37–48, 2002.

Due to the limited processing resources available on a typical host, monolithic multimedia content analysis applications are often restricted to simple content analysis tasks. Multimedia content analysis applications consist of multiple logical levels, such as streaming, filtering, feature extraction, and classification. This complexity makes parallelization and distribution a difficult task, as each logical level may require special purpose techniques. For instance, in [4], it is shown how the filtering in a video based people counting application can be distributed to the sensors, based on a special purpose multimedia surveillance network. Accordingly, a higher frame rate can be achieved or more advanced filtering can be conducted.

In the DMJ (Distributed Media Journaling) project we are developing a component based framework for real-time media content analysis. New sub-technologies (e.g. a new feature extraction algorithm) may be plugged into the framework when available.

The resource requirements for the framework application domain are very challenging and will most likely remain so in the near future, justifying the need for scalability. In this paper we show the framework scalability for a relatively tightly coupled application (components interact with the video framerate frequency) processing a single video stream. A massively distributed application utilizing a large number of cameras (e.g. for traffic surveillance) may require such tight coupling only between some components.

The relative complexity of streaming, filtering/transformation, feature extraction, and classification depends on the application. Therefore the framework should support focusing of processing resources on any given logical level, independently of other logical levels. E.g., if only the filtering is parallelized and distributed (as in the case from [4]), the feature extraction and the classification may become processing bottlenecks.

In this paper we focus on the parallelization and distribution mechanisms of the DMJ framework. In Sect. 2 we describe the general approach for building content analysis applications. We also introduce our application case, tracking of a moving object in a video stream. In Sect. 3 we first give an overview of the DMJ framework. In Sect. 3.1 we shortly describe inter component communication and synchronization. We then proceed to motivate and present the special purpose parallelization and distribution techniques for each logical level in Sect. 3.2 to Sect. 3.5. In Sect. 4 we present the results of an experiment which demonstrate the scalability of our framework. In Sect. 5 we present plans for future work. Lastly, we provide some conclusions in Sect. 6.

2   Content Analysis

A general approach for building content analysis applications is to combine low-level quantitative media processing into high-level concept recognition. Typically, such applications are logically organized as a hierarchy, as shown in Fig. 1. At the lowest level of the hierarchy there are media streaming sources. At the level above, the media streams are filtered and transformed. The transformed media streams are then fed to feature extraction algorithms as media segments (e.g. video frame regions). Feature extraction algorithms operate on the media segments from the transformed media streams, and in the case of a video frame region, calculate features such as color histograms and motion vectors. Finally, results from feature extraction algorithms are reported to classification algorithms higher up in the hierarchy that are responsible for detecting high level domain

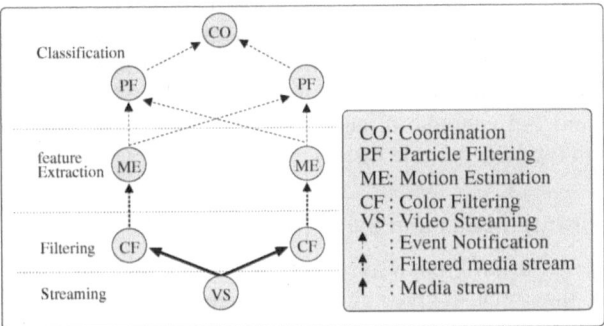

Fig. 1. A specific configuration, out of many possible configurations, of a content analysis application for real-time tracking of a moving object in a video stream

concepts, such as a moving object in a video stream. In other words, classification is interpretation of extracted features in some application specific context.

Fig. 1 illustrates a *possible configuration* of a content analysis application for real-time tracking of a moving object in a video stream, the application henceforth used for illustration purposes. The video stream is filtered by two algorithms, each doing video stream decoding and color-to-grey level filtering. Each filtered video frame is divided into $m \times n$ blocks (media segments) before two motion estimators calculate motion vectors for the blocks. The block motion vectors are then submitted to two so-called *particle filters* (described in 3.5) for object detection and tracking. The coordinator uses the results from all the particle filters to determine the position of the moving object.

Often, the above type of content analysis applications are implemented as monolithic applications making reuse, development, maintenance, and extension by third parties difficult. Such applications are often executed in single processes, unable to benefit from distributed processing environments.

3   The DMJ Framework

As a solution to the inherent problems of traditional monolithic content analysis systems, we suggest a component-based approach. Logically, the media processing hierarchy is similar, but the different algorithms at each logical level are now encapsulated in components - S (Streaming), F (Filtering), E (feature Extraction), and C (Classification) components. The content analysis task is realized as a collection of components, which indirectly monitor other components and react to particular changes in their state.

The resulting content analysis hierarchy can then be executed as a pipeline (each level of the hierarchy is executed in parallel). For instance, the application described in Sect. 2 can be executed on five CPUs, where the streaming is conducted from one CPU, the filtering is executed on a second CPU, the motion estimation is conducted on a third CPU, and so forth. Such distribution allows an application to take advantage of a number of CPUs equal to the depth of the hierarchy. In addition, the DMJ framework also supports independent parallelization and distribution within each logical level. In the current prototype of the framework, each logical level implements special purpose parallelization and distribution techniques, as we will see in Sect. 3.2 to Sect. 3.5. In combination, this opens up for focusing the processing resources on the processing bottlenecks at hand. An example of such parallelization is found in Fig. 1 where the motion estimation (and the particle filtering) can be conducted on two CPUs.

3.1   Component Interaction and Synchronization

Components interact in different ways, such as one-one, one-many (sharing or partitioning of data), many-one (aggregation), and many-many. In [5] we argue that the requirements for our application domain fit very well with the publish/subscribe interaction paradigm, leading to an event-based interaction model. Event-based systems rely on some kind of event notification service which introduces a level of indirection. The responsibility of the event notification service is to propagate/route event notifications from the event producers to interested event consumers, based on content and generally in a many-many manner. A component does not need to know the location, the identity, or if results have been generated by a single or a number of components. The binding between components is loose and based on what is produced rather than by whom. Note that the event notification service should take advantage of native multicast on the network layer for scalability reasons, as will become clear in the following sections.

Some kind of synchronization and ordering mechanism is required in order to support parallel and distributed processing. Such a mechanism is described in [5], in which each media sample and event notification is assigned a timestamp (actually a time interval) from globally synchronized clocks. In other words, the design of our framework is based upon a common knowledge of time in all components. This is realized by synchronizing the computers by e.g. the Network Time Protocol, RFC 1305.

3.2   Media Streaming

Each media source receives its input from a sensor, implemented in software (e.g. a program monitoring files) or as a combination of both hardware (video camera, microphone, etc.) and software (drivers, libraries, etc.). From a scalability point of view, reducing sender side processing and network bandwidth consumption is important.

Some media types may generate large amounts of data, requiring effective encoding in order to reduce bandwidth requirements to a reasonable level. We currently work with live video, a quite challenging media type with respect to processing requirements, the massive amounts of data, and the imposed real-time requirements. E.g., a television quality MPEG-2 encoded video stream, Main profile in the Main Level, 720 pixels/line x 576 lines, may require as much as 15 Mbps [6]. The actual data rate depends on both intra- and inter frame redundancy, i.e. the media content. Real-time encoding is likely to remain costly in the near future too, considering a likely increase in video quality.

A media source should be able to handle a number of interested receivers, belonging to the same or to different applications. A video streaming source which must handle each and every component individually will not scale. Scalable one to many communication is what IP multicast [7] has been designed for. Each packet requires a single send operation and should traverse each network link only once. In the current prototype, we have used IP multicast for streaming video data, as illustrated by label 1 in Fig. 2.

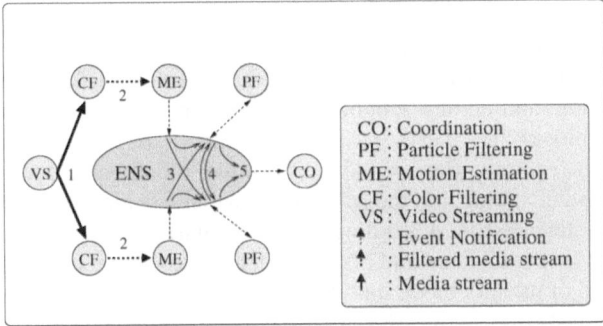

Fig. 2. Inter component communication for the configuration in Fig.1. Feature extraction and classification components interact through an Event Notification Service, labeled ENS

3.3   Filtering and Transformation

Filtering and transformation bridge the gap between what a S component offers and an E component can handle. As an example, filtering and transformation components may be used to convert MPEG-2 to YUV to 32 bit RGB to 8 bit gray level video frames.

An effective encoding of a media stream reduces network bandwidth consumption, but results in increased processing requirements for decoding. If components both receive and decompress each and every frame of a high quality video stream entirely, the number of CPU cycles left for the rest of the processing may be severely reduced. As an example, real-time software decoding of a MPEG-2 TV quality video stream requires a fairly powerful computer. Furthermore, filtering and transformation may be computationally costly by itself. Consequently, our framework should support parallel and distributed filtering and transformation.

In the current prototype the filtering and transformation is executed in the same process as the feature extraction, and data is transferred to feature extraction components by reference passing. This data flow is labeled 2 in Fig. 2.

3.4   Feature Extraction

A feature extraction algorithm operates on media segments from the filtering and trans-formation level (e.g. video frame blocks) and extracts quantititave information, such as motion vectors and color histograms. The features of each media segment are used at the classification level to assign a high-level content class to each media segment.

Feature extraction algorithms may use information from the compressed or partial decompressed domain if available (e.g. utilize the motion vectors in a MPEG-2 video).

Some feature extraction algorithms require relatively small amounts of processing, such as a color histogram calculation which may only require a single pass through each pixel in a video frame. But even such simple operations may become costly when applied to a real-time high quality video stream. In general the algorithms may be arbitrarily complex. In combination with the high data rate and often short period of time between succeeding frames this may easily overwhelm even a powerful computer. A scalable solution necessitates parallelization, which requires a partitioning of the data in the media stream, spatially and/or temporally.

Feature extraction algorithms for video, such as motion vector extraction, color histogram calculation, and texture roughness calculation, often operate locally on image regions (e.g. a block). The DMJ framework supports spatial parallelization and distribution of such feature extractors. As an example, block-based motion estimation is computationally demanding, but the calculation of a single block motion vector is localized to a small image region. Accordingly, the calculation of motion vectors in a single video frame can be parallelized and distributed. For the sake of completeness we give a short description of parallel block motion vector extraction in the DMJ framework.

Block-based Motion Estimation. In order to identify and quantify motion between two consecutive frames, a block-based scheme is used. A block from the previous frame is compared to the corresponding block in the current frame. A block difference value is calculated by summing all the pixel value differences and this value indicates the similarity between the two blocks. If an object or the camera moves between two consecutive frames, the calculated block difference value may become large and a search for a similar block in the current frame is necessary. Searching is done by offsetting the corresponding block in the current frame some pixels horizontally and vertically. A search area is defined by the maximum number of pixels to offset the block. In the worst case, a brute force search must compare the block in the previous frame with all blocks defined by the search area. This searching requires lots of processing and a number of algorithms have been proposed in order to reduce the number of blocks compared [8]. The search is usually terminated whenever a block with difference value below some threshold has been found, introducing indeterminism since the processing requirements depend on the media stream content. The offset $[\delta x, \delta y]$ which produces the smallest difference value, below a threshold, defines the motion vector for this block.

Our implementation allows a component to calculate motion vectors for only some of the blocks in the video frame, defined by a sequence of rectangles, each covering some blocks. In case of parallel processing, such motion estimation components are mapped onto different hosts, each processing some of the blocks in the whole frame.

In Fig. 3, the motion vectors calculated by a single component have been drawn into the left video frame. The figure also illustrates how a component may get configured to process only some regions of the video stream. The blocks processed are slightly darker and they also have the motion vectors drawn, pointing from the center of their respective block. The motion vectors indicate that the person is moving to the left.

The motion vectors calculated for blocks in video frames are sent as event notifications. The event notification service will then forward such event notifications to the interested subscribers, as indicated by label 3 in Fig. 2.

3.5   Classification

The final logical level of the DMJ framework is the classification level. At the classification level each media segment is assigned a content class based on features extracted at the feature extraction level. For instance, if each video frame in a video stream is divided into $m \times n$ blocks as seen in the previous section, the classification may consist of deciding whether a block contains the center position of a moving object, based on extracted motion vectors.

Fig. 3. Left: Block-based motion estimation example. Right: The center position of the tracked object, calculated by the coordinator, has been drawn as a white rectangle

Features may be related spatially and temporally to increase the classification accuracy. E.g., if a block contains the stomach of a person moving to the left, above blocks should contain "person" features. Blocks to the right in previous video frames should also contain such features. When features are related spatially and temporally, the classification may also be referred to as *tracking* or *spatial-temporal data fusion*.

In this section we first discuss how the classification can become the processing bottleneck in a content analysis application, as well as the consequences. We then propose a parallelizable multi-component classifier which addresses this bottleneck problem.

Processing Bottlenecks. The classification may become a processing bottleneck due to the complexity of the content analysis task, the required classification rate, and the required classification accuracy. E.g., rough tracking of the position of a single person in a single low rate video stream may be possible using a single CPU, but accurately tracking the position of multiple people as well as their interactions (talking, shaking hands, etc.) could require several CPUs. Multiple media streams, such as video streams from multiple cameras capturing the activity on an airport, may increase the content analysis complexity even further. In the latter setting we may for instance consider tracking the behavior and interaction of several hundred people, with the goal of detecting people behaving suspiciously. This example would probably require a very large number of CPUs for accurate classification at an appropriate video frame rate. In short, when the classifier is running on a single CPU, the classification may become the processing bottleneck of the content analysis application.

When the classification becomes the processing bottleneck either the content analysis task must simplified, the classification rate/accuracy requirements must be relaxed, or the amount of processing resources available for classification must be increased. Simplifying the content analysis task may be costly in terms of implementation effort. Furthermore, reducing the accuracy of a classifier, in order to reduce the processing resource usage, may be an intricate problem depending on the classifier. Changing the classification rate is easily done, but this may have implications on the other logical framework levels (which also should reduce their operation rate accordingly). In addition, the content analysis task and the classification rate/accuracy requirements are often given by the application and cannot be modified. Consequently, often the only option is to increase the amount of processing resources available for classification. Unfortunately, if the classification cannot be distributed, increasing the available processing resources is only effective to a limited degree.

A Parallel and Distributed Classification Component. To reduce the problems discussed above, the DMJ framework classification level supports: effective specification of content analysis tasks through the use of dynamic Bayesian networks [9], flexible execution of content analysis tasks based on the particle filter algorithm [9], fine grained trading of classification accuracy against classification processing resource usage as a result of using particle filters, and fine grained trading of feature extraction processing resource usage against classification accuracy [10] [11].

In the following we describe our use of the particle filter in more detail. Then we propose a distributed version of the particle filter, and argue that the communication and processing properties of the distributed particle filter allow scalable distributed classification, independent of distribution at the other logical levels of the DMJ framework.

The Particle Filter: Our particle filter is generated from a dynamic Bayesian network specifying the content analysis task. During execution the particle filter partitions the media stream to be analysed into time slices, where for instance a time slice may correspond to a video frame. The particle filter maintains a set of particles. A single particle is simply an assignment of a content class to each media segment (e.g. object or background) in the previously analysed time slices, combined with the likelihood of the assignment when considering the extracted features (e.g. motion vectors). Multiple particles are used to handle noise and uncertain feature-content relationships. This means that multiple feature interpretations can be maintained concurrently in time, ideally until uncertainty can be resolved and noise can be supressed.

When a new time slice is to be analysed, each particle is independently extended to cover new media segments, driven by the content analysis task specification. In order to maintain a relevant set of particles, unlikely particles are systematically replaced by likely particles. Consequently, the particle set is evolved to be a rich summarization of likely content interpretations. This approach has proven effective in difficult content analysis tasks such as tracking of objects. Note that apart from the particle replacement, a particle is processed independently of other particles in the particle filter procedure.

The Distributed Particle Filter: Before proposing the distributed version of the particle filter, we briefly discuss how the classification in some cases can be distributed without any inter-classifier communication. This is the case when the content analysis task can be split into independent content analysis sub tasks. For instance, a particle filter tracking the position of people in unrelated media streams can be replaced by one particle filter for each media stream. These particle filters can then be executed independently on multiple CPUs.

The above distribution approach may be undesirable when the content analysis sub tasks depend on each other; the lack of coordination between the particle filters may cause globally incoherent classification. E.g., a particle filter tracking n people in a single media stream could be replaced by n particle filters, each tracking a single person, but then the sub tasks are dependent. As a result, particle filters tracking different persons may start tracking the same person, resulting in some persons not being tracked.

So, in order to achieve globally coherent classification only a single particle filter is used in our second distribution approach. In short, the particles of the single particle filter are parted into n groups which are processed on n CPUs. An event based communication scheme maintains global classification coherence. The communication scheme is illustrated in Fig. 2 and discussed below.

n particle filter (PF) components and a coordinator (CO) component cooperate to implement the particle filter. Each PF component maintains a local set of particles and executes the particle filter procedure locally. When a new time slice is to be analysed, the components operate as follows. First, m locally likely particles are selected and submitted to the other PF components through the event notification service (label 4 in Fig. 2). Then, each PF component executes the particle filter procedure on the locally maintained particles, except that the local particles also can be replaced by the $(n-1)m$ particles received from the other PF components. After execution, each PF component submits the likelihood of media segment content classes to the coordinator (label 5 in Fig. 2) which estimates the most probable content class of each media segment.

Fig. 3 illustrates the effect of the distributed particle filter when applied to our content analysis application case. The input to the PF components (motion vectors) as well as the output of the CO component (the center position of the moving object) have been drawn into the respective video frames.

In the above communication scheme only $2n$ (from PF components) $+1$ (from the CO component) messages are submitted per time slice, relying on multicast support in the event notification service (and the underlying network). In addition, the size of the messages is controlled by m. Accordingly, this allows scalable distribution of classification on relatively tightly coupled CPUs, independent of distribution at the other logical levels of the DMJ framework. Finally, the classification properties of the distributed particle filter are essentially identical to the classification properties of the traditional particle filter when m equals the number of particles in a single PF component. By manipulating m, classification accuracy can be traded off against the size of the messages.

4   Empirical Results

In this section we present the results of an experiment where the object tracking application was parallelized and distributed based on a prototype of our framework.

A separate PC (700Mhz Celeron CPU) hosted a standard video streaming application (vic [12]) which captured and multicasted a MJPEG video stream (352 x 288 pixels, quality factor of 70) on a switched 100 Mbps Ethernet LAN. The frame rate was varied between 1 f/s and 25 f/s and generated a data rate of approximately 100 kbps to 2.5 Mbps. Java Media Framework [13] was used to implement a motion estimation Java class. We configured the block size to 16 x 16 pixels and the search area to ± 6 pixels, both horizontally and vertically, i.e. a search area of 169 blocks. A "full search" was always performed, even though a perfect match between two blocks was found before having compared with all 169 possible blocks. The number of blocks processed in each frame was 20 x 16 (edge blocks were not processed). A parallel multi-component particle filter has been implemented in the C programming language. For particle filtering 1100 particles were used. Five Dual 1667 Mhz AMD Athlon computers were used as a distributed processing environment. The motion estimation components and the particle

Table 1. The achieved frame rate, in frames/second, for different configurations

	1 CPU	2 CPUs	4 CPUs	8 CPUs	10 CPUs
Ideal Frame Rate	2.5	5	10	20	25
Streaming	2.5	5	10	20	25
Filtering and Feature Extraction	2.5	5	8.5	13.5	16
Classification	2.5	5	10	20	25

filter components communicated across Mbus[14]. In [5] we discuss the suitability of Mbus as an event notification service. Mbus takes advantage of IP multicast.

In order to examine the distribution scalability of our framework we implemented five object tracking configurations, targeting 1, 2, 4, 8, and 10 CPUs respectively. The first configuration, consisting of decoding and filtering components, one motion estimation component, one particle filter component, and one coordination component, was executed as a pipeline on one CPU. In the second configuration the pipeline was executed on two CPUs, that is, the filtering and motion estimation components were executed on one CPU and the particle filter and coordination component were executed on another CPU. This configuration was extended stepwise by adding a motion estimation component (and implicitly also filtering components) as well as a particle filter component, each running on a dedicated CPU.

The configurable parameters of the above components were set so that the feature extraction and the particle filtering had similar processing resource requirements. Then, we kept the content analysis task and the other configurable parameters constant, while we measured the video frame rate of each configuration. If our framework is scalable the frame rate should increase approximately linearly with the number of CPUs. This also means that the operation rate at both the feature extraction level as well as the classification level should increase accordingly.

The achieved frame rate for each configuration is shown in Table 1. From the table we can see that the frame rate increased linearly with the number of CPUs, except for the filtering and feature extraction part of the computation.

In order to find out what caused this effect, we modified the implementation of the motion estimation method in the Java class so that it returned whenever called by the JMF runtime system, without doing any processing. We observed that when streaming at 25 f/s, the filtering and transformation part (depacketization and JPEG to RGB transformation) consumed roughly 30% of the processing power of a single CPU. Each component must decode and filter the complete multicast MJPEG stream, despite the fact that each component only operates on a subpart of each video frame. Scalability is reduced, illustrating the point made in 3.3. Note that the ability of the distributed classifier to handle the full frame rate was tested on artificially generated features.

5   Further Work

Sending a full multicast stream to all receivers wastes both network and receiver processing resources when each receiver only processes some regions in each video frame. In [15], heterogeneous receivers are handled by layered video coding. Each layer encodes a portion of the video signal and is sent to a designated IP multicast address. Each enhancement layer depends on lower layers and improves quality spatially/temporarily. Parallel processing poses a related kind of heterogeneity challenge, but the motivation is distribution of workload by partitioning data. In this respect, using an event notification service for video streaming, as described in [16] and [17], seems interesting. A video streaming component may then send different blocks of each video frame as different event notifications. A number of cooperating feature extraction components may then subscribe to different regions and process the whole video frame in parallel.

With respect to filtering, we consider an approach where (a hierarchy of) filters can be dynamically configured to adapt each media stream to the varying requirements of different receiving components. A similar approach for managing content adaptation in multicast of media streams has been proposed in [18].

The "full search" motion estimation strategy described in Sect. 4 gives deterministic, but also worst case processing requirements. A strategy which terminates the search is more challenging from a load balancing point of view. A moving object increases the processing requirements for a local group of blocks (a processing hotspot), suggesting that blocks processed by a single CPU are spread throughout the whole video frame. The tracking information calculated by a classifier, e.g. the object location and movement direction, can be subscribed to and used as a hint to improve searching.

We will also add resource aware and demand driven feature extraction to the framework [10], i.e., the features are ranked on-line according to their expected ability to contribute to the current stage of the content analysis task. Only the most useful features are extracted, as limited by the available processing resources.

Finally, we will extend our application case and increase the need for scalability by analyzing several video streams concurrently. Content from different video streams can then be related in the classification, e.g. tracking of an object across several cameras. For this purpose, we will add a parallelizable color feature extractor for more robust object tracking, i.e. objects can be identified and tracked based on color features.

6   Conclusion

In this paper we have presented a component based framework which simplifies the development of distributed scalable applications for real-time media content analysis. By using this framework, we have implemented a real-time moving object tracker. The experimental results indicate that the framework allows construction of scalable applications by the means of parallelization and distribution of the main logical application levels, namely streaming, transformation/filtering, feature extraction, and classification.

References

1. Hongeng, S., Bremond, F., Nevatia, R.: Bayesian Framework for Video Surveillance Applications. In: 15th International Conference on Pattern Recognition. Volume 1., IEEE (2000) 164–170
2. Eickeler, S., Muller, S.: Content-based Video Indexing of TV Broadcast News using Hidden Markov Models. In: Conference on Acoustics, Speech and Signal Processing. Volume 6., IEEE (1999) 2997–3000

3. A. Pinz, M. Prantl, H.G., Borotschnig, H.: Active fusion—a new method applied to remote sensing image interpretation. Special Issue on Soft Computing in Remote Sensing Data Analysis **17** (1996) 1340–1359

4. Remagnino, P., Jones, G.A., Paragios, N., Regazzoni, C.S., eds.: Video-Based Surveillance Systems. Kluwer Academic Publishers (2002)

5. Eide, V.S.W., Eliassen, F., Lysne, O., Granmo, O.C.: Real-time Processing of Media Streams: A Case for Event-based Interaction. In: Proceedings of International Workshop on Distributed Event-Based Systems (DEBS'02), IEEE, Vienna, Austria. (2002)

6. Steinmetz, R., Nahrstedt, K.: Multimedia: Computing, Communications & Applications. Prentice Hall (1995)

7. Almeroth, K.C.: The Evolution of Multicast: From the MBone to Interdomain Multicast to Internet2 Deployment. IEEE Network (2000)

8. Furht, B., Smoliar, S.W., Zhang, H.: Video and Image Processing in Multimedia Systems. Kluwer Academic Publishers (1995)

9. Granmo, O.C., Eliassen, F., Lysne, O.: Dynamic Object-oriented Bayesian Networks for Flexible Resource-aware Content-based Indexing of Media Streams. In: Proceedings of Scandinavian Conference on Image Analysis (SCIA2001), Bergen, Norway. (2001)

10. Granmo, O.C., Jensen, F.V.: Real-time Hypothesis Driven Feature Extraction on Parallel Processing Architectures. In: Proceedings of The 2002 International Conference on Parallel and Distributed Processing Techniques and Applications (PDPTA'02), Las Vegas, USA, CSREA Press (2002)

11. Granmo, O.C.: Automatic Resource-aware Construction of Media Indexing Applications for Distributed Processing Environments. In: Proceedings of the 2nd International Workshop on Pattern Recognition in Information Systems (PRIS2002), Alicante, Spain, ICEIS Press (2002) 124–139

12. McCanne, S., Jacobson, V.: Vic: A flexible Framework for Packet Video. In ACM Multimedia'95, pp. 511-522 (1995)

13. Sun Microsystems Inc.: Java Media Framework, API Guide, v2.0. http://java.sun.com/ (1999)

14. Ott, J., Kutscher, D., Perkins, C.: The Message Bus: A Platform for Component-based Conferencing Applications. CSCW2000, workshop on Component-Based Groupware (2000)

15. McCanne, S., Vetterli, M., Jacobson, V.: Low-complexity video coding for receiver-driven layered multicast. IEEE Journal of Selected Areas in Communications **15** (1997) 983–1001

16. Chambers, D., Lyons, G., Duggan, J.: Stream Enhancements for the CORBA Event Service. In: Proceedings of the ACM Multimedia (SIGMM) Conference, Ottawa. (2001)

17. Qian, T., Campbell, R.: Extending OMG Event Service for Integrating Distributed Multimedia Components. In: Proceedings of the Fourth International Conference on Intelligence in Services and Networks, Como, Italy, Lecture Notes in Computer Science by Springer-Verlag (1997)

18. Rafaelsen, H.O., Eliassen, F.: Trading Media Gateways with CORBA Trader, Proceedings of Distributed Objects and Applications. In: Proceedings of the 3rd International Symposium on Distributed Objects and Applications (DOA 2001), Rome, Italy. (2001) 115–124

A Simulation Tool for Dimensioning and Performance Evaluation of the UMTS Terrestrial Radio Access Network

A.B. García, E. García, M. Álvarez-Campana, J. Berrocal, and E. Vázquez

Dept. Ingeniería de Sistemas Telemáticos, Universidad Politécnica de Madrid, Spain
{abgarcia, jurado, mac, berrocal, enrique}@dit.upm.es

Abstract. The efficient support of multiple traffic classes with different quality of service requirements (end-to-end delay, jitter, loss) poses an extraordinary complexity in the design of third-generation mobile networks. This task becomes especially critical for the access network, where radio and transmission resources are usually scarce. In this paper we present a simulation model of the ATM-based UMTS (Universal Mobile Telecommunications System) terrestrial radio access network. The simulator aims to provide a test bed for conducting further research studies on several topics of potential interest. In particular, we intend to use the tool for dimensioning ATM links, for evaluating performance under different mixes of traffic classes, and for investigating quality of service mechanisms. This wide range of applications has led us to develop a very flexible simulation model that captures many low level details. Some preliminary results obtained with the simulator are presented in order to illustrate its capabilities.

1 Introduction

The broad range of services to be offered by 3G (third generation) mobile systems has led to the adoption of flexible multiplexing and switching technologies in the access networks. In the case of the UMTS (Universal Mobile Telecommunications System) access network, the 3GPP (3rd Generation Partnership Project) has selected WCDMA [1] (Wideband Code Division Multiple Access) and ATM (Asynchronous Transfer Mode). The combination of both technologies promises a quite flexible bandwidth allocation and a highly efficient utilization of resources. In practice, however, a number of difficulties arise when trying to exploit these benefits in a real network scenario. The problem lies, essentially, in the multi-service nature of 3G networks.

On the one hand, in spite of the many market studies recently published (for instance, by the UMTS Forum: [2]), the mix of services that will be offered to UMTS networks is still largely unknown. On the other hand, and regardless of the advances in traffic engineering during the last decade, there is still a lack of experience in the design of large-scale multi-service networks with QoS (Quality of Service) differentiation. In the case of UTRAN (UMTS Terrestrial Radio Access Network), the strict QoS

F. Boavida et al. (Eds.): IDMS/PROMS 2002, LNCS 2515, pp. 49-60, 2002.

requirements associated to some user services, together with the goal of optimizing radio and transmission resources, introduce a further degree of complexity to the problem.

During the last few years, several technical papers on dimensioning and performance evaluation of UTRAN have been published (see for instance [3], [4], [5] and [6]). Some of these studies emphasize the difficulty of the problem, and the many aspects that require further research before deploying commercial UMTS networks. A rigorous treatment of the problem requires the appropriate consideration of traffic characterization models (at least for the main expected applications), QoS requirements (tolerance to delay and losses), resource management strategies (e.g. connection admission control), QoS differentiation mechanisms (e.g. giving priority to voice traffic), capacity allocation policies, etc.

The many different aspects of UTRAN requiring further investigation make the analytical approach to the problem impractical, especially when trying to capture low-level details. That is the reason that led us to the development of a simulation model for UTRAN. In this paper, we present the preliminary status of the simulator and the features it currently provides.

Because most of the published works about UTRAN focus on radio planning issues (e.g. [7] and [8]), we have decided to concentrate our efforts on the fixed part of the access network, that is, on the ATM transmission links that connect base stations (called Node-B's) and Radio Network Controllers (RNCs).

The rest of this paper is organized as follows. Section 2 provides an overview of the UTRAN architecture and the use of ATM as the transport technology for delivering QoS. Section 3 describes the traffic modeling approach used by the simulator. Section 4 presents the architecture of the simulation model, and section 5 presents some sample results obtained with it. Finally, in the last section we outline the main conclusions of our work and a brief discussion about our plans in the future.

2   UTRAN Overview

The UMTS terrestrial radio access network allows the connection between the user equipment (UE) and the core network (CN) through a transport infrastructure based on ATM[1]. Fig. 1 shows the architecture of UTRAN, which consists of a set of RNSs (Radio Network Subsystems) each of them being responsible for the resources of a set of UMTS cells. An RNS comprises a radio network controller and the set of Node-B's (or base stations) it controls. The physical topology for interconnecting Node-B's and RNCs may vary according to location criteria and planning issues.

The UMTS specifications define a set of standardized logical interfaces inside UTRAN and between UTRAN and external entities (UE and CN). These interfaces are: Uu (air interface connecting UE and Node-B), Iub (connecting each Node-B with

---

[1] From UMTS Release 5 on, the possibility of using IP as the transport technology in UTRAN has also been considered, as documented in the 3GPP technical report 25.933 [9]. In this paper we only consider the ATM transport option.

its controlling RNC), Iur (interconnecting RNCs) and Iu (connecting RNC to a Core Network access node).

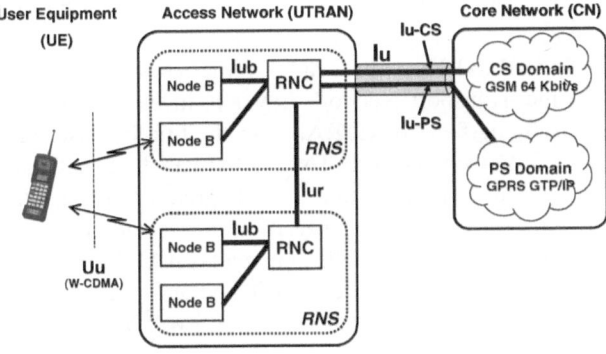

Fig. 1. UTRAN logical elements and interfaces

The 3GPP precisely defines the protocol stacks involved in communications through these interfaces. Fig. 2 shows a slightly simplified view of the protocol stacks defined for UTRAN. For clarity, the Iur interface and some options for the signaling transport are not represented. Nevertheless, even with these simplifications, the complexity of the UTRAN protocol architecture is evident from the figure. Our work focuses on the transfer of user plane information across UTRAN, not explicitly considering signaling.

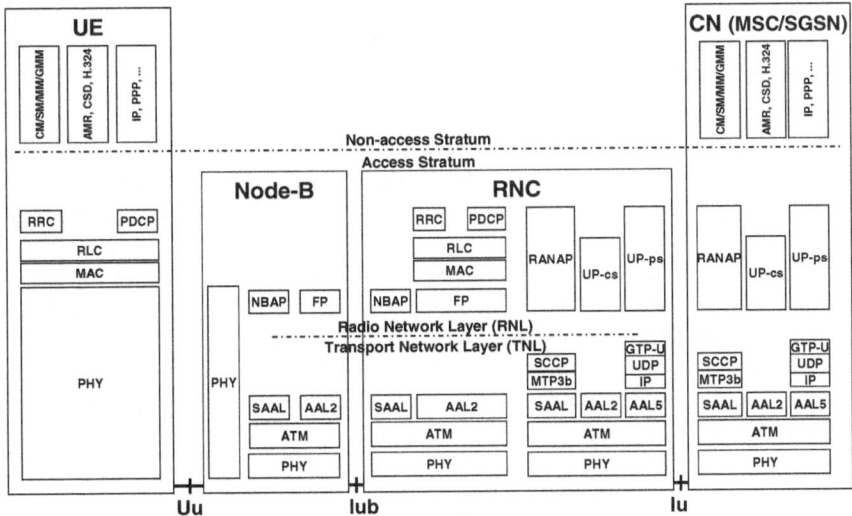

Fig. 2. UTRAN protocol architecture

UTRAN protocols used in terrestrial interfaces are structured in two layers: Radio Network Layer (RNL) and Transport Network Layer (TNL). Inside RNL all the

UMTS-specific protocols for UTRAN are defined, including the so-called radio protocols, RLC (Radio Link Control), MAC (Medium Access Control), and PDCP (Packet Data Convergence Protocol) among them. In the user plane, the Frame Protocol (FP) is defined at Iub and Iur interfaces in order to somehow extend the radio transport channels from Node-B to RNC, where radio frames are to be processed.

Below RNL, the Transport Network Layer is in charge of conveying RNL data across the terrestrial interfaces of UTRAN. For the first Releases of UMTS, 3GPP has decided to adopt ATM technology in TNL. ATM has the benefit of being a relatively mature technology with an exhaustive and integrated QoS and traffic management definition, yet allowing an efficient use of transmission resources. Over ATM an ATM Adaptation Layer (AAL) is used. Concretely, AAL2 is used at Iub and Iur interfaces for all types of user traffic (circuit-switched and packet-switched), and also for circuit-switched data at Iu interface (Iu-CS). AAL5 will be used for conveying packet-switched data at Iu (Iu-PS).

AAL2, specified in ITU-T Recommendation I.363.2 [10], allows the efficient transmission of low-bit-rate services with stringent requirements in terms of delay, such as voice, through an ATM network. This characteristic makes it appropriate for the UTRAN environment. The optional AAL2 error detection and correction mechanisms are not used in UTRAN [11]. [12] indicates that error detection and assured transfer, when needed, are carried out by MAC and RLC protocols.

QoS support at the TNL is essential since performance requirements of applications, as well as some specific radio procedures, pose significant restrictions to delay and losses experimented at UTRAN, including its terrestrial interfaces. This is the general framework of the studies presented in this paper.

3   Traffic Characterization

In order to attain useful results, appropriate traffic models should be used as input for the simulator. These models have to take into account not only the applications' statistical properties, but also the peculiarities of the radio protocols used to convey the data.

There are a number of studies proposing traffic models to be used in 3G access networks. Most of the times only two classes of traffic are considered, usually named voice (with delay requirements) and data (with loss requirements). See for example [4], [13], [5] and [14]. There are also studies dedicated to the modeling of traffic sources in mobile environments (for instance, [15], [16] and [17], being the last one specific to UMTS). Nevertheless, we have found no article in the literature in which all the four traffic classes defined for UMTS are jointly treated and adapted to the terrestrial interfaces of UTRAN.

Since we are not interested in the resource management of the air interface, we would like to abstract as much as possible its specific characteristics. Besides, the peculiarities of radio protocols significantly alter the statistical properties of the sources to be considered. That is why we have avoided using very detailed source traffic models, which in many cases are derived from observations in fixed environments, and hence are probably not well suited for a mobile access network.

Instead, we have tried to represent the four UMTS QoS classes (conversational, streaming, interactive and background [18]) in a uniform and simple way, yet taking into account the most significant parameters of each one. Isnard proposes some guidelines in his Ph.D. Thesis [19] that served us as a basis for our models. He models all the traffic sources as periodic processes, with period equal to the TTI (Transmission Timing Interval) of the transport channel used. Every TTI, a packet of fixed size is generated, thus giving a constant rate for each application type. The use of a constant period may seem a very simplistic assumption, but the pseudo-periodicity inherent to the operation of the low layers of radio protocols makes it quite reasonable for the Iub and Iur interfaces, and we have also used it.

In our case, this basic source model has been enhanced in order to account for variable rate applications. This leads to a more realistic representation of many sources, and allows us to measure the possible benefits of statistical multiplexing.

The procedure we carried out for the traffic characterization is as follows. Each traffic class is represented by a typical application, namely 12.2-AMR (Adaptive Multi Rate) codec (conversational class) [20], interactive web browsing (interactive class), streaming video (streaming class) and e-mail (background class). The main characteristics of each application serve as hints for the parameterization of a general statistical model adequate for the Iub and Iur interfaces. For us, a source includes all the effects of RNL protocols, including the Frame Protocol.

Although in general an application can be considered bi-directional, many applications are clearly asymmetric (for instance, web browsing). Thus, if the traffic pattern of an application type is typically asymmetric, we implicitly model the downstream flow, since this is the direction in which the majority of the traffic is normally observed.

In harmony with several traffic parameterization studies ([15], [17], [21]), we fit each application in a three-level model, trying to give physical significance to each of the levels. Fig. 3 shows its main characteristics.

As shown in the figure, three levels are defined:

- Session level. A user session lasts as long as the user is in "active state". Its real-life correspondence depends on the concrete application. For instance, a session can model a voice call, or a web session (comprising the downloading and reading of several web documents). This level will be typically described by a session arrival process and a session duration statistical function.
- Burst level. This level catches the variability in the traffic generation parameters during an active session. It is given different denominations through the literature (connection-level in [17], page-level in the web model proposed in [15], and packet calls in [21]). The pattern chosen for our sources is based on an ON-OFF model, in which it is possible to generate traffic on both states (it could be called a "High-Low" model). This gives us the possibility of modeling each source as a general bi-rate application. At this level, the relevant parameters are the statistical distributions of each state's duration.

- Packet level. For each state of the burst level, the parameters that govern the packet generation process are described: the statistical distributions of inter-arrival time and packet size for the High and Low states.

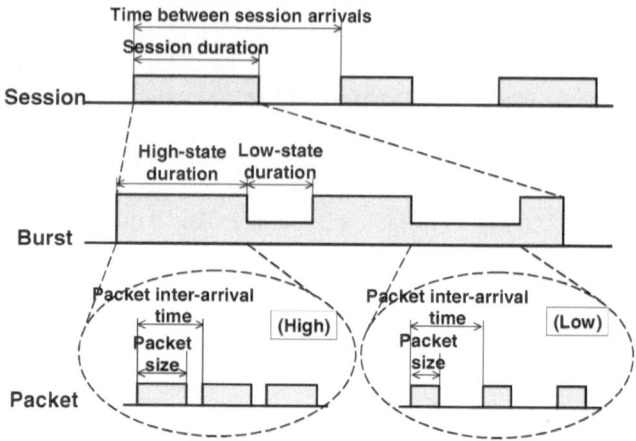

Fig. 3. Application model in three levels

Currently the simulator offers the possibility of creating as many independent active sources as necessary. Since all the sources are considered in an active state, only the burst and packet levels have to be parameterized in the tool. This allows us to study the system behavior in the presence of a precise number of simultaneously active users, possibly of several types. It is also possible to introduce a stochastic time offset between the activation instant of each source, in order to avoid a synchronized behavior between different users (as mentioned in [19] and [4], for instance). All this provides the simulator user with great flexibility when configuring the traffic conditions of the experiments. In section 5 we deduce and justify specific parameters for voice and web users.

4   Simulation Model

This section describes the simulation model we are developing for our research work on dimensioning and performance evaluation of UTRAN. Being initially interested in the analysis of the Iub interface, we have completed a first version of the simulator that is able to model an RNS composed of one RNC and one or several Node-B's, with different interconnection topologies (star, chain, etc.) both at physical (transmission interfaces) and logical levels (ATM Virtual Channels).

The simulator allows us to define one or more groups of users for each Node-B. A group of users, which can be associated to an application type (e.g. voice users), is characterized by a set of parameter values conforming to the traffic model described in section 3, determining the behavior of each single traffic source inside the group.

The detailed modeling of the TNL protocol stack in the Iub interface has also been included in the simulator up to (and including) the AAL2 layer. Special attention has been given to the modeling of the ATM and AAL2 layers. The simulator allows us to define different ATM Virtual Channels (VC) between the RNC and each Node-B. The current version of the simulator only supports CBR (Constant Bit Rate) VCs, being the inclusion of other types of service categories (rt-VBR, nrt-VBR, or UBR) scheduled for the future.

Fig. 4 illustrates the functional architecture of the AAL2/ATM stack block at the transmitter side. As shown in the figure, this block can be viewed as a hierarchy of buffers with their servers. The physical line bit rate, the different buffer lengths and the peak cell rate (PCR) of each VC are all configurable parameters, together with the Timer_CU value (described in ITU-T recommendation I.363.2 [10]).

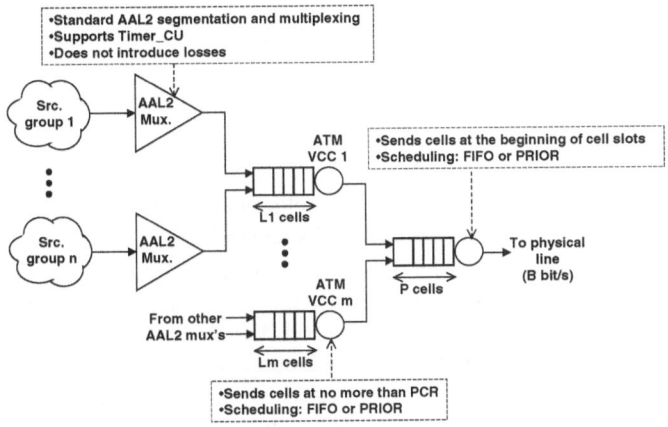

Fig. 4. AAL2/ATM stack modeling (transmitter side)

Devoting a separate ATM virtual channel to each UMTS traffic class is one possible means of giving the necessary QoS to different applications. In this case, ATM Traffic Management (TM) functions will be responsible for the appropriate resource sharing, according to traffic contract parameters. However, some authors have proposed to differentiate traffic classes not at the ATM level, but at a higher level, possibly AAL2 (see, for instance, [13], [5], [14] and [22]), although currently there exists no standard regarding traffic management at AAL2 level. We have included two basic scheduling mechanisms: FIFO and PRIOR. The former considers a single buffer where data units from different group of users (applications) are multiplexed in a first-in first-out basis, without establishing any differentiation among them. In the latter, the data units are served according to the priority of the user group that generated it. Two possible configurations have been considered when using PRIOR: keeping an independent buffer for each group of users, or having a shared buffer for all multiplexed groups.

The simulator offers two different traffic multiplexing strategies, which can be applied at two different multiplexing levels. Different traffic types can be multiplexed at physical level, so that each user group of a Node-B has its own ATM Virtual Channel (VC), or at AAL2 CPS-PDU (Common Part Sublayer Protocol Data Unit) level, so that two or more groups of users (e.g. voice and data users) share a VC. Both multiplexing strategies can be combined so that the performance under different configurations can be evaluated. The above-mentioned scheduling mechanisms can be applied at any (or both) of the multiplexing levels.

The simulator provides a number of statistics at the different levels considered, including the following:

- ATM level: CLR (Cell Loss Ratio), cell transfer delay, and cell delay variation per VC.

- AAL2 level: CPS packet delay and loss ratio, per AAL2 buffer.

- FP level: frame delay, delay variation and loss ratio per group of users.

5 Sample Results

In this section we present several sample results obtained with our simulation tool in order to provide the reader with an idea of its capabilities. The results presented here were obtained with a mix of two kinds of users (two traffic types): voice (AMR codec, 12.2 mode with SID [Silence Insertion Description] frames generation) and data (interactive web browsing). As for the burst level, the High state corresponds to a talk-spurt (voice) or to a downloading of a web document (data). The Low state is associated with SID frames of the codec (voice) or with the reading time between the end of one download and the beginning of the next (data). The parameterization of burst and packet levels is shown in Table 1. The statistical distribution of burst state durations is exponential, while both packet inter-arrival times and packet sizes have a constant distribution.

Burst mean durations (High and Low states) for voice traffic have been extracted from the speech source model present in Annex A of UMTS technical report TR 25.933 [9], where a recommended simulation model framework can be found. On the other hand, the chosen values for web-traffic burst durations can be derived from data published by ETSI in a technical report to be used in evaluation phases for UMTS [21]. The High state mean duration for web traffic is the time it takes to download an average-sized web document (12kB [21]) at the download bit rate (which has been arbitrarily chosen to be 64kbit/s[2]).

The time between packets is in both cases constant and equal to the TTI of the transport channel. The reason of this pseudo-periodicity in the packet generation process is the strict timing with which the physical layer of the radio protocols accept data blocks from the MAC sublayer (see [23] for more details), which greatly affects the packet generation process of Frame Protocol ([24]). As for the concrete values, 20 ms

---

[2] Both the mean web page size and the download bit rate are supposed to be calculated at RLC level for simplicity.

is a very common TTI to be supposed for AMR-codec traffic (see for instance [23] and [19]). 40 ms for web traffic is a value inspired by some examples present in 3GPP report [25].

Packet sizes for voice traffic are easy to obtain from the AMR codec specification [20] and taking into account the relevant protocol overheads. In the case of web traffic, during Low state no packets are generated. During High state, packets of 325 octets (the amount of information generated at 64 kbit/s during a TTI interval, plus FP header) are generated. Although the web application may not generate constant sized packets, RLC segmentation and concatenation functions are in charge of generating "correct-sized" PDUs to be passed to the MAC sublayer (see [26]).

Table 1. Mean values for traffic characterisation parameters

	Voice	Web
Burst level parameters		
High state duration	mean: 3 s	mean: 1.5 s
Low state duration	mean: 3 s	mean: 412 s
Packet level parameters		
Inter-arrival time (High and Low)	value: 20 ms	value: 40 ms
Packet size (High)	value: 40 octets	value: 325 octets
Packet size (Low)	value: 13 octets	value: 0 octets

In all the simulations a single CBR ATM channel was established between the RNC and a single Node-B, over an E1 physical line. The physical buffer size is 10 cells and the ATM VC buffer has a number of cells equal to the total number of end users being multiplexed over it. In all cases the AAL2 Timer_CU value is 1 ms.

The first kind of results presented, exemplified in Fig. 5, is obtained from a set of simulations including a group of identical users each.

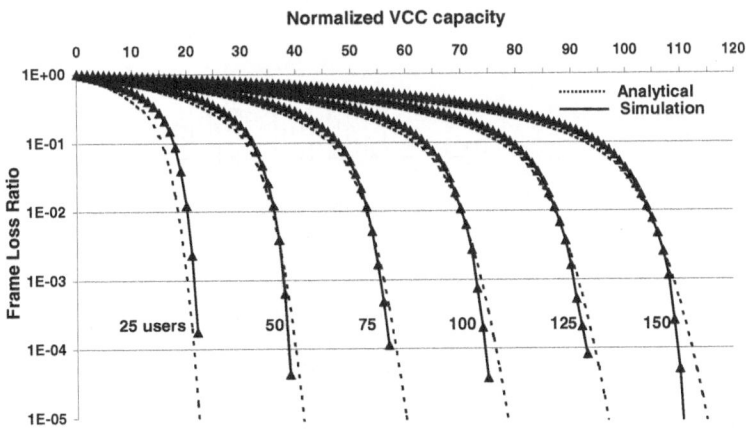

Fig. 5. Frame loss ratio as a function of PCR, voice

By varying the ATM VC capacity (PCR) through the experiments, we can obtain a set of curves that show the variation of a QoS parameter (e.g. frame loss ratio) with respect to the channel capacity. In particular, Fig. 5 represents the FP frame loss ratio as a function of the ATM VC capacity (normalized to the peak bit rate required for a single user at ATM level), for several amounts of voice users. The simulation results are compared with the values obtained via a fluid-flow analytical approximation present in [27], showing a reasonable similarity between both. Analogous results could be obtained with respect to other performance parameters (such as the 95th-percentile of frame delay).

Clearly, if frame loss ratio requirements for the Iub interface are known, these results can be taken as a dimensioning rule provided that an isolated VC is devoted to each traffic class.

Fig. 6 and 7 are example results of traffic mix scenarios.

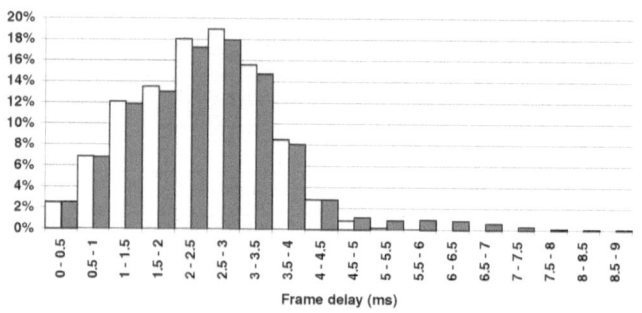

Fig. 6. FP frame delay histograms for PRIOR (white) and FIFO (grey), voice

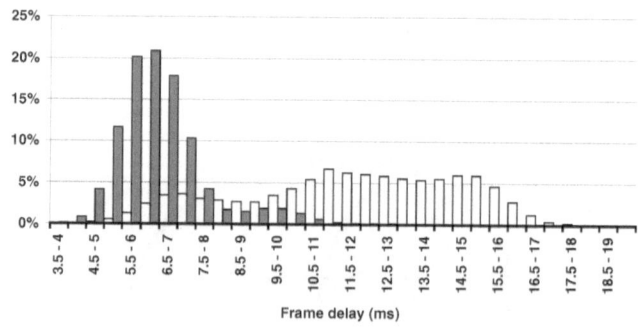

Fig. 7. FP frame delay histograms for PRIOR (white) and FIFO (grey), web

The figures present results for 50 voice and 50 web users sharing an ATM VC of capacity slightly greater than 1 Mbit/s (1 054 800 bit/s). Two simulation runs were executed, one with PRIOR scheduling (voice has priority over data) at AAL2 CPS PDU level, and the other with FIFO, to obtain the FP frame delay histograms for both type of users.

The graphs show that, with FIFO scheduling, data frames experiment significantly higher delays than voice ones. The reason is the difference between data and voice frame sizes (data frames need more cells to be transmitted). With PRIOR scheduling, voice frames experiment a reduction on delay jitter, while for data frames we observe a significant increase of delay. This is qualitatively correct. Since data traffic is considerably more bursty than voice traffic, the benefit that voice frames observe is less than the great growing in data frames delay, if we compare the results with the FIFO case.

6 Conclusions and Future Work

This paper has highlighted the main features of a UMTS Terrestrial Radio Access Network (UTRAN) simulator, as well as a sample of the results that can be obtained with it. The simulator has proved itself as a flexible tool with which useful results may be obtained with a reasonable effort. In the paper several graphs have been shown to illustrate the manner in which our simulation system could help in the task of evaluating the performance and dimensioning the UTRAN interface between a Node-B (or base station) and its controller (RNC).

The simulator allows a wide range of situations to be studied, offering an easy yet powerful way to configure the simulations (in terms of source parameters, number of users, ATM channel configuration, scheduling schemes, etc.). A large number of statistics can be obtained, including ATM CLR of the virtual channels, FP frame loss ratio, frame delay and delay variation.

Regarding future work, it is envisaged to perform simulations including all the four UMTS traffic classes, each with an appropriately modeled statistic behavior. Also, by adding the relevant code, other original (non-standard) traffic scheduling methods (apart from the two already developed) could be tested, possibly mixed with standard ATM-based traffic management. This could help checking the advantages of using different mechanisms inside some UTRAN interfaces. If the platform is upgraded with more UTRAN interfaces and modules, even more general UTRAN parameterization studies could be performed.

References

1. Holma, H., Toskala, A.: WCDMA for UMTS: Radio Access for Third Generation Mobile Communications. John Wiley & Sons. 2000
2. UMTS Forum: The UMTS Third Generation Market Study Update. Report No. 17 from the UMTS Forum. August 2001
3. Pöysti, A.: Blocking in Third Generation Radio Access Networks. M.Sc. Thesis. Helsinki University of Technology, Department of Engineering Physics and Mathematics. 2000
4. Valko, A.G., Racz, A., Fodor, G.: Voice QoS in Third-Generation Mobile Systems. IEEE Journal on Selected Areas in Communications, Vol. 17, No. 1. January 1999. 109-123
5. Eneroth, G., Fodor, G., Leijonhufvud, G., Rácz, A., Szabó, I.: Applying ATM/AAL2 as a Switching Technology in Third-Generation Mobile Access Networks. IEEE Communications, Vol. 37 No. 6. June 1999. 112-122

6. Nananukul, S., Guo, Y., Holma, M., Kekki, S.: Some Issues in Performance and Design of the ATM/AAL2 Transport in the UTRAN. IEEE Wireless Communications and Networking Conference 2000 (IEEE WCNC 2000). Chicago, IL, September 2000

7. Dimitriou, N., Tafazolli, R., Sfikas, G.: Quality of service for multimedia CDMA. IEEE Communications Magazine, Volume 38, Issue 7. July 2000. 88–94

8. Parsa, K., Ghassemzadeh, S.S., Kazeminejad, S.: Systems Engineering of Data Services in UMTS W-CDMA Systems. 2001 IEEE International Conference on Communications (ICC2001). Helsinki, Finland. June 11-15 2001

9. 3GPP: IP Transport in UTRAN. 3GPP TR 25.933. March 2002

10. ITU-T Recommendation I.363.2. B-ISDN ATM Adaptation layer specification: Type 2 AAL. November 2000

11. 3GPP: UTRAN Iur and Iub Interface Data Transport & Transport Signalling for DCH Data Streams. 3GPP TS 25.426

12. Isnard, O., Calmel, J.-M., Beylot, A.-L., Pujolle, G.: Performance evaluation of AAL2 protocol in UMTS Terrestrial Radio Access Network. ITC Specialist Seminar on Mobile Systems and Mobility. Lillehammer, Norway. March 2000. 289-300

13. Isnard, O., Calmel, J.-M., Beylot, A.-L., Pujolle, G.: Handling Traffic Classes at AAL2 / ATM layer over the Logical Interfaces of the UMTS Terrestrial Access Network. 11th IEEE International Symposium on Personal, Indoor and Mobile Radio Communication, PIMRC. London, England. September 2000. Vol. 2, 1464-1468

14. Yoo, S.-K., Park, H.-S.: Quality-of-Service Provisioning for Mobile Voice and Data Services over ATM Network using AAL2. 3rd ICACT. Muju, Korea. Feb. 2001

15. Reyes-Lecuona, A., González-Parada, E., Casilari, E., Casasola, J.C., Díaz-Estrella, A.: A page-oriented WWW traffic model for wireless system simulations. Proceedings of the 16th International Teletraffic Congress (ITC'16). Edinburgh, United Kingdom. June 1999. 1271-1280

16. Staehle, D., Leibnitz, K., Tran-Gia, P.: Source Traffic Modeling of Wireless Applications. International Journal of Electronics and Communications, volume 55, issue 1. 2001

17. Klemm, A., Lindemann, C., Lohmann, M.: Traffic Modeling and Characterization for UMTS Networks. Proc. of the Globecom, Internet Performance Symposium. San Antonio TX. November 2001

18. 3GPP: QoS Concept and Architecture. 3GPP TS 23.107

19. Isnard, O.: Etude du protocole AAL2 dans le réseau d'accès radio terrestre UMTS. Ph.D. Thesis (Université Versailles Saint-Quentin-en-Yvelines). 2000

20. 3GPP: AMR Speech Codec; General Description. 3GPP TS 26.071

21. ETSI: Universal Mobile Telecommunications System (UMTS); Selection procedures for the choice of radio transmission technologies of the UMTS. TR 101 112 V3.2.0. April 1998

22. Lim, H., Lee, S., Lee, D., Kim, K., Song, K., Oh, C.: A New AAL2 Scheduling Algorithm for Mobile Voice and Data Services over ATM. ITC-CSCC 2000, vol. 1. Pusan, Korea. July 2000. 229-232

23. 3GPP: Services provided by the physical layer. 3GPP TS 25.302

24. 3GPP: UTRAN Iub/Iur interface user plane protocol for DCH data streams. 3GPP TS 25.427

25. 3GPP: Channel coding and multiplexing examples. 3GPP TR 25.944

26. 3GPP: Radio Link Control (RLC) protocol specification. 3GPP TS 25.322

27. Hersent, O., Gurle, D., Petit, J.-P.: IP Telephony – Packet-based multimedia communications systems. Addison-Wesley (2000). Chapter 7

Vertical Handover Based Adaptation for Multimedia Applications in Pervasive Systems

Jadwiga Indulska and Sasitharan Balasubramaniam

School of Information Technology and Electrical Engineering
The University of Queensland
St.Lucia, QLD 4072, Australia
{jaga, sasi}@itee.uq.edu.au

Abstract. This paper proposes an architecture for pervasive computing which utilizes context information to provide adaptations based on vertical handovers (handovers between heterogeneous networks) while supporting application Quality of Service (QoS). The future of mobile computing will see an increase in ubiquitous network connectivity which allows users to roam freely between heterogeneous networks. One of the requirements for pervasive computing is to adapt computing applications or their environment if current applications can no longer be provided with the requested QoS. One of possible adaptations is a vertical handover to a different network. Vertical handover operations include changing network interfaces on a single device or changes between different devices. Such handovers should be performed with minimal user distraction and minimal violation of communication QoS for user applications. The solution utilises context information regarding user devices, user location, application requirements, and network environment. The paper shows how vertical handover adaptations are incorporated into the whole infrastructure of pervasive systems.

1 Introduction

The growth of the Internet and wireless networks has seen an increase in the research and development of pervasive computing systems. Pervasive computing allows ubiquitous access to information at any time, from any place, using a variety of devices and allows changing between different networks and devices. An ideal pervasive computing environment should provide minimal user distraction to allow users to interact at subconscious level [1]. Current cellular networks have data transmission capabilities adequate enough for internet applications such as web browsing. However, with the future cellular network expanding to allow access to broadband transmission, users will have the capability to transmit and receive multimedia contents on mobile devices [2] . With the growth of heterogeneous solutions for wireless networking (local wireless networks and global cellular telecommunication networks) it is necessary to provide support

F. Boavida et al. (Eds.): IDMS/PROMS 2002, LNCS 2515, pp. 61–72, 2002.

for dynamic changes between networks in order to support pervasive computing environment for users.

A major requirement for pervasive systems is the ability to adapt to the changes of context in which computational applications operate, such as adaptations of the applications (e.g. the change of accessible services if the user changes location) or their communication streams (e.g. through application of filters) or adaptation in the underlying communication protocols. One area in the adaptation of communication protocols is the ability to dynamically change between heterogeneous networks (between their suites of protocols). Such changes are called vertical handovers and they permit users to change between heterogeneous networks and at the same time maintain connectivity of their applications. So far, research on vertical handovers has concentrated on performing vertical handovers between network interfaces of one mobile device when the user loses coverage of the currently used network (i.e. disconnection happens) but the user is in a range of an overlay network coverage. Pervasive systems, due to their goal of supporting mobile users, devices, and applications, have to be aware of the computational context of each application. Therefore, it is possible to utilise this context information in order to apply vertical handovers as one of the adaptation methods in the system. In pervasive systems, vertical handovers can be used not only to deal with disconnections but can also be applied when network Quality of Service (QoS) degrades or when users want to change their computing devices and still continue their computing applications. One of the important QoS indices is cost, and it can be also taken into account if it is possible to change user communication to a cheaper network when the user moves into the area covered by such a network.

A Mobile Support System (MSS) architecture proposed in this paper utilises context information (user profiles, location, device capabilities, application requirements, network capabilities, and current network QoS) to make decisions about vertical handovers. Vertical handover operations performed by MSS may be due to user migration from one network coverage to another, or degradation in current network QoS while the user is within the coverage of a network with higher resources, or due to discovery, in a new location, of a device that has access to a network with higher QoS. The architecture adaptively performs vertical handover with minimal user distraction and the violation of the QoS required by the application is minimised during such handovers.

The remainder of the paper is organised as follows. Section 2 discusses the related work on vertical handovers. Section 3 presents an overview of the MSS architecture. Section 4 presents the functionality of the Mobile Support Base Agent (MSBA) and the Mobile Support Correspondent Agent (MSCA) which are components of MSS. Section 5 describes the context model utilised for vertical handovers. Section 6 characterizes the functionality of the Adaptation Manager with regards to vertical handovers. Section 7 describes the MSS prototype development, and finally Section 8 presents the conclusion.

2   Related Work

Helal et. al [3], developed the Full Stack Adaptation (FSA) concept to allow both horizontal and vertical handovers between Ethernet, wireless LAN (WLAN), and wireless WAN. In order to allow seamless network interchange, Mobile IP was integrated into the FSA architecture. The architecture allows the application to participate fully in the handover process by providing recommendations in the event of Quality of Service (QoS) changes. Information about the effects of vertical handover is delivered to the Application Adaptation layer in order to perform any necessary adaptation. The vertical LAN/WAN handoff layer in the FSA architecture monitors network characteristics, available power, and application requirements in order to perform vertical handoffs between network interfaces. The FSA architecture is limited to packet transmission that requires TCP/IP. The disadvantage of employing Mobile IP into the architecture is the added latency involved in triangular routing. The Mobile IP specification has a routing process known as triangular routing, where all packets sent to the mobile device must be sent to the mobile's home network and forwarded to the mobile's current location [4]. The FSA architecture requires the detection of signal strength before a vertical handover operation can be performed. The latency involved in discovering disconnections, finding new access points and performing handover will lead to packet losses while changing between network interfaces.

Stemm and Katz developed a vertical handover scheme for wireless networks [5], that provides coverage over a range of geographical areas. The goal of the system is to allow a mobile user to roam among multiple wireless networks in a manner that is completely transparent to applications and that disrupts connectivity as little as possible. The wireless overlay networks used in the architecture include an infrared room network, a WaveLAN network (in buildings), and a Ricochet Wide Area Network. Initial tests revealed that the time needed for vertical handovers is dominated by the time to discover that the mobile has moved in/out of coverage and therefore needs to change the network. This time tremendously affects applications that require low handover latency. Enhancements were later made to minimize this handover latency by either broadcasting beacons at higher frequency or performing packet doublecasting. The project relied heavily on the mobile device making handover decisions based on packet loss thresholds and therefore the handover time is quite long. This approach does not provide QoS support for applications during vertical handover. Similarly to the FSA architecture, this approach only supports vertical handovers due to disconnections and does not support network changes due to QoS degradation.

In ubiquitous/pervasive systems it is possible to use context information to predict many of the necessary vertical handovers. Therefore it is possible to dramatically shorten the handover time as the discovery of network disconnections is eliminated.

3 Mobile Support System Overview

The MSS architecture is built for ubiquitous/pervasive systems and operates above the transport layer in order to support heterogeneous networks using different communication protocols. Pervasive systems have to allow mobility of users, devices, and computing applications and therefore need to provide adaptability if the changes in the computing environment impact on the QoS of applications' communication streams. Pervasive systems utilise context information to discover changes in the computing environment and to make decisions on appropriate adaptability methods. MSS also utilises context information and therefore its architecture includes the Context Repository, the Adaptation Manager, the Mobility Support Base Agent (MSBA), and the Mobility Support Correspondent Agent (MSCA), as illustrated in Fig.1. The Context Repository provides storage and retrieval of context information. It is able to evaluate changes in context information and can notify the Adaptation Manager about context changes if they dramatically affect the application. Context information includes capability profiles of user devices (including available network interfaces), current network QoS, network coverage, application requirements, and user profile and location. Pervasive systems require that the infrastructure gathers context information through monitoring agents such as network environment monitoring agents and location monitoring agents. These agents monitor the network environment and feed the context information to the Context Repository. The Adaptation Manager registers with the Context Repository for event notification about context changes.

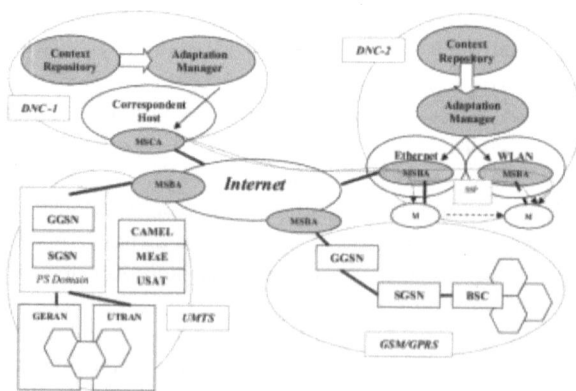

Fig. 1. MSS architecture applied to four heterogeneous networks

The Adaptation Manager processes notification about context changes to select appropriate adaptation methods. Adaptation methods include, among others, vertical handovers between network interfaces of a single device or between different devices. Different networks provide varying levels of resources, especially wireless networks such as cellular networks which are more susceptible to environmental variations than wired connections. The resources in these networks must be shared between varying number of users. The networks also differ in their support for communication QoS. Therefore in designing vertical handovers, QoS support required by applications has to be taken into account. Vertical handovers have to provide QoS mapping between the old and new networks and also minimise QoS violation during handovers.

The MSS architecture applied to four heterogeneous networks is illustrated in Fig.1. The overlaying networks in a particular domain (departmental domain, enterprise domain, etc.) are clustered together into a Domain Network Cluster (DNC). Each DNC is supported by the Adaptation Manager and the Context Repository. It is assumed that MSBA and MSCA reside in each network in DNC. When the Adaptation Manager decides to apply a vertical handover, it is the role of the MSBA to support the handover and minimise QoS violation during the handover. The MSBA uses multicasting to the old and the new network in order to minimise packet losses and minimise packet latency. If the Adaptation Manager decides that in addition to the vertical handover also some adaptations of the communication streams are necessary to adjust it to the current network QoS, it is the role of the MSCA to adjust the communication stream to suit the available network resources and device capability.

The MSBA also supports vertical handover to mobile cellular networks such as General Packet Radio Service (GPRS)/Universal Mobile Telecommunications System (UMTS). The Adaptation Manager, local to DNC, has access to the MSBA which controls the communication streams entering the GPRS/UMTS networks. GPRS is an extension to the Global System for Mobile Communication (GSM) network to provide packet data transmission [6]. The extension to the network is the GPRS support node (GSN), which includes the serving-GSN (SGSN) or a gateway-GSN (GGSN) [7]. The upcoming 3rd generation network, UMTS, will be built on the GSM/GPRS foundation with certain modifications made to the air interface and core network to allow higher data transmission capabilities [8,9]. For both the GPRS and UMTS network, the GGSN of the UMTS network interfaces the external Packet Data Network (PDN). Therefore, as shown in Fig.1, the MSBA is positioned between the GGSN and PDN.

4   Functionality of MSBA and MSCA

The goal of the MSBA is twofold: to receive notifications from the Adaptation Manager about necessary vertical handovers for particular mobile devices and to assist the mobile devices during handover procedures in order to minimise QoS violations during the handovers. Two MSBAs, one from the old network and one from the new network, are involved in vertical handovers. The main methods used by the MSBAs to minimise QoS violations are multicasting by the old MSBA (SSP- Split Stream Packet operation) and buffering in the new MSBA. To accomplish the vertical handover, the packet stream will be redirected to the new network (a new packet stream will be established between the mobile device and

Correspondent Host). During this redirection the old MSBA uses multicasting to the old base station and the new MSBA to minimise packet loss. The purpose of the buffering mechanism in the new MSBA is to minimise packet loss and minimise latency variation during vertical handover. Two solutions have been proposed for the MSBA design, which includes a static MSBA and a dynamic MSBA.

A static MSBA design is shown in Fig.1, where the MSBA is represented as a proxy and directs all incoming packet streams to the mobile device. The disadvantage of employing a static MSBA is that the proxy can be a bottleneck in the network since all streams must pass through this proxy. The advantage of the static MSBA is the simplicity of the architecture, whereby only a single agent residing in each network is required for mobility support.

To avoid congestion and the bottleneck problem at the MSBA, a dynamic MSBA architecture can be used, where an additional Dispatching Agent (DA) is inserted in each base station. All communication streams are directed to the mobile device through the DA instead of going through the MSBA. The MSBA will only be utilised in the event of vertical handover where an SSP operation is performed by the DA, to allow multicasting of packets to the mobile device and to the new MSBA. Similar to the static MSBA, all packets are then directed from the old MSBA to the new MSBA during the vertical handover period.

The MSCA resides at the Correspondent Host and is in charge of transmitting communication streams to the MSBA. The MSCA is involved in additional stream adaptations if adaptations are requested by the Adaptation Manager.

5   Context Description

Context information managed by the Context Repository is organised based on a user profile hierarchy. Namely, context information is divided into two types: Static User Profile and Dynamic User Profile. The Static User Profile includes contextual information which does not change very often, e.g. user personal settings, various user devices and their capabilities. The Dynamic User Profile captures current information about users, such as the current device the user is using, the currently used network interface, network QoS monitoring information, and current user location. Accompanying the Dynamic User Profile is the Impending Network Profile (INP), which holds the QoS information of the next network the user may move to based on the priority set in the personal setting. Certain networks such as cellular networks have varying network conditions between cells depending on the number of users in each cell. Therefore, in order to perform QoS mapping from the current network, QoS information for the new network is required during vertical handovers. QoS information includes current bandwidth, current loss rate, current delay, and delay variation. For devices accessing the UMTS network, such information is obtainable from the Open System Architecture [8].

The **device** profile includes characteristics of various user devices. Each device has an associated device **capability** information, device **software**, user

personal setting for the device, and device **network interfaces**. The device profile information is based on the CC/PP description for mobile devices [10] with some necessary extensions as indicated.

Device capability includes CPU, memory, screen size, operating system, device communication type (eg. wireless or wireline), and content capability (eg. text, images, sound, and video capability).

Device software context information describes software applications for each device. The software applications are grouped based on their communication QoS requirements (Application Traffic Class Requirements - ATCR) into the following classes: Conventional Internet Services class, Playback Streaming class, and Conversational Streaming class. The Conventional Internet Services class includes applications for web-browsing, ftp, e-mails, etc. Playback Streaming class is for stored multimedia applications (eg. radio, audio). The Conversational Streaming class is for real time multimedia applications such as live radio, video conferencing, etc. Each class contains four attributes: delay, jitter, bandwidth, and packet loss. For video and audio streaming in Conversational and Playback Streaming class, context information is also provided with regard to the encoding standard used for multimedia streams (eg. encoding scheme: Mpeg-1, Mpeg-2; encoding method: VBR, CBR). This context information is used when QoS mapping is performed during vertical handovers.

The Personal Setting context allows users to specify their device and network interface priorities. The priority shows the order of devices and the preferred network interfaces for each device. This information is used to perform vertical handover to the user most preferred device or network interface if several options are available.

Associated with each device is context information about network interfaces in order to determine which different networks a particular device can access. Certain devices may have multiple network interfaces allowing access to variety of networks, eg. laptops which may have access to Ethernet, WLAN, Bluetooth, or GPRS networks. Network context also includes specific network information, especially for third party cellular network operators, eg. GSM/UMTS.

To predict possible disconnections based on context description not on signal strength, some information about network coverage has to be provided in the context description. This information is related to wireless networks which have a reasonably static topology (e.g. WLAN with access points attached to a wired network). The information about network coverage for ad-hoc networks (e.g. Bluetooth) can be derived dynamically from the information about devices and their location. There are many ways in which network coverage can be modelled. For simplicity, we model network coverage as a two dimensional geographical grid map. The map provides information with regards to the geographic coverage provided by each network. Segmenting the map into grid blocks provides information about the different networks accessible by users currently located in this grid. The location context information provides user location information with respect to this geographical grid map. The context information also describes the transition zones to indicate the maximum edge of network coverage. This information is analysed by the Adaptation Manager in order to trigger any necessary vertical handovers in the event the user may be disconnected due to the lack of network coverage or has approached a network that can provide better (preferred) network resources.

Our context model also includes **User Cellular Network Profiles** for GPRS and UMTS networks, which contain information from the PDP (Packet Data Protocol) context. The PDP context, created by the GPRS network for each session [11], includes PDP address (IP address for the mobile host, the GGSN uses this to enable packet transmission between the PDN and the mobile device), PDP type (eg. IPv4), the requested QoS, and the address of the GGSN that serves as the access point to the PDN (converting IP packets to GTP (GPRS Tunneling Protocol)) [7].

In GPRS networks, a specific QoS profile, which is part of the PDP context profile, is allocated to every subscriber upon attachment to the network [7]. The user QoS profile includes service precedence class (high, normal, low), reliability class (3 levels), delay class (4 levels), and peak and mean throughput class (8Kb/s to 2Mb/s). To allow for a systematic GPRS QoS adaptation, the context description sets the QoS profile attributes for each ATCR class. The purpose of setting the QoS profile is to provide the quality the user has requested based on billing of the service. Therefore for each ATCR class, the user defines the required QoS class, e.g. video (Playback Streaming – ATCR-2): service precedence:high, packet loss:10^{-9}, delay:0.1ms, mean throughput:64Kb/s (only base layer of scalable flow video). Unlike the GPRS system, where a GPRS QoS is requested by the user or a default profile is assigned, UMTS defines QoS profiles for corresponding applications. The UMTS network organizes application QoS requirements into four classes: Conversational class, Streaming class, Interactive class, and Background class. The QoS parameters for each class are maximum bit rate (Kb/s), guaranteed bit rate (Kb/s), allowed transfer delay (ms), and whether the requested QoS class is negotiable or not.

The context information also describes the address and location of the closest GGSN for the PLMN which is served by the MSS. This information provides for efficient vertical handovers in the event user has moved to a GPRS/UMTS network.

6   Adaptation

Amongst many adaptation methods employed by the Adaptation Manager, there are two methods which use vertical handover as a means of adaptation: handover between different network interfaces on a single device or handover between different devices. In both cases the vertical handover functionality can be divided into two parts: the Vertical Handover Initiation policy and QoS Mapping policy. The first triggers a vertical handover operation between network interfaces or devices after evaluating context information. The second provides QoS mapping policy from the old network to the new one.

Vertical Handover Initiation Policy. The Vertical Handover Initiation policy provides a method to invoke vertical handover operations between interfaces on a single device or inter device vertical handover (handover from one device to another). The vertical handover operation on a single device is invoked based on the location context change, or changes to the current network QoS. The policy evaluates the user location, network coverage, network QoS, and network interface context information to determine to which network the transmission should be handed over. If the user has a device with many network interfaces and is in a geographical area where variety of networks are available, the personal setting context is evaluated to select the most appropriate network. Inter device vertical handover is invoked when a user has no access to any network coverage on their present device. It can also be invoked manually by the user.

QoS Mapping Policy. Once a vertical handover decision is made by the Adaptation Manager, QoS mapping is performed to ensure required QoS for the communication stream and to trigger an adaptation of the communication if QoS cannot be provided. Different networks have varying network resources, therefore adaptation of the communication may be required to suit the new networking characteristics. QoS mapping performed between local networks, such as Ethernet or WLAN, is based on the availability of network resources.

QoS mapping for vertical handovers to cellular networks must take into account the QoS profile (eg. GPRS PDP context) that is set for the specific network. The policy determines the available network resources within the cellular network and maps to the user GPRS QoS profile. The mapping then leads to any required adaptation of the communication stream for the available resources. For the UMTS network, the application QoS profile context produced by the UMTS network is mapped to the external PDN through the QoS Mapping policy.

The Adaptation Manager evaluates the dynamic network QoS context, INP context, device capability context, and ATCR context to perform any necessary adaptation required for the communication stream. Adaptation of the communication stream may involve filtering (eg. jpeg to wbmp format) or scaling (eg. scalable flows for MPEG video) of contents for the new communication stream. The MSBA and the MSCA contain filters that are required for the communication stream adaptation.

7   MSS Prototype

The development of the MSS architecture is part of our ongoing work towards building an infrastructure for pervasive systems [12,13,14]. A prototype for the MSS has been built to test the cooperation of the Context Repository and Adaptation Manager and also functionalities of the MSBA and the MSCA. The scenario used in the prototype is shown in Fig.1 in DNC-2. It assumes a device connected to an Ethernet network and a vertical handover operation is performed to a WLAN network. In the prototype, the Adaptation Manager is notified by the Context Repository about context changes and after evaluating these changes it may trigger vertical handover. The basic part of context information for this scenario is shown in the table in Fig.2. As the resources in the new network are much higher the Adaptation Manager in addition to vertical handover may also trigger an adaptation of the communication stream.

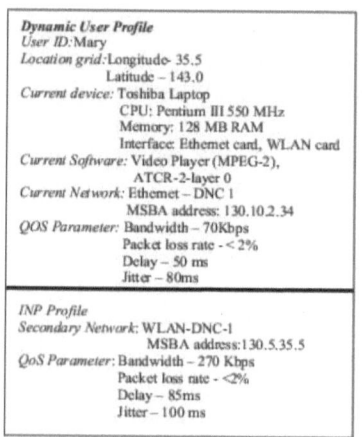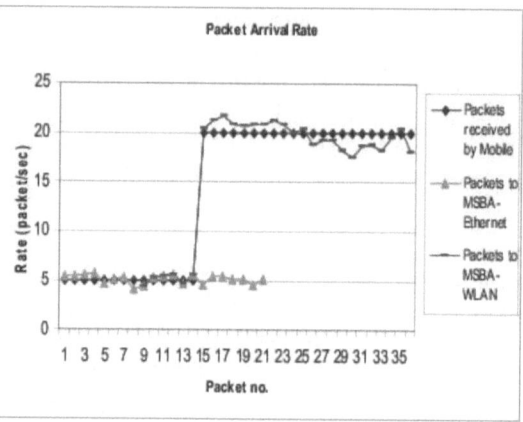

Fig. 2. Prototype Context description scenario and graph of throughput change during vertical handover

The prototype vertical handover is performed for a playback streaming video transmission over the UDP protocol. The video application is based on MPEG-2 standard layered flows. The MPEG-2 layered flows allow video streams to be compressed into multiple layers: a base layer (eg. layer 0(64kpbs)) and one or more enhancement layers (eg. layer 1(256 kbps) and layer 2(1.5 Mbps)) [15]. The base layer can be decoded independently and provides basic quality. However, enhancement layers can also be encoded in parallel with base layer to improve quality. Based on the Dynamic User Profile, the Ethernet QoS bandwidth parameters indicate that the current network resources can only accommodate base layer streams. Therefore, the current software requirement is categorised as ATCR class 2:layer 0, shown in Fig. 2. The personal setting context (the INP profile) is set to a WLAN network as the secondary network for vertical handover. The QoS bandwidth parameters of the INP profile indicates an increase in resources compared to the previous network. The Adaptation Manager discovers that according to the geographical grid, the user location is within the WLAN network coverage. The Adaptation Manager, therefore, triggers a vertical handover operation from Ethernet to WLAN and in the process upgrades the video stream to ATCR class 2:layer 0+layer 1.

The graph in Fig.2, shows the packet stream transmitted to the MSBA-Ethernet, the MSBA-WLAN, and the mobile device. The initial low packet rate indicates the base layer packet stream transmitted to the MSBA-Ethernet. The graph shows the SSP operation activated by the Adaptation Manager starting at packet 9, where the MSBA-WLAN receives the packets from the MSBA-Ethernet at the same rate (this is shown between packets 9 to 14). Once the SSP operation starts, a new data stream is formed between the MSCA and the MSBA-WLAN, where the new data stream is transmitted at a higher rate. During the transparent operation of SSP, the network interface change is performed. The mobile device connects to the MSBA-WLAN and upgrades the packet stream to ATCR class 2- layer 0 + layer 1. Packets transmitted by the MSCA are uniquely identified, allowing the MSBA-WLAN to differentiate and eliminate any repetition packets received from both the MSBA-Ethernet and the MSCA. The packet transmission to the mobile host is performed at a fixed rate as jitter is eliminated during the packet transmission. The prototype has demonstrated the ability of the Adaptation Manager to evaluate context description (user location, network coverage, and network QoS) in order to trigger vertical handover to a network of higher resources. During the vertical handover operation, QoS support was also provided by multicasting packets (SSP) to minimise packet losses and variation of packet delay, and at the same time the video flow was adapted to suit the new networking resources.

8   Conclusion

Future ubiquitous/pervasive systems need to provide adaptations to context changes caused by mobility of users, devices or applications. One kind of adaptations is a vertical handover which allows users to roam between heterogeneous networks with minimal application disruptions. Vertical handover approaches have so far provided solutions for user disconnections. Vertical handovers can, however, play a greater role in future pervasive systems. They can be used to deal not only with disconnections but also with network QoS changes and/or can be used to support user preferences for networking connections and devices when the networking environment changes due to user mobility.

In this paper we presented an architecture which uses vertical handovers as adaptation methods in pervasive systems. The architecture utilizes context information (user profile, user location, device capability, application requirements, network capabilities, and network QoS) in order to select a vertical handover as the most appropriate adaptation method in the given state of the whole system. The proposed MSS architecture includes the Adaptation Manager and the Context Repository which can support multiple heterogeneous networks within one domain. Each of these networks uses the MSBA and the MSCA to carry out vertical handovers and to ensure that QoS violations are minimised during such handovers. The MSBAs use multicasting and packet buffering during vertical handovers to avoid packet loss and minimise variation of packet latency whereas the MSCA can adapt the communication stream to suit the new network resources and device capability. A prototype that demonstrates both the cooperation between the Context Repository and the Adaptation Manager which leads to vertical handovers and the handover procedure between two different networks has been developed for the MSS architecture.

References

[1] Satyanarayanan, M.: Pervasive Computing: Vision and Challenges. IEEE Personal Communications **8** (August 2001) 10–17

[2] De Vriendt, J., Laine, P., Lerouge, C., Xu, X.: Mobile network evolution: a revolution on the move. IEEE Communications Magazine **40** (April 2002) 104–111

[3] Helal, S., Lee, C., Zhang,Y., RichardIII, G.G.: An Architecture for Wireless LAN/WAN Integration. In: IEEE Wireless Communication and Networking Conference (WCNC) 2000, Chicago, Illinois (September 2000)

[4] Perkins, C.E.: Mobile IP. IEEE Communications Magazine **35** (1997) 84–99

[5] Stemm, M., Katz, R.H.: Vertical handoffs in wireless overlay networks. Mobile Networks and Applications **3** (1998) 335–350

[6] Ghribi, B., Logrippo, L.: Understanding GPRS: the GSM packet radio service. Computer Networks **34** (2000) 763–779

[7] Priggouris, G., Hadjiefthymiades, S., Merakos, L.: Supporting IP QoS in the General Packet Radio Service. IEEE Network **14** (September/October 2000) 8–17

[8] Bos, L., Leroy, S.: Toward an All-IP-Based UMTS System Architecture. IEEE Network **15** (January/February 2001) 36–45

[9] Huber, J.F., Weiler, D., Brand, H.: UMTS, the Mobile Multimedia Vision for IMT-2000: A Focus on Standardization. IEEE Communications Magazine **38** (September 2000) 129 –136

[10] Nilsson, M., Hjelm, J., Ohto, H.: Composite Capabilities/Preference Profiles: Requirements and Architectures. W3C Working Draft 21 (July 2000)

[11] Bettstetter, C., Vogel, H., Eberspacher, J.: GSM Phase 2+ General Packet Radio Service GPRS: Architecture, Protocols, and Air Interface. IEEE Communications Surveys **2** (1999)

[12] Henricksen, K., Indulska, J., Rakotonirainy, A.: Modeling Context Information in Pervasive Computing Systems. In Lecture Notes in Computer Science, Mattern, F. and Naghshineh, M., ed.: Proc. of the First International Conference Pervasive 2002. Volume 2414., Zurich, Switzerland, Springer Verlag (August 2002) 167–180

[13] Rakotonirainy, A., Indulska, J., Loke, S.W., Zaslavsky, A.: Middleware for Reactive Components : An Integrated Use of Context, Roles, and Event Based Coordination. In Lecture Notes in Computer Science, Guerraouri, R., ed.: Proc. of the IFIP/ACM International Conference on Distributed Systems Platforms. Volume 2218., Heidelberg, Germany, Springer Verlag (November 2001) 77–98

[14] Indulska, J., Loke, S.W., Rakotonirainy, A., Witana, V., Zaslavsky, A.: An Open Architecture for Pervasive Systems. In: Proc. of the Third IFIP TC6/WG6.1 International Working Conference on Distributed Applications and Interoperable Systems, Krakow, Poland, Kluwer (September 2001) 175–187

[15] Wu, D., Hou, Y.T., Zhang,Y.: Transporting Real-time Video over the Internet: Challenges and Approaches. Proceedings of the IEEE **88** (December 2000) 1855 –1877

Avoiding DAD for Improving Real-Time Communication in MIPv6 Environments

Marcelo Bagnulo, Ignacio Soto, Alberto García-Martínez, and Arturo Azcorra

Universidad Carlos III de Madrid – Dep. Ingeniería Telemática
Avenida Universidad, 30. Leganés, Madrid 28911 – España
{marcelo,isoto,alberto,azcorra}@it.uc3m.es

Abstract. Current specification of address configuration mandates the execution of the Duplicate Address Detection (DAD) mechanism to prevent address duplication. However, a proper support for real time multimedia applications in mobile IPv6 nodes is undermined by the disruption imposed by DAD. In order to overcome this limitation, the usage of randomly generated IPv6 Interface Identifiers without previously performing DAD is proposed, based on the statistic uniqueness of the addresses generated through this method. The address duplication risk is quantified through the calculation of the probability of an Interface Identifier collision among the nodes sharing a link. The calculated probability is deemed to be negligible compared to other causes of communication failure, such as network outages.

1   Introduction[1]

In order to take full advantage of multimedia capabilities of current mobile devices, the network infrastructure must provide an uninterrupted flow of information to appropriately support real time traffic. However, the requirement for performing Duplicate Address Detection (DAD) in the address autoconfiguration mechanism limits the performance of mobility in IPv6, provided by Mobile IPv6 [1]. Using this protocol, a Mobile Node (MN) that joins a subnet must configure an on-link address in that subnet, the Care-of-Address (CoA), before being able to communicate. According to the Stateless Address Autoconfiguration mechanism presented in [2], before using the CoA the MN must perform DAD for that address in order to guarantee its uniqueness on the link. It should be noted that DAD is a time consuming process. Although this it is not an issue for a desktop computer that is booting, the time required for DAD is critical in a mobile environment, since during this time the MN can not communicate and besides, all active communications of the MN are interrupted. The time required to perform DAD has a default value of one second [2], [3], a value subjectively deemed as not acceptable for interactive voice communications [4]. The Mobile IPv6 (MIPv6) specification [1] identifies the aforementioned problem and states that a MN can decide not to perform DAD,

---

[1] This research was supported by the LONG (Laboratories Over Next Generation networks) project, IST-1999-20393 and MobyDick (Mobility and Differentiated Services in a Future IP Network) project, IST-2000-25394 .

F. Boavida et al. (Eds.): IDMS/PROMS 2002, LNCS 2515, pp. 73–79, 2002.
© Springer-Verlag Berlin Heidelberg 2002

pointing this as a trade-off between safety and the time needed for the DAD procedure.

This document proposes the use of random numbers to create the Interface Identifier part of the IPv6 addresses, and assesses the risk of using these addresses without previously performing DAD. It should be noted that this solution is not restricted to a particular data-link layer technology, although it can be optimized in particular cases, such as GPRS, in which collision can be avoided by the GGSN (Gateway GPRS Support Node).

The remainder of the paper is structured as follows: in section 2 the risk of not using the DAD mechanism is quantified in several relevant scenarios. In section 3, implementation issues are discussed, including random number generation and security aspects. In the next section, alternative proposals are considered and finally, section 5 is devoted to conclusions.

2   Avoiding DAD: Risk Assessment

In this section we will asses the risk of using randomly generated Interface Identifiers (IIDs) in IPv6 aggregatable addresses [5] without previously performing DAD. In order to do that, we will quantify the probability of a duplicate address event in several relevant scenarios and we will compare it with the probability of other critical events.

2.1   Duplicate Address Event Probability Calculation and Bounding

In the considered hypothesis, the Interface Identifier part of the IPv6 address is generated randomly, meaning that the node will use a 64 bit long random number as the IID. Actually, only 62 bits of the IID will be generated randomly, since the IID´s semantics defined in [6] imposes that the u bit must be set to "local" and the g bit must be set to "individual".

Considering that n is the number of possible IIDs (i.e. $n = 2^{62}$) and k is the number of interfaces (i.e. mobile nodes) on the same link, we will now calculate the probability of collision of two or more randomly generated IIDs:
We will represent the k IIDs in a link as a sequence of 62 bit long random variables I_i:

$$I_1, I_2, ..., I_k \quad \text{sequence of random integer variables with uniform distribution}$$

$$\text{between 1 and } n \, (k \le n)$$

We would like to obtain the probability that two or more I_is collide, i.e. $I_i = I_j$

The solution for this well known mathematical problem, called the "birthday problem", is presented in Appendix A.
The resulting expression for the probability of the collision of one or more I_i is:

$$P(n,k) = 1 - \frac{n!}{(n-k)! \, n^k} \tag{1}$$

In our particular case, $n = 2^{62}$, and k may vary depending on the considered scenario. We will now obtain an upper bound to $P(n,k)$ in order to simplify calculations (especially to avoid n ! computation)

Performing simple computations in equation (1), we easily obtain:

$$P(n,k) = 1 - \left\{ 1 \cdot \left(1 - \frac{1}{n} \right) \cdot \left(1 - \frac{2}{n} \right) \cdots \left(1 - \frac{k-1}{n} \right) \right\} \qquad (2)$$

Since

$$\forall i \in [1,2,...,k-1] \Rightarrow \frac{i}{n} \leq \frac{k-1}{n},$$

and considering that $k < n$, then

$$1 - \left(1 - \frac{1}{n} \right) \left(1 - \frac{2}{n} \right) \cdots \left(1 - \frac{k-1}{n} \right) \leq 1 - \left(1 - \frac{k-1}{n} \right)^{k-1}$$

Applying this last result to equation 2, we can obtain the following bound B:

$$P(n,k) \leq \frac{n^{k-1} - (n-k+1)^{k-1}}{n^{k-1}} = B \qquad (3)$$

We will next perform some calculations in order to quantify the order of magnitude of the probabilities involved:

We will bound $P(n,k)$ for the following values of k, which we consider to be representative of usual situations

$P(2^{62}, 20) \leq 7.8e - 17$

$P(2^{62}, 100) \leq 2.1e - 15$

$P(2^{62}, 500) \leq 5.4e - 14$

$P(2^{62}, 1000) \leq 2.2e - 13$

$P(2^{62}, 5000) \leq 5.4e - 12$

In order to fully seize the magnitude of the probabilities stated above, we can compare them with the probabilities of some rare events. For instance, according to Table 1.1 in [7], the probability of being killed by a lightning (per day) is about 1.1 e-10. Then, a mobile phone user should be more worried about being killed by a lightning in a given day than to have an interface identifier repeated when he performs a handoff.

Another relevant parameter that can be considered when evaluating the above probability, is the probability of a failure in a network device, since this failure would have similar effects i.e. the user can not continue the communication. So, the probability that a network device were not working properly in a given moment (when the user joins the network, for instance) can be calculated as follows:

$$P_{NEFails} = \frac{MTTR}{MTBF + MTTR}$$

Being MTTR the Meat Time To Repair and MTBF the Mean Time Between Failures.

Good network equipment can have an MTBF of 300,000 hours and if we suppose that some backup device is available, the MTTR stands for the time needed to replace the faulty element, e.g. 0.1 hour (6 minutes). In this case, $P_{NEFails} = 3.3e - 7$.

We can see that $P_{NEFails}$ is several orders of magnitude higher than $P(n,k)$ in the cases calculated above.

2.2 Scenarios

We have quantified the probability of a collision of two or more IIDs. However, this probability is not the most relevant parameter when we try to evaluate and compare the probability of failure of the system, since a mobile user will join multiple links in a given period. So, it is relevant to quantify the probability of at least one collision when a user performs multiple handoffs.

As we stated above, $P(n,k)$ is the probability of a collision of two or more IIDs when there are k interfaces in the same link. Hence, it can be derived that the probability of having at least one collision after joining m links is:

$$P(n,k,m) = 1 - (1 - P(n,k))^m \qquad (4)$$

According to the bound B presented in equation 3 and considering that both $P(n,k)$ and B are lower than 1, we can infer the following bound:

$$P(n,k,m) \le 1 - (1 - B)^m \qquad (5)$$

Therefore, in order to estimate the probability of a collision event during a given period, for instance a year, we must first establish a reasonable number of handoffs per day. If we consider 140 handoffs per day, which seems to be a considerable number, this would mean about 50.000 handoffs per year, i.e. $m=50.000$. Then the probability of having at least one collision over a year during which the mobile node has joined 140 links of 500 nodes per day is:

$$P(2^{62}, 500, 50.000) \le 2.7e - 9 \qquad (6)$$

And, if the considered links have 5.000 nodes each, instead of 500, the probability is:

$$P(2^{62}, 5.000, 50.000) \le 2.7e - 7 \qquad (7)$$

Considering that each time there is a collision there are two users affected, and not taking into account the collision of 3 or more IIDs for this estimation, there will be 6 users out of 1.000.000.000 that will have a communication problem during this year, if users make 140 handovers per day in networks containing 500 interfaces. In the case that users make 140 handovers per day in networks containing 5.000 interfaces, there will be 6 users out of 10.000.000 that will have a communication problem during this year. This probability could be contrasted with some network availability data provided by, for instance, mobile operators, but this data has proven to be extremely difficult to find.

3   Implementation Issues

In this section, we will address some implementation issues regarding random IIDs generation and related security concerns.

3.1   Random Numbers Generation

When considering the usage of random IIDs, the random number generation process must be properly addressed since it is essential to guarantee the statistic uniqueness of the identifier. Several methods have been proposed [8] to generate pseudo-random numbers based on information available in most platforms, such as laptops. However, in some cases, such as mobile phones, the resources required to perform appropriate random number generation may not be available. In such cases, it should be noted that it is not necessary to create the identifier in real time, as long as randomness were guaranteed. This means that when the node joins the network the identifier could have been created already in advance to a network change. It could even be pre-configured in the interface driver with the node using the same identifier without changing the probabilities calculations stated above; this is analogous to the day of birth in the birthday problem. This would reduce the complexity in the nodes, although a mechanism should be provided in order to solve recurrent collisions, caused for example, when two habitual users of the same segment collide.

3.2   Security Concerns

Randomly generated IIDs have also been considered in order to improve security. In particular, its usage has been proposed to ensure anonymity [9] and even to carry cryptographic information when Cryptographically Generated Addresses are used [10]. These proposals are fully compatible with the solution of this document so they can get the benefit of better performance by avoiding DAD.

4   Related Work

The requirement of performing DAD every time a node joins a link imposed by Stateless Address Autoconfiguration mechanisms [2] has already been stated to be a major limitation by the Internet community, resulting in several recommendations and solutions, some of which are discussed below.

The Mobile IP protocol [1] allows not performing DAD when a node joins a link in a trade-off between safety and the time needed for the DAD procedure. Besides, the use of fast handovers [11] allows performing DAD in advance, before the MN arrives to the subnet. In this case, the Access Router (AR) in the subnet is instructed to perform DAD on behalf of the MN before it enters the subnet. But then, the MN has to wait for the time needed to perform DAD before it can accomplish the handover. This is a problem when difficulties in the previous data-link layer connection force the handover. So we will again benefit from avoiding the DAD procedure.

Other solution, specific to 3GPP (3rd Generation Partnership Project), proposed to avoid DAD can be found in [12]. In this case DAD is not performed since every prefix is assigned to only one primary context, preventing from collisions by limiting the numbers of nodes that share the same link. However, this implies reserving a complete prefix of 64 bits to just a couple of interfaces, resulting in an enormous waste of address space.

5 Conclusions

The impact of the time required for DAD during handover on real time multimedia applications can not be underestimated. In this document we evaluate the usage of random numbers to construct the Interface Identifier part of IPv6 addresses and then we asses the risk of using such addresses without previously performing DAD. We conclude that the probability of failure due to a collision is low enough to be acceptable in most cases. Furthermore, we consider that the probability of a failure in a communication due to an IID collision is negligible compared with other quantifiable causes of failure, such as network equipment outage. It should be noted that in this estimation other relevant causes such as operation errors, which are usually considered to be more frequent than the ones presented, have not been included because of the unavailability of hard data. Other possible solutions for avoiding DAD have been presented along with its drawbacks, and we consider that the usage of random IIDs without previously performing DAD is an attractive option since it completely solves the presented problem and it does not incurs in excessive ulterior costs such as waste of address space.

References

1. Johnson, D. and C. Perkins, "Mobility Support in IPv6", Internet draft, Work in progress, July 2001.
2. Thomson, S. and T. Narten, "IPv6 Stateless Address Autoconfiguration", RFC 2462, December 1998.
3. Narten, T., Nordmark, E., Simpson, W., "Neighbor Discovery for IP Version 6 (IPv6)", RFC 2461, December 1998
4. Gruber, J. and Strawczynski, L., "Subjective Effects of Variable Delay in Speech Clipping in Dynamically Managed Voice Systems," IEEE Trans-actions on Communications, Vol. COM-33, No. 8, Aug. 1985.]
5. Hinden, R., O´Dell, M. and S. Deering, "An IPv6 Aggregatable Global Unicast Address Format", RFC 2374, July 1998.
6. Hinden, R. and S. Deering, "IP Version 6 Addressing Architecture", RFC 1998, 1998.
7. Schneier, B., "Applied cryptography", Wiley ISBN 0-471-12845-7,1996.

8. Eastlake, D., Crocker, S., Schiller, J., "Randomness Recommendations for security", RFC 1750, December 1994
9. Narten, T., Draves, R., "Privacy Extensions for Stateless Address Autoconfiguration in IPv6", RFC 3041, January 2001
10. Montenegro, G., Castelluccia, C., "SUCV Identifiers and addresses", Internet draft, Work in progress, November 2001
11. Dommety, G., "Fast Handovers for Mobile IPv6", Internet draft, Work in progress, 2001.
12. Wasserman, M., "Recommendations for IPv6 in 3GPP Standards", Internet Draft, Work in progress, April 2002

Appendix A: The Birthday Problem

The classical formulation of the birthday problem is as follows: we want to calculate the probability that in a group of k people, al least two of them have the same birthday.

We model the birthday as a integer random variable, with uniform distribution between 1 and n (in this particular case n is the number of possible birthdays i.e. $n=365$)

Then, the number N of ways that we can choose k values out of n with no duplicates would be:

$$N = n \cdot (n-1) \cdot ... \cdot (n-k+1)$$

On the other hand, the number of possibilities for choosing k elements out of n, without the restriction of not having any duplicates is n^k

Then, the probability of not having a collision when we select k elements out of n is:

$$P_{NO}(n,k) = \frac{n!}{(n-k)! \cdot n^k}$$

So, the probability of having at least one collision when we select k elements out of n is:

$$P(n,k) = 1 - \frac{n!}{(n-k)! \cdot n^k}$$

Design of OSGi Compatible Middleware Components for Mobile Multimedia Applications

Heinz-Josef Eikerling and Frank Berger

Siemens SBS C-LAB,
Fürstenallee 11, D-33 102 Paderborn, Germany
{heinz-josef.eikerling, frank.berger}@c-lab.de
http://www.c-lab.de

Abstract. This paper studies techniques for the support of user mobility for the delivery of multimedia content like MPEG-2 data in ubiquitous environments. The idea is to devise components forming a service infra-structure for keeping track of the positions of users and display devices in their respective vicinities in order to route content to those devices on demand. The solution though targeted for the domestic environment could be in principal extended to wide area access modalities thus yielding an extended home environment. We describe the service interfaces and validate our findings by showing the OSGi compliant implementation of a follow-me display based on this architecture.

1 Introduction

1.1 Motivation

The enhanced mobility of users is one of the major tendencies in the society even on a world-wide scale. Overcoming ordinary voice communications, the access to value added data communications services comes into a perspective and aside from other applications like distributed gaming, the management of facilities related to the domestic environment through high bandwidth networks becomes imaginable. This is why we refer to the according supportive infra-structure as an *Extended Home Environment* (xHE) which in turn is part of a far broader concept, the *Virtual Home Environment* (VHE)

Within this setup, several issues have to be dealt with. For instance, the user might change the access device and thereby the access modality which has to be accounted for in the environment; on the other hand, the context of the user (e.g., location) may change, thus enforcing the infra-structure to react accordingly. In summary, all these and similar requirements have to be turned into an architectural design for the middleware and the service partitioning which can be generally regarded as a major issue of distributed systems engineering.

Though applicable to a broad range of applications and devices residing in the domestic domain we focus on (in-home) multimedia since the involved devices are rather complex and require the provisioning of sophisticated routing schemes depend-

F. Boavida et al. (Eds.): IDMS/PROMS 2002, LNCS 2515, pp. 80-91, 2002.
© Springer-Verlag Berlin Heidelberg 2002

ing on the positioning of the user. Our solution is based on the OSGi middleware [1] but is likely to be updated to other and forthcoming middleware technologies.

1.2 Related Work

The overall topic can be regarded as a special issue of what is being called ubiquitous or pervasive computing [9]. The major problem is imposed by transparently adapting the users' applications to the environment he or she is currently confronted with. The environment itself can be regarded as being composed of different flavors of context information. Aside from the geographical context itself, the social context of the user (e.g., finding people the user is related to) and the commercial context of the user (e.g., finding a bank in the users vicinity) are currently considered of being of highest interest. Some theoretical work for handling mobility (i.e., handling spatial informa- tion [12] and location contexts [13]) and practical background (i.e., Active Badges for tracking entities in a ubiquitous environment [16]) has been done through partially quite recent research.

Application scenarios implementing follow-me functionality for audio/visual (A/V) content using the aforementioned base technology have been described in [15] (*WWICE*) and [17] (*Audio Aura*), for instance. Employing partially similar base tech- nology, our approach aims at a design which

- targets at the exploitation of and adaptation to web standards, in order to easily extend the system from the private/domestic to the public ambience;
- as result of this, not only the exported components are reachable via web interfaces, but also the system components communicate by http commands thus permitting to easily relocate components to other containers. The environment can be easily ex- tended;
- by contributing certain services, the environment can be accessed by different types of access devices.

1.3 Approach

The paper is organized as follows: we will start by describing some use cases speci- fying the operation modes that are going to be supported and the requirements con- cerning the architectural design. Next we will describe the base system and the tech- nology underlying the system which is going to be extended for the use of location information. Finally, an implementation validating the approach is described and some conclusions on the experiences with the prototype gained so far are drawn.

2 Overview: Use Cases and Requirements

The principal use case is given by controlling and distributing multi-media like MPEG-2 data arriving at a central entity. We refer to this entity as the residential gateway or home server. Assuming the device is readily equipped with digital tuning capabilities, the server may receive and record broadcasts. The user who accesses the server via an appropriate application now is enabled to get notice of broadcasts he / she is interested in and after evaluating the information related to the broadcast (for instance, watching a preview image or clip of the broadcast) he may decide to record the session for future consumption. This use case results in some functional requirements for the core system architecture. Due to space limitations we will only sketch the most important requirements for the core system: consideration of tuning devices (Rc1), secured web-based access (Rc2), support for different kinds of access modes and modalities (Rc3).

Aside from these, there are other, even more fundamental requirements like reuse of already done device integrations (Rg1), and system extensibility and tracking of system configuration (Rg2) which have to be fulfilled by the integrating middleware.

Where the development of these requirements is straight-forward, flexibility concerning system extensions is a major demand. We will focus on one extension which is the support of mobility of users which accounts for conveniently handling location information. In order to ensure a generic tracking mechanism, we have to distinguish two kinds of access modes depending on the location of the user which have a direct impact on the adaptation of the application:

- Local Area Service Access (LAA): here, the user is located within the proximity of the server device. This usually has a significant influence on the access mode since high-bandwidth wired (e.g., IEEE 1394) or wireless RF (WLAN according to IEEE 802.11) connections can be assumed to be readily available.
- Wide Area Access (WAA): in this case the user may access the home-based service while being on travel so that the access has to be done through a WAP enabled phone using a GSM / GPRS connection or via a web browser that is connected to the home server through an Internet connection. The significant difference when compared to LAA is the involvement of an Internet or telecom service provider. Depending on the placement of the location tracking and dispatching service this requires accessibility either from the home server or the operators server.

A general prerequisite for enabling both access modes is the availability of generic interfaces (Rel1) allowing to abstract whether the user operates in LAA or WAA mode. Particularly for the WAA mode the provisioning of interfaces for services to be operated by service providers would be beneficial. Moreover, a service implementation easing the deployment and relocation of the location service (Rel2) and perhaps the federation of location information among several service implementations (either on the operators or the users site) would be rather helpful.

Depending on the access mode (WAA or LAA) for the access device (e.g., mobile phone) different technologies for locating users and devices have to be thought of. For WAA the involvement of the operators data might be of use. For the COO (Cell of Origin) the sensing accuracy may vary between a few hundred and a few kilometers as a result of the cellular network topology. The accuracy can be increased up to 20-150 meters by more advanced technologies like LFS (Location Fixing Schema), Time of Arrival (TOA), E-OTD (Enhanced Observed Time Difference) or the well-known GPS.

In contrast to this, discrete positioning strategies can be used for LAA. Sometimes characteristics of the access protocol can be utilized for this purpose. For instance, the limited range characteristics of Bluetooth-I (around 10 meters) was proposed to be used for tracking the location of a Bluetooth-enabled mobile devices and the associated user. Other location schemes are based on messaging via IR or RF signals.

3   System Design

3.1   Core System

We use the following naming conventions to outline the base system into which the location service has been integrated: a *VHE-Controllable Device* (VHE-CD) can be any device (e.g. TV set, VCR or other domestic appliances) that can be addressed and controlled individually within a *VHE-Network*. A *VHE-Home Server* (VHE-HS) is a computing device that controls access to VHE-CDs within the same local network. It provides a container environment for the basic and advanced services which can be deployed to it. A *VHE-Access Device* (VHE-AD) is a device (e.g., a PDA or a cell phone) that may address and control specific VHE-CDs. It is important to mention that within this notion a physical device can constitute a VHE-CD, VHE-AD and even VHE-HS simultaneously.

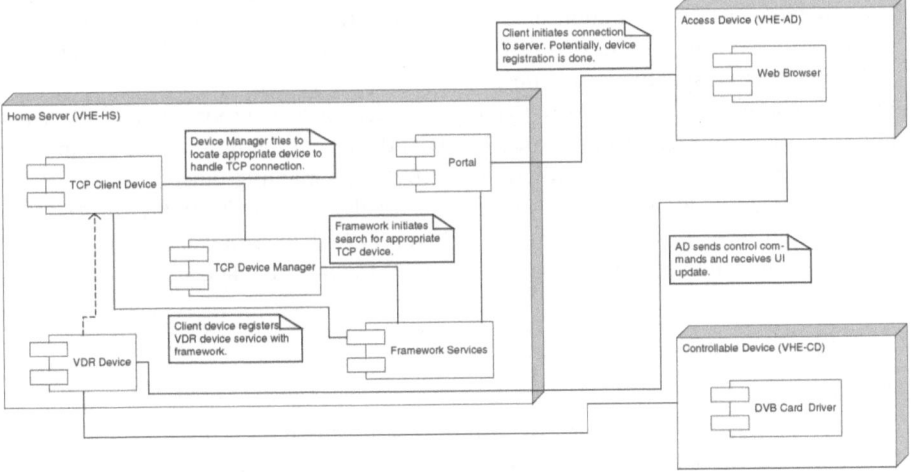

Fig. 1. Architecture of core system.

The VHE-HS constitutes the central entity of the overall system. It is equipped with a set of software components meant to mediate between the VHE-ADs and the VHE-CDs which are connected to it. Independently of the application domain, the following architectural components which are shown in Fig. 1 are usually deployed to the VHE-HS:

- *Portal*: The portal creates and maintains the connection between VHE-AD and the VHE-HS. Proper user session management for a connection can be viewed as a key requirement (Rc2) for handling interactions which span a certain period of time and might be (intentionally or accidentally) interrupted. This forms an additional task of the portal. The portal also manages the hand-over from one to another device if the user changes the type or instance of VHE-AD (Rc3).
- *Devices*: The device services are primarily meant to encapsulate the physical devices (VHE-CD), i.e., to translate the control codes generated by the UI at the VHE-AD into device specific control information and to evaluate and process the return codes coming back from the device for display on the UI. Besides this, device services may also model a virtual device, i.e. combinations of device wrappers thus yielding an extended system (Rc1). For instance, when considering a follow-me mechanism for multi-media content, in which the content is delivered to a display in the vicinity of the user and the display device (VHE-CD) is dynamically changed depending on the location of the user, some buffering of the data is required. The buffering device and the associated control logic is assumed to be also modeled as a device service.
- *Framework*: Since the access is assumed to be mostly done web-based (i.e., through the HTTP protocol), support for the IP protocol in the access service has to be ensured for which the service framework brings some support. For instance, addressing of a certain service wrapping a VHE-CD is performed by providing a URL which also encodes the required parameter sets. For managing these references and for tracking the configuration of the VHE-HS (Rg2), the service framework provides a registry in order to maintain references to the devices (VHE-AD and VHE-CD) and there respective properties.

Fig. 1 also shows the interactions of the above described components and the wrapping of the (here: Video Disk Recorder - VDR) device which in this case comprises a TCP/IP interface. In order to facilitate reuse for implementing other wrappers (Rc1), the VDR device is implemented as an instance of this generic TCP device. Additionally, for each class of devices managers (here: TCP device manager) are provided, handling the insertion of new and the retrieval of already existing drivers.

3.2 System Extensions

3.2.1 Location Service and Display Device

As one of the system extensions, we will devise a web-enabled interface for location service implementation that permits to analyze and restore the locations of the users abstracting from the aforementioned base technologies. For implementing the above described use case (mobile follow-me display), the location service cooperates and another service wrapping the display device which is handled similar to other VHE-CD devices, the location service needs careful examination in order to ensure applicability for a wide range of scenarios requiring the handling of positioning information.

The results of the modeling effort are shown in Fig. 2. In order to permit reuse, the location service is split into two parts, one residing on the VHE-HS maintaining the location information, the other component being external to VHE-HS implements the mapping of potentially technology dependent location information to the syntax of the service interface. This grants at least a high degree of flexibility concerning the to be supported positioning technology (Rel1).

3.2.2 Other Extensions

Several other extensions (like authentication/authorization, profiling of users to handle preferences) have been foreseen to implement the basic use case depicted above. Most notably, a transcoding service is provided which handles the adaptation of the UI to specific VHE-ADs by translating a UI meta-model into a format the VHE-AD is capable to deal with. We assume this to be given by a UIML [7] document. If the input format for the transcoder consists of HTML pages which have to be rendered to a device that supports cHTML, the transcoder has to convert from HTML into cHTML.

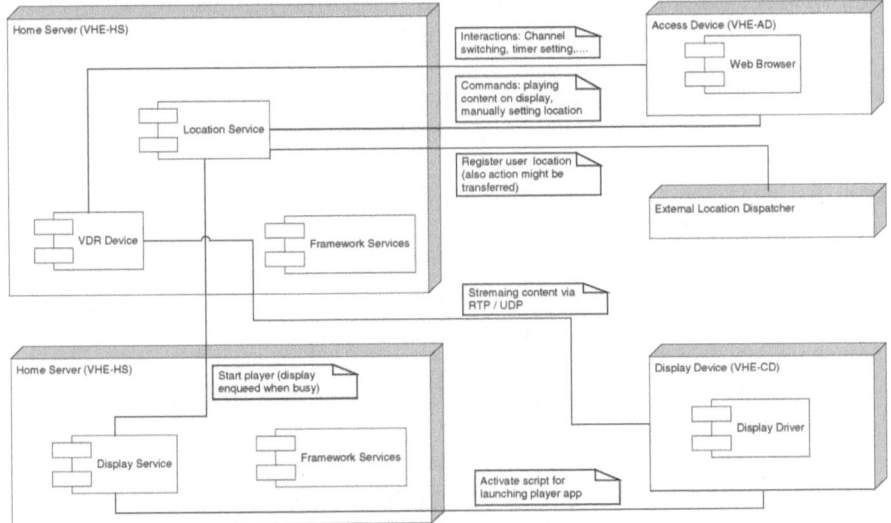

Fig. 2. Deployment of components for mobile display.

4 Implementation and Validation

4.1 OSGi Service Gateway

As mentioned in the introduction, the system presents the application of these VHE architectural concepts to the control of multimedia applications in the home. The example of a standard PC equipped with a DVB (Digital Video Broadcast) card is chosen to show how to configure a Digital Video Recorder through the use of this (software) architecture. Hence, the above architectural components need to be mapped to a supporting infra-structure which supports a variety of platforms, the dynamic deployment of services and a proper set of predefined components for easing application development. In principal, different middleware technologies could be used for this purpose.

For instance, the OSGi [1] defines a Java-technology based framework for developing and deploying components as Java services. It fulfills the constraints concerning the framework component by implementing the according services by Java Servlets, so that services can be addressed using HTTP requests.

The idea of the supporting industry consortium was to provide a software gateway that interfaces the external Internet with internal (domestic) devices. The concept supports service delivery in networked environments, mechanisms for updating and versioning of service implementations and means to discover services and resolve interdependencies between service implementations. An OSGi framework provides a component-based model to encapsulate the functionality of devices and even other middleware models. Component-based means that pieces of software that contribute to the overall functionality can be dynamically installed and uninstalled at runtime in the framework (as opposed to a library-based model in which the ingredients have to be statically linked to the application at compile-time).

As pointed out above, there is a variety of other LAN and device access technologies. What makes OSGi especially appealing is the capability to integrate with other middleware models, i.e., there are bridges to HAVi [3], Jini and UPnP at least in some products.

4.2 System Configuration

Currently, the setup of the prototype system is as follows:
- OSGi 2.0 compliant home server (VHE-HS) based on the Java Embedded Server 2.0 framework [4] by Sun Microsystems.
- Capability for receiving digital video broadcast transmissions utilizing an internal DVB satellite PCI card.
- Provision of a VDR device service as the controllable device (VHE-CD) encapsulating the DVB card. The card driver implements a telnet server which is used to control the card. For the purpose of the demonstration system we have used the software and hardware as distributed by the LinuxTV [11] open source project. For this, the application had to be extended by for instance implementing streaming media capabilities into the VDR application.
- Control of the VDR device by various access devices (VHE-AD) like ordinary PC, PDA and web pad to facilitate channel-switching, rendering, streaming, recording etc. The VHE-AD can be connected via different communication links to the VHE-HS, i.e., wired IP connection through LAN access (desktop), wireless LAN access (PDA) or ISDN connection delivered via DECT or Bluetooth (web pad).

4.3 Service Implementations

4.3.1 Core System Services

One basic task is the registration of new device services as shown in Fig. 1. The OSGi proposes a scheme for this which partially coincides with the idea of reuse as explained in the architectural model. In order to maintain genericity and enable reuse, we have modeled the registration of a generic TCP device (telnet client) which is meant to mediate between the physical device and the framework by maintaining a TCP/IP connection, e.g., by running telnet. The device features are captured in a property file. When the device registers with the framework (either automatically or by manual user intervention through calling a script) this property file is serialized as a set of UDP packets. On the server side (VHE-HS), a listener awaits the arrival of new registration data and acts accordingly.

4.3.2 System Extensions: Location Service

For sake of conciseness, we will solely focus on the implementation of the location service here. In particular, we have considered LAA mode and used discrete localization based on the Active Badge system by ivistar [10].

The Active Badge system is composed of the following components:

- *Infrared Beacon:* Beacons are placed at the positions that are subject to position tracking. The beacons maintain a fixed ID each of which permits to uniquely resolve the position. For discrete and unambiguous positioning the coverage regions need to be adjusted in order to minimize overlapping between beacons.
- *Active Badge*: Badges are approximately credit card size and receive infrared beacon signals from any beacon within visibility range. The badges are worn by users to track movements. They forward the acquired beacon IDs alongside with their own badge ID and button status via midrange 433 MHz RF.
- *Badge Base Station*: Badge base stations receive badge signals from any badge within reach via 433 MHz radio and generate an event whenever a badge enters or leaves the coverage of an infrared beacon, i.e. changes location, or when a badge button is activated. The device has an IP address and connects to an IP network.

Aside from these, other components are available for controlling domestic devices which are also linked to an IP network. For instance, a switchbox is constituted consisting of an embedded CPU and four relay-controlled general purpose power supply outlets for switching on and off connected devices. The embedded CPU executes Java. The device provides remote login and web server capabilities as well as code and data up-/download from a remote HTTP or FTP server.

The web server capabilities are used to interface with the location service on the VHE-HS by implementing a location dispatching procedure. For this, a configuration mechanism is provided which permits to assign beacon Ids to discrete positions (like 'living room'). Similarly, badge Ids are mapped to user names. The user names and position names are then used to create HTTP requests that are forwarded to the location service.

4.3.3 Display Service

The aforementioned use case was explained to constitute a means for relocating the display for output of multi-media content like MPEG-2 streams. The according setup was shown in Fig. 2. Additional to the VHE-HS hosting the VDR device, the display is accommodated by another OSGi server (which is also referred to as a VHE-HS) managing the display device.

4.4 Usage

The location service is capable of interpreting two kinds of requests. The syntax of these requests is rather straightforward and is shown for the `start` command:

    http://<url_of_HS>/locator?<start>;<user>;<location>

By sending this request, the location service is informed that user `<user>` is about to enter `<location>`. Similarly, a `stop` command

    http://<url_of_HS>/locator?<stop>;<user>;<location>

is implemented which indicates that user `<user>` leaves the location (i.e., the range of beacon that is associated with `<location>`). The parameter `<location>` could be skipped if there is a one to one relation between users and locations. However, to increase fault tolerance and ease recovery of inconsistent situations we kept it. Similar to the location service the display service supports two kinds of requests. The `play` command

    http://<url_of_HS>/for_display?<play>;<user>;<resource>

locates the user by retrieving the users location out of the location service and forwards a request for accessing a media resource and playing it. We have foreseen two kinds of resources to support different kinds of uses:

- first, the resource may be given by a previously recorded file or clip that can be replayed on the target display or
- alternatively, the resource parameter might be a multicast channel which is used for streaming MPEG-2 content by the VDR device at the VHE-HS.

Similarly, `for_display` supports a `pause` command

    http://<url_of_HS>/for_display?<pause>;<user>

which stops the rendering on the remote display. As can be inferred from these explanations, another service for remote devices is required which actually launches the viewer process. The `display` service itself resides on a different instance of an OSGi framework which appears as another VHE-HS. The `play` command

    http://<url_HS_disp>/display?<play>;<user>;<resource>

retrieves the media resource and starts the player with the according parameter. Consequently, within this scheme the `pause` command stops the execution of the player. The `<user>` parameter is evaluated for acting in case of blocked devices, i.e., the TV as the display device is blocked by another broadcast which is a quite practical situation.

Up to now we have not focused on this aspect and did not develop any sophisticated preemption and scheduling policies which are likely to be taken over from research on operating systems and digital system synthesis. For the validation prototype we have only focused on one particular use case: if a set of users simultaneously access the same resource, the player application is suspended only after all users left the range of the display and therefore paused their play activities.

5 Findings

5.1 Experiences and Remarks

Facing several refinement stages concerning the architectural design, the system has been continuously operated for 8 months up to now. The experiences with the system can be summarized as follows:

- The implementation of the OSGi services was done without facing any major problems. Surprisingly, there is little support for structuring service implementations in Integrated Development Environments according to the development process. In contrast to this, some concepts of the OSGi middleware coincide with certain methodologies coming with UML (packaging, deployment, sequencing of activities). The base system as described in this paper has been developed by using UML methodology [14].
- The OSGi has also published a specification for a positioning service in its 2.0 release. This concept was not taken into account in our concept because no implementation is currently available and the main purpose of the API is for use within vehicles (e.g., for an accident detection system that informs a management center of the actual location or to a navigation application to guide the user to the nearest pizza parlor).
- Yet, only discrete positioning based on IR / RF messaging via a central base station was examined which is applicable to LAA positioning mode only. For WAA (e.g., the user utilizes a kiosk in his vicinity as a display, the VHE-CD, and a cell-phone, the VHE-AD, to manage access) we plan to investigate other position tracking techniques for WLAN (by analyzing MAC address fields) and operator data (cell id) and combinations of both.
- Especially if the location service is hosted by service providers, scalability issues are of major concern. For this, the performance of the servlet engine has a crucial impact on the overall system. Apparently, performance has not been the major directive when implementing OSGi framework products. However, servlet engines for J2EE containers have been provided which scale up to a few thousand users/requests.
- Particularly the management of the streamed data was recognized to be rather complex. Among others, one objective of the project was to focus on IP technology for the device control and routing of data. We have used MPEG-2 transport streams via RTP for this purpose. To adapt to the capabilities of the access devices in terms of bandwidth and rendering features, a format like MPEG-4 and means to introduce QoS (like reservation based on RSVP) would be preferable. As can be imagined, resource reservation would require a significant interaction with the location system.
- As a major development and deployment platform Linux has been used. Hence, the player had to be enabled to handle streamed data which required a major effort. Moreover, some experiments with the tuning (buffer sizes, frame dropping factor, audio/video synchronization) was required.

- Conceptually, within this setting the influence of changes of location contexts to the timing of operations would be an interesting subject to study. For instance, when the user moves while accessing a broadcast session an automatic pausing of the broadcast and replay with an according time shift on the display within the scope of the user would yield an interesting use case.

5.2 Comparison with Other Approaches

As described in the introduction, there are a few other ventures having similar ambitions (*WWICE, Audio Aura*). The most decisive difference is the focus of this work on modeling of this kind of ubiquitous systems in order to ensure flexibility and reuse of the architectural components for a variety of uses. In contrast to this cited approaches, the support for web-standards and IP not only for the external, but also for the internal component interfaces was a major concern. Also, the structuring of requirements resulted in a layered approach consisting of framework, core and extended system services which we think is essential for this kind of systems. For being widely applicable, the dynamic relocation of components is quite essential. Though designed independently, a proper framework like OSGi permitting to abstract from the platforms of the nodes the services are deployed to helps to fulfill this. The utilization of such technology has not been subject to those former approaches. For the architecture right now, OSGi appears to be a reasonable match. However, mappings to general purpose middleware like RMI, CORBA or web services seem to be feasible.

6 Summary and Future Work

Within our work, we have motivated and exercised the modeling of a system for the convenient redirection of multi-media content to appropriate peers in the users ambience and devised a portable concept for this. In contrast to similar approaches [6, 15, 17] ours is based on a web compliant messaging concept. For validation, it has been implemented based on the OSGi framework concept. It is likely to be extended from the domestic (LAA) to a more ambient environment (WAA).

Right now the base functionality has been realized. For instance, for authentication purposes the BAS (Basic Authentication Scheme) mechanism of the HTTP server in the access service has been employed which gives a rather weak level of security to the end-user. It is planned to optionally support a device (smart card) based authentication mechanism for privileging access to positioning data as part of a personalization mechanism. Currently, the implementation of this personalization mechanism mainly targets a database. It is planned to support a fragmentation and relocation of the personalization data (user/device profiles) between a central directory and the local devices and to sync this with the development of the OSGi approach as part of the contribution to the VHE Middleware [8] project.

Of course and as mentioned in the introduction, there are several other lower and even higher level integration technologies. For the particular field of multi-media broadcasting, the Multimedia Home Platform [5] is worth to be mentioned here. Currently, MHP suffers from changing interfaces (in recent versions of the standard the APIs have been raised to higher logical levels due to performance reasons imposed by the use of Java), comparable high cost even for starter kits and the inability to deal with highly networked environments especially at home. Though appliance integration is foreseen in MHP through the use if HAVi, yet little attention is paid to the consideration of location contexts for routing multi-media content and the combination with emerging services for mobile communications like Multi-Media Messaging (MMS). When it comes to personalized content residing on domestic appliances which has to be delivered via MMS, MHP certainly comes into play and hence needs consideration.

References

1. Chen, K. and Gong, L.: Programming Open Services Gateways with the Java Embedded Server Technology, Addison-Wesley, 2001.
2. Dutta-Roy, A.: Networks for Home, IEEE Spectrum, Volume 36, December 1999.
3. Specification of the Home/Audio Interoperability (HAVi) Architecture, Version 1.1, May 2001.
4. Sun Microsystems, Inc.: Java Embedded Server (TM), Developer Guide, Version 2.0, August 2001.
5. Multimedia Home Platform, http://www.mhp.org
6. Nakajima, T.: System Software for Audio and Visual Networked Home Appliances on Commodity Operating Systems, Middleware 2001, pp. 273 - 294, November 2001.
7. User Interface Markup Language, http://www.uiml.org
8. Middleware for Virtual Home Environments, http://www.vhe-middleware.org
9. Weiser, M.: The Computer for the 21st Century, Scientific American, Vol. 265, No. 3, 1991
10. http://www.ivistar.com
11. http://www.linuxtv.org
12. Beigl, Michael. Using spatial Co-location for Coordination in Ubiquitous Computing Environments. Handheld and Ubiquitous Computing, First International Symposium, HUC'99, Karlsruhe.
13. U. Leonhardt. Supporting Location-Awareness in Open Distributed Systems. PhD thesis, Department of Computing, Imperial College, London, May 1998.
14. H.-J. Eikerling, G. Buhe, F. Berger, and J. Goerlich. Architecting and Prototyping Middleware Components for the Control of Networked In-Home Multimedia Applications. Proc. ITEA Workshop on Virtual Home Environments, Feb. 2002.
15. H. Baldus, M. Baumeister et al.: WWICE – An Architecture for In-home Digital Networks, Philips Research Report.
16. A. Harter, A. Hopper: A Distributed Location System for the Active Office. IEEE Network, vol. 8, no. 1,1994.
17. E. Mynatt, M. Back et al.: Designing Audio Aura, CHI'98.

A Fast QoS Adaptation Algorithm for MPEG-4 Multimedia Applications

Nam Pham Ngoc[1], Gauthier Lafruit[2], Geert Deconinck[1,1], and Rudy Lauwereins[2]

[1]Katholieke Universiteit Leuven-ESAT/ELECTA
Kasteelpark Arenberg 10
B-3001 Leuven-Heverlee, Belgium
Nam.Phamngoc@esat.kuleuven.ac.be
[2]IMEC-DESICS, Kapeldreef 75, B-3001 Leuven-Heverlee, Belgium

Abstract. This paper addresses the QoS adaptation problem in MPEG-4 multimedia applications. This adaptation involves solving a NP-hard optimisation problem, for which an optimal solution is not feasible in real-time. In the paper, we will formulate the problem and present an approximation algorithm called FAQoS to solve the problem in polynomial time by using a number of heuristics. We will show that FAQoS is as fast as the fastest known algorithm in literature (AMRMD [8]) and has a much higher accuracy than AMRMD, especially when the relative importance of objects is considered. Experiments show that solutions found by FAQoS are most of the time as close as 97% of the optimal solution. FAQoS is therefore suitable for use in real-time QoS adaptation in MPEG-4 applications, especially when the number of objects and the number of quality levels for each object are large.

1 Introduction

In MPEG-4 and MPEG-4 like applications, audio-visual objects are encoded and decoded separately. In addition, the quality of an object can be scalable by using scalable coding schemes. This property provides a great flexibility for the applications to adapt to fluctuations in network bandwidth, differences in end system capacity and to user interactions. Typical MPEG-4 applications are multimedia on demand (e.g. video on demand, lecture on demand...), virtual reality, collaborative scene visualisation, infotainment and interactive games [23]. Because of the heterogeneity in receiver decoding capabilities, network bandwidth and quality of service (QoS) requirements, content providers should be able to adapt the contents accordingly. A possible solution is to group receivers in different profiles such as PDA profile, portable computer profile, workstation profile...as proposed in the $2K^Q$ QoS framework [14] and provide the same contents at different levels of complexity to different profiles. However, within one profile, the decoding capabilities of receivers also vary, which leads to the

---

[1] Geert Deconinck is a postdoctoral fellow of the Fund for Scientific Research–Flanders, Belgium.

F. Boavida et al. (Eds.): IDMS/PROMS 2002, LNCS 2515, pp. 92-105, 2002.
© Springer-Verlag Berlin Heidelberg 2002

need of using quality scalable objects for creating the content, which is the task of the content provider and the need for QoS adaptation mechanisms, which is the task of the QoS middleware at end-user systems [5] [15][21].

In this paper, we consider the QoS adaptation problem for deciding at which quality level each object should be decoded in such a way that the overall quality is maximized under resource constraints in MPEG-4 applications where many objects are involved (e.g. up to 32 natural visual objects [1] plus many audio and synthesis visual objects). Unfortunately, this problem is a NP-hard optimisation problem, as we will show in the next section. To allow real-time QoS adaptation, efficient heuristics should be developed, so that decisions can be taken within a few milliseconds of time.

1.1 Related Work

There have been several attempts to find polynomial time approximation algorithms to solve the NP-hard optimisation problem at real-time [8] [11] [13] [15].

ERDoS framework in [11] has considered a similar problem for allocating resource for multiple concurrent objects sharing a single resource. A market-based economic protocol was used to determine the solution for the optimisation problem. The market consists of QoS agents, each agent represents an object. Each agent derives a benefit for consuming resources. For a given amount of resource, an agent tries to maximise the benefit by selecting the maxima on the benefit surface that are within the constraints of the resource usage [11]. With the use of market based methods, the NP-hard problem is reduced to a simple local optimisation problem. The drawback of this approach is the slow rate of convergence and therefore it is only suitable for a small number of objects.

Similarly, the work at University of Colorado [13] has solved the problem for only CPU resource. The authors have proposed different algorithms for the problem of selecting the quality level of each 3D object in 3D rendering applications. However, the proposed algorithms are only suitable for a small number of objects, e.g. 4 objects. Moreover, each object has a limited number of quality levels (typically 10) [13].

In [15] the authors have considered the problem for multiple objects running on multiple resource platforms. [15] presents an approximation algorithm called HEU, which uses the concept of aggregate resource [16] to reduce the complexity of the problem and solve the problem in polynomial time. The use of this algorithm is limited when the number of objects is large, but each object can have many quality levels.

Similar to HEU, [8] has proposed an approximation algorithm called AMRMD, which also uses the concept of aggregate resource to solve the problem for multiple objects running on multiple resource platforms. To the best of our knowledge, AMRMD is the fastest algorithm in the literature for the problem. However, AMRMD, while solving the problem, assumes that the relative importance of all objects is the same, which makes it fail to solve the problem when the relative importance of objects is considered.

We have developed an approximation algorithm called FAQoS (**F**ast **A**lgorithm for **Q**oS adaptation), which, as will be shown in section 5, is as fast as the AMRMD algorithm and has better performances over AMRMD, both when relative importance of objects is and is not taken into account.

The main subject of the present paper is the analysis of FAQoS. The paper is organised as follows. Section 2 presents the system model for MPEG-4 applications. Section 3 formulates the optimisation problem. Section 4 presents in details our approximation algorithm FAQoS. Evaluation and comparison are shown in section 5 and finally section 6 presents our conclusions.

2   System Model

2.1 Application and Resource Model

We consider a MPEG-4 (or similar) application running on a multiple-resource platform. The application consists of N objects O_1, O_2, ...O_N, transmitted in scalable MPEG-4 or similar (e.g. JPEG-2000) format. Characteristics of each object can be modelled by a set of meta data that can be conveyed in an Object descriptor stream (OD). The OD stream is always transmitted from a content provider to a user prior to the transmission of actual data streams. The meta data for each object consists of a relative importance (which can possibly be adapted by the user or calculated on the receiver), a set of object specific QoS parameters, a number of quality levels and for each quality level, a benefit value and the associated values for all QoS parameters.

Let w_i be the relative importance of object O_i, w_i can have a value between 0 and 1. The relative importance parameter represents the relative importance among objects in the application. For example a 3D foreground object should have a higher relative importance than a 3D background object. The relative importance reflects the fact that a more important object should be decoded at a higher quality than a less important one when the resources are insufficient to decode both objects at their highest quality.

Let $Q_i = \{q_{i1}, q_{i2}...q_{i|Qi|}\}$ be the set of QoS parameters[2] of object O_i where $|Q_i|$ is the number of QoS parameters. An instance of Q_i corresponds to one quality level. The number of quality levels of object O_i is denoted by L_i. We refer to the quality level j of object O_i as Q_{ij}, where $L_i \geq j \geq 1$ and $Q_{imax} = Q_{iL_i}$. Among $|Q_i|$ parameters, there are parameters that can be changed to have different quality levels. We call them adjustable parameters. The other parameters are referred to as "content-dependent". For example, in a temporal scalable video object, the frame rate parameter is an adjustable parameter, while the resolution is merely a content-dependent parameter. Associated with each quality level Q_{ij} is a benefit value B_{ij} and a resource requirement vector $R_{ij} = \{R_{ij}^1, R_{ij}^2, ..., R_{ij}^M\}$, where M is the number of resource types, called devices (e.g. CPU, memory, disk bandwidth, network bandwidth...).

---

[2] We consider only discrete parameters. However, continuous parameters can easily be discretized to become discrete ones.

The benefit value represents the degree of satisfaction of the user when receiving a certain quality level. When the user receives the highest quality of an object, the benefit is equal to 1. Lower quality has benefit less than 1. The relation quality-benefit of object O_i is represented by a function of QoS parameters $B_i(q_{i1}, q_{i2}, ...)$. When there is only one adjustable parameter, we have typical shapes of benefit-adjustable parameter function as shown in Fig. 1 (a) and (b). These functions seem to adequately capture the behaviour of many QoS parameters and MPEG-4 object types, for example Fine Grained Scalable (FGS) video objects [4] and 3D objects [19] [20].

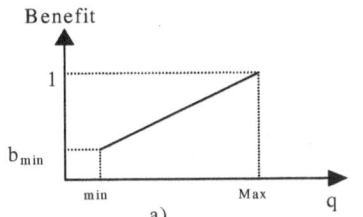
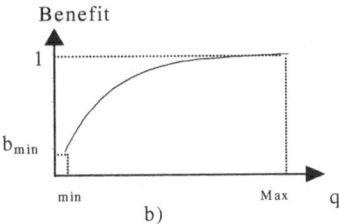

Fig. 1. Typical benefit -adjustable parameter functions

The benefit functions with more than two adjustable parameters are rather complicated since they involve the interdependency between QoS parameters and user perception issues. However, they all have the same property: higher quality corresponds to higher benefit. Our FAQoS algorithm has no problems in the optimisation of such multi-dimensional problems.

The mapping from quality to resource requirements is done by means of resource estimation functions. Similar to the quality-benefit relation, the resource estimation function for object O_i on device k is a nondecreasing function of QoS parameters $R_i^k(q_{i1}; q_{i2}, ...)$. It is very natural that higher quality requires more resources. In [2] we have established a resource estimation model to estimate the decoding and rendering time of 3D objects as a function of adjustable parameters. For 3D rendering, typical adjustable parameters are the number of vertices and triangles of the 3D mesh, as well as the SNR-resolution, width and height of the textures. A content-dependent parameter is the number of pixels rendered on the screen for each object. Our results have shown that the texture decoding execution time is linearly dependent with the number of pixels of the texture, quasi-linear dependent with the number of bitplanes in SNR scalability and non-linearly dependent with the number of levels in spatial scalability mode [2].

2.2 An Example

For better understanding the terminology, introduced in the previous section, a number of examples are described. Consider, for example, an application that consists of 3 objects. The first object is a temporal scalable video object that is encoded in layers, one base layer (BL) to have a frame rate of 10 fps and two enhancement layers EL1 and EL2 to enhance the frame rate to 15 fps and 20 fps respectively. All layers are encoded with a CIF resolution. The second object is a FGS SNR video object that is encoded in a FGS stream that covers the bandwidth ranging from 100 kbit/s to 1 Mbit/s, at a frame rate of 10 fps and with a CIF resolution. The third object is a 3D mesh object that can be rendered with a mesh complexity ranging from 200 triangles to 2000 triangles, with 3 different rendering modes: wire-frame, flat shading, smooth shading.

The first object O_1 has thus $L_1=3$ discrete quality levels Q_{11} ={10 fps, CIF}, Q_{12} ={15 fps, CIF}, Q_{13} ={20 fps, CIF}. Assume that the corresponding benefit values are $B_{11}=0.4$, $B_{12}=0.8$, $B_{13}=1$ and the corresponding resource vectors {CPU load, memory blocks} are R_{11}={5%, 15 blocks}, R_{12}={8%, 20 blocks}, R_{13}={10%, 23 blocks}.

The second object O_2 has almost continuous quality levels. We can discretize the continuous quality to have differently perceived discrete quality levels by a step, for example of 50 kbit/s. We then have $L_2=19$ discrete quality levels Q_{21}={bitrate:100 kbit/s, 10 fps, CIF}, Q_{22}={bitrate:150 kbit/s, 10 fps, CIF}...$Q_{2,19}$={bitrate:1 Mbit/s, 10 fps, CIF}. Suppose that the benefit function B_2(bitrate, 10fps, CIF)) has a shape similar to Fig. 1 (b) and that b_{min} =B_{21}=0.2. We can easily calculate the benefit of other quality levels, for example B_{22} =B_2(150 kbit/s, 10 fps, CIF) which is larger than 0.2.

Because the parameter number of triangles of the third object O_3 can have continuous values, O_3 has three continuous ranges of quality levels according to the three rendering modes. Similar to the second object, we can discretize the number of triangles by a step of, for example 100 triangles, yielding 19 discrete quality levels for each rendering mode and therefore a total of L_3= 57 quality levels. The minimum quality level is Q_{31}={200 triangles, wire-frame} and the maximum quality level is $Q_{3,57}$={2000 triangles, smooth shading}. The benefit function B_3(number of triangles, rendering mode) can be obtained experimentally.

3   Problem Formulation

Given N objects O_1, O_2, ...O_N, the objective of our problem is to assign a quality level for each object in order to maximize the overall benefit of the application given the resource constraints.

The overall benefit of all objects is the weighted sum of the benefit of each object, according to:

$$B = \frac{1}{N} \sum_{i=1}^{N} w_i B_i (q_{i1}, q_{i2}, ...) .$$ (3.1)

For one resource type k (i.e. a device), we have the resource constraint:

$$\sum_{i=1}^{N} R_i^k (q_{i1}, q_{i2}, ...) \le R_{max}^k .$$

The optimisation problem can then be formulated as follows:

Maximize:

$$B = \frac{1}{N} \sum_{i=1}^{N} w_i B_i(q_{i1}, q_{i2}, \ldots) \quad 1 \geq w_i > 0,\ 1 \geq B_i(q_{i1}, q_{i2}, \ldots) > 0.$$

Subject to:

$$\sum_{i=1}^{N} R_i^k(q_{i1}, q_{i2}, \ldots) \leq R_{max}^k \quad k = 1, 2, \ldots, M.$$

It can be easily seen that this optimization problem can be reduced to the 0-1 Knapsack problem and therefore is a NP-hard optimization problem for which an optimal solution cannot be found in real-time [18].

4   The FAQoS Algorithm

4.1   The Algorithm

Before explaining our algorithm, we first introduce a heuristic called *resource cost* for making decisions amongst multiple resources. Consider an example of two objects O_1 and O_2 using CPU and memory resources. Table 1 shows the benefits and resource vectors of object O_1 and O_2 at quality levels Q_{1i}, Q_{1i+1} and Q_{2j}, Q_{2j+1}, respectively.

Table 1.

O_1			O_2		
Quality level	Benefit	Resources (CPU, memory)	Quality level	Benefit	Resource (CPU, memory)
Q_{1i}	0.2	(10%, 20 blocks)	Q_{2j}	0.5	(15%, 80 blocks)
Q_{1i+1}	0.4	(15%, 30 blocks)	Q_{2j+1}	0.7	(18%, 100 blocks)

Assume that at a certain state in the search process, we have to make a decision whether to improve the quality of object O_1 from Q_{1i} to Q_{1i+1} or to improve the quality of object O_2 from Q_{2j} to Q_{2j+1}. For both cases, we will gain a benefit of 0.2. If we improve the quality of O_1, we need 5% more of CPU load and 10 more blocks of memory. If we improve the quality of O_2, we need 3% more of CPU load and 20 more blocks of memory. The decision then depends on whether saving 2% of CPU is better than saving 10 blocks of memory. If the total memory blocks are 500, 10 blocks will correspond to 2% of the total memory. If we know that the application is a memory dominated application, i.e. it requires more memory than CPU resource, saving 2% of memory will be better than saving 2% of CPU. We can see from this example that the cost of using resources depends on the availability of the resources and the resource requirements of the application.

Recall that for quality level Q_{ij} of object $O_{i,}$ the resource vector $R_{ij} = \{R_{ij}^1, R_{ij}^2, \ldots, R_{ij}^M\}$ is needed. If the percentile cost for one unit of resource type (device) k is C_k (e.g a CPU unit can be 1% of CPU load, a memory unit can be 1% of total memory blocks), the cost of using R_{ij}^k units will be $R_{ij}^k * C_k$ and the to-

tal cost of resource vector R_{ij} will be: *Resource cost* $(R_{ij})= \sum_{k=1}^{M} R_{ij}^k * C_k$. C_k should be large (i.e. expensive) when resource k is scarce and it should be small (i.e. cheap) when resource k is abundant. It is obvious that the scarceness of device k depends on the availability of its resources and resource needs of all objects. C_k may therefore be

determined by: $C_k = \sum_{i=1}^{N} \dfrac{R_{iLi}^k}{R_{max}^k}$, where R_{iLi}^k is the amount of resource k needed to decode object Oi at the best quality. $C_k < 1$ means that there are enough resources of type k available to decode all objects at their highest quality level and thus C_k can be set to zero. With this definition of resource cost, higher quality levels correspond to higher resource costs and that the higher the resource cost, the easier the resource constraints are violated.

For each object O_i we define a list *L[i]* of (*benefit, resource cost*) points. The first point in the list corresponds to the lowest quality level of object O_i and the last point in the list corresponds to the highest quality level. *L[i]* is thus a sorted list in the order of increasing resource cost (and also in the order of increasing benefit). The *benefit* value used here is one term of eq. (3.1), i.e. it is the product of the relative importance parameter and the value specified by the benefit function. For example, the *benefit* value of the best quality level (i.e. benefit =1) of an object with relative importance 0.8 is 0.8 (i.e. 1*0.8). The problem in section 3 is equal to finding a point in each list *L[i]* such that the overall benefit is maximized while satisfying the resource constraints. Let:

- L[i].NrOfPoint be the number of point in list L[i]

- L[i][j] be the point j in list L[i]. L[i][j].level, L[i][j].benefit, L[i][j].cost, L[i][j].resvector be the quality level, the *benefit* value, the *resource cost* and the resource vector associated to L[i][j], respectively.

- (q[1], q[2],..., q[N]) be the solution vector. For example, the vector (2, 3, 5) means that object 1 can be decoded at quality level 2, object 2 at quality level 3 and object 3 at quality level 5.

- index[i] represents the current position of a point in list L[i]

- R[k] represents the resource type k.

- slack[k] represents the remaining of resource type k that can be used to improve the quality levels of objects.

The pseudo code of the FAQoS algorithm is given in Fig. 2.

```
Algorithm FAQoS (N, L[1], L[2],...,L[N])

1.    for i=1 to N do
2.    L'[i] = RepresentativeList(L[i]);
3.    index[i]=1;
4.    q[i]=L'[i][index[i]].level; //Initialise the solution with the lowest quality for each object

5.    for k=1 to M do
6.    R[k].AdmissionTest(L'[1][1], L'[2][1],..., L'[N][1], slack[k])
7.    //Now gradually improve the solution with the improvement that corresponds to αₘₐₓ
8.    While (true) do
9.    αₘₐₓ=0;
10.   for i=1 to N do
11.   If (index[i] < L'[i].NrOfPoint)
12.   j=index[i] +1;
13.   feasible=true;
14.   α= (L'[i][j].benefit-L'[i][index[i]].benefit)/ (L'[i][j].cost-L'[i][index[i]].cost);
15.   for k=1 to M do
16.   if (L'[i][j].resvector[k]- L'[i][index[i]].resvector[k]) > slack[k]
17.   feasible=false;
18.   break;
19.   if (feasible) and (α > αₘₐₓ )
20.   αₘₐₓ = α;
21.   i1=i; j1=j;
22.   if (αₘₐₓ=0) break; //No more improvement can be obtained
23.   for k=1 to M do
24.   slack[k]=slack[k]-( L'[i1][j1].resvector[k]- L'[i1][index[i1]].resvector[k]);

25.   q[i1]= L'[i1][j1].level;//Update quality level for object i1
26.   Return (q[1], q[2],....,q[N])
```

The algorithm is based on two heuristics, corresponding to two phases. In the first phase, a heuristic similar to the one in [8] is used, which reduces the number of (*benefit, resource cost*) points in list L for each object to a smaller number of representative points in list L'. This is obtained by calling the RepresentativeList(L) function. This function implements an algorithm similar to Graham-Scan algorithm [22], which finds the convex hull of a set of points. In the second phase, we use the second heuristic, which is based on the *benefit/resource cost* ratio and a nice property of the list L', i.e. L' consists of non-decreasing slope segments. The different steps of the algorithm are summarized as follows:

- The algorithm takes N lists L[1] to L[N] of (*benefit, resource cost*) points corresponding to N objects as the inputs.

- The function RepresentativeList (L) is applied for each list L[i] to get the list L'[i]. Fig. 3 shows an example of two lists corresponding to objects 1 and 2 before and after this step.

- The algorithm starts from the lowest quality for each object (i.e. the first point of L'[i]) and iterates to improve the overall quality until no more improvement can be obtained. At each iteration, only one object is selected and its quality level is improved such that the *benefit/resource cost* ratio is maximum. Fig. 4 shows that if the current quality level is at point A, we have 3 possibilities to improve the quality either to B, C or D. Since $\alpha 1 > \alpha 2 > \alpha 3$, going from A to B always gives us the highest *benefit/resource cost* ratio. Therefore, at each iteration, only the $\alpha 1$ of each object is calculated and compared to this value of other objects. The object with maximum $\alpha 1$ is selected and its quality level is improved by going from the current point in list L' to the next point in the list. This is a very important observation that helps to speed up the algorithm.

The AdmissionTest() function for each resource type implements the corresponding admission test algorithm of that resource type. The FAQoS algorithm can therefore be ported over different platforms with different admission test algorithms.

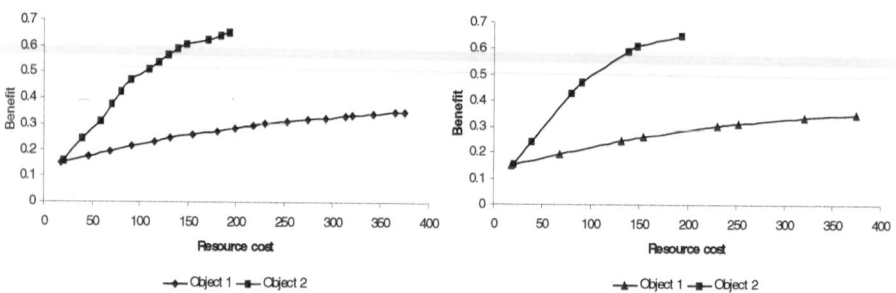

Fig. 3. List L[i] before (left) and after (right) the RepresentativeList() function

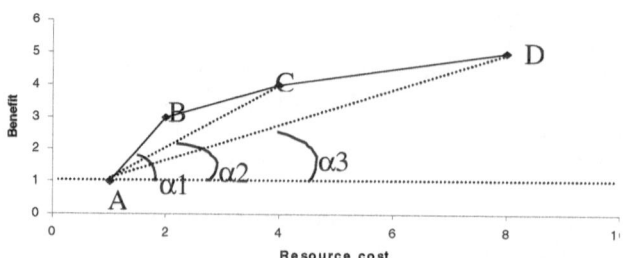

Fig. 4.

4.2 Computational Complexity

Let L= max (Length(L[i]) i=1 to N), L'= max (Length(L'[i]) i=1 to N). We can obtain the worst case computational complexity of the algorithm, excluding the complexity of the admission test algorithms, as follows. The function RepresentativeList(L[]) takes $O(N.LlogL)$ operations for all objects. The while loop can have at most N.L' iteration, each iteration (from step 10 to step 21 in Fig. 2) requires N comparisons and therefore the while loop takes $O\ (N.N.L')$ operations. The total computational complexity of the algorithm is thus $O\ (N.L.logL + N.N.L')$.

5 Evaluation and Comparison

5.1 FAQoS' Superiority

To evaluate the performance of our FAQoS algorithm and to compare it with the existing algorithms, we have run a number of simulations with various data sets and parameters. We also implemented the AMRMD algorithm presented in [8] to compare with the FAQoS algorithm and implemented an optimal algorithm to find the optimal solutions. All the experiments were done on a 866 MHz, Pentium III machine running WinNT 4.0. All data sets, each of which corresponds to one application, were created according to the QoS model presented in section 2.1. In each data set, three kinds of objects were considered. The first kind of objects includes objects that have one adjustable parameter with a linear benefit function (equation 5.1). The second kind of objects includes objects that have one adjustable parameter with a benefit function as in equation 5.2 (which has a shape as in Fig. 1 (b)). The third kind of objects includes objects that have more than two adjustable parameters.

$$
Bf = \begin{cases}
\dfrac{1-b_{min}}{q_{max} - q_{min}} q + \dfrac{b_{min} q_{max} - q_{min}}{q_{max} - q_{min}} & \text{(Fig. 1.a)} & (5.\ 1) \\[2em]
2 - \exp(\dfrac{\ln(2-b_{min})}{q_{min} - q_{max}} q + \dfrac{q_{max}\ln(2-b_{min})}{q_{max} - q_{min}}) & \text{(Fig. 1.b)} & (5.\ 2)
\end{cases}
$$

The parameters b_{min}, q_{min} and q_{max} are randomly generated to obtain different functions by using the rand() function of C, which has a uniform distribution.

For the third kind objects, we generated the benefit values randomly so that higher quality level has higher benefit.

In our experiments only two types of resources were considered, i.e. memory and CPU. The resource requirements were randomly generated in such a way that for each object, higher quality level requires more resources. The CPU resource is the CPU load, while for memory, the resource value is given in the number of memory blocks.

To compare the performance of the approximation algorithm with the optimal algorithm we define: $accuracy = B_{total\_Appro} / B_{total\_opt} * 100\%$,   where B_{total_Appro} and B_{total_opt} are the total benefit of the solution found by the approximation algorithm and by the optimal algorithm, respectively.

Table 2 compares existing algorithms in terms of assumptions and complexity.

Table 2. Comparison of existing algorithms

Algorithm	Resource	QoS parameter	Worst case complexity
Colorado[13]	CPU	1	NA
ERDoS[11]	Single resource	Multiple	NA
AMRMD[8]	Multiple resources	Multiple	$O(N*L*log(N*L) + 2N*L)$
HEU[15]	Multiple resources	Multiple	$O(N^2*L^2)$
FAQoS	Multiple resources	Multiple	$O(N*L*logL + N*N*L')$.

From the table, we can see that the worst-case complexity of the two algorithms AMRMD and FAQoS are very close to each other, while HEU is one order of magnitude slower. We therefore make a comparison between FAQoS and AMRMD.

Fig. 5 shows the runtime of both FAQoS and AMRMD algorithms when the number of objects N varies from 5 to 200, while the number of quality levels of all objects are fixed at 10 and 50. Each point in the graph is obtained by taking an average of 5 different sets of data. Fig. 6 shows the run time of FAQoS and AMRMD when N is fixed at 50 and L varies from 10 to 100.

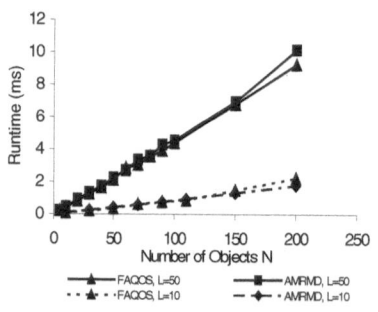

Fig. 5. Fix L, vary N

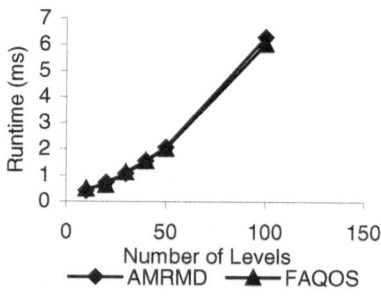

Fig. 6. Fix N=50, vary L

Fig. 7 and 8 shows the accuracy of both FAQoS and AMRMD when the relative importance parameter is and is not taken into account, respectively. The relative importance parameters have been randomly chosen between 0 and 1.

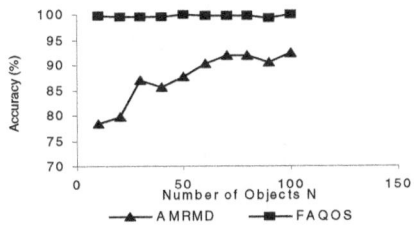

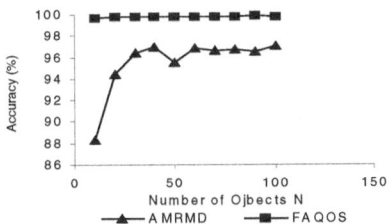

Fig. 7. Relative importance is considered   **Fig. 8.** Relative importance is not considered

From the experiment results, it is clear that the FAQoS algorithm is as fast as the AMRMD algorithm and much better than the AMRMD algorithm in terms of accuracy. When the relative importance of objects is considered, the AMRMD algorithm exhibited a very poor performance. The worst accuracy we found in this case is 72 %. When the relative importance parameters of all objects are equal, the accuracy of AMRMD is improved since it was designed particularly for this case. For both cases, the FAQoS algorithm has much higher accuracy. The average accuracy of FAQoS in all experiments is 99%. The worst accuracy we found for FAQoS is 97% in specific runs.

5.2 Experiments on a 3D Scene Walkthrough Application

We have used the FAQoS algorithm in a MPEG-4-like 3D scene walkthrough application to select the level of detail (i.e. quality level) for each 3D object in such a way that the overall quality of the 3D scene is maximised given the limited total rendering time at each frame. The 3D scene consists of 80 objects, each of which has on average 50 quality levels. In this application FAQoS needs to be executed at every frame to trade off the scene quality for framerate, in order to guarantee a high walkthrough framerate. The run time of the algorithm is less than 5 ms for this application, which is only 10% of the frame time if we want to have a walkthrough framerate of 20 fps. Fig. 9 shows the scene when a) no QoS adaptation is used and b) when FAQoS is used. In the first case, we have the full scene quality but the framerate is only 7fps, which causes jerky and discontinuous walkthrough motions. In the second case, with QoS adaptation we can obtain a higher frame rate (i.e. 15 fps and hence we have a quite smooth motion) with a minimum quality degradation. In this application, the scene may change drastically between two successive frames due to the user interaction. Therefore, the solutions of FAQoS for two successive frames are considered to be independent in the scope of the paper.

The experiments suggest that the FAQoS algorithm is very suited for real-time QoS adaptation in MPEG-4 applications, with a high number of objects (up to 100) and a high number of quality levels for each object (up to 100). In addition, FAQoS works well with different variations of benefit functions (which were randomly generated), i.e. it is not sensitive to changes in benefit functions. The experimental results on the 3D scene walkthrough application have proven the applicability of our proposed algorithm.

a) Original 7fps   b) With QoS Adaptation 15fps

Fig. 9.

6 Conclusions

In this paper, we have addressed the QoS adaptation problem in MPEG-4 applications, with many audio-visual objects, each having a multitude of quality levels. Appropriately adjusting these qualities gives the application more flexibility to adapt to the variations in the CPU/memory/network resource availability. However, this property needs to be handled in a predictable way by a QoS middleware at the end user systems. One important task of the QoS middleware is to determine at which quality level, each object should run such that the overall benefit of the application is maximized, given the limited decoding resources and network bandwidth. We have presented a novel QoS model for MPEG-4 applications and formulated mathematically the optimisation problem. The problem has been recognized as NP-hard, for which an optimal solution is not feasible in real-time. We have presented an approximation algorithm called FAQoS to solve the problem in polynomial time by using a number of heuristics. The most important heuristic is the use of non-increasing slope of the segments in a convex hull set and the benefit/resource cost ratio. We have shown that FAQoS is better than the existing algorithms in terms of speed and accuracy. Typically, the accuracy of FAQoS is larger than 97%.

Acknowledgement. Part of the work presented in this paper has been done in the ITEA-EUROPA project.

References

1.   MPEG-4 ISO/IEC 14496 http://www.cselt.it/MPEG
2.   G. Lafruit, L.Nachtergaele, K. Denolf and J. Bormans, "3D Computational Graceful Degradation", ISCAS 2000 ISCAS - Workshop and Exhibition on MPEG-4, Proceedings, pp. III-547 - III-550, May 28-31, 2000.
3.   S. Fischer, A. Hafid, G. von Bochmann and H. de Meer, "Cooperative QoS Management for Multimedia Applications", IEEE International Conference on Multimedia Computing and Systems, Ottawa, Ontario, Canada, June 3--6, 1997, pp 303 -- 310.

4. H. M. Radha, M. V.D Schaar and Y. Chen, "The MPEG-4 Fine-Grained Scalable Video Coding Method for Multimedia Streaming Over IP", IEEE transactions on Multimedia, Vol. 3,, No.1, pp. 53-67, March 2001.

5. Cristina Aurrecoechea, Andrew Campbell, and Linda Hauw, "A Survey of QoS Architectures", In Proceedings of the 4th IFIP International Workshop on Quality of Service, March 1996.

6. Liu and J. Layland, "Scheduling Algorithms of Multiprogramming in a Hard Real time Environment", Journal ACM, Volume 20, Number 1, 1973.

7. Hafid, G.Bochmann and R. Dssouli, " QoS and Distributed Multimedia Applications: A Review", The Electronic Journal on Networks and Distributed Processing, issue 6, February 1998

8. Lee, J. Lehoczky, D. Siewiorek, R. Rajkumar, and J. Hansen, " A Scalable Solution to the Multi-resource QoS Problem", Proceedings of IEEE RTSS'99, December 1999.

9. J. Huang, P.-J. Wan, and D.Z. Du, "Criticality- and QoS-Based Multiresource Negotiation and Adaptation". Real time Systems Journal, 15(3):249--273, Nov. 1998.

10. T. F. Abdelzaher, E. M. Atkins, and K. G. Shin, "QoS Negotiation in Real time Systems and Its Application to Automated Flight Control", Proceedings of the Third IEEE Real time Technology and Applications Symposium, Montreal, Canada, 1997.

11. Sabata, S. Chatterjee, and J. Sydir, "Dynamic Adaptation of Video for Transmission under Resource Constraints," in Proc. 17th IEEE International Conference on Image Processing (ICIP98), Chicago, Illinois, October 1998.

12. R. Rajkumar, K. Juvva, A. Molano, and S. Oikawa, "Resource kernels: A resource-centric approach to real time systems," in Proceedings of the SPIE/ACM Conference on Multimedia Computing and Networking, January 1998.

13. S. Brandt, G. Nutt, T. Berk, and M. Humphrey, "Soft Real time Application Execution with Dynamic Quality of Service Assurance", Proceedings of the Sixth IEEE/IFIP International Workshop on Quality of Service, pp. 154-163, May 1998.

14. D. Xu, D. Wichadakul, and K. Nahrstedt, "Resource-Aware Configuration of Ubiquitous Multimedia Service," in Proceedings of IEEE International Conference on Multimedia and Expo 2000 (ICME 2000), July 2000.

15. C. Khan, "Quality Adaptation in a Multisession Multimedia System: Model, Algorithms and Architecture", Ph.D thesis, University of Victoria, 1998.

16. Y. Toyoda, "A simplified algorithm for obtaining approximate solutions to zero-one programming problems", Management Science, 21(12):1417--27, August 1975.

17. S. Battista, F. Casalino and C. Lande, " MPEG-4: A Multimedia Standard for the Third Millennium", IEEE Multimedia, pp. 76-85, January-March, 2000.

18. Garey, Michael R., and Johnson, David S., "Computers and Intractability: A Guide to the Theory of NP-Completeness", W.H. Freeman and Company, New York, 1979.

19. T. A. Funkhouser and C. H. Sequin, "Adaptive Display Algorithm for Interactive Frame Rates During Visualization of Complex Virtual Environments", Computer Graphics Annual Conference Series, pages 247--254, August 1993.

20. E. Gobbetti and E. Bouvier, "Time-Critical Multiresolution Scene Rendering", Proceedings IEEE Visualization 1999, IEEE Visualization Conference 1999.

21. Sabata, S. Chatterjee, M. Davis, J. Sydir, T. Lawrence, "Taxonomy for QoS Specifications," proceedings of the IEEE Computer Society 3rd International Workshop on Object-oriented Real time Dependable Systems (WORDS `97), Newport Beach, California, February 1997

22. T.H. Cormen, C. E. Leiserson and R. L. Rivet, " Introduction to Algorithms", MIT Press, McGraw-Hill, 1990.

23. "MPEG-4 Applications", ISO/IEC JTC1/SC29/WG11MPEG 98/N2457

A Genetic Algorithm-Based Segmentation for Automatic VOP Generation

Eun Yi Kim[1] and Se Hyun Park[2]*

[1]College of Internet and Media, Konkuk University,
1 Hwayang-dong, Gwangjin-gu, Seoul, Korea
eykim@kkucc.konkuk.ac.kr
[2]Division of Computer Engineering, College of Electronic and Information, Chosun University,
375 Susuk-dong, Dong-gu, Gwangju, Korea
sehyun@chosun.ac.kr

Abstract. To support the content-based functionalities in the new video coding standard MPEG-4 and MPEG-7, each frame of a video sequence must first be segmented into video object planes (VOPs), each of which represents a meaningful moving object. However, segmenting a video sequence into VOPs remains a difficult and unresolved problem. Accordingly, this paper presents a genetic algorithm (GA) for unsupervised video segmentation. The method is specifically designed to enhance the computational efficiency and the quality of segmentation results than the standard genetic algorithms. In the proposed method, the segmentation is performed by chromosomes, each of which is allocated to a pixel and independently evolved using a distributed genetic algorithm (DGA). For effective search space exploration, except the first frame in the sequence, the chromosomes are started with the segmentation results of the previous frame. Then, only unstable chromosomes, corresponding to the moving objects parts, are evolved by crossover and mutation. The advantages of the proposed method include the fast convergence speed by eliminating the redundant computations between the successive frames. The advantages have been confirmed with experiments where the proposed method was successfully applied to the synthetic and natural video sequences.

1 Introduction

Video segmentation, as related to the extraction and tracking of independently moving objects in a video sequence, has been the subject of intensive research due to its importance in a variety of applications, including vision systems, pattern recognition, and so on [1-4]. In particular, there has been a growing interest in video sequence segmentation mainly due to the development of MPEG-4 and MPEG-7. In the standards, a video sequence is considered to be composed of independent objects, called video object planes (VOPs), and then each the sequence is then processed object by object. Therefore, to support this content-based functionality, each frame of the input sequence must first be segmented into meaningful regions.

Until now, various techniques and algorithms have been proposed for video segmentation. Among these methods, there has been considerable interest in the

---

* Corresponding author

F. Boavida et al. (Eds.): IDMS/PROMS 2002, LNCS 2515, pp. 106–117, 2002.
© Springer-Verlag Berlin Heidelberg 2002

Markov random field (MRF) based segmentation method [1,3,4]. An MRF is effective in representing the spatial and temporal continuity of neighboring pixels in various applications, robust to degradation, and yet computationally involved [1-4]. As a result, genetic algorithms (GAs) have been intensively investigated as a solution to this computational complexity [4,5]. GAs are stochastic search methods based on the mechanics of natural selection and genetics. These algorithms are robust, and can successfully deal with combinatorial problems. They are also attractive because they can achieve an efficient parallel exploration of search space without getting stuck in local optima. However, many research results show that the convergence speed is still the preeminent problem in GA-based segmentation methods, so it is so slow to apply for video segmentation.

Accordingly, this paper presents a new GA-based video segmentation algorithm that can improve the computational efficiency. Each frame in a sequence is modeled by an MRF, and the energy function is then minimized by chromosomes that evolved using DGAs. Usually, a video sequence is highly redundant in the temporal domain. Therefore, in the proposed method, the segmentation of a frame in a sequence is obtained successively using the segmentation result of the previous frame. Moreover, to eliminate any redundant computation among consecutive frames, only unstable chromosomes corresponding to moving object parts are evolved. As a result, these mechanisms prevent any unnecessary waste of computational power and time. Experimental results show that the proposed method can not only reduce the computational time, but also obtain sufficiently good quality segmentation results.

The paper is organized as follows. The next section formulates the segmentation problem as energy function optimization problem. Section 3 describes the proposed method. Experimental results using synthesized as well as natural video sequences are presented in Section 4, and the final conclusions are made in Section 5.

2   Problem Formulation

The input image G was considered as degraded by i.i.d (independent identically distributed) zero-mean Gaussian white noise $N=\{n_{ij}\}$. Let $S=\{(i,j) : 1 \leq i \leq M_1, 1 \leq j \leq M_2\}$ denote the $M_1 \times M_2$ lattice, such that an element in S indexes an image pixel. Let $\Lambda=\{\lambda_1, \ldots, \lambda_R\}$ denote the label set and $X=\{X_{ij} | X_{ij} \in \Lambda\}$ be the family of random variables defined on S. The neighborhood of S can be defined as $\Gamma=\{\eta_{ij}\}$, where η_{ij} is a set of sites neighboring (i, j). Then, X is an MRF on S with respect to Γ because the two conditions of [3] are satisfied. Let ω be a realization of X. The goal is to identify ω which maximizes the posterior distribution for a fixed input image g. That is, to determine

$$\arg \max_{\omega} P(X = \omega | G = g) \approx \arg \max_{\omega} P(g | \omega) P(\omega) \tag{1}$$

Eq. (1) is divided into two components as follows:

$$P(g | \omega) = P(N = g - F(\omega) | \omega) = \prod_{(i,j) \in S} P(n_{ij} = g_{ij} - F(\omega_{ij}) | \omega_{ij})$$

$$= \prod_{(i,j) \in S} \frac{1}{\sqrt{2\pi\sigma^2}} \exp[-\frac{(g_{ij} - F(\omega_{ij}))^2}{2\sigma^2}] \tag{2}$$

$$P(\omega) = \exp(-U(\omega)) = \exp\{-\sum_{c \in C}[S_c(\omega) + T_c(\omega)]\} \qquad (3)$$

In Eq. (2), σ is the noise variance and $F(\bullet)$ is the mapping function that the label of a pixel corresponds to the estimated color vector. In Eq. (3), C is a possible set of cliques, where a clique is defined as a set of pixels in which all the pairs are mutual neighbors. Then the energy function $U(\omega)$ is obtained by the summation of two potentials over all possible cliques: spatial potentials $S_c(\omega)$ and temporal potentials $T_c(\omega)$. The former imposes the spatial continuity of the labels and the latter is to achieve the temporal continuity of the labels. The proposed model assumes that the only nonzero potentials are those corresponding to two-pair cliques, as shown in Fig. 1. Then, $S_c(\omega) = -\alpha$ if all labels in c are equal, otherwise $S_c(\omega) = \alpha$. Similarly, $T_c(\omega) = -\beta$ if all labels in c are equal, otherwise $T_c(\omega) = \beta$. Accordingly, Eq. (1) can be represented by the following equation, which is defined as a posterior energy function.

$$\arg\min_{\omega}\{\sum_{c \in C}[S_c(\omega) + T_c(\omega)] + \frac{[g - F(\omega)]^2}{2\sigma^2} + \frac{1}{2}\log(2\pi\sigma^2)\} \qquad (4)$$

Let ρ_{ij} denote a set of cliques containing pixel (i,j). Since C is equal to the sum of ρ_{ij} for all pixels, the function in Eq. (4) can be rewritten as the sum of the local energy U_{ij} for all pixels.

$$\arg\min_{\omega}\sum_{(i,j) \in S}\{\sum_{c \in \rho_{ij}}[S_c(\omega_{ij}) + T_c(\omega_{ij})] + \frac{[g_{ij} - F(\omega_{ij})]^2}{2\sigma^2} + \frac{1}{2}\log(2\pi\sigma^2)\} \qquad (5)$$

As a result, instead of maximizing the posterior distribution, the posterior energy function is minimized to identify the optimal label.

3   Proposed Method

3.1   Outline of the Proposed Method

In this paper, the segmentation problem of a frame is formalized as an optimization problem of the energy function. For this, GA is used. The computation is distributed into chromosomes that evolve by DGAs. A chromosome consists of a label and a feature vector, which are described in [3]. A set of chromosomes is called as a population and represents a segmentation result. Chromosomes are classified into two groups: stable and unstable chromosomes. When the chromosomes are mapped to an actual video sequence, the stable and unstable chromosomes correspond to the background and moving object parts, respectively.

In the proposed method, the segmentation of the frames in a sequence is successively obtained. For the first frame, chromosomes are started with random value, but for the later frame they are started from the segmentation of the previous frame. The segmentation for the starting frame is determined using Kim et al.'s segmentation algorithm [3]. The remaining frames are processed one at a time. Then, the segmentation algorithm is outlined in Fig. 1.

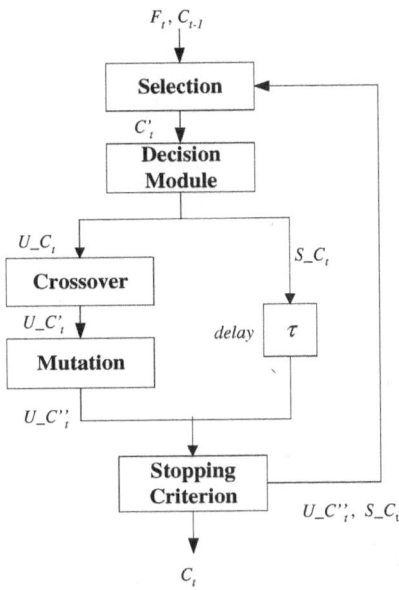

Fig.1. Block diagram of the proposed segmentation method

At intervals of T, the system receives the input $I(t)$ and $C(t-1)$, that is, the current frame and segmentation result of the previous frame, respectively. Starting with the segmentation results of the previous frame, the chromosmes evolve through iteratively performed selection and genetic operations. In DGA, these operations are performed on locally distributed subgroups of chromosomes, called a window, rather than on whole populations. In selection, the chromosomes are updated to new chromosomes, $C(t)$, by an elitist selection scheme [3]. Thereafter, in the Decision Module, the chromosomes are classified into two groups according to their fitness: stable chromosomes, $S\_C(t)$, and unstable ones, $U\_C(t)$. In the current frame, the chromosomes are sorted in an increasing order based on their fitness. Given the probabilites of genetic operations, certain chromosomes with lower fitnesses are selected as unstable in accordance with their probabilities. Only the unstable chromosomes are evolved by crossover and mutation, which are described in detail in [3]. In Fig. 1, $U\_C'(t)$ and $U\_C''(t)$ are chromosomes evolved by crossover and mutation, respectively. $S\_C(t)$ is then delayed for τ, the time taken for genetic operations in a generation. These operations are iteratively performed until the stopping criterion is satisfied. The stopping criterion is described in [3].

3.2 Chromosome

To apply GAs to any practical problem, an appropriate structural representation of the candidate solution is needed. The representation of a solution is an important choice in the algorithm because it determines the data structures that will be modified in the crossover and mutation operators. In this paper, a binary base-2 coding is used. Binary base-2 coding represents each chromosome as a string of elements of the set

{0, 1} (bits), which transforms the m real numbers into integers whose base-2 representations are then stored sequentially in the string. A chromosome consists of a label and RGB color vectors at pixel (i,j), and is located at pixel (i,j). The former is used as the region number for the pixel where the chromosome is located, and the latter is used to assign a fitness value to the chromosome.

Application of the GA to a practical problem requires the definition a fitness function. In this paper, Its fitness is defined as local energy U_{ij}.

In this paper, the chromosomes are classified into two groups based on their fitness values: stable chromosomes and unstable ones. Stable chromosomes have higher fitness values, regardless of the input frame, whereas unstable chromosomes have changing fitness values according to the input frame. When a frame is received as input, the chromosome fitness values may abruptly decrease or increase. When chromosomes are mapped to an actual video sequence, the stable chromosomes correspond to the background, while the unstable ones correspond to the moving object parts. The chromosome classification is performed in the "Decision Module". In the current frame, the chromosomes are sorted in increasing order based on their fitness. Given the crossover and mutation rates, certain chromosomes with lower fitness values are selected as unstable. Fig. 2 shows examples of unstable chromosomes for specific frames in "Table Tennis", a well-known image sequence in the video-coding community. The frames are color images sized at 351×239. The mutation and crossover rates are 0.005 and 0.01, respectively.

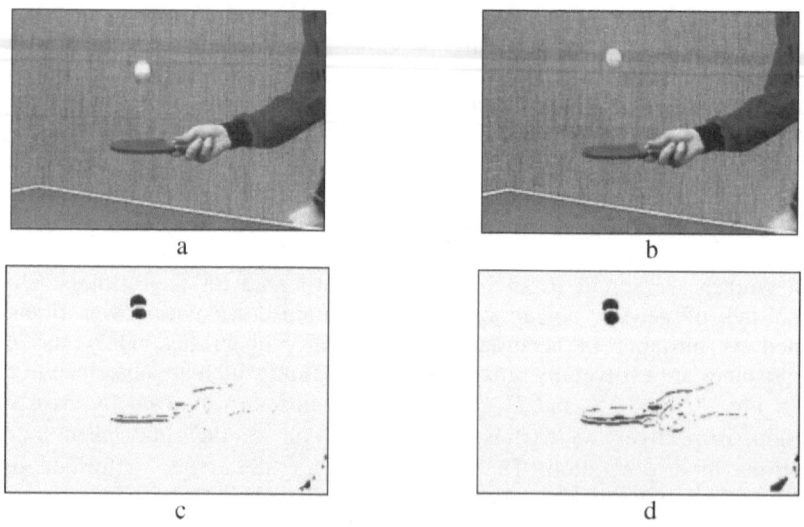

a   b

c   d

Fig. 2. Examples of unstable chromosomes: (a) previous frame; (b) current frame; (c) unstable chromosomes when mutation rate is 0.005; (d) unstable chromosomes when crossover rate is 0.01

In Fig. 3, there are five objects: the background, arm, ball, hand with racquet, and left hand. It is evident that most of the unstable chromosomes correspond to the moving object parts.

3.3 Decision Module

As illustrated in Fig. 1, the chromosomes are classified into stable chromosomes and unstable chromosomes by Decision Module. Let G denote the input image sized at $M_1 \times M_2$. And Let $L = \{L_i \mid 1 \leq i \leq M_1 \times M_2 \}$ denote the list of chromosomes sorted in a decreasing order based on their fitness. Then the unstable chromosomes for crossover, A are determined by the following rule.

$$A = \{L_i \mid 1 \leq i \leq k, \ k = M_1 \times M_2 \times P_c\},$$

where P_c is a pre-defined crossover rate. Similarly, the unstable chromosomes for mutation B are determined as follows.

$$B = \{L_i \mid 1 \leq i \leq k, \ k = M_1 \times M_2 \times P_m\},$$

where P_m is a pre-defined crossover rate. Only the chromosomes corresponding to the list A and B are evolved by crossover and mutation, respectively.

4 Experimental Results

To assess the validity of the proposed method, it was tested on several synthetic video sequences and well-known video sequences. The experiments were performed on a Pentium II-233 PC. The equilibrium threshold was set to 99.5% and the maximal number of generations was set to 1000. In the proposed model, α, β and σ are significant parameters. The value of α has an affect on the number of regions in a frame, and β encourages pixels to have the same label in consecutive frames. Therefore, α and β were empirically determined. The noise variance, σ was obtained as follows: let σ_{ij} be the color variance of the pixels inside the window centered at (i,j) and σ_m be an average of σ_{ij}; then σ is defined as an average of $\{\sigma_{ij} \mid \sigma_{ij} < \sigma_m\}$. Regardless of the input video sequences, DGA parameters were fixed as follows: the label size at 64, mutation rate as 0.005 and crossover rate as 0.05. Finally, the stopping criterion was fixed as in [3]. Due to space constraints, this paper only presents certain sets of results for the two video sequences.

4.1 Segmentation of Synthetic Video Sequences

When dealing with synthetic images, the true segmentation results are perfectly known. Consequently, it is possible to quantitatively evaluate the segmentation results using a numerical criterion rather than simple visual examination. Fig. 3 shows the segmentation result for the synthetic image sequence. All frames in the sequence were color images sized at 240×200. Scenes in the sequence were composed of three objects, which were fast moving to the different directions. Fig. 3(a) and Fig. 3(b) show original frames and the corresponding segmentation results, respectively. As seen in Fig. 3, proposed method can perfectly find the objects boundaries, despite of only unstable chromosomes are evolved by genetic operators.

Two measures were used to evaluate the quality of the segmentation results: the boundary error and misclassification rate. The boundary error was computed according to the distances between the target segmentation result and the segmentation results performed using each method. Then only the pixels corresponding to the region boundary are considered during the distance computation.

Accordingly, the boundary error rate was the sum of all the distances divided by the total number of pixels on the true boundary. The misclassification rate was computed by counting all the mis-classified pixels and then dividing this number by the total number of pixels in the image. When tested using the hand-drawn images, the proposed method showed a $1 \times 10^{-12}(\%)$ misclassification rate and 0.5×10^{-12} $(\%)$ boundary error rate on average.

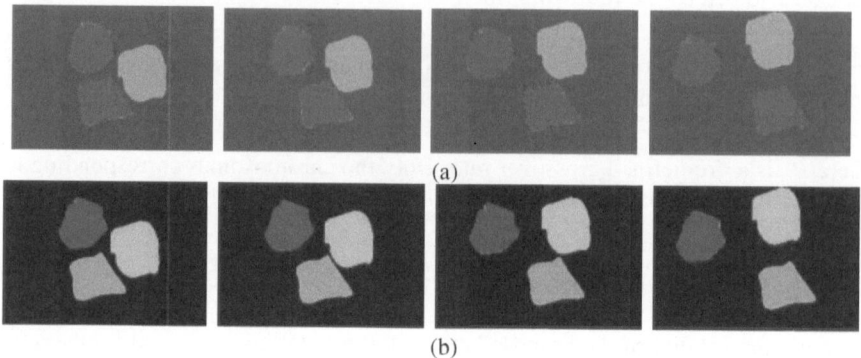

(a)

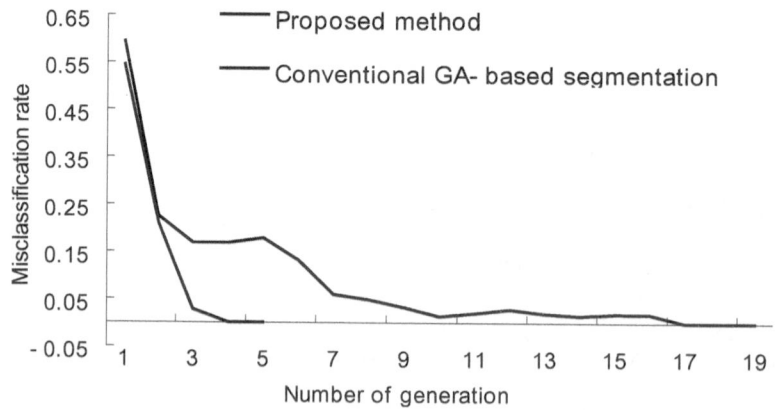

(b)

Fig. 3. Segmentation results for a synthetic video sequence. (a) Original frames, (b) segmentation results

Fig. 4 shows the relation between generation and the segmentation accuracy, for the proposed method and conventional GA-based method. In Fig. 4, the values are the average for the 40 frames, then the number of generations to converge an optimal solution are significantly decreased in the proposed method.

Fig. 4. Performance comparison between the proposed method and conventional GAs

4.2 Segmentation of Well-Known Video Sequences

The video sequences selected for use in this dissertation came from the MPEG-4 library of test sequences and are commonly referred to as *Table Tennis* and *Claire*. Mutation and Crossover rates were set to 0.005 and 0.1, respectively.

Fig. 5 shows the segmentation results for the video sequence *Claire* at time 141, 144, 150 and 156. *Claire* is a simple sequence with an uncluttered, stationary background. The characteristics of the *Claire* sequence are that the head and face include relatively large motions, whereas the chest exhibits only minimal motion during the entire sequence. Fig. 5(a) shows the segmentation result superimposed onto the corresponding frames, and Fig. 5(b) shows the regions, where each region is colored in accordance with its labels. As shown in Fig. 5, the proposed method was able to perfectly determine the boundaries of *Claire*, and tracked her motion even though only unstable chromosomes are evolved.

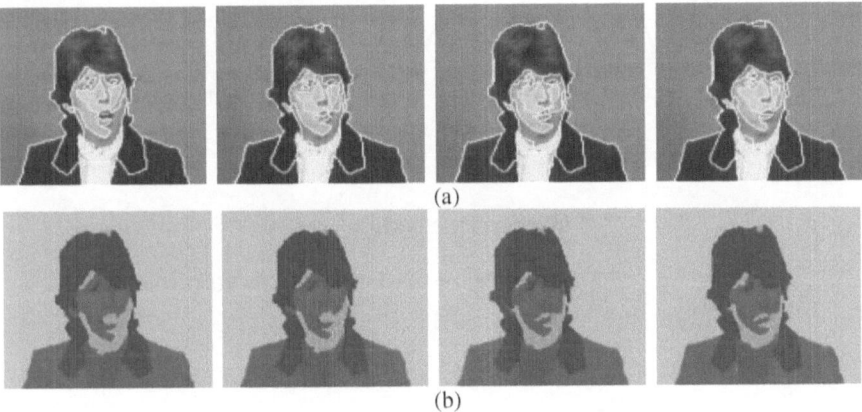

Fig. 5. Segmentation results for the sequence *Claire*. (a) Original frames, (b) segmentation results.

Fig. 6 shows a comparison of the three methods in terms of speed and quality when segmenting the sequence *Claire*. Fig. 6(a) shows the results relative to speed, then it shows the number of generations taken to segment each frame. Note, the number of generations significantly decreased between conventional GA-based segmentation method and our method. Fig. 6(b) shows a comparison between two methods in terms of the quality of the segmentation results. The interesting point observed in these graphs was that the results from the proposed method exhibited a higher quality than the results from conventional GA-based segmentation. Conventional GA-based segmentation method produced a segmentation result with an average function value of around 42.43, and our method produced a function value of around 40.71. On average, the proposed method achieved a F function that was 4% lower than that obtained by the conventional GA-based segmentation method. In addition it also exhibited a remarkable improvement in the convergence speed, which was 5-times faster than the conventional DGA-based segmentation method.

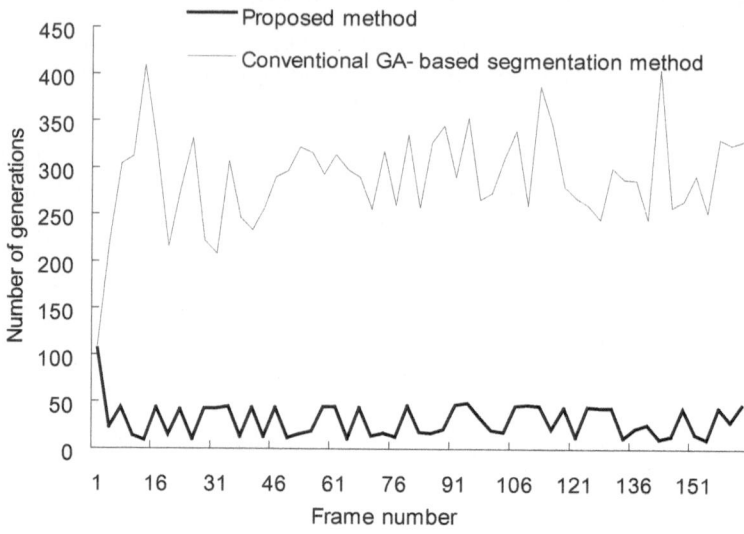

(a)

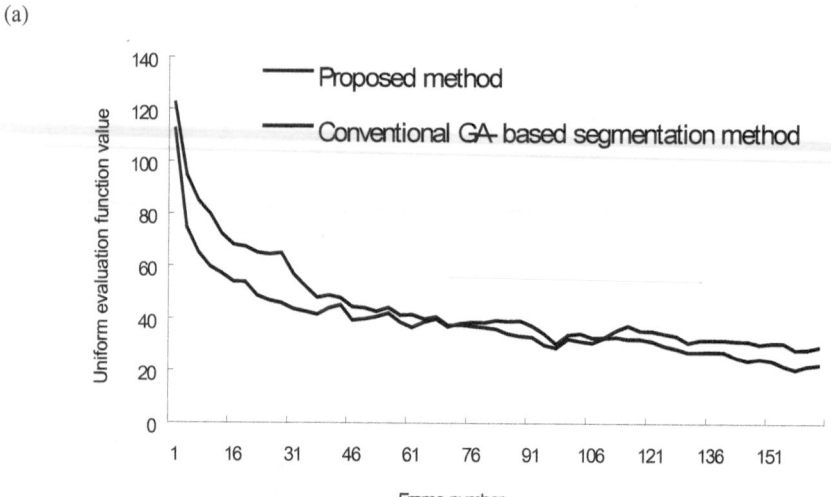

(b)

Fig. 6. Performance comparison for sequence *Claire*. (a) Number of generations required to segment each frame in sequence, (b) uniform function value, $F(\omega)$ for each frame.

To fully demonstrate the validity of the proposed methods for object extraction and tracking, they were applied to a video sequence with more than two objects. Fig. 7 shows the object extraction and tracking results of the video sequence *Table Tennis* at time 11, 12 and 14. The scene was decomposed into four objects: the background, ball, left hand, and right arm with a racquet. The left hand was not explicitly shown in the simulation results as it indeed disappears as the sequence unravels. Fig. 7(a) shows the spatiotemporal segmentation result superimposed onto the corresponding frames, and Fig. 7(b) shows the regions in the segmentation results. The proposed method allowed for this disappearance and kept on tracking the three remaining objects, which were perfectly identified throughout the whole video sequence.

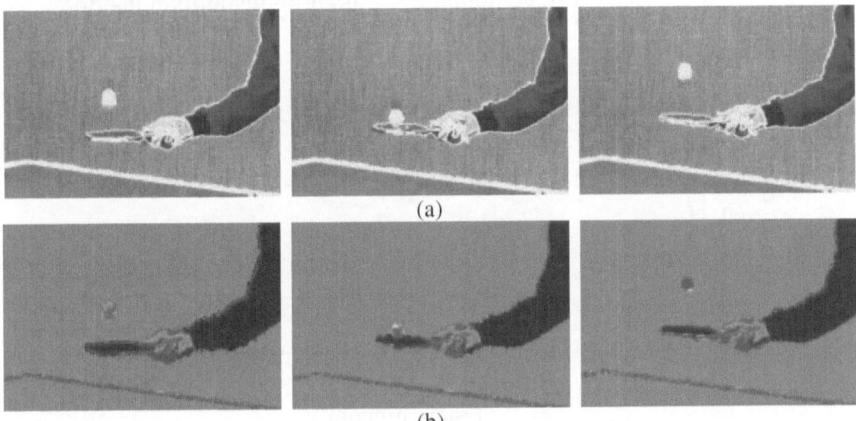

Fig. 7. Segmentation results for the sequence *Table Tennis*. (a) Original frames, (b) segmentation results.

Fig. 8 shows a quantitative comparison between two methods, relative to speed and the quality of the segmentation results. For the sequence *Table Tennis,* the proposed method showed outstanding segmentation results. The number of generations significantly decreased when the segmentation of the current frame was successively obtained using the segmentation result of the previous frame and only unstable chromosomes are evolved by crossover and mutation. Fig. 8(b) shows a comparison of the quality of the segmentation results between the two methods. These figures show that the segmentation results obtained using the proposed method guaranteed better segmentation results than the conventional GA-based segmentation method. Conventional GA-based segmentation method produced a segmentation result with an average function value of around 155.94, and the proposed method produced function value of around 121.00. On average, the proposed method achieved a cost function that was 22% lower than one obtained by the conventional GA-based segmentation method. As shown in Fig. 8, the proposed method also reduced the computational time along with producing the better segmentation results.

In the proposed method, chromosomes are started with the segmentation results of the previous frame, thereafter only unstable chromosomes are evolved by genetic operators. Nonetheless, the method can be accurately tracked the objects, and the object boundaries were virtually perfect. Moreover, the method can improve the convergence speed.

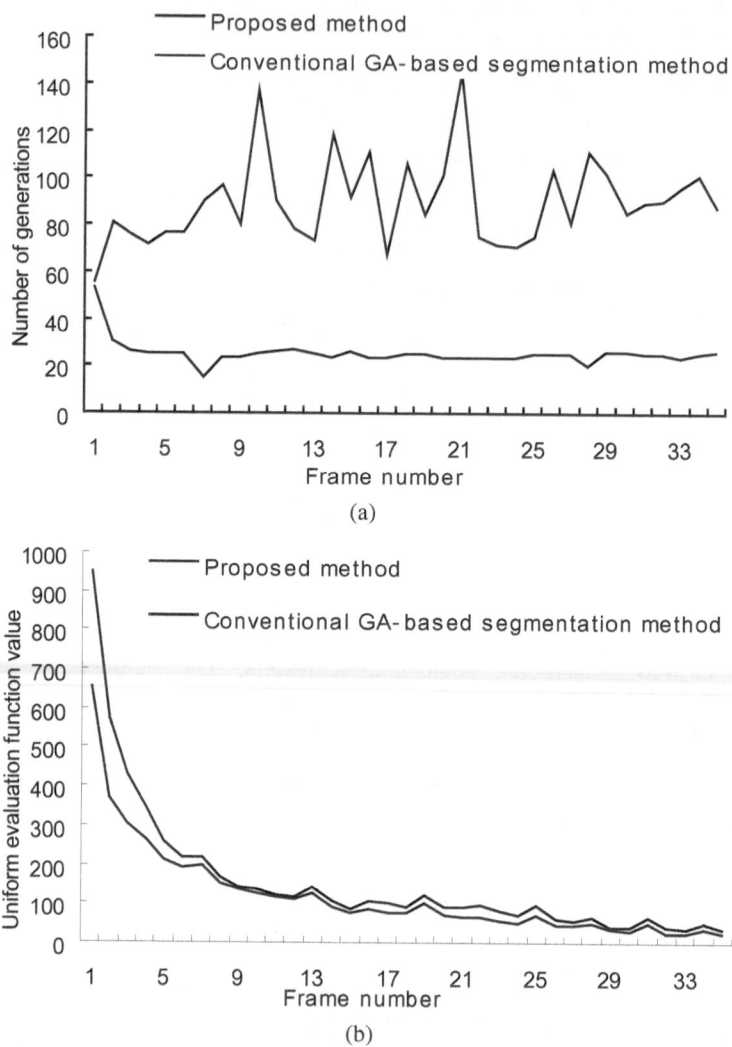

(a)

(b)

Fig. 8. Performance comparison of sequence *Table Tennis*. (a) Number of generations to segment each frame in sequence, (b) uniform function value, $F(\omega)$ for each frame.

5 Conclusion

This paper presented a new unsupervised method for segmenting a video sequence. Each frame in a sequence was modeled using an MRF, which is robust to degradation. Since this is computationally intensive, a new segmentation algorithm based on GA that can improve computationally efficiency was developed. Experimental results demonstrated the effectiveness of the proposed method. However, it is too slow for real-time application, so we are working on that problem now.

Acknowledgement. This work was supported by Korea Research Foundation Grant (KRF-2001-002-E00105)

References

1. Pal, Nikhil R., and Pal, Sankar K.: A Review on Image Segmentation Techniques. Pattern Recognition 26-9(1993) 1277-1294
2. Wu, Gene K., and Reed, T. R.: Image Sequence Processing using Spatiotemporal Segmentation. IEEE Trans. Circuits Syst. Video Technol. 9-5(1999) 798-807
3. Kim, H. J., Kim, E. Y., Kim, J. W., and Park, S. H.: MRF model based Image Segmentation using Hierarchical Distributed Genetic Algorithm. IEE Electronics Letters 33-25(1998) 1394-1395
4. Andrey, P., and Tarroux, P.: Unsupervised Segmentation of MRF modeled Textured Images using Selectionist Relaxation. IEEE Trans. Pattern Anal. Machine Intell., 20-3(1998) 252-262
5. Goldberg, D. E.: Genetic Algorithms in Search, Optimization and Machine Learning. Addison Wesley (1989)

Adaptive Motion Search Based on Block Difference and Motion Magnitude

Dong-Keun Lim and Yo-Sung Ho

Kwangju Institute of Science and Technology
1 Oryong-dong, Puk-gu, Kwangju, 500-712, Korea
{dklim, hoyo}@kjist.ac.kr

Abstract. In this paper, we derive optimal search patterns for fast block matching motion estimation. Since the motion search pattern is important in terms of search speed and correctness of the motion information, we consider various search patterns and search strategies. By analyzing the block matching algorithm as a function of the block size and distance in the search area, we find analytic search patterns for initial motion estimation. We also propose an adaptive motion search algorithm, where we exploit the correlation between block difference and motion magnitude. The proposed idea can provide an analytical ground for the MPEG-4 algorithms for fast motion search. We can improve the prediction accuracy of motion estimation, while reducing the required computational complexity compared to other fast block matching algorithms.

1 Introduction

Block matching motion estimation algorithms are popularly employed in several video coding standards, such as H.261, H.263, MPEG-1, MPEG-2, and MPEG-4. The main objective of motion estimation is to reduce temporal redundancy between successive picture frames. After partitioning the current image frame into non-overlapping rectangular blocks, the block matching algorithm attempts to find the best-matched block in the search area of the reference frame. Its performance is determined by motion prediction accuracy and computational complexity.

Important parameters in motion estimation are: size of block, search area, search pattern, search strategy, and matching criterion. Various algorithms for fast block search have been developed to reduce the computational burden associated with the full-search block matching algorithm (BMA) [1-12]. Since most fast BMAs generally take heuristic approaches to reduce the computational complexity, they sacrifice reconstructed image quality. They mainly focus on the search strategy using heuristic methods. Recently, it is known that the motion search pattern has an important influence on search speed and correctness of the motion information. Since the search strategy depends on search patterns for efficient motion estimation, we analyze search patterns for fast motion estimation.

F. Boavida et al. (Eds.): IDMS/PROMS 2002, LNCS 2515, pp. 118-129, 2002.

Although mathematical modeling and analysis for the block matching algorithm include ill-posed problems, a theoretical approach is possible by simplifying the block matching problem.

In this paper, we derive an optimal search pattern for fast motion estimation analytically. By examining the relationship between block difference and motion magnitude, we propose an adaptive motion search algorithm. Based on statistical correlation between object displacement and frame difference in each block, we change the search pattern for motion estimation adaptively. We also explain how we can generate initial search patterns. The proposed adaptive motion search algorithm can reduce the computational burden substantially relative to full-search block matching algorithm, while providing a good motion prediction. The analysis presented in this paper can support several ideas proposed for the MPEG activities [8-12].

2 Optimal Search Pattern

2.1 Problem Statement

Since the shape and the size of the search pattern in the fast block matching algorithm jointly determine the convergence speed and motion estimation performance, we consider various search patterns: rectangle or diamond of different sizes. Fig. 1(a) and Fig. 1(b) show search patterns for the three-step search (TSS) and the 2-D logarithmic search (TDL), respectively [1-3].

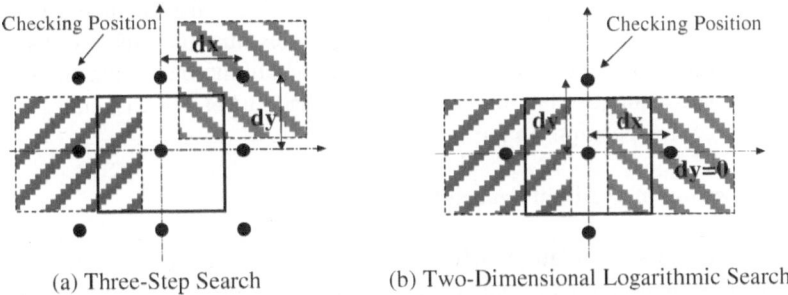

(a) Three-Step Search   (b) Two-Dimensional Logarithmic Search

Fig. 1. Search Patterns for Two Fast BMAs

As shown in Fig. 1, the search pattern for the three-step search algorithm is a rectangle, but that of the two-dimensional logarithmic search algorithm has a diamond shape. In Fig. 1, dx and dy represent distances between adjacent checking positions. In the block matching algorithm, we measure the correlation between the current block and the reference block by shifting the center of the reference block to candidate positions in the search pattern.

In the first step of TSS, block correlations at nine checking positions are examined, as indicated in Fig. 1(a). In the second step, eight new checking positions are spaced less coarsely around the best matched position in the first step. In the third step, the distance between checking positions is further reduced to one pixel, and the minimum distortion position is selected.

TDL tracks the direction of minimum distortion. In each step, five checking positions located in a diamond-shaped search pattern are examined, as shown in Fig. 1(b). If the minimum distortion is observed in the center of the checking positions or at the boundary of the search area, the distance between checking positions is reduced. The final motion vector is determined as the minimum distortion position among all the checking positions of one pixel distance.

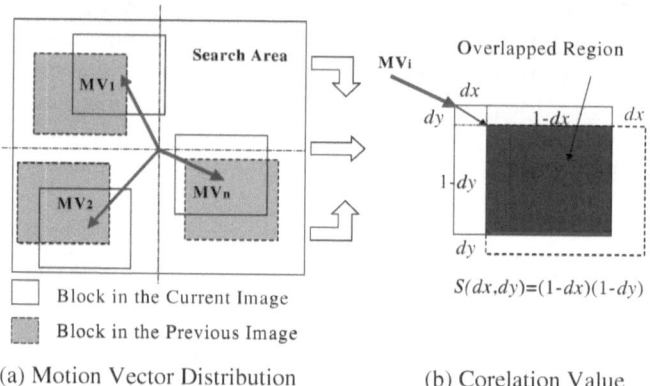

(a) Motion Vector Distribution   (b) Corelation Value

Fig. 2. Correlation of Image Blocks

In order to make a simple analysis, we consider a rectangular image block whose pixel values are unity and its background has all zero values. As shown in Fig. 2(a), motion vectors may locate at any position in the search area. Although we do not know the direction and the magnitude of the actual object displacement MV_i in Fig. 2, we can derive an optimal search pattern for motion estimation. Since we use checking positions to find the candidates of the motion vector in the block matching algorithm, we investigate equi-correlation contours as a function of the distances, dx and dy, between checking positions in the search pattern.

2.2 Derivation of Optimal Search Pattern

In our analysis, the correlation $S(dx,dy)$ between two rectangular image blocks can be calculated as the normalized area of the overlapped region, as shown in Fig. 2(b).

$$S(dx, dy) = (1 - |dx|)(1 - |dy|), \ 0 \leq |dx| \leq 1, \ 0 \leq |dy| \leq 1 \qquad (1)$$

We note that $S(dx,dy)$ has the following symmetry property:

$$S(dx, dy) = S(-dx, dy) = S(dx, -dy) = S(-dx, -dy) \qquad (2)$$

From Eq. (1), we can find locations of distance (dx,dy) having the same correlation value, and draw equi-correlation contours.

$$|dx \cdot dy| - |dx| - |dy| + 1 - S(dx, dy) = 0 \qquad (3)$$

If we represent each point (dx,dy) in the block by a linear function,

$$dy = c \cdot dx, \ c \in \Re \qquad (4)$$

we obtain dx as a function of c and $S(dx,dy)$

$$dx = \frac{(c+1) \pm \sqrt{(c-1)^2 + 4c \cdot S(dx,dy)}}{2c} \quad (5)$$

In order to obtain a distribution of block correlation values, we apply boundary conditions to Eq. (4) and Eq. (5).

Case 1: $S(dx,dy)=0$, two blocks are not overlapped.

$$dx = \frac{(c+1) + \sqrt{(c-1)^2}}{2c} = \begin{cases} \dfrac{c+1+c-1}{2c} = 1, \ c>1, \ dy = c \cdot dx = c \\ \dfrac{c+1+1-c}{2c} = \dfrac{1}{c}, \ c<1, \ dy = c \cdot dx = 1 \end{cases} \quad (6)$$

$$dx = \frac{(c+1) - \sqrt{(c-1)^2}}{2c} = \begin{cases} \dfrac{c+1-c+1}{2c} = \dfrac{1}{c}, c>1, dy = c \cdot dx = 1 \\ \dfrac{c+1-1+c}{2c} = 1, c<1, dy = c \cdot dx = c \end{cases} \quad (7)$$

Case 2: $S(dx,dy)=1$, two blocks are completely overlapped.

$$dx = \frac{(c+1) + \sqrt{(c+1)^2}}{2c} = 1 + \frac{1}{c}, \quad dy = c \cdot dx = c+1 \quad (8)$$

$$dx = \frac{(c+1) - \sqrt{(c+1)^2}}{2c} = 0, \quad dy = c \cdot dx = 0 \quad (9)$$

Since only Eq. (6) and Eq. (9) meet the boundary condition, we know that contour lines converge to rectangular shapes. The same correlation $S(dx,dy)$ exists along the boundaries of the block when there is no overlap between two blocks. By changing the value of c from 0 to infinity in Eq. (5), we can plot equi-correlation contours, as shown in Fig. 3(a).

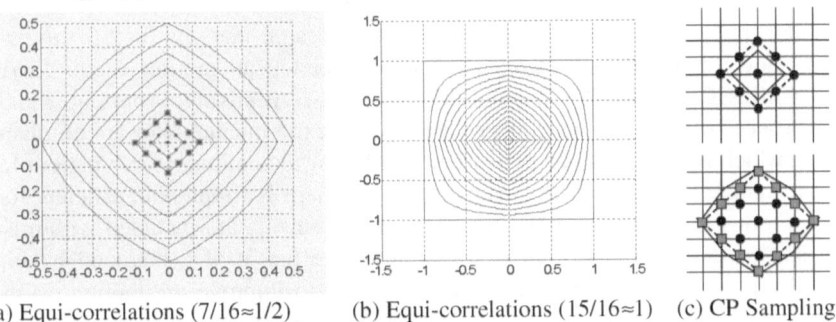

(a) Equi-correlations (7/16≈1/2)   (b) Equi-correlations (15/16≈1)   (c) CP Sampling

Fig. 3. Generation of Search Patterns

In Fig. 3(a), we show the result for limited search area to [-7, 7], or 7/16 ≈ 0.5. Furthermore, when limiting search area to [-15, 15], or 15/16 ≈ 1, we can obtain the derived search pattern in Fig. 3(b). From this result, conventional search patterns can be regarded as subsets of the proposed one.

The analyticallly derived search pattern can be used to analyze search patterns of conventional block matching algorithms. We note that the diamond search [8-9,11] and the advanced zonal search [10-12] have similar characteristics. By sampling checking positions from continuous analytical equi-correlations in Fig. 3(a) and Fig. 3(b), we choose discrete search patterns, as shown in Fig. 3(c). If the contour line is not aligned with a pixel position, we choose the closest pixel position as a checking point. The diamond shape can have different sizes and sampling positions according to motion characteristics in the search pattern. Therefore, there are different trade-off points between search strategy and search pattern. Accuracy and efficiency of motion estimation depend on the selected points.

2.3 Experimental Results for Optimal Search Patterns

In order to verify the derived search pattern, we perform computer simulations on ITU-T mono-chrome test sequences: MISS AMERICA, CLAIRE, CALENDAR, and SALESMAN, each of which contains 88 frames of the CIF format; FOOTBALL, having 88 frames of the ITU-T format. For the full-search block matching algorithm, the block size is 16×16 and the search area is [-7,+7]. In other words, $0 < (|dx|, |dy|) < 7/16 \approx 1/2$.

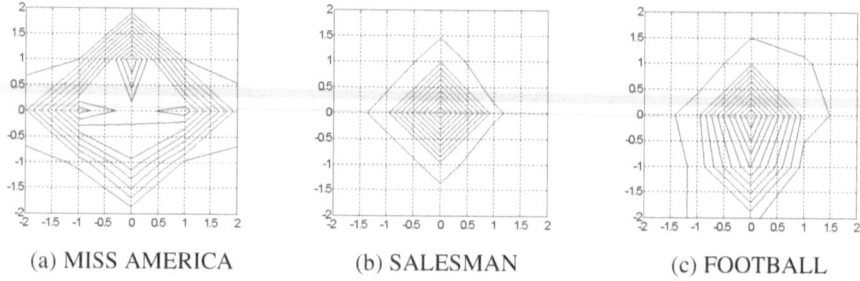

(a) MISS AMERICA   (b) SALESMAN   (c) FOOTBALL

Fig. 4. Experimental Search Patterns

While Fig. 3(a) indicates analytically derived search patterns for $S(dx,dy) > 1/2$, Fig. 4 shows experimental search patterns obtained from motion vector fields for MISS AMERICA, SALESMAN, and FOOTBALL, respectively. From Fig. 3 and Fig. 4, we observe that the derived search patterns and experimental ones are all diamond-shaped, which implies that our derivation is valid for the optimal search pattern for the block matching algorithm. The diamond search pattern is simple, but efficient for fast BMA. From Fig. 4, we can note that most displacements are included within a two-pixel spaced diamond shape. It corresponds to the inside of a diamond having the normalized size of $2/7 \approx 0.29$ in Fig. 3(a). In order to improve the motion estimation accuracy, we can increase the size of the diamond and the number of checking positions, and modify the diamond shape along its external boundary.

3 Block Matching Algorithm Using Optimal Search Pattern

3.1 Criteria for Block Matching Algorithm

The degree of the matching of image blocks can be measured by various criteria [1], including the mean absolute difference (MAD), the mean square error (MSE), and the matching pel count (MPC).

$$MAD(i,j) = \frac{1}{N^2} \sum_{k=1}^{N} \sum_{l=1}^{N} \left| I_t(k,l) - I_{t-1}(k+i,l+j) \right| \tag{10}$$

$$MSE(i,j) = \frac{1}{N^2} \sum_{k=1}^{N} \sum_{l=1}^{N} \left[I_t(k,l) - I_{t-1}(k+i,l+j) \right]^2 \tag{11}$$

$$T(k,l,i,j) = \begin{cases} 1, & if \left| I_t(k,l) - I_{t-1}(k+i,l+j) \right| \leq THS \\ 0, & otherwise \end{cases} \tag{12}$$

$$MPC(i,j) = \sum_{k=1}^{N} \sum_{l=1}^{N} T(k,l,i,j)$$

where $I_t(k,l)$ and $I_{t-1}(k,l)$ be the luminance pixel values in the current frame and in the previous frame, respectively.

In order to reduce the computational complexity of the block matching operation, we define a sum of absolute differences (SAD) by combining MAD and MPC.

$$T(k,l,i,j) = \begin{cases} 1, & if \left| I_t(k,l) - I_{t-1}(k+i,l+j) \right| \geq THS \\ 0, & otherwise \end{cases} \tag{13}$$

$$SAD(i,j) = \sum_{k=1}^{N} \sum_{l=1}^{N} T(k,l,i,j) \left| I_t(k,l) - I_{t-1}(k+i,l+j) \right|$$

The main idea of the new matching criterion is that we only count pixel differences that have significant changes of luminance values. Since pixels that have small changes of luminance values are not included in the computation for SAD, its complexity is reduced substantially. One remaining issue with the new matching criterion is how to select the threshold value THS properly. Since the human visual system (HVS) is sensitive to large changes of luminance values, we can set a just noticeable difference (JND) as THS. For blocks of small displacement, we set the threshold value to 0; then, Eq. (13) is equivalent to MAD.

3.2 Adaptive Motion Search Algorithm

In a teleconferencing video, most image blocks are regarded as stationary or quasi-stationary. Motion vectors for stationary image blocks are mostly around (0,0). In order to decide if a block is stationary, we consider the following situations.

In general, a large object displacement would produce a large block difference (BD) within the search area, as shown in Fig. 5. In Fig. 5, black dots indicate pixel positions having significant changes of luminance values. To calculate the block difference, we use SAD. However, we may have the following exceptional cases.

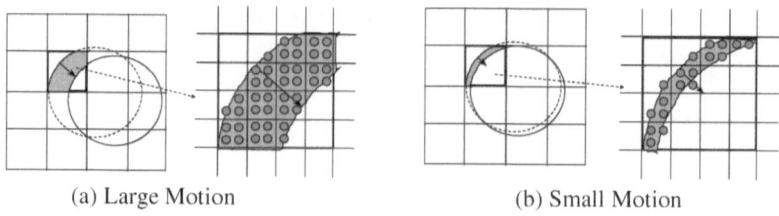

(a) Large Motion   (b) Small Motion

Fig. 5. Object Movement and Block Difference

Case 1: Even if the actual object displacement is large, the block difference is smaller than the threshold value. This situation can occur when similar blocks in the same image object move to the same direction by the same amount. Since it generates an aperture problem [4], we cannot solve it properly. In this case, we simply assume that the block has a small displacement.

Case 2: Even if the actual object displacement is small, the block difference is larger than the threshold value. This case may happen when the background and the object have large luminance differences. If the number of pixels having significant luminance changes is small, we assume that this case occurrs and the block has a small displacement.

Fig. 6 explains the overall procedure of the proposed adaptive motion search (AMS) algorithm, where Ns denotes the number of significant pixels in the block.

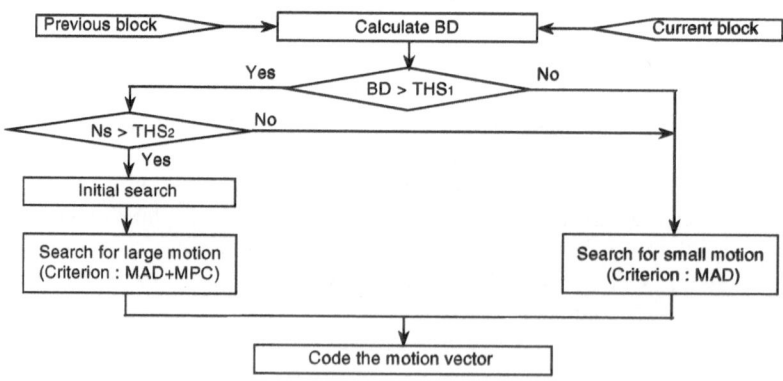

Fig. 6. Adaptive Motion Search Algorithm

If the block difference is large, we use the initial search pattern, shown in Fig. 7(a). The initial search pattern consists of regularly spaced lattice positions that cover the whole or the part of the search area. Once the position of the minimum distortion is selected during the initial search, other positions near the minimum distortion position are examined in the next stages, as illustrated in Fig. 7(c) to Fig. 7(f).

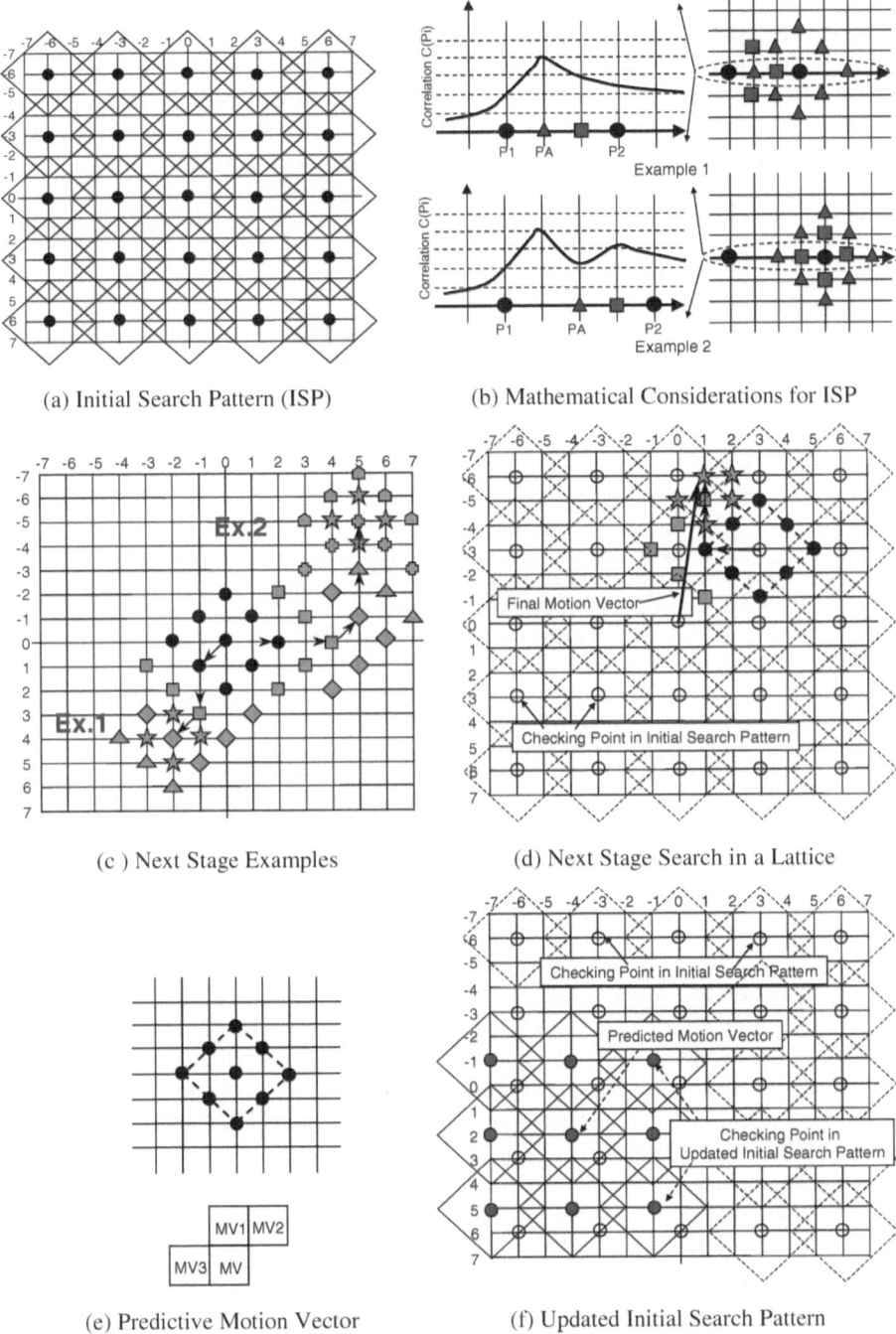

(a) Initial Search Pattern (ISP)

(b) Mathematical Considerations for ISP

(c) Next Stage Examples

(d) Next Stage Search in a Lattice

(e) Predictive Motion Vector

(f) Updated Initial Search Pattern

Fig. 7. Search Strategy and Search Pattern

Now we explain how we obtain the initial search pattern. Fig. 7(b) shows a problem with two examples when we generate the initial search pattern. The problem arises when we use improper resolutions for the center of distributed search patterns, especially when we treat image blocks having large motions. Rounded dots indicate pixel positions in the lattice in Fig. 7(a). In Fig. 7(b), each 1-D graph in the left side is the cross view of the horizontal axis at the center of each 2-D diagram that is drawn in the right side.

We analyze Example 1 in Fig. 7(b) as follows, where $C(\ )$ is a correlation function.

> 1. Initial Search Pattern: $C(P1) < C(P2) \rightarrow$ Choose P2
> 2. Check PA in Diamond Search Pattern:
> $$C(P2) < C(PA) \rightarrow \text{Choose PA}$$
> 3. If $C(P1\text{-}1) > C(PA)$, diamond search will be progressed in (P1-1). (Not in this example)
> 4. One Pixel-resolution Search:
> Final MV is PA, since $C(PA) > C(\ (PA+P2)/2\ )$.
> (Correct Operation)

From Example 2 in Fig.7(b), we have

> 1. Initial Search Pattern: $C(P1) < C(P2) \rightarrow$ Choose P2
> 2. Check PA in Diamond Search Pattern:
> $$C(PA) < C(P2) \rightarrow \text{Choose P2}$$
> 3. One Pixel-resolution Search:
> Final MV is $(PA+P2)/2$, since $C(P2) < C(\ (PA+P2)/2\ )$.
> 4. But $C(\ (PA+P2)/2\ ) < C(\ (P1+PA)/2\ )$
> $\rightarrow$ Global maximum exists (Incorrect Operation).

The output of Example 2 is incorrect. Since the distance between diamond search patterns is too long, the border of each diamond search pattern cannot cover candidate positions properly. In order to solve this problem, we can increase the size of diamond search patterns or reduce the distance between the diamond search patterns. The diamond search pattern resembles a cell in a lattice.

Fig. 7(c) shows two examples of motion search. The role of the initial search pattern is the lattice, as shown in Fig. 7(d). With this lattice, we can reduce the number of search steps in the next stage. This initial search pattern can be generated according to the size of the diamond search pattern. We also consider a predictive motion vector to change the center of the lattice, as shown in Fig. 7(f). In order to find a predictive motion vector, we use a median value among motion vectors of the neighboring blocks, MV1, MV2, and MV3 in Fig. 7(e). Around this predicted motion vector, we generate an updated initial search pattern, as shown in Fig. 7(f).

Fig. 8(a) and Fig. 8(b) explain two different search strategies for large motion. Depending on the last position of the minimum distortion, we add three or five new checking positions. This procedure is repeated until we find the minimum distortion in the center of the search pattern or at the boundary of the search area. The final displacement vector is the position of the minimum distortion among all one-pixel spaced positions around the last position of the minimum distortion.

If the block difference is small, the search area is limited to a local region. The procedure for small motion is similar to that for large motion; however, we start with 3×3 neighboring positions, as shown in Fig. 8(c).

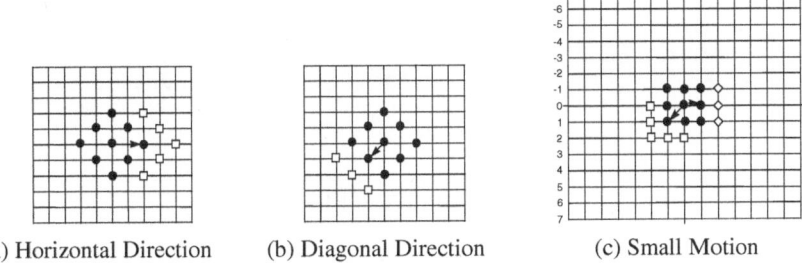

(a) Horizontal Direction   (b) Diagonal Direction   (c) Small Motion

Fig. 8. Search Strategies for Large Motion and Small Motion

4 Experimental Results

Computer simulations have been performed on the monochrome test sequences. In our simulation, the original image of the previous frame was used as a reference frame to generate a motion-compensated prediction image. Quality of the motion-compensated prediction image is measured by the peak signal-to-noise ratio (PSNR), which is defined by

$$PSNR = 10\log_{10}\frac{255^2}{MSE} \quad [dB] \tag{14}$$

$$MSE = \frac{1}{MN}\sum_{m=0}^{M-1}\sum_{n=0}^{N-1}(I_t(m,n) - \tilde{I}_t(m,n))^2 \tag{15}$$

where I_t denotes the original current image frame, and $\tilde{I}_t$ denotes the motion-compensated prediction image frame.

Experimental results with MISS AMERICA and FOOTBALL are depicted in Fig. 9, where the proposed AMS (Adaptive Motion Search) algorithm is compared with FS (full search), TDL (two-dimensional logarithmic search) [1,4], TSS (three-step search)[2,4], 4SS (four-step search) [6], and DSWA (dynamic search window adjust and interlaced search) [7] algorithms. From frame number 60 to 85 in Fig. 9(a), where the image sequence has large motion, the proposed method has good prediction results while the other algorithms fail to estimate large motions. This can be observed in Fig. 9(b), where FOOTBALL sequence has large motions.

Simulation results are summarized in Table 1, where we note that AMS provides better image quality than any other fast BMAs. It also reduces the average number of search points for MISS AMERICA having small motion, while slightly increasing the complexity for FOOTBALL having large motion. The matching criterion defined in Eq. (13) also contributes to reduce the required number of the searching operations.

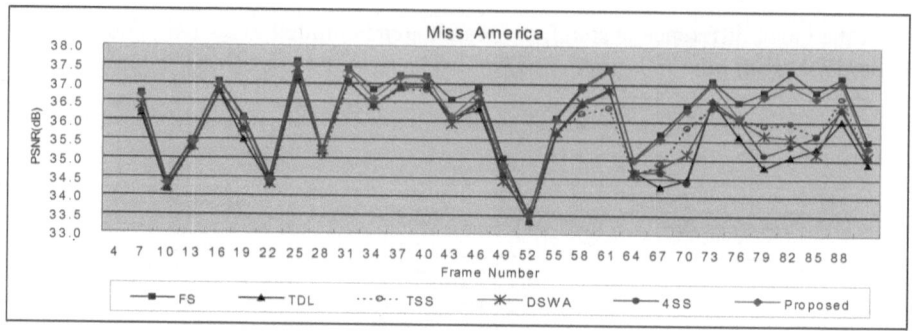

(a) MISS AMERICA

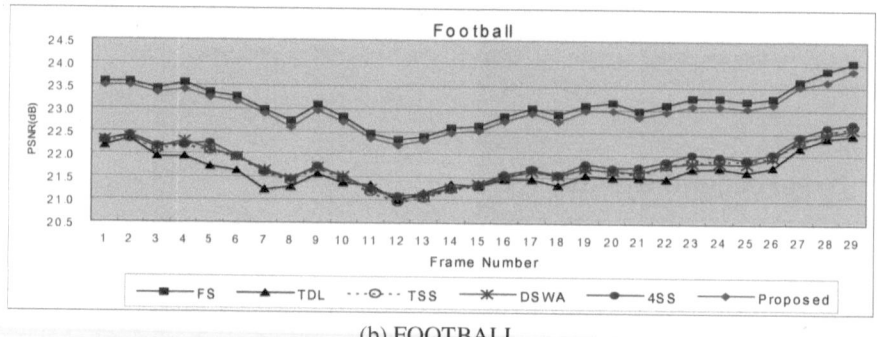

(b) FOOTBALL

Fig. 9. Performance Comparison

Table 1. Average Performance of Block Matching Algorithms

Algorithm	PSNR(dB)		Average Number of Checking Positions	
	MISSA	FOOTB	MISSA	FOOTB
Full Search	36.29	23.12	225.0	225.0
Three Step Search	35.78	21.77	25.0	25.0
4-Step Search	35.81	21.84	20.9	21.9
2-D Logarithmic Search	35.62	21.63	16.6	19.3
Dynamic Search	35.77	21.78	19.8	17.8
Diamond Search	36.08	21.22	17.0	17.2
Diamond Zonal Search	35.99	22.31	16.1	24.0
Adaptive Motion Search (AMS)	36.17	22.99	14.8	29.7

5 Conclusions

In this paper, we have proposed a new algorithm for fast block matching motion estimation based on an optimal search pattern. By a simple analysis, we have shown that the diamond search pattern is compact and optimal in terms of correlation of rectangular blocks. The proposed motion estimation algorithm employs the derived optimal search pattern and a new matching criterion. We also develop an efficient motion search strategy for the given initial search pattern. Performance improvement compared to other fast BMAs is 0.4 dB for MISS AMERICA, and 1 dB for FOOTBALL. The proposed algorithm reduces computational complexity about 6.5% and 13.2% compared to FS BMA for MISS AMERICA and FOOBALL, respectively. It chooses an adaptive search strategy based on the amount of block difference, and reduces the required computational complexity drastically compared to other fast block matching algorithms, while maintaining good prediction accuracy.

Acknowledgements. This work was supported in part by the Korea Science and Engineering Foundation (KOSEF) through the Ultra-Fast Fiber-Optic Networks (UFON) Research Center at Kwangju Institute of Science and Technology (K-JIST), and in part by the Ministry of Education (MOE) through the Brain Korea 21 (BK21) project.

References

1. Jain, J.R., Jain, A.K.: Displacement Measurement and Its Application in Interframe Image Coding. IEEE Trans. Commun., vol. COM-29 (1981) 1799-1808
2. Srinivasan, R., Rao, K.R.: Predictive Coding Based on Efficient Motion Estimation. IEEE Trans. Commun., vol. COM-33, no. 8 (1985) 888-896
3. Ghanbari, M.: The Cross-search Algorithm for Motion Estimation. IEEE Trans. Commun., vol. COM-38 (1990) 950-953
4. Musmann, H., Pirsh, P., Grallert, H.: Advances in Picture Coding. Proc. IEEE, vol. 73, no. 4 (1985) 523-548
5. Liu, B., Zaccarin, A.: New Fast Algorithm for Estimation of Block Motion Vectors. IEEE Trans. Circuit and Systems for Video Technology, vol.3 (1993) 148-157
6. Po, L.M., Ma, W.C.: A Novel Four-step Search Algorithm for Fast Block Motion Estimation. IEEE Trans. Circuit and Systems for Video Technology, vol. 6, no. 3 (1996) 313-317
7. Lee, L.W., Wang, J.F., Lee, J.Y., Shie, J.D.: Dynamic Search-window Adjustment and Interlaced Search for Block-matching Algorithm. IEEE Trans. Circuit and Systems for Video Technology, vol. 3, no. 1 (1993) 85-87
8. Tham, J.Y., Ranganath, S., Ranganath, M., Kassim, A.A.: A Novel Unrestricted Center-biased Diamond Search Algorithm for Block Motion Estimation. IEEE Trans. Circuit and Systems for Video Technology, vol. 8 (1998) 369-377
9. Zhu, S., Ma, K.: A New Diamond Search Algorithm for Fast Block Matching Motion Estimation. IEEE Trans. Image Processing, vol. 92 (2000) 287-290
10. Tourapis, A., Au, O., Liou, M., Shen, G.: An Advanced Zonal Block Based Algorithm for Motion Estimation. ICIP-99, vol. 2 (1999) 610-614
11. Chiang, T., Sun, H.: Report of Ad hoc Group on Encoder Optimization. ISO/IEC/JTC1/SC29/WG11 MPEG99/ M5528 (1999)
12. Tourapis, A.M., Au, O.C., Liou, M.L.: New Results on Zonal Based Motion Estimation Algorithms-Advanced Predictive Diamond Zonal Search, ISCAS, vol.5 (2001) 183-186

Does IPv6 Improve the Scalability of the Internet?

Philippe Owezarski

LAAS-CNRS, 7 Avenue du Colonel Roche
31077 Toulouse cedex 4, France
owe@laas.fr

Absract. The Internet is growing very fast since 10 to 20 years, following an exponential increase. Some scalability issues start to arise in the Internet. A well known one is related to IPv4 addresses exhaustion, that should make the Internet growth stop. Because an access to the Internet is a very strong need for many people, the Internet growth continues thanks to some additional mechanisms as NAT for example. An other important scalability issue, not well known by most of Internet services users concerns the explosion of routing tables that are growing very fast (their size went from 15,000 to 150,0000 entries during the 6 last years), then limiting the Internet performance and scalability by increasing the routing table lookup time, and then reducing routing performances. IPv6 has been designed to cope with such scalability issues (addresses exhaustion and routing table explosion). This paper proposes a monitoring study of some BGP routing tables to analyze the reasons of this huge growth of the number of entries in routing tables. This paper then gives quantitative analysis of the reasons why all routing tables prefixes cannot be aggregated, speaking then of the consequences of NAT, multi-homing, load balancing, broken addresses hierarchy, etc. on routing tables sizes. This paper also presents some of the threats for IPv6 whose deployment in the Internet is so slow, and this point is analyzed in relation with the current strong scalability issues of the Internet.

1 Introduction

The Internet is growing in an exponential way, so following the Moore law[1]. This increase is pushed by the number of new comers that are getting connected to the Internet. This increase is getting more and more important as the Internet is getting more and more popular in new "Internet coming countries", especially in Asia as China, India or Korea. In particular, these new countries are some of the ones that have the largest populations, so increasing again the need for new addresses. The Internet increase is also pushed by new multimedia communication technologies, and related services, as 3rd generation mobiles (3G mobiles) as UMTS[2]. The issues of such an increase are mainly two folds:

---

[1] Initially, the Moore law was stated for the increase of the power of processors, but it also perfectly fits the increase of the Internet
[2] UMTS: Universal Mobile Telecommunications System

F. Boavida et al. (Eds.): IDMS/PROMS 2002, LNCS 2515, pp. 130–140, 2002.
© Springer-Verlag Berlin Heidelberg 2002

1. The amount of IP addresses (meaning the current IPv4 addresses) is (almost) exhausted, and new comers cannot get new address spaces, or at least address spaces that are not large enough to give a native routable IP address to every new host or device that has to be connected to the Internet;

2. The size of BGP[3] [14] routing tables is exploding, meaning that their increase is so large that it creates a big QoS issue: routers are then spending too much time for routing table lookup, then increasing routers and end-to-end delays, and then decreasing the global performance on all connections and of the global network. Just to give an idea about BGP routing table growth, their size went, in average, from 15,000 to 150,0000 entries during the 6 last years.

In order to solve the two issues, expressed just above, IPv6[4] has been proposed by the IETF[5]. At the beginning, IPv6 has been designed for:

1. Providing an increased number of addresses going from 2^{32} to 2^{128}. This change in the number of addresses was supposed to solve the problem of IP addresses exhaustion (providing at least 5 IP addresses by square foot on Earth);

2. Stopping, and even better, reducing the explosion of routing tables. This property can be achieved thanks to a new dynamic mechanism for IPv6 addresses allocation that depends on the real location on Earth of the computer or device to connect to the Internet. This is the auto-configuration mechanism of IPv6. Then, associated to a static process of IPv6 prefixes allocation, with larger enough spaces between adjacent prefixes, IPv6 is supposed to provide a fully hierarchical IPv6 addresses structure, then facilitating the search of IPv6 addresses or prefixes in BGP routing tables.

But IPv6, today, is very far from being widely deployed. One of the reasons is mainly related to the arrival of NAT[6] [11] [12] that provides an alternative solution to IPv6. Of course, NAT is a "dirty" solution that breaks the end-to-end model of the Internet, and in particular not suited for some new kinds of applications as peer-to-peer applications for instance [7]. But NAT has also the strong advantage of being a fast, cheap and available without delay solution. Chinese people that need IP addresses cannot wait for IPv6 to be deployed. So to connect to the Internet they are obliged to chose such a solution, even if it does not provide them with some services and creates some problems with some applications, or for security. The second question about IPv6, not yet answered, and that delays the wide deployment of IPv6, concerns the ability of IPv6 to improve the scalability of the Internet, and in particular if IPv6 is able to reduce the BGP table sizes that are reaching a limit over which the global performance of the Internet is going to decrease. This is one important requirement for Internet carriers.

This paper aims to answer this last question by analyzing the reasons of such an increase of BGP routing tables with IPv4, and then, evaluating (theoretically) if IPv6 is able to provide an improvement for the Internet performance / scalability? Of course, analyzing the BGP tables supposed that the point of view chosen in this paper is the one of an Internet carrier or service provider that has to operate and manage a transport network. This study is based on the monitoring of some routers, especially

---

[3] BGP: Border Gateway Protocol
[4] For an introduction to IPv6, readers can refer to [6] and [10]
[5] IETF: Internet Engineering Task Force (http://www.ietf.org)
[6] NAT: Network Address Translation

analyzing some BGP routing tables publicly available. Tables that have been analyzed are from Telstra[7], RIPE[8], and some public networks as MAE-EAST and MAE-WEST[9,10].

The following of the paper is built as follows: section 2 presents an analysis of the increase of routing table sizes on a very long period (1989-2001). Section 3 tries to explain the reasons of such a behavior. In particular, it analyzes the reasons that make routing table size increase and the ones that make them decrease. Then based on real tables analysis (the ones coming from IP networks monitoring), this section analyzes the prefixes in BGP tables and explains the reasons why the address space is so segmented. Then section 4, based on the results of BGP tables analysis, presents the main threats for IPv6 not to be deployed in the Internet. Finally, section 5 concludes the paper on our opinion about the need to deploy or not IPv6.

2 The Internet Scalability Issue

As presented before, the average size of BGP tables for Internet backbone routers went from 15,000 to 150,0000 entries during the 6 last years. Figure 1 depicts the evolution of this increase, while Figure 2 depicts the evolution of the number of AS[11] in the Internet. The 2 curves have to be analyzed at the same time to provide an explanation of what happened or is happening. This analysis has been made on Telstra traces. The curve of Figure 1 has 3 main periods:

1. From 1989 to 1994, there is an exponential growth of the BGP tables. Compared to the evolution of the number of AS during this period, it is clear that BGP tables are evolving the same way as AS number. The BGP tables growth is then fully due to the increase of the Internet (because of the arrival of the web).
2. From 1994 to 1998 there was only a linear increase of BGP tables. Compared to the increase of AS numbers that was still increasing in an exponential way, it is clear that the scalability of the Internet as well as its performances were getting better and better: BGP table sizes were growing more slowly than AS numbers. The reason of such an improvement of Internet scalability is related to the deployment of CIDR[12] (CIDR will be presented in part 3.1).
3. Finally, since 1998 there is a resume of the exponential growth of routing table sizes, and compared to the evolution of the number of AS during the same period, the routing tables size is increasing much faster than the number of AS, what corresponds to a strong decrease of the Internet scalability and performance. This is this last exponential increase that will be analyzed in the following to find out its reasons, and we will evaluate if IPv6 can stop such an

---

[7] TELSTRA web page: http://www.telstra.com/
[8] RIPE NCC web page: http://www.ripe.net/
[9] BGP tables for MAE-EAST and MAE-WEST are available at the following URL: http://nitrous.digex.net/
[10] Tables of prefixes for MAE-WEST as well as BGP tables are available at the following URL: http://www.rsng.net/rs-views/mae-west/
[11] AS: Autonomous System. It consists of a single Internet domain managed by a single entity.
[12] CIDR: Classless Inter-Domain Routing

increase to make it – at most – follow the curve of the increase of the number of AS.

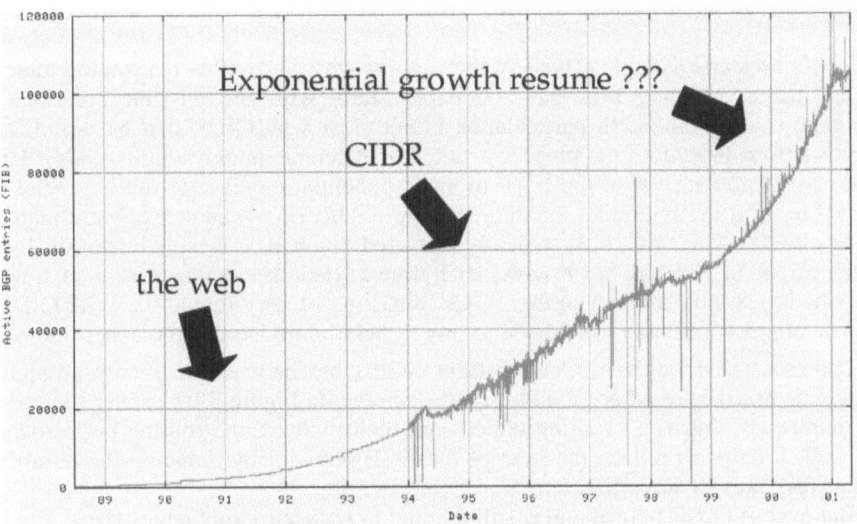

Fig. 1. BGP tables growth (1989–2001)

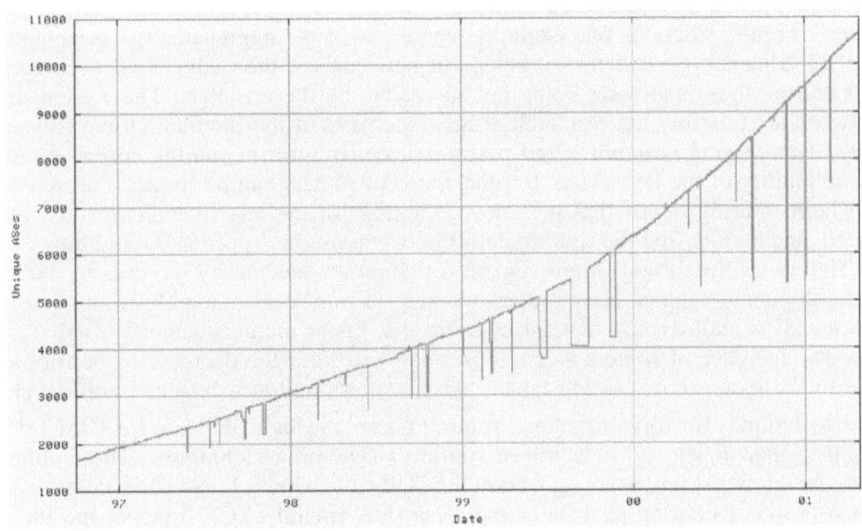

Fig. 2. AS number growth

3 Analysis of the Evolution of Routing Table Sizes

3.1 What Helps to Reduce Routing Table Size and Improves Scalability

This section starts a deep analysis of the reasons why since 1998 the routing table are increasing so rapidly? For that, the paper starts with the possible solutions for reducing routing tables. In particular, it is not clear why CIDR that has so efficient results before 1998 does not provide a suited or efficient enough solution today. CIDR was in 1994 the answer of the IETF to the exponential increase of routing tables that started to limit the Internet scalability. Before CIDR, IP(v4) addresses were managed using classes (A, B or C) [13] statically managed. Such classes were responsible of so much wastes of IP addresses because each time a single IP address is needed, a whole class had to be allocated, even for an AS consisting of very few hosts. With CIDR, it is now (almost) possible to allocate to any system administrator the exact number of IP addresses he requires[13]. And to fight BGP table increase, it is now possible to aggregate prefixes of adjacent addresses (as shown on Figure 3 for carrier #1) to limit the number of entries in routing tables, and then increase the routing performances. As well, it helps to reduce the load of the BGP protocol by reducing the number of routes (prefixes) to advertise.

But even if CIDR helped and is still helping to reduce routing tables sizes, it is now not sufficient. One solution found by carriers to limit routing tables is to force routers to aggregate some addresses segments even if they are not exactly adjacent, so creating some small addresses segments that cannot be reached, also called "black holes". Figure 3 depicts one example where carrier #2 aggregates two segments not exactly adjacent, even if the addresses in between are then advertised by routers of this carrier, these addresses being not accessible by these routers. These addresses in between are possibly not reachable from some parts of the Internet. Of course, such a way of increasing scalability and performances (in term of routing speed) decreases the reliability of the IP service. But the speed of routers can be so much decreased by too large routing tables that it is now essential for carriers to increase this routing speed, and then to find the right trade off between routing speed and reliability.

The other important improvement of Internet scalability is due to the new technologies of routers. New routers working at line speed integrates more and more advanced technologies as optical components, faster memories, new switch fabrics, etc. The increase of routers technologies helps to limit the decrease of performances due to the increase of routing tables. Also, routers builders designed and developed new techniques for forwarding and routing packets. This is the case for CISCO[14] for instance that developed new mixed routing / switching techniques. These solutions were NetFlow [3] few years ago, and CEF (CISCO Express Forwarding) nowadays. It consists in considering packets as part of a flow (mainly TCP flows in the Internet) instead of considering every packet independently. Then, it is just needed to route the

---

[13] This was true as long as the addresses space was not exhausted. Today, it is very difficult to ask for new addresses and to get them adjacent to the segment of addresses that we already got from the organisms in charge of IP addresses allocations: ARIN (American Registry for Internet Numbers), RIPE (Réseaux IP Européens), and APNIC (Asia Pacific Network Information Center)

[14] CISCO web page: http://www.cisco.com

first packet of every flow, to establish a switched path from the ingress to the egress port for this flow, and then to switch all the following packets of this flow. Such kinds of mechanisms avoid to look in routing tables for every packet, so reducing the impact of the increase of routing tables sizes. Also, the way routing tables are organized can improve the performances of research algorithms. For instance, JUNIPER[15] designed a tree based organization of addresses, with bounded depth. Currently, they manage to find any IPv4 address in 16 steps at most. It then makes the process for searching an address in routing tables very fast, with very low variability. Scalability and performances of the Internet are thus well improved.

3.2 What Makes Routing Table Size Increase

Even if a lot of advances have been made since 1994 to improve the Internet scalability, it is not sufficient to stop the current huge growth of routing table sizes. The first reason is certainly due to the growing number of NAT servers used by network / system administrators that do not have enough IPv4 addresses for all their machines. NAT [11] [12] is used to make address translation. It means that a whole computer network behind a NAT server will be addressed by only 1 or 2 public and routable IP addresses. The NAT server is then in charge to deliver packets to the right receiving machines addressed by a private IP address, valid only on this network and not known outside. [5] presents some of NAT issues. But dealing with BGP behavior and routing tables, it means that the increase of NAT servers in the Internet makes the number of 31 bits long prefixes increase very fast in routing tables. Prefixes are then longer and longer, more and more numerous, and less and less easy to aggregate. It makes routing table size increase very fast.

Another large issue making routing tables grow is due to multi-homing. In fact, for improving the availability of their Internet access, to improve dependability and optimize QoS, system administrators, more and more, use several accesses to the Internet, as depicted on figure 3 where a LAN is connected on both carrier #1 (or ISP #1) and carrier #2 (or ISP #2). The issue with such a behavior is that it makes the hierarchical distribution of addresses difficult to maintain as every ISP allocates addresses belonging to its addressing plan. This LAN then belongs to 2 AS, and the initial tree based structure of IP addresses is broken. It then increases routing tables sizes.

The last issue that makes routing tables grow is related to the un-constancy of users that often change from carriers / ISP with their own address space. The problem is that the first time, the address space has been allocated to respect the tree based hierarchical structure of the Internet addressing plan. But when people are changing from carrier or ISP, the hierarchical structure is broken what makes routing tables grow. In fact, the aggregation mechanisms that were working are no more working. The number of entries in routing table increases as well as the length of prefixes, making the research of addresses in routing table more complex and slower.

---

[15] JUNIPER web page: http://www.juniper.net

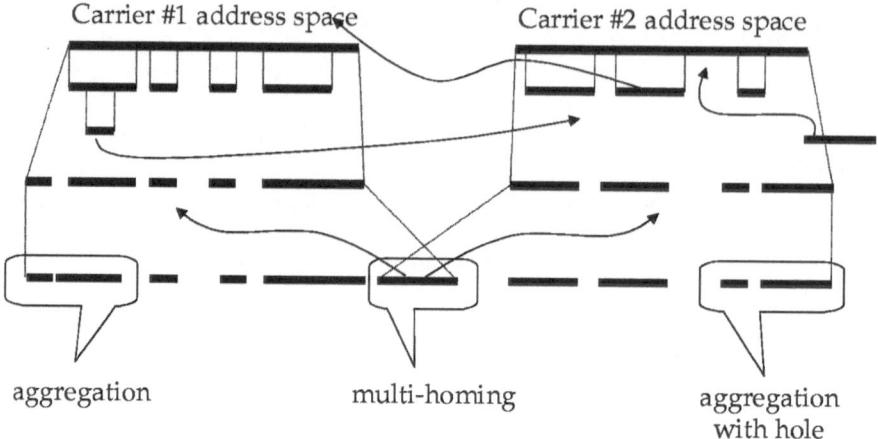

Fig. 3. BGP aggregation with CIDR/Multihoming/Black holes

3.3 Analyses of Prefixes in Routing Tables

Finally, after having analyzed several reasons of the decrease and increase of routing table size, a qualitative analysis of all prefixes in some actual BGP tables has been performed. It is supposed to quantify what are the main reasons of the fragmentation of the IP addressing space. The results we got are the following. Address space fragmentation is due to:

- Multi-homing: between 20 and 30 % (depending on the traces) of BGP tables entries are due to multi-homing.
- Failure to aggregate: between 15 and 20 % of prefixes cannot be aggregated as they do not respect any hierarchical structure. This can be due to people having moved from one ISP to another, or to address allocations not respecting the Internet hierarchical addressing. This problem is also favored by the presence of NAT servers and /31 prefixes difficult to aggregate with other shorter prefixes.
- Load balancing: between 20 and 25 % of prefixes are advertised on several links, then multiplying the number of entries for routing tables. This is mainly the case in core networks and core routers. By definition, the Internet has to be meshed, the more being certainly the best as it improves network availability, dependability and QoS by avoiding to take advantage of congested links. To dynamically solve these kinds of conflicts between several available path, routing protocols integrate load balancing mechanisms. The problem here is that for increasing the dynamic features of traffic engineering processes, it makes routing tables grow, then reducing the Internet scalability and performances.

Finally, this is an average of 75 % of the IPv4 address space that is fragmented. It means that the size of BGP tables could be divided by 4, thus facilitating and speeding-up the research of addresses in routing tables.

4 Threats for IPv6

Recalling that IPv6 has been designed to solve the Internet scalability issues, this part analyzes if IPv6 can provide a suited solution for solving the actual current issues described in section 3. It also indicates all the threats for IPv6 that can delay its global deployment in the Internet.

a) NAT

Even if NAT is a "dirty" solution having many drawbacks [5] (especially dealing with security or peer-to-peer applications[16]) – and in particular the one of making routing tables grow because of many /31 prefixes very difficult to aggregate with other prefixes – it has the strong advantage of being available, easy to deploy, and very cheap. It provides a solution for anybody to be connected to the Internet, even if he does not have enough public addresses. It then solves the problem of IPv4 addresses exhaustion. Even if NAT does not provide any solution against routing tables growth, it does not have only bad sides. For example, it can be useful to improve the Internet performances by contributing to the splitting of connections. In fact, it is then possible to change the parameters of the used transport protocol to adapt to the characteristics of every network crossed with, each time, a dedicated protocol configuration. Such a principle has been described in [2] that also demonstrates the benefits of such an approach.

b) Routers Technologies and Techniques Advances

As described in 3.1, new routers technologies and techniques make routers faster and they are more and more able to cope with very large routing tables. With such new devices, the Internet scalability – in term of performance – will not be an issue anymore. Even if NAT does not help for routing table size, the advances in routers should make things better. Finally, NAT and recent advances in routers could replace IPv6 whose effects do not seem to be fully suited to current problems has shown in section 3.

c) 3G Mobiles and the Ubiquitous Internet

The arrival of 3G mobiles (as UMTS) is often presented as the main reason for deploying IPv6 pretty fast, first because UMTS service providers stated that the growth of UMTS mobiles will be similar to the one of cellular phone. Today this assumption does not seem to be correct. At least, the predictive planning will be strongly delayed. Another reason going in the direction of IPv6 is related to the mobility aspect of UMTS devices and users. And then the auto-configuration mechanism of IPv6 that dynamically allocates IPv6 addresses to users depending on their geographical situation on Earth seem to provide a good solution for mobile users.

But the problem then is to know if the IPv6 auto-configuration mechanism can be fast enough to cope with such mobility, especially if the predictions about 3G mobiles are right and if billions of such devices are available one day. In such a case, the mobile network will have to multiply the number of terrestrial

---

[16] One of the advantage of IPv6 is to be cleaner than NAT, and to maintain the end-to-end IP service, then allowing the use of peer-to-peer applications, for instance, that are very popular applications since few years

equipments – in particular the number of SGSN[17] – to be able to handle all users and all traffic. In such a case, the move from one cell to another that infers the advertising of new routes between equipments in the mobile network and the update of all routing table in SGSN can take up to 45 seconds. Such a duration is of course not suited for interactive, continuous and real-time services or applications. This is mainly a problem of routing / naming tables stability. It could be even worse if the 3G mobile service is extended, one day, between several 3G mobiles operators, thus allowing users to get a seamless service when traveling from one country to another, or more simply, from one area covered by an operator to an other area cover by another operator. In this case, the different mobile networks will be interconnected by the classical wire Internet, and mobility capabilities will be limited by the BGP tables stability. For instance, the current measurements shows that a change in a routing table takes around 5 minutes to be advertised in all routers of a tier 1 network and more than 30 minutes in the global Internet [8] [9]. At the end of this evolution process is the ubiquitous Internet where the Internet service will be provided seamlessly between any kinds of communication infrastructures, ISP and carriers all around the world. The recent "Open Mobile Alliance" consortium [15] between (almost) all the wireless devices vendors to elaborate a set of standards allowing the interoperation of devices of different brands is a big step toward the ubiquitous Internet. In such cases, IPv6 is then not necessarily better suited to provide services requested by 3G mobiles – or several steps forward the ubiquitous Internet – than IPv4. With billions of 3G and or wireless mobile devices connected to the Internet, a huge growth of routing tables – internally to the 3G mobile network as well as in the global Internet – will arise. This growth should be so important that routers will not be able to compute them fast enough to at least maintain the current scalability and performance level. In such a case, IPv6 that can contribute to the explosion of 3G mobiles by allowing the allocation to everybody of native and routable IP addresses, will also necessarily lead to a dramatic routing table increase that can possibly make the global, possibly ubiquitous, Internet stop.

d) *Migration Process*
Another important reason why IPv6 deployment is more and more delayed is related to the complexity and the cost of IPv4 to IPv6 migration, with a risk for a more or less long period to get bad services corresponding to a period where IPv6 services can be of second importance or priority (during the migration period, IPv6 traffic can be tunneled in the IPv4 Internet networks, for example, with software routers on some points of the network). As well, dynamic IPv6 address allocation mechanisms are not yet fully defined, and if you make a choice today there is a big probability that the choice you made will not be the one the IETF or IPv6 forum will do. There is then a risk to redo parts of the migration process many times depending on IPv6 evolutions.

e) *Multi-homing and Users Un-constancy*
The impact of multi-homing and un-constancy of users on routing tables, and then on scalability, has been presented in part 3.2. Up to very recently, there was no solution to "fight" this issue with IPv6. The first proposal for IPv6 multi-homing

---

[17] SGSN: Serving GPRS Support Node

was issued in October 2001 [BLA01]. The problem is that it is just an evolution of
[1] for multi-homing with IPv4, that proved to have a quite limited positive impact
on routing tables growth (cf. Figure 1). In fact, the objectives of this solution is
quite limited. It just uses tunneling techniques (not native IPv6). So, it is not clear
whether this approach can provide an acceptable solution to the general multi-
homing issue? Past experiences with IPv4 seem to prove the opposite. IPv6 seems
then not to be able yet to solve the current scalability issues of the Internet, what
was initially one of its 2 main objectives. This is certainly one of the main reasons
for Tier 1 carriers not to deploy IPv6 yet given the amount of extra entries in
routing tables due to such a characteristic of the Internet topology.

Finally, IPv6 appears as a very suited solution addressing all the Internet issues of the
early 1990's, but 10 years later it seems that it does not bridge the new gaps with the
new current issues of the Internet (as multi-homing for example).

5 Conclusion

This paper presented an evaluation of IPv6 mechanisms compared to the current
Internet problematic, in particular the one of the scalability issues of the global
Internet. More specifically, this paper focuses on the analysis of BGP routing table
whose size has a strong impact on performance, QoS, and scalability of Internet
services.

It then appeared that IPv6 is pushed by 3 main kinds of people:

- 3G mobile operators that need a huge number of addresses without breaking the
  end-to-end IP model;
- New Internet coming countries, especially in Asia that need a huge amount of IP
  addresses because of their huge population (and that were not involved in the
  first rounds for IPv4 addresses allocations);
- New applications as peer-to-peer that require an end-to-end communication
  model at IP level. Such applications are not able to cross NAT servers as they
  are not able to build the tree of users if some of them have non routable
  addresses.

But this paper also showed that IPv6 cannot address the problem of the current huge
growth of routing tables, and is then not able to provide a solution for the Internet
scalability. In addition, core network carriers, mainly located in the US, almost do not
have IPv4 addresses limitations issues, as they where involved in the first rounds for
IPv4 addresses allocation. They do not suffer from IPv4 addresses exhaustion.
Finally, these kinds of issues concern mainly end users and not carriers that are most
of the time at the beginning of evolutions in the Internet in terms of communication
infrastructures.

Finally, this situation seems to show that, at least, the Internet backbone, mainly
located in the US, will remain in IPv4 for a very long time. The IPv4 to IPv6
migration process will be pushed by Asian countries, recently coming to the Internet,
and countries involved in 3G mobiles design and deployment (Japan, western
Europe). The US that got 75% of the IPv4 address space, and that are not really
interested by nationwide 3G mobile services (because of the demographic distribution

of the country) will continue to promote IPv4 for a long time. Between end users that are promoting the arrival of IPv6, and large Tier 1 carriers that have more interest in continuing using IPv4, the IPv4 to IPv6 migration process should last for decades. IPv6 is then not very well engaged because of some issues of the current Internet context. It can finally be the new enhancements in routers technologies and techniques – that make them less sensitive to routing table sizes – that can save IPv6, by solving the scalability issues.

References

1. T. Bates, Y. Rekhter, "Scalable Support for Multi-homed Multi-provider Connectivity", Request for Comments N° 2260, January 1998
2. P. Berthou, T. Gayraud, P. Owezarski, M. Diaz, "Multimedia Multi-Networking: a New Concept", To be published in Annals of Telecommunications, 2002
3. CISCO corporation, "NetFlow Services Solutions Guide", http://www.cisco.com/univercd/cc/td/doc/-cisintwk/intsolns/netflsol/
4. J. Hagino, H. Snyder, "IPv6 Multihoming Support at Site Exit Routers", Request for Comments N°3178, October 2001
5. M. Holdrege, P. Srisuresh, "Protocol Complications with the IP Network Address Translator", RFC 3027, January 2001
6. C. Huitema, "IPv6 - The New Internet Protocol", Prentice Hall, October 1997
7. C. Huitema, "Deploying IPv6", Conference on Deploying IPv6 Networks, Paris, France, November 20th – 23rd, 2001
8. C. Labovitz, A. Ahuja, A. Bose, and F. Jahanian, "Delayed Internet Routing Convergence", Sigcomm 2000
9. C. Labovitz, A. Ahuja, "The Impact of Internet Policy Topology on Delayed Routing Convergence", Infocom 2001
10. P. Loshin, "IPv6 Clearly Explained", Morgan Kaufmann publisher, January 1999
11. P. Srisuresh, M. Holdrege, "IP Network Address Translator (NAT) Terminology and Considerations", RFC 2663, August 1999
12. P. Srisuresh, K. Egevang, "Traditional IP Network Address Translator (Traditional NAT) ", RFC 3022, January 2001
13. W.R. Stevens, "TCP/IP Illustrated, Volume 1: The Protocols", Addison-Wesley, 1994
14. J.W. Stewart, "BGP4: Inter-Domain Routing in the Internet", Addison Wesley Longman, Inc., December 1998
15. The Wall Street Journal, "Open Mobile Alliance hopes to succeed where WAP failed", June 17th, 2002

Deploying New QoS Aware Transport Services

E. Exposito [1,2], P. Sénac [1,2], D. Garduno [2], M. Diaz [2], and M. Urueña [3]

[1] ENSICA, DMI 1 Place Emile Blouin 31056, Toulouse Cedex, France
{ernesto.exposito, patrick.senac}@ensica.fr
[2] LAAS du CNRS, 7 Avenue du Colonel Roche, 31077, Cedex 4, Toulouse, France
{dgarduno,michel.diaz}@laas.fr
[3] Universidad Carlos III de Madrid, Leganés 28911, Madrid, Espagne
{muruenya}@it.uc3m.es

Abstract. Traditional protocols as TCP and UDP propose a very restricted vision of the quality of service notion. These limitations that restrict the spreading out of distributed multimedia application led to us to define a new generic transport protocols generation instantiable from the applicative quality of service requirements. However, the introduction of a new transport protocol has to answer the wide scale deployment questions. This paper proposes a networking architecture based on the concept of active networks that makes possible the automatic and transparent deployment of advanced end to end communications services. The proposed approach has been successfully experimented on top of a large scale European Networking Infrastructure designed in the framework of the GCAP European project.

Keywords: Quality of Service, transport protocols and services, active networks, multimedia applications.

1 Introduction

Advances in software engineering techniques open the door to a promising industry of distributed multimedia applications and software components. However, this parallel and steady evolution of hardware and software has not been followed by a corresponding progress of transport protocols and services. Therefore, there is at the present time a wide gap between applications requirements and services delivered by TCP and UDP that are the transport widely used today on top of IP. Moreover, the introduction of quality of service (QoS) oriented network mechanisms by the Integrated and Differentiated architectures underline the lack of a new generation of transport protocols that would make possible a mapping of application layer QoS needs onto an efficient combination of QoS aware transport-network services. As a result, current multimedia applications implement their own quality of service control mechanisms at the expense of a great increase in programming complexity.

Standard transport protocols (.i.e. TCP and UDP) propose a very restrictive vision of the quality of service notion. Indeed, the quality of service offered by these protocols follows an everything-or-nothing approach, based on two fundamental parameters of the quality of service that are the order and the reliability. However, multimedia flows such as MPEG streams as well as SMIL or MPEG-4 multimedia components, have reliability and continuity constraints which adapt badly as well to a

F. Boavida et al. (Eds.): IDMS/PROMS 2002, LNCS 2515, pp. 141–153, 2002.
© Springer-Verlag Berlin Heidelberg 2002

fully reliable and ordered service, as to a service that offers no guarantee of reliability or order [9]. Indeed, we have previously shown that fundamental QoS parameter of multimedia components and flows can be modeled with partial order relations [10]. We have proposed a formal framework that allows not only the order and reliability constraints associated to the multimedia flows to be modeled, but also the temporal constraints of these media. This formal approach make possible the derivation of fundamental application layer QoS constraints towards transport services and protocols. This new generation of generic transport protocol is formally instantiated from application level requirements and delivers to users a service that complies with application layer requirements while improving, in a very sensible way the use of network resources (i.e. bandwidth and buffers). This new approach has been at the origin of new transport protocols proposed in the context of the IETF, such as SCTP in order to offer a reliable and partial order service [14]. Nevertheless, except the works presented in this article, it does not exist presently a transport protocol that take into account, simultaneously and in a complete way, the fundamental constraints of time, reliability and order associated to the multimedia components and flows.

This new approach that we propose to assure the end-to-end quality of service management led a new generation of generic transport protocols, called "Fully Programmable Generic Transport Protocols" or FPTP, that can be simply and directly instantiated from the applicative quality of service constraints [13]. With regard to the space covering all the services susceptible to be delivered by the FPTP protocol, a specification of service defines the subspace of all the acceptable services that conforms to the service user needs (see figure 1).

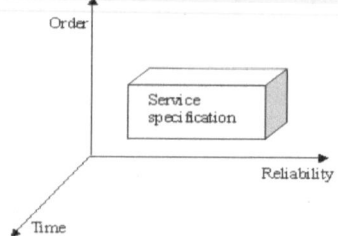

Fig. 1. Services specification in the FPTP protocol space

The gains provided by these new transport protocols generation, compared to TCP and UDP, have been demonstrated by means of two C and Java implementations designed respectively as libraries or packages accessible in the user mode [1]. From an experimental viewpoint, we have shown that the FPTP approach allows the quality of service perceived by a user acceding to MPEG remote flows to be sensibly improved compared to TCP and UDP.

However, the introduction of a new protocol comes along with the critical problem of its dissemination. This paper proposes an original solution to this problem based on the concept of active networks. This approach has the merit of being completely transparent to the applications without demanding any changes of the traditional development technologies.

Next sections are structured as follows. Section 2 gives a short introduction of active networks and introduces the SARA active platform. In section 3, we propose a networking architecture capable to assure the transparent deployment of FPTP services on the SARA active platform. In the last section, we describe several experiments, done in the framework of the GCAP European project (Global Communication Architecture and Protocols), aiming to validate the proposed architecture.

2 Active Networks

Traditional data networks passively transport payload bits from one end-system to another. In the current Internet, the user data is transferred opaquely, i.e., the network applies only routing decisions and checksum processing on the messages it carries between end-systems. Active Networks extend this role by allowing the network to perform customized computation on user data. For example, a user of an active network could send a customized compression program to a node within the network (e.g. a router) and request that the node executes that program for filtering purpose when processing its packets [15]. Another variation could consist of adaptive rate control in active router by dropping some type of packets to adapt to network conditions.

Such networks are "active" in two ways:

- Switches perform computation on the user data flowing through them
- Users can inject programs into the network, thereby tailoring the node capabilities to the user and application profiles.

The implementation of an active network can be done with a more or less important granularity and dynamics of services. From a conceptual point of view, active network architectures are formed by two principal components: Active Nodes and Active Packet (Cell). Active nodes architecture deals with how packets are processed and how local resources are managed. The functionality of the active node is divided among the Node Operating System (Node OS), the Execution Environment (EEs) and the Active Applications (AAs) [4]. The general organization of these components is shown in figure 2.

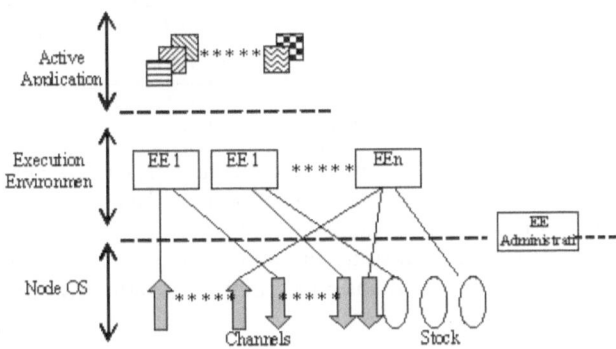

Fig. 2. Active node architecture

For the moment, there exist many implementations of Active Networks which explore different NodeOS, as ANTS [16] or BOWMAN [7]. We have chosen the SARA platform (Simple Active Router Assistant) [19] for dynamically and transparently deploying the FPTP service.

2.1 SARA

SARA implements the NodeOS and the EE over a dedicated processor, called Assistant, linked to an enhanced router. This approach permits to add active node functionalities to the shelf routers in a safe and high-performance way.

The SARA platform can operate over any router in the middle of the network without the explicit knowledge of the user. This means that users send their active packets to the final destination and the routers recognize and process them following the corresponding code, all this while taking normal routing decisions for non active packets.

2.1.1 SARA Active Node Architecture

As explained before, the active applications are not processed by the router, but by a dedicated processor called Assistant, linked to the router. This approach reduces the overhead in the router to the simple identification and redirection of the active packets. SARA is an active node prototype developed using JAVA and is able to process, transparently, the active packets passing through the router.

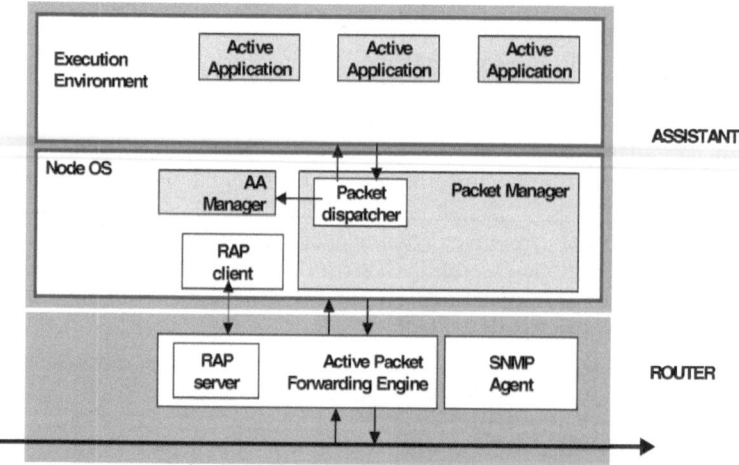

Fig. 3. SARA architecture

In agreement with the active general architecture described above, the SARA platform is formed by two principal modules, the Execution Environment (the execution support for the active applications), and the NodeOS. This NodeOS controls the entire system, administrate the applications and distributes the packets coming from the routing machine to the concerning applications (Figure 3).

2.1.2 SARA Transparency

Transparency of active node implementation is a desirable characteristic for allowing active services to be easily developed without disrupting distributed applications development practices.

The active packet concept in SARA is transparently implemented using the "router alert" bit within the IP header [5]. The active packets are simply UDP datagrams encapsulated into IP packets with the router alert bit activated. The SARA header is shown in figure 4.

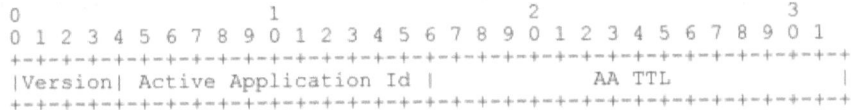

Fig. 4. SARA header packets

SARA provides packet encapsulation for requesting an active service by an UDP socket available in the SARA API.

3 A Proxy Architecture to Ensure QoS

We have explained before how the FPTP approach allows the quality of service for the multimedia applications to be assured more efficiently than with standard transport protocols. However, pragmatic considerations led us to take into account that most of current time critical multimedia applications are developed over the RTP/UDP/IP protocols. So, even if FPTP provides an API similar to the standard socket API, its integration within legacy applications would requires some expensive and dissuasive modifications and adaptations. This problem relates not only to server applications, but also client ones.

In order to facilitate the use of this new family of protocols, it is necessary to design a mechanism able to deliver FPTP services transparently on top of existing network infrastructures. This requirement led us to define an architecture based on a FPTP PEP (Protocol Enhanced Proxy). The FPTP PEP represents a flexible way to extend the actual Internet architecture with new services to solve problems and introduce services not expected in the initial network design [6]. The implementation of a transport level PEP introduces, potentially, certain number of problems related to security and end-to-end principles [3]. According to the end to end principle, for efficiency purpose, the network must have a limited intelligence restricted to packet routing, all complex services and treatments are pushed aside at the network periphery in end systems [11].

Nevertheless, an architecture based on a transport PEP does not try to replace the end-to-end functionality of the applicative layer. Indeed such an approach tries to add a performance optimization in the existing sub-networks between the end systems [3]. This is exactly the goal of our PEP architecture centered on FPTP.

The next subsections explain the architecture of the intermediate transport proxy that aims to improve the multimedia applications QoS; moreover the proposed mechanisms to deploy and maintain such architecture are also detailed.

3.1 Architecture and Basics Mechanisms

We propose an architecture made up of FPTP proxies placed on edge routers at the interface between different QoS domains. For traditional client server applications this approach distinguishes at least three different QoS domain (i.e. the two LANS that support respectively the client and the server applications and the global Internet) interconnected by two edge devices that support the FPTP proxies. In the server side, the proxy offers QoS oriented error, flow, rate and congestion control adaptive mechanisms. In the client side, the proxy makes error detection and synchronization control and enforcement. This additional level of QoS control enforced by the FPTP connection between the two FPTP proxies is based on the partial reliability, ordering and time constraints related to the multimedia flows or components transmitted by the FPTP connection (figure 5).

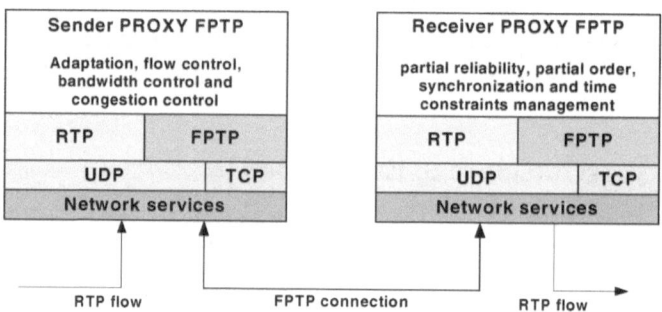

Fig. 5. FPTP proxy architecture

Moreover, transparent protocol translation from RTP to FPTP is done transparently taking account the QoS semantic into the RTP header packets [12]. We have experimentally observed that on flight filtering and analysis of RTP packets induce a negligible delay in active routers. Based on header information, the sending proxy is able to identify the multimedia data type for each packet (H.263 or MJPEG for example), the segmentation of application data units, the order and time constraints, the source address, etc. This set of information is used at the sending proxy level to instantiate a FPTP service compatible with the order, reliability and synchronization requirements of the transmitted application data units.

RTP packets are encapsulated into FPTP packets and the FPTP connection between the proxies allows granting the inferred QoS. The receiving proxy caches the packets and decodes the FPTP packets to reconstruct the multimedia flows to be sent to the receiving application.

As previously mentioned, such architecture supposes that the proxies are located in a strategic place near of the end-users. Therefore, there are not special QoS control mechanisms to be deployed between the end-system and the proxies (Figure 6).

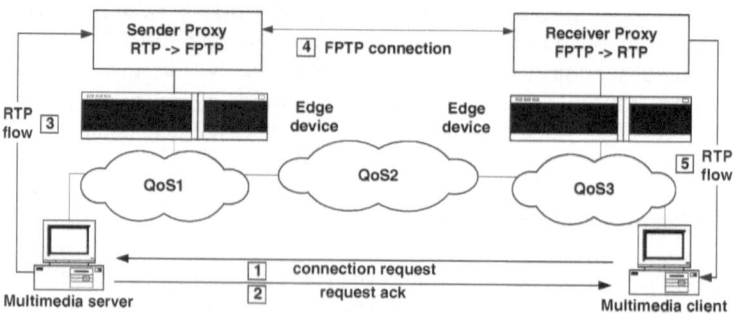

Fig. 6. Proxy architecture deployment

In Figure 6, a multimedia client asks for a video flow from a server placed in the other side of the network. The server answers and starts sending the RTP multimedia data. The sending proxy is able to recognize the flow QoS and to adapt the flow rate to the network behavior so offering the quality of service QoS2. For example, if the video flow is produced at 30 images per second and QoS2 is only 5 images per second capable, the sending proxy adapts the flow to the link possibilities while applying QoS oriented filtering techniques based on ADU semantics. The adapted flow will be transmitted to the receiver through a FPTP tunnel granting a dynamically inferred QoS.

3.2 Proxy Transparency

In order to deploy the PEP architecture described previously, a first option consists in implementing explicitly and statically a connection between each end-system and its respective proxy as well as between both proxies. More exactly, this approach consists on replacing the destination address of the data flow on the server application for the sending proxy address and when the data arrives to the receiving proxy, replace it again by the client proxy and so on.

The shortcoming of this approach is that it breaks the end-to-end view of the server. An appreciable characteristic in a proxy is its degree of transparence [3]. A proxy can operate in a transparent way from the end-user point of view, assuring that no modifications should be done over the existing applications and protocols. In order of taking into account the advantages of the proxy's transparency, we have held this option for the FPTP PEP implementation.

In this approach, the sending proxy has to be deployed in one of the intermediate routing nodes present in the link between the multimedia service provider and the end user. In this node, the multimedia flows are automatically filtered and redirected to the receiving proxy via a FPTP connection (dynamically instantiated from the "on the fly" analysis done to the flow). This connection represents a tunnel carrying out a function of QoS guarantee and adaptation between the network services and the applicative requirements. Finally, the receiving proxy redirects the multimedia flow to the end-user.

In this way, no modifications are done to the multimedia applications and the QoS is guaranteed according to the FPTP approach in a transparent way from the point of view of the end user.

3.3 Deployment

The approach proposed previously raises the problem of the deployment of the FPTP protocol on active nodes. First of all, it is necessary to define the sending proxy location and configuration. The sending proxy may be statically placed and configured by the service provider. Actually, the implementation of this infrastructure can be considered as an add-on service offered by the multimedia provider aiming at improving the QoS delivered to its clients.

On the other hand, the main inconvenient lies in the receiving proxy deployment. In fact, the potential users of the services offered by the FPTP PEP are not known *a priori*. Thus, the router in the receiver side is not necessarily configured to support

FPTP services and QoS control mechanisms. In order to solve this problem we propose an approach based on the dynamic deployment of transport services on receiving active nodes.

Indeed, the implementation of a receiving proxy can be done by sending an active packet over the client-server link. In this way, every active node able to intercept and recognize the packet and being located on a favorable place for the service required, can download, configure and launch the proxy services.

The active packet aiming to configure the receiving proxy can be sent by the client application when opening the connection multimedia. Nevertheless, this method obliges the modification of the receiving application. The same inconvenient results from sending active packet with the connection acknowledgement issued from the server. In contrast, transparency of the dynamic proxy deployment and configuration can be assured by the sending proxy that is in a privileged situation for sending active packets. Furthermore, from the interception of the first multimedia flow packet sent by the server, the sending proxy knows the network address destination where the active packet should be sent to.

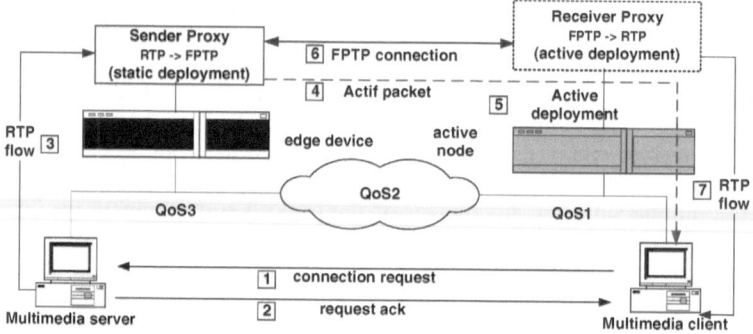

Fig. 7. Active deployment architecture

Figure 7 summarizes this methodology of deployment. First of all, from an application level protocol such a RTSP, a demand of multimedia component is received and acknowledged by the multimedia server. As a consequence of this acknowledgement, the multimedia flow is sent to the client and intercepted by the proxy server which identifies the destination sub-network. Then, the sending proxy produces and sends an active packet to the destination sub-network. If an active node is found in the destination sub-network, the packet is intercepted, the receiving proxy is deployed and a FPTP connection is opened between the client and server proxies. It is advisable to note that the limit of this approach lies in the need of having an active router in the edge of the client sub-network. However, if no active node is found in the path from the proxy server to the multimedia client, the sender proxy can just perform a function of QoS control and adaptation on the multimedia flows delivered to the client.

4 Deployment and Results

Within the framework of the GCAP European project [18], we have performed some experiments at a European Internet scale to evaluate the profits obtained from the proxy architecture described previously. At the application level, a video server and a client application accessing live or stored video flows were developed in JAVA by using the JMF support (Java Media Framework). Java and JMF permit the diffusion of multimedia flows over the RTP protocol, in different standard formats such as H.263 or MJPEG [17][2]. We have chosen JAVA as our development language due to the multi-platform compatibility requirements joined to several concluding performance tests done in preceding studies [1]. Therefore, the receiving and sending proxies, and the FPTP protocols, have been developed in JAVA.

Initially, we have done several tests locally using an emulation environment based on Dummynet [8]. During this emulation based phase, the proxies have been deployed statically over two industrial edge routers [20]. Between these two machines we have placed a third FreeBSD system that routes packets among the two others and support the emulation environment. This test-bed, shown in figure 8, allows, in a simple and powerful way, the fundamental network layer quality of service parameters such as bandwidth, end-to-end delay and distribution of losses to be dynamically modified.

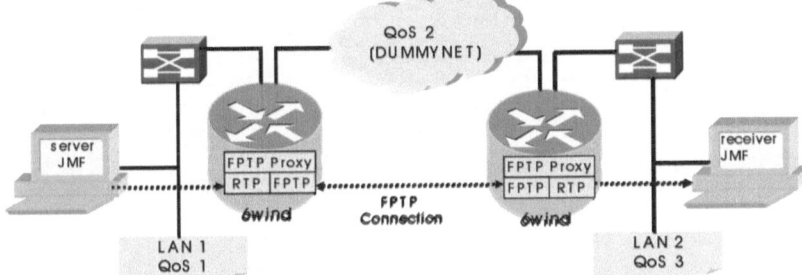

Fig. 8. Local platform

Experiments consisted in transmitting 5 minutes duration MJPEG flows at a approximate rate of 1 frame per second (250 frames per 300 seconds). In a first phase we have emulated a UDP service using a FPTP connection with 0% reliability and no order constraint on the sequence of application data units. This first test has been done by emulating successively a fully reliable network service and an unreliable one that entails between 10 and 30% of losses. The results have been compared with those obtained from a FPTP connection offering a 70% reliable service. The results, summarized in the figure 9, show that FPTP compared to UDP provides systematically, a more important data unit percentage of data delivered on time.

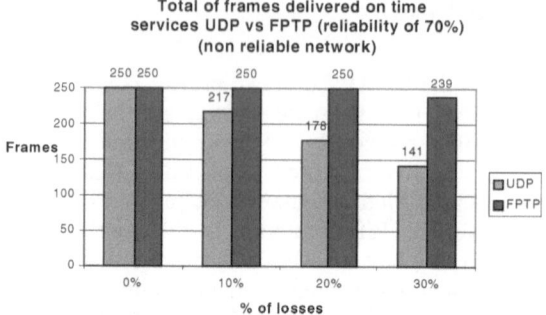

Fig. 9. Comparison of reliable service on UDP and FPTP

Traditionally, time critical multimedia applications such as voice over IP or Video on demand, privilege the use of the UDP protocol because constraints on flow continuity are not compatible with the potentially unbounded discontinuities created by a reliable transport services such as the one delivered by TCP. Figure 10 shows that the partially reliable ordered and timed constraints service offered by FPTP allows an adaptive behavior of the transport mechanisms that result in the increment of the number of frames received by the user in congested network environment.

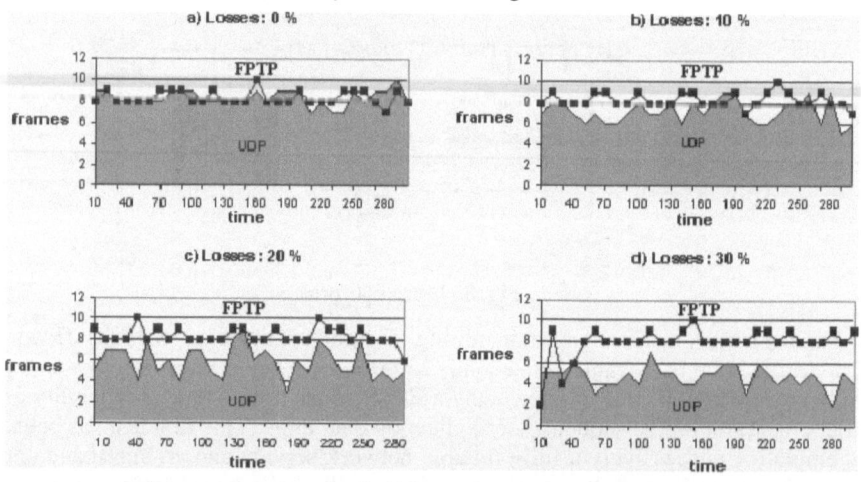

Fig. 10. Number of frames delivered on time (FPTP vs UDP)

In these figures we see that when network conditions are good (case a), FPTP and UDP deliver a similar service which respect the flow continuity. In case of network congestion (cases b, c, and d), FPTP delivers on time a bigger number of frames per unit of time.

In a second time, we have compared the services delivered by the proxy using a FPTP connection ensuring a minimum of reliability of 70% and a TCP connection. This comparison allows to demonstrate that, in any network conditions, the service provided by FPTP offers an optimal trade-off (i.e., in conformity with the application requirements) between the unreliable-unordered service delivered by UDP and the fully reliability-ordered service offered by TCP. In order to reduce the negative impact of the TCP congestion control mechanisms on the experiments, we have emulated TCP by instantiating a fully reliable and ordered FPTP service. Figure 11 shows that in a network with 10% of losses, the partial reliability provided by FPTP allows delivering all the multimedia data in an interval of time that complies with the time constraints of the flow because the difference between the arrival time and the presentation time is positive. On the other hand, the use of TCP in the same network conditions generates a disturbing discontinuous service due to systematic and unbounded packet retransmissions of lost packets. It is important to note that a real TCP implementation in these emulated congestion conditions would have produce a worst service to the user because of the drastic rate reduction entailed by congestion control mechanisms.

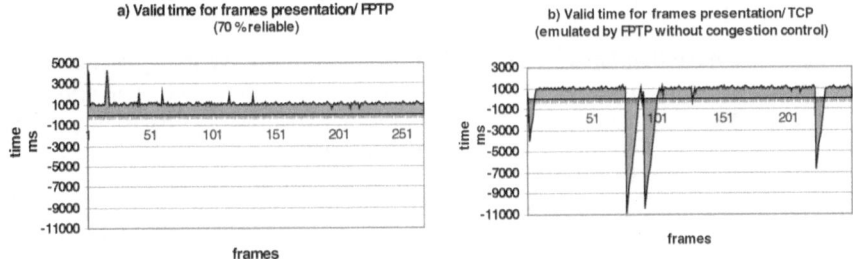

Fig. 11. Arrival and presentation time difference per ADU (FPTP vs TCP)

A second test-bed has been done over the European research Internet between Toulouse (LAAS/CNRS) and Madrid (Carlos III University). In these experiments the multimedia proxy server and application have been placed at Toulouse. The SARA active platform associated to the Telebit router and the receiver application have been placed at Madrid (see figure 12).

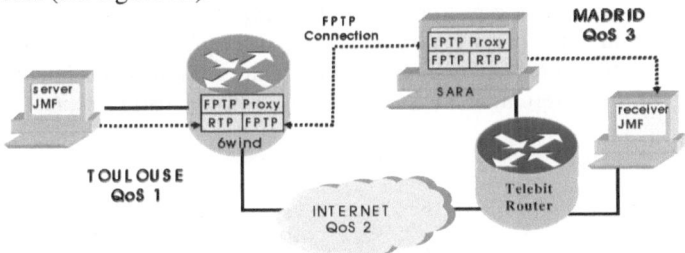

Fig. 12. Active deployment over SARA platform (Toulouse-Madrid)

The receiving proxy has been adapted to be actively deployed over the SARA architecture. The code of the FPTP protocol has been placed on a FTP server working as a repository server. So, after the access demand to the video flow from the client, the sending proxy detects the RTP flows coming from the multimedia server and produces an active packet to be sent to the client. This packet is filtered by the active node placed between the sending proxy and the client (i.e., the Telebit router) who redirects it to the SARA Assistant. The packet is decoded by the assistant who checks whether the corresponding active application is available or whether it is necessary to load it remotely. After the load and execution of the application, the receiving proxy is deployed and the FPTP connection is established with the proxy transmitter. The multimedia flow is so transmitted through the FPTP tunnel and finally directed to the receiving application. After many tests, the results show that the required average time since the active packet is transmitted by the sending proxy till the connection is established with one active node is about of 295 milliseconds, if the code is locally available (i.e. in the active node), otherwise there is an additional time corresponding to the transmission the 42KB of compressed p-code associated to the FPTP protocol (this time is negligible when the code repository is located in the same LAN than the active node).

5 Conclusions and Perspectives

In this paper we have demonstrated that FPTP is able to improve the QoS delivered to the multimedia applications by doing an efficient adaptation between application layer QoS needs and the services offered by the network layer, this is in particular true for Best Effort networks such as the current Internet.

We have also shown how a new generation transport service can be transparently and efficiently deployed in an active network infrastructure. This active deployment represents an efficient and inexpensive approach to implement advanced QoS oriented network services.

The experiments developed in the framework of the GCAP European project have allowed the contributions of this new generation of protocols to be successfully experimentally validated.

Studies should be done to analyse the contribution of this approach in a large scale multi domain network context with different QoS. Additionally, some studies are being done to propose congestion control mechanisms not only fitting to the network behaviour but also in accordance with the QoS required by the applications. The integration of temporal constraints in the error control, flow control, congestion control and even in the order control mechanisms implemented in the routers or active nodes represents another interesting research feature. Some experiments over the new generation of the differentiated network services should also be done.

References

1. Apvrille L., Dairaine L., Rojas-Cardenas L., Sénac P., Diaz M., "Implementing a User Level Multimedia Transport Protocol in Java", The Fifth IEEE Symposium on Computers and Communication (ISCC'2000), Antibes-Juan les Pins, France, July 2000.
2. Berc L., Fenner W., Frederick R., McCanne S., Stewart P., " RTP Payload Format for JPEG-compressed Video", RFC 2435, October 1998.
3. Border J., Kojo M., Griner J., Montenegro G., Shelby Z., "Performance Enhancing Proxys Intended to Mitigate Link-Related Degradations", RFC 3135, June 2001.
4. Calvert K.L., "Architectural Framework for Active Networks".. University of Kentucky; 1999.
5. Katz D., "IP Router Alert Option", RFC 2113, Network Working Group, February 1997
6. Knutsson B., Architectures for Application Transparent Proxys: A Study of Network Enhancing Software. DoCS 01/118, 119 pp. Uppsala. ISSN 0283-0574.

7. Merugu S., Bhattacharjee S., Zegura E., Calvert K., "Bowman: A Node OS for Active Networks". DARPA data base.
8. Rizzo L., "Dummynet: a simple approach to the evaluation of network protocols", ACM Computer Communication Review, Vol. 27, no. 1, January 1997.
9. Rojas L., Chaput E., Dairaine L., Sénac P., Diaz M., "Transport of Video on Partial Order Connections", Journal of Computer Networks and ISDN Systems, 1998.
10. Rojas L., Sénac P., Dairaine L., Diaz M., Towards a new generation of transport services adapted to multimedia applications, published in Annals of Telecommunication, December 1999
11. Salter J.H., Reed D.P., Clark D.D., "End-to-end arguments in system design", In ACM Transactions on Computer Systems. ACM, 1984.
12. Schulzrinne H., Casner S., Frederick R., Jacobson V., "RTP: A Transport Protocol for Real-Time Applications", RFC 1889, January 1996.
13. Sénac P., Exposito E., Diaz M., "Towards a New Generation of Generic Transport Protocols", Lecture Notes in Computer Science 2170, Springer, Eds. S.Palazzo, September 2001.
14. Stewart R., Xie Q., Morneault K., Sharp C., Scwarzbauer H., Taylor T., Rytina I., Kalla M., Zhang L., Paxson V., "Stream Control Transmission Protocol", RFC 2960, October 2000.
15. Tennenhouse D.L., Wetherall D., "Towards an Active Network Architecture".. Multimedia Computing and Networking, 1996.
16. Watherall D., Guttag J.V., Tennenhouse D.L., "ANTS: a toolkit for building and dynamically deploying network protocols".. OPENARCH'98.
17. Zhu C., "RTP Payload Format for H.263 Video Streams", RFC 2190, September 1997.
18. GCAP : Global Communication Architecture and Protocols, IST-1999-10 504, home site: http://www.laas.fr/GCAP/
19. SARA home site. http://matrix.it.uc3m.es/~sara.
20. 6WIND home site. http://www.6wind.com

A Rate Controller for Long-Lived TCP Flows[*]

Peter Dorfinger[1], Christof Brandauer[2], and Ulrich Hofmann[2]

[1] Fachhochschule Salzburg, Schillerstrasse 30,
A-5020 Salzburg, Austria
pdorfing@fh-sbg.ac.at
[2] Salzburg Research, Jakob Haringer Str. 5/III,
A - 5020 Salzburg, Austria
{brandauer,hofmann}@salzburgresearch.at

Abstract. In this paper a new mechanism for providing an assured rate to a long-lived TCP flow is proposed. The mechanism is called TCP rate controller (TRC) and operates as a traffic conditioner at the edge of a network. The TRC seeks to achieve the requested rate by imposing well directed drops and (artificial) delays on the flow's packets. The choice of drop probability and delay is based on an analytical model of TCP sending behavior. It is shown in a simulation study that the TRC performs well over a broad range of requested rates and network RTTs.

Keywords: Quality of Service, TCP rate control, TCP rate assurance

1 Introduction

In the recent years there has been a growing interest in IP Quality of Service (QoS). New applications that have high requirements on network performance are being developed. Some of those applications, for example video conferencing or IP telephony, require some minimum network quality to be useful at all. From the operator's point of view it is hoped that services that deliver high QoS can be profitable.

Currently, a lot of research work is based on the paradigm of Differentiated Services (DiffServ) [1,2]. DiffServ seeks to provide QoS in IP networks in a simple and scalable fashion. It is tried to remove complex tasks from the core and shift them to the edges of the network instead. As an example, traffic controllers that operate on single flows are only acceptable at the ingress/egress of a DiffServ domain.

The focus of this paper is on the topic of rate assurance for TCP flows. Given that TCP is the number one transport protocol [3] in today's Internet, we believe that such a service could be of interest. The topic of assuring TCP rates has been investigated in several other publications, e.g. [4,5,6].

The goal of this work is to develop a traffic conditioning mechanism that can be used to assure a certain level of goodput to long-lived TCP flows. The proposed conditioner could be used in a DiffServ network to enable such a service class. We propose a TCP rate controller (TRC) that regulates the goodput of a TCP flow by controlling packet drops and the round trip time (RTT) of the flow's packets. The TRC is based on a model of TCP sending behavior.

[*] The authors are funded by the IST project AQUILA by contract IST-1999-10077

F. Boavida et al. (Eds.): IDMS/PROMS 2002, LNCS 2515, pp. 154–165, 2002.
© Springer-Verlag Berlin Heidelberg 2002

The remainder of this paper is organized as follows: Section 2 discusses related work. Section 3 summarizes the essential network environment for the TRC. The TRC is described in Section 4. Exemplary simulation results for a variety of network parameter settings are presented in Section 5. Section 6 concludes the paper.

2   Related Work

The Capped Leaky Bucket (CLB) as proposed in [6] is an improved Leaky Bucket traffic conditioner. To take the behavior of TCP into account it is tried to estimate the RTT by measuring the time between two bursts. If the input rate is higher than the target rate one packet each two RTTs is marked as out-profile. Simulations in [6] show performance that is not appropriate to give assurances and a bias against big reservations.

In [4] equations how to set the parameters of a token bucket marker for achieving a requested rate are proposed. The parameter setting depends on the requested rate (R_{req}), drop probability of out-profile packets (p_2) and the RTT. With the equations in [4] it is possible to make correct goodput assumptions for a known value of RTT and p_2. But the crucial aspect in the application of this model is that the RTT and p_2 are not constant for different connections and also strongly vary over time due to changes in the level of congestion.

We therefore believe that it is very difficult, if not impossible, to assure TCP rates by employing a token bucket marker that is configured with a *static* parameter set. A very interesting adaptive marking algorithm has been proposed recently in [5].

3   Network Environment

The TCP rate controller essentially requires some conditions from the network. The first aspect is that at the network edge the TRC must exclusively control single long-lived TCP flows that are not multiplexed with a different kind of traffic (e.g. short-lived TCP flows or UDP flows) [7]. Second, some kind of admission control framework must ensure that the sum of requested rates over all accepted reservations is in fact available. This condition provides an over-provisioned network. Further the used code-point can be different in different domains. In the core netowkr the traffic can be multiplexed with any kind of traffic, but it has to be ensured that drop probability (p) is zero and the network RTT (RTT_{net}) is known and nearly constant.

The TRC does not need any special queue management mechanism, because no packet should be dropped in the network. It has to be established that a few packets can be buffered in the queue.

The receiver window has to be larger than the maximum congestion window (W_{max}) otherwise the achieved rate will be controlled by the receiver and not by the TRC. Further also TCP's Slow Start threshold ($sthresh$) should be larger than W_{max} otherwise the performance during Slow Start will be worse.

The TRC has to be placed at the ingress point of the network. Rate controlling has to be done on a per-flow basis, therefore every flow has to be extracted from an aggregate. Only one TRC can be applied to one flow, because if two TRCs are working on the same flow two times the packets needed to control the flow are dropped.

It has to be ensured that from the receiver to the sender there is no congestion, because RTT_{net} is assumed to be small and constant. Consequently also ACKs have to be marked with the same code-point than packets from the sender to the receiver.

4   TCP Rate Controller

4.1   Goal of the TRC

The goal of the TRC is it to provide the TCP sender with a goodput that was requested (by some means of QoS request) in a prior step. The TRC tries to achieve that goal by imposing well directed drops and delays on the flow's packets. The choice of drop probability p and (artificial) delay RTT_{TRC} is based on an analytical model of TCP sending behavior. We performed our study using the well-known ns-2 simulator, version 2.1b6, and realized that existing TCP models [8,9] do not accurately predict the sending behavior of the TCP SACK implementation we used. In order to exclude errors in the TCP model and to focus on the feasibility of the TRC approach itself, we derived our own model which describes the TCP sending behavior by equations 1-4.

$$time \; per \; cycle = \frac{5}{2} + \frac{W_{max}}{2} \tag{1}$$

$$data \; per \; cycle = \frac{1}{p} = \frac{3}{8} * W_{max}^2 + \frac{5}{4} * W_{max} - 2 \tag{2}$$

$$W_{avg} = \frac{data \; per \; cycle}{time \; per \; cycle} == \frac{\frac{3}{8} * W_{max}^2 + \frac{5}{4} * W_{max} - 2}{\frac{5}{2} + \frac{W_{max}}{2}} \tag{3}$$

$$BW = \frac{W_{avg} * MSS}{RTT} \tag{4}$$

Thus the sending rate (BW) of the TCP sender depends on the average congestion window (W_{avg}) multiplied with the maximum segment size (MSS) divided by the RTT.

The TCP model does not need to take into account timeouts, because losses are exclusively controlled by the TRC and do not force any timeout. From Equation 2 and 3 it is obvious that W_{max} and thus W_{avg} only depend on p and that RTT does not influence W_{max}.

4.2   Principal Idea of the TCP Rate Controller

Now, the basic idea of the TRC is that by controlling the amount of dropped packets and the RTT, the rate of the TCP flow can be pruned to the requested rate. The simple algorithm that has to be executed upon each packet arrival is shown in pseudo code in Figure 1.

The TRC drops packets at the network ingress and thereby enforces the rate of the TCP flow to oscillate around the requested level. Consequently, assuming proper functioning of the resource control framework, TRC-controlled flows experience no

```
for each packet arrival:
    if (packets since drop >= 1/p + E)
        drop packet
    else
        delay packet for RTT_TRC
```

Fig. 1. Pseudo-code for each packet arrival

sustained congestion but merely small and transient queuing delays inside the network. Therefore, the RTT is mainly comprised by RTT_{net} and can thus be well estimated.

Besides dropping, the TRC can add an (artificial) delay RTT_{TRC} in order to control the achieved rate of the TCP flow. The total RTT can then be approximated as the sum of RTT_{net} and RTT_{TRC}.

Consequently for a known value of RTT_{net} the TRC exclusively controls p and RTT. Based on the underlying TCP model the TRC is thus able to make correct assumptions of the achieved rate of a TCP connection.

For a given requested rate there exist several combinations of p and RTT which achieve the same rate. The tradeoffs in the choice of the two parameters are discussed in Section 4.3.

The term E in Figure 1 is used to compensate the drop in the last cycle and has a value of 1. The TRC can however be equally operated in ECN mode which means that packets are not dropped but marked instead. In that case, the term E has a value of 0.

4.3   Tradeoffs in Parameter Setting for Each Request

It has to be ensured that after a drop there are enough packets in the network to receive three duplicate acknowledgements and trigger further packet transmissions during fast retransmit. Therefore the maximum window W_{max} has to be at least 5 packets (1 loss, 3 duplicate ACK, 1 to trigger further transmissions).

Clearly, the accuracy of the TRC is mainly influenced by the ability of the TCP model to accurately predict the flow's sending behavior. The deviation between the model's prediction and the real sending rate increases with the drop probability. A W_{max} of 5 corresponds to a drop probability of 0.0735; we have seen that any p greater than this value results in unacceptably large deviations from the model. Even for some values smaller than 0.0735 (and thus W_{max} larger than 5) we noticed significant deviations in the ns-2 simulations. We tried to find values for p such that the corresponding W_{max} achieves at least the rate that's estimated by the model. We found that if W_{max} is set as an even number plus 0.5 this condition is fulfilled and that the achieved rate is at most 3% higher than estimated.

The second parameter which can be tuned is the RTT_{TRC} and consequently the RTT. As explained above there exist a lot of combinations of setting p and RTT to achieve a requested rate. One choice would be to fix p so that W_{max} is 6.5 and enable different requested rates by imposing different packet delays inside the TRC. This would mean that the greater the requested rate the smaller the RTT would be. For big requests this could lead to the problem that i) small deviations in RTT_{net} have a significant influence on the achieved goodput see Section 5.4 for details or ii) that RTT_{net} is even greater than the total RTT should be. To avoid this, a lower bound for the RTT, called RTT_{min}, has to be fixed. If the required RTT (RTT_{req}) is smaller than RTT_{min} the next greater value of W_{max}, i.e. $W_{max} + 2$ as discussed above, has to be used.

To impose a delay of RTT_{TRC}, packets have to be stored in a buffer. The greater the delay for the same rate the greater must the buffer be. Thus on the one hand the delay should be kept high to keep the influence of a deviation the RTT small; on the other hand the delay should be kept small to keep buffer requirements low. This is a tradeoff that an operator must take into account when choosing RTT and p for a requested rate. It will be further discussed in the next section. Figure 2 shows the pseudo code of the algorithm that computes p and RTT_{TRC} upon each request.

```
for each request:
    set RTTmin min(RTT*min, RTTnet)
    calculate RTTreq for Wmax = 6.5
    if RTTreq > RTTmin
        set drop probability to achieve Wmax of 6.5
        set RTTTRC to (RTT - RTTnet)
    else
        set RTT to RTTmin
        calculate an appropriate Wmax
        recalculate RTT based on appropriate Wmax
        set drop probability to achieve appropriate Wmax
        set RTTTRC to (RTT - RTTnet)
```

Fig. 2. Pseudo-code for parameter computation

4.4   Tradeoffs in Network Parameter Configuration

An operator has to provide two parameters for the initial configuration of the TRC. One is called RTT_{dev} and denotes an operator's estimate on the maximum deviation between RTT_{net} and the real RTT. The second one is called $gput_{error}$ which is the error in the achieved goodput that should be compensated by the TRC. In order to be on the safe side, the rate that is requested by the user is increased by $gput_{error} + 1$ percent.

The smaller RTT_{dev}, the smaller is RTT_{TRC} and thus the smaller the buffer can be. On the other hand, if RTT_{dev} is high, this requires a large buffer space due to the high RTT_{TRC}.

Due to the bursty sending behavior of TCP sources a few packets will be queued at the bottleneck leading to a slight variance in RTT. This occurs especially in high load scenarios. Consequently, RTT_{dev} can generally not be zero.

Equation 5 can be used for determining RTT^*_{min}. As an example assume that a 5% error in the achieved rate is taken into account for TRC configuration and the error in the RTT estimation is not greater than 10ms. In that case RTT^*_{min} would be 200ms. Throughout the rest of the paper this value is used for RTT^*_{min}.

$$RTT^*_{min} = \frac{RTT_{dev}}{gput_{error}} \tag{5}$$

Thus lower bounds for drop probability and for delay are fixed. The other aspect which has to be taken under consideration is the buffer size needed by each connection. The higher the requested rate and the higher the delay the higher the demand of buffer is. The buffer has to be able to store $ceil(W_{max})$ packets from each flow.

To keep RTT_{dev} small not the whole available bandwidth can be sold. We propose that the network is over-provisioned by some amount. In our case using ns-2 it should be over-provisioned by at least 6%. Further the maximum error of the TCP model which is 3% has to be taken into account. To compensate a RTT_{dev} of 5% the achieved goodput is increased by 6%. The sum of requested rates has to be smaller than $\rho * BW$. Where ρ for the above case must not be greater than 0.85 (6% over-provisioned, 3% TCP model error and 6% compensate RTT_{dev}).

In the core network the queue has to be able to store at least one half of the maximum window of the largest possible request. Because during Slow Start packets at the queue are arriving in a burst with a rate that is twice the bandwidth of the bottleneck. Further a few packets have to be stored when a burst of packets from two or more connections arrives at the same time. It is proposed that the buffer size is 50 packets plus one half of the largest W_{max}. This is a topic of further research.

```
for each network:
    set RTT*_min to  RTT_dev/gput_error
    set rate_increase to gput_error + 1%
```

Fig. 3. Pseudo-code for initial configuration

Figure 3 shows the pseudo code of the initial parameterization of the TRC done by each operator. Figure 4 shows examples how to set p and RTT_{TRC} for R_{req} between 50kbps and 600kbps. RTT_{net} is assumed to be zero and RTT_{dev} is assumed to be 10ms. RTT_{min} is set to 200ms.

4.5 Control of Slow Start

Despite the TRC is designed for long-lived TCP flows the Slow Start phase can not be neglected in general. We try to control the Slow Start phase such that the achieved goodput is not significantly lower or higher than during congestion avoidance. At the beginning of Slow Start the window is small. This results in low goodput which has influence on the overall achieved goodput. If the connection stays too long in Slow Start the window will increase significantly above W_{max}. This will have the effect that there is more traffic in the network than estimated and packets of all other TRC-controlled connections might be dropped. Dropping packets inside the network would destroy the whole concept because drops would then be no longer exclusively controlled by the TRC.

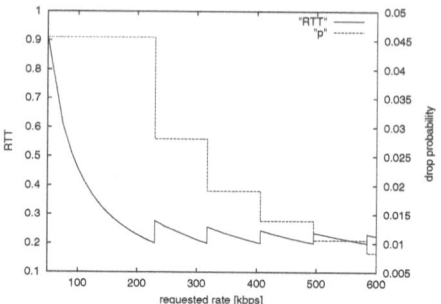

Fig. 4. Exemplary setting of p and RTT_{TRC} based on R_{req}

Consequently an appropriate parameter setting for Slow Start would be to control packet losses so that the window does not exceed W_{max}. The RTT has to be controlled such that as long as the congestion window is smaller than $W_{max}/2$ the TCP sender sends with a constant rate which equals the requested rate. Analyzing the window behavior during Slow Start shows that when $floor(W_{max})$ packets are forwarded and then one packet is dropped the window will be $ceil(W_{max})$ when the loss is detected. Therefore the buffer for delaying packets has to be able to store $ceil(W_{max})$ packets.

If both algorithms work adequately then the Slow Start phase does not significantly influence a connection's performance. This theoretical approach has some restrictions: first, it is not possible to reduce the RTT below RTT_{net} and for small windows it may thus be impossible to achieve the requested rate. Nevertheless this approach of controlling the Slow Start phase is superior to an approach where the Slow Start phase is not particularly taken care of. Second, the influence of the retransmission timeout (RTO) during Slow Start has to be evaluated, because the RTT_{TRC} is increased over time. And thus during Slow Start phase a RTO may occur yielding to a retransmit and a congestion window of one segment. Consequently the rate during Slow Start will be smaller than estimated and thus may influence the overall goodput. This is left for further study. When Slow Start is taken into account the code executed for each packet arrival is slightly modified and can be found in Figure 5.

5   Simulation Study

5.1   Simulation Topology

The behavior of the TCP rate controller is studied by means of network simulations using ns-2 [10]. The simulations were run on a simple dump-bell topology shown in Figure 6(a). FTP senders start sending data from hosts *S1-Sn* at a random point of time within the first 10 seconds to hosts *R1-R5*. The bottleneck bandwidth, access delay and requested rate of the TCP senders are varied for the different scenarios to evaluate different effects. Both routers are using a DropTail queue. Traffic conditioning is done by the TRC on a per-flow basis at each sending host. Unless noted otherwise, simulations last for 1100 seconds where the first 100 seconds are not taken into consideration for

```
init_slowstart=1;
for each packet arrival
    if init_slowstart //connection is in early Slow Start phase
        if packets since drop >= Wₘₐₓ
            drop packet
            init_slowstart=0
        else
            queue packet to achieve requested rate
    else
        code like during congestion avoidance
```

Fig. 5. Pseudo-code of TRC with Slow Start

the statistics. The purpose of the simulation study is it to investigate over a broad range of scenarios to what extent the TRC is able to provide TCP rate assurances. Especially the effect of a mixture of different RTTs and requested rates under maximum load is analyzed. All simulations are run with and without ECN showing equal results.

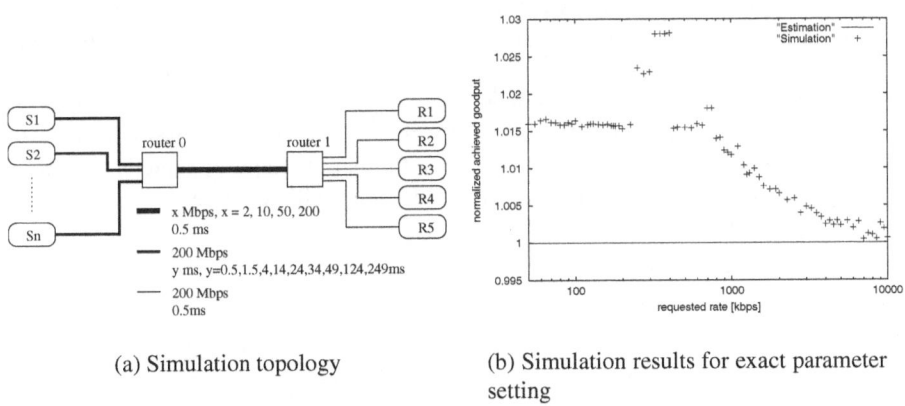

(a) Simulation topology

(b) Simulation results for exact parameter setting

Fig. 6. Simulation topology and first results

5.2   Performance Evaluation for $RTT_{dev} = 0$

In this section we demonstrate that for an exact knowledge of RTT_{net} the TRC is able to give goodput assurances for a wide range of requested rates. Simulations are run on a 200Mbps bottleneck link so that queuing delay can be neglected. All links have a delay of 0.5ms consequently RTT_{net} is 3ms. The requested rates vary between $50 - 10^4$ kbps.

Figure 6(b) shows the normalized achieved goodput over the requested rate. Each flow achieves at least the requested rate. The maximum deviation between simulation and estimation is about 3%.

5.3   Slow Start Behavior

This section provides simulation results for evaluation of the mechanism introduced to control the Slow Start phase. Simulations are run on the topology shown in Figure 6(a) where all links have a capacity of 200Mbps and a delay of 0.5ms.

Simulations are run until the second drop is detected by the sending host. This is chosen for two main reasons. On the one hand the transition from control of Slow Start to Congestion Avoidance should be shown. On the other hand if simulations were stopped after Slow Start only a few packets were transmitted. There are three packets (triggering 3 dupACKs) that have already arrived at the receiver but were not taken into account for statistics, because they are not acknowledged. These packets have great influence on the achieved goodput. The more packets are transmitted the smaller the influence will be.

Figure 7(a) shows normalized achieved goodput for several requested rates. A few earlier discussed effects can be seen in this graphs. The marks in the lower left corner are flows that had a RTO during Slow Start because increasing the RTT_{TRC} during Slow Start does not take into account the value of the RTO. The marks above the estimated goodput come from the effect that for moderate loss rates the achieved goodput is underestimated by about 3%. Simulation results providing values between 0.98 and 1 show the influence of mainly two aspects. The one is that the three packets arrived at the receiver but not yet acknowledged ones, have influence on the achieved goodput. The second aspect is that for a large W in the early phase of Slow Start with small congestion window it is not possible to reduce the RTT so far that the requested rate is achieved. If RTT_{net} increases the achieved rate during Slow Start will decrease.

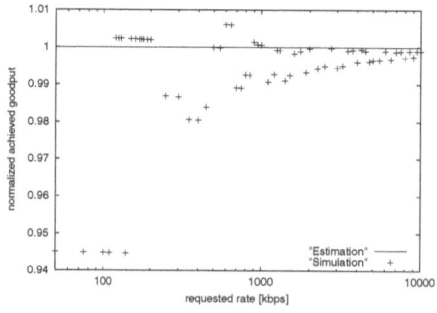

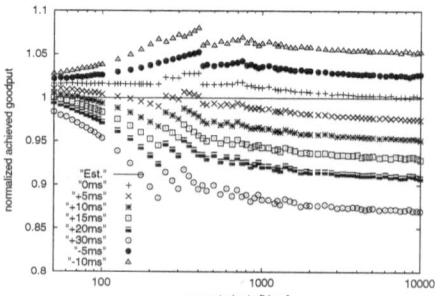

(a) Simulation Results during Slow Start

(b) Simulation results for deviations in RTT

Fig. 7. Simulation results

5.4   Simulations with RTT_{dev} Greater than 0

Simulation results in this section should show the influence of a deviation in the RTT on the achieved goodput. Simulations were run on a 200Mbps bottleneck link consequently the queuing delay can be neglected. The access delay is varied to achieve different deviations. The TRC is configured with an RTT_{min} of 200ms. The parameters of the TRC are not adapted to compensate the RTT_{dev}.

Figure 7(b) shows the normalized achieved goodput over different requested rates for a few RTT_{dev}. RTT_{min} has direct influence on the goodput error for big requests. For an error of 10ms and a RTT_{min} of 200ms the deviation for big requests is 5%. For small requests the influence is smaller, because small requests have a much higher RTT than RTT_{min}. The maximum deviation between simulation results with no RTT error and with RTT error can be approximated by RTT_{dev}/RTT_{min}.

5.5   Simulations Under Maximum Load

This section provides simulation results for maximum load scenarios. The network parameters were set according to Section 4.3 which means that ρ is set to 0.85. The bottleneck bandwidth is set to 2Mbps, 10Mbps and 50Mbps respectively. The access delay is varied to achieve the desired network behavior. Simulations are run 100 times.

The first simulation study should analyze if the TRC has some bias against R_{req}. For evaluating the influence of requested rates the RTT is homogeneous and varied for different scenarios. Simulations are run for an access delay of 0.5, 1.5, 4, 24, 49, 124, 249ms. The requested rates are varied from 50kbps up to 10Mbps within one scenario.

Table 1 provides simulation results for several selected scenarios. Each line shows results from one scenario. It can be seen that there is no bias against big requests. All flows achieve the requested rate.

The rate of a TCP sender is in general heavily influenced by the RTT. Flows with lower RTT are more aggressive. For evaluating the influence of different RTTs the access delays for link S1 router0 is set to 0.5ms up to 249ms for link S7 router0.

Table 2 shows simulation results for different RTTs. It can be seen that the TCP flows achieve nearly the same rate. Thus, the achieved rate of a TRC policed TCP flow has no bias against any RTT and the TRC is able to provide goodput assurances for a wide range of RTTs.

Further simulations are run to evaluate the influence of mixed RTTs and mixed R_{req}. Therefore the bottleneck bandwidth is set to 50Mbps. Table 3 shows simulation results where the parameters are set so that the higher the target rate the higher the RTT and Table 4 for a parameter setting where the higher the target rate the lower the RTT. Each combination of requested rate and RTT achieves the requested rate.

6   Conclusion

In this paper a TCP rate controller (TRC) is proposed. The TRC seeks to achieve goodput assurances for long-lived TCP flows.

Table 1. Simulation results for different requested rates

BW [Mbps]	delay [ms]	50 [kbps]	100 [kbps]	250 [kbps]	500 [kbps]	750 [kbps]	1000 [kbps]	2500 [kbps]	5000 [kbps]	10000 [kbps]
2	1.5	53.229 53.222-53.237	105.64 105.633-105.647	X	517.38 517.348-517.412	X	1024.87 1024.81-1024.93	X	X	X
10	1.5	53.518 53.516-53.519	106.353 106.345-106.361	265.035 265.019-265.051	526.374 526.343-526.405	786.818 786.756-786.88	1043.61 1043.53-1043.69	X	5156.98 5156.4-5157.56	X
10	124	53.475 53.472-53.478	106.238 106.23-106.246	266.73 266.716-266.744	525.35 525.316-525.384	787.662 787.6-787.724	1047.22 1047.14-1047.3	X	5179.03 5178.28-5179.78	X
50	1.5	53.746 53.743-53.75	107.234 107.217-107.251	268.824 268.753-268.895	533.844 533.690-533.998	799.138 798.9-799.376	1063.5 1063.18-1063.82	2638.91 2638.08-2639.74	5261.22 5259.42-5263.02	10495.9 1049.24-10499.4
50	124	53.718 53.713-53723	108.055 108.037-108.073	270.198 270.133-270.263	532.422 532.195-532.649	798.072 797.839-798.305	1061.36 1061.07-1061.65	2639 2638.23-2639.77	5263.32 5261.77-5264.87	10504.5 10500.8-10508.2

Table 2. Simulation results for different RTTs

BW [Mbps]	R_{req} [kbps]	0.5ms [kbps]	1.5ms [kbps]	4ms [kbps]	24ms [kbps]	49ms [kbps]	124ms [kbps]	249ms [kbps]
2	100	105.231 105.179-105.283	105.225 105.172-105.278	105.225 105.172-105.278	105.225 105.172-105.278	105.222 105.169-105275	105.217 105.165-105.269	106.601 106.566-106.636
10	100	107.263 107.176-107.350	107.256 107.170-107.342	107.257 107.171-107.343	107.256 107.170-107.342	107.254 107.168-107.340	107.249 107.163-107.335	108.101 107.998-108.204
10	1000	1048.22 1047.7-1048.74	1048.22 1047.7-1048.74	1048.21 1047.69-1048.73	1048.19 1047.68-1048.7	1048.21 1047.7-1048.72	1049.13 1048.52-1049.74	1052.94 1052.06-1053.82
50	100	105.55 99.901-111.198	105.546 99.898-111-194	105.547 99.899-111.195	105.546 99.898-111.194	105.546 99.898-111.194	105.538 99.890-111.186	105.538 100.612-111.190

Table 3. Simulation results (The higher the requested rate, the higher the RTT)

scenario	50k 3ms	100k 5ms	250k 10ms	500k 30ms	750k 50ms	1M 70ms	2.5M 100ms	5M 250ms	10M 500ms
achieved rate [kbps]	53.719 53.712-53.725	107.115 107.086-107.144	268.21 268.078-268.342	532.809 532.531-533.087	797.508 797.078-797.938	1061.19 1060.62-1061.76	2631.05 2629.49-2632.61	5256.47 5252.28-5260.66	10337.9 10270.3-10405.5

Table 4. Simulation results (The higher the requested rate, the lower the RTT)

scenario	50k 500ms	100k 250ms	250k 100ms	500k 70ms	750k 50ms	1M 30ms	2.5M 10ms	5M 5ms	10M 3ms
achieved rate [kbps]	53.715 53.711-53.720	107.22 107.2-107-24	268.794 268.705-268.883	533.786 533.592-533.98	799.047 798.751-799.343	1063.37 1062.97-1063.77	2638.58 2637.53-2639.63	5260.43 5258.21-5262.65	10494.9 10491.2-10498.6

The task of the TRC is it to control the achieved goodput of a TCP connection by controlling a connections RTT and p. The TRC is based on a TCP model which predicts the sending behavior for known values of RTT and p. The idea of the TRC is it to fix RTT and p of a connection. Therefore the TRC drops packets to control the window size of the TCP connection and delays packets to increase the RTT. Consequently the achieved rate of the connection is controlled. The TRC is a traffic conditioner which has to be placed at the ingress point of the network. A TCP model for `ns-2` TCP SACK implementation was derived. Based on this model the TRC is constructed.

The TRC is evaluated by simulations using `ns-2`. It is shown that the TRC has no bias against any requested rate or RTT. The requested rate is achieved with a very high probability and confidence intervals for the achieved goodput are small.

Overall concluding from the simulation results it seems promising to drop packets already at the ingress point of the network.

The whole concept of the TRC is based on simulations in `ns-2`. So the TRC has to be evaluated by real measurements in TCP/IP networks, because the accuracy of the TRC depends on the TCP model. In real TCP/IP networks there exist a lot of slightly different TCP implementations [11]. Consequently the applicability of the TRC in such an environment has to be evaluated.

The TRC rate controller does not need more suppositions as needed in QoS networks. The diversity of TCP implementations is a general problem of all attempts that try to control or estimate TCP rates based on a TCP model.

There are still open issues which have to be investigated in more detail. For example the dependence of RTT_{dev} on link bandwidth and requested rates has to be analyzed.

References

1. Nichols, K., Blake, S., Baker, F., Black, D.: RFC 2474: Definition of the Differentiated Services Field (DS Field) in the IPv4 and IPv6 Headers (1998)
2. Blake, S., Black, D., Carlson, M., Davies, E., Wang, Z., Weiss, W.: RFC 2475: An architecture for differentiated services (1998)
3. (2002), K.: (Workload Characterization) http://www.caida.org/analysis/workload (May 15, 2002).
4. Sahu, S., Nain, P., Towsley, D., Diot, C., Firoiu, V.: On Achievable Service Differentiation with Tocken Bucket Marking for TCP. In: Proc. of the ACM SIGMETRICS'2000 Int. Conf. on Measurement Modeling of Computer Systems, Santa Clara, CA, USA. (2000)
5. Chait, Y., Hollot, C., Misra, V., Towsley, D., Zhang, H., Lui, J.: (Providing Throughput Differentiation for TCP Flows Using Adaptive Two-Color Marking and Two-Level AQM) to be presented at INFOCOMM 2001.
6. Elizondo-Armengol, A.: TCP-Friendly Policy Functions: Capped Leaky Buckets. In: Seventeenth International Teletraffic Congress (ITC17). (2001)
7. Yilmaz, S., Matta, I.: On Class-based Isolation of UDP, Short-lived and Long-lived TCP Flows. Technical Report BU-CS-2001-011, Boston University (2001)
8. Mathis, M., Semke, J., Mahdavi, J., Ott, T.: The Macroscopic Behavior of the TCP Congestion Avoidance Algorithm. ACM Computer Communication Review **27** (1997)
9. Padhye, J., Firoiu, V., Towsley, D., Kurose, J.: Modeling TCP Throughput: A Simple Model and its Empirical Validation. In: ACM SIGCOMM'98. (1998)
10. Network Simulator ns-2, see http://www.isi.edu/nsnam/ns/.
11. TBIT The TCP Behavior Inference Tool, see http://www.icir.org/tbit/.

Low-Complexity Scalable Video Coding through Table Lookup VQ and Index Coding

Marco Cagnazzo, Giovanni Poggi, and Luisa Verdoliva

Università Federico II di Napoli
Dipartimento di Ingegneria Elettronica e delle Telecomunicazioni
Via Claudio, 21 – 80125 Napoli, ITALY
Fax +39 081 768.31.49,   Phone +39 081 768.31.51
{cagnazzo, poggi, verdoliv}@unina.it

Abstract. The Internet community is very heterogeneous in terms of access band-width and terminal capabilities, hence, there is much interest for low-computation, software-only, scalable video coders that guarantee universal access to video communication. Scalability allows users to achieve a fair quality of service in relation to their resources. Low complexity, on the other hand, is necessary in order to ensure that also users with low computing power can be served.

In this work, we propose a multiplication-free video codec, whose complexity is much reduced with respect to standard coders at the price of a limited increase in memory requirements. To this end we resort to very simple coding tools such as table lookup vector quantization (VQ) and conditional replenishment. We start from the simple coder proposed in [1], which already guarantees high scalability and limited computational burden, and improve upon it by further reducing complexity, as well as the encoding rate, with no effect on the encoding quality. The main innovation is the use of ordered VQ codebooks, which allows the encoder to generate *correlated* indexes, unlike in conventional VQ. Index correlation, in turn, allows us to carry out conditional replenishment (the most time-consuming operation in the original coder) by working on indexes rather than on block of pixels, and to reduce drastically its complexity. In addition, we also take advantage of the correlation among indexes to compress them by means of a predictive scheme, which leads to a 15-20% rate reduction in the base layer, without significant increase in complexity. Thanks to these and other minor optimizations we have obtained improved performance and, more important, a 60-70% reduction of the encoding time (on a general purpose machine) with respect to [1].

1   Introduction

The last decade has witnessed an exponential growth of the information and communication technology, with the huge diffusion of Internet and mobile communications. Yet, expectations about the advent of widespread broadband access have fallen short, long awaited UMTS networks have yet to be deployed, and most end users keep accessing voice and data networks through narrowband channels. On the other hand, not even UMTS, when available, will provide universal wideband access for free, and it is quite likely that bandwidth shortage will keep being an issue, at least for mobile-service users.

F. Boavida et al. (Eds.): IDMS/PROMS 2002, LNCS 2515, pp. 166–175, 2002.
© Springer-Verlag Berlin Heidelberg 2002

In such a scenario, the quest for efficient video coding techniques is more urgent than ever, as they will allow for the provision of interactive video services over the existing networks. In particular, given the wide variety of access channels and terminals that can be envisioned, scalability (spatial, temporal, and SNR) and low computational complexity are very important for such algorithms.

The major current video coding standards, like MPEG-1/2 and H.261/263, guarantee a very good performance in a wide range of conditions but only a fair level of scalability, and present a significant encoding complexity that cannot be reduced too much without a complete change of approach. This is all the more true for MPEG-4, due to the need of complex image analysis algorithms to extract video objects. Under this point of view, wavelet-based techniques (e.g., [2,3]) appear more promising, due to the efficient implementation of the wavelet transform and the availability of high-performance fully scalable coding algorithms such as EZW and SPIHT.

However, wavelet-based techniques still require a 3d transform, which can be too demanding, both in terms of complexity and memory requirements, in certain situations. The mobile-user scenario is a good such example, since all resources, and in particular computing power, are severely constrained by sheer terminal size, and hence simpler symmetric encoding and decoding algorithms are required. This motivates our work towards the development of a symmetric scalable codec that does not require any multiplication at all, thus allowing a real-time video communication on low-power terminals.

To this end we must resort to a very simple compression scheme, even though this entails some performance loss in terms of increased rate or impaired reproduction quality. In particular, our work moves from the all-software video coding system proposed by Chaddha and Gupta in [1], based on conditional replenishment (CR) and hierarchical vector quantization (HVQ) [4,5]. Such a coder, referred to as CG coder from now on, is scalable in space/time-resolution as well as reproduction quality, thus adapting to a wide range of bandwidths, and provides an embedded encoded stream to allow for multicast services. In addition, it has a very limited complexity, because the HVQ coder uses only table lookups, and time-consuming motion compensation is not performed. A different video codec based on HVQ was proposed in [6] but it was definitely more complex, including also motion compensation, although more accurate than [1].

In this work we improve upon the basic CG coder, further reducing both its computational complexity and its encoding rate. The key idea is to exploit the correlation among VQ indexes that appears when an ordered codebook is used [7]. This will allow us to simplify the conditional replenishment check (a relatively complex step in this codec) and to efficiently entropy encode the VQ indexes themselves, thus reducing the encoding rate. Furthermore, even the filtering and interpolation steps, necessary in the pyramidal encoding scheme to guarantee spatial scalability, will be carried out using only table-lookups, all but eliminating computation, at a cost of a negligible performance degradation.

In Section 2 the CG coder is briefly revised, Section 3 illustrates the proposed improvements and, finally, Section 4 shows a few sample experimental results.

2   The Chaddha-Gupta Coder

The CG coder uses conditional replenishment to exploit temporal redundancy and vector quantization to take advantage of spatial redundancy. The choice of CR instead of motion compensation is dictated by the need to reduce complexity, as the accurate estimation of motion vectors is usually quite expensive. Of course, rate-distortion performance suffers from this choice but, if videotelephony and videoconference are the intended applications, where the typical scene has a large fixed background, the performance gap can be quite small. Using VQ in a low-complexity coder, instead, might look paradoxical, as is well-known that VQ's major weakness is just its exceedingly high computational burden.

In vector quantization a set of template blocks (or codewords) called codebook is designed off-line, and for each input block the encoder must single out in the codebook the minimum distance codeword. Once the best matching codeword is found, only its index (a single scalar) is sent and used by the decoder to access a local copy of the codebook and approximate the input block.

Unfortunately, looking for the best matching codeword requires computing a number of vector distances which is quite expensive and hardly affordable in a real-time system. In hierarchical VQ, however, all computation is made off-line and for each possible input block the appropriate codeword is selected at run time only by means of table lookups. Of course, a table with an entry for each possible input block would be prohibitively large, which is why encoding is performed by means of repeated accesses to a hierarchy of small tables. As an example, to encode an 8-pixel block at 0.5 bit/pixel with HVQ only 7 memory accesses (to three 64-kbyte tables) are typically required (see Fig. 1) and no mathematical operation, as compared to the 256 multiplications and additions required in full-search VQ. A thorough description of the table design procedure can be found in [5]. The price to be paid for such a smooth encoding is a limited performance impairment (usually less than 1 dB) with respect to unconstrained VQ.

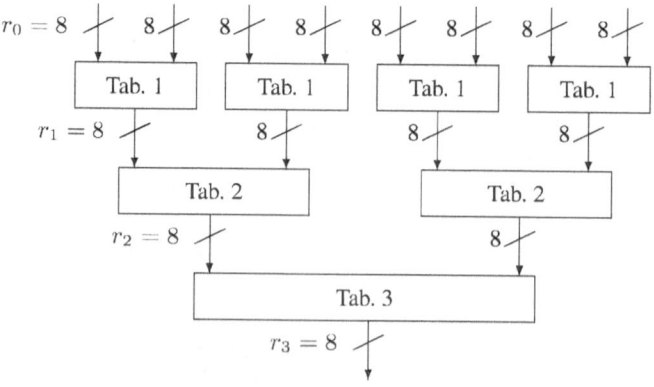

Fig. 1. A 3-stage HVQ encoder

The basic encoder can therefore be described as follows. The input frame X is divided in macroblocks (MBs) and each MB is compared with the homologous MB in the reference encoded/decoded frame $\widehat{X}_R$. If a suitable distance between them (e.g., the euclidean distance) is below a given threshold, the current MB is declared "fixed" and not coded, but reproduced as the reference MB. Otherwise, the MB is further divided in smaller blocks each of which is coded by HVQ and represented by an index in the VQ codebook.

To further reduce the bit-rate, and also to adapt to limited-resolution terminals, the CG coder provides for three types of scalability, briefly sketched here (see [1] for more detail). Spatial scalability is ensured by resorting to a Laplacian pyramid decomposition: low bandwidth/resolution users receive only the base layer of the pyramid, and only when more resources are available an enhancement layer at double resolution is added. A third level of resolution is obtained only by interpolation. Likewise, temporal scalability is obtained by using several embedded layers: low bandwidth users get only every eighth frame, and add intermediate frames (every fourth, every second, etc.) as more bandwidth is available. Finally, SNR scalability is obtained by using tree-structured (hierarchical) VQ and sending only a certain number of bits for each VQ index.

The coder outputs an embedded scalable bit-stream, that is exploited to provide efficiently a multicast video service by means of the multiple multicast groups (MMG) concept, just as is done in [8].

3 Proposed Improvements

A CPU-time analysis of the CG coder (see Table 3 later on), conducted on a general purpose machine, shows that almost 50% of the encoding time is devoted to carry out the conditional replenishment, and almost all the rest is spent on filtering and interpolation required by pyramidal coding. By contrast, HVQ complexity is quite negligible. Our first goal, therefore, is to cut CR complexity, and this is achieved by resorting to ordered-codebook VQ.

3.1 Ordered Codebooks

Usually, when we have to design a VQ codebook, the only goal is to choose a set of codewords $\{\mathbf{y}_1, \mathbf{y}_2, \dots, \mathbf{y}_N\}$ that guarantee the smallest possible average encoding distortion. We impose here an additional constraint, that codewords with close indexes are similar and vice versa, namely

$$|i - j| \text{ small} \qquad \Leftrightarrow \qquad \| \mathbf{y}_i - \mathbf{y}_j \|^2 \text{ small}$$

Such a statement is necessarily vague, as it amounts to requiring some kind of continuity in the codeword-to-index mapping, which is clearly impossible. Nonetheless, the design of ordered VQ codebooks is a well-known and well-understood topic [7], and can be easily accomplished by rearranging a generic codebook or, better yet, by designing an ordered codebook from scratch by the Kohonen algorithm [9]. The algorithm starts with an arbitrary initial codebook; then, a large number of training vectors, $\mathbf{x}(k)$, $k = 1, 2, \dots$, are examined sequentially and, for each of them, all codewords[1] are gradually

---

[1] Not just the best matching as happens with the popular K-means algorithm.

updated according to the rule

$$\mathbf{y}(i) = \mathbf{y}(i) + \gamma(k, d) \left[\mathbf{x} - \mathbf{y}(i) \right]$$

until convergence is reached. Here, $\gamma(k, d)$ regulates the speed of adaptation and the ordering of the codebook and decreases both with time k, to ensure convergence, and with the index distance from the best matching codeword $d = |i - i_{\mathrm{BM}}|$, to ensure the desired codebook ordering. With a careful tuning of parameters, The Kohonen algorithm has proven [7] to guarantee both low encoding distortion and a satisfactory codeword ordering. An example is shown in Fig.2, where a 256-codeword ordered Kohonen codebooks is shown.

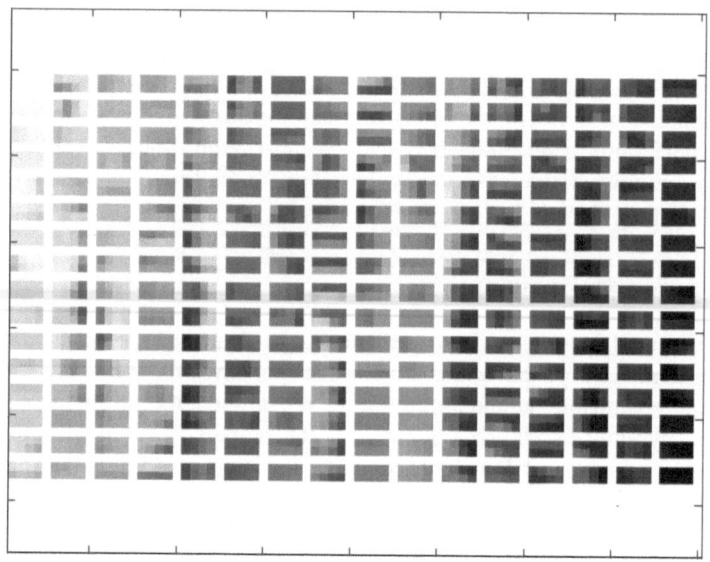

Fig. 2. Kohonen codebook

3.2   Index-Based Conditional Replenishment

Now it is easy to reduce CR complexity. To take a fixed/moving decision for a given block MB we should first evaluate the sum of euclidean (or other) distances of all component VQ blocks from their counterparts in the reference frame,

$$\sum_{k \in \mathrm{MB}} \| \mathbf{x}(k) - \mathbf{x}_R(k) \|^2$$

and then compare it with a threshold.

However if an ordered codebook is available, where the pseudo-continuity holds, than the index distance is a faithful indicator of vector distance, and we can take the decision based only on the few VQ indexes of a MB rather than on all individual pixels. More precisely, for each MB, all component VQ blocks are quantized (only table lookups), their indexes are compared with the corresponding indexes of the reference MB, and a distance measure is computed and compared with a threshold

$$\sum_{k \in \mathrm{MB}} |i(k) - i_R(k)| \leq T$$

Only when this test fails VQ indexes are actually sent, otherwise the reference MB is copied.

Note that, if we did not use an ordered codebook, we could spare transmitting only VQ indexes that remain *exactly unchanged* between successive frames, as proposed in [10] and again in [11]. With our CR technique this would happen for a CR threshold $T = 0$.

3.3   Index-Predictive Vector Quantization

By resorting to an ordered VQ codebook we can also obtain a bit-rate reduction in the spatial domain without any quality loss. In fact, spatially neighboring blocks are strongly correlated and, therefore, their corresponding VQ indexes will be correlated as well if an ordered codebook is used. One can exploit such a correlation through a simple predictive encoding scheme [7]. The index of the current codeword is predicted from some neighboring indexes already known to the receiver. More precisely, the prediction is equal to the index above or beside the current one, based on which one is actually available at the receiver and, if both are present, which one is expected to provide the best prediction. The prediction error is then entropy encoded (another table lookup) by means of Huffman coding.

3.4   Table Lookup Filtering and Interpolation

A further reduction of complexity can be obtained by performing antialias filtering and interpolation via table look-up. In our current implementation, these operations, needed in order to implement pyramidal coding, require only the evaluation of image sample means. For example, we have to compute the mean value of four high-resolution layer samples in order to obtain a base layer sample of the Laplace pyramid, and also our simple bilinear interpolation requires some sample mean evaluation (see figure 3). This can be carried out by using a table in which the means between every possible couple of input values are stored. As the input values are bytes, and the mean is also stored as a byte, this table requires 64KB of memory. Table lookup filtering introduces a small error since we use only 8 bits instead of 9 bits to store the mean value between 2 bytes. However, such error is totally negligible with respect to the error introduced by CR and VQ, as also confirmed by experimental results. Note that table look-up implementation is also amenable for longer filters and some performance improvement can be expected, although more memory will be required.

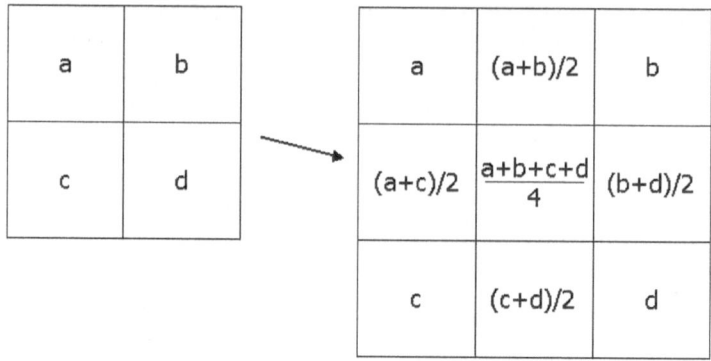

Fig. 3. Interpolation scheme

3.5   Computational Complexity of the Proposed Scheme

As already noted, the proposed improvements make our algorithm multiplication free, but also cause a more intensive use of memory. Therefore, this approach does improve encoding speed only if memory accesses are significatively faster than multiplications. As a matter of fact, even though last years have been characterized by a fast increase in CPU speed and a slower improvement in memory performance, memory access operations are still much faster than multiplications. In addition, one could even develop terminals whose hardware fully exploits the table lookup nature of the proposed algorithm.

In any case, it is interesting to analyze the complexity of the proposed algorithm and of the original CG-encoder, so as to foretell their behavior once the hardware characteristics are known. In table 2 theoretical computational complexity is evaluated for each encoder in terms of how many and which operations are needed for every base level pixel in order to encode both resolution levels. The meaning of all symbol is reported in table 1 ($\bar{c} = 1 - c$). However, note that in the CG coder, CR requires floating point multiplications, while filtering and interpolation need integer multiplications and therefor their cost is quite different.

Although a direct relationship between theoretical complexity and execution time cannot be established, the total elimination of multiplications, and heavy reduction of sums and tests in favor of memory accesses will likely entail a much faster encoding on most hardware platforms.

4   Experimental Results

We have implemented the original Chaddha-Gupta coder as described in [1] and then introduced the variations described in Section 3, based on the use of ordered codebooks designed by means of the Kohonen algorithm. Here we report some experimental results obtained on two 180-frame videoconference-like monochrome test sequence (see Fig.4 and 5).

Table 1. Meaning of symbols in Table 2

Symbol	Meaning
c_b	CR success fraction in base level
c_e	CR success fraction in enhancement level
R	pixel per vector
N	pixel per MB
σ	sum
π	product
μ	memory access
λ	logic operation

Table 2. Operations required for each base level pixel

technique	Filtering	HVQ	CR	Interp.
CG	$15\sigma + 5\pi$	$(\overline{c_b} + 4\overline{c_e})\frac{R-1}{R}\mu$	$5\sigma + 5\pi + \frac{5}{N}\lambda$	$5\sigma + 3\pi$
Proposed	15μ	$\frac{5R-4}{R}\mu + \frac{3}{R}\sigma + \frac{1}{R}\lambda$	$\frac{10}{R}\sigma + \frac{5}{N}\lambda$	5μ

Table 3. Computation time comparison (ms)

technique	I/O	Filtering	HVQ	CR	Interp.	total
CG	1.7	8.6	1.0	17.0	6.3	34.6
proposed	1.7	3.4	1.9	1.5	2.8	11.3

In Table 3 we report the time spent on each encoding step for a single CIF frame (input/output, filtering and decimation, HVQ, CR, upsampling and interpolation) when the original and modified encoder are used[2]. Index-based CR drastically reduces time spent on CR, and only slightly increases time devoted to VQ (because all blocks are now quantized). Table lookup implementation allows for a significative time reduction in filtering and interpolation with an overall time saving above 67%. Extensive experiments (not reported here) show that this computation-time gap remains pretty much the same for a wide range of CR thresholds. As said before, the relationship between theoretical complexity and execution time is strongly implementation[3] dependent, but these example results are nonetheless encouraging. We also compared our algorithm performance with H.261 standard [12], and found that the proposed encoder is almost an order of magnitude faster than the standard one, but the PSNR decreases significatively, up to 5 dB at comparable rates. Although our main focus is on complexity, this performance gap must be reduced to more reasonable values which can be obtained, in our opinion, by suitably tuning the encoding parameters.

Turning to bit-rate reduction, we have evaluated the entropy of the index prediction error and, for a wide range of operative conditions, a reduction of about 20% with respect to the original 8 bits has been observed. Thanks to this improvement, the rate-distortion

---

[2] These results have been obtained using a machine equipped with a 2 GHz *Pentium IV* CPU and Linux operating system.

[3] In terms of both hardware and software.

Fig. 4. Sequence NEWS: original and encoded frames at 35.8 kbps

Fig. 5. Sequence CLAIRE: original and encoded frames at 29.3 kbps

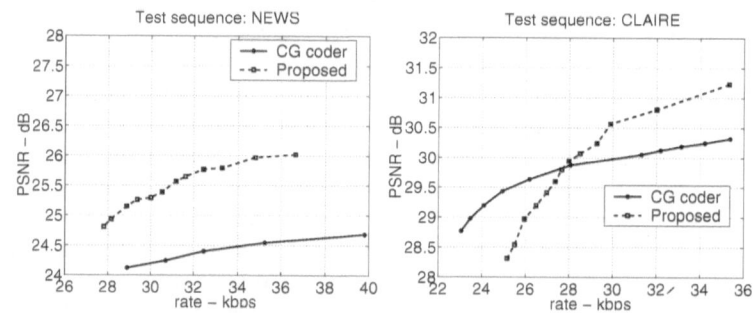

Fig. 6. Rate-distortion performance of CG and proposed coder

performance of the modified coder turns out to be superior to that of the CG coder (see Fig.6) in most operative conditions, despite the loss due to the simplified CR. Note that we apply index prediction only to the lower spatial-resolution layer of the coder where a significant index correlation exists, also because this is exactly the layer received by narrowband users, where rate reduction is especially needed.

In conclusion, the use of HVQ for spatial coding, and the extension of the table lookup approach to all remaining processing steps allow for the implementation of a multiplication-free video coder whose encoding quality, although inferior to that of current standards, is certainly acceptable for users with very low computation power. In future work we will work on fine-tuning the coder to improve its rate-distortion performance and will study its implementation on current low-power hardware platforms.

References

1. N.Chaddha, A.Gupta, "A framework for live multicast of video streams over the Internet," Proc. International Conference on Image Processing, pp.1-4, 1996.
2. B.J.Kim, Z.Xiong, W.A.Pearlman, "Low bit-rate scalable video coding with 3-D set partitioning in hierarchical trees (3-D SPIHT)" IEEE Transactions on Circuits and Systems for Video Technology, Dec.2000, pp.1374-1387.
3. J.W.Woods, G.Lilienfield, "A resolution and frame-rate scalable subband/wavelet video coder," IEEE Transactions on Circuits and Systems for Video Technology, Sept.2001, pp.1035-1044.
4. P.C.Chang, J.May, R.M.Gray, "Hierarchical vector quantization with table-lookup encoders," Proc. International Conference on Communications, pp.1452-1455, Chicago (IL), June 1985.
5. N.Chaddha, M.Vishwanath, P.A.Chou, "Hierarchical vector quantization of perceptually weighted block transforms," Proc. Data Compression Conference, pp.3-12, Snowbird (UT), March 1996.
6. K.Mukherjee, A.Mukherjee, "Joint optical flow motion compensation and video compression using hybrid vector quantization," Proc. Data Compression Conference, pp.541, 1999.
7. G.Poggi, "Applications of the Kohonen algorithm in vector quantization", European Transactions on Telecommunications, March/april 1995, pp.191-202.
8. S.McCanne, M.Vetterli, V.Jacobson, "Low-complexity video coding for receiver-driven layered layered multicast", IEEE Journal on Selected Areas in Communications, Aug.1997, pp.993-1000.
9. T.Kohonen, "Self-Organization and associative memory," 2nd Ed., Springer-Verlag, New York, 1988.
10. M.Goldberg, H.Sun, "Image sequence coding using vector quantization", IEEE Transactions on Communications, pp.703-710, 1986.
11. N.B.Karayiannis, Y.Li, "A replenishment technique for low bit-rate video compression based on wavelets and vector quantization", IEEE Transactions on Circuits and Systems for Video Technology, pp.658-663, May 2001.
12. Anonymous ftp ftp://havefun.stanford.edu:pub/p64/P64v1.2.tar.Z

Accuracy vs. Speed Trade-Off in Detecting of Shots in Video Content for Abstracting Digital Video Libraries

Mikolaj Leszczuk and Zdzislaw Papir

AGH University of Technology, Department of Telecommunications, Al. Mickiewicza 30,
PL-30-059 Kraków, Poland
http://www.kt.agh.edu.pl/
{leszczuk, papir}@kt.agh.edu.pl

Abstract. Two basic requirements for a digital video library to be "browsable" are a precisely indexed content and informative abstracts. Nowadays such solutions are not common in video search engines or generic digital video platforms, therefore, the authors suggest developing some computer applications resolving the problems of at least abstracts' creation. The abstracts cannot be constructed without a deep video content analysis, including some low level processing like a shot detection towards a video sequence segmented to a series of "camera takes". The presented method, aimed at a shot detection, deploys a concept of a Motion Factor (of frame transitions). The basic definition considers the motion factor as a very sudden peak of difference between two successive frames. In some specific areas, the intrashot motion factor may suppress the shot-boundary motion factor. In order to avoid misrecognition of both motion factors during a shot detection process a concept of a differential motion factor was implemented. The full-resolution algorithm achieves the accuracy of up to 80%, however, it is very time-consuming. The shot detection accuracy was measured including true and false shots detected as well as real shots that were bounded visually. The authors' research of a representative number of movies (from various categories) has revealed that the shot detection process can be accelerated up to 500 times without any significant deterioration of shot recognition accuracy. The shot detection algorithm was accelerated in a simple manner by two-dimensional reduction of a frame resolution (in pixels).

1 Introduction

Efficient browsing through the content of voluminous video databases has recently gained importance as a fundamental feature of Digital Video Library. Apart from streaming capabilities, it attracts users to browse through video resources.

A "browsable" library demands both a precisely *indexed content* and an *informative summarization* (abstract) added, Fig. 1.

However, nowadays such solutions are not common in video search engines and generic video platforms. The question is why?

Developers of current video libraries usually assume that basic textual descriptions (data format, file length, filename and so on) should be enough. However, this assumption is no longer true, as the multimedia breakthrough has stimulated a recent growth of users' expectations [11]. A "browsable" digital video library has to support

F. Boavida et al. (Eds.): IDMS/PROMS 2002, LNCS 2515, pp. 176–189, 2002.
© Springer-Verlag Berlin Heidelberg 2002

summarizing and indexing facilities, and in order to enable them, a thorough video file analysis is inevitable. The more information from the video files is extracted, the more complicated an analysis is needed.

Experiments with video saturated databases [24] have revealed that effective browsing has to be supported by content indexing. The automated indexing calls for sophisticated recognition techniques (speech, text, face and even shape).

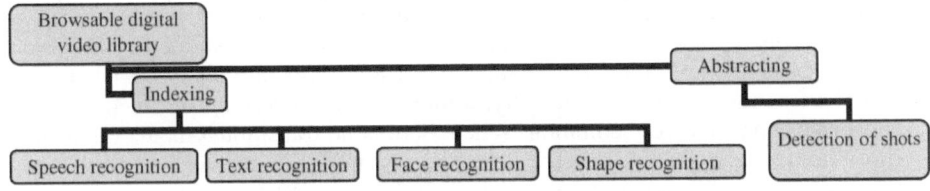

Fig. 1. Browsable digital video library

For example, integrating speech recognition mechanisms into a digital video library to index its content gives satisfactory results [9]. Speech recognition algorithms allow for indexing every video file containing a spoken audio track; they support mainly the English language but some implementations for other languages do exist as well.

Not only can the speech recognition techniques be used for video content indexing. Text recognition (sometimes known as "OCR" – an abbreviation for "Optical Character Recognition") is also a solution worthy to be considered. Text recognition describes the process in which the text is "extracted" from an image. OCR is up to 25 times faster than manual re-typing [3].

As there exist and are available several OCR text recognition engines, suited for a typewritten or a hand-written text [10], it will be possible for digital video libraries of the nearest future, to use them. These software packages support application-programming interfaces (APIs) for C, C++ and Java programmers.

It is important to notice that some face recognition techniques can be used as well. Face recognition is a technique by means of which people could recognise one another, long before the beginning of any civilization. Now, computers have the ability to recognise faces, too [4]. The face recognition technique is a recent invention in the field of recognition techniques. This software allows a computer connected to a video camera to locate human faces in images, extract them from the rest of the image and identify or verify whom they are by matching the facial patterns to the records stored in the database. For many applications, there are benefits of using the face recognition technique that cannot be provided by any other recognition technique (i.e., fingerprint, iris scan). A face recognition engine may be implemented in multimedia indexing systems in future [11]. For example, software packages by Virage or Visionics (Face-It [5]) may be used.

Finally, the shape recognition engines can be used to make digital video libraries easier to browse [11]. Shape recognition is a technique, which can indicate what kind of object appears in the picture. This technique can be used to describe images and videos. Unfortunately, shape recognition solutions are still immature.

The second important issue for digital video library browsing is content abstracting (summarization). The user can inspect the video content (without downloading it) just by watching a trailer.

An automated preparation of a representative movie abstract has to rely on a detailed content inspection including the level of movement and detection of '*shots*' (also known as '*takes*').

A recorded video film consists of a sequence of pictures called frames. It is assumed that 24 frames fit in one second. During the digitalisation process (analogue-to-digital video content encoding), the frame sequence is transmitted to a computer memory. Depending on a TV system, the possible ratios are either 25 (PAL) or 30 (NTSC) frames per second. Currently, a direct digital recording of video frames sequences has become very common. When there is no transitional media (an analogue film) needed and the frames are sent directly to the computer memory any fps (frames-per-second) ratio can be set. The half fps ratio (12.5 or 15 frames per second) is common. This method can be used while reducing the volume of the content but it still does not facilitate the browsing process.

The camera turn-on and turn-off is professionally called a cut, and a group of more than one frame, between cuts is professionally called a shot or a take. Shots usually do not contain rapid changes in the meaning of visual perception [13].

A group of a few, a dozen or even of a few dozens of shots creates "a scene". All the shots in one scene have to be filmed in the same place and more or less in the same time. The concept of a scene will not be discussed in the paper. Terms of "scenes" and "shots" are sometimes confused or even being used interchangeably which is incorrect.

A group of a few, a dozen or even of a few dozens of scenes creates "a movie", that is all the video content.

As the video content itself is outside the scope of this paper and as other authors describe the video streaming issues very well (as in [24] but also in many others), the authors of this article will focus on an analysis of shots (cuts detection), necessary for an abstract preparation.

2   State-of-the-Art

This section presents some current digital video libraries, shows some of their weak points and provides the state-of-the-art level of knowledge related to the issue of shot detection.

2.1   Current Digital Video Libraries

Basic solutions work well for libraries containing still images, but unfortunately, it is not enough for movies.

For example, the AltaVista Entertainment Index (which actually is just a directory of movies, rather than a digital video library, but is considered one of the most voluminous catalogues) presents the content in the way shown in Fig. 2a. As it can be noticed, the user can obtain only some basic information concerning a given movie and only one screenshot. This screenshot, of course, does not represent the whole movie. Moreover, the robot, which creates the screenshot, may sometimes hit at random a black or a smeared frame, which does not give the user any visual information.

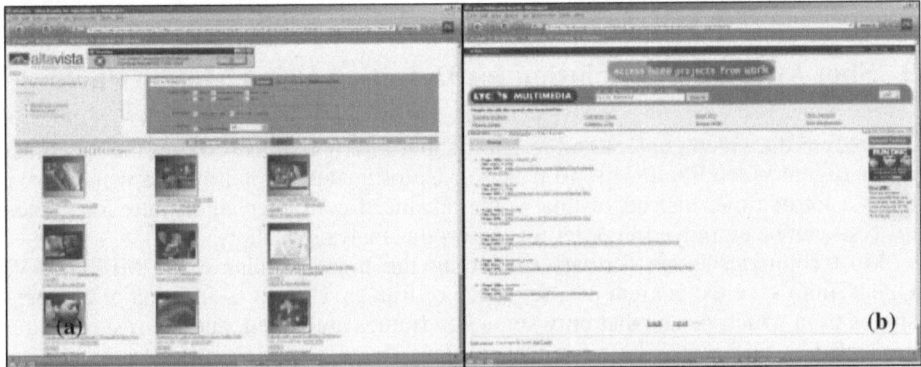

Fig. 2. AltaVista Entertainment Index (a) / Lycos Multimedia Search (b)

The other very popular Lycos Multimedia Search (see Fig. 2b) does not present any screenshots of registered videos at all. Users get only textual information. The same problem appears in the popular search engine: Excite Video Search.

The technique of creating browsable directories is still immature. Only a few solutions have been proposed such as [6] [7]. Therefore, the authors suggest that techniques for the deep video content analysis (shot detection, movement detection) are likely to be useful in future digital video libraries.

2.2 Detecting Shot Boundaries so Far

The issue of automatic shot detection has already been investigated [14]. Several methods have been discovered which, however, is not reflected in market-applications. To the best of the authors' knowledge, only three programs execute this function: [21], [22] and [23]. The authors have tested two of these programs (Scenalyzer and Video Wave) but the results were not satisfactory. Some of the methods employed by these programs, like statistical [14] [15] pixel or block comparison methods, are very simple but relatively effective. Other, more sophisticated methods like histogram-based or dynamic features-based techniques [16] [17] are used as well. Sometimes, parameters such as the dispersion rate [19] [17] [15] [14] or the arithmetic average of the aggregated traffic [20] are considered. Some algorithms even differentiate between abrupt and gradual scene changes [2]. However, the simplest methods still seem to be enough to detect changes between most of shots [1]. These simple methods can be accelerated when not the whole frame but just its thumbnail version is compared [2] [8].

When the shot boundaries have been detected, such fragmented content may be easier analysed. For example, using several concepts, the summarization of the video content can be created.

One of the problems of all of shot detection engines is the speed of the analysis. Usually the more accurate algorithm is used; the more time is spent on the detection.

As the problem seems interesting, the authors decided to investigate it researching one of shot detection engines.

3   Shot Analysis – A Solution for Detection Using Motion Factor

To analyse the video content and to learn about it, a person describing the video clip in the digital video library, has to watch it. Unfortunately, watching the whole movie takes a lot of time. Instead of this, some advanced computer algorithms for content analysis can be employed in order to support the analysis of shots.

Most computer video formats (including the most popular ones: MPEG, AVI, QuickTime) save the content as a sequence of frames. Usually a differential compression is used which means that only some key frames are stored, and the rest of frames are saved as differences between the previous frame and the current frame. Only a few rare formats store the movie as frames separated from each other and compressed independently.

For the current purposes, the authors have to treat the compressed file as a sequence of separate frames, which usually means that partial or total decompression is needed. After finishing the decompression process numerous frames are available, each of them being uncompressed and each of them equal in size. From that moment on, each of the frames is treated separately.

The natural, obvious and intuitive criterion of a shot change is a sudden peak of the difference between the two successive frames.

The difference factor between two frames is called the "Motion Factor" and it has the symbol: *mf* (the symbol *MF* is used as well and it means the average *mf* within a shot (discussed later), to be seen in Fig. 3).[1]

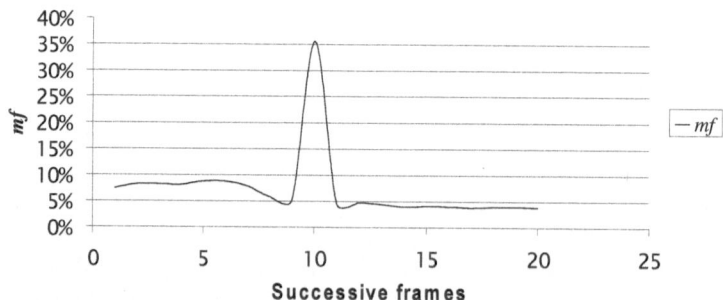

Fig. 3. A sudden peak of the difference (*mf*) between the two successive frames

The method proposed here would be correct, if the "decision point" could be set unambiguously (all frame-pairs having *mf* higher than some value would be considered a shot change).

Unfortunately, quite rarely, it happens that an *mf* inside a shot (when the take contains a lot of action) has a value higher than a take change (when it is made as a soft picture fade between two takes) as shown in Fig. 4.

---

[1] This as well as the following figures concern the real video to be downloaded from [21]

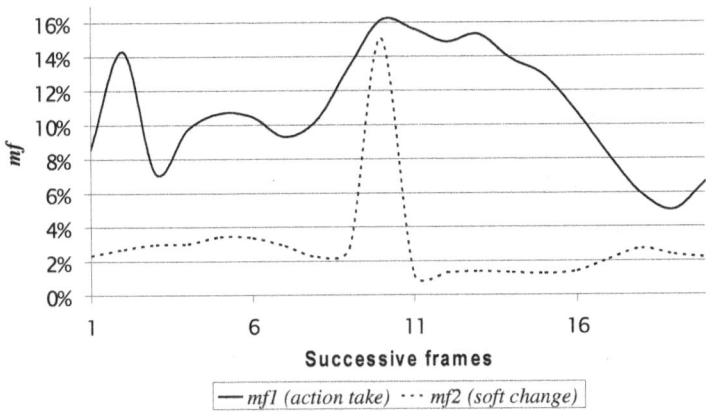

Fig. 4. A "decision point" cannot be set unambiguously

Therefore, a more sophisticated algorithm was developed. The key issue is now not *mf* but *dmf* (being the difference between the current and the previous *mf*). It is observed, that two clear peaks: positive and negative of *dmf* values follow the area of a take change. Therefore, now both *mf* and *dmf* have to meet the conditions mentioned above in order to classify the pair of frames as a take change. This method works well enough and only very "hateful" shot changes (very soft fades) are not detected. In addition, our example shows, that now the take change is clearly visible for the algorithm (Fig. 5).

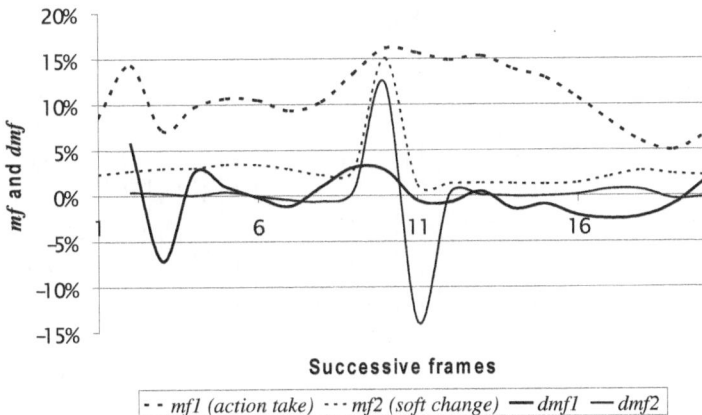

Fig. 5. The shot change is clearly visible for the algorithm

Statistical measurements showed that typical values for minimal mf should be around +13.2% and *dmf* peaks should not be smaller than about ±5.6%.

How to find the "Motion Factor" of the frame? In order to do this it is necessary to compare it with the previous one. Obviously, it is not possible to find this factor for the first frame (there is no frame to compare it with). In other words, this factor can be treated not as the factor correlating to the frame, but to the frame change.

Here, the authors introduce the symbol *mf* as the motion factor of one frame transition and MF_j (used in movement detection) as the average motion factor of frame transitions within movie shot *j* (see Fig. 6)

This value represents changes of a luminance of all the points in the picture. The luminance (*Y*) consists of three mixed colour components: red (*R*), green (*G*) and blue (*B*) ones [12]:

$$Y = 0{,}299R + 0{,}587G + 0{,}114B \tag{1}$$

The general formulas for the *mf* and MF_j could look as follows:

$$mf_{Ri,j} = \sum_{x=1}^{X}\sum_{y=1}^{Y}\left|R_{i,j}(x,y) - R_{i-1,j}(x,y)\right|$$

$$mf_{Gi,j} = \sum_{x=1}^{X}\sum_{y=1}^{Y}\left|G_{i,j}(x,y) - G_{i-1,j}(x,y)\right|$$

$$mf_{Bi,j} = \sum_{x=1}^{X}\sum_{y=1}^{Y}\left|B_{i,j}(x,y) - B_{i-1,j}(x,y)\right| \tag{2}$$

$$mf_{i,j} = 0{,}299mf_{Ri,j} + 0{,}587mf_{Gi,j} + 0{,}114mf_{Bi,j}$$

$$MF_j = \sum_{i=2}^{N_j} mf_{i,j} \Big/ N_j - 1; j = 1,\ldots,J$$

Where:

$mf_{i,j}$ — *mf* of *i*-th frame in *j*-th shot, MF_j — *MF* of *j*-th shot,
$mf_{Ri/Gi/Bi}$ — *MF* in the R/G/B Domain,   *X/Y*   — sizes of the frame,
$R/G/B_i(x,y)$ — intensity of R/G/B component,

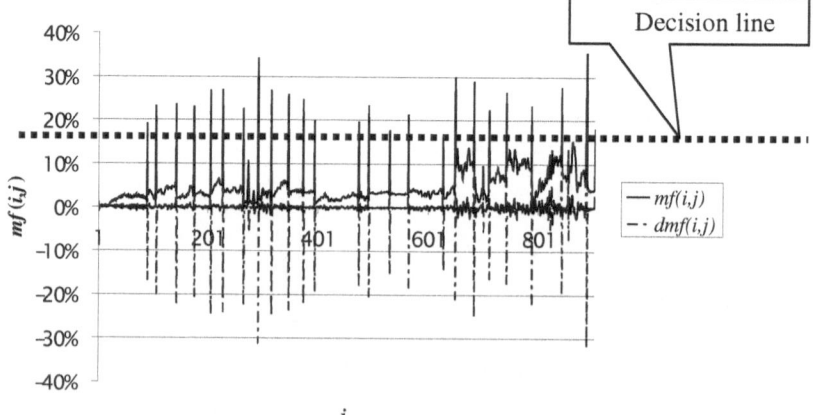

Fig. 6. Example Motion Factor

For each shot not N_j but N_j-1 motion factors are calculated, because one should avoid including $mf_{1,j}$ (the change of the shots), which is likely to be high and which can falsify an MF_j. The motion factor can have some unpredictable values so it seems it would be better to operate on the normalised value: NMF_j. Therefore, the Normalised Motion Factor is introduced. This value can be calculated as follows:

$$MF_{\max} = \max_{1 \le j \le J} \{MF_j\}$$

$$NMF_j = MF_j / MF_{\max} \; ; j = 1, \dots, J \qquad (3)$$

Such a set of motion factors can be used for further shot analysis.

4 Accelerating the Process

Normally, the algorithm analyses all the pixels in each frame. For the CIF resolution (352×288), that gives 101,376 loops. So many loops slow down the whole analysis process. For example, on the Sun Enterprise E-450 Server equipped with a 250 MHz Ultra Spark processor, the analysis of one frame lasts about 18 seconds[2]. Such a length of time is definitely not acceptable, as 90-minute-long movie with fps=25 would be split into shots in… one month!

4.1 Acceleration

The targeted speed of an accurate analysis is the real-time speed[3] that is almost 500 times faster than the speed achieved on the server mentioned above. The rough, ultra fast analysis mode (faster than the real-time) would be expected as well.

Fortunately, there does exist a solution suited well for accelerating the analysis. Instead of comparing all the pixels, it is possible to take only every s-th one in both, horizontal and vertical direction. Then, in case of $s=2$, only ¼ of the pixels will be analysed and the process will be accelerated four times. In case of $s=3$, the process will be accelerated nine times and so on. Generally, the fraction of pixels analysed is equal to $1/s^2$ and the analysis is accelerated s^2 times.

Acceleration of the analysis seems to be an excellent solution. However, one can expect that the accuracy will deteriorate as the number of analysed pixels is decreasing. In order to find out how much the accuracy will decrease, it is necessary to define a proper measure.

The authors analysed about 60 short movies, belonging to one of the following categories: "Action & Adventure", "Comedy", "Documentary", "Drama", "Food", "Horror & Suspense", "Kids & Family", "Motor", "Music & Musicals", "Nature", "News", "Science", "Science Fiction & Fantasy", "Series", "Sports", "Talk show", "Thriller", "War". The categories match the categories of the KaZaA Media Desktop peer-to-peer software[4], used in order to download the movies. Length of the movies varied from a few seconds up to almost 2 minutes, while the average length was about 28 seconds. Each movie contained from 2 up to 45 shots, while the average movie contained a about 11 shots (the average shot length was about 3 seconds which is a very common value). Generally, about 600 shots were analysed.

---

[2] In fact, the analysis may be accelerated a little by a compilation of the analysis script.

[3] The real-time speed means that shot detection process and the playback times are equal.

[4] KaZaA Media Desktop (KMD) is the software for finding, downloading, playing and sharing files with millions of other users [26].

Each movie was analysed 100 times for different s factors reduction, starting with $s=1$ (in case of CIF resolution 101,376 and in case of QCIF resolution 25,344 pixels are analysed) up to $s=100$ (when theoretically, 10 – for CIF – and 3 – for QCIF – pixels should be analysed respectively). It is important to mention, that theoretical numbers of points analysed differ from the real values, as the resolutions are not divisible by all the s values.

These differences are visible especially for larger s values. Differences are shown in Fig. 7.

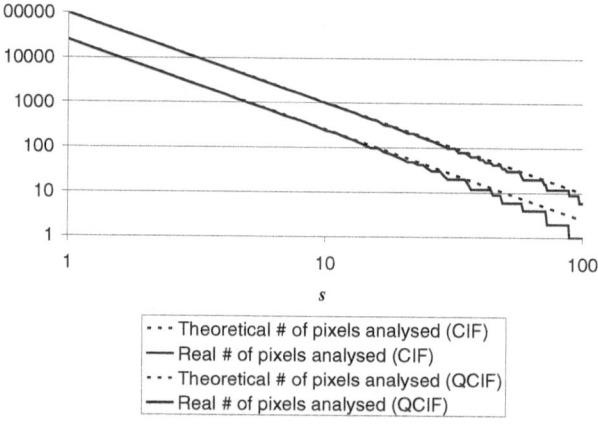

Fig. 7. Numbers of pixels analysed

In order to evaluate the algorithm, the following reasoning was applied. The movie content is segmented perfectly if the number of true shots detected (D) is equal to the number of shots existing in the rough video (R) and no false shots (F) were detected. False shots are shots detected by the software, but which do not exist in the original content.

Since both (D and F) numbers should have an influence on accuracy (A) the formula for the calculation of the accuracy may be written as $A={}^{D}/_{(R+F)}$. Then, the more D number is close to R, the better is the accuracy, unless "overwhelmed" by the high value of the F-number. An example showing how both numbers affect the accuracy, for an imaginary movie with $R=10$ are shown in Fig. 8.

4.2 Experiments

The question is how the D, F and R-values were determined. Firstly, each movie was watched carefully in order to specify the real (reference) number of shot changes appearing in the video content. Then, the shot detecting software segmented each movie 100 times for different s resolutions, producing on its output the number of shots existing ("in its opinion", so it was in fact $D+F$) in the video as well as a mosaic of frames beginning and finishing all detected shots. Those mosaics were investigated again by a human in order to find the number of false shots (if any). Having this number (F) as well as the sum of D and F, there is no problem to get the third missing number – D.

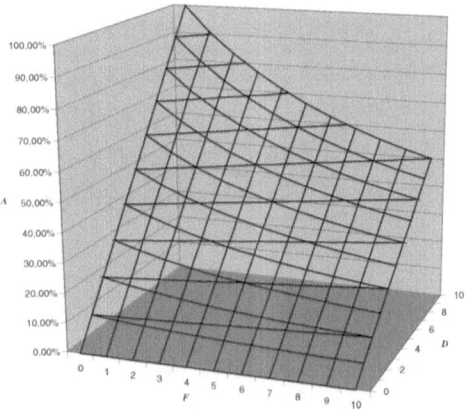

Fig. 8. Influence of D and F-numbers

4.3   Results

The results of a statistical evaluation are optimistic for programmers who want to accelerate their shot detection software by reducing the amount of input data.

The performed measurements show that the accuracy function may be approximated[5] as the quite flat linear function of an analysis time (T): $A = 0.1912T + 0.5942$. A time of analysis, (T) is inversely proportional to s^2. The fractions of properly detected shots ($^D/_R$) as well as false shots ($^R/_{(R+F)}$) are actually constant in the range of the relative $T= [0.10\% \div 100.00\%]$[6] so the accuracy does not drop in this range as well. Fig. 9 depicts the analysis' results.

The s value, which increased from 1 to about 12, has no influence on accuracy. It means, that the real-time segmentation with the maximum or almost maximum accuracy is possible as well as there is no need to slow down the algorithm and analyse more pixels as the accuracy will not grow significantly.

On the other hand, the possibility of further decreasing the number of points being analysed is limited. For the higher s values, some disadvantageous effects start to appear. At first, some rapid picture changes are detected as cuts, which make the F-number grow. An example of such not existing but detected cut is shown in Fig. 10.

For even higher s values, "obvious" shot changes are not detected which in turn lowers D number values. An example for a non-detected cut is shown in Fig. 11.

---

[5] The approximation probably is the best one what was checked using the "R^2" factor-based method.

[6] The relative time ($T[\%]$) is equal to s^{-2} and related to the time of the full-resolution analysis of a one frame (18 seconds in case of the server mentioned before).

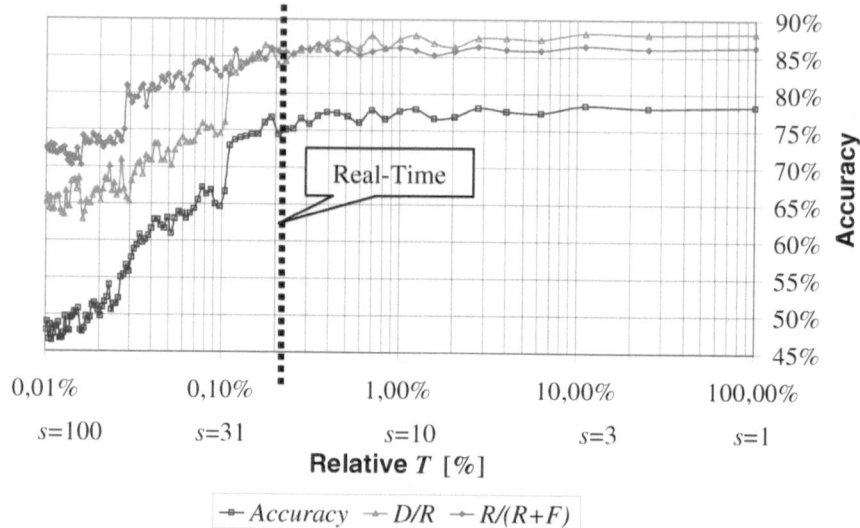

Fig. 9. Accuracy vs. Time

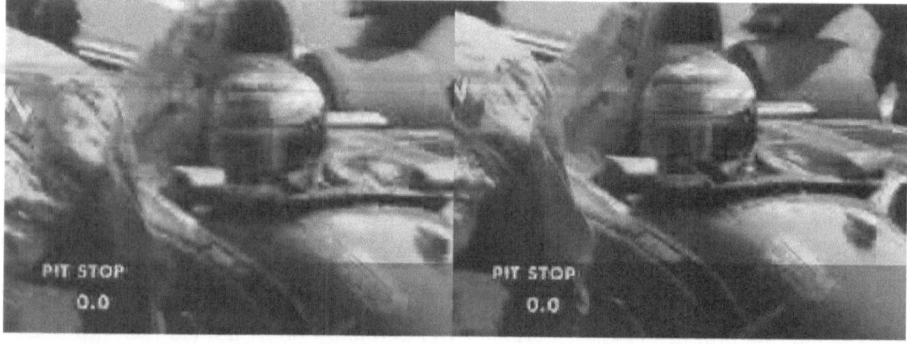

Fig. 10. A false shot change detected

4.4 Comparison

The presented algorithm has been compared to other market solutions ([21] and [22]) with respect to real-time shot detection accuracy (see Fig. 12). Those programs use optical-recognition, which only gives an overview of the cuts. All programs were fed with the same video content. For each program, the number or real (R), true (D) and false (F) shots has been determined.

The results reveal that the presented solution provides improvements in the area of shot detection. However, the algorithm still needs to be tested for a bigger number of movies.

Fig. 11. A shot change not detected

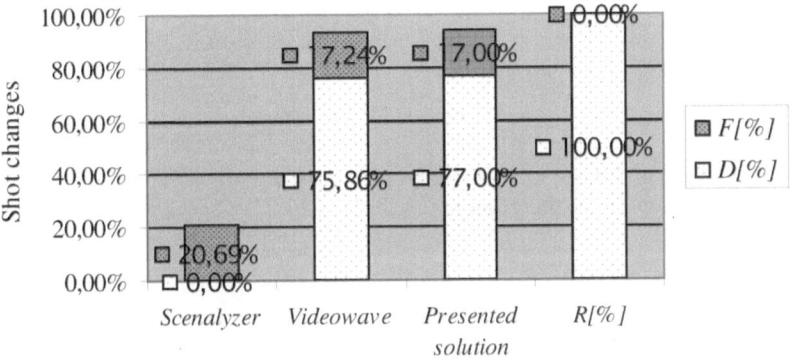

Fig. 12. The results of the comparison

5   Conclusions and Further Work

The issue of video content analysis for indexing digital video libraries deserves a lot of research and development work. The proposed methods of content analysis are based on the algorithmic detection and shots' selection. The information content of any shot is evaluated using motion factors (*MF*). First experiments show that the proposed methods of video content analysis give the results, which are at least comparable with some other solutions.

The issues addressed in this paper will be continued (Fig. 13). The next step will be to develop an application, which would evaluate shots regarding curiosity (using Curiosity Factor – *CF*). This will allow for selecting and including some shots into automatically generated trailers (abstracts).

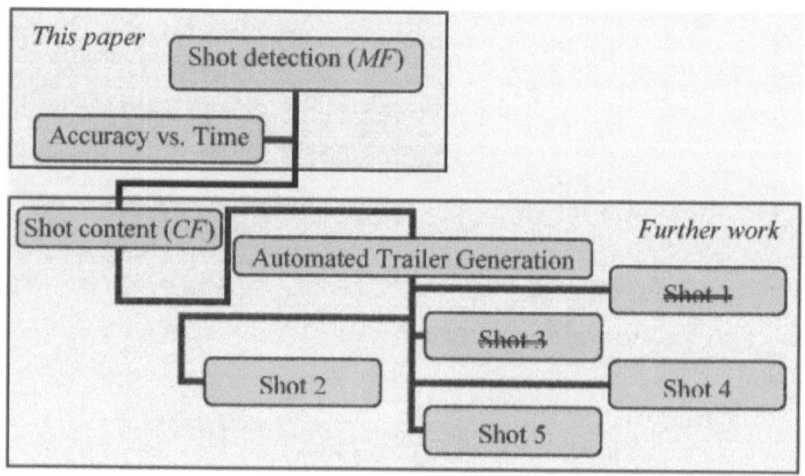

Fig. 13. Workplan

Acknowledgements. This work is supported by the Polish State Committee for the Scientific Research under the grant no.: 7 T11D 023 21.

References

[1] J. R. Smith, "Digital Video Libraries and the Internet", IEEE Communications Magazine, January 1999, pp. 92-97.

[2] B.-L. Ye, B. Liu, "Unified approach to temporal segmentation..." Proc. 2nd Int. Conf. Multimedia Computing and Systems May 1995.

[3] "Office Automation", http://www.irisusa.com/Support, 2000.

[4] P. Kruizinga, "The Face Recognition Home Page", University of Groningen – http://www.cs.rug.nl/~peterkr, 2000.

[5] "Face Recognition Technology", Visionics–http://www.visionics.com/, 2000.

[6] J. R. Smith and S.-F. Chang, "Searching for Images and Videos on the World-Wide Web", CU/CTR Technical Report 459-96-25, 1996.

[7] J. R. Smith and S.-F. Chang, "An Image and Video Search Engine for the World-Wide Web", Proc. EI'1997, San Jose, CA, February 1997.

[8] B.-L. Yeo and B. Liu, "On the Extraction of DC Sequence..." Proc. Int. Conf. Image Processing, October 1995.

[9] M. Leszczuk, Z. Papir, „Integration of a Voice Recognition-based Indexing with Multimedia Applications", Proc. PROMS'2000, Krakow, Poland, Oct. 2000, pp. 375-381.

[10] M. Leszczuk, Z. Papir, „Developing of Digital Video Libraries Indexed by a Speech..." AI'2001, Innsbruck, Austria, February 2001, pp. 107-113.

[11] M. Leszczuk, Z. Papir, „Developing Digital Video Libraries Indexed by a Speech Recognition Engine", ICIMADE'2001, Fargo-ND, USA, June 2001.

[12] J. Mitchell, W. Pennebaker, C. Fogg, D. J. LeGall, "MPEG video compression standard", International Thomson Publishing, New York, 1996, p. 58.

[13] M. Krunz, S. Tripathi, "Scene-based characterization of VBR MPEG-compressed video traffic", Proc. of ACM SIGMETRICS'1997, 1997.

[14] O. Rose, "Simple and efficient models for variable bit rate MPEG video traffic", Performance Evaluation, vol. 30, pp. 69-85, July 1997.

[15] J. Roberts, U. Mocci, J. Virtamo, "Broadband network teletraffic", Springer-Verlag, Berlin 1996, pp. 20-25.

[16] Y. Sang-Jo, K. Seong-Dae, „Traffic Modelling and QoS Prediction for MPEG-Coded Video Services over ATM Networks Using Scene…", „Journal of High-Speed Networks", vol. 8, no. 3, 1999, pp. 211-224.

[17] A. Mashat, M. Kara, "Performance Evaluation of a Scene-based Model…", "System Performance Evaluation…" CRC Press, 2000, pp. 123-142.

[18] D. Heyman, A. Tabatabai, T. Lakshman, "Statistical Analysis of MPEG-2 Coded VBR Video Traffic", sixth Int. Workshop on Packet Video, September 1994.

[19] D. P. Heyman, T. Lakshman, "Source models for VBR broadcast-video traffic", IEEE/ACM Transactions on Networking, vol. 4, no. 1, February 1996.

[20] M. F. Scheffer, K. Wajda, J. S. Kunicki, „Fuzzy Logic Adaptive Traffic Enforcement Mechanisms for ATM Networks", Proc. of ITC, Pretoria, South Africa, 1995.

[21] A. Winter, "Video Capture Software and Scene Detection – Scenalyzer", http://www.scenalyzer.com/, 2001-08-02

[22] MGI Software Corp, "Video Wave", http://www.mgisoft.com/products/vw, 2001

[23] IBM, "DB2 Video Extender", http://www-4.ibm.com/software/data/db2

[24] M. Leszczuk, P. Pacyna, Z. Papir, "Video Content Streaming Service Using IP/RSVP Protocol Stack", IEEE Workshop on Internet Applications WIAPP'99, 7, 1999

[25] L. Sanghoon, M.S. Pattichis, A.C. Bovik, "Foveae video compression with optimal rate control" IEEE Trans. on Img. Proc. Volume: 10 Issue: 7, July 2001.

[26] Sherman Networks, "KaZaA", http://www.kazaa.com/, 2002.

Distributed Video Documents Indexing and Content-Based Retrieving

Ahmed Mostefaoui[1] and Loic Favory[2]

[1] Franche Comté Computer Science Lab.,
4, place Tharradin, BP 71427,
Montbéliard, France
amostefa@pu-pm.univ-fcomte.fr
[2] Information Systems Engineering Lab.
National Institute of Applied Sciences of Lyon,
69621 Villeurbanne Cedex, France
Loic.Favory@insa-lyon.fr

Abstract. In this paper, we present SIRSALE: a set of distributed video documents management tools that allow users to manipulate video streams stored in large distributed repositories. All the proposed tools are based on generic models that can be customized for specific applications using ad-hoc adaptation modules. More precisely, SIRSALE allows users to: (a) browse video documents by structures (sequences, scenes, shots) and (b) query the video database content by using a graphical tool, adapted to the nature of the target video documents. This paper also presents an annotating interface which allows archivists to describe the content of video documents. All these tools are coupled to a video player integrating remote VCR functionalities and are based on active network technology. We then describe experiments of using SIRSALE on an archive of news video and soccer matches. The system has been demonstrated to professionals with a positive feedback. Finally, we discuss open issues and present some perspectives.

1 Introduction

The growing capabilities of today's computers and the availability of large bandwidth networks have made it possible to manipulate digitalized video documents. Distributed video document management systems have became over the last decade an active field of research. The amount of video information stored in archives worldwide is growing fast e.g., conservative estimates state that there are more than 6 million hours of video already stored and this number grows at a rate of about 10% a year [1]. The main objective in such systems is to provide remote users with capabilities to friendly search, access and playback distributed stored video data. This task may be performed in the same way as they do in traditional distributed systems without any restrictions due to the nature of their terminals (PDA, notebook, etc.) or to their network connection (wireless connections for example). However, reaching such objective requires

F. Boavida et al. (Eds.): IDMS/PROMS 2002, LNCS 2515, pp. 190–201, 2002.

to deal with hard issues: (a) video documents repositories generate huge volumes of data, typically of order of terabytes. (b) Video data is time sensitive i.e., streams must be delivered at a specific bit-rate. (c) And more importantly, contents of video data are very hard to be automatically extracted and need to be humanly annotated. Moreover, the contents of a video document could be the subject of several interpretations depending on the context of the target application. For instance, in a soccer document a trainer may be interested by sequences showing collective game play action/combination whereas a fun may want to play sequences related to the apparition of her/his favorite player. (d) Application and user requirements often depend on the application context. Professional users may want to find a specific piece of content (e.g., an audiovisual sequence) from a large collection within a tight deadline whereas the general public may want to browse the contents of a video archive to get a reasonable selection. Mobile users with limited terminal capacities (e.g., PDA that does not support advanced user interface nor high quality video streams) may prefer to use customized interfaces, specifically tailored to their terminals.

Hence, distributed video document management systems must provide functionalities to properly index video documents by content. It will be noted that this task is performed in connection with the context of the target application. Indeed number of multimedia applications impose their own domain-specific customization. For instance, indexing broadcast news is different from indexing soccer archives or educational materials. Therefore, it is essential for the success of a distributed multimedia system to cope with this domain heterogeneity e.g., one may use the same system to search, for example, for course materials as well as for news items. This issue has been studied in the literature by the proposition of generic data models able to support searching and browsing various domains. Although those generic data models could be used to cope with the diversity of domains, they impose however a *training period* for end-users to be able to use the system. In addition, they are not able to fulfill all kinds of requests needed for searching or browsing particular domains. In other words, they facilitate the implementation of the system since the latter has to support only one data model but on the other hand they *impose* adaptation from the end-users.

In this paper, we present a novel approach in designing and implementing distributed video repositories. The key idea behind our approach is to make available for end-users various **modules** that they can download for searching and browsing domain specific video documents. More precisely, we present SIR-SALE system, a complete indexing, searching and browsing distributed video repository system, which allows remote users, through graphical interfaces, to use enhanced searching and browsing tools, specifically tailored to support various domain data models. In practice, users have to choose the domain they want to search or browse (for example soccer matches or news archives); then the system automatically downloads the user interface and the data model related to that domain.

This approach has the advantage of allowing remote users to fully exploit video repositories containing videos of various domains in a more powerful man-

ner since it does not impose any adaptation from their side. However, on the
other hand, the implementation of the system becomes more complex because
of the management of several data models and user interfaces at the same time.
Nonetheless, the usefulness of such system overcomes its complexity. Hereafter,
we describe a full implementation of such an approach and present two practical
examples of its utilization. We have also demonstrated the system to professionals who have given a positive feedback.

The remaining of the paper is organized as follows: section 2 presents related works. Section 3 discusses video indexing and browsing techniques. It also
presents our approach used in the SIRSALE system. Section 4 describes the
architecture of the SIRSALE system. We then discuss the experiments we have
carried out (section 5). Finally section 6 summarizes the contribution of this
paper and points out some future works.

2   Related Work

Many approaches in the literature have addressed the design of distributed video
systems. With regard to the subject area of this paper, these works could be
grouped into two categories: (a) database category [2] which includes data models
and query languages. In this category, the aim is to model video documents
through the management of descriptive meta-data. Data models coupled to query
languages provide powerful tools for content-based access to video documents [3,
4]. More recently, the MPEG-7 standard tends to provide a standard description
meta-data model able to accommodate various description models [5]. Although
a standard approach increases interoperability, the descriptions may be valid
from their own usage point of view, thus motivating the need for contextual
indexing tools.

The second category includes works dealing with image analysis and recognition [6,7]. The objective of these works is to automatically identify the content of
video documents by using low level features. The extraction of low level features
may help to describe the contents of video documents but it does not properly
capture their semantics (see next section).

3   Video Indexing

Although audiovisual information is mainly in digital form, content-based video
retrieval is still a very challenging task. In fact, in order to retrieve the information from a digital collection, we cannot search natively the raw data due to the
nature of audiovisual data but only some kind of descriptions summarizing the
contents. This issue remains an open issue even the research efforts made in this
field.

To support video retrieval applications, the video must be properly modeled
and indexed. Different methods have been proposed in the literature to analyze the structures of audiovisual data. These methods could be grouped in the
following approaches.

3.1   Segmentation Approach: Low Level

In the segmentation approach [8], the video is divided into atomic units called *shots* using low-level features. Each shot consists of a visually continuous sequence of frames. The content of each shot is then described individually. With such segmentation, the retrievable units are low-level structures such as video clips represented by key frames. Although such approach provides significant reduction of data redundancy, better methods of organizing multimedia data are needed in order to support true content-based video information search and retrieval capabilities. A concept structure is normally superimposed on top of the set of shots to provide necessary context information. Hence, a *scene* can be defined as a sequence of shots that focus on the same point of interest, while a *sequence* can be defined as series of related shots and scenes that form a single, coherent unit of dramatic action [9].

Current shot detection algorithms perform fairly well and are able to detect shot boundaries while scene detection remains, however, an open issue. Experts agree that scene detection requires content analysis at a higher level [10].

3.2   Stratification Approach: Semantic Level

Instead of physically dividing the contiguous frame sequences into shots, the stratification approach focuses on segmenting the video's contextual information into a set of strata each of which describes the temporal occurrences of a simple concept such as the appearance of an anchor person in the news video. Since strata are linked to the semantic information within a video, they may overlap and thus the meaning of the video at any instance can be flexibly modeled as the union of all present strata.

The stratification approach is a context-based approach to modeling video content and therefore strongly linked to the domain to be considered. In fact, as noted before, the semantic model used to describe a specific domain (e.g., news, courses, ...) could not be re-used for another domain. Furthermore, the stratification approach imposes human's intentionality early during the semantic extraction stage (indexing stage).

3.3   Multilevel Approach

Multilevel models constitute an alternative solution for searching and browsing video documents by bridging the gap between low-level visual features and high level semantic concepts [11]. Indeed, as noted above, a video can be annotated in two ways: (a) a structural way which organizes the video into a set of sequences, scenes and shots. Though this structuration provides means of browsing the content of the video even the lack of enhanced semantics, it does not allow advanced content-based searching and querying; (b) a semantic annotation which captures the semantic of the contextual contents of the video. Contrary to the structural view, this kind of annotation allows advanced searching and querying capabilities. Figure 1 gives an example of the two views: structural view and stratification view.

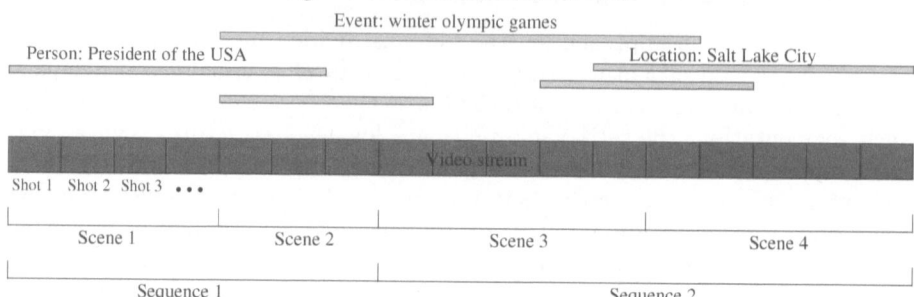

High Level View: stratification view

Low Level View: structural view

Fig. 1. Multilevel view of a video stream

3.4   Our Approach

In our framework, we propose to combine both views: the structural view in order
to support browsing and the stratification view to allow advanced content-based
retrieval. For this purpose, we used the data model of figure 2. It will be noted
that almost all video documents share the same structural view in the sense that
a video stream could be divided into sequences, scenes and shots. We used the
data model of figure 2 (part II) to model the structural part. This model has been
proven to capture well the structures of a video document [12]. Furthermore, in
order to manage the distribution of video documents and taking into account the
fact that a video document could be stored/replicated in different video servers,
we used the data model of figure 2 (part I).

Nevertheless, as mentioned before, the stratification view highly depends on
the semantic of the target domain. For this reason, part III of the proposed
data model (figure 2) is interchangeable from a domain to another in order to
better support domain specific requirements. As presented in the next section,
specific domain data model are derived from this model by specifying part III
(see examples of section 5).

4   System Description

The general outline of the proposed system is illustrated in figure 3. Three main
components can be identified: (a) remote client, (b) servers component and (c)
input data client.

4.1   Remote Client

Remote client component include three main tools: (a) a navigation tool which
allows users to browse the contents of video documents by structures i.e., according to part II of data model of figure 2. (b) A graphical query tool that

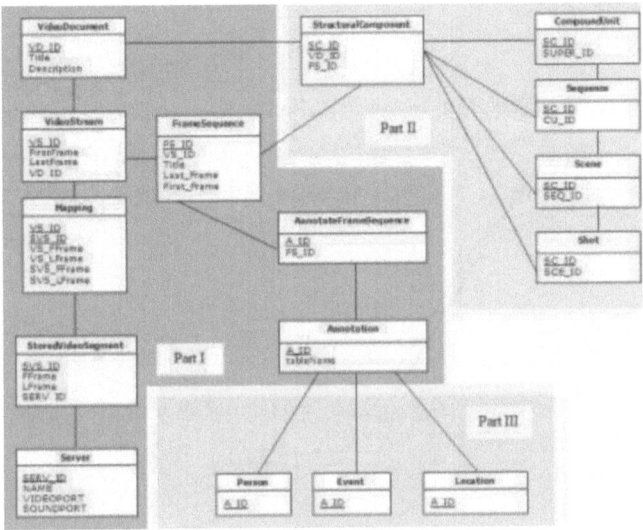

Fig. 2. SIRSALE Data model

allows the construction of complex and nested queries through the use of logical operators like AND, OR, etc and with regard to the domain to be considered (using the appropriate data model). Finally, a remote video player that displays the selected pieces of video streams. A window is used to also display the results of a content based query that might have several corresponding streams (see examples of the next section).

4.2   Servers Component

The server component is composed of three kinds of servers:

Video Servers: we choose to use a video server based on the RTP protocol, that works on the UDP transport protocol because it offers the most adapted services to transport real-time media. The RTP protocol can be used on TCP or UDP. Nevertheless, UDP is more adapted to real-time data transport in long distance context.

The RTP protocol permits to optimize the network bandwidth usage, because it does not need the use of a cache. The client reads the file as the server send it. This model is more adapted to mobile users (PDA, mobile phones, etc.) as it does not require additional cache space.

We developed the video server with JAVA and, specifically, the JAVA Media Framework technology. The server provides a direct access to physical video streams and permits the access to a specified video segment. The beginning and the end of the sequences are specified to the server that sends the corresponding frames to the client.

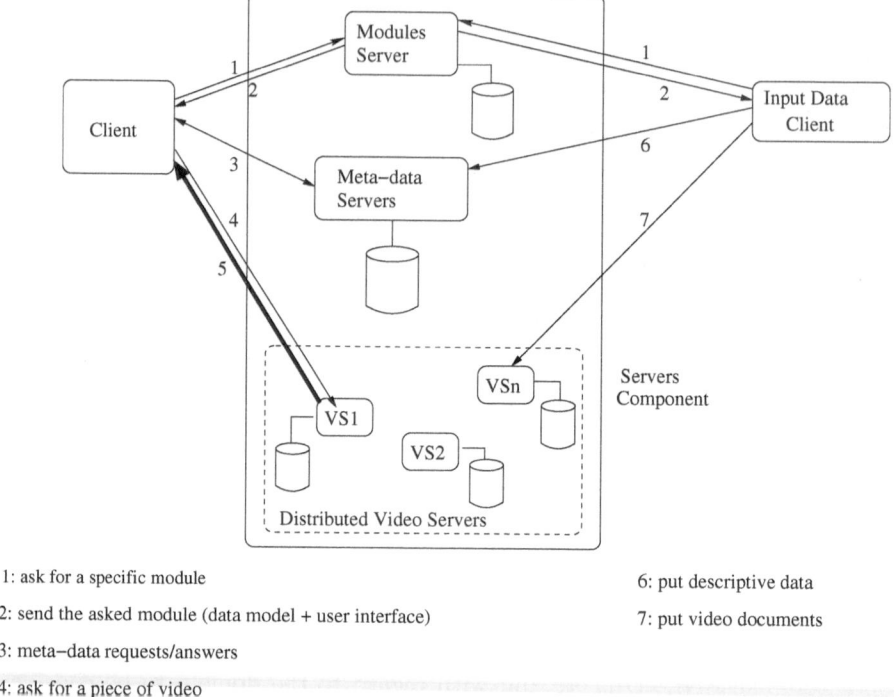

1: ask for a specific module

2: send the asked module (data model + user interface)

3: meta-data requests/answers

4: ask for a piece of video

5: streaming video

6: put descriptive data

7: put video documents

Fig. 3. Outline of the system architecture

Meta-data Servers: the database server contains the video meta-data, like the streams length and the id of the video server used to send video streams. It also manages the low and high level annotations on the video streams. In order to enhance the faut-tolerance and the scalability of SIRSALE we have chosen to use one database per topic of interest (e.g. news, soccer, education...). Meta-data bases can be distributed over several servers.

Module Servers: SIRSALE is based on a set of generic modules like the streaming or meta-data servers and ad hoc modules that can be developed and integrated within SIRSALE in order to deal with the specific features of each kind of application and each topic of interest. For instance, a query interface for basic users for a database of soccer videos is fundamentally different from a query interface dedicated to professional users manipulating video repositories for editing purposes.

In practice, for a specific topic of interest, we group all the functionalities related to annotation activities together into one application package that is stored on the module server. The user interface provides low-level browsing, streaming and displaying functionalities since they do not depend on the video semantics.

However, the basic interface does not include any high level (semantic) functionalities since they are dependent on the topic of interest and the application features. Therefore, after the user has defined his/her target topic of interest, it sends a request to the module server in order to receive the pertinent application package. This latter is then plugged into the interface that the user can deal with a fully functional interface.

This approach combines several advantages. Firstly, it allows providing a lightweight interface that can be adapted to the specific needs of the user. Secondly, it allows limiting the number of connections to the server. Indeed, all the events and the operations such as checking a mouse click, a button press, or requesting the databases for video sequences, are managed by the client interface. Finally, it makes the update and addition of packages, and as a consequence the user interface's update, very easy: the administrator has to put the new packages in a specified directory to make all modifications accessible to the client interface.

4.3   Input Data Client

The purpose of that component is to provide users with an advanced tool to index video document according to the data model used. To define the video sequences, a user needs a dedicated player, with complete VCR functionalities used to create the time sequence, and a set of objects used to annotate the sequence. Video data are firstly downloaded to the user machine before they can be played. We chose this approach because of the intensive use of VCR functionalities especially the fast forward and rewind one during the annotation phase. Remote video playing has been proven to be unsuitable for such use. Obviously, to perform this task, the input data client must dispose of a powerful machine in terms of CPU speed and storage capacities.

Figure 4 shows the annotation interface for the news management domain. It has three parts. On the left, the user selects the video documents and its video sequences he/she is interested in. On the right, the user can define the annotation entities (person, location, . . .) which are concerned using a selection list. In the middle, he/she can view the video document. To get a full control on the video, VCR functions like play, pause, stop, fast and low forward and fast and low rewind are provided.

5   Applications Examples

We have developed a fully functional system that implements solutions described above. This system has been developed in Java, Java RMI and MySQL in order to be portable to various operating systems like Windows and Linux. Two main experiments have been conducted on two different semantic contexts: TV news and soccer archive. These two contexts show different constraints and use different semantic objects.

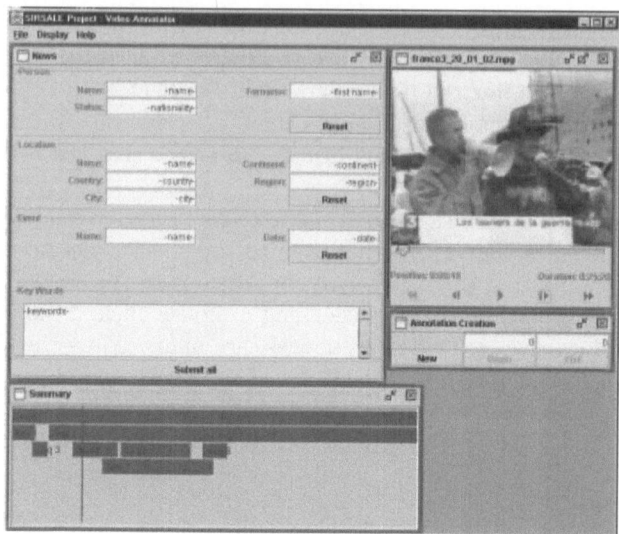

Fig. 4. Annotation interface for News domain

5.1   News Management

The news manager is used to index and retrieve news sequences. In current practice[1], the query result of this kind of manager is not directly linked to the video information. Thus, the retrieval of news items could be very complex and time consuming task. Note that most users of this kind of information are television reporters who need simple and quick retrieval tools (system response time is critical in such application). Hence, the first module we choosed to develop is dedicated to this work: give a complete tool to retrieve and directly visualize news information.

Data model. Figure 2 shows that our model has three different parts. The first part is used to get the physical description of each video document. It is used to retrieve and display the stored video segments in the video servers. The second part is used to structurally cut the video document. This describes all the different structural levels of the cutting process. These two parts, as mentioned before, are common to all the videos and will be the same in all the different module databases.

The third part is used to semantically annotate the video documents. As noted above, such annotations depend on the topic of interest. In the context of a news manager, we used to annotate according to three criteria: **Person**, **Event**, and **Locations** of each frame sequence.

Querying. Figure 5 shows the query interface. On the bottom-left corner, we can see the video document browser with the different parts of the structural

---

[1] Seen in our partners from a broadcast channel

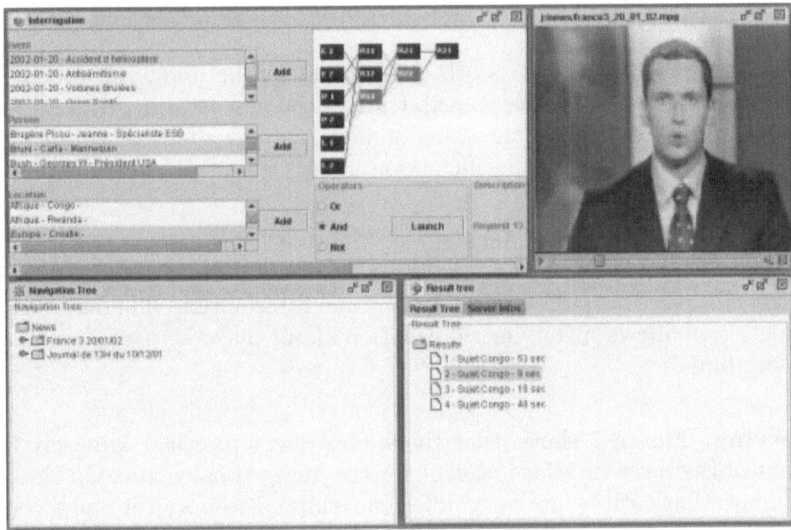

Fig. 5. News Query Interface

cutting. On the top-left corner one can see the request constructor with the various annotation entities. On the bottom-right corner, we can find the result window and on the top-right corner, the video player.

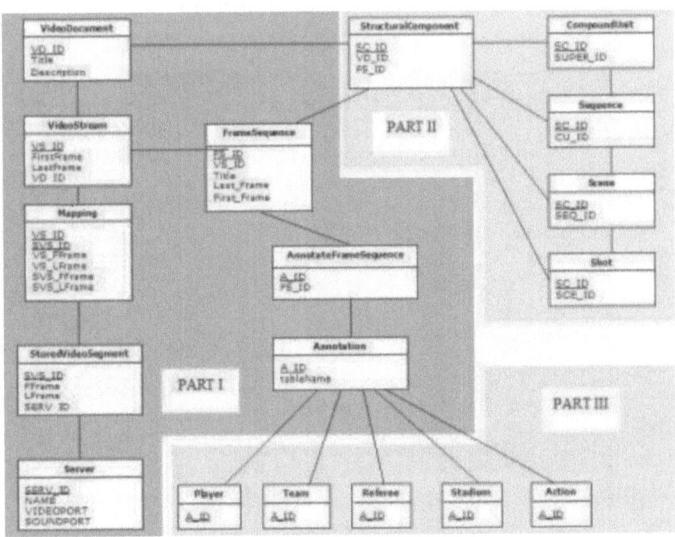

Fig. 6. Soccer annotation model

5.2   Soccer Archive

Soccer archives can interest both the general public and professionals. Soccer clubs use this kind of archive to help train of the players, since video streams are currently used to visualize the game of any opponent team. The video helps the manager to understand a specific action or just visualize the game of a player.

Data model. The soccer data model (figure 6) also has three parts. The two models (news and soccer) use the same first two parts, but the semantic part changes because users do not need the same information. Therefore, the soccer manager tool allows specifying information about players, teams, events, referees and stadiums.

Querying. Figure 7 shows that the soccer query interface is nearly the same as that of the news interface, except for the query constructor. On the contrary, the annotation entities are very different, adapted to a soccer game context.

6   Conclusion and Perspectives

This paper presents a content-based video indexing, searching and retrieving system, called SIRSALE. SIRSALE is based on a multilevel video indexing approach that combines both low level indexing which allows browsing of videos by structures (sequence, scene, shot) and high level indexing that supports content-based video searching. Moreover, SIRSALE, through the management of modules, allows users to use domain specific data-models as well as user interfaces to

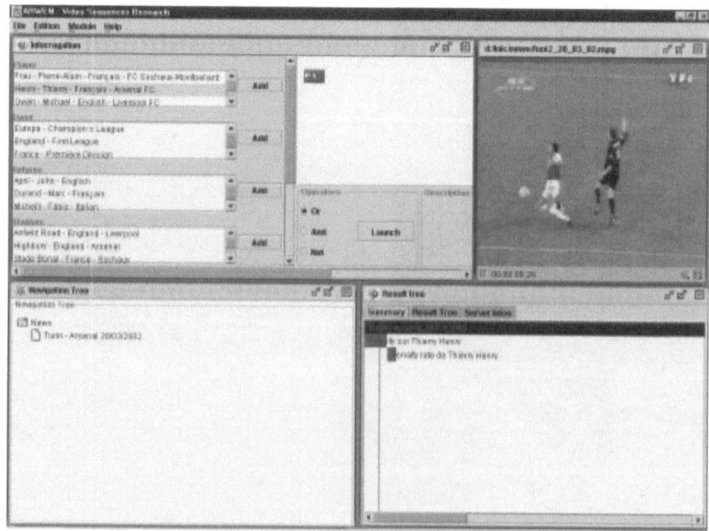

Fig. 7. Soccer Query Interface

search and retrieve video information related to various domains. Although we have made no assumption on the domain specific data models used in SIRSALE (recall that content providers can use their own domain specific data models), we though in future work to use the MPEG-7 standard as a basis for the proposed tools. The customization of the description model for their own requirements is then left to the content providers.

Future evolutions of the SIRSALE system will first include a complete parallel video server that we have developed earlier [13] in order to support the huge volume of the video database as well as the high expected transactional workload. Secondly, we are working to add a presentation tool which will allow users to construct their own multimedia presentations from requested video sequences[14].

References

1. Marques, O., Furht, B.: Issues in designing contemporary video database systems. In: IASTED International Conference on Internet and Multimedia System and Applications, Nassau, Bahamas (1999) 298–211
2. Apers, P., Blanken, H., Houstma, M.: Multimedia databases in Perspective. Springer-Verlag, London (1997)
3. Marcus, S.: Querying multimedia Databases in SQL. In: Multimedia Database System : Issues and Research Direction. Springer (1996)
4. Baral, C., Gonzalez, G., Nandigam, A.: SQL+D : Extended display capabilities for multimedia database queries. In: ACM International Conference on Multimedia. (1998) 109–114
5. Pereira, F., Koenen, R.H.: MPEG-7 : Status and Directions. In: Multimedia Systems, Standards, and Networks. Mercel Dekker, Inc. (2000)
6. Jain, A., Vailaya, A., Wei, X.: Query by video clip. Multimedia Systems **7** (1999) 369–384
7. Bimbo, A.D.: A perspective view on visual information retrieval systems. In: IEEE Workshop on Content-Based Access of Image and Video Librairies, Santa Barbara, California (1998)
8. Rubin, B., Davenport, G.: Structured content modeling for cinematic information. SIGCHI Bulletin **21** (1989) 78–79
9. Konigsberg, I.: The complete film dictionary. New York, Penguin (1997)
10. Zhang, H.J.: Content-based video browsing and retrieval. Handbook of Internet and Multimedia Systems and Applications (1999)
11. Fan, J., Aref, W., Elmagarmid, A., Hacid, M., Marzouk, M., Zhu, X.: Multiview: Multilevel content representation and retrieval. Journal of electronic Imaging **10** (2001) 895–908
12. Hjelsvold, R., Midtstraum, R.: Modeling and querying video data. In: Proceedings of the 20th VLDB Confrence, Chili (1994)
13. Mostefaoui, A., Perez, C., Brunie, L.: Serveur de séquences audiovisuelles parallèle sur réseau haut débit : concepts et expérimentations. In: RENPAR'11, Rennes, France (1999) 127–132
14. Mostefaoui, A., Kosch, H., Brunie, L., Böszörményi, L.: Multi-clip query optimization in video databases. In: IEEE International Conference on Multimedia and Expo., New York, USA, IEEE CS Press (2000) 363–366

Voting Based Bandwidth Management in Multiparty Video Conferences

Mario Zuehlke and Hartmut Koenig

Brandenburg University of Technology Cottbus
Departement of Computer Science
PF 10 13 44, 03130 Cottbus, Germany
{mz, koenig}@informatik.tu-cottbus.de

Abstract. Video conferences are considered as an attractive application in high–performance networks. Nevertheless video conference services are not that broadly used like services such as e-mail or WWW. There are several reasons for this. Most existing conference system solutions do not sufficiently support closed group conferences in a global scales. They also do not provide an appropriate bandwidth management to smoothly play out the audio and video streams at the receivers. This is, however, important for closed multiparty conferences due to the tight relationship among the participants which usually results in the presentation of all partners on each screen independently of their current role (speaker or listener). In this paper we present an approach for managing the bandwidth in global video conferences using a hierarchical system topology and a voting scheme. The approach is based on the use of point-to-point links and a selective transmission of the participants. Measurements substantiate its applicability.

Keywords: Video conferencing, multiparty conferences, closed groups, bandwidth management, QoS, voting procedures

1 Introduction

Video conferences are considered as an attractive application in high-performance networks. Due to improved network, processor, and compression technologies, and reduced equipment and network cost as well video conferences do not any more depend on specialized studio equipment. Video conference systems are available on desktop computers meanwhile. Despite of years of development, however, video conference services are not that broadly used like services such as e-mail or WWW. There are numerous reasons for this. Most existing system solutions do not sufficiently support closed group conferences in a global scales. They do not possess an appropriate bandwidth adaptation to smoothly play out the audio and video streams. This is, however, important for closed multiparty conferences because there is a tight relationship among the participants. Usually all partners are presented on the screens. Their roles (speaker or listener) change constantly. Current systems use a manual tuning. This requires experience by

F. Boavida et al. (Eds.): IDMS/PROMS 2002, LNCS 2515, pp. 202–215, 2002.

the users to find a trade-off between the various QoS parameters. In most cases the achievable QoS depends on the performance of the involved video conference systems and the used network connections. In this paper we focus on the latter and consider the bandwidth management in global network applications. In wide area networks like the Internet the available bandwidth is limited because the links are shared by thousands of users. For global video conferences, an efficient handling of bandwidth is of crucial importance to provide a sufficient audio and video quality to the participants. Adaptations to varying network conditions should be processed automatically.

The solution of this problem is not trivial. It depends on the kind of the video conference. In an open, loosely coupled conference with thousands of participants bandwidth adaptation is less complicated. These conferences use the receiver related multicast as transmission paradigm. Everyone who subscribes to the conference multicast address can join the conference. The sender does not know the actual composition of the conference group. It is therefore not necessary to adapt the sender bandwidth to the receivers' requirements. Needed adaptations can be executed on the way to the receivers, e.g. by scaling down the bandwidth in routers or by using active network mechanisms. Today's video conference applications over the Internet run on the Multicast Backbone (MBone) using the MBone video conference tools. In these systems the sender determines the quality of the outgoing multimedia streams. He mostly adapts to participants with low bandwidth connections. Thus participants with more bandwidth receive worse quality video streams although they are capable to process a higher quality. Further it is not possible in an open multiparty conference group using the MBone tools that a receiver can reject a video stream he/she does not want to receive. A stream from each sender is sent to all receivers and can waste bandwidth.

In multiparty conferences for closed, tightly coupled groups the bandwidth management is more sophisticated. The reason is that closed groups require a sender related transmission paradigm, i.e. the sender always knows the receivers of the data streams. For data transmission, multicast is preferred but it is not always applicable as we discuss later. The sender related scheme allows the sender to take the performance of the receiving systems as well as the network situation into account to avoid overload situations at the receiver hosts. This is important because in a closed group conference the video streams of all conference participants have to be decoded in the end systems. This is usually done in software and requires a large part of the computing power. The regulation of the bandwidth is therefore also important for this aspect. Today's video conference systems for closed groups are mainly based either on the H.320 standard for circuit-switching networks like ISDN or on the H.323 standard for packet-switching networks. Examples of such systems are CU-SeeMe, Intel Pro Share, and Netmeeting. The H.32x standards do not contain a bandwidth regulation. These systems are only applicable in (private or local) networks with a sufficient bandwidth. Their use in global networks is still difficult. QoS models for the Internet like Integrated Services (IntServ) [2] or Differentiated Services (DiffServ)

[3], [4], [5] are promising approaches to guarantee a high throughput for such kind of traffic. These approaches, however, are currently deployed mainly and tested in local environments. It turns out that it is difficult to introduce these concepts into the public core network of the Internet. Routers have to be globally updated. So far only islands of guaranteed QoS exist in public networks. They are connected by best effort links. Active network approaches which try to introduce intelligence into the network and the routers lack the same problem as IntServ and DiffServ [6]. They are still not matured enough to be applied on a large scale. For this reason, these approaches cannot be used as basis for the bandwidth management in global closed group video conferences in near future. Current global video conferences have to cope with best effort services and must adapt their data traffic to this situation.

In this paper we present an approach for managing the bandwidth in global video conferences using a hierarchical system topology and a voting scheme. It tries to overcome the mentioned problems by using dedicated point-to-point links and a selective transmission of participants. The paper is organized as follows. Section 2 discusses topological aspects of the design of closed group video conference systems. Based on this discussion we present in Section 3 a hierarchical topology for the establishment of such conferences on a global scale. Section 4 gives an overview of existing approaches for bandwidth management for long-distance audio and video transmission. The proposed voting approach for bandwidth management is described in Section 5. The next section reports about measurements to demonstrate the applicability of the approach. Finally we give an outlook on further research steps and the application of the approach to practice.

2   Multiparty Video Conference Topologies

The most convenient way for establishing a video conference is the use of multicast. It simplifies the group management, saves bandwidth and supports mostly a good scalability concerning the numbers of participants. In the Internet the receiver based IP multicast is used. It allows the users to participate in a running session without a specific invitation, acceptance or notification by the actual participants. This approach is suitable for open group communication to transmit lectures, conferences, or public events like a shuttle start or a concert.

For closed group conferences, there is the possibility to encrypt the audio and video streams. This, however, requires additional efforts for the encryption/decryption and the key management. These measures also do not prevent that the conference is recorded if the conference address is known. Solutions which use a receiver based transmission paradigm are not suitable for establishing real closed group conferences. For this, the sender related paradigm is required which ensures that the audio and video are only sent to the known group members. The introduction of a sender related multicast service has been proposed with the XCAST approach [7]. The shortage of this solution is the limitation of the number of participants in a session to 8. In addition, it requires that router software is updated to handle XCAST packets. Closed group communication over IP using multicast is therefore currently not possible.

Therefore centralized solutions for group communication are preferred in which all participants are connected to a centralized group server which manages the group composition and delivers the media data to the participants. H.32x video conference systems follow this principle. The main drawbacks of this solution are server failures which terminate the conference and performance bottlenecks in processing the incoming video streams. Commercial products are still pretty expensive. This confines their deployment.

A more flexible approach is the use of a hierarchical system topology which divides the conference group into different local areas. These areas may provide a different Quality of Service. The areas are connected by point–to–point links. Each area possesses a gateway which distributes the incoming streams to the local participants and forwards the outgoing streams to the connected areas. This approach has the advantage that a global multicast environment is not required. H.32x systems use gateways which interconnect standard systems over different media types, e.g. H.323 to H.320 gateways and vice versa. These gateways are passive devices that establish a tunnel for the signaling and media data between both locations. They do not possess any bandwidth management facility. In [6] an intelligent gateway is proposed that decodes the incoming video streams and encodes this stream as a function of the bandwidth on the outgoing links. Each gateway measures the bandwidth to its neighbors based on the RTCP receiver reports. The gateways, however, do not take the relevance of the different streams into account. An important video stream, e.g. the actual speaker, is transmitted with the same QoS as less important ones, e.g. that of the listeners. Each stream is considered as single stream. There is an influence among the video streams that could lead to a strong fluctuation in the sending rates of each single stream out of the gateway. The decoding and encoding at the application level further requires a high performance of the gateway.

3   The OCTOPUS Approach

An approach which implements the above discussed hierarchical topology is the OCTOPUS video conference system [8]. The idea of OCTOPUS was to set up global video conferences by connecting local video conferences over long distances in the Internet. Figure 1 shows an example conference which connects participants in different German universities via the Internet.

OCTOPUS consists of two tiers. The lower tier comprises the local conferences. They run separately. The local systems may have different architectures and organization principles. The upper tier is responsible of the communication between the local conferences. It unites all (local) conference participants into a global conference group with a global floor control for speaker assignment. An intelligent gateway is applied for the interaction between the two tiers. It is called group coordinator. The group coordinator is responsible for the delivery of the media streams and the signaling data to the local conferences. It is able to

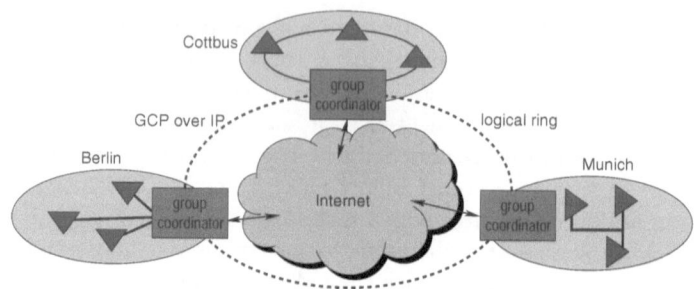

Fig. 1. The OCTOPUS architecture

convert the formats of local video and audio streams into a globally used format if it is necessary. The group coordinator supports different network interfaces, e.g. between ATM in the local network and IP for the global connection. The available bandwidth on the links between the groups is measured by the group coordinators. The bandwidth adaptation is based on the available bandwidth and a voting procedure. It is described in Section 5 of this paper. The conference control comprises the global group management, the floor control, and the exchange of QoS related data. The group management controls the dynamic join and leave of (local) participants. The floor control assigns the access right to the audio channel and to the whiteboard. In OCTOPUS the speaker video is handled with priority in the group coordinators. The continuous exchange of QoS related data ensures that each group coordinator is aware about the network situation within the global conference. For the signalling between the group coordinators, the group communication protocol GCP_{IP} [9] is applied. It provides an atomic, reliable, and ordered data delivery service. GCP also supports a dynamic group management, i.e. the participants can join and leave the conference at any time. Further detailed descriptions of the OCTOPUS concept are contained in [10], [9].

4 Bandwidth Management in Multiparty Conferences

Besides topological decisions bandwidth management plays an important role for the assurance of a good video conference quality. Mechanisms are required to allocate bandwidth and to avoid data congestion during the transmission. In the literature several approaches have been proposed which are used in different topologies.

For the transmission of multimedia streams in the Internet, mostly the Real Time Transport Protocol RTP [11] is applied. RTP does not support bandwidth allocation and congestion control mechanisms. Instead the receiver application of the multimedia streams can measure the packet loss by using the sequence number field of the RTP protocol and returns this information to the sender by means of the RTCP receiver reports (RR). Based on this information the sender application can reduce the sending rate if the losses are too high. The sending rate can be automatically or manually adapted. The latter is used in the MBone tool Vic. An automatic mechanism was proposed by [12]. It works similarly to the TCP slow start algorithm using the following adaptation:

```
if(Congestion)
     rate = max(rate/GAIN, MIN_RATE)
else if(NoCongestion)
     rate = min(rate + INC, MAX_RATE).
```

If the packet loss exceeds a threshold of more than 5 per cent a Congestion is assumed. The sending rate (rate) is reduced either to the current rate divided by the GAIN value or a defined minimum rate with the worst acceptable quality (MIN_RATE). The GAIN value is usually set to 2. If the packet losses are less than 2 per cent (noCongestion) the sending rate is periodically increased by INC until a maximum rate (MAX_RATE) is reached. This maximum rate may be chosen to a value that is either TCP friendly, or that can be provided by the sender, or that can be consumed by the receiver [12].

In multipoint conferences the congestion control is more complicated. Each receiver of the group has to report the received QoS to the sender. Therefore the sender has to decide which receiver he/she takes into account for the adaptation. There are three possibilities to solve this problem: (1) adaptation to the best connection, (2) adaptation to an average connection, or (3) adaptation to the worst connection. The first two possibilities have the shortage that only a subset of participants of a session receives good quality video streams. The other participants receive a worse quality because the lower bandwidth of their connections leads to congestions. This may be unacceptable for some users since especially in video conferences the displayed video image has a high noise due to packet loss. For the third case, the following adaptation procedure has been proposed in [12]. The above given congestion condition is fulfilled if 10 per cent of the group is congested. The sending frame rate is adapted to these connections even if 90 per cent of the participants' connections are not congested. Thus the majority of participants receive an insufficient video quality. On the other hand, if 10 per cent of the group members detect no congestion then the sending rate is incremented. This can lead to an overload of the remaining 90 per cent of the connections after the adaptation. In heterogeneous network environments like in the Internet the trade-off between the participants' connection bandwidth is more obvious than in homogeneous environments. For example, if in a group 10 per cent of the participants are connected with a low bandwidth and 10 per cent with a high bandwidth. Then both subgroups try to adapt the bandwidth in the opposite direction. This does not lead to a stable state.

In open groups such adaptations are difficult to apply because the sender does not exactly know the composition of the group. So it can only estimate the acceptable bandwidth based on the information of the known participants. In a closed group the sender has an exact overview of the demands because it knows all the receivers and their current QoS state.

To solve the problem of insufficient bandwidth adaptation in multiparty conferences and to offer an appropriate QoS to each participant the concept of receiver-driven layered multicast was proposed in [13]. It uses different QoS layers for the transmission of the video streams to which the participants can subscribe. The lowest level contains the worst but still acceptable video quality. The other layers provide an increasingly improved quality. The weakness of this approach is that the coding procedure requires high performance in the end systems and appends additional delays. At receiver side a further delay has to be added by buffering and assembling the different layers because the path through the network of the different layers may be different and can increase the delay.

In open group conference systems the various layers can be transmitted by means of different multicast groups. Each receiver can decide which layer he/she wants to join. The mapping of this approach to closed group conferences is difficult because it is based on the receiver related IP multicast paradigm.

Due to the awareness of the sender about all participants inside the closed group he/she can distinguish a lot of different QoS layers. In the worst case the number of levels equals the number of conference participants. The participants have to announce the desired quality to the sender which assigns them to the respective layer. This solution implies a trade-off between the granularity of the levels and the management efforts of the sender. The finer the quality levels the higher are the additional management and the effort at the sender host for the coding of the different video streams.

5   A Voting Based Bandwidth Approach

In the OCTOPUS system we have introduced a voting based bandwidth management approach on the point-to-point links between the local video conference systems. The voting scheme is based on the observation that in larger conferences it is often not required to play out the video streams at all participants' screens. We call this the visibility problem. There are two reasons for this. First the screen resolution may limit the display of all participants. For example a usual screen resolution of 1024 x 786 pixel is only able to display 4 video images of the QCIF size (384 x 288 pixel). Secondly it is often not required in practice to display all participants because additionally a whiteboard or another joint viewing application is used which covers almost the whole screen.

Therefore it seems useful to display only a subset of the group. Beside the speaker this should be those participants who are relevant for the discussion. But this is a subjective decision of the participants. We apply the following voting procedure. Each participant has a *voting table* on his/her screen which contains the names of all participants. He/she can select the participants he/she wants to see. The actual speaker is always displayed even if he/she is not selected. Figure 2 gives an example for this ballot.

The group coordinators periodically evaluate the voting tables of their local participants and determine by the majority of votes which participants are displayed in the local conference. The voting outcome is stored in the *visibility table* in each group coordinator. The video streams of the participants with the most votes up to the display limit are played out. A participant can change

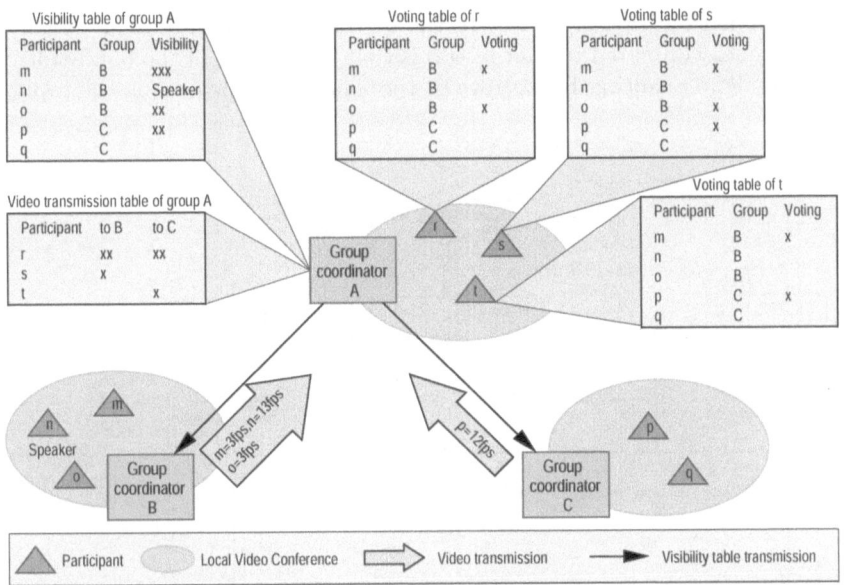

Fig. 2. Example scenario for a voting and bandwidth allocation during an OCTOPUS session

his/her selection every time. The visibility table is updated when the speaker changes. After each update the visibility tables are exchanged between the group coordinators. The selected participants are marked and stored in the *video transmission table*. Only their video streams are transmitted to the other sites to save bandwidth.

The voting outcome is further used to select video streams for transmission when the available bandwidth on the global link is limited. For this, the available bandwidth on these links it is periodically measured. The measurement is carried out at the destination side. The measurement results are returned to the source by GCP. We do not use the RTCP receiver reports here because GCP reduces the signaling overhead compared with RTCP up to 50 per cent [9]. In addition, RTCP reports relate to each stream separately, whereas GCP exchanges all measurement results in one packet. The packet is evaluated by the group coordinators so that each coordinator knows the available bandwidth on its links. For the decision whether a link is congested or not, a similar algorithm like the one described in section 4 is applied. First the algorithm was adapted to the unit frame per second (fps) instead of bits per second used in [12]. We chose the incrementing summand INC to 1 fps. That means the algorithm tries to increase the output frame rate by 1 fps if no congestion occurs. Furthermore, the adapted algorithm takes the whole bandwidth of the link into account and not only the bandwidth of separate streams. Thus influences among the streams are reduced. The last change is that the output frame rate is not reduced to the half of the actual frame rate but to the measured frame rate. The advantage of this approach compared to that in [12] is that the impact of the bandwidth is not so strong. The resulting frame rate of the adaptation process is the input (FR)

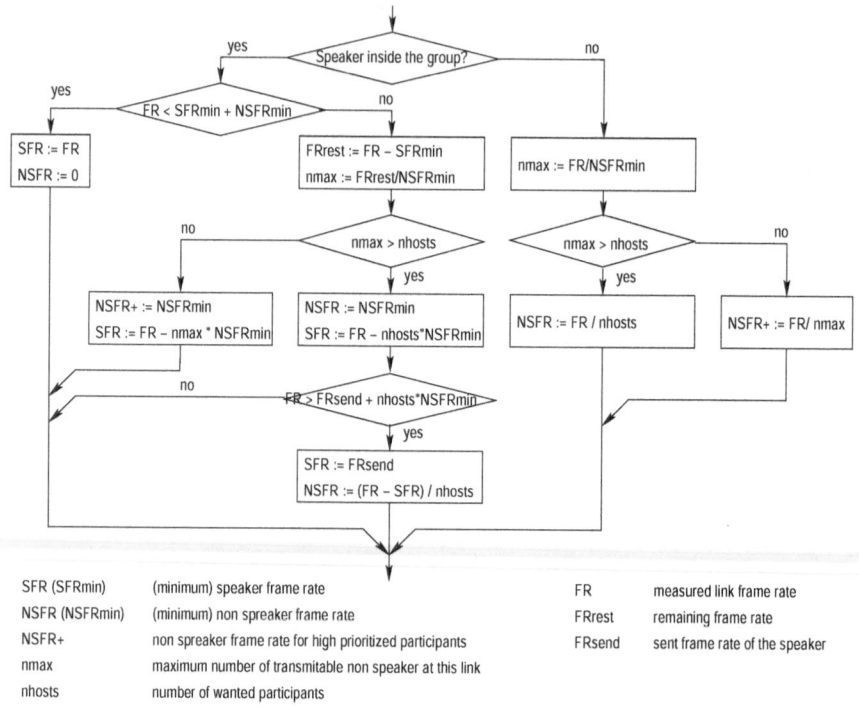

Fig. 3. Bandwidth allocation algorithm based on voting results

for the voting based bandwidth management algorithm presented in Fig. 3. The algorithm distinguishes two modes depending on whether the speaker belongs to the group. The procedure assures that the speaker is always displayed with at least 10 fps. The other participants are displayed with at least 3 fps in the voting order as long as bandwidth is available. Further it might be possible that a video stream is transmitted with different frame rates to different global destinations.

The following example demonstrates the principle based on the voting outcome of Figure 2. We assume that the available bandwidth on the link between A and B is 19 fps and between A and C 12 fps. The group coordinators B and C determine the bandwidth allocation for their group members based on the visibility table of group A. We first consider group B with the three participants m, n, and o. The current speaker is supposed to be n. He/she is displayed with at least 10 fps. Since the remaining frame rate is 9 fps the video streams of participants m and o can be also transmitted with 3 fps each. Additionally, 3 fps can be assigned to the speaker. From group C only participant p is selected by group A. So all 12 fps can be assigned to this video stream. Participant q is not displayed. If the bandwidth between A and B decreases to 14 fps then only the video stream of m (most votes) is transmitted with 3 fps. Speaker n gets 11 fps in this case. Participant o cannot be displayed anymore in A because the available bandwidth does not allow to transmit two video streams with at least 3 fps each.

In order to prevent an overloading of the receiving participants' hosts the following rule for the reception of video streams is applied. Generally the display of remote video streams has priority over the display of the local participants. For example, if a host in group A can process 40 fps then it can receive all video streams of B (19 fps in total) and C (12 fps). The remaining bandwidth of 9 fps is shared by the local participants of A in equal proportions. To prevent visibility problems the voting table can be extended to local participants. This vote does not influence the global ballot.

6   Measurements

In this section we present measurements which prove the applicability of the approach. The measurements comprise the transmission delay, the bandwidth availability on long-distance links, the adaptation behavior, and the delay in the gateways / group coordinators.

Delays. The delay is a very important factor within a video conference. This concerns not only the video and audio transmission but the signaling as well. We measured the delay for different typical packet lengths (see Fig. 4) to different locations based on the round trip time (RTT).

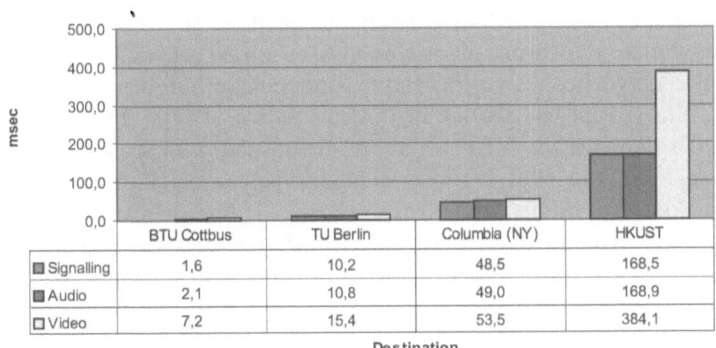

	BTU Cottbus	TU Berlin	Columbia (NY)	HKUST
■ Signalling	1,6	10,2	48,5	168,5
■ Audio	2,1	10,8	49,0	168,9
□ Video	7,2	15,4	53,5	384,1

Fig. 4. Transmission delays for different packet sizes

The measurements were carried out within our campus network in Cottbus (BTU Cottbus), to the Berlin University of Technology (TU Berlin), to the Columbia University New York, and to the Hong Kong University of Science and Technology (HKUST). The latter is connected via a satellite connection to the Internet from Asia to France. The smaller bandwidth and especially the delay caused by a satellite link provide worse conditions for a video conference application. The other universities are connected by wired links. The measurement results are depicted in Fig. 4. They show that the delays are less than 500 msec. Further, they are significant below the typical acceptance threshold for a good quality audio communication. The results also show that related to the delay a global conference as proposed is possible if there is one satellite connection between the locations. Two satellite links cause unacceptable delays.

Bandwidth. Beside the delay the bandwidth is the most important factor to ensure an acceptable video conference quality. For our measurements, we concentrated on links with high delays and limited bandwidth like satellite connections. The German research network G-WiN currently provides a bandwidth of 2.5 Gbps. Bandwidth bottlenecks are currently rare. We measured therefore the bandwidth on the connection to the Hong Kong University of Science and Technology. The measurement scenario applied was the following. The sender continuously increased the frame rate each 30 seconds by 1 fps beginning with 3 fps. At the destination the received bandwidth was measured in fps and kbps. The measurements were repeated several times in the main business time from 8 a.m. to 16 p.m. MEST. The measurements of the direction from Hong Kong to Cottbus result in a bandwidth of only 17 fps (130 kbps) at an error rate of 5 per cent. The opposite direction was less congested. An average frame rate of 100 fps (800 kbps) with a delay of 400 msec and an error rate of 2.7 per cent was monitored.

Bandwidth adaptation. Based on the results of the bandwidth measurement we simulated the following two cases in our local network environment to evaluate the bandwidth adaptation algorithm. We assumed a group of 4 members which have different votes. In case (a) the actual speaker belongs to the group, in case (b) not. The initial bandwidth in both cases was 19 fps. Further we assumed a bandwidth decrease to 5 fps after 35 seconds for a short while due to a TCP data transfer. After that it recovers slowly to the original value. Note that we only consider one single link.

In case (a) the speaker Sp is prioritized (see Fig. 5). When the bandwidth decreases to 5 fps, after 35 seconds, only the speaker can be transmitted with the best possible frame rate. The rate reincreases continuously based on the measured bandwidth. When the available bandwidth is sufficient for the transmission of the speaker and at least one nonspeaker (13 fps), after 75 seconds, the speaker frame rate is set to 10 fps and one nonspeaker is sent with 3 fps. The other nonspeakers are sent when the bandwidth reaches the values of 16 fps and 19 fps, respectively.

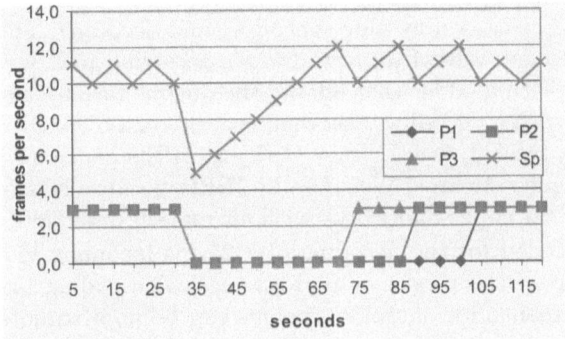

Fig. 5. Bandwidth adaptation with the speaker in the local group

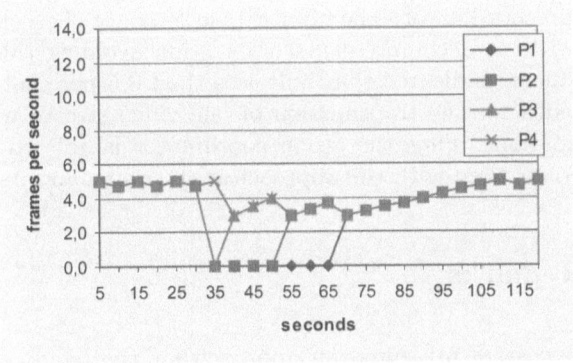

Fig. 6. Bandwidth adaptation without speaker in the local group

In case (b) the bandwidth adaptation procedure treats the voted nonspeakers in the same manner if the available bandwidth is enough to transmit all voted nonspeakers with at least with a minimum rate of 3 fps. As shown as example in Fig. 6 the initial bandwidth is enough to transmit all voted participants *P1* to *P4*. All 4 voted participants share the available bandwidth equally. For worse bandwidth conditions, we assume here that the votes increase from participant *P1* to *P4*. After the bandwidth decrease at 35 seconds only participant *P4* can be sent because there is only bandwidth to transmit one nonspeakers' video stream. The adaptation procedure increases again the sending rate step by step. After a while each participant is resent: *P3* after 40 seconds, *P2* after 55 seconds, and *P1* after 70 seconds.

Processor load at the group coordinator. The main processor load in a video conference is caused by video encoding and decoding. The approach of the intelligent video gateway of [6] introduces a receiving part with a decoder and a sending part with a coder that adapts the output rate to the link bandwidth. We monitored such a decoding/encoding process on a SUN Ultra 10 workstation (433MHz) with the X Image Library (XIL) M-JPEG codec for various incoming and outgoing video streams. We chose M-JPEG because it is less complex than a MPEG or H.261 codec and works without motion detection.

The load needed for the decoding of a 25 fps incoming video stream is less than 1 per cent of the processor performance. The coding load in per cent of the host performance for outgoing streams can be approximated by the sum of output frame rate in fps. For example, a group coordinator which sends 15 fps to one and 20 fps to another group has a processor load of approximately 35 per cent of the processor performance. If we assume that an output rate of 17 fps is sent to each group a group coordinator can only support up to 6 remote groups without any overload. This is insufficient especially if the bandwidth to remote groups is more than 17 fps. Therefore we introduced a frame-dropping filter inside the group coordinator. The filter is able to adapt the video streams based on M-JPEG without decompression/compression avoiding this large processor load. Measurements indicated that only less than 0.5 per cent of the processor power was needed for the transmission of one video stream with 25 fps into 4 different destinations. Thus the group coordinator is able to connect with 10 times more groups than with the approach with coding and decoding.

7   Final Remarks

In this paper we have presented an approach for the bandwidth management of closed group in global video conferences. It is based on the use of dedicated point-to-point links between different local areas and a selective transmission of participants. Point-to-point links simplify the bandwidth management for the transmission between different areas and support a sender related transmission paradigm. This ensures a consistent group composition and allows bandwidth measurements between sender and receiver for allocation decisions. The selective transmission of participants based on voting reflects the practical experience that it often is not necessary in conferences to play out all participants. The voting scheme allows focusing on those participants which are currently relevant for the discussion. In addition, priority is given to the actual speaker who is always displayed.

The proposed approach presents an applicable solution for setting up closed group multiparty video conferences on the existing Internet structure which does not support a sender related sending paradigm and guaranteed bandwidth so far. It is also adaptable to H.323 multiparty conferences. The measurements, especially on fully utilized connections as to Hong Kong, showed that the approach is also applicable for global conferences. In regional or nation wide networks with a much better bandwidth availability this solution already provides a good video conference quality.

The approach was applied in the video conference system OCTOPUS which was developed in a joint project between the Hong Kong University of Science and Technology and our university. It is also introduced in our new system BRAVIS (BRAndenburg VIdeo conference Service) which implements a video conference service over IP for teleteaching applications in the state of Brandenburg. The system uses a similar topology as OCTOPUS, but unlike OCTOPUS it does not use group coordinators. Their tasks are assigned to dedicated participants and to the sender itself what makes the topology more flexible.

References

[1] M. Handley, J. Crowcroft, C. Bormann, and J. Ott. Very large conferences on the Internet: the Internet multimedia conferencing architecture. *Computer Networks (Amsterdam, Netherlands: 1999)*, 31(3):191–204, 1999.

[2] R. Braden. Resource reSerVation Protocol (RSVP) - Version 1 Functional Specification. RFC 2205.

[3] S. Blake, D. Black, M. Carlson, E. Davies, Z. Wang, and W. Weiss. An Architecture for Differentiated Services. RFC 2475, December 1998.

[4] J. Heinanen, F. Baker, W. Weiss, and J. Wroclawski. Assured Forwarding PHB group. RFC 2597, June 1999.

[5] V. Jacobson, K. Nichols, and K. Poduri. An Expedited Forwarding PHB. RFC 2598, June 1999.

[6] O. Spaniol and J Meggers. Active Network Nodes for Adaptive Multimedia Communication. In *Intelligence in Networks. IFIP TC6 WG6.7 5th International Conference, SMARTNET'99*, pages 1 — 18. Kluwer Academic Publisher, 1999.

[7] R. Boivie and N. Feldmann. SGM - Small Group Multicast. Internet Draft Proposal, July 2000.

[8] S. Chanson, A. Hui, E. Siu, I. Beier, H. Koenig, and M. Zuehlke. OCTOPUS – A Scalable Global Multiparty Video Conferencing System. In *7th International IEEE Conference on Computer Communications and Networks (IC3N'99)*, pages 97 — 102, 1999.

[9] M. Zuehlke and H. Koenig. GCP – A Group Communication Protocol for Supporting Closed Groups in the Internet. In *Smart Networks. 7th International Conference on Intelligence in Networks (SMARTNET 2002)*, pages 97 — 102, 2002.

[10] I. Beier and H. König. A Protocol Supporting Distributed Group and QoS Management. In *Proceedings, IEEE Conference for Multimedia Systems – Networking (PROMS-MmNet'97)*, pages 213 — 222, 1997.

[11] H. Schulzrinne, S. Casner, R. Frederick, and V. Jacobson. RTP: A Transportprotocol for Real-Time Applications. RFC 1889, January 1996.

[12] J.C. Bolot, T. Turletti, and I. Wakeman. Scalable feedback control for multicast video distribution in the internet. In *ACM SIGCOMM'94*, pages 58—67, 1994.

[13] S. McCanne, V. Jacobson, and M. Vetterli. Receiver-driven Layered Multicast. In *ACM SIGCOMM '96*, pages 117—130, 1996.

Considering Non-real-time Traffic in Real-Time Packet Scheduling

Yeonseung Ryu

Division of Information and Communication Engineering
Hallym University, Chuncheon, 200-702, Korea
ysryu@hallym.ac.kr

Abstract. Real-time packet schedulers based on EDF policy have been extensively studied to support end-to-end bounded delay for real-time traffic. Since non-real-time traffic could hurt the schedulability of real-time traffic, we need a real-time packet scheduling method considering non-real-time traffic. In this paper, we propose a new admission control algorithm for EDF-based packet scheduling scheme. Proposed scheme consists of two packet schedulers: an *EDF scheduler* servicing real-time traffic and a *Periodic Server (PS) scheduler* servicing non-real-time traffic periodically. Proposed scheme provides good performance to non-real-time flows while guaranteeing the schedulability of real-time flows.

Keywords: Packet scheduling, Real-time scheduling, Admission control algorithm

1 Introduction

Recently a number of real-time packet scheduling algorithms based on *Earliest Deadline First* (EDF) policy have been studied in order to provide end-to-end bounded delay guarantees for real-time traffic [12,7,3,4,1]. EDF is regarded the best choice for providing delay guarantees since it has been proven to be an optimal scheduling policy. However, EDF scheduling algorithm cannot deal with the task systems consisting of a set of real-time tasks and non-real-time tasks since it assumes that all tasks must have hard deadline requirements. In traditional real-time task scheduling researches, *aperiodic server* schemes have been proposed for the task system which consists of real-time tasks and non-real-time tasks to provide non-real-time tasks with fast response time while preserving the schedulability of real-time tasks [9,14,8]. Aperiodic server schemes create a high-priority periodic server for servicing aperiodic (soft real-time) tasks. Since deadline of aperiodic server is assumed the same as its period, it can be adapted to EDF scheduling scheme.

Today's switches must send and receive both *real-time packets* and *non-real-time packets*. If we do not consider non-real-time traffic in the real-time packet scheduling scheme, the schedulability of real-time traffic could be violated by non-real-time traffic. In this work, we also address some sources that make the

F. Boavida et al. (Eds.): IDMS/PROMS 2002, LNCS 2515, pp. 216–228, 2002.

real-time traffic to behave unpredictably. Usually the nodes in the network periodically receive a number of request messages for the purpose of management. For example, manager software at management center can periodically send SNMP messages to query MIB data stored on the node or can send ICMP messages for Ping, and so on. The request messages to setup the real-time flows also could affect the guaranteed transmission of existing real-time traffic if a number of requests arrive at the same time. Therefore, even though the switches service only real-time communications, the real-time flows may experience jitter or loss of data.

In this paper, we study a packet scheduling scheme to provide predictability to real-time traffic by considering non-real-time traffic in real-time packet scheduling. We also present an algorithm to check the schedulability whenever a new real-time flow joins the packet scheduler.

Goals of this work are to:

- guarantee the real-time constraints (end-to-end delay) of the real-time flows.
- service the non-real-time flows as soon as possible while not hurting schedulability of the real-time flows that are already guaranteed.

To achieve these goals, we propose a packet scheduling scheme consisting of two packet schedulers: an *EDF scheduler* for real-time traffic and a *Periodic Server (PS) scheduler* for non-real-time traffic. PS is a periodic packet scheduler that is responsible for transmitting pending packets of non-real-time flows. PS employs the legacy packet management scheme to provide best-effort delivery service. PS is assigned the higher priority than EDF scheduler to provide fast service time to non-real-time flows. And in order not to affect real-time flows, PS is given a reserved time within a period. In this paper, we also present the schedulability condition considering PS and EDF scheduler in an integrated manner. With proposed schedulability condition we give an admission control algorithm that can be executed in pseudo-polynomial time. Through simulations we show that proposed admission control algorithm can be applicable to the practical systems with little runtime overhead.

The rest of this paper is organized as follows. Section 2 presents the background. Researches on traditional real-time scheduling and the recent work on real-time packet scheduling are explained. In Section 3, we give the details of the system model that services two types of flows: real-time flows and non-real-time flows. We also describe the Periodic Server (PS) method to service non-real-time flows. In Section 4, we give the schedulability condition for our system model and present proposed admission control algorithm. Section 5 presents the experimental results to investigate the practicalness of proposed admission control algorithm. Section 6 presents related work and discussion. The conclusions of this paper are given in Section 7.

2   Background

2.1   Real-Time Scheduling for Aperiodic Tasks

There are two types of real-time systems, namely, hard real-time systems and soft real-time systems. In hard real-time systems, tasks must complete before a given deadline. On the other hand, soft real-time systems usually provide statistical guarantee: for example, by providing the probability for a task of finishing before its deadline. A scheduling algorithm is referred to as optimal if it can find a feasible schedule for every feasible task system. Preemptive *Earliest Deadline First (EDF)* scheduling is known as optimal for periodic hard real-time task sets [13]. A task system consisting of just a set of n hard real-time tasks will be schedulable under EDF if and only if

$$\sum_{i=1}^{n} \frac{c_i}{p_i} \leq 1,$$

where c_i is execution time and p_i is period of task i, respectively. Here, $\frac{c_i}{p_i}$ is the fraction of processor time consumed by task i, *i.e.*, the utilization of the processor by task i.

For the systems that have tasks with soft real-time tasks, as well as hard real-time tasks, a number of *aperiodic server* schemes were proposed to schedule soft real-time tasks in a way that does not hurt the schedulability of hard real-time tasks, and provides good response time for soft real-time tasks [9,14,8]. In [8], for example, *deadline deferrable server*(DDS) algorithm was presented, which creates a high-priority periodic server for servicing aperiodic (soft real-time) tasks. At the beginning of each period, DDS receives an execution time budget allocation of a fixed size, C_s. If, after any queued requests are served, the execution time budget is not exhausted, the remaining portion of the budget is retained up to the end of the period, and can be used for requests that come in during that time. So long as a portion of this budget remains, the server is allowed to execute at the priority determined by its deadline. When the budget is consumed, the server is suspend until the next period. The following theorem shows a sufficient condition under DDS algorithm [8].

Theorem 1 *A set of n hard real-time tasks is schedulable under EDF and DDS algorithm if for all k, $(1 \leq k \leq n)$*

$$\sum_{i=1}^{k} \frac{c_i}{p_i} + (1 + \frac{T_s - C_s}{p_k}) \frac{C_s}{T_s} \leq 1 \tag{1}$$

where C_s is the execution time budget and T_s is the period of DDS, respectively.

2.2   Packet Scheduling for Real-Time Traffic

Recently a number of analytical models for Earliest Deadline First (EDF) scheduling were proposed to provide delay bounds for real-time communications

[6,12,4]. EDF is an attractive choice for providing delay guarantees for real-time flows since it has been proven to be an optimal scheduling policy. In general, an EDF scheduler assigns each arriving packet a deadline, computed as the sum of the arrival time at the scheduler and the delay bound. Let d_i be a local delay bound of flow i and $a_{i,j}$ be an arrival time of a packet j of flow i at the scheduler, respectively. Then the deadline of packet j of flow i is assigned as

$$D_{i,j} = a_{i,j} + d_i \tag{2}$$

The EDF scheduler always selects the packet with the earliest deadline for transmission. The packet scheduler needs to know the condition that must hold at the scheduler such that delay bound violations of real-time flows do not occur. These conditions are referred to as *schedulability conditions*. In [6,12], authors presented necessary and sufficient schedulability conditions for a single node under which a set of delay bounds can be met.

Since a network traffic could be distorted and local schedulability conditions will be violated, two mechanisms have been proposed to enforce that traffic entering a packet scheduler conforms to the given traffic constraint function. One mechanism is a *traffic policer* which rejects traffic if it does not comply to traffic constraint function. The other is a *rate controller*, which temporarily buffers packets to ensure that traffic entering the scheduler queue conforms to traffic constraint function. The idea of per-node traffic shaping called RC-EDF (Rate-Controlled EDF) was proposed [7].

Traffic constraint functions can be derived from deterministic traffic models that characterize the worst-case traffic by a small set of parameters. Let $A_i[s, t]$ be the amount of traffic (measured in bits/second) from flow i arriving over interval $[s, t]$. We assume that $A_i[t] = A_i[0, t]$. Let $A_i^*(t)$ be a right continuous subadditive function. $A_i^*(t)$ is said to be an envelope of flow $A_i[t]$, if for all times $s > 0$ and for all $t \geq 0$ we have

$$A_i[s, t] \leq A_i^*(t - s) \tag{3}$$

where $A_i^*(t) = 0$ for all $t < 0$. For example, the traffic constraint function for the (σ, ρ)-model [2] is given by $A_i^*(t) = \sigma_i + \rho_i t$, where σ_i is a burst parameter and ρ_i is a rate parameter of flow i.

Let $R = \{1, 2, ..., N\}$ be a set of flows, where flow $i \in R$ is characterized by the traffic constraint function. Then the schedulability condition for EDF scheduler is given as follows [12,4]:

Theorem 2 *The set R is EDF-schedulable if and only if for all $t \geq 0$*

$$\sum_{i \in R} A_i^*(t - d_i) \leq ct \tag{4}$$

where c is the capacity (maximum rate) of the link (bits/second).

3   System Model

Figure 1 shows the system model in a single node in the network. In our system model, there are two packet schedulers in each node: One is an EDF scheduler, which handles real-time traffic. The other is referred to as a *Periodic Server* (PS) scheduler, which is responsible for servicing non-real-time traffic, including request messages from SNMP agent, RSVP host, and so on. We assume that each node has a rate controller, such as RC-EDF, to ensure that traffic entering the EDF scheduler queue conforms to traffic constraint function, $A_i^*(t)$. In this work, we assume that the real-time traffic is characterized by the (σ, ρ)-model. However, admission control algorithm which will be presented in next section can be used with any other traffic models.

The real-time flows have real-time constraints, such as end-to-end bounded delay. We assume that flow setup protocol such as RSVP is used to provide guaranteed service to the real-time flows. After establishing a flow i, a packet j of flow i arriving at each node has deadline, d_i, as Equation 2. The real-time packets are serviced by EDF scheduling policy. The EDF scheduler selects the real-time packet with the earliest deadline for transmission.

The non-real-time flows do not have real-time constraints and are serviced by the PS scheduler with best effort delivery service. The PS scheduler is a periodic task, which is similar to aperiodic server schemes that were proposed in [14,8]. In order not to affect the real-time flows that are already guaranteed, we need to reserve the capacity of link for the non-real-time flows. The PS scheduler executes periodically and consumes link capacity for a given reserved time within a period. Let T_s and C_s be a period and the amount of reserved time within a period of the PS scheduler, respectively ($C_s < T_s$).

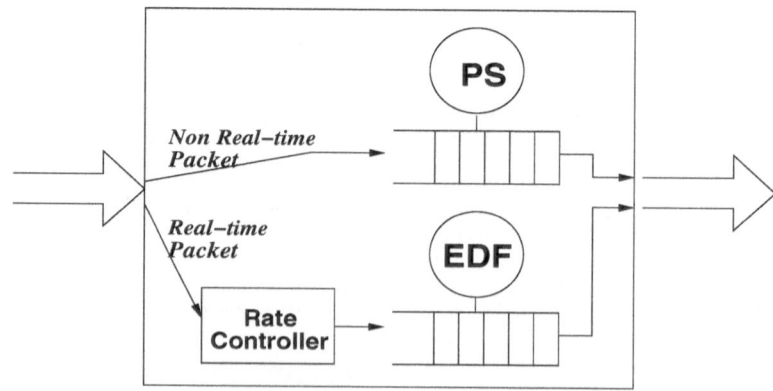

Fig. 1. System Model

The priority of the PS scheduler is given higher than the EDF scheduler to provide good performance to the non-real-time traffic. Note that the schedulability of the real-time flows will not be hurted because the EDF scheduler can consume the link during $(T_s - C_s)$ time interval every period. When the period of the PS scheduler begins, the PS scheduler starts immediately and transmits the non-real-time packets during reserved time interval. If there are no more non-real-time packets to transmit, the PS scheduler stops its work. When the reserved time duration finishes or the PS scheduler completes its work, the EDF scheduler starts its execution. While the PS scheduler is suspending and does not yet spend all its reserved time within the current period, if the non-real-time traffic arrives at the node then the PS scheduler is awakened immediately because its priority is higher than that of the EDF scheduler, and spends the remaining reserved time servicing them. Since the PS scheduler is able to use only specified reserved time within one period, if the PS scheduler spends all its reserved time then it suspends its execution even though it does not yet service all non-real-time traffic.

4   Admission Control Algorithm

In this section, we give the schedulability condition for the system model that consists of the EDF scheduler and the PS scheduler, and present an admission control algorithm.

Let R be a set of real-time flows, where flow $i \in R$ is characterized by the traffic constraint function. The condition that the set R is not schedulable can be easily derived from Theorem 2 by applying the contrapositive rule to Equation 4. That is, the set R is not schedulable if and only if there exists a time $t \geq 0$ such that

$$t < \frac{1}{c} \sum_{i \in R} A_i^*(t - d_i) \tag{5}$$

Informally the condition states that a deadline violation occurs if there exists a time $t \geq 0$ such that the sum of the time for transmitting the real-time traffic that arrived with deadline before or at time t exceeds the available time in the interval $[0, t]$. Equation 5 also means that there exists an upper bound, written B, of t if the set R is not schedulable. It follows thus that the set R is schedulable if there is no time t in the interval $[0, B]$ such that Equation 5 is satisfied.

Next, we discuss the schedulability condition for the set $F = R \cup E$, where E is the set of the non-real-time flows. In our approach the PS is responsible for servicing the non-real-time traffic. The PS executes periodically with higher priority than the EDF scheduler. Let T_s and C_s be a period and the amount of reserved time within a period of PS, respectively. We use $I(t)$ to denote the maximum amount of time available for PS in the interval $[0, t]$. That is,

$$I(t) = \lfloor \frac{t}{T_s} \rfloor C_s + Min(C_s, t - \lfloor \frac{t}{T_s} \rfloor T_s) \tag{6}$$

where $Min(a, b)$ is the smaller value between a and b.

In this case Theorem 3 describes the condition that the set F is not schedulable.

Theorem 3 *A set F is not EDF-schedulable if and only if there exist a time $t \geq 0$ such that*

$$t - I(t) < \frac{1}{c} \sum_{i \in R} A_i^*(t - d_i) \tag{7}$$

where c is the capacity of the link.

Proof: Since the PS scheduler periodically executes with a priority greater than the EDF scheduler, the available amount of link capacity for the real-time flows is $c(t - I(t))$ in the interval $[0, t]$. If the maximum real-time traffic arrivals with a deadline earlier than or equal to t, i.e., $A_i^*(t - d_i)$, exceeds the capacity of the link available for R, a deadline violation occurs. Thus, Equation 7 should be derived from Equation 4 in Theorem 2.   □

Finally we can give the schedulability condition for the set F $(= R \cup E)$. From Theorem 3, the set F is schedulable if and only if there is no time t in the interval $[0, B]$ such that Equation 7 is satisfied, where B is an upper bound of time t when the set F is not schedulable. We define U as

$$\frac{C_s}{T_s} + \frac{1}{c} \sum_{i \in R} \rho_i \tag{8}$$

We assume $U < 1$. The schedulability condition is given as follows:

Theorem 4 *For a given time t, we assign the value of B as followings:*
If $C_s = Min(C_s, t - \lfloor \frac{t}{T_s} \rfloor T_s)$,

$$B = \frac{\sum_{i \in R}(\sigma_i - \rho_i d_i)}{c(1 - U)} \tag{9}$$

Otherwise,

$$B = \frac{(T_s - C_s) + \sum_{i \in R}(\sigma_i - \rho_i d_i)}{c(1 - U)} \tag{10}$$

If for all $t' \in [0, B]$, Equation 7 in Theorem 3 is not satisfied, then the set F is EDF-schedulable.

Proof: From Theorem 3, if the set F is not schedulable, there exists a time t such that Equation 7 satisfies. It also follows that if the set F is not schedulable, an upper bound, written B, of time t can be obtained from Equation 7. So, in order to determine whether the set F is not schedulable or not, we only need to find a time in the interval $[0, B]$ such that Equation 7 is satisfied. If there doesn't exist a time t below B such that Equation 7 is satisfied, then the set F

is schedulable all the time. Therefore, to prove this theorem, we only need to give the value of upper bound B.

First of all, we calculate $A_i^*(t)$ and $I(t)$ in the Equation 7. Since we assume that the real-time traffic is characterized by the (σ, ρ)-model, $A_i^*(t) = \sigma_i + \rho_i t$, where σ_i is a burst parameter and ρ_i is a rate parameter of flow i, respectively. $I(t)$ is obtained using Equation 6. The value of $I(t)$ can be two cases.

In case that C_s is less than $t - \lfloor \frac{t}{T_s} \rfloor T_s$, from Equation 7,

$$t - (\lfloor \frac{t}{T_s} \rfloor C_s + C_s) < \frac{1}{c} \sum_{i \in R}(\sigma_i + \rho_i(t - d_i))$$

$$t - ((\frac{t}{T_s} - 1)C_s + C_s) < \frac{1}{c} \sum_{i \in R}(\sigma_i + \rho_i(t - d_i))$$

$$t(1 - \frac{C_s}{T_s}) < \frac{1}{c} \sum_{i \in R}(\sigma_i + \rho_i(t - d_i))$$

$$t(1 - \frac{C_s}{T_s} - \frac{1}{c} \sum_{i \in R} \rho_i) < \frac{1}{c} \sum_{i \in R}(\sigma_i - \rho_i d_i)$$

By substituting U for Equation 8,

$$t < \frac{\sum_{i \in R}(\sigma_i - \rho_i d_i)}{c(1 - U)}$$

This follows that the upper bound is Equation 9. In case that C_s is not less than $t - \lfloor \frac{t}{T_s} \rfloor T_s$, we can obtain Equation 10 using similar method. This proves the theorem.   □

Using Theorem 4, we can obtain the algorithm for admission control. In Figure 2, we give an algorithm to check the schedulability whenever a new real-time flow joins the packet scheduler. We can easily see that this algorithm can be executed in time $O(Bn)$, where B is the upper bound in Equation 9 or 10, and n is the number of real-time flows. The B is a function of both length and magnitude of the input and hence the complexity of deciding schedulability is pseudo-polynomial time [5]. Since U and B can be computed in time $O(n)$ respectively and hence do not affect the overall complexity of deciding schedulability.

5   Experiments

Since proposed admission control algorithm has pseudo-polynomial time complexity, we need to investigate that it can be used in practical systems with little run-time overhead. We generate a range of traffic patterns that are characterized by the (σ, ρ)-model. In our simulations, we take $\rho = 10^p Kbps$ where p is uniformly distributed in $[1, 3]$. And we take $\sigma = r * \rho Kb$ where r is uniformly

ADMISSION_CONTROL_ALGORITHM(
input : set R of real-time flows with (σ_i, ρ_i, d_i) and the PS parameter (C_s, T_s)
output : schedulable or not)

```
 1. begin
 2.     calculate U;          /* Equ. 8 */
 3.     if U ≥ 1 then
 4.         return(not schedulable);
 5.     endif;
 6.     calculate B;          /* Equ. 9 and 10 */
 7.     for t=1 to B do
 8.         calculate I(t);          /* Equ. 6 */
 9.         if Equ. 7 is satisfied then
10.             return(not schedulable);
11.         endif
12.     endfor
13.     return(schedulable);
14. end.
```

Fig. 2. Admission Control Algorithm

distributed in [0.8, 1.6]. We take a delay requirement $d = 10^s * 30ms$, where s is uniformly distributed in [0, 0.52], thus d ranging in [30ms, 100ms]. The generated traffic patterns include the typical video and audio traffic [11]. We assume the link has a capacity of 155 Mbps.

For PS parameter, we take $T_s = 1000$ ms and $C_s = 100, 300$ and 500 ms. We denote by $U_s = \frac{C_s}{T_s}$ the utilization of PS, thus $U_s = 0.1, 0.3$ and 0.5. U_s means the ratio of time PS is servicing the non-real-time flows to total time. For each U_s, we perform a simulation run. In one simulation run, we generate flows till U in Equ. 8 reaches 1.0 and compute upper bound B using Equ. 9 and Equ. 10. We use mili second as time unit of B because the local delays are usually assigned using mili second time unit (i.e., 50 ms, 100 ms). We use the method of independent replications to generate 90% confidence intervals. We are interested in the value of Bn when the number of admitted real-time flows (i.e., n) is at its maximum.

Figure 3 illustrates the results of our simulation. We can find the flex point, called the knee, beyond which B increases rapidly but the increase in n is small. Before the knee, B does not increase significantly as n increases. Consider that PS is assigned the 10% of the total link capacity (i.e., $U_s = 0.1$). In this case, the maximum number of n is 626 and B becomes 360,913 ms. Hence, in the worst case the algorithm needs the iterations of 626*360913 (=225,931,538). If we limit n to the point less than or equal to the knee, B will be much the smaller value compared with its maximum value and thus we are able to decrease the number of iterations dramatically. To do so, we make the usable link capacity be smaller than the total link capacity. For example, if we want to limit the usable link capacity to 90% of the total link capacity then we modify $U > 0.9$ in line 3 of

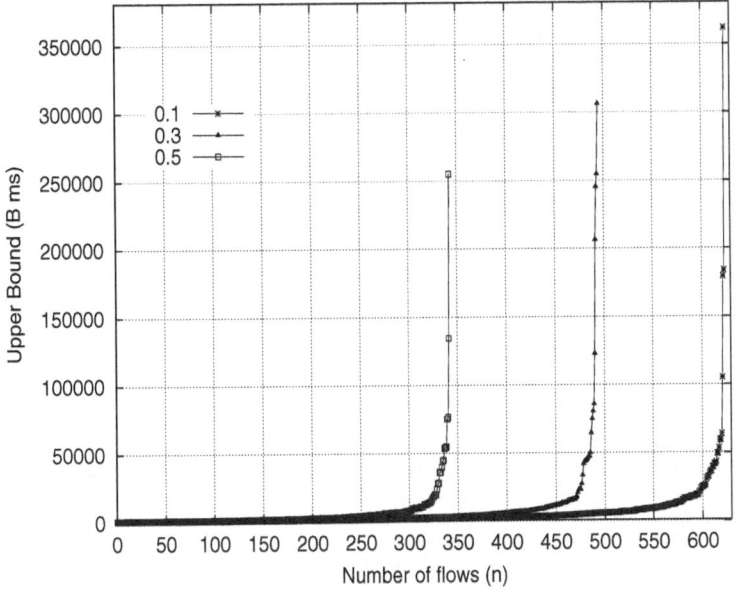

Fig. 3. Experiment result

admission control algorithm. Table 1 (a) and (b) shows the number of iterations (i.e., Bn) when we limit the usable link capacity to 90% and 80% of the total link capacity, respectively.

Table 1. Limiting the link utilization

U_s	0.1	0.3	0.5
n	560	428	274
B	9178	6631	4553
Bn	5,139,680	2,838,068	1,247,522

(a) Limit is 90%

U_s	0.1	0.3	0.5
n	476	358	202
B	4059	2821	1693
Bn	1,932,084	1,009,918	341,986

(b) Limit is 80%

For example, if the link capacity limit is 80% and U_s is 0.3 then the number of iterations is 1,009,918. Hence, there is not much difficulty in finding that the admission control algorithm can be used in the practical systems with little runtime overhead. However, if we limit the maximum utilization of link to a smaller value than 100%, the maximum number of flows decreases. In practice, therefore, we consider tradeoff between the maximum number of admitted real-time flows and the runtime overhead of admission control algorithm.

6   Related Work and Discussion

Recently a number of real-time packet scheduling schemes based on EDF discipline were proposed[12,7,3,4,1]. However, these works did not consider non-real-time traffic since original EDF scheduling algorithm cannot deal with non-real-time tasks. In previous works not based on EDF, there were some packet scheduling schemes to support both real-time packets and non-real-time packets. In [15], *Rate-Controlled Static Priority* (RCSP) was presented. A RCSP scheduler consists of multiple prioritized FCFS queues and services packets using a non-preemptive static-priority discipline: which non-preemptively chooses packets in FCFS order from the highest-priority non-empty queue. Non-real-time packets have the lowest static priority and are serviced only when there are no real-time packets. While RCSP can provide service guarantees to real-time flows at a *low cost*, it cannot provide high-performance to non-real-time traffic. In [10], *Rotating Combined Queueing* (RCQ) was proposed. RCQ uses frame-based scheduling, where each connection is allocated some number of packet slots in a fixed frame time. RCQ can provide good performance to non-real-time traffic by allowing bursty traffic to utilize unused bandwidth. However, it cannot efficiently support communications with low delay bounds requirements since the worst-case packet delay is coupled to the frame size, which is determined by link capacity, bandwidth allocation granularity and packet size.

In this work, we apply aperiodic server method to EDF-based packet scheduling in order to efficiently support both non-real-time traffic and real-time traffic. Proposed scheme consists of two queues, each of which has its own packet scheduler. By reserving the link capacity for each scheduler, it can guarantee the schedulability of real-time traffic. By assigning higher priority to the non-real-time packet scheduler, it can provide good performance to non-real-time traffic. The drawback of proposed scheme is that run-time overhead of admission control algorithm can be high. It highly depends on the value of B that must be computed using traffic parameters. The time unit also can affect the value of B. In the experiment, we use mili second as the time unit. If the time unit should be smaller one, then the value B will be higher. If the run-time overhead becomes too high, we can reduce it dramatically by the sacrifice of a small amount of link utilization (i.e., by the sacrifice of a small number of admittable real-time flows) as seen in Fig. 3.

7   Conclusion

Today's network switches must send and receive *real-time traffic* as well as *non-real-time traffic*. Recently a number of real-time packet scheduling algorithms based on *Earliest Deadline First* (EDF) policy have been studied in order to provide end-to-end bounded delay guarantees for real-time traffic. Even though the switches service only real-time communications, it usually receives a number of request messages for the purpose of management. This could lead to violation of schedulability of guaranteed real-time flows. Therefore, we need a mechanism considering non-real-time traffic in the EDF-based real-time packet scheduler.

In this paper, we propose a new admission control algorithm based on EDF policy considering both real-time flows and non-real-time flows in an integrated way. In proposed scheme, there are two packet schedulers: an *EDF scheduler* for handling real-time flows and a *Periodic Server(PS) Scheduler* for non-real-time flows. Proposed scheme can service non-real-time flows as soon as possible, preserving the schedulability of real-time flows that are already guaranteed. The computation complexity of proposed algorithm highly depends on the value of the traffic parameters and time unit. However, we show through simulations that the proposed algorithm can be used in practical systems with little runtime overhead.

References

1. M. Andrews. Probabilistic end-to-end delay bounds for earliest deadline first scheduling. In *IEEE INFOCOM 2000*, 2000.
2. R.L. Cruz. A calculus for network delay, part i:network elements in isolation. *IEEE Transactions on Information Theory*, 37(1):132–141, 1991.
3. Domenico Ferrari and Dinesh C. Verma. A scheme for real-time channel establishment in wide-area networks. *IEEE Journal on Selected Areas in Communications*, 8(3):368–379, 1990.
4. Victor Firoiu, James F. Kurose, and Donald F. Towsley. Efficient admission control for EDF schedulers. In *INFOCOM (1)*, pages 310–317, 1997.
5. M.R. Garey and D.S. Johnson. *Computing and Intractability, A Guide to the Theory of NP-Completeness*. W. H. Freeman Co., New York, 1979.
6. Leonidas Georgiadis, Roch Guerin, and Abhay K. Parekh. Optimal multiplexing on a single link: Delay and buffer requirements. In *INFOCOM (2)*, pages 524–532, 1994.
7. Leonidas Georgiadis, Roch Guérin, Vinod Peris, and Kumar N. Sivarajan. Efficient network QoS provisioning based on per node traffic shaping. *IEEE/ACM Transactions on Networking*, 4(4):482–501, 1996.
8. T.M. Ghazalie and T.P. Baker. Aperiodic servers in a deadline scheduling environment. *The Journal of Real-Time Systems*, 9:21–36, 1995.
9. J.P. Lehoczky J.K. Strosnider and L. Sha. The deferrable server algorithm for enhanced aperiodic responsiveness in hard realtime environments. *IEEE Trans. Computers*, 44(1):7391, 1995.
10. Jae H. Kim and Andrew A. Chien. Rotating combined queueing (RCQ): Bandwidth and latency guarantees in low-cost, high-performance networks. In *ISCA*, pages 226–236, 1996.
11. Edward W. Knightly, Dallas E. Wrege, Jorg Liebeherr, and Hui Zhang. Fundamental limits and tradeoffs of providing deterministic guarantees to VBR video traffic. In *Measurement and Modeling of Computer Systems*, pages 98–107, 1995.

12. Jörg Liebeherr, Dallas E. Wrege, and Domenico Ferrari. Exact admission control for networks with a bounded delay service. *IEEE/ACM Transactions on Networking*, 4(6):885–901, 1996.
13. C.L. Liu and J.W. Layland. Scheduling algorithms for multiprogramming in a hard real-time environment. *Journal of the ACM*, 20(1):46–61, 1973.
14. B. Sprunt. *Aperiodic task scheduling for real-time systems*. PhD thesis, Dept. of Electrical and Computer Engineering, Carnegie Mellon University, Pittsburg, PA, August 1990.
15. Hui Zhang and Domenico Ferrari. Rate-controlled static-priority queueing. In *INFOCOM (1)*, pages 227–236, 1993.

A Flexible Real-Time Hierarchical Multimedia Archive

Maria Eva Lijding, Pierre Jansen, and Sape Mullender

Fac. of Computer Science, University of Twente
P.O.Box 217, 7500AE Enschede, The Netherlands
lijding@cs.utwente.nl

Abstract. We present a hierarchical multimedia archive that can serve complex multimedia requests from tertiary storage. Requests can consist of multiple request units of streamed and non-streamed data. The request units can have arbitrary synchronization patterns.

Our scheduler *Promote-IT* promotes data from tertiary to secondary storage with real-time guarantees. Promote-IT uses an on-line heuristic algorithm to compute feasible schedules and a separate ASAP dispatcher to increase the efficiency of the resource usage. The heuristic algorithm runs in polynomial time. Schedules are optimized to give short response times to incoming requests.

Three major problems complicate this scheduling problem. First, the fragments of requested real-time data and their synchronization are unpredictable. Second, the medium switching times in tertiary storage are high, and the number of drives and robots is low compared to the number of removable media. Third, the shared resources in the tertiary storage system create resource contention problems.

1 Introduction

We present a flexible *hierarchical multimedia archive (HMA)* that can serve complex requests for the real-time delivery of any combination of media files it stores. Such requests can originate from any system that needs to combine multiple, separately stored media files into a continuous presentation. The HMA can also be used for the more simple case of a Video-on-Demand (VoD) application, where the requests are generally for only a single media file—a movie—to be played from beginning to end. To the best of our knowledge there is no other hierarchical storage system that provides flexible requests and time constraints.

A request can consist of multiple streams and non-streamed data that are synchronized sequentially or concurrently in arbitrary patterns. Examples are queries to multimedia databases to assemble a TV documentary, or a computer generated play list for a huge library of music videos and advertisement that produces a MTV-like program.

The multimedia data is stored in a tertiary-storage jukebox. Tertiary storage can store large amounts of data in a cost-effective way, which makes it eminently suitable for applications handling continuous-media files, large databases and backup data. A jukebox is a large tertiary storage device whose *removable storage media (RSM)*—e.g. CD, DVD, magneto-optical disk, tape—are loaded and unloaded from one or more drives by one or more robots.[1]

---

[1] The acronym RSM stands both for the singular and the plural. In the literature, a jukebox is sometimes called a Robotic Storage Library.

F. Boavida et al. (Eds.): IDMS/PROMS 2002, LNCS 2515, pp. 229–240, 2002.
© Springer-Verlag Berlin Heidelberg 2002

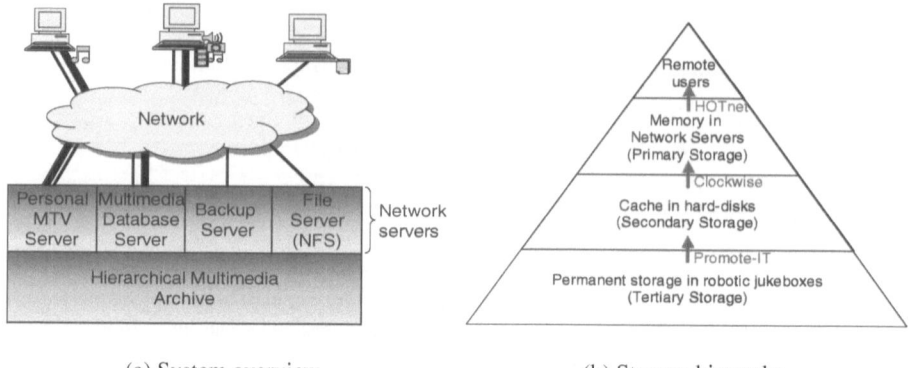

<table>
<tr><td>(a) System overview.</td><td>(b) Storage hierarchy.</td></tr>
</table>

Fig. 1. System overview with various application specific network servers and storage hierarchy showing the promotion mechanisms.

The problem with tertiary storage is that RSM switching times are high and the number of available drives and robots is low compared to the number of RSM. The RSM switching time in a jukebox is in the order of seconds or tens of seconds. This implies that multiplexing between two files stored in different RSM is many orders of magnitude slower than doing the same in secondary storage. Therefore, it is very important to schedule efficiently the use of the jukebox resources. On the other hand, the bandwidth offered by the devices in a jukebox is generally much higher than the one required by the end users. Thus, it makes good sense to stage data in secondary storage buffers from where it is delivered to the applications.

The hierarchical multimedia archive acts as a real-time file system [8] and, thus, does not offer application specific services. We envision multiple *network servers* running on top of the HMA where each provides a specific service to the users as shown in Figure 1(a). In the Distributed and Embedded Systems group at the University of Twente, we are concerned with providing end-to-end quality of service to the users. Our solution is to provide the in-time promotion of data from each level of the storage hierarchy to the next. Figure 1(b) shows the storage hierarchy of the overall system and the mechanisms used to promote data between contiguous storage levels.

The focus of this paper is *Promote-IT (Promote In Time)*, the jukebox scheduler that guarantees the in-time promotion of multimedia data from tertiary storage to secondary storage. In turn Clockwise [2] provides real-time access to data stored in secondary storage, which is used in HMA as cache, and finally *HOTnet* [10] provides real-time guarantees for the use of a local area network.

The main goal of Promote-IT is to guarantee that the data is buffered in secondary storage by the time applications need it and guarantee uninterrupted access to the data. Beyond this, Promote-IT tries to minimize the number of rejected requests, minimize the response time for ASAP requests, maximize the number of simultaneous users, and minimize the confirmation time. The scheduling problem to solve is $\mathcal{NP}$-hard. Therefore, it is not possible to find an optimal solution on-line. So Promote-IT uses an heuristic algorithm that computes near-optimal schedules in polynomial time.

Promote-IT gains part of its efficiency by separating the scheduling and dispatching functionality, because their goals are different. Although separating scheduling and dispatching seems a natural design decision, it has not been used in any other jukebox scheduler. The goal of the scheduler is to find feasible schedules for the requested data. Thus, the scheduler tries to build schedules as flexibly as possible and is not concerned about the optimal use of the resources. The dispatcher, instead, is concerned about utilizing the jukebox resources in an efficient manner. Thus, it dispatches the tasks to the hardware controllers as soon as possible (ASAP). The dispatcher may modify the schedules built by the scheduler as long as no task in the schedule is delayed and the sequence and resource constraints are respected.

To achieve a high degree of flexibility when building the schedules, we model the scheduling problem in a novel way. The model is a *flexible flow shop* [16] with three stages. The first stage is to load the RSM into a drive, the second to read data from the RSM, and the third to unload the RSM. The model uses shared resources to guarantee the mutual exclusive use of shared robots and RSM. Although solving this scheduling problem is far from trivial, it allows to build efficient schedules that deal with the resource contention problem correctly. Another advantage of this model is that it allows us to schedule for any type of jukebox architecture, e.g. one robot, multiple shared robots, dedicated robots, different drive models, etc.

The rest of this paper is organized as follows. Section 2 presents related work. Section 3 gives an overview of the system. Section 4 describes the jukebox scheduler. Section 5 discusses some important aspects of the implementation. Section 6 presents an evaluation of the system. Finally, Section 7 concludes the paper.

2   Related Work

Scheduling of tertiary storage has been studied mainly in the context of Video-on-Demand (VoD) systems and in systems with no time constraints. An assumption in typical VoD systems is that requests are for a single media file to be played continuously from beginning to end. To the best of our knowledge there is no previous work with flexible requests and time constraints.

Lau et al. [14] present an aperiodic scheduler for VoD systems, which can use two scheduling strategies: *aggressive* and *conservative*. When using the aggressive strategy each job is scheduled and dispatched as early as possible, while when using the conservative strategy each job is scheduled and dispatched as late as possible. These two strategies are similar to the strategies EDF (earliest deadline first) and LDL (latest deadline last) that we use in Promote-IT (see Section 4). However, there are very important differences. The most important difference is that their system dispatches the tasks exactly in the same way in which they are scheduled. Thus, they make bad use of the schedules built by the conservative strategy. The schedules they build are less efficient than ours, because they handle the RSM switch (load+unload) as one task and they try to schedule the reads only with the best drive. Furthermore, their scheduler can handle only jukeboxes in which all the drives are identical and the load and unload time are constant for every drive and every RSM. Promote-IT, instead, is able to handle any type of jukebox architecture, including jukeboxes in which the drives are different.

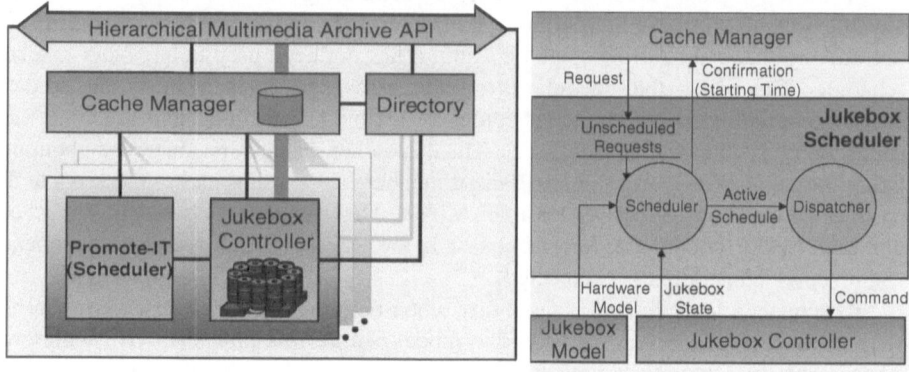

(a) Hierarchical Multimedia Archive.   (b) Jukebox Scheduler.

Fig. 2. Architecture of the Hierarchical Multimedia Archive and the Jukebox Scheduler.

Chan et al. [5] stage a movie completely in secondary storage before it is displayed to the user, because their goal is to provide interactive VoD services. The movies are staged First-Come-First-Serve (FCFS), which in general provides bad response times. This type of algorithm is not appropriate for the flexible type of requests that the HMA handles, because a FCFS approach cannot deal with relative deadlines.

We now discuss briefly other approaches that, although they are interesting, do not deal with the RSM contention problem, which means that they cannot guarantee that an RSM is not assigned to two different drives during the same time period. Therefore, these schedulers cannot be used for jukeboxes with multiple drives and are not suitable to be used with most commercial big jukeboxes, which have multiple drives. Lau et al. [15] propose two algorithms, the round-robin and the least-slack algorithm, which break up the requests into time-slices and try to build a schedule with the time-slices of the different requests. Golubchik et al. [9] propose a periodic scheduler called *Rounds*. Cha et al. [4] use a jukebox scheduler based on a periodic EDF scheduler, which additionally does not deal with the robot contention problem.

Prabhakar et al. [17] and Triantafillou et al. [19] schedule requests without real-time deadlines in order to minimize the mean response time. The conclusion of their work is that as much data as possible should be read from an RSM when the RSM is loaded in the drive. This supports the approach we used in Promote-IT where we read all the data requested from an RSM before the RSM is unloaded. Hillyer et al. [13,12, 11] compare different scheduling algorithms for retrieving data from a magnetic tape without real-time requirements.

3   System Overview

This section gives an overview of the hierarchical multimedia archive (Figure 2(a)). The data of the archive can be stored in multiple jukeboxes. Each jukebox has its own scheduler and controller, thus providing scalability to the system, because the complexity of the scheduler does not increase by incorporating more jukeboxes.

A request arriving at the system is filtered by the cache manager, which checks whether any of the requested data is already in the cache or scheduled for staging. It then consults the directory to find out in which jukebox(es) the remaining data is stored and sends the appropriate requests to them.

The cache manager may be physically distributed, as proposed by Brubeck et al. [3], to avoid becoming a bottle-neck. The directory is a database that contains meta-data about the contents of the jukeboxes and can easily be distributed or replicated. In this paper, we do not address the cache manager and directory any further, but consider only the scheduling of tertiary storage.

Figure 2(b) shows the architecture of *Promote-IT (Promote In Time)*, the jukebox scheduler of our system. Promote-IT schedules incoming requests on-line, re-computing the schedule every time a request arrives. It generates a new schedule to replace the currently *active schedule* only if it can guarantee that including the new request does not lead to missed deadlines. The dispatcher uses the active schedule to send commands to the jukebox controller to move RSM and stage data into secondary storage. The dispatcher guarantees that the tasks are sent to the controller in time.

Once the HMA accepts and confirms a request from a user, it is committed to provide the service requested by the user. The confirmation includes the starting time assigned to the request. The user can start consuming the data at the starting time, with the system's guarantee that the flow of data will not be interrupted. The request and the confirmation are the contract between the user and the system.

3.1   Requests

The requests consist of a deadline and a set of request units u_{ij} for individual files, or part of files. The requests can represent any kind of static temporal relation between the request units. Formally we represent a request r_i with l_i request units as:

$$r_i = (\tilde{d}_i, asap_i, maxConf_i, \{u_{i1}, u_{i2}, \ldots, u_{il_i}\})$$
$$u_{ij} = (\Delta\tilde{d}_{ij}, m_{ij}, o_{ij}, s_{ij}, b_{ij})$$

The deadline $\tilde{d}_i$ of the request is the time by which the user must have guaranteed access to the data. The flag $asap_i$ indicates if the request should be scheduled as soon as possible. The maximum confirmation time $maxConf_i$ is the time the user is willing to wait in order to get a *confirmation* from the system, which indicates if the request was accepted or rejected. The relative deadline of the request unit $\Delta\tilde{d}_{ij}$ is the time at which the data of the request unit should be available, relative to the starting time of the request. The other parameters of the request unit m_{ij}, o_{ij}, s_{ij} and b_{ij} represent the RSM where the data is stored, the offset in the RSM, the size of the data, and the bandwidth with which the user wants to access the data, respectively.

The confirmation to the user indicates if the request is accepted or rejected. If the request is accepted, the confirmation contains the starting time st_i assigned to the request. The starting time must be less or equal to the deadline of the request ($st_i \leq \tilde{d}_i$). If the request is ASAP the scheduler tries to find the earliest value of st_i that will allow it to accept the request. The system must provide a confirmation before $maxConf_i$.

3.2   Hardware Model

Tertiary-storage jukeboxes are composed of the following hardware: *drives* to access the data in the RSM, *shelves* where the RSM are kept and *robots* to move the RSM from the shelves to the drives and vice versa.

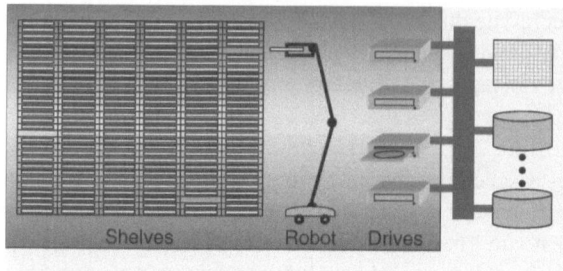

In big jukeboxes the number of shelves is at least two orders of magnitude larger than the number of drives and the number of robots. Our jukebox, for example, has 720 shelves, 4 drives and 1 robot. Jukeboxes are available for different types of RSM, for example CD, DVD, magnetic tape or magneto-optical disk.

Fig. 3. Jukebox architecture.

Figure 3 shows the architecture of a generic jukebox with four drives and one robot. The data from the drives can be transferred directly to secondary storage through a high-bandwidth connection.

The time it takes to load and unload a drive depends on different factors: opening and closing time of the drive, spin-up/-down time in the case of disks, rewind time for tapes, and the distance between the drive and the shelf where the RSM is kept.

We use a model of the hardware to predict the time that the system will need for operations on robots and drives. We have validated the model against our actual hardware and use it both for constructing the schedules and as a simulator in our experiments.

4   Promote-IT

Promote-IT is the jukebox scheduler of the hierarchical multimedia archive. It guarantees that the data is promoted to secondary storage in time. Promote-IT schedules the incoming requests on-line, building a new schedule that includes all the request units that still need scheduling plus the request units of the new request. Promote-IT provides short response times, short confirmation times and makes good use of the jukebox resources.

We now formalize the scheduling problem. Let us assume that at time t_0 request r_k arrives at a jukebox scheduler. At time t_0 the jukebox scheduler has a set of request units from previous requests, $\mathcal{U}$, that have not yet been dispatched to the jukebox. The goal of the scheduling algorithm is to find a feasible schedule for the new set $\mathcal{U}'$, which includes the request units of the new request r_k.

$$\mathcal{U} \subseteq \{u_{ij} \mid i < k, j \leq l_i\}$$
$$\mathcal{U}' = \mathcal{U} \cup \{u_{k1}, u_{k2}, \ldots, u_{kl_k}\}$$

The starting time of the request must not be later than its deadline, so $st_k \leq \tilde{d}_k$. If the request is ASAP, the scheduler assigns the request the earliest possible starting time st_k that will allow it to be incorporated into the system. Thus, the scheduler must find the minimum starting time st_k that makes $\mathcal{U}'$ schedulable. The scheduler tries different candidate starting times st_k^x and selects the earliest feasible st_k^x. If the request is not

ASAP, the scheduler assigns it the starting time corresponding to its deadline. If the deadline of the request cannot be met, then the scheduler rejects the request.

Determining if the set $\mathcal{U}'$ is schedulable is an $\mathcal{NP}$-hard problem and so is finding the the minimum starting time that makes $\mathcal{U}'$ schedulable. We use a polynomial heuristic algorithm to schedule the requests. In order to simplify the problem we assume that the user can start consuming the data of a request unit only·once all its data has been buffered. In this way we can compute a deadline for each request unit in a request, namely, $\tilde{d}_{ij} = st_i + \Delta\tilde{d}_{ij}$.

The scheduler uses an iterative algorithm to schedule a request. The algorithm keeps a list of candidate starting times already analyzed and the schedules produced for them. The structure of the algorithm is the following:

1. Generate a candidate starting time st_k^x and update the deadline of each request unit so that $\tilde{d}_{kj} = st_k^x + \Delta\tilde{d}_{kj}$. The algorithm uses a variation of the bisection method for finding roots of mathematical functions.
2. Compute the *medium schedules* for the RSM corresponding to the request units in $\mathcal{U}'$. The medium schedule determines the sequence in which the requested data of an RSM is read.[2] We read all the requested data of an RSM at once. Therefore, there is at most one medium schedule per RSM. As there may be different drive models in the jukebox, we compute a medium schedule for each drive.
3. Model as a *flexible flow shop* scheduling problem with three stages (FF_3) [16]. The first stage is to load an RSM to a drive, the second stage is to read the data from the RSM and the third is to unload the RSM. The scheduling problem is represented as a set of jobs $\mathcal{J}$, where each job J_j must execute one task corresponding to each stage $(J_j = \{T_{1j}, T_{2j}, T_{3j}\})$. There is at most one job for every RSM, because the read task (T_{2j}) involves reading all the requested data from the RSM.
4. Compute the resource assignment. The algorithm must incorporate each job $J_i \in \mathcal{J}$ into the schedule. If the algorithm succeeds in finding a valid resource assignment, the output of this step is a feasible schedule S^x; otherwise $S^x = \emptyset$. The pair (S^x, st_k^x) is incorporated into the list of analyzed solutions.
5. Repeat from step 1 until the bisection stop-criteria is fulfilled for the list of candidates, i.e. the time difference between the last unsuccessful and first successful candidate is smaller than a threshold.
6. Select the best solution. The algorithm selects the earliest candidate starting time for which step 4 could compute a feasible schedule $(\min\{st_k^x \mid S^x \neq \emptyset\})$. If there is no such st_k^x the request r_k is placed in the list of unscheduled requests to be scheduled at a later time. Otherwise the scheduler confirms the starting time st_k to the user and replaces the active schedule with the new feasible schedule.

The problem model we use allows us to to represent any kind of jukeboxes (e.g. jukeboxes with one shared robot, multiple shared robots, multiple dedicated robots). We use additional shared resources to guarantee the mutual exclusive use of the robots and drives. The model imposes the restriction that all the data requested from an RSM must be

---

[2] Finding the optimal sequence is equivalent to solving the *asymmetric traveling salesman problem with time windows* [1], and is thus an $\mathcal{NP}$-hard problem. We use an algorithm that finds a near-optimal sequence.

read before the RSM is unloaded. This restriction results in a good system performance, because with each switch effective bandwidth is lost. Prabhalkar [17] shows that reading all the requested data from an RSM at once is good even when the access time in a loaded RSM dominates over the switching time.

In step 4 we use a branch-and-bound algorithm to prune the tree of possible assignments of jukebox resources to the jobs in $\mathcal{J}$. The branch-and-bound algorithm uses the *best-drive heuristic* to choose which drive will be tried first to schedule a job and prune from the tree the branches corresponding to drives which offer a worse solution. When pruning the tree, the algorithm may be throwing away a feasible solution that an optimal scheduler would find. But searching the whole tree of solutions is computationally impossible. For comparison, we have also implemented an optimal scheduler, but it can take up to several days to compute a feasible schedule for one new request, in contrast to the few milliseconds needed by Promote-IT. The complexity of our algorithm is $O(m!\, n)$, where m is the number of drives and n is the number of jobs in $\mathcal{J}$.

We have defined four strategies to incorporate the jobs to the schedule: *earliest deadline first* (EDF), *earliest starting time first* (ESTF), *latest deadline last* (LDL) and *latest starting time last* (LSTL). They are classified by two axes indicating the way in which the jobs are incorporated to the schedule: *Front-to-Back* and *Back-to-Front*, and the parameter of the tasks to use for sorting the jobs: *deadline* or *latest starting time (LST)*. The LST of a task is the latest time at which a task should start in order not to miss its deadline. None of the strategies is absolutely better than the others, because each strategy can find schedules that cannot be found by the others. However, their performance varies considerably depending on the usage scenario.

Using the F2B strategy each job is scheduled as early as possible and the jobs are incorporated to the front of the schedule in increasing order of 'restrictiveness', in such a way that the most 'restrictive' jobs are incorporated to the schedule first. In addition the tasks are also incorporated F2B, scheduling first the load T_{1j}, then the read T_{2j} and finally the unload T_{3j}. When using the B2F strategy, each job is scheduled as late as possible and the jobs are incorporated to the back of the schedule in decreasing order of 'restrictiveness'. The tasks in turn are incorporated B2F, scheduling first the unload T_{3j}, then the read T_{2j} and finally the load T_{1j}. In both cases, the goal is that the most restrictive tasks should be at the front of the resulting schedule, while the less restrictive tasks should be at the back. We determine the 'restrictiveness' of a job using either the deadline or the LST of the read tasks.

Figure 4 shows an example of the schedules built for a set of four jobs with EDF and LDL, and a jukebox with one robot and two identical drives. Both drives and the robot are initially empty. For the sake of simplicity we assume in this example that the load and unload time is constant for all drives and shelves.

Both strategies can build feasible schedules, but these schedules are quite different. Many times LDL is more successful in finding feasible schedules than EDF because it delays unloads as much as possible. In that way, the unloads tend to interfere less with other jobs, as illustrated by the unloading of J_1 in the example. If J_2 would have only a slightly earlier deadline, EDF would no longer find a feasible schedule because its load would overlap J_1's unload. The LDL-schedule would not be affected by the change.

The graphic at the bottom shows the resource utilization resulting from using the LDL-schedule with the ASAP dispatcher. This schedule is very compact and makes excellent use of the resources, specially of the shared robot. The dispatcher can easily fill the holes in an LDL-schedule by successively moving tasks to the front. The holes in an EDF-schedule allow no such optimization, except by small amounts when a task finished earlier than predicted. In the dispatched schedule there are two places where the dispatcher created a 'jump', changing the order of the tasks in the robot schedule.

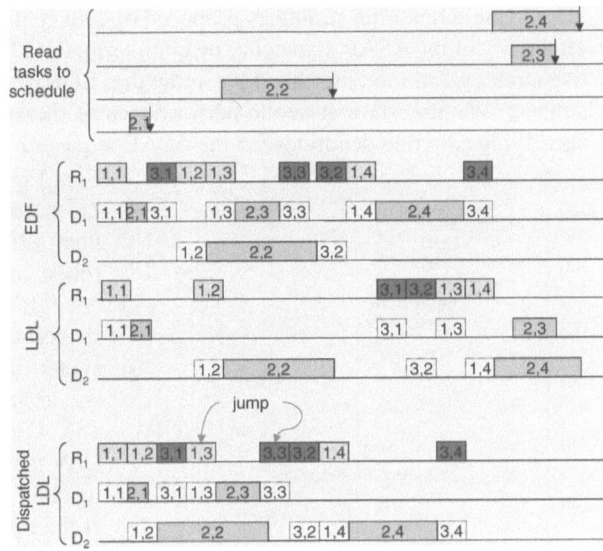

Fig. 4. Example of an EDF and LDL schedule. (i, j of T_{ij} shown in the boxes)

5   Implementation and Simulation

We have implemented the HMA in Java 1.3 on Linux. The system can run the same code when using a real jukebox and a simulation of a jukebox. When using a real jukebox, the jukebox controller sends commands to the jukebox and waits for the replies. When using simulated hardware, it places an event on the event queue simulator indicating the time at which it should be woken up. The drive controller uses the Java Native Interface (JNI) to call C functions in order to open and close the drives and get drive specific information. We use the same hardware models to simulate the behavior of the jukebox and to estimate the processing time needed for the different tasks to schedule.

At present the cache manager uses a Linux file system to store the data, which does not provide real-time guarantees. However, it seems to be good enough for the applications we have tested and it is of no relevance when simulating. The network servers use the Java Media Framework [18] to stream data to the remote users. Although JMF cannot provide real-time guarantees, it is useful for building prototype network servers. The next step is to integrate Clockwise and HOTnet into the HMA.

6   Evaluation

In this section we present a brief evaluation of the jukebox scheduler. We compare the different scheduling strategies used in Promote-IT and show the superiority of Promote-

IT over the scheduling strategies proposed by Lau et al. [14].[3] On one hand we show the effectivity of the ASAP dispatcher by comparing the LDL strategy against the conservative strategy. On the other hand we show that EDF performs better than the aggressive strategy. We also show how the performance of the system improves considerably by specifying concrete deadlines for the ASAP requests.

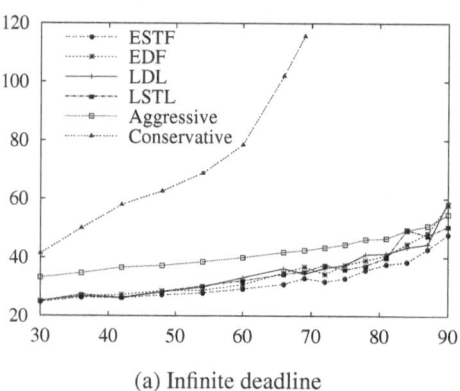

(a) Infinite deadline

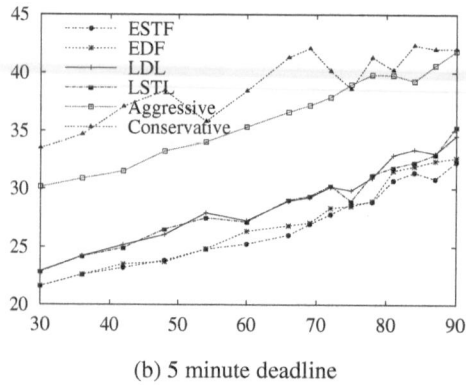

(b) 5 minute deadline

Fig. 5. Mean response time (y-axis; seconds) over system load (req./hour) with CD jukebox.

For Figures 5(a) and 5(b) we used the hardware model of our DAX jukebox [7], which has 720 shelves, 1 robot and 4 drives—three CD readers (1.75 MBps) and one 8X CD reader/writer (1.17 MBps). The average switch time is 44 seconds. For Figure 6 we assume that the jukebox has four 16X DVD drives. The DVD drives use CAV technology (constant angular velocity) and the transfer speed is 6.45 MBps at the inner track and 19.53 MBps at the outer track.

The test set used consist of 1000 ASAP requests for audio, video and discrete-data. The data requested follows a Zipf distribution, because this type of distribution represents correctly the pattern of requests on storage systems [6]. In the first case the deadline of the requests is infinite, so the system does not reject any request and the response times can become very high. In the second and third case the requests have a deadline of 5 minutes and a maximum confirmation time of 30 seconds, so if the scheduler does not succeed within that limit it rejects the request.

The cache manager uses *least recently used* (LRU) policy. The capacity of the cache is 10% of the jukebox capacity. The cache is preloaded with the results of another simulated run. The requested data produced in average 57% cache hits when using the CD jukebox and 60% when using the DVD jukebox. This did not change significantly when varying the system load or the scheduling strategy.

Figure 5(a) clearly shows that the conservative strategy performs very badly, even when the system load is not very high, because it makes a poor use of the jukebox resources by dispatching as late as possible. The graphic also shows that EDF performs

---

[3] We have extended their aggressive and conservative strategies for jukeboxes with different drive characteristics.

better than the aggressive strategy. This is mainly noticeable when the system load is low, because the aggressive strategy leaves the drives loaded until they are needed again by the system. Thus, when the system load is low, the robot is left idle while it could be unloading an RSM and freeing a drive. Leaving the drives loaded could be a good idea if the probability of receiving new requests for an RSM loaded in a drive would be high, but given the big number of RSM in the jukebox the probability is very low.

Figure 5(b) shows a considerable improvement in the response time of Promote-IT when the requests have deadlines and the scheduler is able to reject some requests. The improvement is considerable, even if the percentage of rejected requests is less than 2%. The aggressive strategy does not improve much, because it leaves the drives loaded. The rejection ratio of the conservative strategy is high (between 1 and 11%).

Figure 6 shows the performance of the different scheduling strategies of Promote-IT and the aggressive strategy when using the DVD jukebox. This graphic does not show the conservative strategy, because its rejection ratio is so high, that the mean response time is not comparable to the others. In this architecture the robot is the clear bottleneck in the system. The utilization of the robot reaches nearly 95%, while the utilization of the drive is less than 35%. The two Back-to-Front strategies show the best performance as the load increases, because Back-to-Front makes better use of the robot.

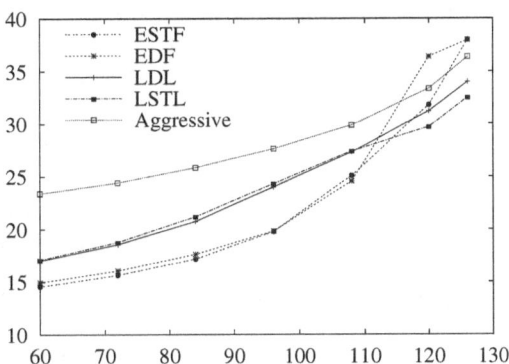

Fig. 6. Mean response time (y-axis; seconds) over system load (req./hour) with DVD jukebox and 5 min deadline.

7   Conclusions and Future Work

We present a hierarchical multimedia archive that provides flexible real-time access to large volumes of data stored in tertiary storage. Promote-IT guarantees the in-time promotion of data from tertiary to secondary storage. Promote-IT is a key component in the end-to-end real-time delivery system that spans from tertiary storage to end-user applications.

We describe a polynomial heuristic algorithm to solve the scheduling problem, whose optimal solution is $\mathcal{NP}$-hard to find. Promote-IT provides short response times while using the jukebox resources efficiently and performs better than comparable schedulers. At present we are comparing the performance of Promote-IT against that of an optimal scheduler. The results obtained so far indicate that Promote-IT performs very near the optimal. We are also comparing the performance of Promote-IT against a new periodic scheduler that uses the robot in a cyclic way, called *cached early quantum scheduler (CEQS)*. Promote-IT performs clearly better that CEQS with all jukebox architectures and request sets we have tested so far.

A distinguishing feature of Promote-IT is the separation of scheduling and dispatching. The scheduler can build flexible schedules with holes in which the resources are scheduled to be idle, while the ASAP dispatcher dispatches each task as soon as possible. This feature makes the Back-to-Front strategy, where each task is scheduled as late as possible, a competitive strategy.

References

1. N. Ascheuer, M. Fischetti, and M. Grötschel. Solving the asymmetric travelling salesman problem with time windows by branch-and-cut. *Math. Program.*, 90(3):475–506, 2000.
2. P. Bosch. *Mixed-media file systems*. PhD thesis, University of Twente, June 1999.
3. D. W. Brubeck and L. A. Rowe. Hierarchical storage management in a distributed vod system. *IEEE Multimedia*, 3(3):37–47, 1996.
4. H. Cha, J. Lee, J. Oh, and R. Ha. Video server with tertiary storage. In *Proc. of the Eighteenth IEEE Symposium on Mass Storage Systems*, April 2001.
5. S.-H. G. Chan and F. A. Tobagi. Designing hierarchical storage systems for interactive on-demand video services. In *Proc. of IEEE Multimedia Applications, Services and Technologies*, June 1999.
6. A. L. Chervenak. *Tertiary Storage: An Evaluation of New Applications*. PhD thesis, Dept. of Comp. Science, University of California, Berkeley, December 1994.
7. Chess Engineering bv. *DAX Software Architecture Manual, Version 0.5*, March 1998.
8. D. Gemmel, H. Vin, D. Kandlur, P. Rangan, and L. Rowe. Multimedia storage servers: A tutorial and survey. *IEEE Computer*, 28(5):40–49, November 1995.
9. L. Golubchik and R. K. Rajendran. A study on the use of tertiary storage in multimedia systems. In *Proc. of Joint NASA/IEEE Mass Storage Systems Symposium*, March 1998.
10. F. Hanssen, P. Hartel, T. Hattink, P. Jansen, J. Scholten, and J. Wijnberg. A Real-Time ethernet network at home. In M. G. Harbour, editor, *Research report 36/2002*, pages 5–8, Vienna, Austria, June 2002. Real-Time Systems Group, Vienna Univ. of Technology.
11. B. K. Hillyer, R. Rastogi, and A. Silberschatz. Scheduling and data replication to improve tape jukebox performance. In *Proc. of International Conference on Data Engineering*, pages 532–541, 1999.
12. B. K. Hillyer and A. Silberschatz. Random I/O scheduling in online tertiary storage systems. In *Proc. of the 1996 ACM SIGMOD International Conference on Management of Data*, pages 195–204, June 1996.
13. B. K. Hillyer and A. Silberschatz. Scheduling non-contiguous tape retrievals. In *Proc. of Joint NASA/IEEE Mass Storage Systems Symposium*, pages 113 – 123, March 1998.
14. S.-W. Lau and J. C. Lui. Scheduling and replacement policies for a hierarchical multimedia storage server. In *Proc. of Multimedia Japan 96, International Symposium on Multimedia Systems*, March 1996.
15. S.-W. Lau, J. C. Lui, and P. Wong. A cost-effective near-line storage server for multimedia system. In *Proc. of the 11th International Conference on Data Engineering*, pages 449–456, March 1995.
16. M. Pinedo. *Scheduling: Theory, Algorithms and Systems*. Prentice Hall, 1995.
17. S. Prabhakar, D. Agrawal, A. E. Abbadi, and A. Singh. Scheduling tertiary I/O in database applications. In *Proc. of the 8th International Workshop on Database and Expert Systems Applications*, pages 722–727, September 1997.
18. Sun Microsystems. *Java Media Framework API Guide*, November 1999.
19. P. Triantafillou and I. Georgiadis. Hierarchical scheduling algorithms for near-line tape libraries. In *Proc. of the 10th International Conference and Workshop on Database and Expert Systems Applications*, pages 50–54, 1999.

Tradeoffs between Signaling and Resource Utilization in DiffServ Networks with Hierarchical Aggregation

Susana Sargento and Rui Valadas

University of Aveiro/Institute of Telecommunications, 3810 Aveiro, Portugal,
`susana@ua.pt, rv@det.ua.pt`

Abstract. In this paper, we analyze the tradeoffs between signaling and resource utilization in DiffServ networks partitioned in areas (hierarchical domains) using flow aggregates that can be dynamically adjusted. These tradeoffs are studied using two analytical models. In the first model, based on multidimensional birth-death processes, the offered load is detailed at the flow level, which allows accurate assessment of the signaling overhead. The second model accommodates time-varying offered loads, which allows studying the tradeoffs between the time-scale of the aggregate demand and the time-scale of signaling. Our results show that structuring a network domain in areas achieves high performance gains, which can contribute to reduce significantly the cost of core routers.

1 Introduction

In the IntServ architecture [1] resources are reserved for individual flows, i.e., on a per-flow basis, using the RSVP protocol. This implies that every time a new flow requests admission in the network, there must be signaling messages exchanged between the various network elements (hosts and routers) in the flow's path; moreover a state for each flow needs to be maintained at all routers along the flow's path. Both these factors contribute to the lack of scalability attributed to the IntServ architecture.

The reservation of resources for aggregates of flows (instead of individual flows) has been proposed in the context of DiffServ architecture [2,3,4,5,6], as a means of reducing significantly the signaling load and the state information stored at routers, while still providing the same QoS for real time flows. To support aggregation, an extension to RSVP that allows RSVP signaling messages to be hidden inside an aggregate, was recently defined in [3].

In the simplest case, all edge routers reserve bandwidth end-to-end, i.e., between ingress and egress routers of a network domain; this reservation can be updated in bulks much larger than the individual flow's bandwidth. Whenever a flow requests admission at an ingress router, the router checks if there is enough bandwidth to accept the flow on the (end-to-end) aggregate leading to the egress router. If resources are available, the flow will be accepted, without any need for signaling the core routers. Otherwise, the core routers will be signaled in an attempt to increase the aggregate's bandwidth. If this attempt succeeds, the flow will be admitted; otherwise, it will be rejected. Thus, with aggregation, signaling messages are only exchanged when the aggregate's bandwidth needs to be updated. The efficiency of aggregation depends heavily on the matching between the aggregate reservation and the aggregate demand.

F. Boavida et al. (Eds.): IDMS/PROMS 2002, LNCS 2515, pp. 241–254, 2002.
© Springer-Verlag Berlin Heidelberg 2002

If the bulk size is too large, the signaling load will be minimal but either reserved resources will be under-utilized or there will be unnecessarily blocked flows. Otherwise, with a too small bulk size the signaling load may approach that of per-flow signaling.

Within a large network domain, the need to set-up a lot of end-to-end aggregates can lead to poor resource utilization. One way to alleviate this problem is to partition the domain in areas and to have end-to-end aggregates between the area border routers. The resource utilization can be increased since an area aggregate can now be shared by flows coming from different domain edge routers. However, the signaling load also increases, since the area border routers need to be signaled on a per-flow basis. In fact, every time a new flow arrives at a domain edge router, there is the need to check if there are sufficient resources in every aggregate that the flow traverses within the domain. We recall that the facility for partitioning a domain into areas is already included in several routing protocols, e.g. OSPF and ISIS, and also in MPLS, again motivated by scalability reasons.

In this paper we analyze the tradeoffs between signaling load and resource utilization in a network domain that can be partitioned in areas. For this purpose we develop two different analytical models. In the first model, called per-flow load model, the offered load is detailed at the flow level. It assumes flow arrivals according to a Poisson process and exponentially distributed flow durations, such that a multidimensional birth-death process can describe the number of flows in a domain. Note that, although a Poisson model may not be appropriate for packet level traffic, it is widely used for flow level traffic, given that flows are usually generated by a large number of independent users. The second analytical model, called aggregate load model, accommodates an offered load whose average aggregate bandwidth is time-varying. In particular, we will assume a sinusoidal variation. In addition, we assess the impact of a measured data via discrete-event simulation.

This paper is organized as follows. Section 2 presents the system model. Sections 3 and 4 present the two analytical models: the per-flow load model and the aggregate load model. Section 5 discusses the results obtained with the analytical models, and the ones obtained with discrete-event simulations with a measured trace. Finally, section 6 concludes the paper.

Our contribution is the following. First we develop a per-flow load model that allows detailed characterization of the signaling load and the resource utilization in hierarchical network domains using aggregation. In particular, we introduce a signaling metric that is well adapted to the case of flow aggregates. Then, we develop an aggregate load model that permits studying the tradeoffs between the time-scale of the aggregate demand and the time-scale of signaling. Third, we carry out numerical studies that clearly show the advantages of structuring network domains into areas.

2   System Model

Consider a network domain partitioned in areas (Fig. 1). We refer to the routers in the edge of the domain as Domain Border Routers (DBRs), and the routers in the edge of each area as Area Border Routers (ABRs). DBRs also play the role of ABRs.

Sessions of packet flows are offered between DBRs and can be aggregated in pipes of reserved bandwidth called aggregates. We consider two cases, where the bandwidth is reserved end-to-end between DBRs (called end-to-end aggregates) or reserved end-to-end between ABRs (called area aggregates). In the first case, sessions traverse a single aggregate (between DBRs) whereas, in the second case, they traverse a concatenation of area aggregates. Each aggregate (end-to-end or area) will have ingress and egress routers and will (possibly) traverse several other routers, called internal routers. We assume that the aggregate's bandwidth can be adjusted over time through appropriate signaling. The ingress router of each aggregate will process signaling messages on a per-flow basis, whereas the internal routers will only process signaling messages when the aggregate's bandwidth is to be updated. Aggregates traverse one or more areas; in each area, they travel through an ABR pair (an ingress and an egress ABR). Let $\mathcal{J} = \{1, 2, ..., J\}$ be the set of ABR pairs in the domain. We consider that each ABR pair has a bottleneck capacity C_j, which corresponds to the lowest capacity among the links that belong to the route between the two ABRs. While the bandwidth of an aggregate can vary over time, it is limited by the bottleneck capacities of the ABR pairs it traverses. Let $\mathcal{H} = \{1, 2, ..., H\}$ be the set of aggregates. Aggregates are defined by (i) their bandwidth $r_h(t)$, (ii) their origin and destination ABRs, (iii) their route $\mathcal{R}_h \subseteq \mathcal{J}$ described by the ABR pairs they traverse and (iv) the number of internal routers m_h (i.e. not including ingress and egress routers) traversed by the aggregate.

As mentioned before, the traffic is offered between ingress and egress DBRs. Let $\mathcal{K}$ = $\{1, 2, ..., K\}$ be the set of sessions. We consider two offered traffic models. In the first one, called per-flow load model, a session k is characterized by (i) ingress and egress DBRs, (ii) route $\mathcal{H}_k \subseteq \mathcal{H}$ described in terms of the aggregates it traverses, (iii) the bandwidth of each packet flow b_k, (iv) and the traffic intensity $\rho_k = \lambda_k/\mu_k$. Specifically, to allow Markov modeling, we assume that packet flows arrive according to a Poisson process with rate λ_k and have exponentially distributed durations with mean $1/\mu_k$. We also consider that the bandwidth of an aggregate can be adjusted in steps of a bulk bandwidth, which we denote by q_h. The second model, called aggregate load model, considers a time-varying aggregated offered load. Session k is simply characterized by (i) ingress and egress DBRs, (ii) route $\mathcal{A}_k \subseteq \mathcal{J}$ described in terms of the ABR pairs it traverses and (iii) bandwidth $r_k(t)$. In this case, a session is meant to represent an aggregate of flows. We consider that the bandwidth of an aggregate is adjusted at the beginning of fixed time intervals, matching exactly the requirement for the interval (i.e. the maximum $r_k(t)$ over the interval).

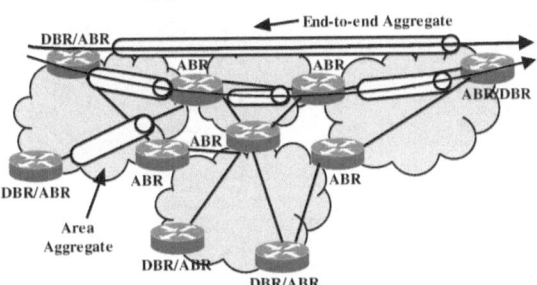

Fig. 1 System model.

We further define $\mathcal{K}_h \subseteq \mathcal{K}$ as the set of sessions that traverse aggregate h, and $\mathcal{H}_j = \{1, 2, ..., H_j\} \subseteq \mathcal{H}$ as the set of aggregates that traverse ABR pair j. Note also that different aggregates can be used for different service classes.

3   Per-Flow Load Model

In this section, we develop a continuous-time Markov process (more specifically, a multi-dimensional birth-death process) that characterizes the system state under the assumption of flow arrivals according to a Poisson process and exponentially distributed flow durations. The system state is characterized by vector $n = (n_1, n_2, ..., n_K)$, where n_k represents the number of flows of session k in the system. New flows requesting admission in the domain can be accepted if there is enough bandwidth in each of the aggregates they traverse; they can also be accepted if the bandwidth in all aggregates that do not observe previous condition can be increased to accommodate the flows.

We consider as a metric for assessing the signaling overhead and the amount of state information, the (total) rate of signaling messages processed by all routers in a domain. The signaling messages correspond to attempts of updating the reservation state at a router. In particular, a signaling message may attempt installing (or uninstalling) a flow or aggregate, or may attempt increasing (or decreasing) the bandwidth of an aggregate. With this metric we capture not only the number of reservations at routers but also the frequency of their updates, which is an important factor in terms of router cost. For example, the metric considered in [4] was the average number of flows in a domain. This only captures the amount of state information, which is clearly insufficient, especially when dealing with flow aggregates.

In a domain without aggregates (i.e., using only per-flow reservations), upon a flow arrival all routers in the flow's path will process a signaling message. In a domain with aggregates, signaling messages will always be processed by the ingress router of each aggregate, but the internal routers of the aggregates only process signaling messages if there is an attempt of updating the bandwidth of the aggregate. Note that, in the case of a session traversing multiple aggregates, as in the case of a domain with areas, a flow arrival may provoke attempts of bandwidth updates in more than one aggregate.

Consider the simple example of Fig. 2, that corresponds to a domain partitioned in 3

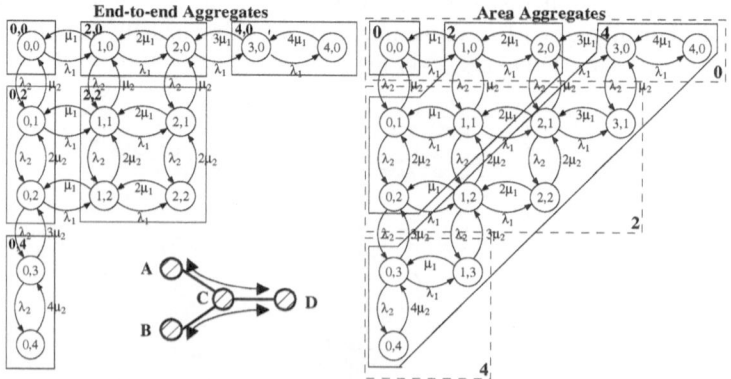

Fig. 2 Domain with 3 areas and respective state diagram with end-to-end and area aggregates.

areas. There are two sessions, one offered between DBRs A and D and the other between DBRs B and D. Fig. 2 represents the Markov chains for the cases of end-to-end aggregates and area aggregates. In the first case, there are 2 end-to-end aggregates; in the second one, there are 3 area aggregates. We consider that the flow's bandwidth of both sessions is $b_1 = b_2 = 1$ unit, the bulk size is $q_h = 2$ units in all aggregates and the bottleneck capacity of all ABR pairs is $C_j = 4$ units.

In Fig. 2, states are grouped according to the bandwidth of the corresponding aggregates; each group is enclosed in a polygon and its respective bandwidth is indicated in one of the polygon's corners. In the case of area aggregates we show polygons for areas CD (fixed line) and BC (dotted line). For example, in the case of end-to-end aggregates, in state $(2,1)$ both aggregates have 2 units of reserved bandwidth; the first aggregate from A to D is utilized at 100% and the second one, from B to D, at 50%. States $(3,1)$ and $(1,3)$ are only allowed in area aggregates, since there is a single aggregate in area CD shared by both sessions, whose bandwidth can grow up to the limit of 4 units; this illustrates the higher utilizations that can be achieved with this type of aggregation. Signaling messages attempting to update an aggregate's bandwidth are driven by transitions between states belonging to different polygons. Take the example of the state $(1,1)$ and area aggregates. Transitions to either state $(2,1)$ or state $(1,2)$, drive signaling messages in the aggregate of area CD, but not in the aggregates of other areas. However, the transition from state $(0,2)$ to state $(0,3)$ drive signaling messages both in area CD and in area AC (or BC).

In the general case, the state space of the Markov chain, is defined by:

$$S = \left\{ n \in I^K : \sum_{h \in \mathcal{H}_j} \left\lceil \sum_{k \in \mathcal{K}_h} n_k b_k \right\rceil_h \leq C_j, j = 1,...,J \right\} \tag{1}$$

where I is the set of non-negative integers and $\lceil x \rceil_h$ is the lowest multiple of q_h higher than x. The inner sum in the state space definition corresponds to the bandwidth reserved for each aggregate, which is always a multiple of the bulk bandwidth q_h. The outer sum corresponds to the overall bandwidth, reserved for all aggregates, in ABR pair $j \in \mathcal{J}$.

From the state space the limiting state probabilities can be easily calculated through standard techniques. We denote by π_n the limiting probability of state n. The reserved resource utilization, i.e., the percentage of the reserved bandwidth that is utilized by the admitted traffic in all ABR pairs is given by

$$U = \frac{1}{J} \sum_{n \in S} \sum_{j \in \mathcal{J}} \left[\frac{\sum_{h \in \mathcal{H}_j} \left(\sum_{k \in \mathcal{K}_h} n_k b_k \right)}{\sum_{h \in \mathcal{H}_j} \left\lceil \sum_{k \in \mathcal{K}_h} n_k b_k \right\rceil_h} \right] \pi_n \tag{2}$$

To model the signaling load, let n_k^+ be a state (possibly not belonging to S) reached from $n \in S$ through increasing the number of session's k flows by one unit, i.e., $n_k^+ = (n_1, ..., n_k+1, ..., n_K)$, and let $\left(n, n_k^+ \right)$ represent an (upward) transition (possibly not allowed within the state space) from state n to state n_k^+. There are two types of upwards transitions: allowed and forbidden within the state space. The sets of allowed transitions, $\mathcal{A}$, and forbidden transitions, $\mathcal{F}$, are defined by

$$\mathcal{A} = \left\{(n, n_k^+): n, n_k^+ \in \mathcal{S}\right\} \text{ and } \mathcal{F} = \left\{(n, n_k^+): n \in \mathcal{S}, n_k^+ \notin \mathcal{S}\right\} \tag{3}$$

In order to describe an aggregate's bandwidth adjustment we introduce the indicator function $I_h^{(n,n_k^+)}$ that equals 1 whenever there is an allowed or forbidden transition, driven by an arrival of a session's k flow that can no longer be accommodated in the bandwidth currently reserved for the aggregate h it traverses, i.e.,

$$I_h^{(n,n_k^+)} = \begin{cases} 1, & \sum_{k \in \mathcal{K}_h} n_k b_k + b_k > \left\lceil \sum_{k \in \mathcal{K}_h} n_k b_k \right\rceil_h \\ 0, & otherwise \end{cases} \tag{4}$$

If $I_h^{(n,n_k^+)} = 1$ for $(n, n_k^+) \in \mathcal{A}$, i.e., for an allowed transition, there will be a successful reservation update; otherwise, if the transition is forbidden, the reservation update fails. In both cases, signaling messages will be processed at routers of the aggregate. The number of routers of an aggregate h that suffer an attempt of reservation update upon an (n, n_k^+) transition is $1 + m_h I_h^{(n,n_k^+)}$ (we do not consider the egress router of the aggregate). A transition in the opposite direction provokes reservation updates in the same number of routers. Thus, the rate of signaling messages processed at routers is then

$$\gamma = \sum_{(n,n_k^+) \in \mathcal{A}} \left(\lambda_k \pi_n + (n_k + 1)\mu_k \pi_{n_k^+}\right) \sum_{h \in \mathcal{R}_k} \left(m_h I_h^{(n,n_k^+)} + 1\right) + \\ \sum_{(n,n_k^+) \in \mathcal{F}} \left(\lambda_k \pi_n\right) \sum_{h \in \mathcal{R}_k} \left(m_h I_h^{(n,n_k^+)} + 1\right) \tag{5}$$

The first part in the equation corresponds to signaling messages resulting in successful reservations; the second part corresponds to unsuccessful reservation attempts. Note that per-flow reservation is a particular case of previous model, when there is one end-to-end aggregate per session and a bulk size equal to the session's flow bandwidth.

4   Aggregate Load Model

In this section we present a model that considers a time-varying offered load, which is an extension to multiple areas of the model described in [6]. In particular, we consider that the aggregate traffic of session k is characterized by a sinusoid with random phase

$$r_k(t) = d_k + e_k \cos\left(\frac{2\pi}{T} t + \theta_k\right) \tag{6}$$

where d_k is the mean bandwidth of the aggregate, e_k is the amplitude of the sinusoid, T is the sinusoid period, and θ_k is the random phase uniformly distributed in $[0, 2\pi]$. This model is motivated by the behavior of a large number of observed traces of traffic aggregates that exhibit a near-deterministic periodic long-term trend. Consider, for example, the trace of Fig. 3, which corresponds to traffic observed at the ingress router of Qbone "PSC" [7]. The period T corresponds to 24 hours.

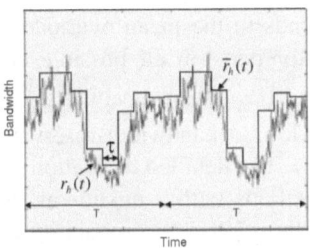

Fig. 3 Traffic observed at the ingress router of Qbone "PSC".

As mentioned before, we also assume that (i) the reservation of aggregate h is updated at the beginning of fixed time intervals of duration τ, and that (ii) the amount of bandwidth to be reserved in the beginning of time interval matches exactly the requirement for that time interval. The desired bandwidth reservation, at time interval x_h = 1, 2, ..., T/τ, in aggregate h, corresponds to the maximum offered bandwidth calculated over this interval, i.e.,

$$r_{h,x_h} = \max_{(x_h-1)\tau \le t < x_h\tau} \sum_{k\in\mathcal{K}_h} r_k(t) \tag{7}$$

Note that at the beginning of time interval x_h the bandwidth of the aggregate (i.e. the bandwidth effectively reserved) may or may not be adjusted to r_{h,x_h}, depending on the bandwidth available at the ABR pairs traversed by aggregate h. This is illustrated in Fig. 3 where $r_h(t)$ and $\bar{r}_h(t)$ represent the offered load and the bandwidth effectively reserved to the aggregate, respectively. To avoid trivialities we assume that T/τ is an integer.

We define the probability of overload of session k, P_k, as the fraction of bandwidth of session k that cannot be admitted. To calculate this metric we consider a reduced load approximation [9], where the traffic offered to an ABR pair is reduced according to the overload suffered by the sessions using that ABR pair in the other ABR pairs traversed by those sessions. Denoting the probability of overload at ABR pair j as L_j, the reduced load offered to ABR pair j at time interval x_h is

$$\hat{r}_j(t) = \sum_{h\in\mathcal{H}_j}\sum_{k\in\mathcal{K}_h} r_k(t) \prod_{l\in\mathcal{A}_k-\{j\}}(1-L_l) \tag{8}$$

and the reduced desired bandwidth reservation is

$$\hat{r}_{j,x_h} = \sum_{h\in\mathcal{H}_j}\hat{r}_{h,x_h} = \sum_{h\in\mathcal{H}_j}\max_{(x_h-1)\tau\le t<x_h\tau}\left(\sum_{k\in\mathcal{K}_h} r_k(t)\prod_{l\in\mathcal{A}_k-\{j\}}(1-L_l)\right) \tag{9}$$

The overload probability at ABR pair j is the ratio of the overload bandwidth (bandwidth that cannot be reserved, calculated over the set of aggregates of ABR pair j) and the desired bandwidth reservation. This probability is approximated by

$$L_j \approx \frac{\left(\frac{\tau}{T}\right)^{H_j}\left[\sum_{x_1=1}^{T/\tau}\cdots\sum_{x_{H_j}=1}^{T/\tau}\left(\sum_{h\in\mathcal{H}_j}\hat{r}_{h,x_h} - C_j\right)^+\right]}{\frac{\tau}{T}\left(\sum_{h\in\mathcal{H}_j}\sum_{x_h=1}^{T/\tau}\hat{r}_{h,x_h}\right)}, \quad j=1,2,...,J \tag{10}$$

The numerator corresponds to the mean overload bandwidth in ABR pair j. The summations in the numerator perform all possible combinations of relative phases between aggregates and $(\tau/T)^{H_j}$ is the probability of each combination. The denominator represents the mean desired bandwidth reservation, calculated over the set of aggregates in the ABR pair j. The detailed derivation of this result is presented in [8]. The set of J non-linear equations with J unknowns in (10) can be solved using the method of repeated substitutions [9]. The probability of overload of session k is then given by

$$P_k \approx 1 - \prod_{j \in \mathcal{A}_k}(1 - L_j) \tag{11}$$

The reserved resource utilization is defined as the ratio of average offered load to average reserved bandwidth:

$$U \approx \frac{1}{J}\sum_{j \in \mathcal{J}}\frac{(1 - L_j)E\left[\displaystyle\sum_{h \in \mathcal{H}_j}\sum_{k \in \mathcal{K}_h} r_k(t)\prod_{l \in \mathcal{A}_k - \{j\}}(1 - L_l)\right]}{\left(\dfrac{\tau}{T}\right)^{H_j}\left[\displaystyle\sum_{x_1 = 1}^{T/\tau}\cdots\sum_{x_{H_j}=1}^{T/\tau}\min(\hat{r}_{j,x_h}, C_j)\right]} \tag{12}$$

where $E(x)$ represents the expected value of x.

5 Numerical Investigations

In this section we present numerical examples and simulations to study the tradeoffs between signaling load and utilization. We consider a Dumbbell network topology with two peripheral areas in each side of the domain and a central area (Fig. 4). Experiments with other topologies are presented in [8]. There are 4 sessions, ACDE, ACDF, BCDF and BCDE, all traversing the central area, denoted by r_{xy}, where x is the origin and y is the destination. The number of routers inside each area is 4. Thus each session travels through 15 routers (not including the domain egress router). Except the case of real aggregate simulations, the bandwidth of all ABR pairs is 32 Mb/sec. We compare two types of network domains: (i) domains with only end-to-end aggregates and (ii) domains with only area aggregates.

In the figures presented bellow, we denote end-to-end aggregation by "End-to-end" and area aggregation by "Area". In area aggregation we consider domains with one service class, denoted by "1 class", and two service classes, denoted by "2 classes". In the case of two service classes, we consider that sessions r_{AE} and r_{AF} belong to one class and sessions r_{BE} and r_{BF} belong to another, leading to one aggregate in the left peripheral areas and two aggregates in all other areas. We will consider two cases

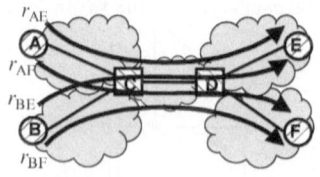

Fig. 4 Dumbbell topology.

regarding the bulk size or τ/T, the normalized time interval: the same bulk size (or τ/T) for all aggregates in the domain, called fixed bulk size (or fixed τ/T), and bulk size (or τ/T) proportional to each aggregates' offered load, denoted by "Prop. bulk" (or "Prop. τ/T"). In the later case, the *xx*-axis will represent the bulk size (or τ/T) of peripheral areas. We will consider as the metric for assessing the signaling load, the signaling gain of end-to-end and area aggregation over per-flow signaling.

5.1   Per-Flow Load Model

In these studies we assume that sessions are characterized by $b_k = 1$ Mb/sec, $\lambda_k = 8$ sec^{-1} and $1/\mu_k = 1$ sec. Thus the session's average offered bandwidth is 8 Mb/sec.

Fig. 5 (a) shows the signaling gains with both end-to-end aggregation and area aggregation, considering all routers in the domain. We present signaling gains considering (i) all reservation attempts (solid lines, denoted by "All") and (ii) only successful reservations (dashed lines, denoted by "Successful"). When the bulk size equals the flows' bandwidth the signaling rate is the same as in per-flow signaling (so a unitary gain is obtained). Results show that the gains over per-flow signaling increase with the bulk size. For a bulk size of 8 Mb/sec the gains considering only successful reservations are approximately 15 with end-to-end aggregation and 4 with area aggregation. These gains will approach 15 and 5, respectively, which are obtained in the limit, as the bulk size increases, when no signaling takes place in internal routers. Note that the number of routers that process signaling messages on a per-flow basis (i.e., every time a flow arrives or departs), is 1 with end-to-end aggregation (the ingress DBR), 3 with area aggregation (the ingress ABRs of each area) and 15 without aggregation, which explains the referred gains. The gains in end-to-end aggregation almost reach the limit when the bulk size is 8 Mb/sec. Given that in the central area there are 4 aggregates, each with an average offered load of 8 Mb/sec, and that the bandwidth of the ABR pair is 32 Mb/sec, the system trend is to have the bandwidth of all aggregates adjusted to the bulk size at all times. This leads to very few bandwidth update attempts and, therefore, very few signaling messages in internal routers. The gains obtained with the three cases of area aggregation are very similar, the one in the case of one service class and proportional bulks being slightly larger (in this case, the bulk size in the central area is twice the bulk size in the peripheral areas).

Consider now the difference between the signaling gains of (i) all reservation attempts and (ii) successful reservations. For a 8 Mb/sec bulk size, with end-to-end aggregation, the signaling gain decreases from 15 to 8.5, reflecting the significant number of reservation requests that cannot be established, i.e., a relatively high blocking probability. With area aggregation, the signaling gains are almost the same, showing that almost all reservation attempts turn into successful reservations.

Fig. 5 (b) considers the signaling gains achieved by internal routers, i.e., not including DBRs, in the case of end-to-end aggregation, and not including DBRs and ABRs, in the case of area aggregation. This metric is very important, as it represents the gains that can be achieved by the routers that are supposed to have the lowest cost. As seen before, the gains corresponding to all domain routers are biased by the number of routers that need to perform per-flow signaling and router costs are most certainly not a linear function of the signaling load. We first notice that the signaling gains of internal routers are higher than the domain ones. Considering only successful reservations and fixed bulk sizes, we observe that the signaling gains in area aggregation with one and two service classes are similar (recall that with one service class there is only one aggregate in the central area, and with two service classes there are two). There are two opposite effects. First, with one service class the aggregates are always shared by more than one session; the overall traffic inside an aggregate becomes smoother, which contributes to reducing the signaling rate. On the other hand, the resource sharing in area aggregation with one service class increases the number of admitted flows, which contributes to increasing the signaling rate. These two opposite effects balance out, which explains the similarities in terms of gains. Considering proportional bulk sizes, we notice that the signaling gains increase. This is due to the larger bulk size of the central area, which provokes a reduction in its signaling load. The signaling gains in end-to-end aggregation are higher for bulk sizes larger than approximately 4 Mb/sec. This is again explained by the system trend, to have the bandwidth of all aggregates adjusted to the bulk size at all times, for large bulk size values.

Fig. 5 (c) depicts the reserved resource utilization. The resource utilization increases in area aggregation because the resource sharing is larger, compared with end-to-end aggregation. In area aggregation with one service class, the four sessions share the same aggregate in the central area. Consider the cases of area aggregation with one service class, with fixed and proportional bulk sizes. The utilization achieved with proportional bulk size is slightly smaller, but quite close to the one obtained with fixed bulk size. This reflects the good tradeoff between signaling and utilization that can be

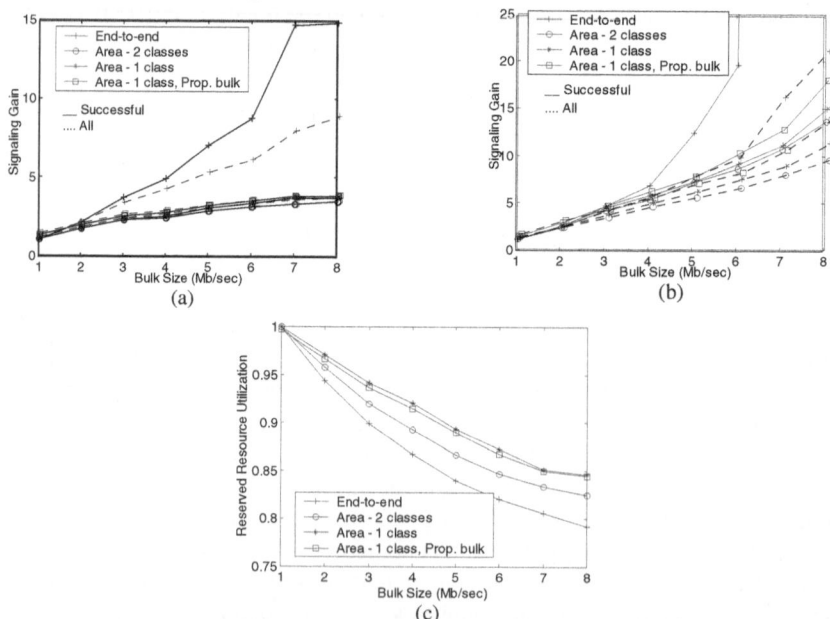

Fig. 5 Signaling gains of (a) all routers in the domain, (b) internal routers and (c) reserved resource utilization (per-flow model).

achieved in this case. As an example, to achieve 84% of resource utilization, the bulk size must be lower than 5 Mb/sec in end-to-end aggregation, 6 Mb/sec in area aggregation with two service classes, and 8 Mb/sec in area aggregation with one service class and with proportional and fixed bulk sizes.

5.2 Aggregate Load Model

In these experiments the mean bandwidth of the cosine wave is $d_k = 5.3$ Mb/sec and the amplitude is also $e_k = 5.3$ Mb/sec, so as to reproduce an overload situation.

Fig. 6 depicts the reserved resource utilization and the overload probability in the domain. The results concerning the case of area aggregation with one service class and a proportional τ/T are presented only for $\tau/T \leq 1/2$. Note that the τ/T values of the central area are twice the ones of the peripheral area, and the xx-axis is representing those of peripheral areas.

As τ/T increases, the frequency of reservation updates decreases, leading to lower resource utilization and higher overload probabilities.

For small τ/T, the reserved resource utilization and overload probabilities obtained with all types of aggregation are approximately the same. We recall that with end-to-end aggregation there are four aggregates in the central area (one aggregate per session) and with area aggregation and one service class there is only one aggregate (whose resources are shared by all four sessions). With end-to-end aggregation the four sessions will only share resources when their aggregates do so, while with area aggregation the four sessions will always share resources irrespective of τ/T. For small τ/T, the aggregates are adjusted frequently (in relation to the time-scale of the offered load), and significant resource sharing takes place in both types of aggregation. This is done at the cost of a high signaling rate. As τ/T increases, and the signaling rate decreases, the reservations are made for longer time intervals, leading to a decrease in the resource utilization (and higher overload probabilities). This affects more a system with end-to-end aggregation because, as mentioned before, in area aggregation the four sessions still share resources. As an example, to reach an utilization larger than 75% and an overload probability smaller than 4%, $\tau/T \leq 1/2$ in area aggregation with one service class and $\tau/T \leq 1/6$ in end-to-end aggregation. The case of area aggregation with one service class and a proportional τ/T achieves a resource utilization slightly smaller (and a slightly larger overload probability), when comparing with the

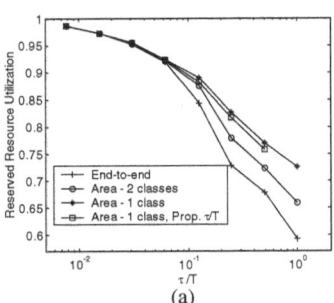
(a)

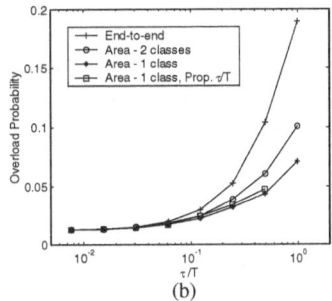
(b)

Fig. 6 (a) Overload probability and (b) reserved resource utilization (aggregate model).

case of a fixed τ/T. This is due to the decrease in the frequency of the reservations updates in the central area. However, the differences between the utilization and overload results achieved in these cases are very small, reflecting that the increase in the τ/T of the central area has little impact in the resource utilization and overload probability. The increase in the number of service classes increases the number of aggregates required in each area. Therefore, the case of two service classes is an intermediate case between end-to-end and area aggregation with one service class.

Although this model does not detail the offered load at the flow level, it is still possible to derive a (rough) approximation for the signaling gains, by noting that a unitary reserved resource utilization is achieved when using per-flow signaling. From Fig. 6 (a), it can be seen that a unitary utilization is approximately obtained when $\tau/T=1/256$. Thus, as an example, the signaling gains will be 32 when $\tau/T=1/8$, and 128 when $\tau/T=1/2$.

In general, the results obtained with this model confirm the ones obtained with the per-flow load model. Although this model accommodates a time-varying offered load, it does not allow the determination of the exact signaling load. In the next section, we will present a simulation study, based on measured aggregates, that determines the signaling gains for time-varying offered loads.

5.3   Simulations with Measured Aggregate

We consider now a traffic trace measured at NLANR on December 1, 1999 [10] and evaluate the system performance via discrete event simulation. This trace is characterized by a very large variance and noise. The information available includes the arrival time, the duration, and the number of bytes of each flow. The total number of flows is 64087. The average flows' bandwidth is 19.6 Kb/sec, but approximately 80% of the flows have a bandwidth bellow the mean. The total average bandwidth is 1.43 Mb/sec and the variance is 0.144 Mb/sec. In order to study a scenario with overload, we decreased the bandwidth of all areas to 10 Mb/sec. The simulation results correspond to averages taken over a total of 20 runs; in all runs, the phase (time instant of beginning) of each aggregate was chosen randomly.

Fig. 7 (a) shows the signaling gains with both end-to-end and area aggregation, considering (i) all reservation attempts and (ii) only successful reservations. The results confirm the ones obtained with the per-flow load model.

Fig. 7 (b) shows the signaling gains of internal routers. In all types of aggregation, the signaling gains increase sharply with the bulk size reaching much higher values than in the per-flow load model case. With a 1.25 Mb/sec bulk size and only successful reservations, the signaling gains reach 900 in end-to-end aggregation, 1100 in area aggregation with two service classes, 1600 in area aggregation with one service class and fixed bulk size, and 1800 with one service class and proportional bulk sizes. This is essentially due to the larger ratio between the bulk size and the flow's bandwidth. We also notice that the signaling gains are always larger with area aggregation than with end-to-end aggregation. This is explained by the higher burstiness of the traffic and the larger resource sharing that is possible with area aggregates. The overall traffic in the aggregate becomes smoother and the number of signaling attempts decreases. Note also that we are still far from the limiting situation of the per-flow load model case, since the maximum bulk size value considered in the experiments still allows sufficient granularity in the bandwidth adjustment process. This, in fact, represents a more realistic scenario. When taking into account non-successful reservation attempts, it can be seen that the gains of area aggregation over end-to-end aggregation are effectively higher. This can be explained by the lower blocking with area aggregation, which reflects in a lower number of unsuccessful signaling attempts. Area aggregation with two service classes is again an intermediate case between the other two.

We also notice from Fig. 7 (b) that signaling gains of 124 in area aggregation with one service class and fixed bulk sizes, and 160 in area aggregation with proportional bulk sizes, are obtained when the ratio between the bulk size and the mean flows' bandwidth is 8 (i.e. with a bulk size of 156.8 Kb/s). For the same ratio in the per-flow load experiments (i.e. a bulk size of 8 Mb/sec), the gains were 15 and 18, respectively. This difference can be explained by the asymmetry of the distribution of the flows' bandwidth in the real aggregate, which is 80% bellow the mean (recall that in the per-flow load model the flow's bandwidth is fixed). Thus, in this case, the bandwidth update attempts are provoked by a much smaller number of flows (mostly the flows with larger bandwidth), leading to a decrease in the signaling rate.

The reserved resource utilization is depicted in Fig. 7 (c). Results show again that area aggregation achieves higher resource utilization, slightly decreasing with proportional bulk sizes. As an example, to achieve an utilization larger than 90%, the bulk size should be lower than 800 Kb/sec in area aggregation with one service class (with fixed and proportional bulks), 400 Kb/sec in area aggregation with two service classes, and 300 Kb/sec with end-to-end aggregation. For these bulk sizes, the signaling gain in

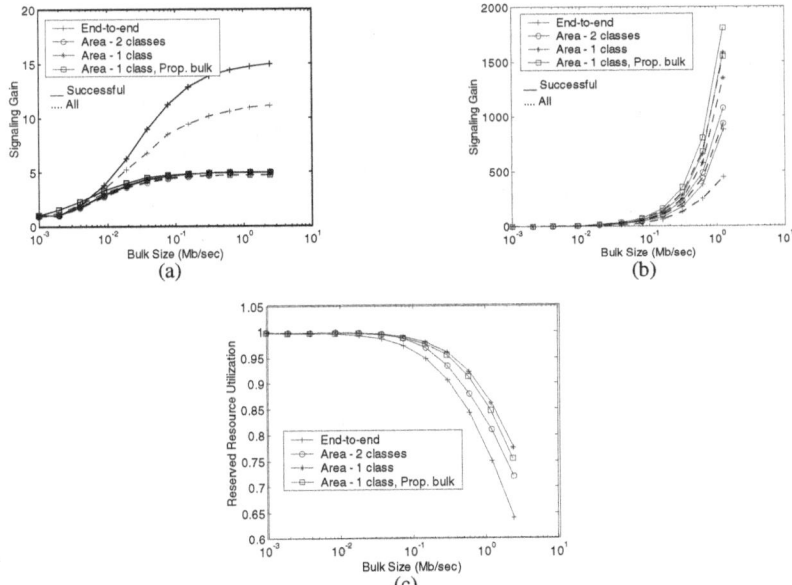

Fig. 7 Signaling gains of (a) all routers in the domain, (b) internal routers and (c) reserved resource utilization (measured aggregate).

internal routers with end-to-end aggregation is 150, with area aggregation, one service class and fixed bulk size is 1250, and with area aggregation, one service class and proportional bulk sizes is 1500.

The results of these studies show that area aggregation, compared with end-to-end aggregation, can achieve larger signaling gains and larger utilizations. They also show that area aggregation with proportional bulk sizes can raise the signaling gains with very little impact on the utilization.

6   Conclusions

We analyzed the tradeoffs between signaling and resource utilization in DiffServ networks partitioned in areas (hierarchical domains) using flow aggregates that can be dynamically adjusted. These tradeoffs are studied using two analytical models. In the first model, based on multidimensional birth-death processes, the offered load is detailed at the flow level, which allows accurate assessment of the signaling load. The second model accommodates time-varying offered loads, which allows studying the tradeoffs between the time-scale of the aggregate demand and the time-scale of signaling. Our results show that structuring a network domain in areas achieves high performance gains, which can contribute to reduce significantly the cost of core routers.

References

1. R. Braden et al., "Integrated Services in the Internet Architecture: An Overview", IETF RFC 1633, June 1994.
2. D. Awduche et al., "RSVP-TE: Extensions to RSVP for LSP Tunnels", IETF RFC 3209, December 2001.
3. F. Baker el al., "Aggregation of RSVP for IPv4 and IPv6 Reservations", IETF RFC 3175, September 2001.
4. P. Pan et al., "BGRP: A Tree-based Aggregation Protocol for Inter-Domain Reservations", Journal of Comm. and Networks, 2(2), pp. 157-167, June 2000.
5. O. Schelén and S. Pink, "Aggregation Resource Reservations over Multiple Routing Domains", In Proceedings of IWQoS'98, Napa, CA, May 1998.
6. H. Fu and E. Knightly, "Aggregation and Scalable QoS: A Performance Study", In *Proc. of IWQoS '01*, June 2001.
7. Internet Page of Qbone, http://tombstone.oar.net/sitemap.html.
8. S. Sargento and R. Valadas, "Aggregation Performance in Hierarchical Domains", University of Aveiro Technical Report, May 2002.
9. K. Ross, "Multiservice Loss Models for Broadband Telecommunication Networks", *Springer*, 1995.
10. Internet Page of NLANR, http://moat.nlanr.net/Traces/ Kiwitraces/auck2.html.

Robust Delay Estimation for Internet Multimedia Applications

Kyung-Joon Park[1], Won Jong Jeon[2], Klara Nahrstedt[2], Tamer Başar[3], and Chong-Ho Choi[1]

[1] School of Electrical Engineering and Computer Science and ASRI
Seoul National University, Seoul 151-742 KOREA
{kjpark, chchoi}@csl.snu.ac.kr
[2] Department of Computer Science
University of Illinois at Urbana-Champaign, IL 61801 USA
{wonjeon, klara}@cs.uiuc.edu
[3] Department of Electrical and Computer Engineering and Coordinated Science Laboratory
University of Illinois at Urbana-Champaign, IL 61801 USA
tbasar@decision.csl.uiuc.edu

Abstract. Traffic estimation and modeling has been a crucial issue in many research areas of communication networks. For example, intermediate routers in networks estimate the rate of packet flows via queue size information in order to maximize throughput and provide fairness between flows. Also, many senders in the end system such as multimedia applications estimate end-to-end delay between a sender and a receiver to reduce dropping probability of packet. In this position paper, we propose a robust adaptive estimation scheme for Internet multimedia applications. The proposed scheme adopts an autoregressive (AR) model for the process and identifies the parameters of the AR process via a robust identification algorithm. This robust identification algorithm usually leads to better performance when the noise is correlated and/or non-stationary, and it is also more robust to modeling uncertainties. Here, we consider the problem of end-to-end delay estimation for audio playout mechanisms. We rigorously formulate the proposed scheme in the realm of audio playout mechanisms and give some preliminary simulation result which shows effectiveness of the proposed scheme. Even though we apply the proposed scheme to the estimation of end-to-end delay in audio applications, the scheme itself is very general and we expect that it can be applied to many other estimation problems in Internet multimedia applications.

1 Introduction

Recently, there has been a significant increase of interest in Internet multimedia applications, i.e. video conferencing, Internet telephony, video-on-demand etc. This kind of applications require quality of service (QoS), such as throughput, packet loss, delay, and jitter. However, the current Internet multimedia applications commonly employ the UDP transport mechanism, which is not capable of

F. Boavida et al. (Eds.): IDMS/PROMS 2002, LNCS 2515, pp. 255–262, 2002.

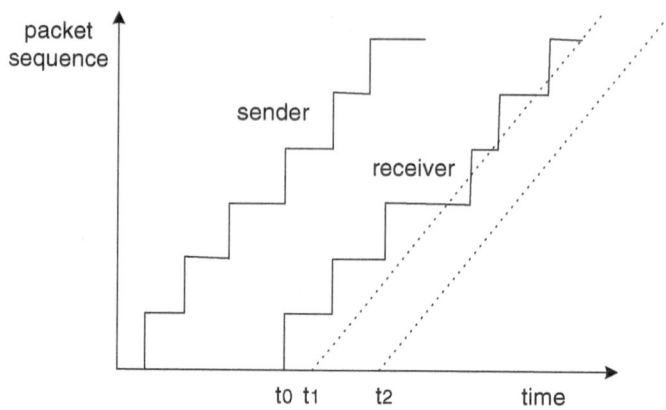

Fig. 1. Playout Jitter Problem.

congestion control. Consequently, QoS is usually provided by application-level end-user adaptation [1], [2], [3].

In many applications, the problem of traffic modeling and estimation at the end users is a crucial issue for providing QoS [2], [3], [4]. One of the applications is the estimation of packet delay for audio playout mechanisms [5]. In Internet audio applications such as real-time voice communication and packet radio service, delay jitter are the most crucial factor for QoS. In order to alleviate the problem caused by unpredictability of delay and delay jitter in the Internet, the receiver usually needs to buffer some amount of packets before it actually plays them. Small buffering delay cannot tolerate severe delay jitter and also lead to significant packet loss, whereas large buffering delay causes large startup delay. Therefore, the amount of buffered packets and timing of playout are very important for the performance of audio applications. Figure 1 shows the sample sequence of operations on a sender and receiver of an audio application. Two solid lines represent the sequence number of audio packets sent and received respectively, and two dotted lines represent the sequence number of packets played by the receiver. Delay jitter during transmission causes the uneven arrivals of the packets at the receiver. In order to reduce such delay jitter, the receiver delays the initiation of playout of received packets. t_1 and t_2 represent two different playout times. In case of t_1, some of packets are delivered to the receiver after their playout time, therefore they are dropped without playing. In case of t_2, the receiver has larger delayed startup time, i.e. $t_2 - t_0$ than that in case of t_1, which is $t_1 - t_0$. Consequently, the main objective of playout algorithms is to choose a small startup time which can also keep acceptable packet loss rate.

The basic algorithm of delay estimation used in audio conferencing tools such as NeVot 1.4 [6] has been influenced by RFC 793 TCP RTT estimation [7]. The estimate of average packet delay d_i is as follows:

$$d_i = \alpha d_{i-1} + (1 - \alpha)n_i \tag{1}$$

where n_i is the delay suffered by the i-th packet in the network, and α is a weighting factor which controls the rate of convergence of the algorithm. The variation in this delay, v_i is estimated by

$$v_i = \alpha v_{i-1} + (1 - \alpha)|d_i - n_i|. \tag{2}$$

This is used to fix the end-to-end delay, ted for playing out the next packet as follows:

$$ted = d_i + \beta v_i \tag{3}$$

where β is called a safety factor used to guarantee that the estimated delay is larger than the actual delay with a high probability. The most significant shortcoming of this basic algorithm is that it does not adapt to network traffic efficiently. Once the value of α is given, the model is fixed and this can degrade estimation performance. We should not ignore that TCP can somehow adapt itself to networks, but it does not adapt itself efficiently, especially when there is an abrupt change of network condition.

Many researchers have suggested modified algorithms for better performance [1], [5], [8], [9], [10]. However, most of the proposed schemes were not based on estimation theory, but some kind of heuristics. Recently, P. DeLeon and C. Sreenan [11] have proposed a scheme which used a simple normalized least-mean-square (NLMS) algorithm in adaptive filter theory [12].

In this paper, we propose a robust adaptive estimation algorithm based on recent development in robust control [13]. The proposed scheme is not only adaptive in its nature, but also robust to non-stationary noise and modeling uncertainties. We will also explain that most of the existing schemes correspond to special cases of the proposed scheme. We further expect that the proposed scheme can be applied to many estimation problems in Internet multimedia applications. The rest of the paper is organized as follows: In Section II, we will formulate the delay process as an autoregressive (AR) model and give a design criterion which is of H^∞ type [14]. In Section III, we derive the update rules for the estimate of α and the estimate of the variance σ^2. We give some preliminary simulation result in Section IV. Finally, conclusion and future work follows in Section V.

2   Problem Formulation

Here, we will closely follow the methodology introduced in [15]. This methodology is a discrete-time version of the original algorithm in [13]. The AR model we adopt is as follows:

$$d_{n+1} = \sum_{i=1}^{p} \alpha_i d_{n+1-i} + \phi_n \tag{4}$$

where d_i is the i-th packet delay, α_i's are parameters of the AR process to be identified, and ϕ_n is an unknown noise sequence. Here, p is called the order of the AR process. Note that the complexity and the computational burden of the algorithm is determined by p. The AR model (4) is a generalization of (1) since the model (1) corresponds to the special case of $p = 1$ of (4). Furthermore, while the basic algorithm (1) uses a fixed weighting factor α, the proposed algorithm identifies the parameters α_i's via a robust identification method as in the next section.

We can express (4) with the following vector notation:

$$d_{n+1} = \boldsymbol{\alpha}^T \eta_n + \phi_n \tag{5}$$

where $\boldsymbol{\alpha} := (\alpha_p, ..., \alpha_1)^T$ and $\eta_n := (d_{n+1-p}, d_{n+2-p}, ..., d_n)^T$. What we are going to do is to identify $\boldsymbol{\alpha}$ based on the previous data, i.e. η_n.

We wish to obtain a sequence of estimates for $\boldsymbol{\alpha}$, denoted $\hat{\boldsymbol{\alpha}}_n$ at step n, so that $\hat{\boldsymbol{\alpha}}_n$ would depends on all the past and the present value of $d_{(\cdot)}$, i.e. $\hat{\boldsymbol{\alpha}}_n = \hat{\boldsymbol{\alpha}}(d_n, d_{n-1}, ..., d_0)$. The criterion to be minimized is of the H^∞ type [14], which is the gain from the energy of the unknowns to a weighted quadratic identification error:

$$J(\{\hat{\boldsymbol{\alpha}}_n\}_{n=0}^\infty) := \sup_{\{\phi_n\}_{n=0}^\infty, \boldsymbol{\alpha}} \frac{\sum_{n=0}^\infty (\boldsymbol{\alpha} - \hat{\boldsymbol{\alpha}}_n)^T Q_n (\boldsymbol{\alpha} - \hat{\boldsymbol{\alpha}}_n)}{\sum_{n=0}^\infty |\phi_n|^2 + (\boldsymbol{\alpha} - \overline{\boldsymbol{\alpha}}_0)^T \overline{Q}_0 (\boldsymbol{\alpha} - \overline{\boldsymbol{\alpha}}_0)} \tag{6}$$

where $\overline{\boldsymbol{\alpha}}_0$ is some initial estimate for $\boldsymbol{\alpha}$, $\overline{Q}_0 > 0$ is a fixed weighting matrix, and $Q_n \geq 0, n = 0, 1, ...$ is a sequence of weighting matrices which will be specified later. Intuitively, the criterion J is an index that measures worst-case attenuation from additive disturbance and error in the initial estimate to the estimation error over an interval of interest. Consequently, our objective is to find a sequence $\hat{\boldsymbol{\alpha}}^* := \{\hat{\boldsymbol{\alpha}}_n^*\}_{n=0}^\infty$, with the properties that

$$J(\hat{\boldsymbol{\alpha}}^*) = \inf_{\hat{\boldsymbol{\alpha}} = \{\boldsymbol{\alpha}_n\}_{n=0}^\infty} J(\hat{\boldsymbol{\alpha}}) =: (\gamma_{id}^*)^2 \tag{7}$$

and $\lim_{n \to \infty} \hat{\boldsymbol{\alpha}}_n^* = \boldsymbol{\alpha}$.

3   Robust Identification Algorithm

3.1   Update Rule for Estimation of α

Now, from [15], we derive update rules for estimate of $\boldsymbol{\alpha}$. First we introduce Σ_n, which is a sequence of $p \times p$-dimensional positive-definite matrices. Note that Σ_n is necessary in the way of estimation of $\boldsymbol{\alpha}$ and does not have significant physical meaning. The following is the update rule for Σ_n:

$$\Sigma_{n+1} = \Sigma_n + \eta_{n-1} \eta_{n-1}^T - \frac{1}{\gamma^2} Q_n, \tag{8}$$

$$\Sigma_1 = \overline{Q}_0 - \frac{1}{\gamma^2} Q_0. \tag{9}$$

Here, if we let $\overline{Q}_0 = Q_0 = I_p$, where I_p is the $p \times p$ identity matrix, and $Q_n = \eta_{n-1}\eta_{n-1}^T$ in which case $\gamma_{id}^* = 1$ in (7), then we get the following update rule for Σ_n:

$$\Sigma_{n+1} = \Sigma_n + (1 - \gamma^{-2})\eta_{n-1}\eta_{n-1}^T, \tag{10}$$
$$\Sigma_1 = (1 - \gamma^{-2})I_p. \tag{11}$$

Here γ is a parameter of the algorithm and should be larger than 1.

Now, we have the following update rule for $\hat{\boldsymbol{\alpha}}_n$:

$$\hat{\boldsymbol{\alpha}}_{n+1} = \hat{\boldsymbol{\alpha}}_n + (d_{n+1} - \hat{\boldsymbol{\alpha}}_n^T\eta_n)(\Sigma_{n+1} + \eta_n\eta_n^T)^{-1}\eta_n, \tag{12}$$
$$\hat{\boldsymbol{\alpha}}_0 = \boldsymbol{\alpha}_0. \tag{13}$$

Here $\hat{\boldsymbol{\alpha}}_n$ denote the estimate of $\boldsymbol{\alpha}$ for n-th iteration and $\boldsymbol{\alpha}_0$ an initial value. Note that $\hat{\boldsymbol{\alpha}}_n$ is a p-dimensional vector.

Remark 1: The estimator (12) is a generalized LMS filter [13]. Hence, the NLMS estimator in [11] corresponds to a special case of the proposed algorithm. Furthermore, if we let $\gamma \uparrow \infty$, the proposed algorithm will be precisely the least-squares (LS) estimator [13], [15]. In general, the proposed estimator ranges from the LS estimator to the generalized LMS estimator for certain choices of γ.

Remark 2: The proposed algorithm has been derived based on H^∞ optimal control theory [14]. Hence, it usually shows better performance when the noise is correlated and/or non-stationary, and it is also more robust to modeling uncertainties. Consequently, unlike the NLMS estimator, the proposed algorithm does not require pre-filtering methods such as Discrete Wavelet Transform (DWT) in [9] for decorrelation.

3.2   Update Rule for Estimation of the Variance

Here we obtain an estimate of the variance σ^2 of ϕ_n. We need the variance σ^2 when we calculate the playout time as in (3). First we define the autocorrelation function estimator at step n as follows:

$$\hat{R}^n[k] = \frac{1}{n+1}\sum_{i=k}^{n} d_i d_{i-k} \tag{14}$$

where $k = 0, 1, ..., p$. Then we have the following recursive relation:

$$\hat{R}^{n+1}[k] = \frac{n+1}{n+2}\hat{R}^n[k] + \frac{1}{n+2}d_{n+1}d_{n+1-k}. \tag{15}$$

Now we have the following equation for the estimate of variance σ_n^2:

$$\hat{\sigma}_n^2 = \hat{R}^n[0] - \sum_{i=1}^{p} \hat{l}_n^i \hat{R}^n[i]. \tag{16}$$

Here $\hat{l}_n^i$ is the i-th element of $\hat{l}_n$, where $\hat{l}_n$ is the LS estimate of α at time n. Note that $\hat{l}_n$ is a p-dimensional vector. $\hat{l}_n$ can be obtained as follows:

$$\hat{l}_{n+1} = \hat{l}_n + (d_{n+1} - \hat{l}_n^T \eta_n)(\sum_{i=0}^{n} \eta_i \eta_i^T + I_p)^{-1} \eta_n. \tag{17}$$

3.3   Robust Playout Algorithm

Now, the overall playout algorithm for Internet multimedia applications can be summarized as follows:

For each talkspurt,
  For every i-th packet,
    Calculate $\hat{\alpha}_i$ and $\hat{\sigma}_i^2$ by (12) and (16).
  End
  Next playout time $t_p = \hat{d}_{n+1} + \beta \hat{\sigma}_n$, where $\hat{d}_{n+1} = \hat{\alpha}_n^T \eta_n$.
End

Here, instead of calculating $\hat{\sigma}_n$ by (16), we can simply use (2) to lessen the computational burden caused by (16).

4   Simulation

In this section, we give some preliminary simulation result. We compare the proposed algorithm with the basic algorithm (1). In both cases, we used (2) for simple calculation of the variation. Here, we adopted the traces used in [5]. We only show simulation result for trace 2 in [5] for space limitations.

We used $\alpha = 0.99802$ for the basic algorithm and $\beta = 4.0$ for the variation as in [5] and we set $p = 2$ for the AR model (4) . Here, we compare the estimation error, i.e. the error between the estimated delay and the actual delay for all

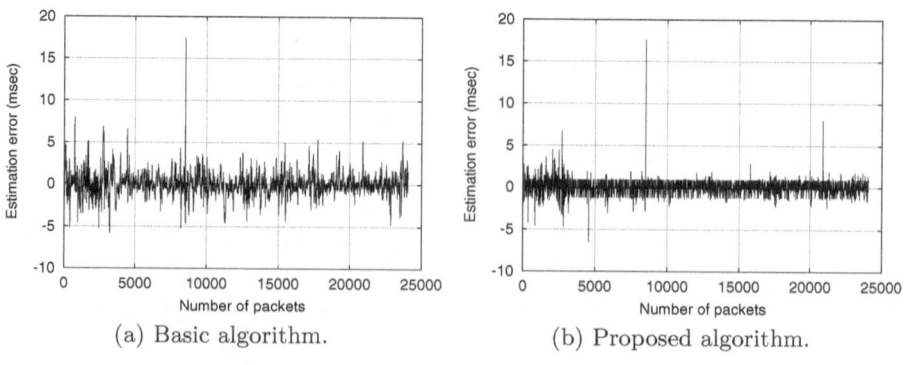

(a) Basic algorithm.   (b) Proposed algorithm.

Fig. 2. End-to-end delay estimation for audio application.

packets at the receiver. As we can see from Figure 3.3, the estimation error of the proposed scheme is kept smaller than that of the basic algorithm and also the variation of the proposed scheme is much smaller than that of the basic algorithm. Hence, we can verify the potential effectiveness of the proposed algorithm.

5   Conclusion and Future Work

We have proposed a robust adaptive estimation algorithm which adopt an AR model. The parameters of an AR model are identified by a robust identification algorithm which is based on recent development in robust control [13]. This identification algorithm is not only more effective when the noise is correlated and/or non-stationary, but is also more robust to model uncertainties than the usual estimation schemes. We have applied the proposed scheme to the problem of Internet audio playout mechanisms. Our preliminary simulation result shows the potential effectiveness of the method. We are currently working on performance comparison between the proposed algorithm and other adaptive schemes such as those in [5], [8], [9], [11]. Since the most salient feature of the proposed scheme is its robustness, we are also working on extensive simulation to show the robustness of the proposed scheme over the existing algorithms. We expect that the proposed algorithm can be applied to many estimation problems in Internet multimedia applications.

Acknowledgements. The work of K.-J. Park and C.-H. Choi has been partly supported by the BK21 SNU-UIUC Collaborative Program. The work of W. J. Jeon and K. Nahrstedt has been partly supported by the Kodak fellowship.

References

1. X. Wang and H. Schulzrinne, "Comparison of adaptive Internet multimedia applications," *IEICE Transactions on Communications*, vol. E82-B, no. 6, June 1999.
2. B. Li and K. Nahrstedt, "A control theoretical model for quality of service adaptations," in *Proceedings of the IEEE International Workshop on Quality of Service (IWQoS)*, Napa, CA 1998.
3. B. Li, "Agilos: a middleware control architecture for application-aware quality of service adaptations," *Ph.D Dissertation*, Department of Computer Science, University of Illinois at Urbana-Champaign, May 2000.
4. V. Paxon, "Measurements and analysis of end-to-end Internet dynamics," *Ph.D Dissertation*, Department of Computer Science, University of California, Berkeley, 1997.
5. R. Ramjee, J. Kurose, D. Towsley, and H. Schulzerine, "Adaptive playout mechanisms for packetized audio applications in wide area networks," in *Proceedings of IEEE INFOCOM*, 1994, pp. 680–686.
6. H. Schulzrinne, "Voice communication across the Internet: a network voice terminal," *Technical Report*, Department of Computer Science, University of Massachusetts, Amherst, MA, July 1992.

7. V. Jacobson, "Congestion avoidance and control," in *Proceedings of ACM SIG-COMM*, 1998.
8. C. J. Sreenan, J. C. Chen, P. Agrawal, and B. Narendran, "Delay reduction techniques for playout buffering," *IEEE Transactions on Multimedia*, vol. 2, no. 2, pp. 88–100, June 2000.
9. A. Kansal and A. Karandikar, "Adaptive delay estimation for low jitter audio over Internet," in *Proceedings of IEEE GLOBECOM*, 2001.
10. S. B. Moon, J. Kurose, and D. Towsley, "Packet audio playout delay adjustment: performance bounds and algorithms," *Multimedia Systems*, vol. 6, pp 17–28, Jan. 1998.
11. P. DeLeon and C. J. Sreenan, "An adaptive predictor for media playout buffering," in *Proceedings of IEEE ICASSP*, Phoenix, AZ, March 1999, pp. 3097–3100.
12. S. Haykin, *Adaptive Filter Theory*, Prentice Hall, 3rd edition, Englewood-Cliffs, NJ, 1998.
13. G. Didinsky, Z. Pan, and T. Başar, "Parameter identification for uncertain plants using H^∞ methods," *Automatica*, vol. 31, no. 9, pp. 1227–1250, September 1995.
14. T. Başar and P. Bernhard, H^∞*-optimal Control and Related Minimax Design Problems: A Dynamic Game Approach*, Birkhäuser, Boston, MA, August 1995.
15. Omar Ait-Hellal, Eitan Altman, and Tamer Başar, "A robust identification algorithm for traffic models in telecommunications," in *Proceedings of the IEEE International Conference on Decision & Control*, 1999, pp. 3071–3076.

Supporting Mobile Multicast in Mobile Networks by Considering Host Mobility

Jin Park[1], Young-Joo Suh[2], and Shin-Gak Kang[1]

[1]Electronics and Telecommunications Research Institute, 161 Kajeong-Dong, Yuseong-Gu, Deajeon 305-350, Korea
{pj63450, sgkang}@etri.re.kr
[2]Department of Computer Science & Engineering
Pohang University of Science & Technology (POSTECH)
San 31 Hyoja-Dong, Pohang 790-784, Korea
yjsuh@postech.ac.kr

Abstract. Mobile computing and multimedia application are two emerging trends in computer systems. 'Multicast' reduces the number of multimedia traffics by delivering a single stream of information to thousands of recipients simultaneously. Since multicast routing protocols being used in a wired network were originally designed for stationary host, they do not consider the dynamic location changes of mobile hosts. Therefore, the naive deployment of existing multicast routing protocols is not suitable. In this paper, we present a new mobile multicast routing protocol. The proposed protocol uses Foreign Multicast Agent (FMA) to maintain the group membership. The service range defined by the timer of a mobile host may efficiently take advantage of the characteristics that mobile multicast has according to the speed of mobile hosts. Various performance evaluation results illustrate that the proposed protocol shows distinct performance enhancements over existing protocols.

1 Introduction

Mobile computing and multimedia application are two emerging trends in computer systems. Since 'multicast' reduces the number of multimedia traffics by delivering a single stream of information to thousands of recipients simultaneously, there will be more needs for multicast in order to transmit multimedia traffic efficiently to mobile hosts. Providing multicast support for mobile hosts in the IP Inter-network, however, is a challenging problem for several reasons. First, existing multicast protocols (DVMRP, MOSPF, CBT, PIM-SM, PIM-DM, etc.) have been designed for static hosts. Second, a mobile multicast protocol must deal with not only dynamic group membership [1] but also dynamic member location [2]. Third, the IETF Mobile IP [3,4,13] concentrates on unicast delivery to mobile hosts. Thus, a new additional mechanism must be added to support mobile multicast.

Two traditional approaches for mobile multicast are the Bi-directional tunneling and Remote subscription [5,6,7]. The Bi-directional tunneling is the HA (Home Agent) based protocol because the HA is responsible for managing group membership for its away mobile hosts. The HA subscribes to a required multicast group, and may forward received multicast datagrams for its away mobile hosts using the unicast

F. Boavida et al. (Eds.): IDMS/PROMS 2002, LNCS 2515, pp. 263–272, 2002.

tunneling. This scheme has some drawbacks as follows. First, a routing path for a multicast datagram delivery becomes far from being optimal because of the triangular routing. Second, scalability is limited because the HA must replicate multicast datagrams and deliver them to each of its away mobile hosts by the unicast tunneling. Third, when multiple mobile hosts in a foreign network require the same group membership, duplicated datagrams may be forwarded by multiple HAs, which is called *tunnel convergence problem*.

On the other hand, the Remote subscription is the FA (Foreign Agent) based protocol, where the FA manages the group membership for visiting mobile hosts, and directly joins the multicast tree. The scheme is simple, and the routing path may become optimal by SPT (Shortest Path Tree). The scheme works well when a mobile host spends relatively longer time in a foreign network. However, the scheme does not work if no multicast router exists in the foreign network. A number of tree reconstructions may lead to high overhead for the network. The latency for a new tree reconfiguration may cause data loss for roaming mobile hosts.

A new approach for mobile multicast is the hybrid style of protocols, such as [9,10,16]. In this approach, a new multicast agent may be defined to maintain the group membership. The tree reconfiguration and unicast tunneling may be performed in parallel. The former is usually used for better route optimality, and the latter for less tree reconstruction overhead. The multicast agent is called various names such as MA (Multicast Agent), MHA (Multicast Home Agent), etc. It may forward multicast datagrams by the unicast tunneling, if any mobile host in its service requires.

In this paper, we propose a new hybrid routing protocol for mobile multicast. The proposed protocol takes advantage of the characteristics that mobile multicast has according to the speed of mobile hosts.

2   Related Work

The MOM (MObile Multicast) protocol [7,8] is one of the HA-based protocols. Two main features introduced are the DMSP (Designated Multicast Service Provider) selection algorithms and the link-level multicasting by the FA (Foreign Agent) for one hop wireless link. The DMSP is one or more HA selected by an FA. The DMSP is used to solve the *tunnel convergence problem*. It has the responsibility of forwarding multicast datagrams to the FA where its mobile host is attached. The DMSP selection algorithm includes random, age-based, count-based, proximity-based algorithms. The DMSP handoff means that an FA reselects its DMSP. It occurs when a new mobile host moves in and out of the foreign network in order to find a more suitable DMSP. Since IETF Mobile IP does not support an explicit re-registration mechanism, the FA is only able to notice a mobile host's handoff out of its network by the re-registration timeout. Therefore, as long as the stale DMSP information of the FA is not updated, mobile hosts in the foreign network suffer data loss until the FA selects a new DMSP. In general, frequent DMSP selections lead to more data loss.

The MMA [9] protocol is one of the hybrid style protocols. The multicast agent entity is called MA (Multicast Agent). With the 'JOIN option' on, a mobile host tries to join a multicast tree every time when it visits a new foreign network. In order to compensate the data loss during the latency of tree reconstructions, the FA receives datagrams by the unicast tunneling from the MA. In many cases, the MA information of a mobile host is informed to the FA by a mobile host's registration with the previous foreign agent notification. With the 'JOIN option' off, a roaming mobile host does not try to make extra multicast group join. It only triggers the MA selection in each foreign network to receive multicast datagrams by the unicast tunneling. If a mobile host encounters a foreign network already subscribing to the multicast group, its MA information is simply updated. Although the JOIN option provides optimal path, the protocol is susceptible to large tree reconstruction overhead. Likewise, when the JOIN option is not used, the data delivery path can be far from being optimal, because no more extra tree reconstruction occurs.

The RBMOM [10] protocol is also one of the hybrid style protocols. The multicast agent entity is called MHA (Multicast Home Agent). The RBMOM targets the tradeoff between the shortest routing path and the tree reconstruction by controlling the service range of a MHA. The service range is determined by the maximum hop distance value that the MHA allows. If a mobile host resides within the service range of the MHA, the MHA joins the multicast group as a proxy, and may forward the multicast datagrams to the FA where its mobile host is attached. When a mobile host moves out of the current MHA's service range, it selects a new MHA. The major role of the service range is to restrict the maximal length of the tunnel between a mobile host and its MHA. The RBMOM, however, has difficulty in deciding the hop distance of the service range, because two neighboring foreign networks can have various hop-distance values in the real network. Moreover, the MHA forwards multicast datagrams in its service range, regardless of how long the mobile host reside in the service range. If a mobile host reside in a foreign network, which is within the service range, for a long time, the data delivery path continues to remain sub-optimal during this time, leading to relatively large tunneling overhead and low scalability. On the other hand, when a high-speed mobile host passes many foreign networks in a short time, the small service range may still lead to large tree reconstruction overhead.

3 Proposed Protocol Overview

The important observation from the previous work is that the FA-based approach is advantageous in terms of the route optimality when a mobile host resides in a foreign network for a relatively long time (low mobility). And the HA-based approach is advantageous when a mobile host's handoff rate (high mobility) is high in terms of tree reconstruction overhead and data delivery latency. Accordingly, we defined our protocol design goal to take advantage of the characteristics that the mobile multicast has according to the speed of mobile hosts, which means that low tree construction overhead is advantageous for high-speed mobile hosts and route optimality is advantageous for low-speed mobile hosts.

The proposed protocol, TBMOM (Timer-Based Mobile Multicast), is a new hybrid style protocol, and uses a mobile host's JOIN-timer. The new multicast agent entity is called FMA (Foreign Multicast Agent). While a mobile host travels foreign networks, it dynamically selects the FMA and requests the FMA to join a multicast tree if the mobile host's timer expires. When the FMA completes the joining procedure and starts to receive multicast datagrams from the multicast tree, it takes the responsibility of delivering the multicast datagrams for the mobile host within a certain time interval. The FMA may forwards the multicast datagrams using the unicast tunneling, if mobile hosts reside in the service range of the FMA.

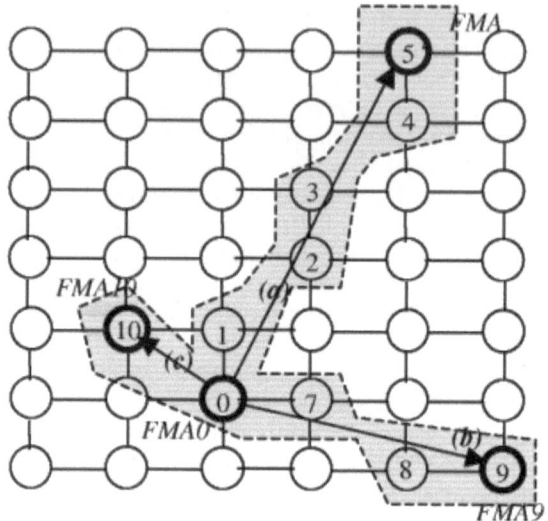

Fig. 1. The Service Range of TBMOM

Note that the service range is made by periodic JOIN operations and it looks different every time a timeout occurs. Figure 1 shows the service range. Each circle shows a foreign network where an FA is located. The bold circle shows a foreign network with FMAs. Each FMA is joined to the multicast tree directly. It manages its own multicast membership and may forward multicast datagrams to another FA where a mobile host in its service might be attached. Note that the service range of the proposed protocol is fluid form according to the mobility of a mobile host. When it is compared with the solid circle form of the service range in RBMOM [10], we believe it efficiently limits the tunneling path length and reduces tree construction overhead, according to the speed of mobile hosts.

In Figure 1, for example, three mobile hosts start at the lan0. It is assumed that each mobile host has the same time interval value, six seconds, and the multicast tree source resides in the lan0 here. Then, within six seconds of the time interval, the mobile host with high mobility (a) may move from the lan0 to lan5; the mobile host with intermediate mobility (b) moves from the lan0 to the lan9; the mobile host with low mobility (c) moves from the lan0 to the lan10. For the high-speed mobile host (a), joining a multicast tree occurs after its 5th handoff, while for the intermediate-speed mobile host (b) after 3rd handoff, and for the low-speed mobile host (c) after 1st handoff. This means that the service using the time interval makes tree reconstruction overhead remains constant for a high-speed mobile host at the cost of the route optimality, and the data delivery path optimal for a low-speed mobile host at the cost of tree reconstruction overhead. The cost of latter case, however, may be very low because it visits a few local foreign networks. Therefore, we can take advantage of the characteristics that the mobile multicast has according to the degree of mobility, which is the design goal of the proposed protocol as mentioned above.

When compared with two old schemes of the mobile multicast, the Bi-directional tunneling and Remote subscription, the time interval of the proposed protocol can be explained, for instance, as follows. We assume here that a mobile host receives multicast datagrams for sixty seconds and spends at least one second in a foreign network. If the time interval of a mobile host is set to longer than sixty seconds and the mobile host does not encounter any joined local foreign network while its roaming, TBMOM is similar to the Bi-directional tunneling scheme except the DMSP scheme. In this case, the HA is the only entity that forwards multicast datagrams to mobile hosts. If the timeout interval of a mobile host is shorter than one second, TBMOM is similar to the Remote subscription because the mobile host will require each FA that it visits to join a multicast tree and become its FMA. By determining a proper intermediate time interval value (1<time interval<60), tree reconstruction overhead can be restricted constantly even when a high-speed mobile host passes hundreds of local networks for a relatively short time. If a mobile host moves with low mobility and visits a few foreign networks for a relatively long time, a FA's tree joining by its mobile host's timeout will provide route optimality.

4   Event Handling and Data Structure of FMA

Two main events are when a mobile host moves into a foreign network and when the JOIN-timer of a mobile host expires. For simplicity, we assume each FA is enabled to be the FMA and has ability to process the registration including multicast service request. We will call an FA as the FMA only when it joins a multicast tree and it is able to support forwarding service as a proxy for mobile hosts. As a software module, the FMA module may be ported on an FA or HA. In Mobile IPv6 [11,12], however, FA may be no longer needed, in which case the FMA modules can be ported on HA module. Just as selecting one HA as the DMSP in MOM protocol, selecting the FMA as the DMSP also occurs in TBMOM. The DMSP selection algorithms in MOM protocol can also be deployed to the FMA selection for the DMSP.

4.1   Operation on MH Handoff

When a mobile host moves in a foreign network and requests a multicast group membership, it registers with the corresponding FA. For the registration, one of the reserved bits in the registration message is assigned for the M bit. We assume that the requested group information including the required multicast address can somehow be piggy-backed in the registration message in such a way as defining a new multicast extension. The group information also includes the remaining timer value of the mobile host. If the registration procedure completes, the FA copies the group information into memory, and starts to decrease the timer value synchronously with the timer of a mobile host. If the visited foreign network already has the requested membership, the FA will immediately serve as the FMA for the mobile host. Otherwise, the FA tries to send the FORWARD request message to the FMA of the mobile host. If the FA was already receiving the required multicast datagrams forwarded from another FMA, the FA selects a more suitable FMA considering the FMA of the new mobile host. If more suitable one is found, the FA performs DMSP FMA handoff.

4.2 Operation on Timeout

If any timer of the visiting mobile hosts expires, the FA of the foreign network becomes the FMA for the requested multicast group. The FMA starts to join the multicast group. At this time, the FA of the foreign network joins the multicast group as a proxy for the mobile hosts, and the FA is assumed to have a routing function. When the FA starts to receive multicast datagrams from the tree, all mobile hosts in the foreign network are informed of the change of FMA information. Subsequently, all visiting mobile hosts update their FMA information. Note that FMA handoff for DMSP selection occurs only for the time before one of visiting mobile hosts' JOIN-timer expires. Once one of JOIN-timers expires and FA completes the join procedure, no more FMA selection occurs. The decreasing timer value of a mobile host turns around to the initial value. The turning around continues as long as the mobile host is alive. If any timeout occurs in a foreign network that has the requested membership already, the mobile host timer turns around to its initial value and no further action is taken by the timer expiration.

4.3 Data Structure

Figure 2 illustrates the data structure of the proposed protocol. When the foreign network has the required multicast group, the FMA module maintains the *forwarding lists* to forward multicast datagrams to its away mobile hosts. When a foreign network does not have the required multicast group, the FMA module maintains the *group information lists* to receive the multicast datagrams forwarded from its DMSP FMA. One or more DMSP can be selected from the FMA lists. Once the FMA joins a multicast membership, the *group information list* is deleted, and the corresponding *forwarding list* is allocated. The FMA list of the *forwarding lists* may be deleted by the FORWARD stop message.

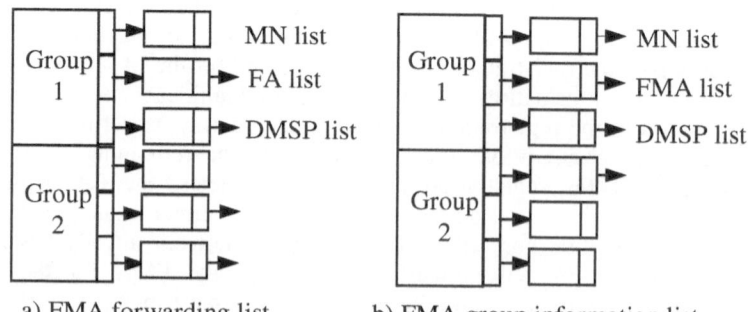

a) FMA forwarding list   b) FMA group information list

Fig. 2. The Data Structures of FMA module

Table 1. Simulation Parameters

Parameters	Description	Value
Time	Total simulation time unit	10000
Test	Total number of tests	9
N	The number of LANs	100
T	The number of initially joined LANs	10
M	The number of multicast group	1
G	The number of multicast group member	20
S	The mobility rate of a mobile host	1~100%
α	Timeout interval	4 tick
β	Hop distance	1 hop

5   Performance Evaluation

Performance evaluation of the proposed protocol was performed by discrete-event simulation using simulation time tick. As network topology, we assumed that 100 LANs are located on x-y coordinate system. The x-y coordinate of each LAN was selected randomly and fixed for entire simulation time. The initial multicast tree was established by ten of randomly selected LANs. The multicast source was selected randomly every 10000 simulation time tick. We also assumes the multicast tree is SPT and shortest path length between LANs is measured by Dijkstra's shortest path. The speed of a host was measured by the mobility rate, or handoff rate, ranging from 1 (low) to 100 (high). Random-walk mobility model was used as the pattern of a host's mobility. All member mobile hosts of the multicast group are assumed to be receivers and all LANs to have multicast routers for simplicity. For the DMSP FMA selection policy here, the closest-to-FA algorithm was used. Table 1 summarizes the parameters used in the simulation study.

The average number of tree reconstructions in Figure 3 means the average number of JOIN and PRUNE operations by mobile hosts during total simulation time. Although higher tree reconstruction overhead means shorter data delivery path length by SPT, it also implies higher processing overhead and longer latency before receiving multicast datagrams after handoffs. As mentioned earlier, the primary goal of the TBMOM protocol is to lower the high tree reconstruction overhead when the speed of mobile hosts is high. For comparison purpose with the RBMOM protocol, we found the time interval value of four matches the hop-distance range of one in the RBMOM protocol. As shown in the figure, the TBMOM protocol shows smaller number of tree reconstructions than the RBMOM protocol, when the handoff rates are about 60% or more.

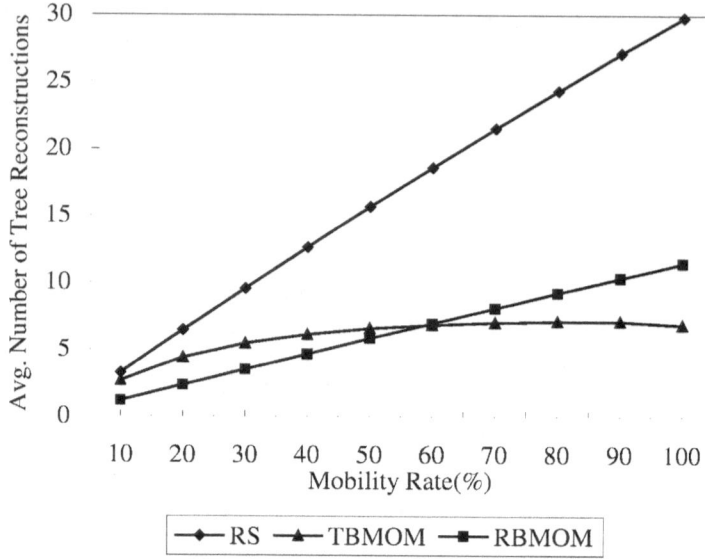

Fig. 3. Avg. Number of Tree Reconstructions per Mobility Rate

Figure 4 shows the average tunnel length as a function of handoff rate of mobile hosts. The RBMOM and TBMOM protocol have shorter tunnel length than the MOM or MMA protocol. The TBMOM protocol has shorter tunnel length in relatively low speed mobile hosts, when compared with the RBMOM protocol. In high mobility, however, TBMOM has slightly longer tunnel length in compensation for the lower tree reconstruction overhead. In the simulation, the crossover point of the two protocols appears at handoff rate 40.

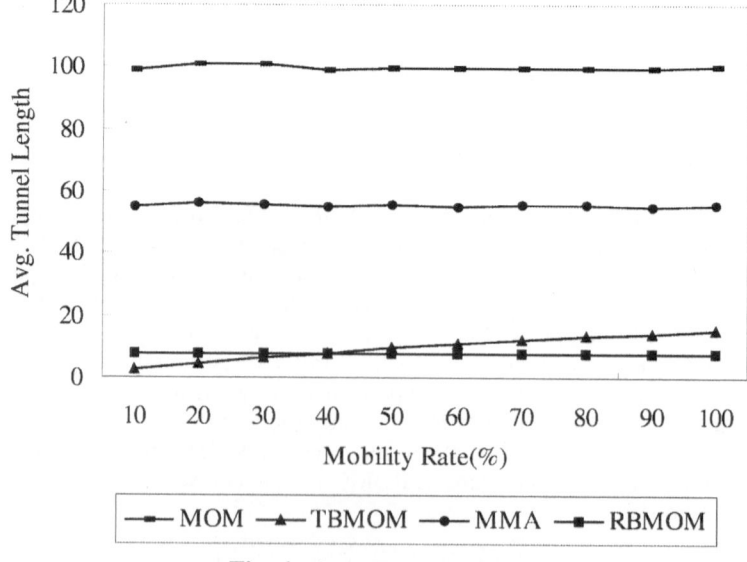

Fig. 4. Avg. Tunnel Length

As mentioned earlier, DMSP (Designated Multicast Service Provider) was first introduced to solve the *tunnel convergence problem*. The DMSP handoff means that an FA, which is not joined to the multicast tree, reselects its DMSP when it finds more suitable one. It is caused by a mobile host's handoff. Since frequent DMSP handoffs may cause data loss, the smaller number of DMSP handoffs provides better service for mobile hosts. When we compare TBMOM with RBMOM, the TBMOM protocol obtains the smaller number of DMSP handoffs when mobility rates are below 60 because it performs more JOIN operations than the RBMOM protocol, as shown in Figure 5.

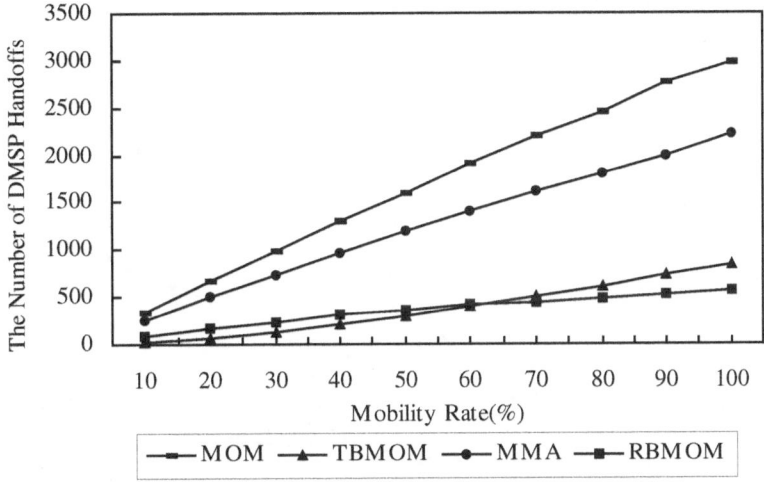

Fig. 5. The Number of DMSP handoffs per Mobility Rate

Average delivery latency due to handoffs in Figure 6 means the latency from the time when a mobile host is attached to an FA, to the time when multicast packets are delivered to the new location of the mobile hosts. In the HA-based scheme, such as the MOM protocol, the disruption is computed as the length of the path through which the registration message passes from the mobile host to the HA via the newly visited FA. In the FA-based scheme, the latency is computed as the length of the branch added to the multicast tree. However, adding a branch to the multicast tree is generally more costly than sending a message using unicast on the same path because of the extra processing at each multicast router on the path, leading to the longer latency. In Figure 6, 1.3 and 1.5 in RS (1.3) and RS (1.5) mean cost factors that are the ratio of the cost for constructing a branch to the multicast tree to the cost of sending a unicast message along the same path. In hybrid schemes, such as MMA, RBMOM, and TBMOM, both the latencies must be considered at the same time. The average delivery latency due to handoffs can also be called as the disruption of multicast service due to mobility, which is illustrated in [16]. As shown in Figure 6, TBMOM shows better performance than RBMOM in all of the mobility rate, or handoff rate. This is because the RBMOM protocol allows a mobiles host to reselect a new MHA and attempt to join multicast tree every time when the mobile host moves out of the service range of its previous MHA. Therefore, in this case, the latency of adding a branch must be added. If the mobile host roams within a service range, only the unicast path length between the mobile host and its MHA is computed for the latency. In TBMOM, however, a mobile host's timer expires while the mobile host is receiving multicast datagram by the unicast tunneling. The mobile host changes its FMA only if it is notified by it new FMA and receives multicast datagrams from the new FMA. Thus, TBMOM enables a mobile host to receive seamless multicast service even while it is changing its FMA. If the mobile host moves out of the local network before it actually receives multicast datagram from a new FMA, the mobile host does not change its FMA. By this smooth operation in changing a new FMA, TBMOM achieves the lowest average values of Data Delivery Latency due to Handoffs during the total simulation time. This mechanism can be more useful for a mobile reliable multicast [14,15].

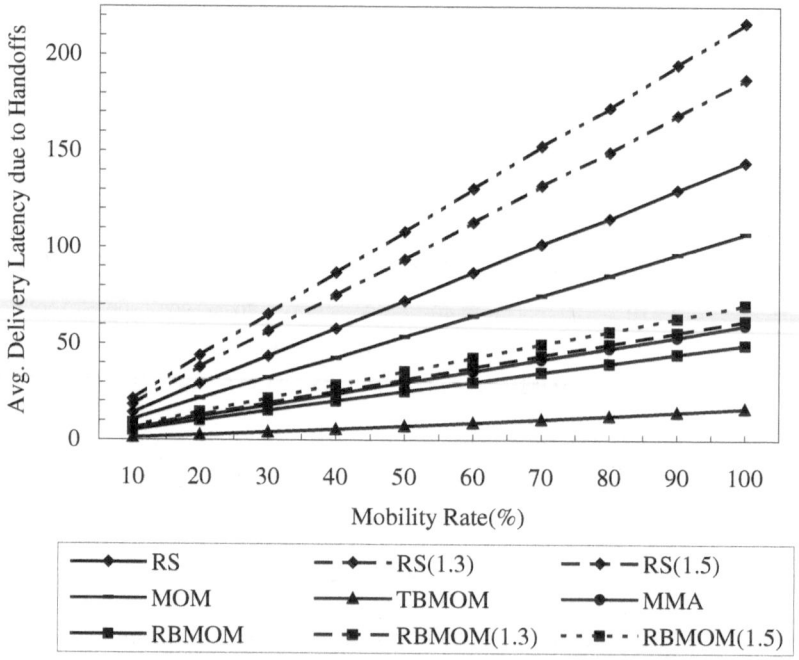

Fig. 6. Avg. Delivery Latency due to Handoffs

6 Conclusion

In this paper, we proposed an efficient mobile multicast routing protocol considering the speed of mobile hosts. In TBMOM, a foreign network joins a multicast tree periodically by a mobile host's timeout. This means that when a mobile host spends a relatively longer time in a foreign network, the foreign network comes to join a multicast tree, and when a mobile host moves fast passing many foreign networks in a relatively shorter time, it receives multicast datagrams forwarded from other entities, FMAs, to reduce the tree reconfiguration overhead.

The proposed protocol provides the better route optimality and smaller number of DMSP handoffs compared with MOM [7], MMA [9], and RBMOM [10] (in low mobility), and less tree reconstruction overhead when compared with remote subscription, MMA [9] and RBMOM [10] (in high mobility). In addition, the proposed protocol shows the least disruption of multicast services due to handoffs when compared with existing protocols.

References

1. C. K. Miller, "Multicast Networking and Applications", Addison Wesley, 1998.
2. S. Deering, "Multicast Routing in Datagram Internetworks and Extended LANs", ACM Trans. On Computer Systems, Vol. 8, No. 2, pp.85-110, May 1990.
3. C. Perkins, IP Mobility Support, RFC 2002, Mobile IP networking group.
4. C. Perkins, "Mobile IP Design Principles and Practices", Addison Wesley, 1997.
5. G. Xylonmenos, "IP Multicast for Mobile Hosts", IEEE Communications Magazine, pp. 54-58, January 1997.
6. V. Chikarmane, C. L. Williamson "Multicast Support for Mobile Host Using Mobile IP: Design Issues and Proposed Architecture", ACM/Baltzer Mobile Network and Applications, Vol. 3, no. 4, pp. 365-379, 1999.
7. T. G. Harrison, C. L. Williamson, "Mobile Multicast (MOM) Protocol: Multicast Support For Mobile Hosts", ACM MobiCom'97, pp. 151-160.
8. V. Chikarmane and C. L. Williamson, "Performance Evaluation of the MOM Mobile Multicast Protocol", ACM/Baltzer Mobile Networks and Applications, pp. 189-201, 1998.
9. Young-Joo Suh, Hee-Sook Shin, and Dong-Hee Kwon, "An Efficient Multicast Routing Protocol in Wireless Mobile Networks," ACM Wireless Networks, vol.7, no.5, pp.443-453, Sep. 2001.
10. Chunhung Richard Lin, Kai-Min Wang, "Mobile Multicast Support in IP Network", INFOCOM 2000 Vol.3, pp.1664 –1672.
11. C.E. Perkins, D.B. Johnson. "Mobility support in IPv6", ACM MobiCom'96, Nov. 1996.
12. David B. Johnson, C. Perkins, "Mobility Support in IPv6", Mobile IP Working Group INTERNET-DRAFT, June 1996.
13. David B. Johnson, Charles Perkins, "Route Optimization in Mobile IP", Network Working Group, Internet Draft(work in progress), July 7. 1995.
14. Wanjiun Liao, Chien-An Ke, Jiunn-Ru Lai, "Reliable Multicast with Host Mobility", GLOBECOM, Vol. 3, pp. 1692 -1696, 2000.
15. Chunhung Richard Lin, Chang-Jai Chung, "Mobile reliable multicast support in IP network", ICC 2000, vol 3, pp. 1421 –1425, 2000
16. Yu Wang, Weidong Chen, "Supporting IP Multicast for Mobile Hosts", Mobile Networks AND applications 6, pp. 57-66, 2001.

Fast Asynchronous Streaming Handoff

Jinsong Lin, Glenn Glazer, Richard Guy, and Rajive Bagrodia

University of California, Los Angeles
{jinsong, glenn, rguy, rajive}@cs.ucla.edu

Abstract. In this paper[1], we present a new signaling protocol that enables real-time audio/video viewing to transfer from one device to another, extending Application Session Handoff (ASH) to streaming media. ASH is a novel system service that provides seamless and uninterrupted data access across heterogeneous devices in the mobile, asynchronous computing environment. We discuss our architecture in detail, provide a sample application and present experimental results that show handoff latencies on the order of 10^{-2} to 10^{-3} seconds.

1 Introduction

Every day, more and more applications are joining the sphere of ubiquitous computing[2]. These applications face many challenges, including varied network environments, heterogenous platform/operating environments and the high availability demanded of "always-on" and realtime applications. Currently, such applications are limited by the software offerings of the cellular phone and pager companies. It is our goal to empower the user to easily and transparently utilize heterogenous devices and media without chaining themselves to a particular application or set of applications. We do this by providing the user with the ability to move a session. Note that by session, we mean a single, off-the-shelf, media application running on the user's desktop, allowing a finer grain of control over what is transferred than if the entire desktop or X session was transferred as in [3]. We refer to this ability to move sessions from device to device as Application Session Handoff (ASH)[4]. Thus, we achieve our goals by creating this new functionality of a fast handoff and in this paper we focus on streaming MPEG video as our media.

The solution space in which we to work is that of middleware servers and unaltered, legacy application servers. In this space, powerful server machines do work on behalf of less powerful clients machines to enable these clients to present media that they would not have otherwise been able to handle due to limitations of bandwidth, CPU power, display, and so forth. Note that with the exception of a small client wrapper on the client device, we have left unaltered both client and application server. This property gives us both a large degree of transparency to

---

[1] This project is an extension to the iMASH middleware architecture[1] and is supported by NSF grant ANI-9986679. An extended version of this paper is available at ftp://pcl.cs.ucla.edu/pub/papers/FASH.ps.gz

F. Boavida et al. (Eds.): IDMS/PROMS 2002, LNCS 2515, pp. 274–287, 2002.

and an easy, graceful insertion into the current network environment. In doing so, we impose a set of additional criteria aimed at providing the best possible user experience. The first is that we must support heterogeneous clients and networks, from high-powered desktops connected via high-speed LAN's to low-powered palmtops connected via wireless networks, and everything in the middle. Secondly, the ASH must be natural to the user experience. The delay between stopping on one device and starting on another should be minimal. There should be no loss of semantic data introduced by the ASH and no information should be presented twice. Another constraint is the desire to leave both server and player untouched so as to facilitate the use of commercial off-the-shelf products and ease of integration with legacy Application Servers (AS). This has the added benefit of generalizing our solution so that different applications such as audio-video players can be added as modules to the suite.

Heterogeneity of network and clients applies the requirement of content adaptation on the architecture. We approach this problem by introducing a modular, chained pipeline of adaptations we call a Content Adaptation Pipeline (CAP)[5]. Each module, or Media Processing Unit (MPU), may be called on any appropriate data stream and each one can accept the output of another and be used to create input for another. The CAP parses the stream and provides the appropriate adaptation. Thus, we see that executing an ASH for an audio-video presentation becomes significantly more complex than a simple sluicing or re-routing of the stream from one client to another.

2   Related Work

Moving applications among many hosts has been studied in several research areas, however none of them address all of the problems and enable all of the features that iMASH does. Mobile agents[6] is a related research area that was stimulated by the popularity of the Internet. In mobile agents, both the code and the state are moved along with the agent, and thus requires the applications to be written in one language and operate in a uniform run time environment.

The teleportation work done at Olivetti (now AT&T) in the early 1990's[3] tried to move entire X Windows or Windows sessions using a similar structure. However, this is a heavyweight protocol that seeks to transfer the entire desktop of the host operating system onto the client, rather than selected applications and our feeling that tremendous bandwidth and computation are being abused here is confirmed by the high-bandwidth requirements and low scalability of the SunRay[7] technology that Sun Microsystems implemented from the Olivetti model. Furthermore, all of the computation from accepting graphical interface events to adapting content is done at the proxy. This treats all clients uniformly as thin, dumb clients and deprives the system of useful computation that can be done local to the client.

BARWAN[8] exploits the heterogeneity of networks by providing a "vertical handoff" functionality, which allows a mobile client to dynamically change its connections to the servers among network interfaces. Their mechanism to support vertical handoffs relies on mobile-IP[9]. Comparing iMASH with BARWAN, we see several key differences. First, an iMASH handoff among different devices is more general than vertical handoff in BARWAN, therefore more challenging to implement. Second, we believe that handoff among multiple devices will be more commonly used in nomadic environment than vertical handoff, because a mobile device with two or more wireless interfaces are still rarely seen these days, and will probably still be the case in the near future due to the consideration of the power consumption and the weight of the device. Finally, using middleware servers as an infrastructure to support handoff is more flexible and easier to deploy than mobile-IP, because the implementation can built on existing network protocol stacks as demonstrated in our implementation (see Section 3.4).

Using a proxy architecture to perform distillation or transcoding of multimedia data has been investigated[10][5] by multiple research groups. However, our architecture goes one step further by incorporating session control and management with the content adaptation mechanism. Also, IETF has proposed a family of standards[11][12][13] to support session initialization and set up for applications like multimedia conferencing, but they do not address the issue of session transfer among different devices.

In a wireless network, disconnection or intermittent connection is the norm rather than the exception, and the Coda[14] file system tries to address the connection issue in the context of file systems by introducing disconnected operations. We believe such type of functionality should be easily supported in iMASH by leveraging the power of middleware servers to resolve the possible conflicts between multiple updates from mobile clients during disconnection. Coda's successor, Odyssey[15], provides application-aware adaptation by allowing the application to adapt the fidelity of its data contents based on the availability of system resources. The iMASH approach is similar to Odyssey in concept, but instead of building the complex adaptation mechanism on the mobile device OS, we push it to the middleware layer, which has almost unlimited resources compared to its mobile counterparts. This will greatly reduce the complexity of the client software, in turn reduce the energy consumption and increase the battery life of mobile devices.

3   Audio/Video ASH Architecture

3.1   Introduction to the iMASH Architecture

Figure 1 depicts our basic architecture. A client sends a request for a stream to the Application Server (AS) via the Middleware Server Service (MSS) for a video stream which is sent to the client back through the MSS. The MSS consists of distributed Middleware Servers (MWS) and a lightweight application router we call the Multiplexor. ASH considers as its start point a data flow currently streaming from the AS to the client application coupled with the desire to switch the application to a different device. At the time of the handoff, the session state is transferred via the MSS from the source client to the second and in doing so, a similar or identical application is spawned on the target client.

The important detail is that while session state and data flow from client to middleware to client, actual process code does not. Thus, an application with ASH is no longer bound by the constraints imposed by a single device or vendor and may choose the best of several available options at any given moment. In the sequel, we will show examples of a handoff that is triggered by a request from the user and also a handoff that can be triggered by other concerns such as mobility and fault tolerance. Note now that this use of the term "handoff" is

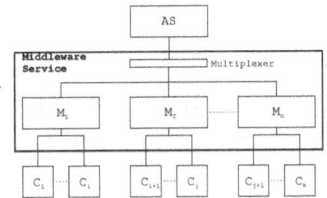

Fig. 1. Basic iMASH Architecture

different than what is typical in the cellular community, where the user device is constant and the base stations change, usually due to varying signal strengths or load-balancing policies. In our simplest case, the middleware is constant and the device changes. Notably, our architecture is based on multiple middleware servers (MWS) combined into a single MSS so that an ASH transfer can include transferring to a new MWS either as a policy choice internal to the MSS or as a means to execute the transfer between two clients. Further, cellular handoff is an OSI Layer 2 handoff and utilizes techniques and information only available deep within the protocol stack. ASH is a much more challenging project, since on one hand we must respect the entire stack[2] and yet our being at the Application Layer means that we cannot easily use any of the specialized techniques below us.

3.2   iMASH Audio/Video ASH Architecture

The key component in the iMASH architecture is a Middleware Server Service (MSS) strategically deployed between the application server and the clients. Acting as a proxy, the MSS mediates the communication between the clients and the server in order to facilitate the handoff of the multimedia sessions among varied devices in wired and wireless networks.

Figure 1 shows the general architecture with multiple MWS, using three MWSs and six clients as an example. In the most general case, the connections between the clients and the MWS form a fully connected graph, as are the connections between each MWS. However, policies such as security, cost, power and traffic management may reduce this. Such connections may be lazily instantiated as well. In order to work with multiple middleware servers, we have added a lightweight piece into the picture: a Multiplexor running at the application

---

[2] E.g., we must allow for TCP and UDP to both work equally well.

server or on a separate machine which functions as an application level router for the MSS. Looking at this figure, we can construct three example scenarios for ASH. First is the simple case of a handoff from Client 1 to Client 2 while retaining MWS 1. We will call this the client-only case, or CASH. The second case is similar to the standard mobility handoff in which a Client 2 hands off "to itself" and changes MWS from MWS 1 to MWS 2 in the process. We will call this the middleware-only case, or MASH. The third case is that of handoff from Client 1 to Client 3, but with a change of MWS as well. Since this case is, in fact, the composition of the first two, we will call this the full handoff case, or FASH.

A/V Handoff Architecture: Multiplexor. The purpose of the Multiplexor is simply to sluice the AS traffic it outputs from one MWS to another. If an ASH does not result in a change in MWS (as in the client-only case), the Multiplexor is never notified of any change and the AS keeps pumping data through the Multiplexor to the MWS involved. If the ASH requires a change in middleware server, the Multiplexor is informed by the old MWS to immediately stop sending to the old MWS and begin sending to the new MWS regardless of where in the data stream the transmission happens to be, allowing the Multiplexor to maintain total simplicity and full generality. After the redirection, it is then up to the old and new MWS to perform any synchronization or reconstruction of the data stream.

The Multiplexor is completely media independent and does not examine or modify the data, so that it may be utilized by different application servers and minimizes the alteration to the legacy servers. This also allows for the Multiplexor to be on a separate machine if the legacy machine is fully immutable.

A/V Handoff Architecture: Middleware Server. Figure 2 depicts a detailed view of the lower half of the architecture. For clarity, only one MWS and one client are shown. Off the diagram, the legacy application server retains its traditional role as the source of media stream. It is optimized for transmitting multimedia data in the wired high-bandwidth network setting and does not pay any potential cost of supporting session handoff and handling client and network variations. All of the complexities and intelligence are pushed into the middleware service. A middleware server is assumed to be a powerful computer with a fast CPU and large amounts of storage and memory space. The software architecture contains the following components, following the datapath from top to bottom (See Figure 2).

1. ServerProxy: The ServerProxy manages the communication channels between a middleware server and various application servers. It retrieves the data from the application server and exchanges control messages on behalf of the' clients. These control messages can include messages to the Multiplexor, authentication information, switch and fetch or start/pause/stop commands. In combination with the Multiplexor, the ServerProxy effectively hides the existence of the middleware infrastructure from the legacy server.

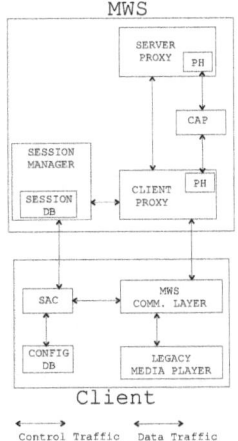

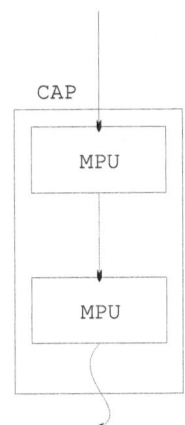

Fig. 2. A/V Session ASH Architecture   **Fig. 3.** A/V CAP Architecture

2. Protocol Handler (PH): The Protocol Handler acts as a wrapper around the CAP, freeing the CAP of the job of determining transmission protocols and data types. At the top, it strips off protocol information and insures that the CAP only receives data objects. On the bottom, the PH takes the transformed objects and re-wraps a protocol around them for shipment. The top end of the PH resides in the ServerProxy and the bottom end in the ClientProxy.

3. Content Adaptation Pipeline (CAP): The media stream arriving at the middleware server must go through the data path between ServerProxy and ClientProxy. Within the data path is a Content Adaptation Pipeline (see figure 3), which is composed of multiple Media Processing Units (MPU) configured as a sequence of modules connected together. A MPU is a software algorithm that can retrieve the structure information (such as macroblocks or bidirectionality) from the raw byte stream and then possibly manipulate the contents of the stream if content adaptation is required. A MPU pipeline structure can implement complex distilling and transcoding algorithms: for instance, assume that one MPU can reduce the frame rate of MPEG video stream and another can drop the color from the stream. By combining these two into a single CAP, we are able to dramatically reduce the size of the data transmitted to low power clients. Thus, the ability of the CAP to reconfigure itself on the fly by adding or removing MPUs dynamically for content adaptation proves to be an important feature in the context of session handoff. When a user transfers a multimedia session from one client to the next, the ASH may result in numerous changes in the needed adapation within a few seconds. This is handled by swapping MPU's in and out of the pipeline.

4. Session Manager(SM) and Session Database(SD): Each middleware server has a Session Manager to manage the session initialization and handoff process including all communication between MWSs of both control messages and data. The SD includes an unique Session ID for each session, the URN of the stream,

the UID/authentication, the client device address, and the session state which includes whether a session is in handoff and if another MWS is involved. This state may also include media metadata.

5. ClientProxy: ClientProxy serves as a contact agent for the application clients. It takes the clients' data requests and forwards them to ServerProxy and is also responsible for delivering data from the middleware server to the clients.

A/V Handoff Architecture: Clients. To support ASH, an application client must be MWS and session aware. All of the software running on the clients are lightweight and only communicate with the middleware and forward data to the player. The thin client wrapper consists of three major components. The first component is the Session Access Control (SAC). The SAC is always running on the client device and listens for incoming handoff requests. It manages the entry of a new session and the clean up of old ones. The Media Configuration Database contains a list of media types that the underlying platform supports and application information for type. This information is used by the CAP to decide which MPUs to use. The Middleware Aware Communication Layer (MACL) provides a set of API's that a client's application code calls to communicate with the MSS and the local SAC service. It is this piece which receives the data from the client's network buffers and passes it on to the appropriate child player. As discussed below, there may be times during a MASH in which the client will receive two streams of data for a short period of time and a small demultiplexor that is part of the MACL will reconstruct the original stream order.

3.3   A/V Handoff Protocol

The handoff protocol assigns responsibilities to each architectural component during the session handoff process and it also specifies the syntax and semantics of the control messages exchanged among the different subsystems. An ASH is initiated by the user in control of the session. In these protocol algorithms a message is received by a process either as a network or local user event and passed to the client wrapper.

CASH: The Client-Only ASH. We now present the process algorithms for the MACL and the MWS, followed by an outline of the CASH algorithm. Note that there are only two algorithms, since the client algorithm is identical on both source (C_1) and target (C_2) clients. These entities interact as follows:

1. the client application on the source client (C_1) sends a HANDOFF request (`Line 05`) to the Session Manager on the middleware server, along with the session ID and the IP address of the target device.

2. After receiving the HANDOFF request (`Line 33`), the Session Manager on the MWS internally notifies the ClientProxy associated with the session to stop sending data and buffer any data from the AS. Meanwhile, it connects to the Session Access Control (SAC) on the target and sends a SETUP request, along with the session ID and the media type (`Line 34`).

```
00 process Client {
01   while(true) {
02     wait(msg) //from UI or MSS
03     switch(msg) {
04       case(USER-REQUEST) {
05         Send: HANDOFF → MWS
06         wait(stream completed)
07         Send: DROP → MWS }
08       case(SETUP) {
09         if(media ∈ SAC)
10           launch(player)
11           Send: SUCCESS → MWS
12           Send: JOIN → MWS
13         else {
14           Send: FAILURE → MWS
15           STOP } }
16       case(SERVICE_UNAVAILABLE) {
17         Notify User Interface } } } }
```

```
30 process MWS {
31   while(true) {
32     switch(msg) {
33       case(HANDOFF) {
34         Send: SETUP → C₂ }
35       case(JOIN) {
36         reconfigure CAP
37         ClientProxy connects to Client
38         Send: Buffered data → C₂
39         Send: New data → C₂ }
40       case(DROP) {
41         Disconnect ClientProxy from Client }
42       case(FAILURE) {
43         if(MediaType)
44           Send: SETUP → C₂
45         else
46           Send: SERVICE_UNAVAILABLE } } }
```

Fig. 4. CASH Process Models: Client and Middleware

3. After receiving a SETUP, the SAC on the target client queries its database (**Line 8**) to obtain the name and path of the client application that can play this media type. If the query succeeds, SAC will instantiate the player and return SUCCESS to the MWS (**Line 11**).

4. After the new player is launched on the target device by the target's SAC, it uses the session ID to send a JOIN request (**Line 12**) to the MWS.

5. Upon receiving JOIN command (**Line 35**), the Session Manager will ask ClientProxy to set up the connection with the new client. It reconfigures the CAP (**Line 36**) based on the profile of the target device and composes a new data segment that has the proper header, followed by the sequence of block data not yet played by the source client. This data is buffered on the MWS until the player on the old client has emptied its buffer. Then, the middleware aware layer on that client notifies the middleware that it is time to start sending it to the new client.

6. The client that originates the handoff sends a DROP command (**Line 07**) to the middleware server, finishes cleaning up the process, and closes all its connections with middleware server.

7. After the MWS receives the DROP command from the source client and the JOIN request from the target, the ASH procedure is done. The ClientProxy will then start delivering stream data to the new client (**Line 39**).

MASH: The Middleware-Only ASH. MASHs are triggered by conditions within the network and the architecture, and thus may exhibit a very fine granularity. Figure 5 presents a visualization of the architecture's state transitions in which time moves forward from left to right and Figure 6 shows the protocols. In these protocols, MWS_S is the client's source MWS and MWS_T is the target MWS that accepts the handoff from MWS_S. The protocol begins with the optional sending of the MW-HANDOFF message (**Line 65**). This message is only required if the client wants to change middleware servers, rather than a change

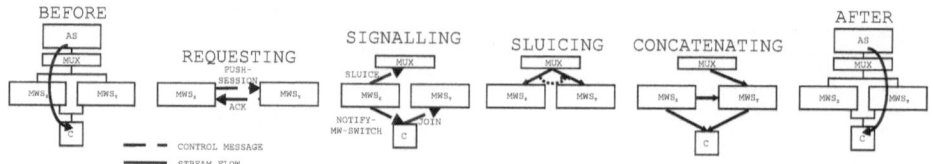

Fig. 5. MASH State Transitions

initiated by an internal policy of the MSS as discussed above. When MWS_S either receives the message or decides on its own that a handoff is required (**Line 84**), it sends a PUSH SESSION request message to its first choice of another MWS (**Line 85**).

Assuming that MWS_S gets an ACK from some MWS, let us denote this new MWS as MWS_T. MWS then informs the client Demultiplexor of the identity of the new MWS via a NOTIFY-MW-HANDOFF message (**Line 92**). As soon as the client receives this message, it sends a JOIN message to MWS_T. Simultaneously with contacting the client, MWS_T sends a SLUICE command to the Multiplexor (**Line 100**). The Multiplexor, in response to this message, immediately stops sending the stream to MWS_S and starts sending the stream to MWS_T, regardless of where in the data stream it is or how the stream is formatted. It does this by merely remapping the (IP,port) pair for the given stream.

During the time between MWS_S getting the ACK and the reception of the SLUICE command at the Multiplexor, data will still be flowing from the AS through the Multiplexor and on to MWS_S. MWS_S then makes another policy decision as to what to do with this fragment of the stream and any part of the stream it has buffered so far. Note that this buffer contains data distinct and "after" the data in the client wrapper's buffer which the wrapper always empties prior to sending the DROP command. Now, MWS_T is starting to receive the stream from the Multiplexor and possibly, from MWS_S. MWS_T takes in the entire fragment of the stream from MWS_1, and concatenates the stream from the Multiplexor behind it. Similarly, the Demultiplexor takes the fragment it gets from MWS_S, and concatenates the stream consisting of the previous concatenation to the fragment. The stream is now fully reconstituted and the situation is as before the protocol began, excepting only the new MWS. It should be noted that at all times during this protocol, the data stream is continuously flowing down to the Demultiplexor. This means that efficiency and synchronization are key, but also that some of the aforementioned concatenations may be null operations. An example of when this may occur is when the fragment from MWS_S to MWS_T is very small and is forwarded to the client before the stream from the Multiplexor begins to arrive.

FASH: The Full ASH. One of the elegant features of a modular architecture is that if the pieces are well-designed, then composing them to produce new effects should be nearly trivial and so it is with a FASH. Thus, a "full handoff" is the simple composition of the previous two cases, and so doing a FASH amounts

```
60 process Client {
61   while(true) {
62     wait(msg)
63     switch(msg) {
64       case(USER): {
65         Send: MW-HANDOFF → MWS₁
66         wait(msg) }
67       case(NOTIFY): {
68         Recv: NOTIFY-MW-HANDOFF ← MWSₜ
69         Send: JOIN → MWS
70         Order-Concatenate streams
71         Send: stream to player }
72       case(SERVICE_UNAVAILABLE) {
73         Notify User Interface } } }
```

```
80 process MWS {
81   while(true) {
82     wait(msg)
83     switch(msg) {
84       case(MW-HANDOFF || POLICY): {
85         Send: PUSH-SESSION → MWSₜ
86         wait(rmsg)
87         switch(rmsg) {
88           case(NACK): {
89             select another target MWS
90             CONTINUE }
91           case(ACK): {
92             Send: NOTIFY-MW-HANDOFF → Client
93             Send: MW-HANDOFF → MWSₜ
94             Stream per policy to Client
95       case(PUSH-SESSION): {
96         if(status=NO-ACCEPT) {
97           Send: NACK → MWSₛ
98           CONTINUE }
99         Send: ACK → MWSₛ
100        Send: SLUICE → Mux
101        Order-Concatenate streams
102        Send: stream → client } } }
```

Fig. 6. MASH Process Models: Client and Middleware

to doing a MASH with the NOTIFY-MW-HANDOFF being sent to a different client. This new client will treat it as a SETUP message and send the JOIN and so forth. From the perspective of the source client, it is though it had asked for a MASH and from the target client, as if it had been the recipient of a CASH. From the perspective of the MSS, we perform a MASH first and a CASH second.

In this way, MWS_T handles the asynchrony of stream blocks forwarded over different paths and we see that a Full Application Session Handoff protocol is the culmination of our Fast Asynchronous Streaming Handoff protocol.

3.4   Concrete Implementation

Based on the complete architecture proposed above, we have built a prototype as a proof of concept and also as a testbed for measuring the ASH latency. Both the client communication layer and the middleware are written in C/C++, and have been ported to Linux and Solaris. The client application wrapper is a daemon application and graphical user interface written in Java. The Multiplexor and Demultiplexor are also in Java.

Inside the middleware server, the ServerProxy is an HTTP client, which is able to connect to the Web servers on the Internet to retrieve MPEG video streams via the standard HTTP protocol. The only MPU currently implemented is a MPEG-1 stream parser that breaks up the MPEG video stream into a stream header and a sequence of Group of Pictures(GOPs)[16]. The output of the stream parser is stored in a FIFO queue that is later read by the ClientProxy. When ASH of any kind occurs, the stream data remaining in the FIFO queue will be redirected to the target.

We use MpegTV[17] as the client application. A user can request an MPEG video by entering the URL and then a user can send a handoff command by choosing the target client from lists of available dynamically discovered clients and MWSs.

4   Experiments and Measurement

We tested our architecture for both stability and efficiency. Our experimental setups, as detailed below, mirrors the setup shown in Figure 1, for the case of two MWSs and four clients. We ran each video a large number of times and randomly chose handoff times within each run of the video, exercising all three ASH types extensively and the results are presented below.

4.1   Initial Experimental Setup

As a sample environment, we set up a wired network of Dell Inspirons. The AS, Multiplexor, one of the MWSs and one of the clients were hosted on distinct model 8000s. The other three clients and the remaining MWS were run on distinct model 4000s. As an initial setup, two clients were assigned to each middleware, e.g. C_1 and C_2 to MWS$_1$ and C_3 and C_4 to MWS$_2$. A result of this is that there were only four permutations of CASH handoffs (C_1 to C_2, C_2 to C_1, C_3 to C_4, and C_4 to C_3). There were four permutations of MASH handoffs (one for each client) and sixteen permutations of FASH handoffs, resulting in 24 distinct handoff possibilities.

In order to rigorously test the client and middleware software, we designed and implemented an automated controller program. This controller exercised each permutation 15 times for a total of 360 test runs. During each run, the given type of ASH was exercised at three random intervals in the stream, for a total of 1,080 handoffs. Within each run, two clients, A and B were randomly chosen and the three handoffs consisted of $A \to B$, then $B \to A$ and back by $A \to B$. Further, it randomly selected the order in which these 360 runs would occur, eliminating any possible hysteresis effects from running the same handoff twice or more times in a row. This randomization is also a powerful statistical technique to eliminate the effects of covariates and the large number of repetitions eliminates experimental error. The controller itself ran on another machine, remotely directing which handoffs would occur when by directly communicating with the appropriate MWS and impersonating the client to request a handoff. Lastly, we performed the experiment twice, once with a live action video and once with an animated presentation. Figure 7 describes the videos we used.

	size (K)	frame width	frame height	framerate	time
animation	18,758	240	144	30	5:45
live action	9,000	240	160	30	3:03

Fig. 7. Experimental Data Stream Characteristics

To investigate how long an ASH would take, the clients included a local times-tamp along with any messages sent to the middleware. To solve the distributed clock problem, we used NTP[18] over the same links as the data to synchronize the times of all of the machines. However, we found that some small clock skew did occur, generally around the order of 10^{-4} seconds (or less) and thus we only report data up to an accuracy of 10^{-3} seconds. This is also the maximum level of resolution that NTP claims for LAN environments. We measured the interval duration from the point in time in which the handoff is first requested until the time the new client is ready to receive data. [3]

Throughout our analysis below, we use an $\alpha = 0.05$ for the mean, normalized standard deviation and error to remove the few outliers present. The behaviors seen in the live action experiment and in the animation experiment are essentially the same and therefore we only present the animation results for lack of space. This also allows us to conclude that our experiments are independent of the specific MPEG presentation and server.

4.2   Single Middleware Results

We report a mean CASH handoff time of $\mu = 0.008$ seconds; the standard deviation and error were both 0 to three digits and thus formally below our level of significant digits.[4] The data clearly shows that we have time invariance as well. Thus, we see that if we have the luxury of a single middleware server (i.e., few enough clients that one middleware can support them all), we obtain extremely fast (well below the threshold of human perception) and extremely consistent results. In our actual viewing of the test in progress, the only visible delay after signaling a handoff was the time it took to load the buffer of the player on the new client and this is strictly dependent on a user-tunable environment variable. While these results are good, a single middleware solution does not not scale and this brings us to the multiple middleware case.

4.3   Multiple Middleware Server Results

Multiple middleware servers introduce two kinds of handoff. In the MASH case, the client remains constant and the session is passed from one middleware server to the next. In the FASH case, both middleware server and client change. To remove as much clock skewing from our data as possible, we used a standard procedure for measuring link latency using a full RTT and took the last two handoffs of the three handoffs per run and averaged them. If H is the wall clock time and Δ is the clock skew, then the mean μ of two handoffs in opposite directions is given by $\mu = \frac{(H+\Delta)+(H-\Delta)}{2} = H$. We chose the last two handoffs rather than the first two handoffs as to avoid any possible initial conditions. For

---

[3] This would be Step 5 (**Line 12**) in the CASH client process and **Line 71** in the MASH/FASH client process.

[4] The "actual" value for the normalized standard deviation was 3.5E−4 and the "actual" value for the error was 2.7E−5.

the MASH case, we observed that the mean handoff time was $\mu = 0.063 \pm 0.006$ with a standard deviation of $\sigma = 0.035$. For the FASH case, we obtained $\mu = 0.016 \pm 0.001$ with $\sigma = 0.008$. We see that the cost of a FASH is not much greater than a CASH, both being on the order of 10^{-2} seconds.

Initially, it concerned us that the MASH times were significantly larger than the FASH times. What we found, after some investigation and review is that our implementation contains a minor performance hit. Our client wrapper for the video player uses a single threaded client and so when it comes time to do a handoff, the request waits at the client while it to handles whatever MPEG data it has. It is this wait time that became incorporated in our measurements for the MASH timing. This then explains why this problem occurs in MASH, but not in CASH or FASH, since in the latter two cases we re-create the session on a new client, effectively multi-threading the client. Thus, we believe that writing a multi-threaded client would fix this problem completely and some informal testing with our new architecture (see Section 5) has born out this conclusion.

4.4   Wireless Results

We re-ran a subset of the previous experiment with one client's wired NIC replaced with an 11Mbps Orinoco WaveLAN card. Since we have shown that the results were media independent, we randomly selected the animated (versus the live) presentation from before. These choices resulted in a data set of 60 CASHs, 30 MASHs and 60 FASHs. For CASH, we obtained $\mu = 0.017 \pm 0.002$ with a $\sigma = 0.006$; for MASH $\mu = 0.076 \pm 0.012$ with a $\sigma = 0.039$; and for FASH $\mu = 0.021 \pm 0.008$ with a $\sigma = 0.029$. These mean values are remarkably consistent with the previously obtained values and confirms our hypothesis that this protocol can operate in the restricted mobile environment. There is an increase in the latency of approximately 0.01 seconds which is constant across all handoffs and it is our conjecture that traversing between subnets and the contention for the wireless is as much or more responsible for this as is the change of bandwidth. The errors values are also slightly higher, but consistent with the reduced sample size.

5   Conclusions, Work in Progress, and Future Work

In this paper, we have proposed a general middleware framework to support the session handoff of real-time audio/video media stream among heterogeneous clients. We also developed an application-independent handoff protocol to manage the complexity of the handoff process. As a prototype, we built a middleware and client software suite that supports real-time MPEG video stream transmission and session handoff across heterogeneous devices. The measurements on the prototype show that our middleware architecture is a viable solution to support the novel transfer of complex multimedia services in the nomadic environment.

Our future work involves a more generalized implementation that will integrate a fully functional CAP, encryption and a MWS cache, along with more application types.

The authors would like to thank Vitaliy Dykhne and Vadim Olshansky for their assistance on this project in crafting a very early version of the prototype. We would also like to thank George Zorpas for his valuable input on CAP functionality.

References

1. "Interactive mobile application support for heterogenous clients," http://pcl.cs.ucla.edu/projects/imash.
2. Mark Weiser, "The computer for the 21st century." *Sci.Am.*, pages 94–110, September 1991.
3. "AT&T laboratories cambridge: The teleporting system." http://www.uk.research.att.com/teleport/.
4. T. Phan, K. Xu, R. Guy, and R. Bagrodia, "Handoff of application sessions across time and space." *IEEE International Conference on Communications*, 2001.
5. T. Phan, G. Zorpas, and R. Bagrodia, "An extensible and scalable content adaptation pipeline architecture to support heterogeneous clients." The 22nd International Conference on Distributed Computing Systems (ICDCS 2002).
6. D. Kotz and B. Gray, "Mobile agents and the future of the internet." *ACM Operating Systems Review*, 33(3):7–13, 1999.
7. "Products & Solutions - SunRay Information Appliances." http://www.sun.com.
8. E.A. Brewer and R.H. Katz, et al, "A network architecture for heterogeneous mobile computing." *IEEE Personal Communications*, October 1998.
9. C. Perkins, "IP mobility support, October 1996." IETF RFC 2002.
10. R. Han and P. Bhagwat, et al, "Dynamic adaptation in an image transcoding proxy for mobile web browsing." *IEEE Personal Communications Magazine*, December 1998.
11. M.Handley, et al, "SIP: Session initiation protocol." IETF RFC 2543.
12. M.Handley, et al, "SDP: Session description protocol." IETF RFC 2327.
13. M.Handley, et al, "Sesssion announcement protocol." IETF RFC 2974.
14. J.J. Kistler and M. Satyanarayanan, "Disconnected operation in the coda file system." *ACM Transactions on Computer Systems*, 10(1), February 1992.
15. B. Noble and M. Satyanarayanan, et al, "Agile application-aware adaptation for mobility." In *Proceedings of the 16th ACM Symposium on Operating System Principles*, October 1997.
16. Joan L. Mitchell, William B. Pennebaker, Chad E. Fogg, and Didier J. LeGall, *"MPEG Video Compression Standard."* Chapman and Hall, 1996.
17. "MpegTV - MP3, MPEG, VCD software for Windows, WinCE, Linux, Unix etc," http://www.mpegtv.com.
18. "Time server," http://www.eecis.udel.edu/ ntp/index.html.

Power Constraints: Another Dimension of Complexity in Continuous Media Playback*

Jungwan Choi and Youjip Won

Division of Electrical and Computer Engineering, Hanyang University,
17 Hangdangdong Seongdongku, Seoul, Korea
{chrys, yjwon}@ece.hanyang.ac.kr

Abstract. In this paper, we address the issue of minimizing the power consumption in retrieving the continuous media data from the disk drive for real-time playback purpose. Different from the legacy text based data, real-time multimedia playback requires that the storage supplies the data block *continuous* fashion. This may put immense burden on the power scarce environment since the disk is required to be *active* for the entire playback duration. We develop elaborate algorithm which carefully analyzes the power consumption profile of the disk drive and which establishes the data retrieval schedule for the given playback. It computes the amount of data blocks to read, the length of *active* and *standby* period. According to our simulation result, the ARM algorithm exhibits superior performance in continuous media retrieval from the aspect of power consumption to legacy playback scheme.

Keywords: Disk Scheduling, Power Management, Multimedia, Playback, Mobile Device

1 Introduction

1.1 Motivation

Due to the rapid deployment of the mobile devices and the concern of environmental impact of electronic systems, reducing the power consumption of the system becomes one of the most important issues. The disk portion of the power consumption has decreased in past few years from 25% to 10%[13]. However, it is still one of the major components which take up significant fraction of power in entire system. While the disk based storage device, e.g. hard disk and optical disk becomes small enough to be used in mobile devices, the practical usage of which leaves much to be desired due to the stringent power consumption restriction of the mobile device.

Typical approach to reduce the power consumption for hard disk drive is to shutdown the disk when there is no outstanding I/O requests[7]. Disk shutdown algorithms can be classified into two categories: *predictive*[3] and *stochastic*[2]

---

* This work is supported by KOSEF through Statistical Research Center for Complex System at Seoul National University.

F. Boavida et al. (Eds.): IDMS/PROMS 2002, LNCS 2515, pp. 288–299, 2002.

schemes. State transition from *standby* state to operational state entails extra power consumption. Thus, it is required to elaborately model the energy consumption profile for a given workload and to establish the disk operation schedule.

Different from general purpose computer, mobile handheld device usually has dedicated purpose. This leaves us great chance of optimization in various aspect of system design since the workload exhibits rather unique and predictable behavior. Continuous media retrieval from low power disk is not an exception. We believe that it is possible to achieve greater reduction in power consumption by effectively exploiting the workload characteristics and by incorporating it into I/O scheduling.

In this work, we like to address the problem of minimizing the power consumption of the disk drive for real-time multimedia data playback. The major issue in supporting the real-time playback of multimedia data in the local storage is *how to guarantee the continuous flow of data*. Round based disk scheduling algorithm has been widely used to support the continuous flow of the data[5, 10]. Preceding works assume that the disk drive operates always in the *steady* state. However, disk drive controlled by dynamic power management can adaptively change the state of operation, e.g. *active* or *standby*, with respect to the state of workload [11,13]. While this feature can significantly extend the battery life, it adds another dimension of complexity in scheduling of the multimedia data retrieval. We elaborately model the power consumption behavior of the low power disk drive and develop an algorithm which guarantees real-time multimedia playback while minimizing the power consumption involved in operating the storage device. We presently assume that the multimedia file is constant bit rate(CBR) encoded.

1.2   Related Works

There have been a number of works regarding the hard disk power management. A set of hard disk requests are grouped into a number of distinct sessions, and disk is shutdown between the sessions. The prime issue here is how to detect the session termination. Simunic et al.[11] used semi-Markov decision process model. Lu et al.[7] adaptively changes the threshold value for detecting session termination. By increasing the number of disk states, it is possible to reduce the power consumption of the disk[13]. Greenawalt[4] et al. formulates the relationship between the number of disk state transitions, power consumption, and system performance.

There have been a number of power management approach from the operating system's point of view[1,9,6,12]. Helmbold et al.[8] introduced an algorithm that decides when to spin down the disk of a mobile computer in order to reduce the power consumption. The algorithm called the *share algorithm* dynamically chooses a time-out value as a function of recent disk activity. The above mentioned power management strategy assumes that the device operates in the *generic* workload. When the device(or embedded system) is designed to perform specific task, e.g. MP-3 player, digital camera, personal video recorder, etc., it is possible to further effectively exploit the characteristics of the underlying workload to minimize the power consumption of the storage drive.

2   Power Consumption Profile of Low Power Drive

We first examine the power consumption profile of the low power disk drive[1]. Figures in Fig. 1 illustrate the power consumption profile of the lower power disk

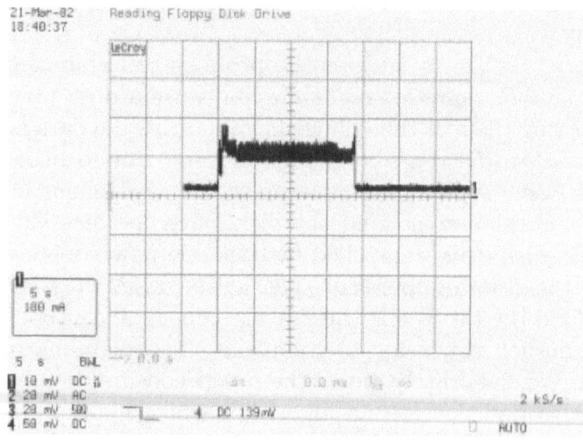

(a) Power Consumption Profile for entire play-back duration

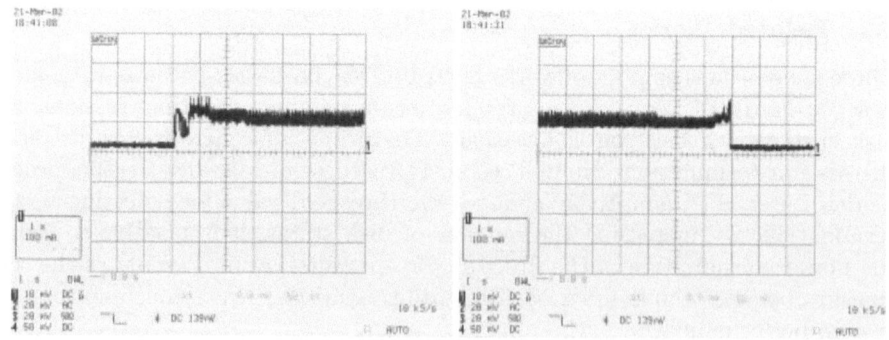

(b) Power Consumption profile dur-ing Startup phase

(c) Power Consumption profile dur-ing Finish phase

Fig. 1. Power Consumption Profile of IBM MicroDrive(DMDM-10340)

---

[1] It is measured using WavePro 950 from LeCroy. Sampling rate is 16 Gigasamples/sec

drive. We measure the power consumption of real-time playback of MP3 file(1.5 Mbits/sec, 20 sec) in the IBM MicroDrive(DMDM-10340). It was measured on Compaq Notebook(ARMADA M700) loaded with Windows XP. Windows media player is used for music playback. Fig. 1(a) shows the power consumption during entire playback. Fig. 1(b) magnifies the power consumption behavior during the start of the playback. We find that spinning up the disk requires extra overhead in power consumption and it takes approximately 1.7 sec before the disk reaches the steady state. Fig. 1(c) illustrates the power consumption profile during the disk shutdown. Disk platter stops rotating when there is no outstanding I/O requests for a certain period of time. According to our experiment(Fig. 1(c)), the length of *finish* phase is approximately 0.8 sec[2]

We model the power consumption behavior of the disk drive as in Fig. 2. Retrieving data blocks from the disk drive consists of five phases: *Startup, Read, Idle, Finish* and *Standby* phases. The device is initially in *Standby* state. In the standby mode, it goes into startup mode when the device interface accepts the commands, e.g. I/O requests. Startup phase includes the operation of *spin up, focus* and *tracking*. In *Read* phase, the disk drive transfers data from the disk. When all outstanding I/O requests are serviced, disk drive state changes from *Read* state to *Idle* state. In idle phase, the disk head is in the parking position and the spindle is still rotating at the full speed. Disk drive state changes to *read* when new command arrives. Power saving algorithm has *time-out* value for *idle* phase. If no request arrives for *time-out* period of time, disk drive goes into *finish* phase where the platter spins down and which eventually goes into *standby* state. In standby phase, disk head is in the parking position. The spindle stops rotating and all circuitry except host interface are in power saving mode. It is important to note that commodity small size disk based storage device retrieve the data based on *startup, read, idle, finish,* and *standby* phases.

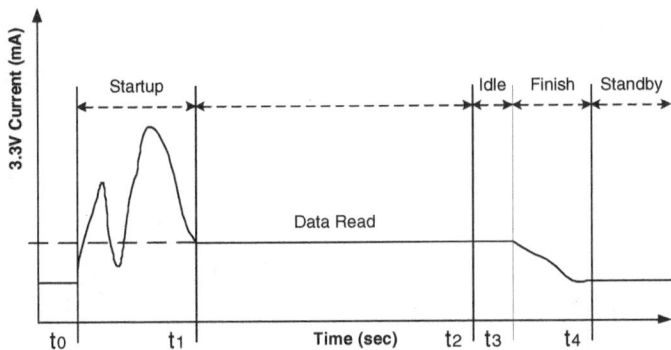

Fig. 2. Schematic View of Power Consumption Profile of Data Read Operation

---

[2] We will use the term *phase* and *state* interchangeably.

For real-time multimedia playback, an application issues burst of reads periodically and the disk supplies the data block in periodic fashion conformant to the playback rate. The size of read burst and the interval between the adjacent read bursts need to be carefully determined based upon the available buffer size, tolerable startup latency, disk overhead such as seek and rotational latency[15]. The power saving feature of low power disk drive introduces another dimension of complexity in determining these value due to the existence of *standby* period. *Standby* period should be effectively incorporated into retrieval schedule in order to minimize the power consumption for multimedia playback.

3   Adaptive Round Merge(ARM) Scheduling

3.1   Problem Formulation

Fig. 3 illustrates the multimedia data retrieval operation in desktop environment and mobile environment. The term "desktop environment" is used to denote the disk drive which does not have dynamic power management feature. In desktop environment, the disk stays active during entire playback period. In the low power disk drive equipped with dynamic power management feature, it is possible that the disk drive retrieves the data block in burstier manner and goes into the standby state(right-hand side of Fig. 3). This is primarily to reduce the fraction of *active period* in entire playback.

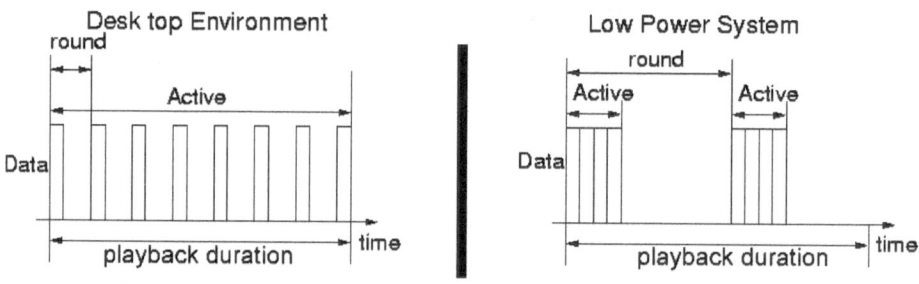

Fig. 3. Multimedia Data Retrieval: Desktop environment vs. Mobile Environment

The Adaptive Round Merge algorithm proposed in this work is designed to minimize power consumption to retrieve multimedia data from the disk. We first formulate the power consumption behavior in multimedia playback. Without power management algorithm(left-hand side of Fig. 3), disk drive is in *read* state during the entire playback period. We define it as *Normal Playback*.

Let B^* be the size of buffer. R and r denotes the maximum transfer rate of the disk and the playback rate. The term L denotes the playback length. The length of read phase, T_p, corresponds to $\frac{B^*}{R-r} + \frac{Lr-B}{r}$. This is because the transfer rate from the disk is bounded by the playback rate once the buffer is full. P_s

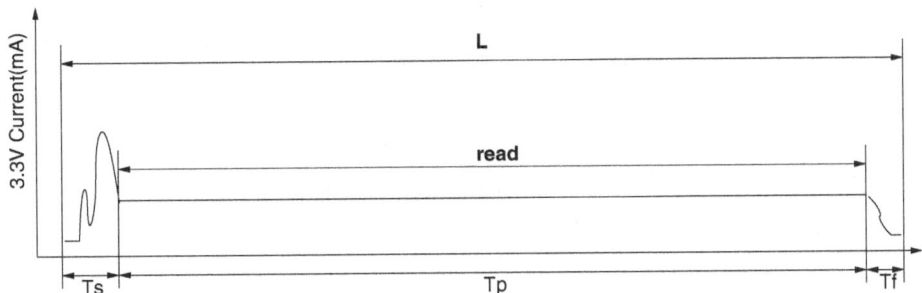

(a) Power Consumption Profile in Normal Playback Strategy

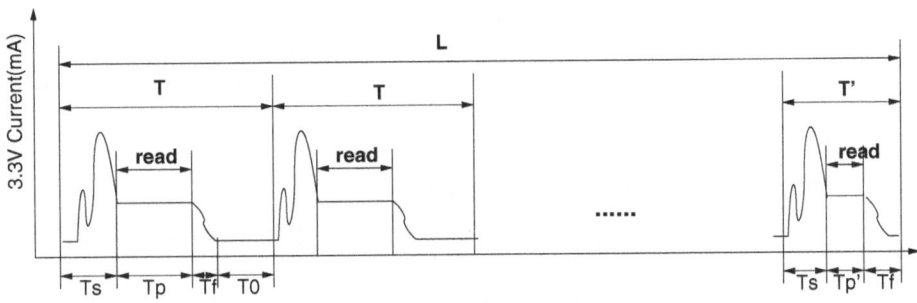

(b) Power Consumption profile in Full Buffering Strategy

Fig. 4. Multimedia Data Retrieval and Power Consumption Profile

and P_f denote the power consumption in *startup* and *finish* phases, respectively. The term α denotes the power consumption rate in read phase. Fig. 4(a) shows the power consumption profile in retrieving the multimedia data using normal playback strategy. We can formulate the total power consumption in normal playback, $\mathcal{P}_\mathcal{N}$, as Eq. 1

$$\mathcal{P}_\mathcal{N} = P_s + P_f + \alpha T_p$$
$$= P_s + P_f + \alpha(\frac{B^*}{R-r} + \frac{Lr - B}{r}) \tag{1}$$

Another way of retrieving the multimedia data is *Full Buffering* strategy. In *full buffering* strategy, the disk reads the data blocks until the buffer is full and immediately goes into *standby* state. In this strategy, entire playback is made up of sequence of *rounds*. In each round, active period consists of *startup*, *read* and *finish* phase. The read phase ends when the buffer is full. Fig. 4(b) illustrates the power consumption profile in retrieving the multimedia data using *Full Buffering* strategy. Length of read phase in each round, T_p, corresponds to

$\frac{B^*}{R-r}$. T_s, T_p, T_f and T_0 denotes the length of *startup, read, finish* and *standby* phase, respectively. Let T be the length of a round. If the length of read phase is T_p^*, we can compute the length of a round, T, as large as $\frac{T_p^* R}{r}$. Let us formulate the total power consumption in Full Buffering strategy. All the rounds except the last one have the same length and the last round in the playback can be shorter than the preceding ones. Let N be the number of rounds of the same length. We can compute the total power consumption in Full buffering, $\mathcal{P}_{\mathcal{F}}$, as in Eq. 2.

$$\mathcal{P}_{\mathcal{F}} = N(P_s + P_f + \alpha T_p) + (P_s + P_f + \alpha T_p')I \tag{2}$$

$$= \left\lfloor \frac{Lr}{\frac{B^* R}{R-r}} \right\rfloor (P_s + P_f + \alpha \frac{B^*}{R-r}) + (P_s + P_f + \alpha T_p')I \tag{3}$$

T' and T_p' denotes time to read the remaining data in the last round and the length of read phase in the last round. I is an index function, which is 0 if $L \bmod T = 0$ and 1, otherwise. If playback length, L, is integer multiples of T, i.e. $I = 0$, *Full Buffering* yields minimum power consumption.

3.2 Adaptive Round Merge Algorithm

In *Full Buffering*, the disk drive stops reading when buffer is full and then goes into standby phase. This is because efficiency of the power consumption is significantly degraded when the disk continues reading after the buffer is full. However, restarting another rounds accompanies *start* and *finish* phase which is just an overhead. If the amount of remaining data is *small*, it may not be worth reading the remaining blocks in separate round which accompanies *startup* and *finish* phase from the perspective of the power consumption. When the buffer is full, we need to decide whether to keep reading the remaining data block in the current round or to enter *finish* phase. We develop a framework which determines whether to read the remaining data blocks in the current round or in the separate round. We assume that the power consumption during the *standby* phase is negligible.

The length of the *standby* period, T_0, can be computed as $\frac{T_p * R}{r} - (T_s + T_f + T_p)$. It takes $\frac{B^*}{R-r}$ to fill the empty buffer. Once the buffer is full, disk can retrieve the data block only at the rate of consumption. Thus, the amount of data blocks read during T_p can be represented as in Eq. 4.

$$B = \begin{cases} T_p R & , \ if \ T_p \leq \frac{B^*}{R-r} \\ \frac{B^*}{R-r} R + (T_p - \frac{B^*}{R-r})r, & otherwise. \end{cases} \tag{4}$$

Let B the amount of data blocks retrieved during a single round. Then, the amount of remaining data blocks read in the last round, B_l is corresponded to $L \cdot r - N \cdot B$. Power consumption in the last round corresponds to $P_s + P_f + \alpha \frac{B_l}{R}$. If we merge the last round with its immediately preceding one(round merge), we can save the power consumption of *startup* and *finish* phases of the

Table 1. Adaptive Round Merge Algorithm

Algorithm: Adaptive Round Merge Algorithm() {
```
  i=0;
  compute N;        /* N denotes the number of equal length rounds. */
  compute P_N;      /* P_N is total power consumption in Normal playback */
  compute P_F;      /* P_F is total power consumption in Full buffering */
  compute P*;
  IF( P_N ≤ P_F ) {
      startup();          /* spin up, focus and tracking */
      continue reading;   /* Disk is in read state during the playback */
      finish();
  }
  ELSE {
      WHILE(N≠ 0) {
          D_r = L · r − i · B;
          startup();
          read();
          IF(D_r < B AND P* < 0) {
              continue reading;
              finish();
              N--;
          }
          finish();
          N--; i++;
      }
  }
}
```

last round. However, *read* phase in the preceding round is extended by $\frac{B_l}{r}$ and additional power consumption, $\frac{\alpha B_l}{r}$ is ensued. We can finally establish function $\mathcal{P}^*$ to determine whether to merge the last round to its immediately preceding round or not as in Eq. 5.

$$\mathcal{P}^* = \underbrace{P_s + P_f + \alpha\frac{B_l}{R}}_{without\ Merge} - \underbrace{\alpha\frac{B_l}{r}}_{with\ Merge} \qquad (5)$$

If $\mathcal{P}^* > 0$, the last round is merged with the preceding one. Otherwise, last B_l data is retrieved in the separate round. This algorithm achieves the minimum power consumption in retrieving given multimedia data. Table 1 illustrates the details of the algorithm.

4   Simulation

We examine the effectiveness of our algorithm via simulation based experiment. The disk parameters are modeled after IBM microdrive DMDM-10340. *Startup* phase is 1 sec long and consumes 0.858 Joule. *Finish* phase is 0.4 sec long and consumes 0.7 Joule. Power consumption in steady state read operation is 0.924 Watt. Disk transfer rate is 41.6 Mbits/sec. The playback rate is 1.4 Mbits/sec[14].

4.1   Buffer Size vs. Power Consumption

We first compare the power consumption under different buffer sizes, B^*. The X-axis and the Y-axis in Fig. 5 denotes playback length and the power consumption, respectively. As shown in Figures in Fig. 5, power consumption is inversely proportional to the buffer size. With the larger buffer size, the disk can fetch larger amount of data in each round and subsequently power efficiency improves. Let us consider 10 sec playback. With 512 KByte buffer, merging the round with the preceding one in *Adaptive Round Merge* brings approximately 9% reduction in power consumption against the Full Buffering strategy. The effect of round merge manifests itself typically when the playback length is relatively short, typically less than 60 sec.

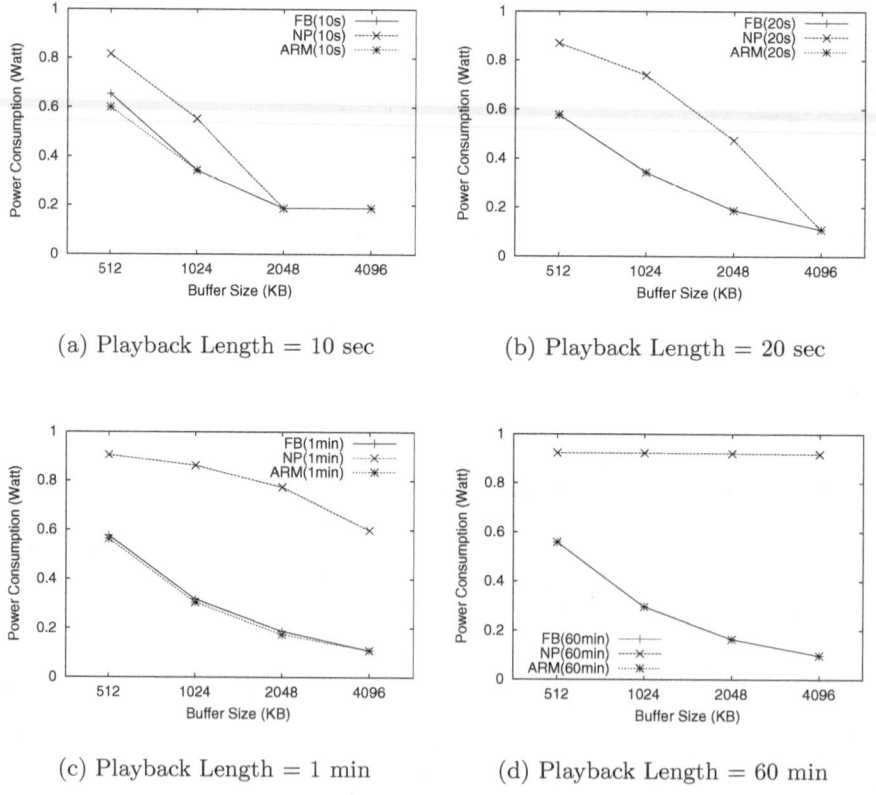

(a) Playback Length = 10 sec   (b) Playback Length = 20 sec

(c) Playback Length = 1 min   (d) Playback Length = 60 min

Fig. 5. Buffer Size vs. Power Consumption

In *Normal Playback* strategy, effectiveness of using larger buffer greatly depends on the length of playback. With short playback (Fig. 5(a), Fig. 5(b)), using the larger size buffer improves power consumption behavior. This is because significant portion of the file can be loaded on to memory when playback length is short. However, when playback is long, e.g. 1 min or beyond, using the large size buffer(upto 4 MByte) does not bring any improvement in power consumption.

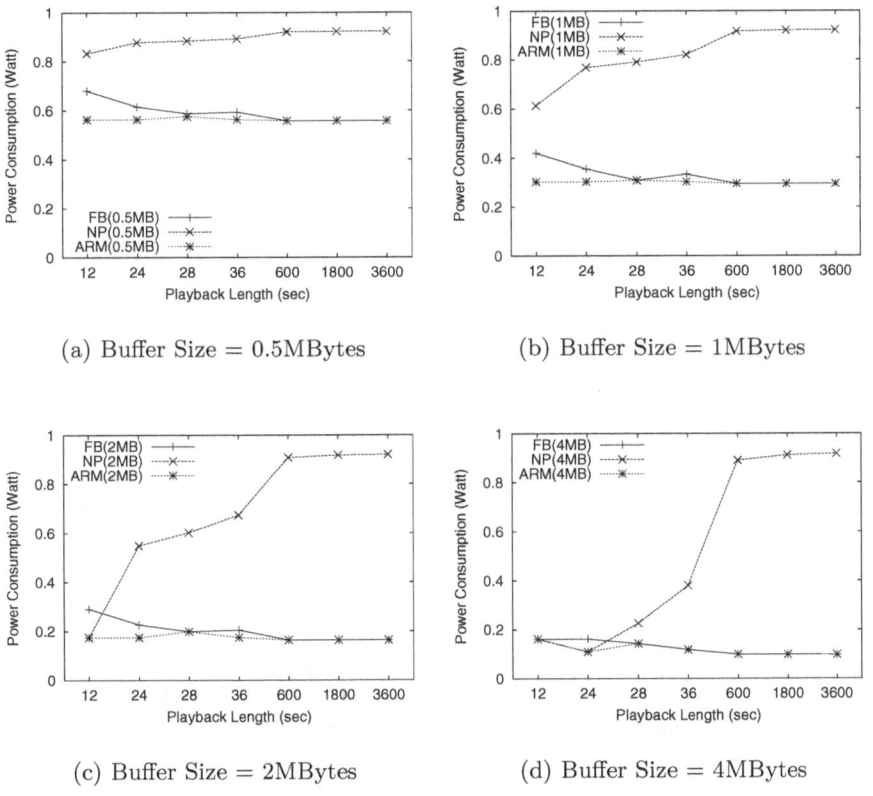

(a) Buffer Size = 0.5MBytes

(b) Buffer Size = 1MBytes

(c) Buffer Size = 2MBytes

(d) Buffer Size = 4MBytes

Fig. 6. Playback Length vs. Power Consumption

4.2   Effect of Playback Length

Fig. 6 illustrates the relationship between the playback length and the power consumption. The X and Y axis denotes the playback length and the power consumption, respectively. We consider four different buffer sizes, 0.5, 1, 2 and 4 MByte. In *ARM* algorithm, it makes the decision of merging the last round with preceding one based upon Eq. 5. We can observe the advantage of using power saving feature in retrieving the data blocks. In Full Buffering and Adaptive Round Merge scheme, disk drive goes into *standby* mode when the buffer becomes full. The disk drive remains in *standby* mode until buffer becomes empty. In Normal Playback mode, there is no notion of *standby* mode and therefore the power consumption rate converges to the power consumption rate of *read* phase. The advantage of merging the last round with the previous one becomes more visible when playback length is relatively short. With the playback length of 12, 24 and 36 sec, ARM reduces the power consumption by 18%, 28% and 40% against Full Buffering strategy, respectively, with 0.5 MByte Buffer. These values correspond to 9%, 15% and 23% with 1 MByte buffer.

5   Conclusion

Realtime playback of multimedia data puts unique demand on the disk subsystem. Retrieval of data blocks needs to be scheduled properly so that it can meet the playback deadline of individual data blocks and also minimizes the various overheads, e.g. service startup latency, buffer requires, etc. Power management feature of low power disk drive opens up a new chance to develop further power efficient multimedia player. However, it adds another dimension of complexity in determining the block retrieval schedule. In this paper, we analyze the power consumption behavior of the low power disk drive and propose scheduling algorithm, *Adaptive Round Merge*, which guarantees continuous retrieval of data blocks and which minimizes the power consumption for the given data retrieval. Given the power consumption profile of disk drive, data transfer rate of the disk, and playback rate, ARM algorithm computes the size of read burst in a round and the length of *standby* period. Our algorithm generates the disk operation schedule which determines when to *start* and when to *stop* the spindle. In the simulation based experiment, we observe that the ARM algorithm makes significant improvement on power consumption for the given playback. Compared with Normal Playback which does not have power management feature, ARM algorithm can decrease the power consumption by 60% with 1 MByte buffer. With larger size buffer, the reduction becomes even more dominant. While our simulation parameter is based upon IBM microdrive, this algorithm can be applied to any disk based storage device with power management feature.

References

1. L. Benini, A. Bogliolo, S. Cavallucci, and B. Ricco. Monitoring system activity for os-directed dynamic power management. In *Proceeddings of IEEE International Symposium on Low Power Electronics and Design*, pages 185–190, 1998.
2. E.-Y. Chung, L. Benini, A. Bogliolo, and G. D. Micheli. Dynamic power management for non-stationary service requests. In *Proceedings of Design Automation and Test in Europe*, 1999.
3. F. Douglis, P. Krishnan, and B. Bershad. Adaptive disk spin-down policies for mobile computers. *Computing Systems*, 8:381–413, 1995.

4. P.M. Greenawalt. Modeling power management for hard disks. In *Proceedings of the Second International Workshop on Modeling, Analysis, and Simulation of Computer and Telecommunication Systems(MASCOTS '94)*, pages 62–66, 1994.
5. D.R. Kenchammana-Hosekote and J. Srivastava. Scheduling Continuous Media on a Video-On-Demand Server. In *Proc. of International Conference on Multi-media Computing and Systems*, Boston, MA, May 1994. IEEE.
6. Yung-Hsiang Lu, Luca Benini, and Giovanni De Micheli. Operating-system directed power reduction. In *Proceedings of the International Symposium on Low Power Design, 2000*. ACM, New York, NY, USA, 2000.
7. Yung-Hsiang Lu and Giovanni De Micheli. Adaptive hard disk power management on personal computers. In *Proceedings of the IEEE Great Lakes Symposium on VLSI, 1999*. IEEE, Los Alamitos, CA, USA, 1999.
8. David P.Helmbold, Darrell D.E.Long, Tracey L.Sconyers, and Bruce Sherrod. Adaptive disk spin-down for mobile computers. *Mobile Networks and Applications*, 5(4):285–297, Dec 2000.
9. Dinesh Ramanathan, Sandra Irani, and Rajesh K. Gupta. An analysis of system level power management algorithms and their effects on latency. *IEEE Trans. on Computer-Aided Design of Integrated Cirtuits and Systems*, 21(3):291–305, March 2002.
10. A. L. N. Reddy and J. Wyllie. Disk Scheduling in a Multimedia I/O system. In *Proc. ACM Multimedia Conf.*, pages 225–233. ACM Press, New York, 1992.
11. T. Simunic, L. Benini, P. Glynn, and G. De Micheli. Dynamic power management of laptop hard disk. In *Proceedings of Design, Automation and Test in Europe Conference and Exhibition 2000*, page 736, 2000.
12. T. Simunic, L. Benini, P. Glynn, and G. De Micheli. Event driven power management. *IEEE Transactions on Computer-Aided Design of Integrated Circuits and Systems*, 20(7):840–857, July 2001.
13. IBM Storage Systems Division. Adaptive power management for mobile hard drives. Technical report, IBM Co. Storage Systems Division, San Jose, CA, USA, 1999.
14. IBM Storage Systems Division. Oem hard disk drive specifications for dmdm - 10340/10170 ibm microdrive revision 1.0. Technical report, IBM Co. Storage Systems Division, USA, 1999.
15. Youjip Won and Jaideep Srivastava. "smdp: Minimizing buffer requirements for continuous media servers". *ACM/Springer Multimedia Systems Journal*, 8(2):pp. 105–117, 2000.

Replica Striping for Multi-resolution Video Servers

Minseok Song and Heonshik Shin

School of Computer Science and Engineering
Seoul National University, Seoul 151-742, Korea
mssong@cselab.snu.ac.kr, shinhs@snu.ac.kr

Abstract. Multi-resolution video compression techniques are used for the efficient support of heterogeneous clients with different quality of service (QoS) parameters. However, data rates for high- and low-resolution video streams can vary widely; so the number of admitted clients may be limited due to the unbalanced use of server resources (i.e., disk bandwidth and buffer). Thus, the server may not accommodate new users although there is sufficient buffer or disk bandwidth. To remedy this problem, we propose a new replication scheme called Splitting Striping units by Replication (SSR) for multi-resolution video servers. To increase the number of admitted clients, we define two striping unit sizes of data which are stored on the primary and backup copies in different ways. In addition, we present a new admission control algorithm which adaptively decides whether to read data from the primary or the backup copy in order to make the best use of disk bandwidth and buffer of the video server. The effectiveness of the proposed scheme is evaluated through simulations.

1 Introduction

Recent advances in multimedia and network technologies make it feasible to provide video-on-demand (VOD) services. Unlike traditional broadcasting services, clients subscribing to VOD services will control quality of service (QoS) parameters such as resolution, frame rate and display size according to their requirements. For example, clients with high-definition television (HDTV) will want much higher resolution video services than clients with mobile phones. Meanwhile, some clients may prefer lower quality video services in order to pay a lower rate. To satisfy these requirements, the service provider can take advantage of multi-resolution compression techniques [1,4]. Multi-resolution video streams permit the extraction of lower resolution streams as a subset of full-resolution streams, so they eliminate the need for storing multiple copies of the video at different resolutions on the server.

Video servers typically employ disk arrays to store hundreds of movies as well as to transmit video data to thousands of users. A central issue in the design of disk-array-based video servers is how to locate video data across disks so that the number of concurrent users is maximized. In addition, since large-scale disk arrays are highly vulnerable to disk failures, fault-tolerant mechanisms are needed to prepare for degraded mode (i.e., when a disk has failed). To achieve fault tolerance, parity-based and replication-based schemes are used [8]. In parity-based schemes, a parity is computed by an exclusive-or operation and used for data reconstruction in degraded mode. In replication-based

F. Boavida et al. (Eds.): IDMS/PROMS 2002, LNCS 2515, pp. 300–312, 2002.

schemes, original data is duplicated on separate disks; in this case, we refer to the original data as the primary copy (PMC) and the duplicated data as the backup copy (BCC), respectively. As disk storage costs continue to decrease rapidly, replication becomes a promising approach to the implementation of fault tolerance and the improvement of system throughput. Our video server employs the replication technique [3].

Generally, round-based scheduling is used for data retrieval: Time is divided into equal-sized intervals, called rounds, and each admitted client is served once in every round. In addition, to utilize disk bandwidth efficiently, a video object is distributed over multiple disks. We refer to a scheme that partitions a video object into blocks and distributed these blocks on different disks as *striping*. The unit of data striping, referred to as *stripe unit*, denotes the maximum amount of logically contiguous data that will be stored on a single disk. Two striping schemes, periodic interleaving and balanced placement, have been proposed for multi-resolution VOD servers [1,7]. In the balanced placement scheme, data is striped in very small chunks across all available disks [7]. By contrast, in the periodic interleaving scheme, the amount of data retrieved during a round for the full-resolution video stream is the same as the striping unit size; thus, only one disk is involved in each data retrieval during a round [1]. We will adopt the periodic interleaving scheme as our striping method, because it is able to utilize disk bandwidth effectively [1,6]. Moreover, in order to provide high data throughput and fault tolerance, we combine striping and replication, and call the resulting scheme *replica striping*.

The choice of round length is important because it has a great impact on the maximum number of admitted clients [5,6]. Likewise, since the striping unit size is equal to the data retrieval size for the full-resolution video stream during a round, the choice of striping unit size also greatly affects system performance. For example, since video streams for high data rate applications (e.g. HDTV) require large buffer space, a small striping size will show better performance. On the other hand, low data rate video streams require relatively a small buffer with frequent disk accesses, and thus a large striping size is preferred [5,6,10]. Since the data rates for high- and low-resolution video streams can be very different in multi-resolution video, the choice of an inappropriate striping unit size may degrade the system performance greatly due to the unbalanced use of the disk bandwidth (BW) and buffer.

In this paper, we present a new replica striping scheme called Splitting Striping units by Replication (SSR) for multi-resolution video servers with the aim of increasing the number of concurrent users. In SSR, the server has two striping unit sizes and stores them on the primary and backup copies in a judicious way to efficiently utilize server resources (i.e. disk BW and buffer). In addition, we propose a new admission control algorithm which dynamically decides whether to read data from the primary or the backup copy. To achieve the balanced use of the disk BW and buffer, this algorithm characterizes the system resources in terms of utilization of the disk BW and the buffer, and adaptively selects whether to read data from the PMC or the BCC. This prevents either buffer or disk BW from becoming saturated while the other remains under-utilized. Additionally, a disk scheduling algorithm is presented to support our scheme.

The rest of this paper is organized as follows: In Section 2, we survey the conventional replica striping schemes. In Section 3 and 4, we propose a new replica striping scheme and a retrieval scheduling technique. In Section 5, we propose an adaptive admission control algorithm. We validate the proposed schemes through simulations in Section 6 and conclude the paper in Section 7.

2   Conventional Replica Striping Schemes

Recently, several replica striping schemes (i.e. mirrored declustering, chained declustering, and interleaved declustering) have been proposed to increase system throughput as well as to provide fault tolerance [3,8]. Let us assume that the disk array consists of D homogeneous disks. Mirrored declustering simply duplicates primary copies of each disk on to another disk, and thus causes load imbalance in degraded mode [3]. To overcome this problem, interleaved declustering uniformly distributes backup copies to all remaining disks. In chained declustering (CD), the primary copy in disk i has a backup copy in disk $(i + 1)$ mod D. It is noteworthy that the interleaved declustering scheme expects to access $D - 1$ disks to retrieve data from BCC, so it may degrade system performance due to the disk latency overhead. Thus, in our scheme, we place the backup copy on one disk as in the CD scheme. An illustrative data placement with the CD scheme is shown in Figure 1.

Disk NO.	0	1	2	3	4	5	6
PMC	S_0 S_7 ...	S_1 S_8 ...	S_2 S_9 ...	S_3 S_{10} ...	S_4 S_{11} ...	S_5 S_{12} ...	S_6 S_{13} ...
BCC	S_6 S_{13} ...	S_0 S_7 ...	S_1 S_8 ...	S_2 S_9 ...	S_3 S_{10} ...	S_4 S_{11} ...	S_5 S_{12} ...

Fig. 1. An illustrative data placement with a CD scheme.

Note that, in the CD scheme, the server can use approximately $\frac{D-1}{D}$ of the entire disk BW in degraded mode, because it can share the additional workload between PMC and BCC in degraded mode [3]. Instead of wasting server resources to prepare for the degraded mode, various schemes have been proposed for the enhancement of the system throughput in normal mode (i.e. when all disks are operational) [8,9]. Hence, we assume that the server will use the entire disk BW in normal mode instead of reserving some disk BW to prepare for the degraded mode.

3   SSR Data Placement for Replica Striping

The choice of round length is important because it greatly affects the maximum number of users [1,5,6]. Increasing round length enhances the disk efficiency, but increases the buffer size. Thus, in terms of disk efficiency, a long round is preferred, whereas in terms of buffer cost per user, a short round is more appropriate. To balance this tradeoff, the round length which minimizes the sum of disk and buffer cost per user is usually selected, and we will refer to this round length as the optimal round length [1,6]. Since the striping unit size is equal to the data retrieval size for the full-resolution video stream during a round in our placement, the optimal striping size is equal to the data retrieval size for the full-resolution video stream during the optimal round length.

To determine the round length, we should consider the distribution of users' requested video bit rates. High-resolution video streams require relatively a large buffer, and thus a short round is preferred; whereas a long round shows better performance for low-resolution video streams [5,6]. Since it is difficult to accurately determine the requested resolution of future clients, selecting the optimal round length at system design time is not possible. For example, suppose that we select the optimal round length for the low-resolution video streams. However, if the actual requests are concentrated on the high-resolution video streams, the number of admitted clients may be limited due to the excessive use of the buffer, even though further disk BW is available. Since only one striping unit size is supported in the CD scheme, a wrong estimation of striping unit size may greatly degrade the system performance. To overcome this problem, we now introduce an SSR scheme.

In the SRR scheme, the striping unit is divided into two parts. Striping units of the original size are used for the PMC and split striping units for the BCC. To determine an appropriate striping size, SSR first finds an optimal round length R_f for full-resolution video streams. We will call data for the full-resolution video stream retrieved during $2R_f$ and R_f as the segment and the sub-segment respectively. Then, multi-resolution video streams can be modeled as follows [4]: A given video V has P segments such that $V = \{S_0 \bigcup ... \bigcup S_i \bigcup ... \bigcup S_{P-1}\}$. Then, we can see that the video can be composed of $2P$ sub-segments such that $V = \{s_{0.0} \bigcup s_{0.1} ... \bigcup s_{i.0} \bigcup s_{i.1} \bigcup ... \bigcup s_{2P-1.1}\}$.

Let us assume that each segment S_i and sub-segment $s_{i.k}$ $(k = 0, 1)$ has up to Q display resolutions such that

$$S_i = \{S_i^0 \bigcup ... \bigcup S_i^j \bigcup ... \bigcup S_i^{Q-1}\}, s_{i.k} = \{s_{i.k}^0 \bigcup ... \bigcup s_{i.k}^j \bigcup ... \bigcup s_{i.k}^{Q-1}\},$$

where S_i^j and $s_{i.k}^j$ represent the jth component $(0 < j \leq Q - 1)$ of the segment S_i and sub-segment $s_{i.k}$, respectively.

We will refer to S_i^0 and $s_{i.k}^0$ as the *base resolution* of the segment S_i and the sub-segment $s_{i.k}$. To display a video stream at a resolution of m, it requires the data at the base resolution as well as all the data from the first component to the mth component. For example, to view S_i or $s_{i.k}$ at a resolution of m, we need to retrieve $\{S_i^0 \bigcup S_i^1 \bigcup ... \bigcup S_i^m\}$ during $2R_f$ or $\{s_{i.k}^0 \bigcup s_{i.k}^1 \bigcup ... \bigcup s_{i.k}^m\}$ during R_f, respectively. Let each $s_{i.k}^j$ be composed of b_j bits; then the total number of bits that should be retrieved during R_f, to obtain $s_{i.k}$ at a resolution of m is $\sum_{j=0}^m b_j$. Since twice the number of bits need to be retrieved for the segment as for the sub-segment, the total number of bits retrieved during $2R_f$, to obtain S_i at a resolution of m is $2\sum_{j=0}^m b_j$. Figure 2 shows a segment and associated sub-segments of the video stream at a total of 5 resolutions.

SSR stores each segment S_i onto the PMC in a round-robin fashion across disks, and each sub-segment $s_{i.k}$ $(k = 0, 1)$ is stored as part of the BCC on the disk after the disk where S_i is stored. For example, if S_i is stored on disk m, then $s_{i.k}$ $(k = 0, 1)$ is stored as part of the BCC on disk $(m + 1) \bmod D$. Figure 3 shows an illustrative SSR data placement. By employing SSR, we can adaptively retrieve the video streams from either the PMC or the BCC and thus balance the use of disk BW and buffer.

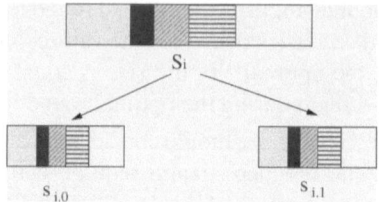

Fig. 2. A segment and sub-segments of the video stream at 5 resolutions.

Disk NO.	0	1	2	3	4	5	6
PMC	S_0 S_7 ...	S_1 S_8 ...	S_2 S_9 ...	S_3 S_{10} ...	S_4 S_{11} ...	S_5 S_{12} ...	S_6 S_{13} ...
BCC	$s_{6.0}, s_{6.1}$ $s_{13.0}, s_{13.1}$ ...	$s_{0.0}, s_{0.1}$ $s_{7.0}, s_{7.1}$ ...	$s_{1.0}, s_{1.1}$ $s_{8.0}, s_{8.1}$ ...	$s_{2.0}, s_{2.1}$ $s_{9.0}, s_{9.1}$ ...	$s_{3.0}, s_{3.1}$ $s_{10.0}, s_{10.1}$ ...	$s_{4.0}, s_{4.1}$ $s_{11.0}, s_{11.1}$ ...	$s_{5.0}, s_{5.1}$ $s_{12.0}, s_{12.1}$ ...

Fig. 3. An illustrative data placement with an SSR scheme.

4 A Retrieval Scheduling Algorithm

4.1 Description of the New Disk Scheduling Algorithm

To provide two round lengths simultaneously, we divide every round into two sub-rounds. We will refer to the round and sub-round as the *major* and *minor* cycle, respectively. Let R_{mj} and R_{min} be the length of the major and minor cycle, respectively. Let us assume that there are N clients C^m ($m = 1, ..., N$) to be serviced by the server, each of which requests a video stream with resolution res^m. Video streams can be retrieved from either the PMC or the BCC, and thus we define two service modes for the client C^m. If C^m is in PR mode, C^m receives its video stream from the PMC, whereas a video stream from the BCC is retrieved for C^m in BR mode. Every client in PR mode receives its stream once in every major cycle, whereas every client in BR mode receives its stream once in every minor cycle. Thus, we observe that $R_{mj} = 2R_f$ and $R_{min} = R_f$. We assume that SCAN scheduling is used during each minor cycle. Then, every client in PR mode is assigned to a certain minor cycle (the first or second minor cycle), and serviced every other minor cycle. Thus, we can see that grouped sweeping scheduling (GSS) with two groups [11] is used for the clients in PR mode with a round duration of R_{mj}. On the other hand, the SCAN scheduling is used for the clients in BR mode, where a round duration is equal to R_{min}. We refer to our scheduling as Mixed GSS and SCAN (MGS) scheduling.

Let us consider the variation of the load on every disk when MGS scheduling is used. Every client accesses a single disk during a major cycle, and each segment is placed in round-robin fashion across the disks as shown in Figure 3. Thus, the clients receiving video streams from the same disk will all move to the following disk during the next major cycle. To express such a load-shifting property succinctly, we will refer to the clients accessing the same disk during a major cycle as a client group; then, we can partition clients into D client groups (say CG_1, CG_2,...,CG_D). We refer to the set of clients in CG_i which receive their video streams from the PMC as CIP_i. We can also divide CIP_i into two groups: clients which receive their video streams during the first minor cycle and the second minor cycle, respectively (say CIP_i^F and CIP_i^S). Since every client in PR mode is assigned to a certain minor cycle, $CIP_i^F \cap CIP_i^S = \phi$ always holds. We also refer to CIB_i^F and CIB_i^S as sets of clients in CG_i which receive their video streams from BCC during the first and the second minor cycles respectively.

4.2   Resource Requirements for Each Service Mode

Disk BW requirement. To ensure jitter-free playback, the service time, which represents total read, seek and rotation times requested by the clients in one round, must not exceed the round duration. Let us assume that the server disk array is characterized as shown in Table 1, and we use a typical seek time model as described in [1], in which every client requires a seeking overhead (seek time + rotational delay) T_s for one read. If C^m is in PR mode, then a service time of $T_s + 2(\frac{\sum_{j=0}^{res^m} b_j}{r_t})$ is required for C^m during R_{mj}. On the other hand, if C^m is in BR mode, then a time $2T_s + 2(\frac{\sum_{j=0}^{res^m} b_j}{r_t})$ is required, because two disk seeks are needed during R_{mj}.

Table 1. Notation and parameter values for a video server.

Transfer rate	r_t	14 MB/s
Typical disk seek and rotation time	T_s	14 ms
Total buffer size	B	500 MB

Buffer requirement. To estimate the buffer usage in MGS scheduling, we need to know the buffer requirement of the GSS and SCAN disk scheduling algorithms. Since, in the SCAN scheme, the stream serviced first in the current minor cycle may be retrieved last in the next minor cycle, double buffering is used [10]. Thus, the buffer requirement for the client C^m in BR mode is $2\sum_{j=0}^{res^m} b_j$. But, using the GSS scheme, the maximum time between two reads is $R_{mj}(1 + \frac{1}{g})$, where g is the number of groups [10]. Since the number of groups is 2 in MGS scheduling, the buffer requirement for C^m in PR mode is $\frac{3}{2}\sum_{j=0}^{res^m}(2b_j) = 3\sum_{j=0}^{res^m} b_j$. Table 2 summarizes the resource requirements for C^m according to the service modes.

5   An Adaptive Admission Control Algorithm

5.1   Admission Control Condition

Disk BW utilization. We consider two constraints, disk bandwidth and buffer, for admission control. Let n_i^{PF}, n_i^{PS}, n_i^{BF} and n_i^{BS} be the number of clients *to be serviced*

Table 2. Resource requirements for C^m

	Service time	Buffer
PR mode	$T_s + 2(\dfrac{\sum_{j=0}^{res^m} b_j}{r_t})$	$3\sum_{j=0}^{res^m} b_j$
BR mode	$2T_s + 2(\dfrac{\sum_{j=0}^{res^m} b_j}{r_t})$	$2\sum_{j=0}^{res^m} b_j$

in the $CIP_i^F, CIP_i^S, CIB_i^F$ and CIB_i^S, respectively. Disk BW utilization for CG_i, U_s^i is the sum of the utilization for the 1st minor cycle, U_1^i, and the utilization for the 2nd cycle, U_2^i, each of which is defined as:

$$U_1^i = \frac{(n_i^{PF} + n_i^{BF}) \times T_s + 2(\sum_{C^m \in CIP_i^F} \frac{\sum_{j=0}^{res^m} b_j}{r_t}) + \sum_{C^m \in CIB_i^F} \frac{\sum_{j=0}^{res^m} b_j}{r_t}}{R_{mj}},$$

$$U_2^i = \frac{(n_i^{PS} + n_i^{BS}) \times T_s + 2(\sum_{C^m \in CIP_i^S} \frac{\sum_{j=0}^{res^m} b_j}{r_t}) + \sum_{C^m \in CIB_i^S} \frac{\sum_{j=0}^{res^m} b_j}{r_t}}{R_{mj}}.$$

Buffer utilization. From Table 2, we observe that the buffer requirement for the clients in CIB_i^F is $2\sum_{C^m \in CIB_i^F} \sum_{j=0}^{res^m} b_j$. Since every client in CIB_i^F is a member of one of CIB_i^S or $CIB_{(i+1) mod D}^S$, the buffer requirement for every client in BR mode is $2\sum_{i=1}^{D} \sum_{C^m \in CIB_i^F} \sum_{j=0}^{res^m} b_j$. We can easily obtain $3\sum_{i=1}^{D} \sum_{C^m \in CIP_i} \sum_{j=0}^{res^m} b_j$ for the buffer requirement for all clients in PR mode from Table 2. Let B be the total buffer size, and the buffer utilization, U_B, is defined to be:

$$U_B = \frac{\sum_{i=1}^{D}(2\sum_{C^m \in CIB_i^F} \sum_{j=0}^{res^m} b_j + 3\sum_{C^m \in CIP_i} \sum_{j=0}^{res^m} b_j)}{B}.$$

Admission Test. When a client requests a video stream, *the new client is assumed to be in PR mode*, which is definitely advantageous as regards disk efficiency. Then, the server assigns the new client to the appropriate client group. Due to the load shifting property of our placement, we can balance disk loads across disks by delaying the admission of new clients such that each new client is assigned to the client group with the minimum service time. In the worst case, D major cycles of delay may be introduced by the load balancing. We assume that the server is able to delay the admission by D major cycles, because it is valuable to increase the number of admitted clients at the expense of service latency in VOD servers [2]. Detailed description of the admission test algorithm (ATA) is shown in Algorithm 1.

5.2 Service Mode Conversion

Since a new client is assumed to be in PR mode, there may be situations that the service mode for clients should be converted to BR mode in order to acquire buffers. Thus,

---

Algorithm 1 ATA: Admission Test Algorithm

1: Boolean $TEST \leftarrow FALSE$;
2: A set of U_S^is $(i = 1, ..., D)$: X;
3: Find the least value $U_S^u \in X$ and recalculate U_1^u and U_2^u;
4: **if** $U_1^u \leq U_2^u$ **then**
5:    **if** $U_1^u \leq 0.5$ **then**
6:       $TEST \leftarrow TRUE$; { passes the disk BW test }
7:    **end if**
8: **else**
9:    **if** $U_2^u \leq 0.5$ **then**
10:       $TEST \leftarrow TRUE$; {passes the disk BW test}
11:    **end if**
12: **end if**
13: **if** $TEST = TRUE$ and $U_B \leq 1$ **then**
14:    the new client passes the admission test;
15: **else**
16:    reject the new client;
17: **end if**

---

we should find an appropriate client group for the client whose service mode has been changed. To find an appropriate group for the clients in CIP_i^F after conversion, we assume that S_k is retrieved for the client C^m in CIP_i^F. Since the next blocks of data ($s_{(k+1).0}$ and $s_{(k+1).1}$) are located on the disk accessed by the clients in $CG_{(i+1)modD}$, C^m becomes a member of $CIB_{(i+1)modD}^F$ and $CIB_{(i+1)modD}^S$ after conversion.

For the clients in CIP_i^S, we assume that segment S_k is retrieved for the client C^m in CIP_i^S during the second minor cycle of the jth major cycle. Then, we should retrieve $s_{(k+1).0}$ during the second minor cycle of the $(j + 1)^{th}$ major cycle. Since $s_{(k+1).0}$ is located on the disk accessed by the clients in $CG_{(i+1)modD}$, C^m becomes a member of $CIB_{(i+1)modD}^S$. In contrast, at the beginning of the first minor cycle in the $(j+2)^{th}$ major cycle, $CG_{(i+1)modD}$ shifts to the next disk, and $s_{(k+1).1}$ is located on the disk accessed by the clients in CG_i. Thus, C^m becomes a member of CIB_i^F after conversion. To summarize, Table 3 shows the client group to which clients in CIP_i^F and CIP_i^S belong after conversion.

Table 3. Transition of the client group after conversion.

Before conversion	After conversion
CIP_i^F	$CIB_{(i+1)modD}^F$ and $CIB_{(i+1)modD}^S$
CIP_i^S	CIB_i^F and $CIB_{(i+1)modD}^S$

5.3   Resolving Excessive Use of the Buffer

After admission, the server checks that there is enough buffer space for the next client. In other words, if the available buffer space is below a threshold value α, which represents the maximum buffer requirement of one video stream ($3\sum_{j=0}^{Q-1} b_j$), we need to create buffer space for the next client. Definition 1 shows a condition for the conversion from PR to BR mode.

Definition 1 *The conversion from PR to BR mode is required if $U_B > 1 - \frac{\alpha}{B}$.*

When conversion is required, we convert a client from each CIP_i ($CIP_i \neq \phi$) ($i = 1, ..., D$), to BR mode. Since $CIP_i^F \bigcup CIP_i^S = CIP_i$, a client can be converted from one of CIP_i^F or CIP_i^S. Let SIP_i denote the group from which a client will be converted. If $CIP_i = \phi$, then $SIP_i = \phi$. Otherwise, SIP_i can be one of CIP_i^F or CIP_i^S. For example, CIP_i^F becomes SIP_i when $n_i^{PF} > 0$ and $n_i^{PS} = 0$, whereas CIP_i^S becomes SIP_i when $n_i^{PF} = 0$ and $n_i^{PS} > 0$. If $n_i^{PF} > 0$ and $n_i^{PS} > 0$, the server can select one of CIP_i^F or CIP_i^S for SIP_i. From Table 3, we observe that U_i^1 and $U_{(i+1)mod D}^2$ increase after conversion if $SIP_i = CIP_i^S$. On the other hand, $U_{(i+1)mod D}^1$ and $U_{(i+1)mod D}^2$ increase if $SIP_i = CIP_i^F$. We select SIP_i with the aim of balancing disk loads across disks. Thus, if $U_i^1 \leq U_{(i+1)mod D}^1$, then CIP_i^S becomes SIP_i. Otherwise, CIP_i^F becomes SIP_i.

Since extra buffer space is acquired at the cost of additional disk BW, the conversion should maximize buffers while minimizing the sacrifice of disk BW. We will thus define the mode conversion problem ($\mathcal{MCP}$) in Definition 2. In addition, we introduce an algorithm, called the mode conversion algorithm (MCA), which is executed when conversion is required. Detailed description of the MCA is shown in Algorithm 2. If conversion would not violate the disk BW constraint (line 8 and 13), then MCA chooses a client with the largest resolution (bit rate) V_i^L from each SIP_i ($SIP_i \neq \phi$), and converts it to BR mode. Theorem 1 states that the MCA produces an optimal solution to the $\mathcal{MCP}$.

Definition 2 The Mode Conversion Problem ($\mathcal{MCP}$)
If conversion is required, the $\mathcal{MCP}$ is to convert one client from each SIP_i ($SIP_i \neq \phi$) ($i = 1, ..., D$), to BR mode, which minimizes U_B.

Theorem 1 *When conversion is required, if one client with the largest resolution is converted from every SIP_i ($SIP_i \neq \phi$) ($i = 1, ..., D$) to BR mode, U_B can be minimized.*

Proof: We prove the theorem by contradiction. Let us assume that converting a client fv from SIP_i to BR mode minimizes the buffer requirement, and there exists a certain client V_i^m in SIP_i whose resolution res_i^m is greater than that of the client fv. This implies that a client with the largest resolution from every SIP_i is not converted to BR mode. Let the current buffer usage and the resolution of fv be B_f and res^{fv} respectively. Then, by including fv in SIP_i, and V_i^m in BR mode, we obtain the buffer requirement $B_t = B_f - \sum_{j=0}^{res_i^m} b_j + \sum_{j=0}^{res^{fv}} b_j$ from Table 2. From our assumption $res_i^m > res^{fv}$, we obtain $\sum_{j=0}^{res_i^m} b_j > \sum_{j=0}^{res^{fv}} b_j$. This leads to $B_t < B_f$, which contradicts to our assumption that converting a client fv from SIP_i to BR mode minimizes the buffer requirement. Hence, MCA minimizes the buffer requirement.   □

Algorithm 2 MCA: Mode Conversion Algorithm

1: Boolean: $TEST \leftarrow TRUE$;
2: Boolean: $DONE_i$ $(i = 1, ...D)$;
3: **while** $(U_B > 1 - \frac{\alpha}{B}$ and $TEST = TRUE)$ **do**
4:     **for** each SIP_i where $SIP_i \neq \phi$ **do**
5:         $DONE_i \leftarrow FALSE$;
6:         Find a client with the largest resolution (the highest bit rate), $V_i^L \in SIP_i$;
7:         **if** $V_i^L \in CIP_i^F$ **then**
8:             **if** $U_1^{(i+1)modD} \leq 0.5$ and $U_2^{(i+1)modD} \leq 0.5$ **then**
9:                 V_i^L becomes a member of $CIB_{(i+1)modD}^F$ and $CIB_{(i+1)modD}^S$;
10:                 $DONE_i = TRUE$;
11:             **end if**
12:         **else if** $V_i^L \in CIP_i^S$ **then**
13:             **if** $U_1^i \leq 0.5$ and $U_2^{(i+1)modD} \leq 0.5$ **then**
14:                 V_i^L becomes a member of CIB_i^F and $CIB_{(i+1)modD}^S$;
15:                 $DONE_i = TRUE$;
16:             **end if**
17:         **end if**
18:     **end for**
19:     **if** for every CIP_i $(i = 1, ...D)$, $CIP_i = \phi$ or $DONE_i = FALSE$ **then**
20:         $TEST \leftarrow FALSE$;
21:     **end if**
22: **end while**

6   Experimental Results

To evaluate the effectiveness of our schemes, we have performed simulation-based experiments. Arrival of client requests is assumed to follow a Poisson distribution, and the mean arrival rate is assumed to be 20 arrivals/minute. Our server has 14 disks, and the characteristics of our disk array is shown in Table 1. Each segment as well as sub-segment has 11 display resolutions whose bit rates are shown in Table 4 [1], and we refer to video streams with resolution indices $0 - 2$, $3 - 6$ and $7 - 10$ as low-, medium- and high-resolution video streams, respectively. The length of each video clip is 100 minutes.

Table 4. Scalable video data rates

Resolution index	0	1	2	3	4	5	6	7	8	9	10
Current bit rate (kb/s)	190	63	63	64	126	127	127	127	126	127	190
Total bit rate (kb/s)	190	253	316	380	506	633	760	887	1013	1140	1330

In order to compare SSR with CD schemes, we assess the number of admitted clients for 10 hours under various sets of clients' requested resolutions. In the SSR scheme, let R_{min} and R_{mj} be 2 and 4 seconds respectively. We compare SSR with three CD schemes with round length of 2, 2.5 and 2.8 seconds. Figure 4 shows the number

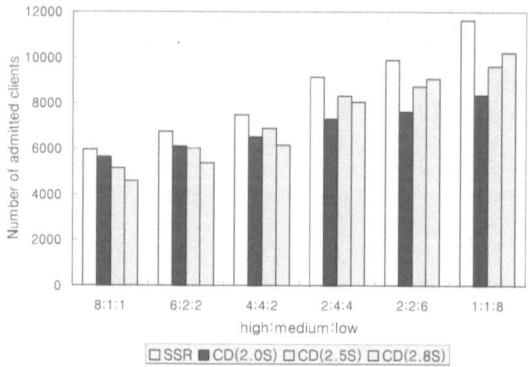

Fig. 4. Comparison between CD and SSR.

of admitted clients according to the proportion of high-, medium-, and low-resolution video streams requested by the clients. As the number of low-resolution video streams increases, the number of admitted clients also increases, because low-resolution video streams require less resource than high-resolution video streams. Our scheme outperforms the CD schemes under all workloads. This is because our scheme adaptively finds appropriate striping units to balance disk BW and buffer utilization while minimizing the usage of resources. Table 5 illustrates this fact by showing the largest values of U_S^i, namely U_S^{max}, and U_B for the CD and SSR schemes, just before admission of the new client fails. As can be seen in Table 5, both resources are fully utilized in SSR; on the other hand, the disk BW is always saturated in the CD scheme (round length = 2.0 S) although the buffer is available. In the CD (round length = 2.5 S) scheme, the disk BW becomes a bottleneck when the low-resolution video streams are in the majority. In contrast, as the number of high-resolution video streams increases, the number of admitted clients is limited by the shortage of buffer.

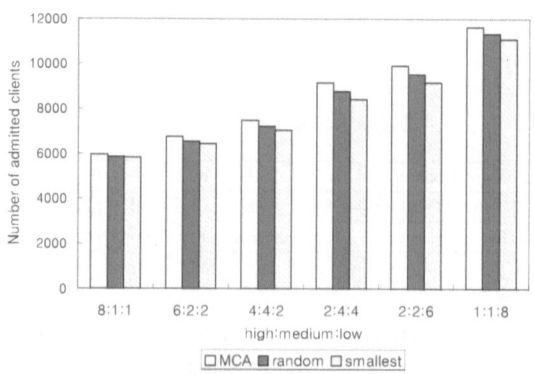

Fig. 5. Effectiveness of MCA.

Table 5. U_S^{max} and U_B for SSR and CD schemes.

high:medium:low	SSR		CD (2.0S)		CD (2.5S)	
	U_s^{max}	U_B	U_s^{max}	U_B	U_s^{max}	U_B
8:1:1	0.99	0.99	0.99	0.88	0.82	0.99
6:2:2	0.99	0.99	0.99	0.80	0.88	0.99
4:4:2	0.99	0.99	0.99	0.75	0.94	0.99
2:4:4	0.99	0.99	0.99	0.66	0.99	0.92
2:2:6	0.99	0.99	0.99	0.61	0.99	0.87
1:1:8	0.99	0.99	0.99	0.51	0.99	0.73

To investigate the effectiveness of MCA, let us consider two algorithms which convert a client from PR to BR mode with smallest resolution first and randomly. Figure 5 illustrates the number of admitted clients according to the proportion of high-, medium- and low-resolution video streams requested by clients. As can be seen in Figure 5, MCA shows better performance under all workloads.

7 Conclusions

In this paper, we have proposed a new replica striping method for multi-resolution video servers to increase the number of clients admitted. The proposed method defines two striping units and stores them on the PMC and the BCC, respectively. Thus, it enables the server to select an appropriate striping size dynamically in order to cope with heterogeneous properties of multi-resolution video streams. In addition, for the balanced use of disk bandwidth and buffer, we present an adaptive admission control scheme, which adaptively decides whether to read data from the PMC or the BCC by considering both system resource usages and clients' bit rates. Thus, it prevents either buffer or disk bandwidth from becoming saturated while the other remains under-utilized. Experimental results show that our schemes enable the server to admit a much larger number of clients. They also reveal that the utilization of disk bandwidth and buffer is balanced for various workloads.

References

1. E. Chang and A. Zakhor. Disk-based storage for scalable video. *IEEE Transactions on Circuits and Systems for Video Technology*, 7(5):758–770, October 1997.
2. Y. Huang, J. Ding, and S. Tsao. Constant time permutation: An efficient block allocation strategy for variable-bit-rate continuous media data. *The VLDB Journal*, 8(1):44–54, 1999.
3. C. Chou L. Golubchik, R. Muntz and S. Berson. Design of fault-tolerant large-scale vod servers: with emphasis on high-performance and low-cost. *IEEE Transactions on Parallel and Distributed Systems*, 12(4):363–386, 2001.
4. K. Law, J. Lui, and L. Golubchik. Efficient support for interactive service in multi-resolution vod systems. *The VLDB Journal*, 24(1):133–153, January 1999.
5. K. Lee and H. Yeom. A dynamic scheduling algorithm for large scale multimedia server. *Information Processing Letters*, 68(5):235–240, 1998.

6. B. Ozden, R. Rastogi, and A. Silberschatz. Disk striping in video server environments. In *Proceedings of IEEE ICMCS'96*, pages 580–589, 1996.
7. S. Paek, P. Bocheck, and S. Chang. Scalable mpeg2 video servers with heterogeneous qos on parallel disk arrays. In *Proceedings of NOSSDAV95*, pages 363–374, April 1995.
8. P. Shenoy and H. Vin. Failure recovery algorithms for multimedia servers. *ACM/Springer Multimedia Systems Journal*, 8(1):1–19, January 2000.
9. M. Song, H. Shin, and N. Chang. A qos negotiation scheme for efficient failure recovery in multi-resolution video servers. In *Proceedings of IDMS'01*, pages 62–73, 2001.
10. Y. Won and J. Srivastava. Smdp: Minimizing buffer requirements for continuos media servers. *ACM/Springer Multimedia Systems Journal*, 8(2):105–117, 2000.
11. P. Yu, M. Chen, and D. Kandlur. Grouped sweeping scheduling for dasd-based multimedia storage management. *ACM/Springer Multimedia Systems Journal*, 1(1):99–109, 1993.

On Availability QoS for Replicated Multimedia Service and Content

Giwon On, Jens Schmitt, and Ralf Steinmetz

Multimedia Communications (KOM), Darmstadt University of Technology, Germany
Tel.: +49-6151-166150, Fax: +49-6151-166152
{Giwon.On, Jens.Schmitt, Ralf.Steinmetz}@KOM.tu-darmstadt.de

Abstract. Recently, it has been realized that the importance of satisfying service availability is becoming one of the most critical factors for the success of Internet-based services and applications. In this paper, we take an availability-centric view on QoS where the availability is treated as a new controllable QoS parameter and focus on the issues of providing availability guarantees for distributed and replicated multimedia services and contents. We especially tackle the replica placement (RP) problem and study the effects of number and location of replicas on the achieved availability. From a simulation study, we find that (1) the location of replica is a more relevant factor than their number for satisfying the availability QoS requirements for all individual users, and (2) the heuristic methods, in general, cannot give any guarantee for their achieved availability QoS, while they are very efficient for large size graphs.

1 Introduction

1.1 Satisfying Availability - The Key for Successful Services in Internet

Even though there are many significant research results, technology advances and solutions in *quality of service* (QoS) since the last 20 years [1,2], their application to commercial products or systems was not so successful, in comparison to their attention in the research arena. One critical reason probably is that, as H. Schulzrinne pointed out in [3] and an interview statistic mentioned in [4], the main research focus for QoS was to control transmission characteristics like bandwidth, delay, and loss. This is because applications on the Internet typically assumed in need for QoS support, such as video-on-demand (VoD), tele-teaching, Internet telephony, strongly motivated the development of QoS technologies. While for these the control of the transmission characteristics is certainly important it seems likely by now that, on the one hand, for them this may not be the most pressing need with regard to QoS requirements, and on the other hand that there are other applications having quite different requirements. Indeed, the perceived QoS may be much more influenced by how available a certain service and its data are. In the context of QoS, the availability issue has so far seldom been mentioned, and there is no work known to us which tries to treat availability as a controllable QoS parameter.

F. Boavida et al. (Eds.): IDMS/PROMS 2002, LNCS 2515, pp. 313-326, 2002.
© Springer-Verlag Berlin Heidelberg 2002

1.2   Differentiation of Service Classes and Availability Requirements

While most research efforts in high availability and fault-tolerant systems areas have their focus on achieving the so-called 'five nines' (99.999%) availability [5], there is a demand for service differentiation from service consumers and providers due to costs and competitive nature of the marketplace, which derives for the mechanisms that support different levels of services and their availability. In fact, the need for service differentiation can be observed from different services, such as VoD or news-on-demand over the Internet, as wells as different users' requirements which depend on the service type they demand, on the service time when they access, on the peripherials they have, and on the service price they pay.

From the service system provider's point of view, on the other side, not all system components need to have the same redundancy level, i.e., availability level to offer. The availability level required for individual system components depends on the fact of how much they should be reliable and are critical for offering the service. For example, in developing replication mechanisms for increasing availability of services and their data in a distributed multimedia system *medianode* [6], we analysed the characteristics of multimedia contents and their meta-data and could identify that not all service operations and not all data access functions require the same availability level of the 'five nines'.

1.3   The Main Focus and Approach

The work in this paper is strongly motivated by the two aspects mentioned above. So, the main focus is building a model and mechanisms to study the problem of how to satisfy and guarantee different availability requirements for distributed and replicated multimedia services in a wide-area internetwork like the Internet, and to evaluate the achieved availability QoS. In many existing works, it has been shown that the availability of distributed services and their data can be significantly increased by replicating them on multiple systems connected with each other, even in the face of system and network failures. Thus, we especially tackle the replica placement problem (RPP) and study the effects of number and location of replicas on the reached availability QoS. For this purpose, we develop a concept called *quality of availability* (QoA) in which the availability is treated as a new controllable QoS parameter. Based on the QoA concept, we model the distributed multimedia system as a stochastic graph where all nodes and edges elements are parameterized, statistically independently of each another, with known availability and failure probabilities. We decompose the RPP in three questions: (1) finding a "good" placement for fixed number of replicas, (2) checking the reached QoA with a selected replica placement, and (3) determining the number and location of replicas for satisfying a required QoA with absolute guarantees. Thus, the main focus of the paper is not developing additional, new algorithms for the RPP, but instead specifying the QoA concept and model. For each RP question, we review some solution algorithms from heuristic and exact methods and evaluate their achieved QoA. Based on a simulation study, we find that (1) the location of replica is a more relevant factor than its number for satisfying the required QoA, and (2) the heuristic methods do not give any guarantee for their achieved QoA, even though they are very efficient for large size graphs. Note that we do not address the replica selection and update distribution issues in this work. These issues are handled in our previous work [6] where we also give a comprehensive survey on existing solutions for these problem.

1.4 Outline

The rest of this paper is organized as follows. In Section 2, we develop the concept of quality of availability and describe the QoA metrics to be used in this work. Section 3 presents the replica placement problem and details the algorithms that we reviewed and modified for our problem. In Section 4, we present our implementation methods including the experimental simulation environment and in Section 5 we evaluate the results. Section 6 discusses related work. Finally, Section 7 concludes the paper.

2 The Concept of Quality of Availability (QoA) and Its Metrics

2.1 Basic Idea

The basic idea of the QoA concept is that the availability can be defined as *a new controllable, observable QoS parameter*. Indeed, we move the focus of the objective function for the resource and performance optimization problems of the QoS field from satisfying transmission-dependent characteristics such as minimizing transmission delay, jitter, and/or loss to satisfying the availability requirements such as minimizing failure time of service systems and their components and to maximizing the total time amount in which the required service functions as expected and its data are reachable. Given a set of different levels of availability requirements and a network topology with a finite number of possible replica locations, we are then interested in how many replicas are needed, where should they be placed, whether their placement on the given topology satisfies the individually required availability QoS and how they affect the overall service availability quality.

2.2 The QoA Metrics and Parameters

A service is said to be *available* when it functions as expected and its data is reachable. Commonly we distinguish between two levels of available services: *basically available* (BA) and *highly available* (HA). At the BA level, a service delivers correct functionality as long as no faults occur, but it neither offers any redundancy for its system components and data, nor fault detection and recovery mechanisms, while a HA service, in addition to the BA level's feature, provides a certain level of redundancy and eventually the mechanisms for fault-tolerance support [5].

Availability is usually defined either as (a) the percentage of time during which the service is available or (b) the probability of service systems' reachability where each system has an independent failure probability [5]. We use these definitions to specify our availability metrics used in both defining QoA requirements and evaluating reached QoA for networked services. Using these availability metrics - the *percentage of successful service time* and the *failure probability* of underlying systems and network connections, QoA guarantees can be specified in various forms like the cases in network QoS [2]:

- *deterministic* - a service (or its data item) is reachable all the time with an availability guarantee of 99.99 percent. This means for a service that the time duration where the service is unreachable should be absolutely no longer than 53 minutes for a year (1 year = 525600 minutes).
- *probabilistic (or stochastic)* - a service availability probability is guaranteed to be at least, e.g., 90 percent of the whole service access requests.

Actually, the exact form of QoA parameter can be specified both by applications and service providing systems. The QoA evaluation conditions that we use for evaluating satisfied QoA in the evaluation part of this work are as follows:

- *reachedQoA(v)* - it indicates for each demanding node how much the availability requirement has been fulfilled by the selected placement R. For example, the required and satisfied availability values are 95% and 94%, respectively. Then, the reachedQoA is 0.99.
- *minQoA* - it is the minimum of the reachedQoA for all demanding nodes with the selected placement R.
- *avgQoA* - it is the average value of the reachedQoA .
- *guaranteedQoA* - it indicates for how many demanding nodes the selected placement R satisfies the QoA requirement.

Parameter	Notation	Definition
reachedQoA(v)	$QoA_{rch}(v)$	the ratio of satisfied availability to required availability for node v, $\forall v \in V_R$ with $V_R = V$ without R
minQoA	QoA_{min}	min { $QoA_{rch}(v) : \forall v \in V_R$ }
avgQoA	QoA_{avg}	$1/n(\sum QoA_{rch}(v))$ with $\forall v \in V_R$ and $n = (\|V\| - \|R\|)$
guaranteedQoA	QoA_{gua}	the ratio of $\|V_{rch}\|$ to $\|V\|$, where $V_{rch} = $ set of nodes with $QoA_{rch}(v) \geq 1$

3   The Replica Placement Problem

Distributed, networked service systems that consist of storage/server nodes and network connections between them can be modelled as a graph, *G(V,E)*, where V is the set of nodes and E the set of connection links. This graph is *static* if the members and the cardinality of V and E do not change else it is *dynamic*. The graph is said to be *stochastic* when each node and link are parameterized, statistically independently of each other, with known failure or availability probabilities. The following sections introduce three replica placement (RP) sub-problems that are explored in this work. For all three sub-problems, we model the RP problem as a *static and stochastic* graph.

3.1 Finding a "Good" Placement for a Fixed Number of Replicas

As input, a stochastic graph G (V, E) is given. As the second parameter, a positive integer number k may also be given. The objective of this problem is to place the k replicas on the nodes of V, i.e., find R with $|R| = k$ such that a given optimization condition $O(|R|, R, a)$ is satisfied for given availability requirement for service demanding nodes. How well the optimization condition is satisfied depends on the size of $|R|$ and the topological placement R. Because the main goal associated with placing replicas on given networks in our work is satisfying availability QoS which can be required in different levels, we take the availability and failure parameters as our key optimization condition, i.e., $O(|R|, R, guaranteedQoA)$. Thus, with the use of 100% of all clients', 90%-tile, and mean clients' required availability value, the optimization condition can be denoted as $O(|R|, R, 1.0)$, $O(|R|, R, .90)$, $O(|R|, R, avgQoA)$, respectively. For these conditions, the replica set R must be chosen such that the maximum, average or any given failure bound for service and its data access meets the QoA requests for any demanding node (client node) of V.

The RP problem can be classified as NP-hard discrete location problem[8,9]. In literature, many similar location problems are introduced and algorithms are proposed to solve the problems in this category. The heuristics such as *Greedy, TransitNode, Vertex substitution*, etc. are applied to many location problems and have shown their efficiency [10,12,13]. In this work, we take some basic heuristic algorithms as follows. But, different variants of these heuristics and any such improvement can be used with light modifications to enhance the efficiency and performance of our basic heuristics:

- *Random (RA)*. By using a random generator, we pick a node v with uniform probability, but without considering the node's supplying availability value, and put it into the replica set. If the node already exists in the replica set, we pick a new node, until the given number reaches k.
- *HighestFirst (HF)*. For each node v, we calculate v's actual supplying availability value by taking the availability values of all adjacent edges of the node into account. The nodes are then sorted in decreasing order of the actual availability values, and we finally put the best k nodes into the replica set.
- *TransitNode (TR)*. The basic principle of the *TransitNode* heuristic is that nodes with the highest (in/out) degrees, i.e., the number of connection links to adjacent nodes, can potentially reach more nodes with smaller latency. So we place replicas on nodes of V in decending order of (in/out) degree. This is due to the observation that nodes in the core of the Internet that act as transit points will have the highest (in/out) degrees [12].
- *HighestFirst+TransitNode (HF+TR)*: a combination of the *HF* and *TR* algorithms.

We applied the *HR+TR* algorithm to an example stochastic graph which represents a model of a virtual network topology (Figure 1). In this example graph G(V,E) with $|V|=10$ and $|E|=20$, nodes and links are parameterized with randomly generated probability values, e.g., the demanding and supply availability values of nodes are between 90% and 99%, and the failure probability values of links are between 1% and 10%. For a given number $k = 1$, the candidate replica nodes are {4}, {9}, {8}, {3} and {0}. By considering only the availability value (*Sup.QoA*), the algorithm choices {4} as the replica set.

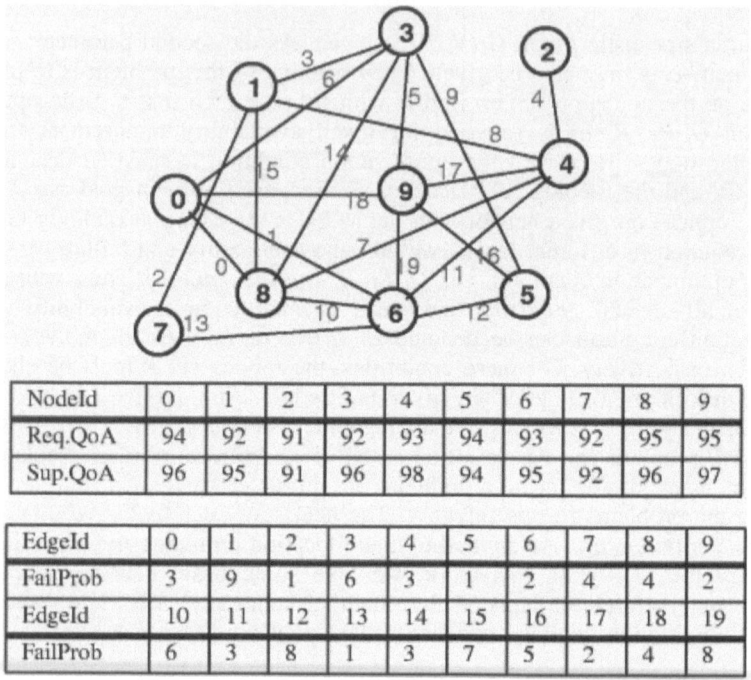

NodeId	0	1	2	3	4	5	6	7	8	9
Req.QoA	94	92	91	92	93	94	93	92	95	95
Sup.QoA	96	95	91	96	98	94	95	92	96	97

EdgeId	0	1	2	3	4	5	6	7	8	9
FailProb	3	9	1	6	3	1	2	4	4	2
EdgeId	10	11	12	13	14	15	16	17	18	19
FailProb	6	3	8	1	3	7	5	2	4	8

Fig. 1. An example stochastic graph: the demanding and supplying availability values for all nodes are independent and decoupled. To each edge a failure probability value is assigned. The values are in percentage.

3.2 Calculating the Reached QoA

Given a stochastic graph $G(V,E)$ and a replica set R. The objective of this problem is to check for all demanding nodes whether the reached availability satisfies the required QoA for them, i.e., whether $\overline{A}(R)$ is 1 or 0. In comparison to the problem of finding a good placement decribed in Section 3.1, this problem requires a solution which exactly tests whether the result is 1 or 0. Some similar works are introduced in the literature, which are devoted to the problem of *network reliability* [11]. The methods that provide an exact reliability are called exact methods, in contrast to the heuristic methods which provide an approximate result.

Enumerating all possibilities without skipping any solution case requires to take exact methods for solving this problem. From some exact methods which are proposed in the literature, we adopted the state enumeration method [11] and modified it for our problem [7]. In the state enumeration method, the state of each node and each edge are enumerated: the state value is either *1* when it functions or *0* when it fails. Indeed, there are $2^{|V|+|E|}$ states for a graph $G = (V,E)$, i.e., $2^{|V|+|E|}$ partial graphs for G. We then check the QoA for all partial graphs with the replica set given as input.

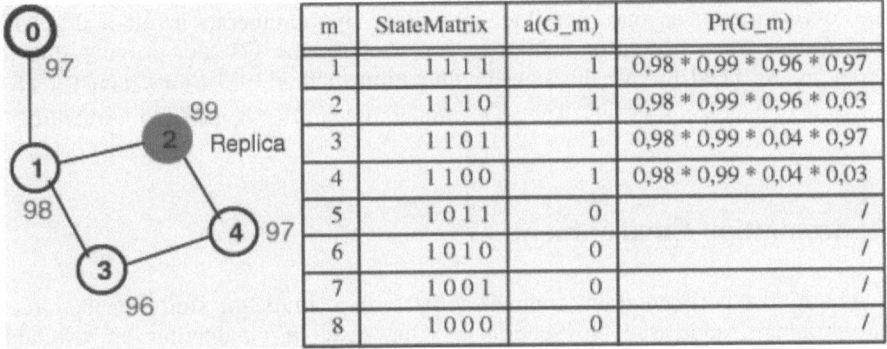

m	StateMatrix	a(G_m)	Pr(G_m)
1	1 1 1 1	1	0,98 * 0,99 * 0,96 * 0,97
2	1 1 1 0	1	0,98 * 0,99 * 0,96 * 0,03
3	1 1 0 1	1	0,98 * 0,99 * 0,04 * 0,97
4	1 1 0 0	1	0,98 * 0,99 * 0,04 * 0,03
5	1 0 1 1	0	/
6	1 0 1 0	0	/
7	1 0 0 1	0	/
8	1 0 0 0	0	/

Fig. 2. An example graph G=(V,E), |V|=5, |E|=5 (left). Only the node states are enumerated and the cases where the node 1's state is 0 are skiped (right).

We applied the *StateEnumeration* algorithm [7] to an example stochastic graph G(V,E) with |V|=5 and |E|=5, placement R={2}, |R|=1, as shown in Figure 2. As test node, we take the node 0 which has the availability requirement value 97%. Figure 2 (right) presents the state matrix, the availability and the sum of availability probability value for each partial graph. In this example, we only encounter the states of nodes to reduce the time complexity, i.e., from $2^{|V|+|E|}$ to $2^{|V|}$. The first column means number of the partial graphs to be tested. Instead of considering all partial graph cases of $2^{|V|+|E|}$, we only have the half size of them by skipping the cases in which the node 1 is 'not available', i.e., (the state value of the node 1 is 0), because the node state 'zero' of the node 1 causes no further possible connection for the test node 0 to build any path to the replica node 2. After building a state matrix for the nodes 1,2,3 and 4 at the second column, we check whether there is any path between the node 0 (test node) and the node 2 (replica node) at the third column. According to the result of this check, we calculate the availability probability values for each partial graph of which the availability check value is 1: as shown in the fourth column, we calculated the *Pr(G_m)* just for the first 4 partial graphs (m = 1,2,3 and 4). The summation of the availability probability values of the four satisfied states is: A_node0(G) = Pr(G_1) + Pr(G_2) + Pr(G_3) + Pr(G_4) = 0,97135624, and this availability value is greater than the availability value required by the node 0. Indeed, the QoA for the node 0 is: A_node0({2}) = 1.

3.3 Determining the Number and Location of Replicas for Satisfying Required QoA

As input, only a stochastic graph *G(V,E)* is given. It has to be determined (a) how many replicas must be deployed and (b) where these replicas should be placed to guarantee the required QoA.

Satisfying a certain, required QoA value with a guarantee means that we have to offer always a replica set which fulfils the given QoA requirements in any case. Heuristics are not proper approaches for solving this problem, because they give not always a solution with QoA guarantee. To solve this problem, we generally can use the exact methods, one possible case may be enumeration method such as *StateEnumeration* algorithm which is described in the [7]. For solving this third problem, we need to call the state enumeration method $2^{|V|}$ times, i.e., for all the possible replica solution sets. The algorithm complexity is then $O(2^{|V|} \cdot 2^{|V|+|E|})$.

4 Simulation Environment

We built an experimental environment to perform a simulation study for the three RP sub-problems addressed in Section 3. Our goal in conducting an availability evaluation is to determine exactly the replica set R for given QoA requirements, and to study the effect of changing R and $|R|$ on the required and reached QoA which is given as the optimization condition $O(|R|, R, a)$, on the other side. For our availability evaluation, we conducted simulations on random network topologies.

By using Leda graphic library [14] several random topologies in different sizes can be generated at run time. We also used graph files which are generated by the topology generator Tiers[15]. To reflect the actual Internet topology, we used several different network trace data from NLANR[16], which describe the Autonomous System (AS) topology on a different day, and associated in/out-degree of the AS with each node of the randomly generated graphs. But, because we had no access to any real data concerning the availability or failure probability parameters, we simply assign the values from a certain range to each node and each edge.

The availability and failure probability parameters for nodes and edges of the graphs are single values: for example, 50, 80, 90 or 99% as availability values and 10, 5, or 1% failure probability values. We decoupled the availability values between the demanding and supply nodes, i.e., all nodes have two availability parameters assigned: one value as the demanding availability parameter and the other as the supplying. Thus, when a node is a demanding node (client node), then its demanding availability value is used, while for supplying node the actual supplying availability value is, for example, calculated by multiplicating the availability values of its supplying own and the average value of its adjacent edges. At the replica set building phase, each node is evaluated according to its supplying availability value. Thus, to be elected as a replica node, for example in the *HA* algorithm, a node should have a high supplying availability value.

As replication model, we assume the *full replication* in which the whole data items of an origin server system are replicated to other nodes located within the same network. *Mirroring* is a typical case of the full replication model. The simulation program is written in C/C++ and runs on Linux and Sun Solaris 2.6 machines.

5 Evaluation of Reached QoA

In this section, we present our experiment results. We evaluated the reached QoA of our heuristics and the exact enumeration method using topologies of different sizes. We ran each basic heuristic and the exact state enumeration method on each topology using different value ranges for the availability and failure probability parameters of nodes and edges. The demanding and initial supplying availability values of the nodes and the failure probability values of the edges are assigned randomly, from a uniform distribution where we varied the parameter values as Table 1 shows. To evaluate the QoA offered by our heuristics and *StateEnumeration* algorithm, we used the QoA metrics defined in Section 2.2.

Table 1. QoA parameters and their values for our simulaiton

Type	Parameter	Notation	Value
Graph	node and edge size	$|V|:|E|$	G1(20:30), G2(100:300)
Edge	edges' failure probability	q_l	1 ~ 10 %, 0%
Node	nodes' required availability	p_{nReq}	90~99%, 50~99%, 50-90-99%
	nodes' supply availability	p_{nSup}	$p_{nSup} \geq p_{nReq}$

5.1   Relative Comparison of Reached QoA by Heuristics

We evaluate at first the reached QoA by our simple heuristics. The baseline for our experiment is an initial placement R_0 which is obtained by randomly selecting k nodes from V. We then compare the reached QoA of each heuristic to this baseline and present the relative QoA improvement obtained with each heuristic.

5.1.1   Effects of R and |R| on Reached QoA

The first experiment was to find good locations of a replica set R with $|R| = k$ for given graphs G with maximal replica number k. The conditions that we assumed for this problem were: (1) $QoA_{min} > 0.9$, 0.95, and *0.99,* respectively, and (2) $QoA_{avg} > 1.0$. In this case, there was no constraints on the topological location of the replicas and replicas may be placed at any node v in G.

Figure 3 (*top*) shows the results from this experiment with $G2$. We plot the number of k on the x-axis and the reached QoA on the y-axis. In each graph, we plot different curves for different heuristics and different ranges for required availability values. From Figure 3 (*top*), we can see that our heuristics *HA* and *HA+TR*, although they are very simple, reach significantly higher QoA in comparison to the baseline placement. Even though the improvement of 12% QoA guarantee rate with replicas 5 to 25 (totally, 20% of the whole nodes are replicas) may not seem much, it is important to note that the number of replicas is really a relevant factor for improving QoA: the lager the replica number is, the better is the reached QoA.

5.1.2   Effects of Varying Availability Requirement Value Ranges on QoA

In the second experiment, to study the effects of different ranges of the required availability values on the reached QoA, we varied the ranges of required availability values (p_{nReq}) from 50~99% to 80~99% and 90-99% for the same graph G2. We took also p_{nReq} as different single values like 50-80-99%. As Figure 3 (*bottom*) shows, the improvement rate of the reached QoA is better when the p_{nReq} is distributed in wider ranges.

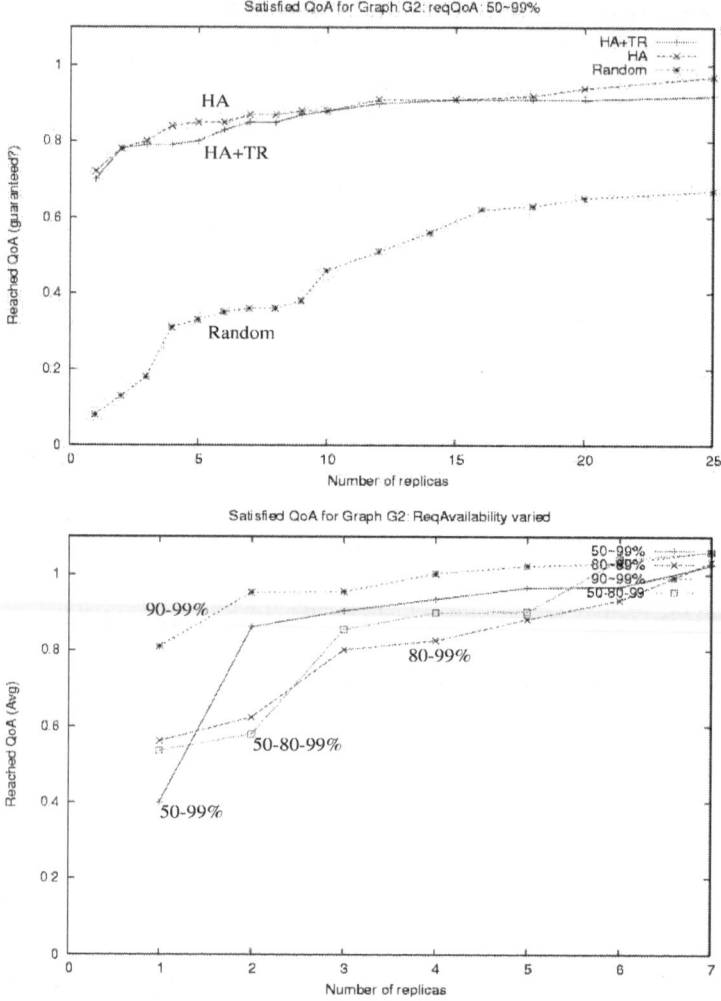

Fig. 3. Reached QoA values by our heuristics: (*top*) different heuristics, (*bottom*) different ranges for required availability values

5.2   Exact Evaluation of Reached QoA by Heuristics

We now evaluate the QoA reached by our heuristics in an exact form and check whether the reached QoA can really satisfy the required QoA for all demanding nodes (*test for guaranteedQoA*). We test also how many replica nodes do the heuristics need to give a QoA guarantee, i.e., *guaranteedQoA* = 1. For this purpose we ran our *StateEnumeration* routine with replica sets produced by our heuristics *HA* and *HA+TR* as input. Due to the exponentially growing runtime complexity and the memory requirements with growing graph sizes, we limited our experiments for the *StateEnumeration* to a small graph, the test graph *G1* with |V| = 20 and |E| = 30. Table 2 shows the detailed test result from *HA+TR*. For the calculation of the average (*avgQoA*) and minimal reached QoA (*minQoA*), we excluded the QoA values for replica nodes.

Table 2. A detailed result for *HA+TR* with *G1*, : *0%*, and p_{nReq} range: *90-99%*

|R|	Replica locations, R	Avg QoA	Min QoA	QoA_{gua}	QoA_{gua} by exact test
1	8	1.0118	0.9100	0.75	**0.80**
2	8,10	1.0194	0.9100	0.75	not checked
3	8,10,12	1.0226	0.9193	0.75	not checked
4	8,10,12,11	1.0355	0.9496	0.85	not checked
5	8,10,12,11,13	1.0399	0.9496	0.85	not checked
6	8,10,12,11,13,0	1.0487	0.9591	0.90	**0.95**
7	8,10,12,11,13,0,16	1.0556	0.9900	0.95	**1.00**
8	8,10,12,11,13,0,16,1	1.0577	0.9900	0.95	not checked
9	8,10,12,11,13,0,16,1,2	1.0610	0.9900	0.95	not checked
10	8,10,12,11,13,0,16,1,2,5	1.0711	1.0000	**1.00**	**1.00**

Even though *HA+TR* could reach the average QoA (1.0118) greater than 1 with one replica node, it could not offer the QoA guarantee: 10 replicas were needed to satisfy the QoA guarantee for the small graph.

5.3 Finding the Optimum - |R| and R

In the last experiment, we considered the case of finding the optimum, i.e., the minimal number of replicas and their geographical placement which satisfies the availability QoS with guarantee. We re-used *StateEnumeration* and the test graph *G1* with the same values for availability and failure probability parameters. We started the routine with a replica degree of 1, i.e., k=|R| = *1*, and selected each node as replica node. We then incremented the replica degree, until we reached the QoA_{gua} = 1.0 (a QoA with guarantee). Table 3 shows the reached QoA values at each *k* *(k=1,2,3)*. Figure 4 plots the reached QoA that *StateEnumeration* algorithm calculated exactly with each instance for the given *k*. The wider spectrum of the left part is for highlighting the reached QoA from all of the instances for k=1 and the choosen instances for k=3. The right part of Figure 4 shows how the reached QoA varies in the case of k=2, and how big is the gap between good and bad QoA rates reached by the instances.

5.4 Discussion

The following observations could be identified from our experiment results: (1) the location of replicas is a relevant factor for the availability QoS. Even though the QoA improvement could be achieved by increasing replica numbers, replicas' placement and their dependability affected the QoA more significantly; (2) using a heuristic method is more efficient than the exact method, at least in terms of the runtime complexity, to find a good placement for large graphs. But, the replica degree of their placement results are in most cases higher than those of exact methods. Furthermore, the heuristics give no guarantee for availability QoA; (3) in opposite to the heuristic method, the exact method guarantees the availability QoS with its placement results, although the runtime complexity is very high: $O\ (|V_R| \cdot 2^{|V|+|E|})$ and $O(2^{|V|} \cdot |V_R| \cdot 2^{|V|+|E|})$ for the availability checking (Section 3.2) and the guaranteed QoA problems (Section 3.3), respectively.

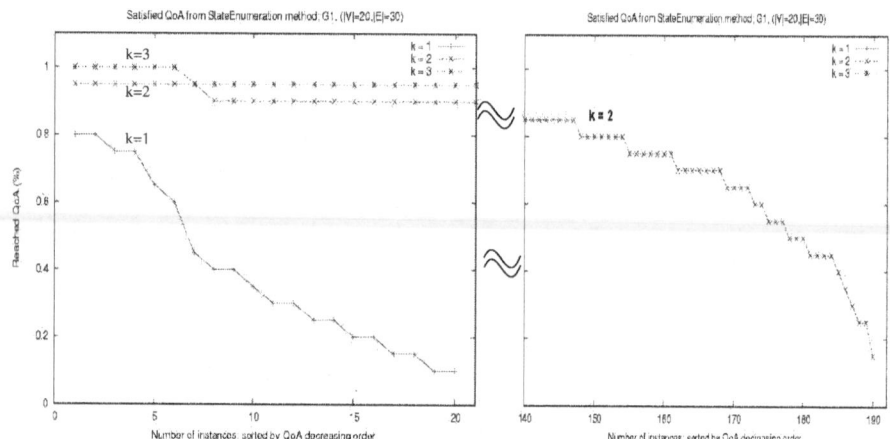

Fig. 4. Reached QoA that was checked exactly by *StateEnumeration*

Table 3. A test result from *StateEnumeration* with *G1*, failure probability *(q_l)*: 0%, and req. availability *(P_{nReq})* range: *90-99%*

No. of replicas	Best QoA value	Worst QoA value	Mean QoA value	Instances achieved the best QoA value
1	0.80	0.10	0.3345	{0},{8}
2	0.95	0.15	0.8078	{0,11},{0,18},{8,11},{8,18},{11,13}, {12,16},{13,16}
3	1.00	not checked	not checked	{0,11,16},{0,16,18},{8,11,16}, {8,16,18},{11,12,16},{11,13,16}

6 Related Work

The key ideas on which our work on QoA concept in this paper bases are (i) an availability-centric view on QoS and (ii) satisfying different levels of QoA values required by individual users. Since the common goals associated with placement problems in exsisting studies are reducing clients' download time and alleviating server load, the main feature of the problem solving approaches for this problem category is that they usually addressed the cost and resource minimization issues, but not the question how to guarantee the required availability. Furthermore, we can find an "good" upper bound, if the selected placement meets the required availability QoS, but it is not guaranteed that the selected placement always meets the availability requirement.

7 Conclusion

In this paper we took an availability-centric view on QoS and focused on the issues of providing models and mechanisms to satisfy availability requirement for replicated multimedia services and contents. We developed a concept called *quality of availability (QoA)* in which the availability is treated as a new controllable QoS parameter. Based on the QoA concept, we modelled a distrbuted multimedia system as a stochastic graph where all nodes and edges are parameterized with known availability and failure probabilities. We especially tackled the replica placement problem in which we specified different placement problems with different QoA metrics such as *minQoA*, *avgQoA*, and *guaranteedQoA*. The primary result shows already that (1) the location of replicas is a more relevant factor than their number for satisfying the availability QoS for different users, and (2) the heuristic methods could not give any guarantee for their achieved QoA, even though they are very efficient for large size graphs. Our proposed QoA concept and model can be used as a base mechanism for further study on the availability and reliability QoS with dynamic replication problems and mobile storage planning problems.

References

[1] Zheng Wang. *Internet QoS: Architectures and Mechanisms for Quality of Service.* Lucent Technologies, 2001.
[2] J. Schmitt. *Heterogeneous Network QoS Systems.* PhD thesis, Darmstadt University of Technology, December 2000.
[3] H. Schulzrinne. "QoS over 20 Years". Invited Talk in *IWQoS'01.* Germany, 2001.
[4] SEQUIN project. "Quality of Service Definition" *SEQUIN Deliverable D2.1,* April 2001. Available at <http://www.dante.net/sequin/QoS-def-Apr01.pdf>
[5] G. Coulouris, J. Dollimore, and T. Kindberg. *Distributed Systems.* 3rd Ed., Chapter 1, 8, 14 and 15, Addison-Wesley, 2001.
[6] G. On, J. Schmitt and R. Steinmetz. "Design and Implementation of a QoS-aware Replication Mechanism for a Distributed Multimedia System", in *Lecture Notes in Computer Science 2158* (IDMS 2001), pp.38-49, Sep. 2001.

[7]   G. On, J. Schmitt and R. Steinmetz. "The Quality of Availability: Tackling the Replica Placement Problem", *Technical Report*, KOM-TR-2001-11, Darmstadt University of Technology, December 2001.

[8]   M.R. Garey and D.S. Johnson. *Computers and Intractability: A Guide to the Theory of NP-Completeness*. Freeman, 1979.

[9]   Christos H. Papadimitrio and Kenneth Steiglitz. *Combinatorial Optimizatioon: Algorithms and Complexity*. Prentice-Hall, ISBN 0-13-152462-3, 1982.

[10]   N. Mladenovic, M. Labbe and P. Hansen: "Solving the p-Center Problem with Tabu Search and Variable Neighbourhood Search", July 2000.

[11]   C. Lucet, J.-F. Manouvrier. "Exact Methods to compute Network Reliability". In *Proc. of 1st Inter'l Conf. on Math. Methods in Reliability*, Bucharest, Sep. 1997.

[12]   S. Jamin, C. Jin, A. R. Kurc, D. Raz, Y. Shavitt. "Constrained Mirror Placement on the Internet", In *Proc. of IEEE INFOCOM'01*, pp. 31-40, 2001.

[13]   P. Krishnan, D. Raz and Y. Shavitt. "The Cache Location Problem", In *IEEE/ ACM Transactions on Networking, 8(5)*, pp. 568-582, Oct. 2000.

[14]   Leda. software available from <http://www.algorithmic-solutions.com/>

[15]   Tiers. software available at <http://www.isi.edu/nsnam/dist/topogen/>

[16]   NLANR measurement and operations analysis team. <http://moat.nlanr.net>

An Open Middleware Architecture for Network-Integrated Multimedia

Marco Lohse, Michael Repplinger, and Philipp Slusallek

Computer Graphics Lab, Department of Computer Science
Saarland University, Im Stadtwald, 66123 Saarbrücken, Germany
{mlohse, repplix, slusallek}@graphics.cs.uni-sb.de

Abstract. Today, we are surrounded by a constantly growing number of networked multimedia devices. These devices offer high-quality input and output capabilities often together with enough computing power and programmability to perform a variety of multimedia operations. However, integrating and controlling these distributed devices from an application is difficult because of the variety of underlying technologies.

In this paper we present a network-integrated multimedia middleware especially designed for this heterogeneous environment. Our architecture allows for a flexible usage of different networking technologies and offers the extensibility to transparently use various existing infrastructures. Distributed devices can be discovered, inspected, and then integrated into a common media processing graph. We demonstrate our approach with a distributed camera control application and a multimedia home entertainment center.

1 Introduction

Today's common multimedia middleware such as DirectShow from Microsoft [1] or the Java Media Framework from Sun [2] adopt a PC-centric approach. Applications can only access directly connected devices and the network is used as a source of data only. With the increasing number of networked multimedia devices like video recorders, set-top-boxes, TVs, hi-fi systems, multimedia PCs, or small screen devices like PDAs, support for distributed multimedia applications is becoming increasingly important. The goal of our work is to design and develop a multimedia middleware that considers the network as an integral part and enables the intelligent use of devices distributed across a network.

Several approaches for multimedia middleware supporting distributed computing have been proposed. These frameworks typically directly extend existing middleware for distributed object environments (DOE), namely OMG's CORBA or Microsoft's DCOM. The Multimedia System Services (MSS) [3] offer an architecture for building distributed multimedia application using CORBA. MSS is the basis for the ISO Presentation Environment for Multimedia Objects (PREMO) [4]. Like the Reference Model of Open Distributed Processing (RM-ODP) [5], PREMO is restricted to a high-level conceptual description rather than an approach for implementation. Other frameworks focus on specific problems

F. Boavida et al. (Eds.): IDMS/PROMS 2002, LNCS 2515, pp. 327–338, 2002.

in distributed multimedia environments and propose sophisticated extensions for QoS management and adaption, e.g. the Multimedia Component Architecture (MCA) [6] or CINEMA [7]. The Toolkit for Open Adaptive Streaming Technology (TOAST) examines the use of reflection and open programming in distributed multimedia [8]. The approach described in [9] extends the standard CORBA Event Service to support multimedia and includes data types for multimedia data flows. In [10] an extension for the CORBA Event service is described which offers different levels of reliability, congestion control mechanisms and jitter suppression strategies. An architecture which allows mobile computers to use resources in a distributed environment is described in [11]. Like the above mentioned frameworks it is based directly on CORBA.

In contrast, our approach offers an integrating open architecture that does not rely an a particular technology or middleware. Instead, it allows the flexible usage of different networking and middleware technologies. The network-integrated multimedia middleware (NMM) [12] presented in this paper offers following advantages.

- **Heterogeneity.** In heterogeneous environments one cannot assume the availability of a certain DOE technology on all platforms. Instead, with mediating proxy objects and parameterizable communication strategies, different technologies can be combined. By recursively using this approach, even different technologies without a directly connecting communication channel can be used together, if some other technology can be used as mediator.
- **Optimized communication strategies.** The tight coupling of a multimedia middleware to an existing middleware for DOE might incur significant overhead, which is often permanent even for locally operating applications. The possible usage of optimized communication strategies allows to chose an appropriate technique depending on the current context or the locality of components. Furthermore, with this explicit binding mechanism, suitable strategies and QoS parameters can be chosen independently for the transmission of multimedia data and the controlling of components.
- **Extensibility.** Different extensions to existing DOE middleware as well as new multimedia middleware technologies will emerge in the future. Our middleware can take advantage of this progression by using these DOE technologies as new communication channels or by integrating new multimedia middleware functionality with suitable proxy objects.
- **Unified messaging system.** By providing a unified event system components can dynamically be queried for their supported functionality. Furthermore, application can register to be notified by components. Method invocation on interfaces exported by components have the same semantics as event passing.
- **Resource consumption.** On platforms with restricted resources like PDAs or set-top boxes, traditional DOE middleware often require too much computational power and memory capacity. By using light-weight transport strategies these platforms can still be integrated transparently.

2   Locally Operating Middleware

This section will describe the architecture and services offered for building multimedia applications operating on a single host. The next sections will then show how these aspects are extended for a network-integrated environment.

2.1   Flow Graph-Based Architecture

Within the network-integrated multimedia middleware (NMM), which is implemented in C++ under Linux, hardware devices (e.g. a DVD-ROM drive) as well as software components (e.g. a decoding module) are modeled by so called *nodes* (see Figure 1). A node represents the smallest entity of processing. In order to be able to extensively reuse specific nodes in different application scenarios, nodes should represent fine-grained processing units. The innermost loop of a node produces data, performs a certain operation on the data, or finally consumes data.

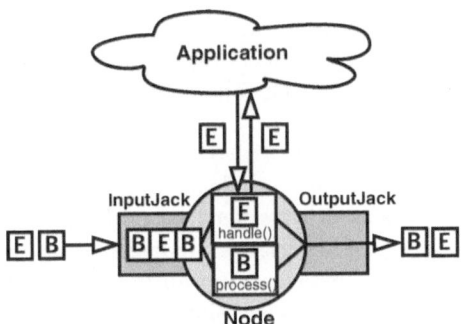

Fig. 1. NMM node with in-stream events and buffers, and out-of-band events sent from or to an application ('E' event, 'B' buffer). Buffers are processed inside the node and events are handled with registered methods.

A node has potentially several input and output ports, each represented by a *jack*. Associated with each jack are its supported *formats*, which precisely describe the supported type of multimedia data with type, subtype, and format specific parameters as key-value pairs. Multimedia formats can be described recursively. This allows for arbitrary complex formats. Formats characterize nodes with their capabilities in the registry and XML descriptions of formats can be exported during runtime and (see Section 2.4).

To perform a specific type of multimedia processing, nodes are connected to a directed graph, the *flow graph*. This is done by connecting output jacks to input jacks. The structure of this graph then specifies the operation to be performed.

Synchronization is performed by *Controller*-objects attached to nodes, which are in turn monitored by a *Synchronizer*-object. Several other services are provided by NMM that cannot be covered in detail in this paper.

2.2   Format Negotiation

Although a flow graph can be created by hand, our multimedia middleware provides support for setting up complex flow graphs. Instead of having to provide a valid and fully configured flow graph, only a high-level description of the wanted functionality has to be specified that is independent of possible connections and supported formats: the *user graph*. A format negotiation procedure then transforms the user graph into a valid and fully configured flow graph following a well-defined quality measurement as optimization criterion. The quality of a media presentation is defined as the quality perceived by a user. Solutions which provide the same quality, are ranked according to their costs. More details can be found in [13].

2.3   Messaging System

All communication within the NMM architecture is performed through an unified message system. This aspect is especially important because it allows to extend locally operating middleware like the one described in this section to incorporate distributed nodes without relying on a particular DOE middleware.

The message system consists of two types of *message* objects. Multimedia data is generated at source nodes and placed into messages of type *buffer*. Buffers are forwarded along connected jacks between nodes and can be enqueued before being processed (see *process()* in Figure 1). Jacks use a *transport strategy* that is responsible for forwarding messages from an input to an output jack. In a local application the transport strategy is a simple pointer forwarding. In Section 3.4 the role of transport strategies in distributed environments is described.

Messages of type *composite event* can be used to control node behavior. This can be done in two ways. Nodes can create *in-stream* composite events that are forwarded between nodes and possibly enqueued the same way as buffers. In addition, an application can communicate with its instantiated nodes by sending *out-of-band* composite events. This mechanism is mainly used for setting node specific parameters. A composite event consists of an ordered set of single events (or commands). Each event is identified by a key and contains additional parameters. To be able to handle a specific event, a node has to register a method. Events are then dispatched automatically (see *handle()* in Figure 1).

The unified event system allows to dynamically add and remove the ability to handle certain events. In addition, listener objects can transparently register to be informed when a certain event reaches a node. For example, an application can register to be notified when an "end-of-stream" event reaches a certain node. Furthermore, the event system provides reflection: nodes can be asked for all events they can handle together with the parameter types. For example, this is useful for applications providing a GUI for creating flow graphs and setting node specific parameters. Here, the GUI elements for event parameters can be generated automatically from the parameter type.

During its lifetime, a node can be in different states. After being instantiated (*constructed* state), a node might require specific parameters to be set before its supported formats can be announced (*initialized* state). After the jacks of a node are connected, a node reaches the next state (*activated* state) where it is ready to start processing. A call to start() will then finally set the state of the node to *started*. In order to take the properties of these different states into account, the event system allows to specify two additional parameters to be set when registering an event handling method. First, the states in which an event can be handled; and secondly, the states in which the particular event must have been received and successfully handled before the next state can be reached.

Together, we consider the reflection property together with the possibility to register additional listeners and to restrict event handling to certain states to be essential parts of a multimedia middleware. This is especially important in distributed environments where new devices with unknown properties may become available at any time.

However, compared to a method call, sending an event to a node requires additional programming effort since the event must be created and filled with parameters explicitly. Additionally, since events are identified by strings, type-safety is not guaranteed at compile time. Therefore, our architecture adds interface classes on top of the event system. This step will be explained in detail in Section 3.

2.4   Registry Service

The basis for device discovery is a registry service. On each host, a unique *registry server* object administrates all local resources represented by NMM nodes. Here, information about all available NMM nodes are stored in internal data structures, which can be exported in XML format. Locally running application send queries in XML format to the registry server. After searching its database, the registry server returns a reply and eventually performs reservations of resources (including network and CPU). Objects are then instantiated by a *node factory* object. If the search was not successful, the request can be forwarded to other registries in the network using different peer-to-peer protocols. Details for this step are not covered in the scope of this paper.

The registry server not only administrates nodes. It can also include other specialized registries which are then requested recursively. These registries are useful for the management of devices with special properties (like Firewire devices, which may be connected to more than one host at a time) or for integrating devices from other multimedia frameworks (like the Java Media Framework).

3   Distributed Middleware Architecture

Within the architecture described in the previous section, the nodes connected to a flow graph are restricted to be in the same address space on a single host. In order to be able to control and connect distributed nodes, a network-integrated multimedia middleware needs to provide several services [5].

3.1   Requirements

In the scope of this paper we focus on fulfilling the following requirements.

- **Network- and technology-transparent control.** An intermediary infrastructure has to be established that allows control of all distributed devices and components independent of their physical location and underlying technology.
- **Open components and reflection.** Due to the dynamics and the heterogeneity of distributed environments, components have to provide a self-describing notation of their capabilities and supported interface during runtime. Furthermore, application need to be able to register with components independently of their location and technology.
- **Network-wide cooperation.** Connections for streaming continuous multimedia data between distributed nodes as well as between different technologies must be possible to allow seamless cooperation.
- **Migration-transparency.** Nodes should be allowed to be relocated. This relocation process should be transparent to the application.

The network-integrated registry service described in Section 2.4 provides information about all available nodes and can instantiate nodes on the specific host upon request.

3.2   Proxy Objects

By providing a *proxy architecture*, our multimedia middleware is able to fulfill the above mentioned requirements. The term proxy object is generally used to describe an object that acts as a surrogate for another object to enable access to it [14].

The essential point in using proxy objects is that they allow to separate method invocation and execution. This allows for redirecting an invocation to a remote object. Migrating this remote object only requires updating the way in which communication is performed and not the proxy object itself. Furthermore, proxy objects can be used as translators between different technologies. Section 4 shows the integration of NMM and the Java Media Framework as an example. In addition, proxy objects can be used as interface classes on top of the event system. Section 3.3 will describe this step in detail. Method invocations on these proxy interfaces have the same properties as sending an event. Remember, events allow nodes to be queried for their supported functionality, additional listeners can be registered, and event handling can be restricted or required for certain states of a node. Therefore, local nodes and jacks as well as distributed nodes and jacks are represented as proxy objects within applications.

In order to represent the communication between two objects as a first class data type, we use *communication channels*, which are binding objects according

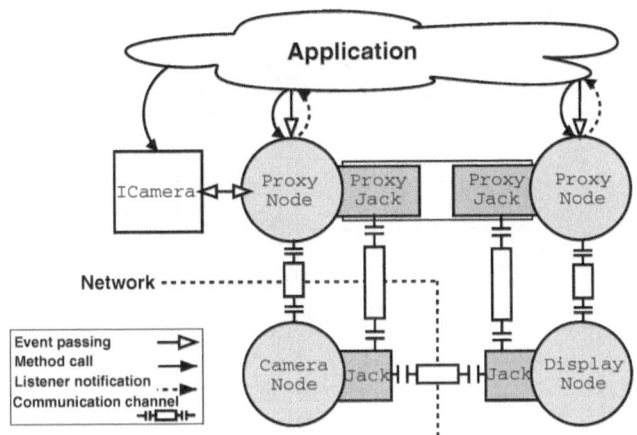

Fig. 2. An application controls a remote camera and a local display node through their proxies and communication channels. An interface object for the camera interface is also provided. Nodes are connected with a communication channel for streaming media.

to the RM-ODP [5]. The design of communication channels as a first class data type allows for a flexible plug-and-play design were the application can choose or change the *transport strategy* of a communication channel depending on its requirements. Communication channels are used in two ways. First, proxy objects control possibly remote objects by sending out-of-band events that were generated by an application or an interface. Secondly, communication channels can be used to transfer multimedia buffer objects or in-stream events between connected nodes.

Figure 2 shows the overall structure of a distributed flow graph. Here, a remote camera (CameraNode) is connected to a local display (DisplayNode). These two nodes are accessed by the application via their proxy nodes. Similarly, the jacks of the nodes are controlled through corresponding proxy jacks.

All these proxy objects are connected to their implementation objects by communication channels. Since the camera is a remote object in this example, a network transport strategy is negotiated for the camera node and its jack upon requesting the node from a remote registry. Jacks represent the binding between two nodes. If the application connects the two proxy jacks, a network transport strategy is negotiated because the two nodes are not collocated. Details on this process are described in Section 3.4

In addition to the general node interface, the camera provides a specific interface. This interface is requested by the application and an interface object is dynamically created (e.g. ICamera). The application can control these proxies by passing an event directly or by invoking the corresponding method on the interface object. Method calls are forwarded as events to the corresponding proxy node. Furthermore, the application can register to be notified for received events.

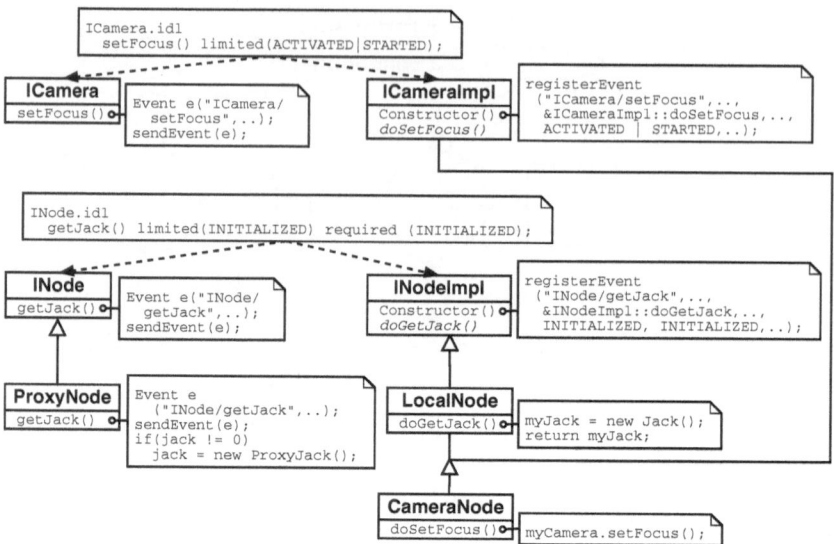

Fig. 3. Simplified IDL notation for interfaces and UML diagram for proxy classes and implementation classes.

3.3   Interface Definition

As mentioned above, the unified event system offers reflection and the possibility to register additional event listeners. Furthermore, event handling can be restricted to certain states of a node and events can be specified as required to reach another state. In order to provide type-safe interfaces for application development, our architecture offers automatically generated interfaces that provide the same semantics as sending an event.

Interfaces are described in an interface definition language (IDL) which is an extended subset of CORBA IDL. Methods can additionally be restricted to a certain state or marked as required to reach another state (limited or required). For each interface, a proxy class and an implementation class is generated. The proxy class (prefix I) contains public methods which internally generate the corresponding event. The implementation class (suffix Impl) contains a protected do-method for each public method in the proxy class. These methods are to be implemented by subclasses. Within the constructor, do-methods are registered for handling the corresponding event.

Figure 3 shows as a simplified example the corresponding classes for NMM nodes and for a camera interface in UML notation. The setFocus-method in ICamera.idl is limited to two states and the getJack-method in INode.idl is limited to the initialized-state and must also be called in this state. The CameraNode inherits from LocalNode and ICameraImpl and finally implements the setFocus-method. Notice, that ProxyNode re-implements the getJack-method: instead of a local jack, a ProxyJack-object is returned.

3.4   Object Binding and Communication Channels

Within our architecture, communication channels are used to transport objects. Objects are mainly of type message but it general any user-defined type can be transferred.

As mentioned above, our architecture allows the flexible usage of different transport strategies within a communication channel. Communication between objects in the same address space is implemented as pointer forwarding. Communication over a network can be performed using different transport strategies. In any case, serialization of objects on the sender side and deserialization on the receiver side is needed.

For these steps our architecture uses so called *ValueStreams*. The ValueStream interface provides input and output operators (i.e. the $\ll$ and $\gg$ operators in C++) for classes of type *Value*, which include classes for basic types and for sequences of Value-objects. With these types, arbitrary complex objects can be built, which are automatically serialized and deserialized without additional programming effort. For instance, the buffer class and the event classes are subclasses of Value. A buffer is a sequence, which includes an array of bytes for the multimedia data and additional value types for information like the size and timestamp. For user-defined classes the ValueStream operators have to be implemented or a mapping between user-defined types and the generic value types has to be provided.

By choosing different subclasses of ValueStream for serialization and deserialization the data format for transmission is selected. One option we are currently providing is to generate an XML representation, another is a representation with "magic numbers" for different data types. Both representations can be directly transferred over a socket using protocols like TCP, UDP, or RTP. Another option is a transport strategy together with a ValueStream subclass that uses CORBA any-types for transmission. We currently use The Ace Orb (TAO) [15] which also provides real-time extensions. Other possible middleware technologies we are planning to evaluate are the Multimedia Communication Protocol (MCOP) [16] and the Desktop Communication Protocol (DCOP) [17] used in the KDE project.

Our architecture supports explicit binding where the strategy of a communication channel and the ValueStream class to be used can be selected or automatically negotiated. In order to simplify this process we use *binding factories* that try to negotiate a connection with wanted properties like QoS requirements. If a direct connection to a distributed object fails the factory searches the network for available proxy objects and communication channels. Based on this result the factory tries to negotiate a connection through more than one proxy objects. If the negotiation process is successfully completed the factory requests the necessary resources and configures them depending on the given requirements. This process is repeated if a node is migrated during runtime.

Communication channels provide interfaces which can be used to realize the mapping of QoS requirements to certain network settings. They also allow the registration of event handlers that are called if certain settings are no longer maintained. Upon these facilities, advanced services like dynamic QoS adaption can be built.

3.5 Discussion

Although CORBA and other DOE systems also offer a proxy architecture, our framework only uses these facilities as one possible solution among others for realizing access to remote objects. Our approach provides an open architecture that offers the transparent and flexible usage of different networking and middleware technologies.

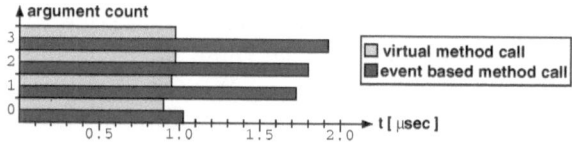

Fig. 4. Execution time per call: dynamic cast plus method invocation compared to event handling (measured for 10,000,000 invocations, 1 GHz Linux PC).

With the unified event system, nodes can be queried for their supported functionality, additional listeners can be registered, and event handling can be restricted or required for certain states. Despite this extra functionality, our current non-optimized implementation shows good performance compared to a virtual method call with a preceding dynamic cast (see Figure 4). We added the dynamic cast to simulate the typical usage of interfaces.

4   Applications

Within the NMM framework, we have implemented a distributed control application for Firewire cameras in C++ that allows to access all cameras registered in the network. The upper half of Figure 5 shows the user interface of this application running on a Linux PC. The features of the currently activated camera are requested dynamically and the user interface is configured appropriately. A distributed camera source node is connected to two sink nodes for rendering the video image. The lower part of Figure 6 shows the image captured by the currently activated camera as rendered by these two different video output nodes. On the left side, the video is rendered with a NMM video display node for the X window system. On the right side, the video is rendered with the Java Media Framework (JMF). To integrate this middleware, we provide the node and jack implementation classes and communication channel based on sockets in Java. Messages that were sent from the connected jack or the corresponding proxy

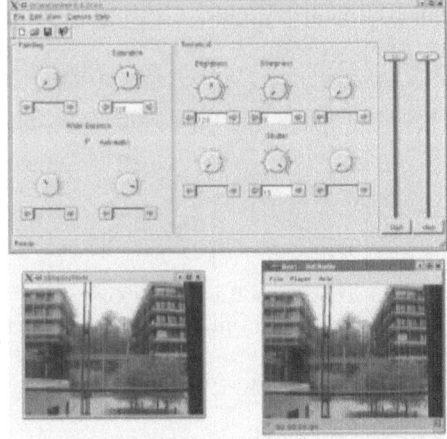

Fig. 5. Distributed camera control application with X display and JMF display.

Fig. 6. The Multimedia-Box, a multimedia home entertainment PC.

object are received by this communication channel and then mapped to JMF buffers or control commands, respectively.

Based on NMM, the Multimedia-Box application offers an extensible application framework for a home entertainment center based on a Linux-PC (see Figure 6). The Multimedia-Box provides the following functionality: TV and video recorder with time-shifting, DVD replay, audio-CD replay, and MP3 encoding and replay. All these features are realized as flow graphs of NMM nodes. Furthermore, the Multimedia-Box can extend its functionality by using devices distributed across the network, e.g. a remote DVB-board can be used as a new data source or time-consuming tasks like video transcoding can be distributed to other devices or specialized hardware.

5   Conclusions and Future Work

In this paper we presented a network-integrated multimedia middleware (NMM) for heterogeneous distributed environments. Our middleware offers network-transparent control and network-wide cooperation of components with different underlying technologies. Based on a unified messaging system, distributed components can be queried for their supported capabilities and interfaces. An open and extensible design allows to integrate new technologies and existing middleware solutions. Two applications were demonstrated; one using distributed components of the NMM architecture together with components of the Java Media Framework.

Future work will include the study of different communication strategies in terms of performance and network bandwidth. Quality of Service monitoring and probing together with advanced QoS negotiation and adaptation will complete our approach. The locally operating middleware and a number of plug-in nodes is already available as Open Source; other parts will follow.

Acknowledgements. This research has been supported by Motorola, Germany, and the Ministry of the Saarland.

References

1. Microsoft: DirectShow Architecture. http://msdn.microsoft.com/ (2002)
2. Sun: Java Media Framework API Guide. http://java.sun.com/products/java-media/jmf/ (2002)
3. Hewlett-Packard Company and IBM Corporation and SunSoft Inc.: Multimedia System Services (1993)
4. David Duke and Ilvan Herman: A Standard for Mulimtedia Middleware. In: ACM International Conference on Multimedia. (1998)
5. Gordon Blair and Jean-Bernard Stefani: Open Distributed Processing and Mulitimedia. Addison-Wesley (1998)
6. Waddington, D., Coulson, G.: A Distributed Multimedia Component Architecture. In: IEEE International Workshop on Enterprise Distributed Object Computing. (1997)
7. Rothermel, K., Dermler, G., Fiederer, W.: QoS Negotiation and Resource Reservation for Distributed Multimedia Applications. In: IEEE International Conference on Multimedia Computing and Systems. (1997)
8. Tom Fitzpatrick and Julian Gallop and Gordon Blair and Christopher Cooper and Geoff Coulson and David Duce and Ian Johnson: Design and Application of TOAST: An Adaptive Distributed Multimedia Middleware. In: International Workshop on Interactive Distributed Multimedia Systems. (2001)
9. Chambers, D., Lyons, G., Duggan, J.: Stream Enhancements for the CORBA Event Service. In: ACM International Conference on Multimedia. (2001)
10. Orvalho, J., Boavida, F.: Augmented Reliable Multicast CORBA Event Service (ARMS): A QoS-Adaptive Middleware. In: International Workshop on Interactive Distributed Multimedia Systems and Telecommunication Services. (2000)
11. Seitz, J., Davies, N., Ebner, M., Friday, A.: A CORBA-based Proxy Architecture for Mobile Multimedia Applications. In: International Conference on Management of Multimedia Networks and Services. (1998)
12. Network-Multimedia Workgroup: Network-Integrated Multimedia Middleware. http://www.networkmultimedia.org (2002)
13. Lohse, M., Slusallek, P., Wambach, P.: Extended Format Definition and Quality-driven Format Negotiation in Multimedia Systems. In: Multimedia 2001 – Proceedings of the Eurographics Workshop. (2001)
14. Gamma, E., Helm, R., Johnson, R., Vlissides, J.: Design Patterns. Elements of Reusable Object-Oriented Software. Addison-Wesley (1995)
15. Douglas C. Schmidt et al.: The Ace Orb(TAO). http://www.cs.wustl.edu/~schmidt/TAO.html (2002)
16. Stefan Westerfeld: Multimedia Communication Protocol (MCOP) documentation. http://www.arts-project.org/doc/mcop-doc/ (2002)
17. Preston Brown et al.: Desktop Communication Protocl (DCOP) documentation. http://developer.kde.org/documentation/library/dcop.html (2002)

Security Attributes Based Digital Rights Management

Cheun Ngen Chong[1], René van Buuren[2],
Pieter H. Hartel[1], and Geert Kleinhuis[3]

[1] Dept. of Computer Science, Univ. of Twente, Enschede, The Netherlands
{chong, pieter}@cs.utwente.nl
[2] Telematica Institute, Enschede, The Netherlands
Rene.vanBuuren@telin.nl
[3] KPN Research, Groningen, The Netherlands
G.Kleinhuis@kpn.com

Abstract. Most real-life systems delegate responsibilities to different authorities. We apply this idea of delegation to a digital rights management system, to achieve high flexibility without jeopardizing the security. In our model, a hierarchy of authorities issues certificates that are linked by cryptographic means. This linkage establishes a chain of control, *identity-attribute-rights*, and allows flexible rights control over content. Typical security objectives, such as identification, authentication, authorization and access control can be realized. Content keys are personalized to detect illegal super distribution. We describe a working prototype, which we develop using standard techniques, such as standard certificates, XML and so forth. We present experimental results to evaluate the scalability of the system. A formal analysis demonstrates that our design is able to detect a form of illegal super distribution.

1 Introduction

Annual losses to the film and music industry due to illegal distribution of content on the Internet amount to billions of dollars annually [1]. Digital Rights Management (DRM) provides a potential solution to the problem of illegal content distribution on the Internet. DRM systems manage copyrights on digital content in untrusted cyberspace.

Commercial DRM platforms for selling digital contents on the Internet are available from SealedMedia, InterTrust and Microsoft etc. Some music and movie industries have adopted online business models for instance subscription-based music sales and pay-per-view movies, such as Sony Music Entertainment and Universal Music Group. Some companies have identified the opportunity to protect intellectual property within enterprise or organization instead of business-to-consumer model, such as Authentica and Alchemedia. These systems are proprietary or include key components that are proprietary. We propose an open system, and analyse how effective it is to provide management flexibility.

F. Boavida et al. (Eds.): IDMS/PROMS 2002, LNCS 2515, pp. 339–352, 2002.

Our system has components for identification, authentication and authorization to achieve a standard level of access control. However, this provides only limited flexibility, for example the in terms of the variety of permissions offered. More flexibility is needed because we cannot foresee which types of permissions and rights will be needed in future. For example, in a standard access control system when a new permission type is added to the system, the associations of all subjects and objects with their permissions must be revisited. This creates management problems. Therefore, we introduce a second level of management and control, which has a dual purpose: (1) the second level *refines* the first level control by specialising it, and (2) the second level provides facilities for the secure distribution of content. We could sloganise our contribution by: $SABDRM = AccessControl + DRM$.

Section 2 introduces our design of a DRM system and elaborates on the aforementioned flexibility of management with a real-life example. Section 3 discusses the state of the art and related work. Section 4 describes our prototype system, a performance evaluation of the implementation, and a SPIN model of the system. Finally section 5 concludes the paper and briefly explains future work.

2   The Idea

We consider a client-server setting in which a user downloads content, where her rights on the content are carefully controlled, say by the content providers or by DRM service providers. We assume that each user has a unique identity. A standard public key certificate [2] can then be used to bind the identity to a public key. The public key certificates are issued and distributed by a Certificate Authority (CA) [3]. We assume that the server can establish the validity of the public key certificate, so that the server can identify and authenticate the user. Additionally by using the server public key certificate, the user is able to authenticate the server.

For maximum flexibility, we assume that different security attributes can be associated with each identity. Security attributes are information, other than cryptographic keys, that is needed to establish and describe the security properties of a user in the system. These security attributes may include role, group membership, time of day, location to access resources, password etc. A security attribute is encapsulated in an attribute certificate [4,5]. The latter has a similar structure to the public key certificate but the attribute certificate does not carry a public key. The Attribute Authority (AA) [6], is responsible for issuing, assigning, signing, distributing and revoking attribute certificates. Note that the CA and AA could be the same authority, but for maximum flexibility, the CA and AA would be different parties. An attribute certificate is signed with the AA's private key to ensure the integrity of the attribute certificate. Having established the identity of a user, and her security attributes we are now able to decide: (a) What content is accessible to the user, and (b) What rights the user may exercise on that content.

The separation of deciding *what content is accessible* from *what can be done with the accessible content* is a key aspect in our system; it creates flexibility, and at the same time simplifies the implementation. For example, consider a document that contains both aggregate and detailed business data. Users with appropriate security attributes may obtain the detailed data, whereas others may only obtain the aggregate data. Establishing the particular rights (i.e. the ability to view, print, save, edit etc) for any of these users holding their respective attributes is still a separate, orthogonal issue.

We use a digital license to capture the rights of a user on a particular item of content. The digital license carries information about the content, the license holder, the payment status (if payment is involved), as well as other terms and conditions of using the content. The digital licenses are described by using XrML [7]. XrML provides a detailed syntax for encapsulating fine-grained control information on a digital content. The Clearing House (CH) is responsible for issuing, managing payment, and distributing and revoking digital licenses. Again, the CH could be the same as one of the CA or AA but would be different from either for maximum flexibility.

The licensing mechanism we have sketched above is not vastly different from other DRM mechanism. However, there are two innovations:

1. Identity, attribute and rights are decoupled to allow for maximum flexibility.
2. Digital licenses are generated on demand at a time after the identity and the security attributes have been verified. This is the earliest moment when the system is able to decide which (partial!) content must be delivered, and what the associated rights should be.

2.1   Certificates and License

The difference between the public key certificate and attribute certificate and why we use a digital license can be shown from an illustration in real life here: A Malaysian resident wishes to enter The Netherlands. She would like to stay in the country for more than a year. Therefore, she needs (1) a passport, (2) a visa and (3) a residence permit.

- The Malaysian Immigration Department issues the passport. The Malaysian government has a policy to decide which of its citizens can be issued passports. This step effectively establishes the identity of a party in the system, and is a prerequisite for access control.
- The Netherlands Embassy grants the visa. The visa is a proof of permission for the passport holder to enter the country. An Embassy also works to policy to decide whom to grant a visa. This step is akin to the first level access control we mentioned in the introduction.
- The Alien Police Department in The Netherlands distributes the residence permit. The residence permit is granted according to Dutch government policies. This step corresponds to the second level access control we described in section 1. Three trusted authorities with three different policies are thus involved in this process.

The immigration system is manageable from the Malaysian government perspective because the Malaysian government does not have to know about Dutch government policy. The policies involved in issuing a residence permit are primarily concerned with what the visitor intends to do (study, work, vacation etc). The Malaysian government is not involved and does not even care.

A public key certificate can be seen as a passport - it identifies the owner, it tends to be valid for a long period, it is difficult to forge and it has a strong authentication process to establish the owner's identity. Our attribute certificate is like an entry visa. A different authority issues it, and in most cases, a passport has a longer validity than a visa. Consequently, acquiring the entry visa becomes a simpler and more manageable procedure. The entry visa will refer to the passport as a part of how that visa specifies the terms under which the passport owner is authorised to enter the country. Once the passport owner is identified and authenticated, the visa may authorise her to enter the country. Once in the country, the traveller may apply for a residence permit, which is then an analogue to our digital licence.

2.2   Association of Authorities

There must be a relationship between the authorities involved to establish a chain of control. For example, the visa is a stamp in the passport; therefore, the link between visa and passport is difficult to break. In the digital world, the public key certificate, attribute certificate and digital license are linked using cryptographic techniques.

An identity may be associated with several attributes, that an attribute may be associated with other attributes, and that an attribute may be associated with several rights. For example, Alice (*identity*) is an editor (*attribute*) and she belongs to an administrative group (*attribute*). The editor is only allowed to enter the system at a given time (*attribute*). The editor can print (*rights*) an annual report and she can view (*rights*) some confidential document.

Because of the interposition of attributes between the identities and the actual rights we call our system a security attribute based digital rights management (SABDRM) system. The association between these three properties identity, attribute and rights represents a chain of control. The distinctive features of the SABDRM are:

1. The use of public key certificate, attribute certificate, content identification and a source of randomness to generate a secret, unique, personalized content key. This should allow multiple use of the same key to be detected with high probability.
2. A hierarchy of authorities that is able to provide for flexibility in the rights management.

3   Related Work

Horne, Pinkas and Sander [8] present a fair exchange protocol for peer-to-peer file sharing which encourages people to comply with the rules by providing incentives, such high quality of service, status or even air miles. Kwok and Lui [9] have proposed a license management model to provide peer-to-peer sharing domain. They implement two types of services, one at the server side and one at the client side, to handle consumer registration, payment, and license issuing processes and to deal with licensing in peer-to-peer distribution model.

Just regulating the distribution of digital content cannot solve the illegal distribution problems alone; it is also necessary to check that rights violations do not happen. Techniques to achieve this include watermarking and fingerprinting [10]. Dittman et al [11] present a technology for combining collusion-secure fingerprinting schemes based on finite geometries and a watermarking mechanism with special marking points for images. Fridrich [12] introduces the concept of key-dependent basis functions and discusses the applications to secure robust watermarking. Brin and Davis [13] describe a copy detection server which identifies copies of digital content, even for partial copies. Shivakumar and Garcia-Molina [14] have introduced a centralized server that can detect copy or reuse (either part or whole) of digital documents. In our system, we are able to detect super distribution thanks to key personalization.

Silbert et al propose a self-protecting container, which they call a DigiBox for protecting the digital content by providing a cryptographically protected environment for packaging content and enforcing rights. The approach proposed by Durfee and Franklin [15] investigates trustworthiness of the distribution chain (i.e. from the Producer to the Consumers), which includes middlemen. Their approach allows trusted middlemen to alter rights but prohibits attackers from tampering with rights.

Voloshynovskiy et al [16] investigate various existing attacks on digital watermarking systems. They show the fundamental limits of the current watermarking technologies and argue that the present technologies are still in their adolescent stage.

Our idea of the personalized key contains the characteristic of watermarking, which embeds the user's identity, her security attribute information, the data of the content and the license. The personalized key is unique (depends on the collision-resistant one-way hash function we use to generate the key) and closely related to the content and the user. The user needs the key to access the protected content. Therefore, we believe that by keeping track of the key, we can keep track of the digital content to some extent.

Finally, yet importantly, proprietary and trustworthy client-side DRM is another problem that has been researched. The main goal is to achieve application- and platform-independence, i.e. using different software applications to access the same protected digital content. Mourad et al [17] implement an application, namely WebGuard that enables existing Internet Explorer Browser and the browser's plug-ins to handle protected content. They use a technique dubbed 'Windows sub classing', which bypasses the Windows message passing within the operating system and application. We share their objective for application-independence but we work at the application level instead of the operating system level. Horne et al [18] use software tamper resistance (by code obfuscation) to protect the client side. Lie et al [19] suggest architectural changes in the hardware that will execute only encrypted code. Their contributions have inspired our future work of applying tamper-resistant security token in a DRM system.

4 Prototype: SUMMER

We have developed a prototype of our DRM system in the context of the Secure Multimedia Retrieval (SUMMER) project. The main objective of SUMMER is to design a secure distributed multimedia database management system for efficient multimedia retrieval from distributed autonomous sources. Figure 1 shows the overview architecture of the SUMMER system. The present paper focuses on the right part. The left part (IAA-QM) is described only briefly below.

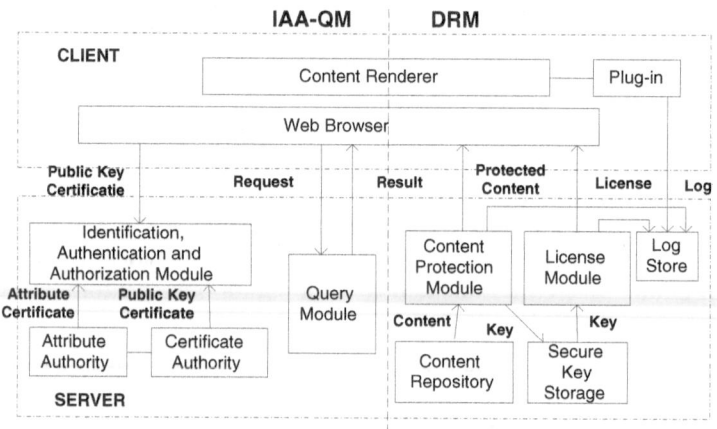

Fig. 1. The overview architecture of SUMMER.

The Identification, Authentication and Authorization (IAA) module decides the identity of the user and then establishes the security attributes for that identity. Therefore, the IAA begins the chain of control of identity-attribute. As described in section 2, attribute certificates and public key certificates, which are generated and distributed by AA and CA respectively, are used as means to achieve IAA.

The Query Module (QM) enforces access control in the system. The QM acts as a filtering and monitoring environment on requests from the client and results from the server. The requests and the results are described using XML. A security policy file and the attribute of the client are fed in to the module. The result displays a list of digital content accessible according to the attribute of the client. The details are beyond the scope of this paper. Further information on IAA-QM can be found in Damian et al [20,21], Bertino et al [22], as well as Kudo and Hada [23].

The DRM part (right half of Figure 1) is composed of four components, namely the Content Module, the License Module, the Content Renderer and the

Plug-in. The DRM part completes the chain of control started by IAA-QM, by linking the digital rights to identity-attribute. The Content Module is composed of the following sub components:

1. Content protection: generates, personalizes, and stores the digital content encryption key in a secure fashion. We hash the public key certificate, attribute certificate, content identity and some random data to generate a key that is unique with a high probability.
2. Raw content repository: securely stores the unencrypted digital content.
3. Secure key storage: stores the content key generated by the Content Protection module.

The License Module implements the CH (Clearing House). The License Module generates digital licenses. The module also retrieves the associated digital content key from the key storage, encrypted by using the client's public key, and embeds in the digital license. The security attributes of the user, the identity of the digital content are fed into the License Module for license generation. The License Module needs the security attributes to retrieve a list of access rights the user possesses for the content. A digital license is generated on-demand and stored. The digital license is signed by using the server's private key.

The Log Store is used to store records of all transactions. The Log Store is assumed to be secure [24,25]. The Log records the content protection time and license generation time on the server side as well as license interpretation process and time by the Plug-in on the client side. The Log Store provides a complete overview of all actions the client has exercised on the digital content. The purpose of the Log Store is to achieve non-repudiation, for audit trailing, and if necessary for billing. All records from the Plug-in are signed by using client's private key to prevent the client from denying any of the messages.

At the client side, a Web browser, i.e. Internet Explorer is used as an interface to communicate between the client and the server. We use Adobe Acrobat (adobe.com) as our Content Renderer to access the digital content in the form of PDF files. We have created a Renderer specific plug-in to interface our server with Adobe Acrobat as a proof of concept. For future work we plan to build a format/Renderer independent client side application that interfaces to arbitrary Renderers via much smaller Renderer specific plug-ins. The development of the plug-in to the Adobe Acrobat gave us first-hand experience of application customisation and extension. The client side code plays an important role on:

1. Understanding and interpreting the protected digital content structure.
2. Validating the digital licenses (signature verification and time validity etc.).
3. Decrypting and retrieving the digital content key from the digital license.
4. Upholding and enforcing the client's access rights (triggering on/off the functions on the Renderer application) on the digital content according to the digital rights stated on the digital license.
5. Logs all the client's actions exercised on the digital content.

The Renderer and plug-in run in an insecure environment, which makes it possible for unencrypted content to be leaked. This problem occurs with most

DRM systems. The problem can be solved to an extent by using tamper resistant hardware at the client side, and with watermarking techniques (See Section 3).

The security features of the prototype are as follows:

1. The digital content is kept protected (encrypted) at the client-side. Only when the user has the proper digital license and certificates, can the protected digital content be decrypted and accessed by Adobe Acrobat (using the plug-in).
2. The digital content key is personalized to the user (as described in Section 4). Therefore, the key can be traced back to the user. The owner of the key may thus be held responsible if a rights violation is detected – detecting such violations is outside the scope of this paper. The content key should never leave the confines of the user's machine.
3. The server (CH) is the only entity able to sign a license. Every client can verify the signature on a License.
4. Clients are not anonymous.
5. Clients can exercise rights multiple times. To control this, secure timers, counters and the like may be needed. This is an area of future work.

4.1   Performance Evaluation

We have performed some experiments on our content server to measure the overhead at the server side due to the on-demand content encryption and licence generation. The measurements would allow us to determine the limitations of the server, and the extent to which the system is scalable.

We used Apache (`apache.org`) on a Pentium III 650 MHz, 128 MB RAM machine as a server. We have installed the Jakarta Tomcat (`jakarta.apache.org`) servlet container to interface with Apache. The client is a Pentium III 850 MHz, 256 MB RAM, which is connected to the server via an intranet 10Mbps Waveland.

The encryption algorithm we employed in the prototype is Blowfish [26] with 128bits key. We implement the Blowfish encryption using the JCE library. We have varied the block size for encryption to see the possible influences on the performance. The two block sizes we have chosen are 1KB (1024 bytes) and 8KB (8192 bytes). We have not tested with larger block sizes, because a larger block size makes it harder to hide the patterns of the plaintext securely [27]. Timings were generated by executing the target code block in a tight loop and by using `System.currentTimeMillis()` to capture (wall clock) timing information. We have run two sets of tests on the prototype, measuring *time as a function of content size* for content protection, as well as *time as a function of the number of users* for content protection, as shown in Figure 2.

A typical video is 700MB (this just fits on a 700MB CD-R); a typical MP3 is 3MB. All other digital document (TXT, PDF, DOC and so on) and digital pictures (BMP, JPEG, GIF, and so on) can be as small as 1KB, or as large as 10MB (or even bigger). To cover a significant variety of sizes of digital content, we have chosen the range 7B, 70B, 700B, ... 7MB, 70MB, 700MB. We assume a 10Mbps

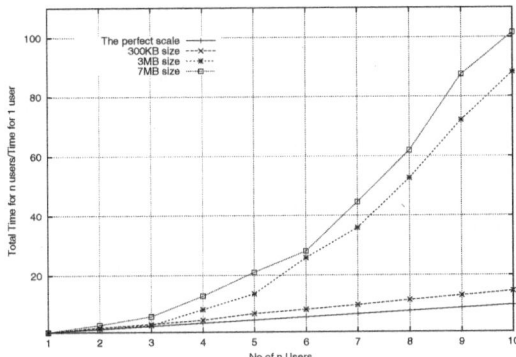

Fig. 2. Scaled time needed for content protection as a function of the number of user activating the content encryption simultaneously.

network (typical cable modem for home user). An MP3 can be downloaded in about 2 s, while a video takes 9 min.

The time spent downloading content is nearly a linear function of the content size. The time taken to encrypt the content with 1kB block size and 8kB block size hardly differs. We infer that varying encryption block sizes does not show a significant difference. We found that the time encryption for content size ranges from 7B to 100KB is less than 100 ms, which is imperceptible to users. The time spent for an MP3 is approximately 1 s, which is 50% of the time needed to download the content. A typical 1 hour video of 700MB takes about 5 min to encrypt; this represents a 55% time overhead. However, by overlapping encryption and downloading using streaming techniques [28] [29], the time taken to encrypt can be completely hidden from the user.

Figure 2 shows how the performance of the server degrades gracefully when there is more than one concurrent user. For each of three file sizes 300KB, 3MB, and 7MB, and for each of $n = 1, 2, ...10$ concurrent users we have made a number of measurements, and plotted the average of these measurements in the figure. We have scaled the averages, dividing the average time for n users by the average time for one user. The line indicating perfect scalability is also shown. The performance of the server is not affected by small content sizes, but it becomes overloaded if the content size increases and/or if the number of concurrent users increases beyond a certain point.

To avoid degrading the service beyond the point where content encryption time can no longer hidden from the user, the server could to decide when to accept and when to reject further demands for content could on the basis of these measurements. We have evaluated the license generation time. The size of a digital license is around 10KB, and it can be generated in 60±20ms per license. This is negligible with respect to the download times for small content size.

4.2 SPIN Model

Designing correct security protocols is notoriously difficult [30]. Many tools and systems are available to help the designer to analyse the protocols [31]. Our system includes some moderately complex protocols. Therefore, we have used the SPIN model-checking tool [32] to help us explore a key property of the protocol: preventing the re-distribution of content. SPIN is able to explore the state space of a model looking for undesirable states. An example of such an undesirable state is one where content is intercepted by a Thief, and redistributed.

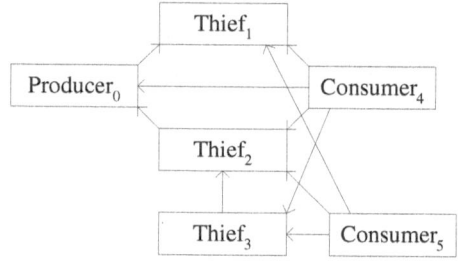

Fig. 3. Network with a Producer, three Thieves and two Consumers showing arrows in the direction of Request message flow; License and Content messages flow in the opposite direction.

Figure 3 Shows a network of six processes, where the server (labelled as Producer) supports five clients. Three clients play the role of Thieves; the remaining clients (labelled Consumers) are honest, the Producer is also honest. Only the Producer is able to create original Packaged Content and Licenses. Thieves acquire Packaged Content and License from the Producer or from each other. Thieves would do this in order to earn money: purchasing content for a certain price from the Producer, then selling it for less money to many Consumers would enable Thieves to earn arbitrary amounts of money. Consumers and Thieves can either download Packaged Content and License from the Producer or from one of the Thieves. Thief 3 demonstrates that another middleman can be involved in a transaction. Of course, there are many networks involving any number of Producers, Consumers and Thieves. We believe that the network show in Figure 3 represents the essence of all such networks. The processes shown in Figure 3 exchange three different types of messages:

- Request messages identify the desired content.
- Packaged Content messages contain the actual content encrypted under a unique content key.
- License messages contain a content key, which is signed by the Producer. The signed key is then encrypted under the public key of the process requesting the license, i.e. a Consumer or a Thief.

Request messages flow in the direction of the arrows, response messages flow in the opposite direction. In response to reach Request message, a Packaged Content and a License message are sent. For example in the simplest scenario, Consumer 4 sends a Request message to the Producer, which returns the appropriate Packaged Content and License messages to the Consumer.

To keep the model simple and yet to make it sufficiently expressive, we have made the following simplifying assumptions:

- A private key is truly private, and public keys are universally known.
- A Thief must re-encrypt a License because every client requires that a License be encrypted with her public key.
- The Producer and Consumer are honest; the Thieves are not. No parties collude.
- The Producer never reuses a content key. This allows the Consumer to check keys received for duplicates. A duplicate content key indicates the involvement of a Thief.
- Encryption is modelled by including the key in a message. Decryption then becomes comparing keys.

The model is limited and could be extended in the number of ways:

- It is possible to eavesdrop on a channel; to model this is future work.
- The Thieves are really middlemen [15] with bad intentions. A generalization to middlemen with good intentions would be valuable.
- Billing is not taken into account, this would rely on non-repudiated logging [24].

The key property of any DRM system is to prevent illegal super distribution: Anyone other than the Producer trying to redistribute content without permission or agreement from the Producer will eventually be caught. To ensure this we rely on two assumptions: that all content keys are unique, and that customers when receiving content keys are able to check that the key received is fresh. We will show below that our SPIN model satisfies this property. The SPIN model is of course an abstraction of the real system, and as such provides no guarantees about the prototype. However, the fact that the model satisfies the prevention of illegal super distribution property demonstrates that the design of the system is sound.

We have run the model checker twice; once with the assertion by the Consumer that every key is fresh commented out and once with the assertion taking effect. No assertion violations were found with the assertion on fresh keys commented out. With be fresh keys assertion effective, a problem was found, as follows.

Firstly, a Consumer sends a Request message to a Thief, which in turn sends a Request message to the Producer. The Producer responds with Packaged Content and License message to the Thief, which caches the Packaged Content and License, then sends it along to the Consumer. The Thief takes care to re-encrypt the License with Consumers public key.

When the Consumer asks for the same content a second time, the Thief has no choice but to resend the cached Packaged Content and License again, and thus is caught. The price we have to pay for this level of security is that the Clients have to be able to cache all license keys. This requires in principle an unbounded amount of store. However, with an appropriate hashing technique the storage requirements could be curtailed, as hashing the same key twice is guaranteed to give a collision. The question then remains how to deal with falls positives. This is an area for future research.

5   Conclusions and Future Work

We propose a Digital Rights Management system for multimedia content that separates the authorities involved in three categories: Identity, Attribute and Right. This separation creates flexibility because each authority has a significant degree of autonomy. The link between the authorities is established using cryptographic means to build a chain of control (*identity-attribute-rights*). Hashing the public key certificate, attribute certificate, license identity and some random data generates the content key.

We describe a prototype implementation of the system, with a performance evaluation from a users perspective. We have measured the average time needed for content encryption and license generation when simultaneously serving several users and the average time needed for content encryption while varying the size of the content. The measurements indicate that the system is scalable for digital documents, digital pictures and MP3 (of size around 3MB-7MB). A SPIN model of the system is used to validate the main protocols. Our validation result with the SPIN model asserts that super distribution is prevented when content keys are unique.

The server side DRM of our prototype is document and Renderer independent. The prototype uses Adobe Acrobat to render content. An Acrobat specific plug-in is responsible for the client side DRM. The DRM client functions as a validator for the chain of control constructed by the server, as a detector for key/license violation. The DRM client also acts as a secure store for licenses (akin to installing certificates on Web browsers).

References

1. F. Hartung and F. Ramme, "Digital rights management and watermarking of multimedia content for m-commerce applications," *IEEE Communications Magazine*, vol. 38, pp. 78–84, Nov 2000.
2. International Telecommunication Union, Place des Nations 1211 Geneva 20 Switzerland, *ITU-T Recommendation X.509, Information Technology, Open Systems Interconnection, The Directory: Authentication Framework*, July 1997. http://www.itu.int.
3. D. Henry, "Who's got the key?," in *Proceedings of the 27th annual SIGUCCS Conference on Mile high expectations*, (Denver, Colorado, United States), pp. 106–110, ACM Press, 1999.

4. S. Farrell and R. Housley, *An Internet Attribute Certificate Profile for Authorization, IETF Draft.* PKIX Working Group, January 2001.
   http://search.ietf.org/internet-drafts/draft-ietf-pkix-ac509prof-09.txt.

5. B. Gelbord, H. Hut, G. Keinhuis, and E. Kwast, "Access control based on attribute certificates." Email: {b.s.gelbord, d.h.hut, g.kleinhuis, e.kwast}kpn.com, 2002.

6. J. Linn, "Attribute certification: An enabling technology for delegation and role-based controls in distributed environments," in *Proceedings of the 4th ACM Workshop on role-based access control on Role-based access control,* (Fairfax, Virgina, United States), pp. 121–130, ACM Press, 1999.

7. H. Guo, "Digital rights management (drm) using xrml," in *Telecommunications Software and Multimedai TML-C7,* 2001.
   http://www.tml.hut.fi/Studies/T-110.501/2001/papers/.

8. B. Horne, B. Pinkas, and T. Sander, "Escrow services and incentives in peer-to-peer networks," in *Proceedings of the 3rd ACM Conference on Electronic Commerce,* pp. 85–94, October 2001.

9. S. H. Kwok and S. M. Lui, "A license management model to support b2c and c2c music sharing," in 10th *International World Wide Web Conference, Hong Kong,* pp. 136–137, May 2001.

10. D. Sellars, "An introduction to steganography," tech. rep., University of Cape Town, Computer Science, May 1999.
    http://www.dsse.ecs.soton.ac.uk/ techreports/99-4.html.

11. J. Dittman, A. Behr, M. Stabenau, P. Schmitt, J. Schwenk, and J. Ueberberg, "Combining digital watermarks and collusion secure fingerprints for digital images," in *IEE Electronics and Communications, London,* pp. 6/1–6/6, 2000. UK ISSN 0963-3308 - Reference No:2000/39.

12. J. Fridrich, "Robust digital watermarking based on key-dependent basis functions," in *Proceedings of Second International Workshop on Information Hiding, USA,* pp. 143–157, 1998.

13. S. Brin, J. Davis, and H. Garcia-Molina, "Copy detection mechanisms for digital documents," in *Proceedings of the ACM SIGMOD Annual Conference San José,* pp. 398–409, May 1995.

14. N. Shivakumar and H. Garcia-Molina, "Building a scalable and accurate copy detection mechanism," in *Proceedings of the 1st ACM International Conference on Digital Libraries,* pp. 160–168, ACM Press, March 1996.

15. G. Durfee and M. Franklin, "Distribution chain security," in *Proceedings of the 7th ACM Conference on Computer and Communications Security,* pp. 63–70, ACM Press, New York, 2000.

16. S. Voloshynovskiy, S. Pereira, T. Pun, J. Eggers, and J. Su, "Attacks on digital watermarks: Classification, estimation-based attacks and benchmarks," in *IEEE Communications Magazine (Special Issue on Digital Watermarking for Copyright Protection: a communications perspective),* vol. 39, pp. 118–127, IEEE Press, 2001. M. Barni, F. Bartolini, I.J. Cox, J. Hernandez, F. Pérez-González, Guest Eds. Invited paper.

17. M. Mourad, J. Munson, T. Nadeem, G. Pacifici, and M. Pistoria, "Webguard: A system for web content protection," in 10th *International World Wide Web Conference, Hong Kong,* pp. 142–143, May 2001.

18. B. Horne, L. Matheson, C. Sheehan, and R. E. Tarjan, "Dynamic self-checking techniques for improved tamper resistance," in *Workshop on Security and Privacy in Digital Rights Management 2001,* February 2002.

19. D. Lie, C. Thekkath, M. Mitchell, and P. Lincoln, "Architectural support for copy and tamper resistant," in *Architectural Support for Programming Languages and Operating Systems*, pp. 168–177, 2000.
20. E. Damiani, S. de Capitai di Vimercati, S. Paraboschi, and P. Samarati, "Design and implementation of an access control processor for xml documents," in *Proceedings of WWW9 Computer Networks*, 1–6, pp. 59–75, 2000.
21. E. Damiani, S. de Capitai di Vimercati, S. Paraboschi, and P. Samarati, "Securing xml documents," in *Advances in Database Technology - EDBT 2000, 7th International Conference on Extending Database nology, Konstanz, Germany, March 27-31, 2000, Proceedings*, vol. 1777 of *LNCS*, pp. 121–135, Springer, 2000.
22. E. Bertino, S. Castano, E. Ferrari, and M. Mesili, "Controlled access and dissemination of xml documents," in *Proceedings 2nd ACM Workshop on Web Information and Data Management (WIDM99)*, pp. 22–27, 1999.
23. M. Kudo and S. Hada, "Xml document security based on provisional authorization," in *Proceedings of the 7th ACM Conference on Computer and Communications Security*, pp. 87–96, 2000.
24. B. Schneier and J. Kelsey, "Cryptographic support for secure logs on untrusted machines," in *The 7th USENIX Security Symposium Proceedings*, pp. 53–62, USENIX Press, January 1998.
25. C. N. Chong, Z. Peng, and P. H. Hartel, "Secure audit logging with tamper-resistant hardware," tech. rep., Universiteit Twente, Enschede, The Netherlands, August 2002. ISSN: 1381-3625.
26. B. Schneier, "Description of a new variable-length key, 64-bit block cipher (blowfish)," in *Fast Software Encryption, Cambridge Security Workshop Proceedings*, pp. 191–204, Springer-Verlag, December 1994.
27. B. Schneier, *Applied Cryptography, Second Edition*, ch. 15, pp. 357–368. John Wiley & Sons, Inc., 1996. ISBN: 0-471-11709-9.
28. C. Shi and B. Bhargava, "A fast mpeg video encryption algorithm," in *Proceedings of the 6th ACM International Conference on Multimedia*, (Bristol, United Kingdom), pp. 81–88, ACM Press, 1998.
29. F. LaMonica, "Streaming media," *Linux Journal*, vol. 81es, January 2001.
30. G. Lowe, "Breaking and fixing the Needham-Schroeder Public-Key protocol using FDR," *Software Concepts and Tools*, vol. 17, pp. 93–102, 1996.
31. P. H. Hartel, M. Butler, A. Currie, P. Henderson, M. Leuschel, A. Martin, A. Smith, U. Ultes-Nitsche, and B. Walters, "Questions and answers about ten formal methods," in *4th Int. Workshop on Formal Methods for Industrial Critical Systems, Vol II* (S. Gnesi and D. Latella, eds.), (Trento, Italy), pp. 179–203, ERCIM/CNR, Pisa, Italy, Jul 1999. www.dsse.ecs.soton.ac.uk/techreports/99-1.html.
32. G. J. Holzmann, "The model checker SPIN," *IEEE Transactions on software engineering*, vol. 23, no. 5, pp. 279–295, 1997. http//cm.bell-labs.com/cm/cs/who/gerard/.

An Active Network Approach to Support Multimedia Relays

Manuel Urueña[1], David Larrabeiti[1], María Calderón[1], Arturo Azcorra[1],
Jens E. Kristensen[2], Lars Kroll Kristensen[2], Ernesto Exposito[3],
David Garduno[4], and Michel Diaz[4]

[1] Universidad Carlos III de Madrid. 20, Av. Unidersidad, Leganés 28913, Spain
{muruenya,dlarra,maria,azcorra}@it.uc3m.es
[2] Ericsson Telebit A/S. Skanderborgvej 232, DK-8260 Viby J., Denmark
{jens.kristensen,lars.k.kristensen}@lmd.ericsson.se
[3] ENSICA, DMI 1 Place Emile Blouin 31056, Toulouse Cedex, France
ernesto.exposito@ensica.fr
[4] LAAS CNRS. 7, Avenue du Colonel Roche, 31077 Toulouse, France
{dgarduno,diaz}@laas.fr

Abstract. This paper summarizes a pragmatic technical approach to
active networks that supports prototyping of multimedia transport protocols. One of the targets of the architecture defined is the extension
of the processing capabilities of existing routers trying to keep up the
forwarding performance of regular packets. This work presents practical
results obtained from the development of a Java execution environment
based on the design principles presented and proposes a method for the
transparent deployment of multimedia relays over a source-destination
path, tested in several experiments.

1 Introduction

Processing multimedia flows inside the network is known to be a rather convenient way to support multi-QoS (reflectors) or multi-coding (translators) in
multipoint sessions. Usually the approach followed is to locate such relays in
servers. This has the major drawback that the users usually have not the ability to choose the optimum place to run these services (usually this optimum
place is in the heart of the network) nor the possibility to adapt the server behaviour to their specific needs (new codecs, specific bitrates, partial reliability,
etc). The former problem can cause suboptimal delay and bandwidth usage, and
the latter, simply prevents the development of new ways of processing multimedia flows, if the server is not open to this possibility. This could be overcome by
bringing in to scene some concepts developed in the light of the active network
paradigm, namely, actually locating relays on the nodes on the source-destination
path rather than on a remote off-the-way host. The main drawback for this is
that multimedia flow processing is a CPU-intensive task and currently available
routers are not designed for such work.

This paper summarizes the experience obtained from a design process aimed
at building an active network framework useful for new multimedia services.

F. Boavida et al. (Eds.): IDMS/PROMS 2002, LNCS 2515, pp. 353–364, 2002.

This framework was developed and applied to multimedia processing in the context of the IST project GCAP [1] [1] [2]. Two outputs of this project were directly related to active network support of multimedia flows. One of them was a software/hardware prototype designed to demonstrate the way commercial routers could be easily enhanced to support a few active processing capabilities. The second one was the practical application of this system to support the deployment of multimedia multicast protocol entities running as active applications.

This paper has the following structure: the second section reviews the currently available Java extensions for multimedia applications over IP and its relationship with active networks. The next section describes SARA, an architecture defined to integrate only practical principles from active networks technology, including innovative solutions to keep most router's architecture unchanged. This third section also includes a description of a prototype developed to demonstrate the feasibility of this approach. The fourth section discusses a case study to apply this framework to the deployment of multimedia processing, in particular to multimedia relays. Finally, some conclusions are drawn.

2   Java for Networked Multimedia Applications

The Java language [2] developed by Sun Microsystems has achieved a noticeable success among application developers. Initially marketed as "the Internet language" with its "Write Once, Run Anywhere" slogan, it was employed to develop "applets", small programs embedded in web pages to be downloaded and executed by browsers. This phase lost momentum and most of current Java applications do not reside in desktops but in servers, as Java, plus XML technologies as SOAP, turned to be the ideal platform to develop web applications and services.

Standard Java libraries have been in continuous growth and nowadays includes many packages that ease multimedia development:

- Java Media Framework (JMF) [3] is an extension package to develop multimedia applications and services using the Java language. This package is cross-platform as it has been implemented in pure Java. However there are some other implementations for widely deployed operating systems (Windows, Solaris and Linux) with native code to enhance capture and playback performance.
- The Real-Time Specification for Java had been also released [4]. It defines the javax.realtime package that extends the Java language so it can be appropiate to develop real-time applications by adding predictable scheduling

[1] This work has been funded by the IST project GCAP (Global Communication Architecture and Protocols for new QoS services over IPv6 networks) IST-1999-10 504. Further development is being supported by the Spanish MCYT under project AURAS TIC2001-1650-C02-01.

[2] Disclaimer: this paper reflects the view of the authors and not necessarily the view of the referred projects.

models, memory management, synchronization and resource sharing, asynchronous event handling and many others mechanisms needed by real-time applications, as multimedia processing ones.

However, Java has been designed as a high level language, that is, to develop applications, not to offer a system programming platform, although some efforts as the above mentioned Real-Time Specification may change that in the next future. Moreover, Java programs must be able to run in a variety of platforms from different vendors, thus only the common features of all platforms can be offered by the standard API.

These factors had led to a limited Java networking API. The standard library version 1.4, recently released, supports IPv4, IPv6, TCP, UDP and multicast sockets. Enough for most of networked applications but quite constrained for low-level advanced network programming. For example, the current API provides socket options but IP options still cannot be set. During the community process that led towards the latest release, raw socket support was discussed but it was later dropped off from the final specification due to security considerations.

To overcome the lack of several features needed for the development of advanced multimedia services and, in particular, the target packet processing capabilities of the active network platform here described, a new Java networking library was needed. That is the motivation of a raw socket library, which is described later in this article.

Due to its multiplatform design, Java has always been heavily associated with mobile code, such as agents and active applications. That feature, absolutely vital in such an heterogeneous environment as an active network, is able to overtake other Java drawbacks such as its limited networking API and lower performance. This, together with Java's enhanced multimedia capabilities, made it the choice to prototype the system described in the next section.

3   Simple Active Router Assistant Architecture

As already introduced, our aim is the definition of a pragmatic framework to implement basic active networking functions, valid both for IPv4 and IPv6, and realistic in an industrial context. This section defines this framework which we will refer to in the remainder of the paper as the "router-assistant" approach. This way of building active networks is based on a set of techniques selected according to its industrial applicability.

3.1   Motivations

The key features of the defined framework and the rationale behind them are:

- **Current Routers have been designed to forward packets, no to process them up.** Most high speed commercial routers have a distributed architecture controled and supported by a CPU with a capacity far below today's hosts' capacity; in principle, they needn't have it because a CPU's main function is system management and routing, and most of a router's performance is due to its interface processors specialised in packet forwarding. Therefore, a router CPU cannot spare so much horsepower itself to CPU-intensive processes as e.g. multimedia transcoding is. Thus an Execution Environment with Active Applications cannot be run without disrupting forwarding performance for both, active packets and 'regular' ones.

- **Can you add capacity without buying a new router?** Active Applications should, by definition itself, be able to make a broad set of operations, from traffic probing to multimedia flow transcoding. Therefore resource requirements of active nodes should be able to be changed in a very dynamic fashion. Scalability must be considered as a primary issue in order to evaluate active network proposals.
- **Internet is not active.** Most of current Active Networks platforms rely on overlay networks, that is, building an parallel active Internet [5] with its own routing protocols. Clearly this effort requires a lot of work to be added to the development of active network entities, a quite complex task by itself. The experience with current middleware devices (NAT, firewall,...) shows that most intelligent services should be transparent to the end user. Therefore, explicit addressing, as overlayed active networking is, should be allowed but not mandatory.
- **Active Capsules poses a great security risk.** Capsules, that is, active packets carrying the code to process them, allow end users to inject its own protocols. This mechanism provides the greatest level of flexibility in protocol deployment ever seen for the price of security checking. Mobile code must be checked for security and safety reasons before being executed. Many mechanisms have been proposed, from signed code [6] to safety checking [7], each one has advantages and drawbacks but none has been able to fulfill all requirements. Capsules cannot be justified as they are inherently harmful, as they could compromise the security of the whole network. This problem limits in practice the degree of dynamism of active code.
- **Active Applications must be dynamically deployed... but what is dynamic enough?** Current network services and protocols are 'static'; the deployment of a new protocol is really a painful task (IPv6 is a perfect example). Preventing this problem is one major objective of the active network community and the reason for the theoretical capsules approach. However, dynamic code deployment requirements can be lowered considering that service and protocol deployment are not tasks to be done on a daily basis.

3.2   Design Principles

Considering these facts and introducing practical constraints, an architecture named Simple Active Router Assistant Architecture (SARA) has been defined with the purpose of giving a pragmatic approach to the most important services provided by active networks.

A summary of architecture characteristics follows:

- **Active node = Router + Assistant.** Legacy routers can be upgraded to active nodes by delegating active processing to an attached host (or host

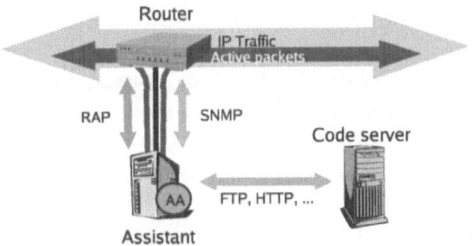

Fig. 1. Simple Active Router Assistant Architecture.

cluster) called Assistant via a high speed interface. The assistant host runs the NodeOS, Execution Environment and Active Applications, thus avoiding such process to consume router's resources. This architecture allows administrators to increase active processing capacity by adding more assistants, thus adapting nodes to the resource requirements of active applications deployed on them.

- **Router diverts packets to Assistant.** In order to adapt easily routers to this architecture, its requirements are reduced to simply forward certain packets to its assistant, in particular those defined as active. Hence, router's performance cost is limited to just to identifying such packets. To accomplish this task without a severe performance penalty, the Router Alert IP option [8] [9] should be employed. This option forces routers to get the packet off the fast-path and deliver it to the appropriate software entity to handle it.

- **Transparent active processing.** As it can be inferred from the previous paragraphs, packets to be processed are not explicitly addressed to active nodes but captured as they are forwarded to their final destination. An overlay network of active nodes is not necessary as they are truly integrated with real network nodes. Adding an active node to the network requires no routing protocols other than the one running on the network itself. Of course, active nodes may be made aware of other active nodes in the network and build an overlay if necessary, to override the routing tables. Nevertheless transparency is a desirable property for the sake of end-system simplicity.

- **Assistant processes diverted packets.** Packets diverted by the router are dispatched by the assistant's Execution Environment and put on the input queue of the corresponding active application. An active application can alter anything in the packet from network to application level and may reinject the packet to the router so that it can be routed as any other packet.

- **Dynamic Active Application deployment.** Any code loading/execution approach can be applied under SARA architecture. However, the recommended method is that active packets carry references to active code that processes them (and security credentials if necessary). If code has not been yet loaded it can be retrieved on demand from code servers by existing methods (e.g. ftp), and then loaded dynamically onto the Execution Environment as a new active application.

- **Monitoring the router state.** One of the drawback of this approach is the need for greater interaction complexity between router and assistant as they reside in separate hosts. This communication is necessary to provide active applications with the sense of actually being run on the router. In order to make it possible to adapt the active behavior to the real-time network status, active applications need to access the router's state. As one of SARA objectives is to cooperate with legacy routers, the Simple Network Management Protocol (SNMP) [10] was selected, as it is the standard management protocol, supported by most of network devices. However, a more efficient management protocol could be used instead, to avoid some problems associated to SNMP. In order to avoid the router performance hit when the router's state is constantly polled. A small cache, managed by the Execution Environment, storing recent state variables may improve both router performance and applications response time.
- **Router-Assistant Protocol.** Two conformance levels have been defined for routers supporting SARA. Level 1, for routers that only divert active packets and accept SNMP queries, and level 2, for routers that also support Router-Assistant Protocol (RAP) operations. This protocol allows assistants to configure somehow its attached router. Some examples of RAP operations may include setting tunnel endpoints or configuring firewall rules. One of the most important operations requested by assistants to level 2 conformant routers is to divert non-active flows as it is done with active ones. This mechanism enables active applications to capture and process non-active packets; that is, to enhance communications without modifying current applications and services. At this scenario active packets are relegated to the control plane.
- **Trusted code.** From the authors' viewpoint, end users freely injecting mobile code in the network is not a realistic scenario. Instead of evaluating mobile code safety techniques, a more pragmatic approach has been taken. Each network administrator must be able to control exactly what active applications are allowed to execute into his domain and never load untrusted ones. In this scenario trusted active applications may be provided by the network administrator itself, by customers or by any trustable third party. Active Applications stored in code repositories of a certain administrative domain are allowed to execute in that domain as they have trusted code. Code safety can be checked in advance by multiple techniques as auditing source code or just trusting the application supplier. In fact, this is the common procedure of today's mobile code, as it is the casew of software packages downloaded from internet: applications from known vendors are trusted and installed directly.
- **Latency.** SARA architecture is not well suited to support applications that require a tight interaction with low level router resources (e.g. selective dropping of packets buffered at the router queues). Although latency might be reduced by increasing the bandwidth of the link between the router and the assistant, the fact is, that most diverted packets need to be routed twice. Depending on the platform chosen, this may be an important issue for some real-time multimedia applications. However, it should be noted that a sim-

ilar delay is found when we choose the alternative server-based approach, as packets are forwarded to the server and sent back to the network once processed.

– **Active processing isolation.** As the Execution Environment and the Active Applications are executed on a separate host, the router is quite shielded from many kinds of active processing errors. In the worst case scenario a buggy active application could crash the assistant host, and diverted packets may get lost; however any other flow passing through the router will remain unaffected. To reduce the packet loss due to assistant's crash, the RAP protocol defines a heartbeat mechanism to detect when an assistant has become unreachable.

3.3   Implementation

To demonstrate the feasibility of the proposed architecture, a SARA prototype has been developed [11]. Two testing platforms are available today. One fully based on linux (playing both roles: router and assistant as a development/testing scenario) and a hybrid platform where the router used is an Ericsson-Telebit AXI462 running a modified kernel adapted to interwork with an active assistant. As already mentioned, a main goal of this latter platform, currently under conformance level 1, is to demonstrate that it is possible to build an active network platform based on commercial routers without a significant drop of performance on regular packets.

Active applications and the developed execution environment are based on Java. However, given the limitiations of the current JVM interface reviewed in section 2, a small native extension was needed. In particular, `java.net` package does not contain any object that allows Java applications to open raw sockets or set IP options. Both characteristics are needed by SARA prototype, the first one to capture active-packets while the second one is needed to add the router alert option to active packets. To fulfill these requirements, a networking library for Java providing support for IPv4, IPv6, UDP and TCP sockets with advanced options was developed. This library defines a number of classes, resembling standard API ones, that actually wraps system calls to the standard BSD C socket API, using the Java Native Interface (JNI). Multiplatform capability is somewhat kept as SARA native code is small and easily portable.

Although the current implementation is still at an early development stage and there is much room for performance improvements, the basic throughput measures look promising. As it can be seen in figure 2, flows up to 10 Mbps of mid-sized active packets can be processed by the current SARA prototype.

4   Multimedia Relay Deployment

Several authors have highlighted the benefits obtained from applying the active network paradigm to multimedia flows. Many research initiatives propose the deployment of active relays inside the network to provide solutions as transcoding [12] [13] or multimedia multicast [14] [15]. However the problem related to where these proxies must be deployed has been scarcely addressed.

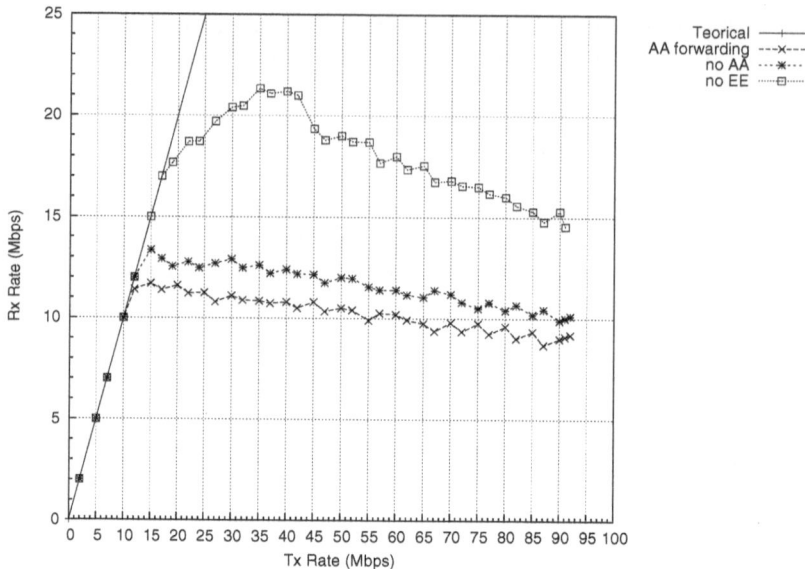

Fig. 2. Effective throughput for EE and simple AA with 1024-byte packets.

4.1 Relay Location

First of all, the "right places" for relay deployment need to be studied. As a rule of thumb, it can be said that network nodes with some sort of discontinuity are ideal points to set up a multimedia relay or, in general, an active entity. Its behavior depends upon what kind of gap is found. A list with some examples:

- Border routers or ISP gateways. This is the most obvious place, and many existing technologies as NAT or firewalls need to be deployed into such nodes. An active node deployed at an edge device could build automatic tunnels to forward multicast flows whenever its ISP does not provide multicast service.
- Bandwidth discontinuity, as a router with different speed interfaces, such as a pool of modems, an ATM interface with several channels configured with different service categories and rates, etc. This can be a good candidate to deploy for example a multimedia codec translator.
- Lossy links, as wireless access segments, and high delay links, as satellite segments. Buffering packets until the corresponding acknowledgement is received prevents longer delayed end-to-end retransmissions, in fully and partially reliable transport services.
- Nodes involved in a muticast delivery tree branching to several destinations, specially in the case of multi-QoS support. Network processing in these nodes could resolve many problems of reliable multicast protocols as ACK/NACK implosion.
- Congested nodes. Selective packet discarding could dynamically adapt multimedia flows traversing congested links to achieve a better quality, for example by dropping video frames and priorizating sound packets.

Many of these discontinuities are rather static, therefore the requirement to deploy a proxy dynamically is lowered as active applications can be continuously running at such places. However, some others services, as automatic tunnels, multicast nodes or congestion spots have a very variable nature, and hence relay deployment must be more flexible, and the framework that supports such proxies should be able to detect the best place to run these applications. Active networks can provide such deployment framework, as well as the mechanisms to compute optimal relay placement.

4.2   Relay Deployment Methods

By definition, all existing active network platforms provide dynamic code deployment, however not every platform may be suitable to detect the optimum active location, mainly due to the need of defining an overlay network. Overlay networks hide underneath path characteristics as all links between two active nodes are aggregated as a virtual circuit. Another problem is the deployment of short-lived proxies, as the overlay network needs to be reconfigured to add new nodes.

SARA architecture allows the transparent deployment of active entities while avoiding these problems. As SARA does not require defining an overlay network, overlay routing is not an issue, and, thanks to SNMP, an assistant could have an influence area around its attached router. By setting SNMP traps, active applications can react more quickly to network changes. SARA ability to inject any kind of IP packet could be used to monitor flow paths by sending pings to check response times, packet loss or any other parameter interesting for active applications. For instance, tools like *A-clink* [16] can be very useful to optimize the placement of multimedia proxies. This active application is a path characterization application based on the freely available *clink* tool, enhanced with active support to improve the efficiency and accuracy of estimations yielded by existing end-to-end performance estimation tools such as *pathchar*, *pchar*, *clink* and *nettimer*.

5   A Case Study

While the previous section refers to theoretical aspects of proxy deployment using active networks, the following describes an experiment carried out in the context of GCAP, with a real active application running over a SARA implementation. Firstly, we describe the active application involved: a proxy running the FPTP protocol, and then the setup is described.

5.1   Fully Programmable Transport Protocol (FPTP)

FPTP is transport protocol sub-layer located between the application and the traditional transport protocols. Multimedia applications are able to access to the FPTP API directly (FPTP sockets) or using an XML-based, QoS configuration. In both cases applications have to specify the QoS transport required in terms of order, reliability, bandwidth, time and synchronization constraints. FPTP protocol is able to instantiate standard transport protocols or to deploy new protocol mechanisms and services, following the QoS transport constraints specified by the application.

FPTP protocol consists of 2 kinds of transport connections:

- The multimedia connection control allows communicating both sides of the multimedia connection. This connection is a bidirectional connection and based on XML messages exchanged (SOAP).
- The monomedia connections allow transferring the media data following the QoS constraints required. Each monomedia connection is a unidirectional connection.

A FPTP monomedia session is established between a sender and a receiver entity. In both sides the transport protocol mechanisms can be instantiated and/or programmed according the QoS constraints required. If the QoS constraints can be assured by the standard transport protocols, the FPTP monomedia connection will be instantiated using these available protocols. If the requirements are applications specific, the transport protocol services can be instantiated using the available FPTP transport protocol services or programming and deploying new mechanisms and services.

5.2   Deploying FPTP Proxies with SARA

An experiment was held to stream video between two sites connected across the Internet. The FPTP protocol was employed to adapt video quality to QoS offered by such a connection. As the video server and the client were executing traditional RTP multimedia applications, intermediate proxies were needed to issue the QoS enhancements. The SARA prototype did provide active network support for such proxy deployment as well as path QoS characterization between sites.

The video server run at Ensica (France) while the client application was running in Universidad Carlos III de Madrid (Spain). Proxies were deployed over two different platforms, a 6Wind edge device located at France and an active node formed by a Ericsson-Telebit AXI462 router and a linux box running SARA Execution Environment where the FPTP-RTP proxy was automatically loaded on demand by downloading code from a local server via HTTP.

As seen in figure 3, three sessions were established, an traditional RTP session between server and the French proxy, a FPTP session between both proxies and another RTP session as the Spanish proxy received FPTP packets and sent the video flow to the client using RTP. An asymmetrical deployment method was used (transparent and explicit deployment respectively) and the experiment succeed in demonstrating cross-platform interoperation of FPTP proxies and dynamic code deployment thanks to SARA platform.

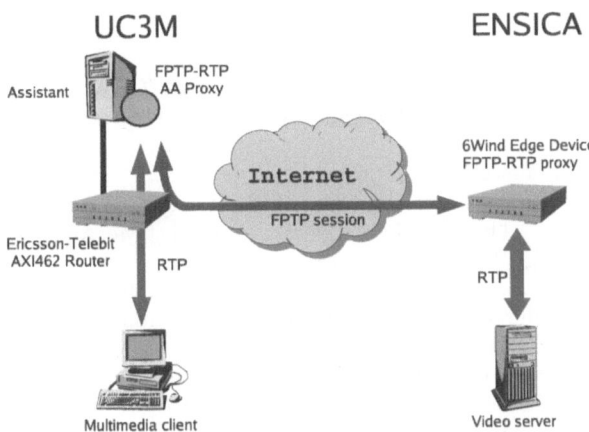

Fig. 3. FPTP-RTP proxy deployment.

6   Conclusions

This paper has reviewed the preeminent position of Java as a multiplatform language to develop active network applications, along with the multimedia framework it provides. Both features converts Java platform in the ideal tool to develop active applications to handle multimedia flows, in spite of some drawbacks as performance and lack of low level communication facilities. That is why Java was the chosen language to implement the Simple Active Router Assistant Architecture (SARA).

SARA is an architecture that allows upgrading legacy high-speed routers to work as active nodes by delegating active processing to an external entity called assistant. This design is based on a set of existing network technologies, that were selected because they could be applied in a production environment oriented to multimedia flow processing. The experience has shown that, such a pragmatic approach is a suitable way to support multimedia relays, and also to compute accurately the optimum places to deploy them, a problem partially addressed nowadays. Transparent processing of active packets is the most important feature claimed by this system. It avoids the need of defining an overlay network as many other active network platforms have to do. To accomplish that task, a new library has been designed to overtake certain limitations of Java networking API.

The feasibility of SARA architecture has been demonstrated by running several multimedia experiments employing active FPTP-RTP proxies. These entities ran over a prototype of SARA assistant working together with a commercial router. The router was an Ericsson-Telebit AXI462, slightly modified to divert active packets containing the router alert IP option, both for IPv4 and IPv6.

References

1. GCAP IST project home page: http://www.laas.fr/GCAP
2. J. Gosling, B. Joy, G. Steele: The Java Language Specification. Addison-Wesley 1996.
3. Java Media Framework home page: http://java.sun.com/products/java-media/jmf/index.html
4. G. Bollella et al.: The Real-Time Specification for Java. Addison-Wesley 2000.
5. Abone home page: http://www.isi.edu/abone/
6. L. Gong, R. Schemers: Signing, sealing, and guarding Java objects. In Mobile Agents and Security, volume 1419 of Lecture Notes in Computer Science. Springer-Verlag, 1998.
7. P. Fong, R. Cameron: Proof linking: An architecture for modular verification of dynamically-linked mobile code. Proc. of the 6th ACM SIGSOFT International Symposium on the Foundations of Software Engineering (FSE-6), pages 222-230, Orlando, Florida. November 1998.
8. D. Katz: IETF RFC 2113: IP Router Alert Option. February 1997.
9. C. Partridge, A. Jackson: IETF RFC 2711: IPv6 Router Alert Option. October 1999.
10. J. Case, M. Fedor, M. Schoffstall, J. Davin: IETF RFC 1157: A Simple Network Management Protocol (SNMP). May 1990.
11. SARA home page: http://enjambre.it.uc3m.es/ sara.
12. E. Amir, S. McCanne, R. Katz: An Active Service Framework and its Application to Real-time Multimedia Transcoding. Proc. of ACM SIGCOMM '98. 1998.
13. I. Kouvelas, V. Hardman, J. Crowcroft: Network Adaptive Continuous-Media Application Through Self Organised Transcoding. 1998.
14. B. Banchs, W. Effelsberg, C. Tschudin, V. Turau: Multicasting Multimedia Streams with Active Networks. Proc. of the 23rd. Annual Conference on Local Computer Networks. 1998.
15. S. Kang, H. Yong Youn, Y. Lee, D. Lee, M. Kim: The Active Traffic Control Mechanism for Layered Multimedia Multicast in Active Network. Proc. of the 8th International Symposium on Modeling, Analysis and Simulation of Computer and Telecommunication Systems. 2000.
16. M. Sedano, B. Alarcos, M. Calderón, D. Larrabeiti: Caracterización de los enlaces de Internet utilizando tecnología de Redes Activas. III Jornadas de Ingenería Telemática. Barcelona. September 2001.

Internet Multimedia – Streaming Media (Tutorial)

Henning Schulzrinne

Columbia University, USA
hgs@cs.columbia.edu

Abstract. Over the past decade, a set of protocols have been developed that support a variety of multimedia applications on the Internet, ranging from streaming media to Internet radio and TV to Internet telephony. All of these require new protocols and algorithms. The tutorial will review the principal components of the current multimedia architecture and outline how the challenges posed by a largely best-effort network can be met. It will also highlight some of the on-going developments such as fresh attempts at scalable resource reservation protocols. Topics: Types of Internet multimedia (streaming, continuous media, interactive media); Challenges of Internet multimedia (differences to other Internet traffic types; summary of codecs); Components of the Internet multimedia architecture; Multimedia transport (RTP; loss compensation and recovery; scalable feedback); Session setup and control for streaming media (RTSP); Internet telephony (session initiation: SIP and H.323; address mapping: ENUM; gateway location: TRIP; convergence with IM, presence and events); Future challenges: content distribution networks.

F. Boavida et al. (Eds.): IDMS/PROMS 2002, LNCS 2515, p. 365, 2002.
© Springer-Verlag Berlin Heidelberg 2002

Internet Middleware (Tutorial)

Mikhail Smirnow

Fraunhofer Institute, FOKUS, Germany
smirnow@fokus.gmd.de

Abstract. This talk covers in depth only one- though mostly important - part of the Internet middleware (IMW) - policy, and provides some in-depth study of one aspect of it - a policy-based programming of network elements to support advanced Internet services. We start however with other IMW parts as a background constraining and motivating the agenda. The talk will be concluded by a discussion of scalability design methodology for the policy-based programming. First, following popular but hard to accept practice, we introduce IMW as an unstructured set of services and resources between Internet application programming interfaces and the Internet Protocol. Then we examine IMW core components (APIs, AAA, Policy, Directories, resource management, discovery and retrieval, QoS, security, operational tools) and observe that they all are organically using a concept of *a group* and a concept of a *policy*. We conclude this introductory part with a conclusion that a *combined* use of middleware services and resources is a hot a research issue, providing several examples of research challenges. We then make a big picture of existing Internet as a patchwork of dedicated client-server protocols, while Internet services, especially those with call features (SIP, RSVP, RTSP, mobility, AAA) and QoS demands require co-ordinated behaviour (known as midcom - middle box communication) from several dedicated protocols, almost always including a policy protocol. To achieve required co-ordination one can either develop yet another client server protocol (that clearly does not scale to a number of emerging combined usage scenarios), or use application level middleware (explicitly non-goal for this talk), or extend the very notion of policy to meet the co-ordination requirement. This extension asks for a broader view on policy. Rather than plain "device configuration" [IETF, DMTF], a policy is "a rule that defines a choice in the behaviour of a system" [M. Sloman]. A policy-controlled component in turn needs to have Externalised Behaviour Choices (EBC). Once this is done consistently and safely, one can: separate EBC and policy rules design concerns, one can influence behaviours by changing rules, compose rules from components originating in multiple sources (combined use of IMW components), thus achieving policy-based self-organisation. We demonstrate a practical example of self-organising behaviour. Policy conflicts, similar to feature interaction, are detected mainly at policy enforcement points, while conflict resolution is possible mostly during policy computation or adaptation to an enforcement environment. We show how early conflict resolution can be done with yet another extension of a policy by a meta-data. Finally, we claim that policy programming together with event based interaction and group communication of IMW components enable design of evolvable systems. We show a snapshot of emerging design methodology that keeps complexity under strict control, yet allows very high level of flexibility. The tutorial will be concluded by an overview of an Internet research frontier.

F. Boavida et al. (Eds.): IDMS/PROMS 2002, LNCS 2515, p. 366, 2002.
© Springer-Verlag Berlin Heidelberg 2002

IP Network Monitoring and Measurements:
Techniques and Experiences (Tutorial)

Philippe Owezarski

LAAS-CNRS, France
owe@laas.fr

Abstract. The Internet tends to become the universal network for transmitting all kinds of information, from simple computer data to voice, video, and many interactive real-time information. There is then a strong need for the Internet to provide new kinds of services suited to the requirements of all the Internet applications and all the data they transmit. In addition, the Internet is growing rapidly in size (number of users, computers connected, etc.) as well as in complexity, in particular because of the need to provide new services, and to optimize the use of communication resources to improve the Quality of Service (QoS) provided to users. Because of the Internet complexity increase, the evolution of this global network is tied to an accurate knowledge and understanding of network traffic. Consequently, the development of tools and techniques to capture Internet traffic and its characteristics is now a research and engineering topic of first importance. This tutorial then addresses several techniques for monitoring, measuring and analyzing Internet traffic. In the first part of this tutorial, we will provide a survey of existing approaches and techniques for IP monitoring, in particular dealing with active and passive measurements. This state of the art on IP monitoring and measurements includes the description of basic tools (ping, traceroute, etc...) as well as more advanced devices as OCx-MON, IPANEMA, etc. It also provides a survey on pioneering projects in the domain of IP network monitoring. In the second part of the tutorial, we will show on some actual examples from operational networks how measurements can help in the design, engineering, management of IP networks, as well as in designing new protocols and architectures for next generation Internet, especially addressing the issues of QoS and scalability in large scale IP networks. The following topics will be addressed: Traffic characterization; Traffic modeling; Congestion analysis; Delays in routers; Traffic matrices; Routing table explosion; Summary on QoS. Finally, the tutorial will finish by giving the main issues – not well known – that have to be solved in the Internet, and some research directions to achieve them.

F. Boavida et al. (Eds.): IDMS/PROMS 2002, LNCS 2515, p. 367, 2002.
© Springer-Verlag Berlin Heidelberg 2002

Media Representation Standards for the New Millennium (Tutorial)

Fernando Pereira

Instituto Superior Técnico, Portugal
fp@lx.it.pt

Abstract. The fast evolution of digital technology in the last decade has deeply transformed the way by which information, notably visual information, is generated, processed, transmitted and stored. The need for standards comes from an essential requirement relevant for all applications involving communication between two or more parts: interoperability. Interoperability is thus the requirement expressing the user's dream of exchanging any type of information without any technical barriers, in the simplest way. Without a standard way to perform some of the operations involved in the communication process and to structure the data exchanged, easy interoperability between the terminals involved would be impossible. Having said that, it is clear that a standard should specify the minimum number of tools to guarantee interoperability since it is important that as many as possible non-normative technical zones exist, to allow the incorporation of technical advances, and thus to increase the life time of the standard, as well as to stimulate the industrial technical competition. The existence of a standard has also important economical implications since it allows the sharing of costs and investments and the acceleration of applications' deployment. Among the most relevant standardization achievements are those by ISO/MPEG and ITU-T for media representation, some of them developed in close collaboration such as MPEG-2/H.262. The ISO/MPEG standardization committee has been responsible for the successful MPEG-1 and MPEG-2 standards that have given rise to widely adopted commercial products and services, such as Video-CD, DVD, digital television, digital audio broadcasting (DAB) and MP3 (MPEG-1 Audio layer 3) players and recorders. More recently, the MPEG-4 standard is aimed to define an audiovisual coding standard to address the emerging needs of the communication, interactive and broadcasting service models as well as of the mixed service models resulting from their technological convergence. The MPEG-4 object-based representation approach where a scene is modelled as a composition of objects, both natural and synthetic, with which the user may interact, is at the heart of the MPEG-4 technology. With this new coding approach, the MPEG-4 standard opens new frontiers in the way users will play with, create, re-use, access and consume audiovisual content. Following the same vision underpinning MPEG-4, MPEG initiated after another standardization project addressing the problem of describing multimedia content to allow the quick and efficient searching, processing and filtering of various types of multimedia material: MPEG-7. The need for a powerful solution for quickly and efficiently identifying, searching, filtering, etc., various types of multimedia content of interest to the user, human or machine, using also non text-based technologies, directly follows from the urge to efficiently use the available

F. Boavida et al. (Eds.): IDMS/PROMS 2002, LNCS 2515, pp. 368–369, 2002.
© Springer-Verlag Berlin Heidelberg 2002

multimedia content and the difficulty of doing so. Following the development of the standards mentioned above, MPEG acknowledged the lack of a "big picture" describing how the various elements building the infrastructure for the deployment of multimedia applications relate to each other or even if there are missing open standard specifications for some of these elements. To address this problem, MPEG started the MPEG-21 project, formally called "Multimedia framework" with the aim to understand if and how these various elements fit together, and to discuss which new standards may be required, if gaps in the infrastructure exist. Once this work has been carried out, new standards will be developed for the missing elements with the involvement of other bodies, where appropriate, and finally the existing and novel standards will be integrated in the MPEG-21 multimedia framework. The MPEG-21 vision is thus to define an open multimedia framework to enable the transparent and augmented delivery and consumption of multimedia resources across a wide range of networks and devices used by different communities. The MPEG-21 multimedia framework will identify and define the key elements needed to support the multimedia value and delivery chain, as well as the relationships between and the operations supported by them. This open framework guarantees all content creators and service providers equal opportunities in the MPEG-21 enabled open market. This will also be to the benefit of the content consumers who get access to a large variety of contents in an interoperable manner. In a similar manner, ITU-T defined standards such as H.261 and H.263 for videotelephony and videoconference over different types of channels and it is now developing the so-called H.26L/JVT or MPEG-4 Advanced Video Coding (AVC) standard in collaboration with MPEG; this new standard should provide further significant improvements in terms of coding efficiency. These ITU-T/MPEG collaborations highlight the convergence of technologies for media representation, independently of the transmission and storage media and many times of the application and business models involved. This tutorial will address the evolution and current status in terms of media representation technologies and standards as well as the most relevant emerging developments.

Author Index

Lecture Notes in Computer Science

For information about Vols. 1–2446

please contact your bookseller or Springer-Verlag

Vol. 2487: D. Batory, C. Consel, W. Taha (Eds.), Generative Programming and Component Engineering. Proceedings, 2002. VIII, 335 pages. 2002.

Vol. 2488: T. Dohi, R. Kikinis (Eds), Medical Image Computing and Computer-Assisted Intervention – MICCAI 2002. Proceedings, Part I. XXIX, 807 pages. 2002.

Vol. 2489: T. Dohi, R. Kikinis (Eds), Medical Image Computing and Computer-Assisted Intervention – MICCAI 2002. Proceedings, Part II. XXIX, 693 pages. 2002.

Vol. 2490: A.B. Chaudhri, R. Unland, C. Djeraba, W. Lindner (Eds.), XML-Based Data Management and Multimedia Engineering – EDBT 2002. Proceedings, 2002. XII, 652 pages. 2002.

Vol. 2491: A. Sangiovanni-Vincentelli, J. Sifakis (Eds.), Embedded Software. Proceedings, 2002. IX, 423 pages. 2002.

Vol. 2492: F.J. Perales, E.R. Hancock (Eds.), Articulated Motion and Deformable Objects. Proceedings, 2002. X, 257 pages. 2002.

Vol. 2493: S. Bandini, B. Chopard, M. Tomassini (Eds.), Cellular Automata. Proceedings, 2002. XI, 369 pages. 2002.

Vol. 2495: C. George, H. Miao (Eds.), Formal Methods and Software Engineering. Proceedings, 2002. XI, 626 pages. 2002.

Vol. 2496: K.C. Almeroth, M. Hasan (Eds.), Management of Multimedia in the Internet. Proceedings, 2002. XI, 355 pages. 2002.

Vol. 2497: E. Gregori, G. Anastasi, S. Basagni (Eds.), Advanced Lectures on Networking. XI, 195 pages. 2002.

Vol. 2498: G. Borriello, L.E. Holmquist (Eds.), UbiComp 2002: Ubiquitous Computing. Proceedings, 2002. XV, 380 pages. 2002.

Vol. 2499: S.D. Richardson (Ed.), Machine Translation: From Research to Real Users. Proceedings, 2002. XXI, 254 pages. 2002. (Subseries LNAI).

Vol. 2501: D. Zheng (Ed.), Advances in Cryptology – ASIACRYPT 2002. Proceedings, 2002. XIII, 578 pages. 2002.

Vol. 2502: D. Gollmann, G. Karjoth, M. Waidner (Eds.), Computer Security – ESORICS 2002. Proceedings, 2002. X, 281 pages. 2002.

Vol. 2503: S. Spaccapietra, S.T. March, Y. Kambayashi (Eds.), Conceptual Modeling – ER 2002. Proceedings, 2002. XX, 480 pages. 2002.

Vol. 2504: M.T. Escrig, F. Toledo, E. Golobardes (Eds.), Topics in Artificial Intelligence. Proceedings 2002. XI, 432 pages. 2002. (Subseries LNAI).

Vol. 2506: M. Feridun, P. Kropf, G. Babin (Eds.), Management Technologies for E-Commerce and E-Business Applications. Proceedings, 2002. IX, 209 pages. 2002.

Vol. 2507: G. Bittencourt, G.L. Ramalho (Eds.), Advances in Artificial Intelligence. Proceedings, 2002. XIII, 418 pages. 2002. (Subseries LNAI).

Vol. 2508: D. Malkhi (Ed.), Distributed Computing. Proceedings, 2002. X, 371 pages. 2002.

Vol. 2509: C.S. Calude, M.J. Dinneen, F. Peper (Eds.), Unconventional Models in Computation. Proceedings, 2002. VIII, 331 pages. 2002.

Vol. 2510: H. Shafazand, A Min Tjoa (Eds.), EurAsia-ICT 2002: Information and Communication Technology. Proceedings, 2002. XXIII, 1020 pages. 2002.

Vol. 2511: B. Stiller, M. Smirnow, M. Karsten, P. Reichl (Eds.), From QoS Provisioning to QoS Charging. Proceedings, 2002. XIV, 348 pages. 2002.

Vol. 2513: R. Deng, S. Qing, F. Bao, J. Zhou (Eds.), Information and Communications Security. Proceedings, 2002. XII, 496 pages. 2002.

Vol. 2514: M. Baaz, A. Voronkov (Eds.), Logic for Programming, Artificial Intelligence, and Reasoning. Proceedings 2002. XIII, 465 pages. 2002. (Subseries LNAI).

Vol. 2515: F. Boavida, E. Monteiro, J. Orvalho (Eds.), Protocols and Systems for Interactive Distributed Multimedia. Proceedings, 2002. XIV, 372 pages. 2002.

Vol. 2516: A. Wespi, G. Vigna, L. Deri (Eds.), Recent Advances in Intrusion Detection. Proceedings, 2002. X, 327 pages. 2002.

Vol. 2517: M.D. Aagaard, J.W. O'Leary (Eds.), Formal Methods in Computer-Aided Design. Proceedings, 2002. XI, 399 pages. 2002.

Vol. 2518: P. Bose, P. Morin (Eds.), Algorithms and Computation. Proceedings, 2002. XIII, 656 pages. 2002.

Vol. 2519: R. Meersman, Z. Tari, et al. (Eds.), On the Move to Meaningful Internet Systems 2002: CoopIS, DOA, and ODBASE. Proceedings, 2002. XXIII, 1367 pages. 2002.

Vol. 2521: A. Karmouch, T. Magedanz, J. Delgado (Eds.), Mobile Agents for Telecommunication Applications. Proceedings 2002. XII, 317 pages. 2002.

Vol. 2522: T. Andreasen, A. Motro, H. Christiansen, H. Legind Larsen (Eds.), Flexible Query Answering. Proceedings 2002. XI, 386 pages. 2002. (Subseries LNAI).

Vol. 2525: H.H. Bülthoff, S.-Whan Lee, T.A. Poggio, C. Wallraven (Eds.), Biologically Motivated Computer Vision. Proceedings 2002. XIV, 662 pages. 2002.

Vol. 2526: A. Colosimo, A. Giuliani, P. Sirabella (Eds.), Medical Data Analysis. Proceedings 2002. IX, 222 pages. 2002.

Vol. 2527: F.J. Garijo, J.C. Riquelme, M. Toro (Eds.), Advances in Artificial Intelligence – IBERAMIA 2002. Proceedings 2002. XVIII, 955 pages. 2002. (Subseries LNAI).

Vol. 2528: M.T. Goodrich, S.G. Kobourov (Eds.), Graph Drawing. Proceedings 2002. XIII, 384 pages. 2002.

Vol. 2529: D.A. Peled, M.Y. Vardi (Eds.), Formal Techniques for Networked and Distributed Sytems – FORTE 2002. Proceedings 2002. XI, 371 pages. 2002.

Vol. 2534: S. Lange, K. Satoh, C.H. Smith (Ed.), Discovery Science. Proceedings 2002. XIII, 464 pages. 2002.

Vol. 2535: N. Suri (Ed.), Mobile Agents. Proceedings 2002. X, 203 pages. 2002.

Vol. 2536: M. Parashar (Ed.), Grid Computing – GRID 2002. Proceedings 2002. XI, 318 pages. 2002.

Vol. 2540: W.I. Grosky, F. Plášil (Eds.), SOFSEM 2002: Theory and Practice of Informatics. Proceedings 2002. X, 289 pages. 2002.